MODERN APPLIED SELLING

ALLAN L. REID

*International Sales Consultant; Formerly Vice-President, Sales
Prentice-Hall, Inc. and Prentice-Hall International*

Prentice Hall
Englewood Cliffs, New Jersey 07632

Library of Congress Cataloging-in-Publication Data

Reid, Allan L.
    Modern applied selling / Allan L. Reid.
        p.   cm.
    ISBN 0-13-597618-9
    1. Selling.   2. Selling--Case studies.   I. Title.
    HF5438.25.R43   1990
    658.8'5--dc20   89-36479
                                                            CIP

Editorial/production supervision: *Jacqueline A. Jeglinski*
Interior design: *Lorraine Mullaney*
Cover design: *20/20 Services, Inc.*
Cover art: © *Peter Plagens,* Untitled (50-85), *acrylic on canvas/Nancy Hoffman Gallery, N.Y.*
Manufacturing buyer: *Laura Crossland/Pete Havens*

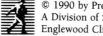 © 1990 by Prentice-Hall, Inc.
A Division of Simon & Schuster
Englewood Cliffs, New Jersey 07632

Printed in the United States of America
10 9 8 7 6 5 4 3 2 1

ISBN 0-13-597618-9

Prentice-Hall International (UK) Limited, *London*
Prentice-Hall of Australia Pty. Limited, *Sydney*
Prentice-Hall Canada Inc., *Toronto*
Prentice-Hall Hispanoamericana, S.A., *Mexico*
Prentice-Hall of India Private Limited, *New Delhi*
Prentice-Hall of Japan, Inc., *Tokyo*
Simon & Schuster Asia Pte. Ltd., *Singapore*
Editora Prentice-Hall do Brasil, Ltda., *Rio de Janeiro*

To my wife
Bessie

CONTENTS

2 Selling in the Marketing Environment 33

3 Buyer Behavior and the Psychology of Selling: To Individual Consumers and to Organizational Buyers 71

10 The Presentation, Part II: Arousing Desire and Securing Conviction   246

Six Essentials of a Good Presentation 247   How to Explain and Show Your Product to Its Best Advantage 251 *Features–Advantages–Benefits Technique 251 Role-Playing Helps 253 Discussion (Talking) 254 Demonstration (Showing) 255 Participation (Doing) 257*   How to Help Your Prospects Recognize and Accept Your Proposal 258 Arousing Desire 258   Persuasion and Motivation Are the Keys to Desire, Conviction, and Buying Action 261 *Motivation by Logic (Selling Through Logical Reasoning) 261 Motivation by Suggestion (Suggestive Selling) 262*   Suggestive Techniques That Can Help Prospects Convince Themselves 263   Summary 265

CASE STUDY 10
Convincing Proof Through Demonstration Wins the Sale of Electronic Jet-Engine Component 267

11 Principles and Techniques of Handling Objections   272

Why Are Objections Raised? 273   What Should Your Attitude Toward Objections Be? 274   Prior Planning Can Anticipate or Forestall Many Objections 275   Basic Strategy and Psychology for Handling Objections 276   How to Turn Objections into Sales 278   Six Techniques for Handling Objections 280 *Yes–But (Indirect-Denial) Technique 280 Question (Interrogation) Technique 280 Boomerang (Capitalization) Technique 281 Offset (Compensation or Superior-Point/Fact) Technique 282 Direct-Denial (Contradiction) Technique 282 The Pass-Over (Pass-By) Technique 283*   Points to Consider in Handling Objections 283   Standard or Common Objections You May Encounter 284   Price Objections 284 *Benefits That Help Justify Price 286 Techniques That Help Prove Value and Justify Price 286 Standard Replies to Common Specific Price Objections 288*

12   How to Close the Sale   305

13   The After-Sale Follow-Up and Follow-Through   326

15   In-Store Retail Selling   374

18   Sales Management and Selling   449

21 How to Program Your Career Toward Higher Earnings and Management 522

PREFACE

This can be one of the most personally helpful texts you have ever studied, or will study! Reason: A knowledge of how to sell your ideas and yourself as a person can help you attain success in sales or any other career, or in nonwork avocations involving close association with other people whom you hope to persuade or lead throughout your life.

This book is addressed to *you*—the individual student or reader, in a way that will unfold in the pages to follow. What you get out of it is strictly up to you. If you underline key passages and make notes on the pages to help study and restudy points presented, you will find this book useful to keep in your personal library and refer to time and again for years to come.

The following paragraphs will give you an overview of the approach and key concepts of the book, and show the many pedagogical aids designed to help students and instructors.

APPROACH AND KEY CONCEPTS OF THIS EDITION

Modern Applied Selling, is a carefully revised and updated new edition of the originally titled *Modern Applied Salesmanship*, first published in 1970 by Goodyear Publishing Company, then a wholly owned subsidiary of Prentice-Hall, Inc.

New reorganization and new topics introduced in this edition follow recommendations of many lecturers in personal selling from both two- and four-year colleges and universities in the United States and Canada. Among the major improvements resulting from this feedback are the following:

- Focus is increased throughout on a "how to sell" sales training approach.
- We integrate throughout the selling of products and services, both tangible and intangible, including products such as cause, person, idea, or anything else of value.
- Chapter 2, "Selling in the Marketing Environment," has been completely rewritten and updated.
- Chapter 3, "Buyer Behavior and the Psychology of Selling: to Individual Consumers and to Organizational Buyers" has been completely rewritten and expanded.
- A complete sales presentation example serves as lead-in to Part III's "Working the Plan: Steps in the Selling Process."
- Chapter 14, "Selling to Organizational Buyers," is new to this edition. It covers selling to buyers in the industrial, reseller, government, and services markets. It builds on Chapter 3 by stressing "how to sell" applications.
- Two chapters in this edition are devoted to the broad field of direct-to-consumer retailing and retail selling in this way: Chapter 15, "Instore Retail Selling," and Chapter 16, "Nonstore Retail Selling by Telemarketing, Direct Selling, and Service Providers; Trade Show, Sales Seminar, and Exhibition Selling."
- Far more dialogue illustrations are provided throughout in chapters and sales problems suited to classroom role-playing, and other types of in-class activities.
- Several chapters have been extensively reorganized, revised, and updated.

Overall, this edition remains a globally oriented, reader-centered career guide, covering both the "why" (theoretical) and "how-to" (applied) principles, practices, and techniques of modern selling in general and personal selling in particular.

The modern salesperson of the 1990s will have to be better educated and more managerially oriented in order to earn maximum financial rewards and greater opportunities for promotion. At all levels, he or she is playing an ever more important role on company or organizational marketing-management teams that start their planning with end-customers' needs, wants, and problems in mind. To help salespeople prepare, this edition offers the following features:

Managerial orientation is stressed throughout. The reader is taught that from the start he or she must learn to think like a manager by scientifically and practically learning to forecast, plan, establish procedures and programs, schedule work efficiently, and follow through in every way.

Principles with practical applications are carefully explained and illustrated through real-life examples and case studies. Although mostly presented from the point of view of those outside salespeople of any field who are concerned mainly with closing sales, the material is equally valuable to sales promotion or in-store retail salespeople, or to marketing representatives of not-for-profit organizations.

The modern international sales/marketing approach of customer/society oriented problem solving is emphasized. This concept starts with the needs, wants, and problems of the end-customer and works backward, seeking to create products or services that will be profitable and offer value and benefit to the individual consumer and to society. Numerical currency figures throughout the book are expressed in American dollars ($) unless otherwise noted.

Concepts from the behavioral sciences are discussed. What causes both individual consumers and organizational buyers to buy what they do when they do? Can research really anticipate individual and group buying behavior? The behavioral sciences, though not yet exact, have given us many valid generalizations about individuals, groups, social processes, and interactions over the years. These are presented so that the reader may recognize and know how to apply, whever possible, relevant, scientific principles of buyer behavior.

PEDAGOGICAL AIDS

This book employs the following pedagogical aids to help readers and instructors:

1. *Learning Objectives.* A short list of *learning objectives* precedes each chapter. These are target guides to the key concepts to be learned in each chapter, and they provide general checklists to use when you have finished that chapter.

2. *End-of-Chapter Summaries.* Each chapter ends with a summary that outlines the chapter's major contents.

3. *End-of-Chapter Questions.* Eight questions follow each chapter, serving to test comprehension of the material covered in that chapter.

4. *Case Studies and Sales Problems.* One case study and two sales problems follow each chapter, serving as a basis for written reports or class discussion. These add up to 21 case studies (nine of them new to this edition) and 42 sales problems (including four new to this edition). All retained case studies and sales problems have been revised and updated as necessary. Most are real-life examples from the business world, but some are fictional. Some are more detailed in concept than others.

   These case studies and sales problems are not presented in order of increasing difficulty, but rather to illustrate points covered in the preceding chapter. However, most also build on earlier chapters, so you will find that overall they offer progressive illustration of our unfolding study of principles, practices, and techniques of modern applied selling. Complete or partial answers to most of the sales problems can be found in the chapter material that they follow.

5. *Glossary of Sales Terms.* A comprehensive glossary of the most important and commonly used sales terms is provided for quick reference.

6. *Index.* An unusually comprehensive subject index to aid readers in quickly tracking down information within the text appears at the end of the book.

7. *Instructor's Manual.* A separate detailed instructor's manual is available to instructors who use this book as their class text.

ACKNOWLEDGMENTS

A text such as this is the product of years of experience working with others and in researching the writings of countless book authors and contributors to journals and periodicals. I can only hope that I have contributed my own 10 percent plus to what has been learned from them and that others in turn will build on this endeavor.

My first specific acknowledgments go to a handful of men who, in their own time, place, and way, taught me so much of what is at the heart of this book. They include the late Paul W. Ivey, Ph.D., whose inspiring classes in salesmanship (as it was then called) at the University of Southern California first opened my eyes to selling as a career; the late George L. McNelley, a grand ex-railroad engineer turned direct salesperson who taught me that cold-call selling is really "that adventure on the other side of the door"; and Richard P. Ettinger, Jr., the most conscientious and helpful field sales supervisor I ever worked under. The listing continues with Kenneth C. Matheson, of Australia, the most all around capable professional salesperson I ever had the pleasure of working closely with; Hillard H. McMullen, of New Zealand, whose high ethical principles and goals in selling and business serve as constant personal inspiration; and Kenneth Thurston Hurst, from whom I learned much about scientific management applications to selling and sales management.

My second special acknowledgments go to the following companies and organizations and their busy executives who were kind enough to help provide practical and meaningful case study materials: CBS News; CPC International, Inc., Electrolux Canada; Electrolux Corp.; Four Seasons Travel Agency, Inc.; Holland America Line Westours, Inc.; IBM Corporation; R.T. Reid Associates, Inc.; Shaklee U.S., Inc.; Singer Sewing Company; The Coca Cola Company; Thomas J. Lipton, Inc.; Tupperware Home Parties; and Volkswagen United States. I also wish to acknowledge assistance provided by permissions editors of the several book, magazine, and other type publications cited as sources of quoted material, and by columnist Ann Landers.

Acknowledgments are also due:

- To the following individuals who assisted in providing useful real-life text or case study material: Donald T. Caldwell, Laura M. Carter, George E. Frim, Tom Pih, Paul A.B. Poynton, and Robert L. Young.
- To the many able, talented Prentice Hall inhouse editors and specialists, and outside freelance copyeditors and designers, who worked so hard to produce this beautiful edition; and to the several academics who reviewed the manuscript. Also, and especially, to the two dynamic individuals who coordinated all that effort: Whitney Blake, Marketing Edi-

tor; and Jackie Jeglinski, Production Editor—both of Prentice Hall's College Book Division.

- To former undergraduate students of my evening "Principles of Selling" course at Rockland Community College, Suffern, N.Y., and "Sales Management" and "Organizational Behavior" courses at Saint Peters College, Englewood Cliffs, N.J., and graduate students of my evening M.B.A.-level "Sales Management and Distribution" courses at Fairleigh Dickinson University, Teaneck, N.J.—from whom I learned much.

My last and most heartful acknowledgment goes to my wife, Bessie, whose inspiration, encouragement, and long hours of critical reviewing, typing, and proofing helped make this book possible—and to whom it is lovingly dedicated.

Allan L. Reid
Colorado Springs,
Colorado, U.S.A.

PART ONE

CONCEPTS
OF
MODERN SELLING

Part One of our book shows how a knowledge of personal selling principles and techniques can lead to greater success in anyone's personal life and career, describes how selling and personal selling fit into the "big picture" of business and marketing, and explains how salespeople may affect the buying-decision process of both individual consumers and organizational buyers.

This information will help you better understand the managerial approach to our study of personal selling and the "how to" applications that follow.

1 The Challenge of Personal Selling in the 1990s

2 Selling in the Marketing Environment

3 Buyer Behavior and the Psychology of Selling: To Individual Consumers and to Organizational Buyers

The Challenge of Personal Selling in the 1990s

After studying this chapter you will be able to:

Explain the terms *selling, personal selling, persuasion,* and *sales/marketing.*

Describe how a knowledge of personal selling will help you attain success in either a sales or nonsales career throughout the 1990s, or in nonwork avocations involving close association with other people.

Summarize the kinds of careers available in selling and the advantages and monetary rewards each might offer in terms of your own interests, educational and experience background, age and career aspirations.

Answer the question, "What do I stand to gain from studying selling?"

Let us begin by talking about you, the reader—wherever you live in the world, whatever your age, sex, race, religion, or educational or experience background.

What kind of personal relationships with others do you hope for—to be liked, to influence others? What kind of career ambitions do you have—do you seek wealth, an interesting and challenging profession or job occupation, status, career advancement, an opportunity through your work or your nonwork avocational activities to make a contribution to society?

Have you ever been puzzled or confused by friends, family members, fellow students, or fellow workers' refusing to accept your ideas or opinions, or to behave or react in the way you expect? Have you secretly envied the success of others in any of these areas noted so far and wondered why success came to them and not to you? Would you like to be as popular or successful as they are?

Why begin a book on selling with questions like these? Simply because most of these things involve getting along with, working with, or leading other people, and selling, especially personal selling, as a study is basically concerned with influencing and persuading others. In fact, a course in selling, or your study of this book, could well be one of the most helpful and practical studies you will ever encounter, since it specifically relates to achieving personal, social, and career success.

PLANNING AND SELF-MANAGEMENT: KEYS TO GOAL ATTAINMENT

We are going to talk in this book about how you can plan your future work so as to achieve your personal goals—whether they be wealth, status, career advancement, or leadership. Our framework is personal selling; you must be interested in the possibilities of selling as an avenue for achieving your ambitions, or you would not have chosen to read this book. The principles we talk about relate to the achievement of success in business, industry, government, nonprofit organizations, and in any other occupations or avocations involving close association with other people. Along the way we constantly stress the importance of planning and self-management as keys to goal attainment.

In this first chapter we further discuss what you stand to gain from a study of personal selling as applied to any type of career or avocation you may follow, business or nonbusiness, and then consider the advantages of a possible professional sales career for achieving your goals.

But first, a word of warning! In spite of its very personal "you approach," this is a serious textbook on personal selling. You will have to think and study, and start putting into practice immediately many of the principles, practices, and techniques we discuss, if they are to mean anything to you. A good way to start, if you are not in selling already, is to try to get a part-time sales job now, so you can start practicing and developing skills. Personal selling is like swimming; you can read all about it yet know little about it until you have jumped into the water, started kicking, and developed skill through practice.

Another good way to get quickly involved in selling, provided that you are currently an American college student, is to join a local collegiate chapter of Pi Sigma Epsilon. This professional undergraduate collegiate fraternity, as of 1990 had 110 chapters in the continental United States, Hawaii and Puerto Rico. Membership is comprised of students interested in selling, sales management and marketing. Students from colleges or universities anywhere in the world who would like to start a chapter on their campus can find out how to do so by writing The Executive Director, Pi Sigma Epsilon, 155 East Capitol Drive, Hartland, Wisconsin 53029, U.S.A.

If you are unable to get a part-time sales job, or join a local Pi Sigma Epsilon chapter, then at least get in the habit, starting today, of observing retail salespeople at work whenever you buy anything and evaluating their actions in terms of your current study of personal selling. At the same time you can observe your friends and others "selling" their ideas, and practice the principles and techniques of personal selling that we will be studying in "selling" your own ideas to friends.

WHY STUDY SELLING, ESPECIALLY PERSONAL SELLING?

While we have already answered this question in part, let us consider the fact that literally everyone "sells" something—themselves, their ideas, services, or products. Actually, you started selling yourself immediately after birth, with your first lusty howl for attention. Throughout your life up to this point you have consciously and unconsciously sold yourself in many ways. And you must keep selling yourself—possibly proposing marriage, landing the career job of your choice, maybe even getting a loan at the bank, and in countless other ways—for the rest of your life.

Everyone sells. The politician trying to win an election has to sell voters on the idea that he or she is the best person to represent them; a minister or priest has to sell his or her religion (and sell the flock on the need for continued financial support).

The end result of any business venture, personal or corporate, is to profitably sell its products or services. Nonprofit organizations have to sell their ideas if they want public acceptance.

This "selling" takes place in literally every aspect of life where people have to live or work together—with subordinates, peers, bosses, customers, or anyone else with whom you personally or the company, organization, or group you represent has to collaborate or work with.

If selling is so important, how does one go about it? Answering that question is what the study of personal selling, and this book, is all about. You will learn how to sell—yourself, your ideas, and things—in the pages to follow, as we consider principles, practices, and some proven techniques of modern selling in general, and personal selling in particular, that apply not only to a sales career, but to any other career or noncareer associations involving other people with whom you might be associated in your lifetime.

WHAT DO WE MEAN BY SELLING AND PERSONAL SELLING?

Traditionally, most definitions of *selling* have been in the strictly commercial sense. The American Marketing Association, for example, defines selling as "the personal or impersonal process whereby the salesperson ascertains, activates and satisfies the needs of the buyer to the mutual, continuous benefit of both buyer and seller."[1]

Since selling is, as we have already noted, concerned with far more than things of commercial significance, here is a definition better suited to our needs.

> *Selling:* the process of analyzing potential buyers' needs and wants and assisting them in discovering how such needs and wants can best be satisfied by the purchase or acceptance of a specific product, service, idea, or anything else of value.

Authors have defined *personal selling* (formerly called salesmanship) in various ways: one definition holds that personal selling is the art of teaching or helping others to buy; another, that personal selling is the persuasive leadership that influences people to buy goods and services. A third and broader definition asserts that personal selling is learning customers' viewpoints and making them see yours by getting them to think or act. Here is a more precise definition for our purposes.

> *Personal selling:* selling that involves a face-to-face interaction with one or more prospective purchasers for the purpose of making sales.

PERSUASION IS CENTRAL TO PERSONAL SELLING

All the above definitions clearly indicate that *persuasion* is at the core of selling and personal selling. In fact, persuasion is central to decision making in most areas of life: professional, social, business, or political. A sale is made whenever two people disagree on a subject that is eventually resolved; one has persuaded, or sold, the other on his or her point of view. *Persuasion* means to move a person or persons to a belief, a position, a point of view, or a course of action.

Personal selling is the practice of selling, and if mere persuasion is the end objective, it can either be harmful or beneficial. But, as we shall discuss more fully in Chapter 2, modern selling and personal selling goes far beyond merely persuading another to accept your ideas or buy your product or service. It is also concerned with offering something of value and benefit that will result in *buyer satisfaction* and the *welfare of society*—highly desirable, worthwhile objectives.

[1] Peter D. Bennett, Ed., *Dictionary of Marketing Terms* (Chicago: American Marketing Association, 1988), p. 183.

IMPORTANCE OF KNOWLEDGE OF PERSONAL SELLING FOR NONSALES CAREERS

It Can Help You Land a Job of Your Choice in Any Career Field

One of the most important problems facing many college students is whether to pursue a college course that will train them for a specific job-related career field, or one that will provide a general liberal arts education. Many feel it more important to gain a broad background, yet as they begin to recognize that graduates who major in social sciences and the humanities often have difficulty in finding desirable jobs in those fields, they wonder if they might not have been better off to major in a job-related field.

United States Department of Labor reports and other services indicate that almost one out of five recent American college graduates are working in jobs unrelated to their major fields of study. As examples, one might cite cases such as a 1988 sociology major who is now an office receptionist in Chicago, an art history major who is working as an aide in a New York City law office, and an American studies major who is working as an assistant buyer in a Miami department store. Competition for choice positions in many career fields is likely to become increasingly fierce throughout much of the world during the 1990s due to probable continued international economic, energy, and political problems.

Many authorities blame colleges and universities for inadequate guidance and counseling in helping students learn more about the working world. A leading American Labor Department executive in a major city was quoted as saying, "Regrettably, many college youngsters today learn about career opportunities in the same way they learn about sex, through a peer process which differs only, perhaps, in that the classroom is not the street but the campus."

What do *you* stand to gain from studying personal selling? At the very least, a knowledge of how to *sell yourself* for a job of *your choice*; in Chapter 19 we discuss specifically how to accomplish that highly desirable objective. The examples relate to obtaining a sales position of choice, but the how-to-principles are the same for obtaining a job of your choice in any career field, regardless of college major.

It Can Help You Achieve Success in Many Nonbusiness Activities

Just as knowledge of personal selling can help you sell yourself for a job of your choice, so can it help you sell yourself or your ideas in many other ways throughout your life. The same basic principles of selling a product or service in a business sense also apply to the marketing or selling of other things, such as political, organizational (private or governmental), cultural, social, and cause ideas or programs. Let us consider a few such activities in which personal selling applies:

Political.   Candidates have to sell themselves to their constituents in order to get elected. They are the product, voters are the prospects (potential buyers), and the sales job is to persuade the voters that a particular candidate is the best one to provide leadership for putting into effect the type of laws they desire.

Organizational.   Churches, as an example of private organizations, spend a great deal of time and effort not only selling their faith, but also in persuading members to give financial support. The Billy Graham organization is well-known for its highly successful sales methods in selling its brand of religion worldwide. Many government organizations also actively sell ideas; the United States Travel Service, for example, was set up to sell foreigners on the idea of visiting the United States, as one means of earning dollars to help offset the flow of dollars spent abroad by American tourists.

Cultural.   Organizations, such as local symphony orchestras, have to seek basic financial support from government, business, and the general public. Their "sales presentation" in some countries may stress that donations from the latter two sources are tax-deductible. Private colleges and universities also constantly seek continued financial support by selling the long-term value of the institution to the local community.

Social.   Programs that will benefit society in general often have to be sold to the general public in order to gain widespread acceptance and support. Well-known campaigns in the United States include "Keep America Beautiful," "Smokey the Bear," and "Buy Bonds and Support America."

Cause.   Campaigns to warn of the health dangers associated with cigarette smoking, and antipollution campaigns mounted both by governmental and private organizations in many nations of the world are but two examples.

It is quite likely that sometime during your lifetime you will be engaged, individually or as part of an organized group, in "selling" one or more such nonbusiness ideas. This "selling" may embrace a "mix" (meaning the relative proportions of each type necessary to achieve success) of sales/marketing methods—advertising, publicity, sales promotion, and personal selling. Success will depend on persuading others to your point of view. Your current study of modern applied personal selling will help equip you to effectively participate in such activities and possibly even lead them to success.

It Can Help You Achieve Success in All Nonsales/Marketing Areas of Business

The purpose of any business, from a Mom and Pop corner delicatessen to a major corporation such as General Motors, is to make a profit. *Profit*, to any individual business person, is the difference between income received from *sales* and all *costs and expenses.*

If you eventually enter your own business, whether it be a shoe store or motel, or professional practice, such as accounting, brokerage, or management consulting, you will be vitally concerned with sales. If you work for a large firm or corporation, in whatever capacity, you should constantly be aware of, and help to attain, the overall profit-goal—the end result of the business enterprise.

Whether you enter into a business career on a self-employed basis or work for a small firm or large corporation as a manager, accountant, computer technician, or in production or in any other capacity, your current study of modern applied personal selling will help give you more awareness and understanding of the vital sales/marketing end of the business.

THE PROBLEMS OF CAREER SELECTION IN TODAY'S WORLD

The average young college student of today encounters a bewildering number of choices in making a career decision. Job counselors advise and common sense dictates that one plan a career in a growth industry in order to gain financial and material rewards. In 1900 the leather and buggy industries were excellent growth industries. Today, however, the electronic, scientific, and precision-equipment industries, to name but a few, have surpassed leather and buggies in growth potential.

The normal problems of career selection are compounded because we live in an unprecedented age of technological explosion and distribution revolution, affected by increasing world population, changing age structure with emphasis on youth, increasing population mobility, and in many of the world's countries, rising levels of income, education, and leisure. This means that the needs and wants of an expanding world population will continue to increase, and private or nationalized companies or organizations will be fulfilling the marketing function of supplying those needs. Marketing, as we further define in Chapter 2, is concerned with the many things that fall between manufacturing or producing goods or services and the ultimate consumer, with personal selling as perhaps its most important function.

Sales/Marketing. This is the term we shall use often throughout this book to integrate marketing and personal selling; it describes a growth area, providing unlimited career opportunities for you.

In order to take advantage of these opportunities, however, you will have to develop your knowledge and skills through study and practical application, and become managerially oriented. A major purpose of this book is to help you accomplish this. But first, let us see whether or not the possibilities of a sales/marketing career hold any real interest for you.

OVERALL THE SALES FIELD IS LARGE AND GROWING

The number of men and women engaged in sales or sales-related occupations worldwide is very large. In the United States, for example, out of a 1989 population of slightly over 246 million, over 13 million were so employed. And in Canada, out of a 1989 population of slightly over 26 million, some 1.1 million were employed in sales occupations. In most of the world's countries, current-year sales occupation employment figures and growth projections for the future can easily be obtained either from government sources or private industry trade associations. Worldwide, trends indicate that a sizable increase in the number of salespeople will be needed during the 1990s.

QUESTIONS TO BE CONSIDERED IN EVALUATING A CAREER IN SELLING

Let us start relating some of the previously mentioned trends to your specific desires and interests, to ascertain whether you should spend your remaining working years in the field of selling. If you are seriously interested in selling as your pathway to career success, you should seek answers to these questions:

1. What kind of careers are there in selling?
2. What kind of rewards and opportunities does a sales career offer?
3. What kind of education is necessary for success in selling?
4. What future economic and marketing trends will affect a sales career?
5. What are the advantages and disadvantages of a sales career?
6. What personal attitudes and characteristics are essential to success in selling?
7. Does a career in selling appeal to you?

In discussing these questions in this chapter, we are assuming (1) that you are ambitious and desire increased compensation and promotion during your working career, and (2) that you are interested in working as a real salesperson— one who will contact buyers, purchasing agents, or the public in order to sell products or services—or in retail selling.

WHAT KINDS OF CAREERS ARE THERE IN SELLING?

Various systems have been devised to classify sales occupations. One way is to classify specific types of selling by market type, such as to the consumer market, to organizational markets (industrial, reseller, and government), or to the service market. We shall learn more about these markets in due course.

Another method of classification is by the type of sales activity performed, such as (1) *order takers* (such as outside milk or bread route delivery salespeople or in-store sales clerks), (2) *missionary salespeople* (those who educate or build goodwill but don't actually sell), and (3) *real salespeople* (those why try to get new orders during sales calls).

Within these various classifications, men and women who sell are called by various names such as salesperson (the official U.S. Department of Labor term used to denote male and female sales workers), sales representative (or sales rep), sales consultant, marketing representative, or account representative.

For our purposes in this book, we will break the field of selling into two broad categories—*inside* and *outside*—in order to better treat some of the differences in approach and techniques between the two, and to place emphasis on the latter. The distinction between these two broad classifications is not always clear; some salespeople, for example, work on the floor in retail establishments part of the time and call on customers in their homes the rest of the time. But basically we can outline the following differences between these two broad categories as follows:

1.   *Inside salespeople* normally work inside stores, where customers come to them, or engage in selling by telephone from an inside central location.
2.   *Outside salespeople* call on customers or potential customers (called *prospects*) in their homes or offices.

We can make a further distinction between outside *real salespeople*—who are vitally concerned with closing sales on most calls—and those outside missionary, route, or promotions salespeople, whose company or organization policy may not require them to try to close a sale during every call or interview. While most of the specific techniques and examples in this book are addressed to real salespeople, much can be applied by the others to their own specific work.

In order to more clearly describe some of the major types of business-oriented selling careers, we will consider the following four generally accepted broad classification categories of salespeople: (1) manufacturers, (2) wholesalers, (3) retail, and (4) specialty.

Manufacturers' Salespeople

This category includes different types and specializations of salespeople calling on industrial concerns, on wholesalers, distributors, and dealers, and on direct consumers. Some specialize in pioneering new products or brands, and, since good producers are always in demand, they can earn excellent compensation if they can overcome the challenge of stiff competition. The following sales groups are included in this category.

Dealer-servicing salespeople call regularly on retail outlets in their territory, trying to write larger orders on each visit. For example, a salesperson for a hardware manufacturer brings new samples, checks stock, writes new orders, and even sets up window displays.

Sales-promotion salespeople specialize more in sales promotion than in taking on-the-spot orders. This category includes sales representatives of pharmaceutical houses, often referred to as *detailers*, who call on doctors, and publisher's representatives, who present information about new or future books to university professors.

Merchandising salespeople include those who arrange newspaper and television publicity, hold product demonstrations for distributors' salespeople, and even work with them in the field. Counselors for cosmetics companies are of this type.

Missionary salespeople work through wholesalers, jobbers, or distributors, whose own salespeople sell to the ultimate customers. An example is a home economist for a dairy cooperative, who sponsors demonstration classes for chain-store route or retail sales personnel.

Technical salespeople are often highly trained specialists or engineers who call on old or new customers to help solve their technical problems. The sales representative of a computer company, for example, has to be able to discuss entire systems and types of technical equipment that will best meet a customer's need.

Wholesaler's Salespeople

These men and women represent the jobber or wholesaler who carries stocks of many items from several different manufacturers. They serve the many retailers of other customers who find it more convenient to place one consolidated order for small quantities of many items than to send individual orders to all the manufacturers. Such a salesperson may represent a book jobber, who carries stocks of books from all publishers. He or she calls on libraries and perhaps displays a carefully indexed stock list or copies of publishers' catalogues; from these the librarian may order one copy of each of 100 books from 30 different publishers.

In-Store Retail Salespeople

The bulk of that portion of any national work force engaged in "sales occupations" is made up of in-store retail salespeople. They are behind the counters in retail establishments all over the world. Often low-paid and untrained, most can be classed as order takers rather than as salespeople in the true sense. Others, however, are highly trained, earn excellent income, and enjoy favorable opportunities for advancement to store or corporate-chain management. We discuss in-store retail selling at greater length in Chapter 15.

Specialty Salespeople

These men and women usually represent a single product or service, or a line of products or services that they sell by going directly to consumers, organizational end-users, or resellers. Here are some of the more common classifications of specialty salespeople:

- *Product or service salespeople* specialize in selling products or services used in the office or in the factory. They call on business or governmental purchasing officers or department heads, selling such things as computers, insurance, industrial or office machines, and training courses. Many salespeople in this area earn very high incomes, although in some cases they may have to work for years to make one large sale.
- *Inside-outside salespeople* are in a broad category that includes both those working from a showroom or office and outside, such as automobile or insurance salespeople, and those operating a personalized route or direct-mail service from their home. Many retail stores have outside salespeople who call either on the store's existing customers to sell them more, or on entirely new customer prospects at their homes. They usually try to sell by telephone expensive durable goods such as furniture, washing machines, vacuum cleaners, and television sets—

often bringing the interested customers back to the store to see the product. Most of the men and women in this sales category work on a straight commission or draw against commission, many of them earning very high incomes.

- *Direct salespeople* take their products directly to consumers' homes and workplaces, where they make sales presentations, frequently with demonstrations, for individual consumers or groups of prospective customers.

Throughout the world, direct selling adds up to big business. In 1989, by some estimates, direct selling worldwide accounted for over $35 billion in retail sales made by nearly nine million salespeople on six continents. Table 1.1 illus-

TABLE 1.1 *Direct Selling Was Big Business in these Countries During 1987*

Country	Approximate Total Retail Sales (in U.S. $)	Number of Full and Part-Time Direct Salespeople Employed
Argentina	$ 200 million	108,000
Australia	$ 450 million	160,000
Belgium	$ 70 million	25,000
Brazil*	$ 165 million	350,000
Canada	$ 325 million	275,000
Chile	$ 20 million	24,000
Finland	$ 35 million	900
France	$ 1 billion	240,000
Germany	$1.44 billion	145,000
Hong Kong	$ 20 million	15,000
Indonesia	$ 100 million	25,000
Ireland	$ 7.5 million	2,000
Italy	$1.76 billion	120,000
Japan	$17.5 billion	1 million
Malaysia	$ 240 million	209,000
Mexico	$ 233 million	359,000
Netherlands	$ 93 million	11,000
New Zealand	$ 100 million	25,000
Norway	$ 200 million	8,000
Philippines	$ 40 million	200,000
Singapore	$ 35 million	22,000
South Africa	$ 150 million	60,000
Spain	$ 380 million	82,000
Sweden	$ 150 million	22,000
Switzerland	$ 150 million	7,500
Taiwan	$ 60 million	150,000
Thailand	$ 22 million	140,000
United Kingdom	$ 765 million	255,000
United States	$8.79 billion	3.606 million
TOTAL	$34,500,500,000	7,646,400

Source: World Federation of Direct Selling Associations, WFDSA Secretariat, 1776 K Street, N.W., Washington, D.C. 20006.
* Brazil figures are from 1985.

trates the number of direct salespeople at work in 29 of the world's nations, and the sales volume (in U.S. dollars) they generated in 1987.

Direct selling offers great opportunity to men and women of all ages, no matter what their amount of education. Minor physical handicaps are no barrier. Direct salespeople can set their own goals and objectives, and work as much or little as they choose. They can elect to work year-around or on a temporary or seasonal basis. How they sell, via person-to-person and via party-plan methods, is discussed in Chapter 16, and in Case Study 1 at the end of this chapter.

Direct Selling Association, an American national trade association headquartered in Washington, D.C., has estimated that in 1988 their 100 member firms employed over 3.6 million full and part-time independent direct salespeople in the United States, whose domestic retail sales totaled $8.8 billion.

SELLING OFFERS MANY INTERESTING AND REWARDING CAREER POSSIBILITIES

Opportunities are there for you in any of the above traditional areas of selling, providing you are willing to put forth the effort and to follow the principles of personal selling outlined in this book. Good salespeople are constantly being sought by nearly every type of profit or nonprofit firm or organization, but it will pay to look carefully into the career opportunities offered by each.

Perhaps the most important thing to consider is the future growth potential of any given sales area. Many areas will experience tremendous growth during the 1990s. For example, sales of computers and office machines may triple; sales of industrial instruments and controls may double, and the chemical industry is expected to boom. Countries with expanding populations and rising income levels will see unheard-of new demands for housing, furniture, and household appliances of all types. And countries such as the United States and Canada, where increased life expectancy and rising income combine, will see far greater spending on sports, hobbies, entertainment, and vacations.

Selling during the 1990s offers a wide variety of interesting, worthwhile, and financially rewarding career possibilities. Successful salespeople in growth industries and areas will have unusually good opportunities for promotion to sales management and top executive rank. Much more is said about such opportunities and how to reach them via the sales/marketing route in Chapter 21.

WHAT KIND OF REWARDS AND OPPORTUNITIES DOES A SALES CAREER OFFER?

Intangible Rewards

Many employers have wisely observed that for many people money is not the chief motivating factor in life or in work; they would rather be happy in their work with a reasonable income than to work for money alone. Perhaps you should seek to combine both—work you enjoy in a financially rewarding area.

Most salespeople enjoy their work because they like the relative freedom of action, the fact that sales increases are a direct reflection of their own abilities, the quick recognition of such abilities, and the fact that opportunities for advancement in earnings or promotions are great. The sales-minded person enjoys the opportunities that such work offers to meet interesting people, to see what is going on in his or her industry or work area, and to be a participant rather than a desk-bound observer.

Opportunities to travel, the advantage of a probable expense account, and above all the challenge of matching wits with the prospective customer are all forms of compensation not readily found in nonselling vocations. Perhaps above all, truly motivated salespeople engaged in worthwhile, creative work they enjoy have the feeling that personal efforts can accomplish something now.

Monetary Rewards

The amount of money you can earn as a salesperson depends largely on what kind of selling area you enter, your educational background, the country, region, or area in which you work, and the compensation plan offered by your employer. It also depends on your level of experience.

One of the best sources of information on the earnings of American salespeople, as well as other interesting profile information, is compiled every two years by Dartnell Corporation, a well-known Chicago-based business publisher.

Figure 1.1 presents national averages on American salespeople from their 24th Biennial Survey published in 1988. This survey covers more than 300 companies with some 12,000 salespeople in 36 industrial classifications throughout the United States. Most of the companies represented by this survey sell to businesses rather than direct to end-consumers.

In comparing 1988 average incomes versus those of 1985 for salespeople representing three levels of experience, the Dartnell survey revealed that in 1988 *sales trainees* earned an average of $23,000, a 13.9 percent increase over 1985's level. *Semi-experienced salespeople* with one to three years of experience averaged $31,000 (a 5.1 percent increase over 1985), and *experienced salespeople,* with three or more years of experience, averaged $40,000 in 1988 (an 8.1 percent increase over 1985).

The "average range" figures in Table 1.2 do not include extreme range figures. In industries such as paper and allied products, textiles and clothing, primary metals, chemicals, and petroleum, earnings for experienced salespeople can run as high as $100,000 or more per year.

In general, the highest beginning wages tend to be paid to those having technical experience. Also, many areas within that collection of vocations loosely called the service industry offer potentially high salaries, especially at the experienced stage. Real estate sales is but one example of such areas; it is one where many salespeople earn very large incomes.

FIGURE 1.1   *Dartnell Profile: The American Sales Professional*[2]

Dartnell Profile
The American Sales Professional
National Averages

- 36 years old

- 82% male

- 18% female

- 81% some college or degree

- Most likely to leave after 4.7 years

- Average length of service—7.3 years

- Incentive Payment Frequency:
  Annual—15%
  Semi-Annual—5%
  Quarterly—26%
  Monthly—54%

- Automobiles:
  Company—29%
  Leased—21%
  Personal—54%

- Length of training— 6 months

- Sales call costs $56.68

- Sales calls per day— 5.5

- Number of calls to close—5

- Field expenses cost $14,666

- Value of benefits— $8,218

- Average sales volume—$1,579,707

- Spends 45 hours per week in selling activities

- Spends 15 hours per week in nonselling activities

- Trainee makes $23,000

  Semi-experienced makes $31,000

  Experienced makes $40,000

- Costs $14,435 to train

Copyright 1988. Compiled from *Sales Force Compensation— Dartnell's 24th Biennial Survey:* The Dartnell Corporation 1988.

[2] From "Sales Force Compensation—Dartnell's 24th Biennial Survey" @ The Dartnell Corporation, Chicago, Ill. 1988, p. 2.

Compensation Plans

There are three general compensation plans in selling. The first is the *straight-salary plan,* in which an annual fixed salary is paid, plus perhaps an annual bonus or prizes or merchandise not directly related to individual sales efforts. Second is the *straight-commission plan*, in which the salesperson is paid at a fixed or sliding rate in proportion to his or her sales or profit volume. This includes plans that offer a draw against commission.

The third and most widely used is the *combination-salary-and-commission plan*, which can have many variations. Such a plan may offer a salesperson two-thirds of his or her total compensation in salary and one-third in commissions or bonus in direct relation to sales or profit volume. Other combinations include a fixed salary plus a bonus for profitable sales above a fixed ceiling, or a salary plus profit-sharing. In 1989, well over half of all American and Canadian companies used some form of combination plan.

Expense accounts and fringe benefits must be taken into consideration when incomes from various sales positions are compared. Most companies and nonprofit organizations pay travel expenses; many provide automobiles; many reimburse salespeople for entertainment and other expenses. Fringe benefits can include paid vacations; free hospitalization; life, accident, and medical insurance; stock options; pension plans; superannuation; and profit-sharing. In the face of the high national income taxes in most countries, fringe benefits can be worth more than a larger salary. For example, profit-sharing funds, which may enjoy favorable capital-gains tax rates, may be more important to you on a career basis than more pay now.

Higher income can be earned by an American salesperson in some parts of the country than in others. For example, salaries are generally higher on the eastern seaboard in the New York to Boston region than in North or South Dakota. Also, many companies pay higher salaries at certain overseas posts than they do at home. The cost of living versus the take-home pay is an important consideration. A salesperson may enjoy a better standard of living in Sioux City, South Dakota than in crowded New York City, even though his or her income is considerably less.

Wherever they live, whatever area of selling they are engaged in, American salespeople earn better than average income; in fact, 50 percent better than the typical male worker, according to latest Census Bureau reports. It is not at all uncommon for a good salesperson to earn $50,000 per year or more, and the more one earns, the better it is for the company. The average income, incidentally, is higher than that for engineers, accountants, and those in many other business categories.

Readily available in North American college and large public libraries, and in many foreign libraries as well, is the excellent monthly *Sales & Marketing Management* magazine. Its annual special Survey of Selling Costs issue (normally published each February) especially, presents statistical comparisons about salary levels in different industries and many other items on the preceding year. These are then compared against same-type figures of earlier years. For college students and others considering selling as a career, or for anyone currently employed as a real, outside salesperson, this magazine should be a must reading.

IN THE UNITED STATES, SPECIAL OPPORTUNITIES EXIST IN SELLING FOR BLACKS, HISPANICS, ASIANS AND OTHER MINORITIES

In spite of the fact that in 1989 blacks numbered approximately 12 percent of the 246 million American population and Hispanics approximately 8 percent, these two minority groups were statistically underrepresented in the nation's sales-worker occupational category, especially at the "real salesperson" level. Greatly increased minority recruiting efforts by many business firms and nonprofit organizations, and federal laws and regulations calling for positive action to ensure equal employment opportunities have not produced the desired effect. In part, this situation stems from the fact that many blacks and Hispanic Americans view selling as a low-status career occupation. The same applies to Asians who in 1989 numbered just over 5 million and represented 2 percent of the population.

While equal and even exceptional opportunities are there, a sales career may present some psychological problems for some American minority-group individuals, apart from status. To be successful in selling, one must have a positive mental attitude. Personal selling works on a percentage basis; a salesperson hears "no" far more often than "yes." If, due to past psychological blocks, an inexperienced minority-group salesperson reacts to a "no" by attributing it to racial bias, then it may create a hostile potential buyer, or other problems, to the extent that initial failure can lead to more failures and even to rapid dissatisfaction with sales work. Success in selling for a minority-group person depends to a great extent on personal reaction to failure and a positive attitude toward life and work.

Studies indicate that minority-group members resent showcase hirings; they want to be hired, paid, and promoted on performance. Since higher earnings and promotion in selling are so dependent on results, selling offers you, if you are a minority-group American, unparalleled opportunities for rapid personal recognition and career success.

FOR WOMEN

In many of the world's industrialized countries, the 1980s will long be remembered as the decade of the emerging saleswoman. In no country has this been more evident than in the United States where, during this period, the proportion of women in sales increased from around 7 percent to over 18 percent.

While American women had long been visible in lower paid instore retail sales positions, they began to be hired in large numbers during the 1980s for countless other types of selling. They have rapidly filled sales positions from field salesperson to sales vice-president in such record numbers, and with results so encouraging, that by the mid-1990s nearly half the nation's sales managers may be women. Many have become leading performers in their fields, filling top corporate sales slots and earning six-figure incomes.

Increasingly today, ambitious young American and Canadian women especially are entering full-time selling due to the fast track promotional opportunities offered. U.S. Department of Labor statistics show that companies in the service and consumer products fields so far offer them the best sales career opportunities. Among these are the real estate, advertising, publishing, securities and financial industries. Many other industries, especially in the industrial area are still heavily male oriented, with few, if any, female salespersons. These include those such as aerospace, fabricated metal products, automotive parts, industrial chemicals and machine tools.

The decision to enter outside, on-the-road full time selling is often especially difficult for women who want to combine sales work with a somewhat normal family life. For women who wish for both children and a sales career, the direct selling field may provide the answer. In the United States, for example, Direct Selling Association figures show that during the late 1980s nearly 80 percent of active American salespeople in the industry were women. Their figures also show that over 88 percent of all active American direct salespeople work on a part time basis (less than 30 hours per week).

Regardless of whether they engage in full or part time selling, experts agree on what makes successful American saleswomen tick. The consensus is that they tend to be "highly motivated, detail oriented, flexible, creative, hard working individuals with outgoing personalities." Just the sort of words the experts also use to describe successful men in selling!

FOR MATURE ADULTS

As is the case in most Western European countries and Japan, the population of the United States is getting increasingly older. The U.S. Bureau of the Census projections show that by the late 1990s 10 percent of the American population will be over 65, including 100,000 people over the age of 100. As the labor pool of younger workers in the United States dries up, a result of the so-called "birth dearth" that began in the mid-1960s, ever more job opportunities are opening up for older men and women.

Although there is no legal or mandatory retirement age for workers in the United States, an increasingly high percentage of age 55 or older Americans are taking early retirement with the goal of a more interesting full- or part-time second career. Many of these men and women wish to continue working, not only to increase their income, but also to keep mentally and physically active. Certain 1988 U.S. Department of Labor studies showed that of the 2.8 million American workers who were 65 and older that year, about half held part-time jobs because they wanted to, not because they really needed the money earned.

Many American employers try to hire seniors whenever they can. One example is Home Depot, an Atlanta, Georgia-based chain of home improvement stores, which by 1989 employed 10 to 20 senior citizens as salespeople in each of its 90 stores. Another example is Texas Refinery, which has over 500 mostly part-time "seniors" among its salesforce of 2000, selling roof repair jobs to homeowners, and earning from $6000 to $30,000 annually on a commission basis.

As one executive put it, "Hiring older men and women for many types of sales positions makes good business sense. They are easily trainable, reliable, seldom get sick, don't have attitude hangups, make excellent supervisors, and have a stablizing role-model influence on younger employees."

WHAT KIND OF EDUCATION IS NECESSARY FOR SUCCESS IN SELLING?

We have already observed that certain industries pay higher starting salaries than others do. Most of these are in technical fields, so they naturally try to employ college-educated engineering or science graduates, to whom they have to pay high wages. But it is not only the technical fields that seek well-educated salespeople. Most industries seem willing to pay more for better education, and most companies within these industries are looking for applicants with at least some college or university background.

Media articles of recent years concerned with campus recruiting activities of well-known American business and industrial companies reflect a consensus that companies are looking for "outstanding achievers" with academic majors directly related to various specialized jobs for the better career positions being offered. Engineering, accounting, chemistry, math/statistics, sales/marketing, and economics/finance majors are reported in greatest demand. General business majors are acceptable and are being hired in large numbers, as in previous years, and late 1980s trends showed that interest in liberal arts majors is on the increase.

For sales positions, trends indicate a preference for applicants with a broad liberal education plus a good background in the behavioral sciences and business, marketing, and advertising. Study of quantitative methods, statistics, and applied mathematics may be necessary for future key managerial positions.

What is the future in selling for those who have not had or will not have a higher education? For those who do not have the time or money to spend on a four-year college or university degree, there is also hope. Community colleges, technical schools, and universities are all offering adult night classes geared to the needs of local business, government, and industry. Executives of local institutions or firms teach many of these courses. Programmed instruction has speeded up the learning process in many areas, and many of these courses can be studied at home. Company training programs are increasing, and more companies than before are paying all or part of evening-course tuition for ambitious employees.

Sales opportunities that do not require a high level of education exist in the expanding areas of direct selling, service agencies of all kinds, and franchise plans, in which management is provided for a self-owned and self-run business.

WHAT FUTURE ECONOMIC AND MARKETING TRENDS WILL AFFECT A SALES CAREER?

We have already noted some of the major changes that will affect selling in North America and the rest of the world throughout the 1990s and into the twenty-first century. These include the continued technological and communications revolution, increased automation, and fast-moving changes in the world's marketing and distribution environment. Most of these trends involve bigness in everything—larger and more complex marketing programs by fewer big companies and more complex and sophisticated roles for salespeople.

Business itself will be only one of the factors or institutions in this environment that will change or affect marketing. Government, for example, affects economic and marketing trends. High-level government officials in many countries are increasingly assigned the task of organizing groups of executives from business and industry to tour the world seeking new markets for national products, new areas for investment, and new ways to export national knowledge and skills. In effect, these teams are selling their national products to a world market, and their leaders have to be sales representatives in a very real sense.

In all these areas, personal selling will continue to play a vital and important role. Some economists feel that personal selling plays a key role in the world's economy. The spotty success of discount houses in the United States is but one proof that price alone is not the secret of successful selling. Offering real economic value helps, but just as important is the communication between salespeople and customers. The need and opportunities for good salespeople will continue to increase simply because people still do the buying, and people like to interact with other people. Vending machines and computers cannot do this, but you, as a salesperson, can.

ADVANTAGES AND DISADVANTAGES OF A SALES CAREER

The proper choice of a career is one of the most important steps you will ever make. A major purpose of this book is to help you decide wisely whether selling is the best vocation through which you can reach your own career goals. Different people have different needs and abilities, and if you enter a profession or vocation in which you will not find personal job satisfaction, then you probably will not be successful. You will waste your time, that of your employer, and that of prospective customers you may call upon. With this in mind, let us briefly examine some of the disadvantages as well as review the advantages offered by a sales career.

Disadvantages: Why Do Some Salespeople Fail?

Surveys indicate that in a high percentage of American, British, Canadian, and Australian industries and companies about 20 percent of the salespeople produce about 80 percent of the business. In addition, 10 to 30 percent of the sales force

What Personal Attitudes and Characteristics Are Necessary for Success in Selling?

21

does not even pay its own way. Many of the salespeople in this latter group either have to be dismissed or leave the selling field of their own volition—failures in either case.

Why do so many salespeople fail at such great cost to their employers and loss of time and self-confidence to themselves? Here, in descending order of importance, are the major reasons:

Primary Factors

1. Lack of planning ability and time utilization; that is, poor work habits.
2. Lack of industriousness and drive.
3. Lack of resourcefulness and aggressiveness.
4. Lack of observation, an eye for sales possibilities, and vision.
5. Lack of self-evaluation and self-development.
6. Lack of self-confidence and enthusiasm; that is, too easily discouraged.
7. Lack of ambition or desire to succeed.
8. Ineffective calls; could not develop interest-getting sales presentations.
9. Inability to handle objections; slow, uncreative thinker.
10. Inability to develop successful closing techniques.

Secondary Reasons

1. Would not work hard or steadily enough.
2. Had an unstable or immature personality.
3. Could not assimilate training.
4. Needed more money now.
5. Lacked good human relations abilities.
6. Felt that a different type of job offered more security.
7. Did not like to sell.
8. Had too many outside interests apart from work.

In view of the above facts, let us be honest, not negative, and review a few of the personal reasons why some people do not enjoy selling as a career and fail as salespeople. Many men and women, for example, prefer a 9 A.M. to 5 P.M. job in which they can follow a set plan or procedure established by others. Many of them do not like to make constant decisions on their own, and many more want a job they can forget except during working hours. Many people dislike travel, even in a restricted territorial area, and even if the individual does like it, his or her spouse may not. Many do not like the constant pressure of meeting or even thinking about meeting sales budgets or planned objectives.

Perhaps the basic cause of most individual failure in selling, however, is a psychological inability to meet the challenge of constant face-to-face contact with people in a situation in which the salesperson is trying to persuade the other to make a decision. Personal selling is not visiting and talking about weather; it is hard physical and mental work. Most people basically do not want to make decisions, to change their attitudes or routines, or to buy anything. They constantly object to doing this or that. A face-to-face sales presentation can basically end in only two ways: the salesperson sells the prospect—persuades him that it is in his or her interest to buy—or the prospect sells the salesperson on the idea that he or she is not buying. If you get discouraged easily and cannot keep up your positive, optimistic, cheerful, desire-to-be-helpful attitude after days of no's, then selling is not the career for you.

Advantages

The advantages of a sales career, some of which were noted earlier, are just the opposite of the disadvantages cited above. If you enjoy being your own boss, like having relative freedom of action to do the job your own way, like the constant challenge of meeting people, thrive on personal challenge, enjoy travel, and appreciate the idea of your own abilities being recognized more rapidly through increased income and possible chances for promotion, then selling may be just the career for you. If you want to get to the top in business and industry, selling is perhaps the best vehicle, because the decisions you make in managing your sales territory are very closely akin to those faced by top executives and decision makers in the professions, government, industry, and business.

WHAT PERSONAL ATTITUDES AND CHARACTERISTICS ARE NECESSARY FOR SUCCESS IN SELLING?

By now you should have some idea of whether or not a career in selling appeals to you. If so, you may wonder whether or not you have the necessary personal attitudes and characteristics to achieve success in this career.

The basic key to success in selling or in any other career field, of course, as in life itself, is within you. If you have a strong desire to succeed, and a positive approach to life and work, then you probably can and will succeed. If you really want to get ahead via a sales career, it can be done—regardless of your age, sex, educational level, social or financial position, national or racial origin. It can be done provided that your attitudes toward life and work are realistic, and that you possess certain basic personal character and human qualities. Among these are the following:

Basic Character Qualities	*Basic Human Qualities*
Ambition	Personality
Self-discipline	Loyalty
Persistence	Empathy and tact
Dependability	Sincerity
Courage	Cheerfulness
Initiative	Willingness to cooperate
Stability	Positive mental outlook
Thoroughness	Enthusiasm

To be truly successful in any career, you must have a positive attitude toward life in general and toward your work in particular. In selling especially, you must believe strongly in the value of the work you do. If you do not, it will show in your attitude—and in your sales volume. In the final analysis you are the only one who can honestly rate your personal attitudes in light of the basic character and human qualities we have noted. Table 1.2 is a sales aptitude self-

TABLE 1.2 *Sales Aptitude Self-Evaluation Chart*

	Needs Improving	Average	Strong Asset	Very Strong Asset
Pleasant personality				
Even temperament				
Good appearance				
Analytic ability				
Memory for faces and details				
Vocabulary and word usage				
Harder than average worker				
Self-confidence				
Persuasiveness				
Ability to make friends				
Original and creative ideas				
Competitive attitude				
Persistence				
Accepts criticism and advice				
Problem-solving ability				
Practical-minded				
Poised and self-assured				
Adaptability				
Sincerity				
Sales ability				
Determination to succeed				
Reliability				
Enthusiasm				
Ability to learn quickly				
Good listener				

The table includes many of the basic personal attitudes and characteristics essential to success in personal selling. You can rate yourself by filling out the self-evaluation blanks alongside each one listed. Based on those, does your overall self-image evaluation indicate that you might be successful as a salesperson? It is important that you first ask this question of yourself, since you are the only one who knows the real you.

evaluation chart. If you take the time now to honestly fill in its blanks, it may help you assess your aptitude for a sales career.

DOES A CAREER IN SELLING APPEAL TO YOU?

The choice of whether or not to consider a sales career is up to you—the opportunities, advantages, disadvantages, and what it takes to succeed have been fairly presented. From here on we will study the history and development of sales/marketing and the principles, practices, and techniques of modern applied personal selling. Even if you do not elect to follow a sales career, this study will help you in many ways throughout your life and work, as we have indicated. If you are interested in selling as a career, you will learn how to become a truly professional salesperson—plus, if you have the ability, drive, and determination, how to get right to the top as a highly paid salesperson or executive.

SUMMARY

In this chapter we have defined *selling* and *personal selling* and indicated the importance of a knowledge of personal selling in attaining success in both sales or nonsales careers, or in nonwork avocations involving close association with other people whom you might hope to persuade or lead throughout your life. We considered the kinds of professional careers available in selling, the rewards (both intangible and monetary) to be expected, the special opportunities in selling for women, minorities, and older people, and the advantages and disadvantages of a sales career.

Questions for Analysis and Discussion

1.   What is the meaning of the word *persuasion* as it applies to selling in general and to personal selling in particular?

2.   At this point, what do you feel you personally stand to gain from your current study of personal selling, as related to your past experience in life and work, and your future plans?

3.   Describe the selling activities of any two nonbusiness organizations in your local community with which you are personally familiar, or have read about or heard about from parents or friends. What additional selling activities do you feel each could do to enjoy greater success?

4.   Assuming that your father owns a retail business in your local community that you plan to enter and eventually take over and manage, what do you feel you can gain from your current study of selling that might help you increase profitability of the business?

5.   Define, in your own words, the meaning of *selling, personal selling,* and *sales/marketing.*

6.   Job counselors advise that in order to achieve personal happiness and the best chances of financial security and professional growth in any specific career field, one

should consider the intangible as well as tangible rewards that the career field offers. What is the meaning to you of the terms *intangible* and *tangible* rewards, in terms of your own objectives and expectations?

7.   We have said that responsible sales positions in the United States today are opening rapidly for women, blacks, and other minority-group members. If you are an American, have you observed this happening in your local community over the past two years? If so, explain. If not, why do you feel it has not happened in your area, since national trends clearly show the statement to be true?

8.   Do you feel at this point that a sales career might interest you? What opportunities through selling do you now see for yourself? What type of selling appears of most interest to you now, and why?

Successful Tupperware, Shaklee, and Electrolux Canada Salespeople Illustrate Direct Selling's Profitable Career Potential

Direct selling is big business worldwide, with nearly 9 million full and part-time salespeople on six continents accounting annually for over $35 billion in retail sales. It is a field of selling that offers great opportunity for men and women of all ages and levels of education to quickly become well compensated, self-employed, independent businesspeople. To learn more about this industry, let's take a brief but factual look at the following three internationally respected direct sales companies: Tupperware Home Parties, Shaklee Corporation, and Electrolux Canada.

TUPPERWARE HOME PARTIES

Kissimmee, Florida-based Tupperware Home Parties, the world's largest party plan sales company, is also the world's leading manufacturer of high-quality plastic housewares such as food-storage and serving containers. Each of the company's over 200 products, including toys, comes with a full life-time warranty for normal noncommercial use that supports the well deserved tradition of quality of Tupperware.

All sales are made through the company's worldwide independent direct sales force of an average 89,000 dealers and managers in the United States, and an average 325,000 dealers and managers in 42 other countries. Tupperware today, as it has for many years, continues to outsell all American competitors combined by a two-to-one margin in the over $1 billion U.S. plastic-food-container market. Over half the company's more than $900 million total sales comes from outside the United States.

The key to the success of Tupperware is a highly motivated sales force composed of distributors, franchised in the United States, and dealers and managers who are independent contractors. Front-line spark plugs in the sales effort are the dealers and managers who organize "Tupperware parties" in homes, offices, at fund-raising events of all types, and via neighborhood or shopping center "tailgating parties" where they make "demonstrations" to passersby from their cars.

For home parties, dealers prospect (look) for individuals who agree to "date a party" (arrange one) for both male and female friends in their homes in return for a gift of Tupperware products based on attendance and sales. The Tupperware dealer puts on a "demonstration" (sales presentation), gives out plastic items like spoons or orange peelers to everyone attending, and writes up orders to be fulfilled a few days later.

Since so many North American women now work, more and more selling of Tupperware brand products in the United States and Canada is being done via alternative party formats and locations. "Office parties," for example, are those held physically on premises in the work environment, and "rush hour parties" are those held after work. "Stop and shop parties" are those where demonstrations to individuals are given as they drop in or stop by to look at the product line.

Selling Tupperware products is considered fun, as well as financially rewarding. American dealers, as an example, average from $7.00 to $12.00 per hour, and can qualify for valuable gifts. Their income is based on the time they commit, level of effort, and selling skills. Since each dealer is his or her own boss, dealers can increase their income at any time—just by holding another demonstration!

American dealers can qualify to "promote-out" to manager by meeting these three requirements: (1) have three active dealer recruits, (2) have $3000 in total unit sales (personal sales plus sales of all active recruits) during the four weeks prior to "promoting-out," and (3) have a solid personal party lineup. Some American Tupperware managers have six-figure incomes, and qualify for a variety of performance-based awards including use of a car or van, trips, furniture, and other gifts.

In addition to a good income and valuable gifts, Tupperware dealers and managers alike are able to set their own hours, and own their own businesses.

SHAKLEE CORPORATION

Shaklee Corporation, with overall annual sales in the $600 million range, is a highly regarded international family of companies consisting of Shaklee, U.S., Inc., Shaklee Japan, K.K., Shaklee Canada, Inc., and Bear Creek Corporation. The first three of these sell a broad range of nutritional, household, and personal-care products, plus other specialty lines, directly to consumers by a sales force of male and female independent distributors located in their respective countries.

Bear Creek Corporation, a Shaklee subsidiary, includes Harry and David, the largest American direct mail marketer of fine fruits and gourmet foods, and Jackson & Perkins, the leading direct mail rose plant company in the United States.

The late Dr. Forrest Shaklee, a chiropractor, who founded the company in 1956 to gain wider distribution for "natural" nutritional food supplements he had developed, based his business philosophy on the Golden Rule. Integrity and fairness are thus stressed in the code of ethics to which company salespeople are expected to adhere. Those wishing to join the U.S. company (as a Member) have to

be "sponsored" by someone who is already a Member of the sales force, called the Shaklee Family. The only entry requirement is a $6 two-year membership fee, which includes a subscription to *ALIVE!* magazine, product catalogues, and discounted prices for catalogues.

Distributors are urged to use Shaklee products before selling them, based on the theory "One cannot successfully sell a product he or she does not believe in."

Advancement progression for a new Member, based on sales and recruitment of new Members, follows this progression: Member Distributor, Supervisor, Coordinator, Senior Coordinator, Key Coordinator, Senior Key Coordinator, and Master Coordinator. In order to make life a little simpler, all title-holders from Supervisor through Master Coordinator are called "Sales Leaders." In the late 1980s Shaklee, U.S. had around 225,000 Member Distributors, mostly part-timers, and some 6500 full-time Sales Leaders. Everyone up through Master Coordinator is an independent businessperson as opposed to being company employees. Top national and regional sales managers are company employees.

The company does not have assigned sales territories; Shaklee distributors are free to sell when and where they like. Their selling is done one-on-one to individuals or to groups—in homes, schools, health clubs, and elsewhere—with a soft-sell "educational" approach.

Salespeople buy products from Shaklee distribution centers at an average 30 percent discount. Besides profit on sales, the company offers generous bonuses and life and medical insurance at low group rates. Credits toward the leasing of bonus cars are based on purchase volume. A sizable number of the Master Coordinators of the U.S. Shaklee family earn gross income well into six figures. Usually, these top earners are husband-and-wife teams.

Shaklee Corporation is especially proud of the fact that many of Shaklee Japan's 4500 dedicated and hardworking "Sales Leaders" are women. Direct selling in that country offers one of the few ways for a woman to pursue an independent, financially rewarding career.

ELECTROLUX CANADA

Electrolux had its North American beginnings back in 1924 when Gustaf Sahlin, an immigrant, brought a vacuum cleaner from his native Sweden to the United States in search of an importer. Today, from its headquarters in Atlanta, Georgia, the company offers a complete line of floor-care products, including vacuum cleaners, combination rug shampooer/floor polishers, a central vacuum cleaning system, and other associated products for home and commercial or industrial use. All products are manufactured in the United States. It also provides the industry's largest North American maintenance/repair service network to back these products.

Electrolux floor care products in North America are sold direct to the consumer by approximately 23,000 company-trained field sales representatives (approximately 40 percent of whom are women), operating through nearly 750 branch stores in the United States and Canada. Since 1987 Electrolux has been owned and managed by senior managers, most of whom have spent their entire working careers with the company.

Electrolux Canada, with approximately 5000 full- and part-time salespeople, is one of the largest direct sales forces of its kind in Canada, which has a population of around 26 million people. Since establishment of its door-to-door sales force in 1930, the direct sales approach is still the company's main focus of merchandising, and still the most successful (accounting for some 70 percent of sales).

Its sales representatives have independent dealer agreements and operate out of nearly 200 retail store branch offices located across Canada. Each branch has a sales manager, service technician, and secretary. Along with a fully equipped service department, the branch has both a sales meeting room and a display room. After-sale follow-through service has always been a key element in Electrolux's sales success—offering service directly to the consumer's home. This has led to repeat sales and referral leads adding up to over 40 percent of sales year after year.

The company's carefully designed sales training programs at sales representative, branch sales manager, and divisional sales manager levels have helped Electrolux achieve a much greater long-term employee retention percentage than is common in the direct sales industry. Annual gross earnings for full-time sales representatives average CAN $30–70,000, with the leaders earning CAN $100,000 or more. Average branch sales managers' annual gross earnings fall within the CAN $50–160,000 range.

Thorough training, along with excellent commission income potential, bonuses for increased sales and recruitment of new people, and other ongoing incentives, has consistently enabled the company to attract many college graduates to make Electrolux their career.

Electrolux Canada, as the leader in its industry, prides itself on the quality of its products and service, and on the quality of the sales organization that drives it.

Questions for Written Reports or Class Discussion

1. If, as a Tupperware dealer, you drove "cold" to a community street fair with a car full of Tupperware products and rented space from the fair organizers for a "Tailgate Tupperware Party," how

would you go about setting it up and attracting prospects (possible buyers) from among the fairgoers?

2. How would you, as a part-time Tupperware dealer or Shaklee distributor, go about organizing an after-work "rush hour party" aimed at selling your company's products to fellow office or factory workers?

3. Do you feel that direct salespeople should be granted "exclusive sales territories" by their company, or be allowed to sell when and where they like in competition with fellow company salespeople? Explain your reasons.

4. Based on material presented in this case study, which one of the three direct sales companies discussed do you feel that you would prefer to represent? You must select one of them, and explain your reasons.

Sales Problem 1.1   Will my liberal arts degree be worthless in a job market that is increasingly technically oriented?

Linda Brady, a senior psychology major at a well-known California, U.S.A. state college, has just asked this question of a business executive friend of her father's. Let's listen to his answer, and a bit more of their conversation.

Executive: A liberal arts degree represents a well-rounded education, plus a lot more. But will it help you land any particular job? The answer to that is not so simple. Your psychology degree can work for you—if you make it work for you.

Linda: I don't quite understand what you mean.

Executive: Your first task is to uncover the *hidden skills* implicit in your degree, skills that are useful—even crucial—to most businesses. Then you must determine who needs those skills, and *sell* them to the highest bidder, emphasizing that you are the prize.

Linda: With so many of my college friends graduating with degrees in business administration, what skills can I, as a psychology major, hope to offer business firms with whom I might seek employment, in order to be able to compete?

Executive: Well, let's try to jot a few ideas down on this piece of paper under the heading "Selling Points." I'll start with these two (he writes down the following):

1. Adaptability—the general and broad-based nature of my liberal arts degree program has trained me to think critically and reflectively in ways that can be useful in almost any type of job situation.

2. Problem-solving ability—my liberal arts training has given me the ability to define and to solve problems.

Linda: I see what you are getting at. How about these additional two "selling points?" (she writes the following):

3. Broad perspective of life—in my psychology courses, I studied the dynamics of interpersonal relationships; and in the sociology courses I took, I learned to understand group dynamics.

4. Ability to communicate—through training in English courses and practice in my liberal arts classes, I learned good written communication skills. And through training in two speech classes, plus participation in several student organizations, I also learned techniques of effective oral communication.

Executive: The ability to communicate effectively is very important to prospective employers, Linda. The transmission of growing masses of information has become a major problem of business life. Job applicants may have all sorts of degrees, but if they can't speak good English or write a clear, concise memo, letter, or report, forget it! Your good written and verbal skills may prove to be your strongest selling point.

Linda: You've really helped me come up with specific selling points that can help me sell myself for some position with either a business firm or nonbusiness organization. The best jobs in this area seem to be with business firms. The question now is, what kind of job should I go after? I haven't had any business experience.

Executive: We have a good list of selling points to start with, but—how well do you like people? You belonged to several student organizations, and that's good. But would you like to work with people constantly, or would you rather work pretty much alone at an inside office job?

Linda: Oh, I want to work with people. I enjoy meeting new people.

Executive: Linda, I think you should aim for a career in the sales/marketing field. The large number and broad diversity of tasks to be done—marketing is the total activity of getting a product or service to the buyer—make it an area that offers, I feel, unusually good career opportunities for you.

Linda: That sounds interesting. But what specific types of position should I apply for?

Executive: I would suggest a sales position. It's the best place to learn about the total business process. Later on, you might go into more specialized areas such as a marketing product manager, or advertising associate.

Linda: Okay, now that I have something specific to go after—a sales position—how do I get one?

Executive: Later I'll suggest some growth areas and specific firms within them to check out. For now, however, I must stress that the best way to get a job of choice is to "sell yourself." Due to your limited work experience, potential—your potential for growth—is what you must sell now.

Linda: You've been very helpful. Thank you.

Questions for Written Reports or Class Discussion

1.   What other "selling points" can you add to Linda's list that a college liberal arts major background might offer in helping her obtain a desirable sales position with a business firm?

2.   Do you agree with the executive's comments that a sales position might be perhaps the best place to start a business career? Explain your reasons.

3.   From what other sources can Linda now explore possible need by business firms for "hidden skills" implicit in her liberal arts degree?

4.   How might Linda "prove" her written communication skills to a prospective employer when she appears for employment interviews?

Sales Problem 1.2	In evaluating applicants for sales positions, which of the following characteristics would you, as a sales manager, consider the most important?

The point was made on page **23** that "if you really want to get ahead via a sales career, it can be done—regardless of your age, sex, educational level, social or financial position, national or racial origin. It can be done provided that you possess certain basic personal character and human qualities" (some of which were listed).

To carry this line of thought further, let us assume that you are a sales manager now judging a number of applicants for an open position on your sales force. You have listed the following ten characteristics that you consider to be the most important in a new salesperson. This listing is in random order, so you are now trying to rate them in descending order of importance on a scale of 1 to 10. You have already rated the four lower ones (as shown below), and are now engaged in filling out your rating-rankings for the remaining ones.

_____ High persuasiveness	__9__ Follows instructions
__10__ Apparent sociability	__8__ Highly recommended
_____ Enthusiasm	_____ High verbal skill
_____ Well organized	_____ General sales experience
_____ Obvious ambition	__7__ Specific sales experience

Questions for Written Reports or Class Discussion

1.   How will you complete the ranking? Do so by filling in the blanks.

2.   If you had to choose from among the applicants on the basis of only *one* of the above attributes, which would it be? (Note: your answer here need not necessarily be the same as your number 1 in the list above.)

Selling in the Marketing Environment

After studying this chapter, you will be able to:

Explain important sales/marketing and management terms such as *market, marketing, marketing concept, market potential, sales potential, marketing/mix, management by objectives,* and *sales* and *expense budgets.*

Identify three major types of organizational customer markets, and describe some key ways that consumer markets can be segmented.

Name the four parts of the "promotion mix" of marketing, and describe the role and basic employment of each.

Describe how business firms go about planning, organizing, directing, and controlling their sales/marketing activities.

Relate key concepts of modern management theory to the role of a salesperson acting as a "market manager" of his or her own sales territory.

ow does selling, especially personal selling, fit into the big picture of business in general, and marketing (a function of business) in particular? How do business firms plan, organize, direct, and control their selling activities in today's fast-changing marketing environment? These are questions that must be considered before we can talk about personal how-to-sell principles and techniques. This is especially true since one of the goals of this book is to help you learn to "think like a manager" right from the start in our study.

Your initial reaction as a reader may be to wonder why we start certain sections in this chapter with some quite basic aspects of economics, business, marketing, and management when this is a book about personal selling. If you have taken basic college courses in such subjects, these aspects may already be familiar to you. For readers who have not taken such courses, however, knowledge of these will aid understanding of the managerial concepts and applications that will fill many of the pages to follow.

MARKETING—A FUNCTION OF BUSINESS

The science of and the study of *economics* is concerned with the production, distribution, and consumption of goods and services. It is also, in the political economic sense, concerned with the welfare of mankind.

The term *business* in the economic sense relates to the buying and selling of goods and services; in the commercial sense it relates more to a person, partnership, or corporation engaged in manufacturing, commerce, or service. In both senses the term *business* technically relates to profit-seeking activities, although nonprofit organizations are commonly described as "in the business of" delivering whatever service they are organized to provide. For example, The Bureau of the Census, a common governmental agency in most countries, is in the business of collecting and disseminating population statistical information.

In practice, business (in the profit-making sense) is the whole system of interrelated activities acting together to make goods and services available in the marketplace. These activities are conducted both within the business enterprise, called a "firm," and between the firm and the environment.

The marketplace is the central focus of all business activities. It is here, in competition with other sellers, that a seller presents his goods and services to customers. It is here that consumers register their "votes" (through buying or not buying) and register changing wants and preferences. Over three-fourths of all the goods and services produced by business in the United States, for example, are in response to consumers' demands expressed by over 246 million Americans in the marketplace. These consumers, allocating their incomes to fulfill their needs and wants, provide basic signals to business producers telling what consumers want produced.

Business is carried on via several functional areas—production, marketing, finance, purchasing, planning, and administration. Of these, marketing activities are particularly vital, since they are so directly concerned with sensing, stimulating, serving, and satisfying consumer demands.

THE NATURE, DEVELOPMENT, AND FUNCTIONS OF MARKETING

Marketing can be defined in several ways. One definition holds that it is the performance of business activities that directs the flow of goods and services from producer to consumer or user. Another broader definition describes it as involving those activities necessary to assure that the right goods and services are moved efficiently to satisfied customers through the right channels, at the right price, and that the right promotional combinations are used.

Professor Philip Kotler, one of today's most globally respected authorities on marketing, goes further by reasoning that marketing occurs when people decide to satisfy needs and wants through "exchange"—in his opinion, the key concept of marketing. In this view, "exchange" is the act of offering something (goods or products, services, ideas, or other objects) in return for something desired. He favors, and we will accept, the following definition—one rooted in human behavior:

> *Marketing* is a social and managerial process by which individuals and groups obtain what they need and want through creating and exchanging products and value with others.[1]

Markets and Market Segmentation

To sales/marketing people, the marketplace is made up not of one single market for goods and services, but rather of many different types of markets and market segments. A *market* can be described as the total or aggregate demand of actual and potential buyers of a product, service, or anything else of value; *aggregate* is the composite demands of many consumers for a specific item. Within the total or aggregate demand are *market segments*, or groups of potential buyers who demand specific different requirements for the same item.

For example, the aggregate demand for automobiles is made up of several market segments—sports cars, small economy cars, large luxury sedans. Thus a market is not only an aggregate demand for a product or service, but the sum total of demands of several different market segments.

In trying to fulfill customers' needs and wants, sales/marketing people carefully study changing market and market segment demands and trends in order to produce and effectively sell what will satisfy different groups of current and potential buyers. This is done within the broad framework of two separate types or divisions of markets: (1) *consumer markets* and (2) *organizational markets*. Since there are differences in approach necessary for effective selling to each of these broad market divisions (which we shall consider in later chapters), we need to explain the differences between them.

[1] Philip Kotler, *Marketing Management*, 6th ed. (Englewood Cliffs, N.J.: Prentice-Hall, 1988), p. 3.

Consumer Markets. The overall consumer market is composed of all the individuals and households that buy or acquire goods and services for personal or family consumption. This overall consumer market can be broken down or segmented in several ways, such as by:

- *Demographic data* (family composition, occupation, race, family income, geographic location, or marital status).
- *Psychological traits* (intelligence level, avocational interests, personality characteristics, or psychological needs).
- *Physical characteristics* (age, sex, or health).
- *Behavior patterns* (brand loyalty, religion, social class, amount of previous consumption of a given product, or language spoken).
- *Marketing conditions* (channels of distribution or competition).

Organizational Markets. There are millions of different types of business organizations and many, many types of not-for-profit organizations that buy all sorts of goods and services for their own use, use in further production, resale, or redistribution. Marketing authorities have classified these into the following three major types of customer markets:

- *Industrial Markets:* Composed of those profit and nonprofit organizations (other than government ones) that buy goods and services to be used in producing other goods and services, increasing sales, cutting costs, or meeting other requirements. An automobile manufacturer, for example, is likely to buy individual components (such as tires or batteries), from several independent subcontractor firms. A not-for-profit church-owned hospital or senior citizen care home has to buy medical supplies and food for clients and residents.
- *Reseller Markets:* Composed of those organizations that buy goods and services in order to resell them at a profit. Wholesaling firms and retail chains are examples.
- *Government Markets:* Government buying organizations exist in every nation of the world and are frequently found not only at the national (or federal) level, but also at state (or provincial) level, and at local (county, city, or municipal) level. At national or federal level buying centers can be found within both civil and military departments or agencies. State or provincial and local buying agencies include such entities as hospitals, school districts, and police departments.

International markets can technically either be considered separately or included, as we are doing, within the broad consumer and organizational market groupings just described. International markets include all types of foreign buyers—consumers as well as producers, resellers, and governments.

In this book, we are considering sales/marketing from an integrated, global point of view. The view from a top sales/marketing executive's office today is somewhat like the view of the world from a satellite orbiting 885 kilometers (550 miles) out in space. The problems of reaching the global market are greater than those involved in covering a neat little upstate or provincial sales territory, but the sales/marketing principles of reaching it are basically the same.

Before we go into details of how business firms organize for and implement selling to these various markets, let's first trace the evolution of marketing and personal selling over the years, and its probable future direction, as it affects salespeople.

Historical Development of Marketing

As a national economy develops, its functions change. The first stage, in the face of scarcity, is to increase production; engineers are the chief innovators at this time. As production increases during the second stage, production is consolidated to maximize efficiency and profitability.

Then, as production increases to a high level and initial wants and needs are satisfied, a third stage—that of finding new and different market outlets or customers—is reached. The problem then is not so much a scarcity of goods but a scarcity of markets.

In this third sales-oriented stage, faced with a shortage of customers, companies increase advertising budgets and sales forces to stimulate demand for existing products, and wage all-out competition for increased market share. In the United States, it was toward the end of this stage (in the 1930s and 1940s) that market research became highly developed, and sophisticated promotion and merchandising techniques were created.

This concentration on selling led to what is known as the *selling concept* (or sales concept), described as follows:

> The *selling concept* holds that consumers, if left alone, will not buy enough of the organization's products. The organization must therefore undertake an aggressive selling and promotion effort.[2]

Most of today's business firms around the world still base their sales/marketing on this selling concept. It is a concept that is practiced hardest by direct-selling firms offering "unsought" consumer products or services, such as insurance or encyclopedias, or by telephone or television sales organizations. Fund-raising promotions and political campaigns are examples of unsought non-profit products or ideas marketed via the selling concept. Since emphasis under this concept is on seeking out new customers and persuading them to buy the seller's specific offering, salespeople play the key role.

The Customer-Oriented Marketing Concept

By the mid-1950s business attitudes in the highly developed United States began to change. Prospective customers became more sophisticated, and marketing executives became aware that changing customers' wants to fit existing products

---

[2] Kotler, *Marketing Management*, 6th ed., p. 15.

and services was not good enough. They realized that they should adjust the goods before they were produced to fit the customers' wants or needs.

This resulted in articulation of a more sophisticated business philosophy than the earlier, narrower selling concept. Called the *marketing concept*, it has been defined by Professor Kotler as follows:

> The *marketing concept* holds that the key to achieving organizational goals consists in determining the needs and wants of target markets and delivering the desired satisfactions more effectively and efficiently than competitors.[3]

This truly creative American-oriented concept rapidly caught the attention of companies, institutions, and nations where marketing as a definable, systematic discipline had seldom if ever been seriously considered. Under this concept literally all functions of business, from research and development to production, through advertising, selling, and customer service, became oriented not only toward the needs and wants of customers but toward their after-purchase satisfaction as well. By putting customers in the center, and by using market research efficiently to identify new market trends rapidly, firms were able to plan and compete more efficiently.

The new marketing concept was welcomed also by nonbusiness institutions and organizations, such as educational institutions, hospitals, political parties, and governmental agencies. They realized that many of their problems of product or service development, information, persuasion, distribution, and customer service were similar to those that were being resolved so successfully by marketing management in business firms.

Nowhere was this new marketing concept adopted more quickly, widely, and enthusiastically than in Japan, a nation which proceeded during the 1970s and 1980s to show Americans and other foreigners how to put it into successful practice worldwide.

EMERGENCE OF A NEW CUSTOMER/SOCIETY-ORIENTED MARKETING CONCEPT

Some of the critics of business and marketing have pointed out what they consider a serious flaw in the customer-oriented marketing concept. They have noted that while customers are at the heart of all business and marketing planning activities, the end result is to "give customers what they want" with little consideration of whether "what they want" is really beneficial either to them or to society. Are smoky, noisy "dirt track" sport motorcycles, which pollute clean country air and stampede wildlife even in the most remote areas, or throw-away aluminum beer and soft drink cans that litter the countryside beneficial to society?

Is it beneficial to society for business to cater solely to want-satisfaction of some individuals, when pursuit of such may be in conflict not only with their

---

[3] Kotler, *Marketing Management*, 6th ed., p. 17.

personal long-term best interest, but with society's as well? Is the concept actually not immoral—in an age of resource shortages, environmental concerns, and an ever-widening gap between rich and poor nations, and between incomes of people within many of these nations?

Many sales/marketing leaders, recognizing that the public is increasingly holding them responsible for choices offered the consumer, are fast accepting a newer, still-developing marketing concept. Called the *societal marketing concept,* its aim is not only to fulfill consumer needs with something of value and benefit that will bring lasting satisfaction at a profit to the seller (the heart of the older customer-oriented marketing concept), but to provide as well "in a way that preserves or enhances the consumer's and the society's well-being.[4]

Under this new concept, business plays a positive and vital role in society through a careful sales/marketing policy balance between company profits, consumer need and want satisfaction, and public interest. What greater a challenge for free-enterprise business than to satisfy the consumer at a profit and enhance the overall welfare of society at the same time!

Functions of Marketing

Nearly 50 percent of what a consumer pays for an item in a retail store goes to cover marketing costs. On the surface, this percentage cost seems high, yet when we consider all the marketing functions that take place as goods move from producer to consumer, it is easy to understand. These functions include market research, product planning, financing, buying, standardization and grading, pricing, storing, transporting, risk bearing, and promotion and selling.

Merchandising is the overall term used to describe most of these marketing functions or activities. It can be defined as the planning and promotion of sales by presenting a product to the right market at the proper time, by carrying out organized, skillful advertising and sales promotion. It involves nearly every activity that influences consumers to buy the product except personal selling (but even here a salesperson often sells merchandising plans).

In most of today's business firms worldwide salespersons are playing an increasingly important role on the integrated marketing-management team. Salespeople are becoming ever more involved in helping determine market needs and in finding production and marketing solutions to them. Thus, while engaging in the primary task of face-to-face selling, they must be informed on all the other marketing functions not only to provide feedback to their firms, but also to consult with prospects or customers about these functions in a truly professional manner. Here are just some of the ways salespeople are involved in five of the above noted marketing functions:

■ *Market research.* While most large firms have their own staff-level market research departments, they rely heavily on outside professional market research organizations for market surveys and testing. The sales

[4] Kotler, *Marketing Management*, 6th ed., p. 28.

force can assist by providing ideas internally and field checking or testing research findings.

- *Product planning.* This is concerned with decisions like the type of product or service to be offered, the number of items to produce, the design of the item, and periodic modifications or changes that may be necessary. Feedback from the sales force is highly important to such planning.

- *Risk-taking.* For a high percentage of businesses, a major part of their working capital is tied up in inventory. If they are overstocked, and styles or models change or a new and better product comes out, they may have to return their stocks to the producer (if allowed to do so) or be unable to pay for them if credit has been extended. The salesperson, through observation or knowledge of the buyer's situation, can help his or her firm's credit department decide whether to extend credit in the first place and help the customer with returns or credit extension where necessary. And the salesperson can help both firm and customer by recommending proper buying and stock control so as to increase highest possible profitable turnover at least risk.

- *Transporting.* Since most products have to be physically moved from producer to buyer, speed and cost of transportation are important. Salespeople keep these elements in mind in advising their customers, and they follow through after the sale to see that items ordered were delivered safely and to ensure customer satisfaction.

- *Promotion and selling.* This is the function of marketing entailing the most activity and requiring the greatest amount of personal and financial effort. From our point of view in studying personal selling, it is by far the most important of all the marketing functions, and the one that we consider next in greater detail.

Promotion and Selling—The "Promotion Mix" of Marketing

Promotion and selling is a major function of marketing. In the attempt to communicate with, inform, persuade, and sell goods, services, or ideas to consumers, the firm or organization employs a four-part "promotion mix" (sometimes called "marketing communications mix") consisting of *advertising, publicity, sales promotion,* and *personal selling.* These four activities have separate yet overlapping capabilities and are carefully managed to produce optimum results as part of an overall sales/marketing program.

Historically, personal selling was the first of these separate activities; then came advertising, with publicity still later. It was not until the 1950s that sales promotion was considered, studied, or employed as a fourth distinctive activity of promotion and selling. We shall now consider these briefly and separately, listing personal selling last only because from that point on we will be discussing it in depth. Definitions of the four activities are those endorsed by the American Marketing Association.[5]

[5] Bennett, Ed., Dictionary of *Marketing Terms,* 1988.

- *Advertising:* Paid, nonpersonal communication through various media by business firms, nonprofit organizations and individuals who are in some way identified in the advertising message and who hope to inform and/or persuade members of a particular audience; includes communication of products, services, institutions and ideas.

   Advertising is a varied activity. It employs many kinds of media, such as newspapers, magazines, radio, television, outdoor advertising (billboards, and the like), direct mail, directories and circulars, and novelties (such as book matches and calendars). It is used in different forms for different goals; national advertising, for example, asks consumers to buy a specific brand, and mail order or direct mail advertising asks customers to mail in their orders for the item or items advertised.

   Four broad classifications of advertising are *institutional*, to build up a company image or name ("You're in good hands with Allstate," used by Allstate Insurance Company, or "the Chase Advantage," used by Chase Manhattan Bank); *brand*, to build up long-term brand image; *classified*, to tell about an event, a service, or a sale; and *sales advertising* of various types.

   Chief advantage of advertising is that it can be repeated publicly often in many different and dramatic ways; its chief disadvantage lies in its impersonal nature. Advertising can "talk to" people but not "talk with" them as can a salesperson.

- *Publicity:* Non-paid-for communication of information about a company (or organization) or product, generally in some media form.

   Many business firms and other organizations spend a lot of time and money creating "significant news" about which the press or television will give free coverage. America's United Airlines, for example, received excellent publicity by sending 2500 executive secretaries a fresh rose, under a "Roses to a First Lady" program, each Friday for several weeks. The Bicycle Institute of America, a booster of safe cycling paths and cycling for health and fun, gained national publicity by persuading the Secretary of the Interior of the United States to lead a bike parade of congressmen from the White House to the Capitol.

   Advantages of publicity are that many people are more inclined to accept or believe news stories about a product or company than paid advertisements, or than hearing about it from a salesperson. Disadvantages are that many potential buyers, suspicious of systematic efforts by public relations departments of firms to get "free publicity" through contrived "news," may react negatively.

- *Sales Promotion:* Media and non-media marketing pressure applied for a pre-determined, limited period of time at the level of consumer, retailer or wholeseller in order to stimulate trial, increase consumer demand or improve product availability.

   Sales promotions are usually short-term or temporary activities designed to support normal advertising and sales-force activities. Those supporting advertising often involve the offer of "more for your money," like temporary price reductions. They fall into these three broad categories:

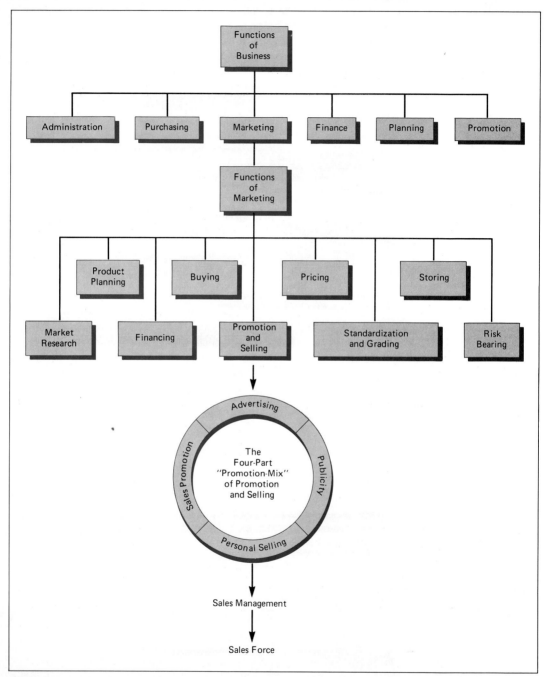

FIGURE 2.1 *How Sales Management and Sales Force Fit into the Big Picture of Business*

1. *Trade promotions* include such things as cooperative advertising, where retailer and manufacturer split costs of a retailer's newspaper ad featuring the manufacturer's product.

2. *Free goods or special discount promotions* are offered for specified quantity purchase within a given period of time, such as a publisher's offering booksellers one free copy for every ten books purchased by a certain date.

3. *Sales contests,* where prizes are offered the sales staff of the distributor or retailer in order to encourage them to promote the manufacturer's product.

■ *Sales-force promotions:* Aimed by a firm at its own sales force, include such things as cash bonus payments for sales above quota, contests in which prizes (normally durable goods such as luggage, or holiday trips) are given for extra sales during a given period, and enthusiasm-building sales meetings, often held at famous resort centers.

■ *Consumer promotions:* Aimed at the end-consumer, they include such things as the giving away of free samples; coupons which, whether mailed, on display at point-of-sale, or inside product packaging, are redeemable either from the retailer or the manufacturer for cash or other awards; premiums, which are special gift items given free or at low cost, provided the consumer buys a particular product; trading stamps, which are given in proportion to size of purchase and are redeemable for merchandise; and public demonstrations, which either feature a product or how to use it, such as a fashion show during a luncheon period at a large hotel, private club, or group meeting.

Personal selling, you will recall, was defined earlier as "selling that involves a face-to-face interaction with one or more prospective purchasers for the purpose of making sales."

Personal selling is considered by many the most important element of the whole marketing process, as producer meets potential buyer face-to-face in the marketplace. Figure 2.1 shows how sales management and the sales force fit into the big picture of business.

Since our book is about personal selling, let us trace for a moment the historical development of personal selling and consider in greater detail what role the salesperson will play throughout the 1990s and into the twenty-first century.

HISTORICAL DEVELOPMENT OF PERSONAL SELLING

If persuasion is at the core of selling, salespeople have been at the heart of trading (buying and selling) since the first long-distance trade in sea shells occurred in what is now France over 10,000 years ago. Priests of Sumeria in 5000 B.C. were the first to keep written records of goods acquired through barter. As early as 4000 B.C. Arab traders traveled by caravans to market centers in the Near East, Middle East, and Egypt. Early Greek and Roman traders traveled widely on land and sea.

The ancient Egyptians in about 2000 B.C. were quite advanced in the fields of administration, diplomacy, and trade, and left us many written records of their activities. With a little imagination, we can conclude that these quotes from their scrolls contain advice on how to handle a persuasive salesperson of the time.

> If thou art one to whom petition is made, be calm as thou listenest to what the petitioner has to say. Do not rebuff him before he has swept out his body or before he has said that for which he came. . . . It is not (necessary) that everything about which he has petitioned should come to pass, (but) a good hearing is soothing to the heart.
> Proclaim thy business without concealment. . . . One ought to say plainly what one knoweth and what one knoweth not.[6]

We certainly know that trader-salespeople were active during the Bronze Age, about 1000 B.C., since archeologists have unearthed "sample cases" dating from that period. And we know from ancient sagas and paintings that the Aztecs of Mexico honored a colorful "god of the commercial travelers" named Yacate-cuhtli.

In the early days goods were sold on a barter basis after much haggling. By the Middle Ages, especially during the thirteenth and fourteenth centuries, trading became more refined, and great Italian merchant princes especially ranged widely throughout Europe, selling an increasingly sophisticated variety of products. Spices and other exotic goods from far-off lands were brought back by adventurous sea captains and eagerly purchased by royalty and the wealthy.

British Take the Lead in Global Selling

With the advent of the Industrial Revolution in England around 1760, British salespeople traveled the world, successfully selling their country's high-quality textiles and manufactured items from Europe, to China, to the new world. In 1791, Alexander Hamilton, the first Secretary of the Treasury of the United States, called upon Congress to study the way Great Britain had spread "her factories and agents over the four quarters of the globe." By agents, he meant salespeople. Hamilton was thus one of the earliest American officials to publicly recognize the importance of salespeople in both national and international commerce.

Growth of Selling in North America

Selling in North America was initially carried on inland by traders and peddlers and via sea by the captains of the great ships that traded throughout the world. These latter men were far more than master mariners. They were also international traders of a very high order. When a ship was dispatched, no advance arrangements had been made for sale of the cargo abroad; the captain had to negotiate the best price for his cargo and use the money to obtain goods that

---

[6] Quoted in Adolf Erman, *The Literature of the Ancient Egyptians*, trans. Aylward M. Blackman (London: Methuen & Co., 1927), pp. 55–60.

could be sold at the next port. Since voyages often lasted months, markets could disappear while the ship was at sea, and fortunes were made and lost on the voyage of a single successful trip.

Yankee peddlers was the name given to the earliest "traveling salespersons" in what later became the United States. These peddlers carried goods inland by backpack, by horse, or by boat. As trails were blazed, they employed carts or wagons to carry items essential to frontier life, such as cloth, tinware, flints and bullets, other household necessities, and primitive luxuries. Many of them stayed at settlements along the way to open trading posts or general stores, carrying civilization with them wherever they went. From these early roots, direct selling has grown into a modern and effective distribution system.

Credit investigators were the earliest forerunners of modern salespeople in North America. During the early 1830s some eastern firms began sending credit investigators to western frontier areas to collect past-due accounts and to report back credit data and other business information. They often sold goods along the way, and in time these sales functions became more important than the financial ones. Later on credit agencies or other financial institutions took over credit matters, but the investigators' sales efforts were so useful that they were kept on the road primarily for that purpose.

Drummers, or greeters, were next on the North American scene, followed by "traveling salesmen." Prior to 1860 there were relatively few real salesmen in the United States and Canada and no real saleswomen to speak of. The custom was for retailers to visit manufacturers or wholesalers in the major trading cities once or twice a year. To make it easy for them to see goods fast, groups of firms or jobbers often jointly rented display rooms at one location and sent drummers, or greeters, to show the customers around, to entertain them, and of course to try to sell to them.

As new trading centers spread westward to Cincinnati, St. Louis, Toronto, and Chicago, many eastern jobbers and wholesalers began to send out traveling salespeople to meet the competition. The growth of the railroads accelerated the use of this system; U.S. census figures record the growth in the number of traveling salespeople: 1000 in 1860, 7762 by 1870, 28,158 by 1880, 58,691 by 1890, and 92,919 by 1900.

The two systems—retailers coming to visit the trading city and wholesalers and traveling salespeople going out—existed side by side for several years. But the drummers and greeters were generally replaced in the early 1900s, and traveling salespeople were busy everywhere. The railroads sped them and their samples about the United States and Canada, and the telegraph enabled them to keep in touch with their home offices to obtain rapid decisions regarding price quotations and delivery dates.

Continued Evolution of Personal Selling

In time, personal selling became more customer-oriented. Slowly but surely, during this historical evolution, the manufacturers, the jobbers, and the wholesalers and their drummers and traveling salespeople began adding utility or value to their products in order to win customer acceptance and beat the competition. They improved product styling, added new lines for increased selection, made products readily available, and even commenced educating customers on the use of newly developed products. The selling process thus became a truly useful and productive area of marketing.

We in the modern age owe much to these early-day salespeople, who played such a vital role in speeding world exploration and trade. They helped open the frontiers of the New World and break down the trade barriers of the Far East. Their sales tactics and strategies, crude as they often were, were accepted ones during the period.

Many of our modern merchandising and selling methods grew out of their collective experience. Salespeople, not marketing professors, originated such standard techniques as mail-order selling, installment buying, market research, and sampling. Much of our modern sales sophistication is a direct result of the trial and error, ingenuity, and tenacity of the early salespeople.

THE CHANGING ROLE OF MODERN-DAY SALESPEOPLE

The half-century between the end of the drummer era and the major North American economic and marketing changes of the mid-1950s led to increased professionalism in selling worldwide. During this period, new developments in the areas of physical distribution, such as communication, transportation, and materials handling were made, changing the structure of retailing and wholesaling. The growth of information processing following World War II (1939–1945) has led to the continued development of new mass-marketing techniques and near instantaneous worldwide communication via computers and relay satellites hovering in space.

As the size and complexity of business and marketing have increased, the sheer magnitude and cost involved in making major marketing decisions have brought new responsibilities to salespeople. By helping their producer firms understand and respond to evolving market requirements, ever more salespeople help stimulate industrial innovation and speed the distributive process. This enables their firms to maximize output and improve efficiency, and their customers to spend their money wisely and more effectively.

Unfortunately, far too many companies and organizations still fail to bring their salespeople into the planning of their frequently costly and risky major new marketing ventures. This can be illustrated by the great story about the American dog-food company that spent millions on marketing strategy, a host of comprehensive marketing research studies, and a spectacular national advertising and sales promotion campaign designed to overwhelm the competition—without bringing their salespeople into the planning process. Failing to sell any more dog food as a result, the company belatedly got the explanation why from one of their humble field salesmen. "The dogs don't like it," he said!

Salespeople Are Becoming True Market Managers

Especially for salespeople who represent the world's larger business firms, these changes and increased responsibilities have led to a rapid role change from that of being a mere seller of products or services to that of being a proficient territorial business manager out in the marketplace.

Increasingly in such firms salespeople are becoming ever more vital members of a customer-oriented, marketing-management team that starts its planning with customers' needs or wants in mind. Technical research, product design, manufacturing decisions, marketing, and physical distribution are all based on market research. Striking changes constantly alter buying habits and patterns, and the salesperson, as the link between firm and customer, has acquired new importance in interpreting one to the other.

Each change presents a management problem, and the modern day salesperson in effect has become a problem solver in approaching them. As part of such management teams, salespeople have to think analytically and systematically about the problems they encounter. They have to help plan, forecast, establish procedures and programs, fix schedules, and finally coordinate all these activities to achieve customer satisfaction.

What Does the Future Hold?

Trends indicate that the salesperson's job will continue to increase in importance, with each individual handling more of the business of smaller as well as the larger firms, and playing a more important role in the overall plan of the organization than he or she does now. Along with this increasing management role will come higher compensation and greater opportunities for promotion. Also will come increased responsibilities for which salespeople will have to be better educated and trained. Here are just some of the areas in which salespeople of the 1990s will have to be even better prepared than those of today:

An Understanding of Customer Needs and Problems. Salespeople will increasingly have to know customers thoroughly—what they want, how they buy, how they use the product, and how they react to it. They will also have to understand more deeply the buying process—why their customers buy. Such knowledge will require a more sophisticated understanding of economics and psychological and sociological behavior than that possessed by many of today's salespeople.

An Ability to Speak the Customers' Language. Ever-expanding new technologies will result in having products on the market that can be explained or sold only by technically trained salespeople. With the increasing use of EDP (electronic data processing) at all levels, the salesperson will have to be capable of relating the firm to the customer and vice versa, at all levels in an ever more professional way.

A Thorough Understanding of Customers' Operations and Facilities. Since far more salespersons will be required to serve as true account managers, they will have to be able to serve as indepth consultants on all aspects of their customers' business. For this role they will need a deeper and more intelligent understanding of finance, credits and collections, inventory controls, purchasing, automation, advertising, government regulations, and tax and legal matters.

An Ability to Work at Management Level. Growth of the team concept in management has increased the trend toward executive and group buying decisions. Salespeople of the future will increasingly be expected to intelligently meet with, advise, and negotiate with such groups. To be successful, they will need to more thoroughly understand their customers' methods of operation, marketing problems, and those of the customers they serve. Above all, salespeople of the 1990s, like those of today, must understand how their customers make their profits.

HOW DO COMPANIES GO ABOUT PLANNING, ORGANIZING, AND MANAGING THEIR SALES/MARKETING ACTIVITIES?

Now that we have placed marketing in proper perspective as a function of business, and described the role and importance of personal selling as a key part of the "promotion mix" of marketing, we turn our attention to the managerial aspects of sales/marketing activities.

Setting and meeting *goals* and *objectives* are the keys to success in every sales/marketing program, just as they are for any business or nonbusiness, group, or individual action program of any type. Here are helpful definitions of these two often confused terms.

> *Goal*—a broad-based, long-range, desirable but not always attainable statement of purpose or mission.
> *Objective*—a quantifiable, time-minded (usually one-year, but no more than five-year), measurable statement of intended output, purpose, or target.

In order to achieve success, any type of sales program—business firm, nonprofit organization, or that of a salesperson in his or her own personal sales territory—has to be built around two essential elements: *products* and *markets*.

> A *product* is what a seller has to sell; it can be physical objects, services, persons, places, organizations, ideas, or anything else of value.

In terms of physical objects *goods* and *products* mean the same thing in marketing terminology; while product is the term most frequently used, they are used interchangeably in this book.

Ensuring that goods and services desired by consumers are produced and supplied to consumers at the right time, in the desired amounts, and at an acceptable price, is the role and responsibility of business management. We can define "management" as follows:

> *Management* is the process whereby resources are combined into an integrated system in order to accomplish the objectives of the system.

In both business firms and nonprofit organizations, management, at its many levels, plans and sets goals and objectives and strives to ensure that they are met.

How Do Companies and Organizations Divide and Organize Managerial Activities?

From a managerial point of view, each individual in a business firm or other type of organization plays a specific part in the overall team effort. Direction in any group activity starts at the top, or policy-making level. Thus the chairperson of the board, or the chairperson of directors, as the post is called in some countries, leads in establishing overall company or organization policies and charges the president, managing director, or executive director, with their overall implementation. This person in turn delegates responsibility to various department heads in the functional areas such as research and development, personnel, finance, operations, production, and sales.

The degree of centralization of *decision making* in business firms varies from company to company. Some companies organize their functional sales policies and planning in a highly centralized fashion. The head, or home, office does most of the planning for their sales activities. An executive committee decides which products are to be sold and their prices and also plans advertising, sales promotion, training aids, budgets, and specific territorial sales policies and procedures. If a company is highly centralized in this manner, the principal sales task of a salesperson in a territory may be to merely carry out the established sales program as effectively as possible rather than to generate new ideas.

Many modern companies favor more decentralized sales policies; that is, they allow the various branches or individual salespeople as much freedom as possible to manage sales activities on a local level. The theory here is that the local salesperson on the spot is better able to plan for, to judge, and to solve local problems than anyone at the head office. Even in highly decentralized companies, however, the head office always makes these important decisions: (1) products to be sold and (2) prices for these products.

Actually, nothing is inherently wrong in either centralization or decentralization. Many companies use a varying combination of both to suit their needs. Even in highly centralized organizations, the limitations can spur an individual salesperson to work creatively to succeed within the guidelines.

How Does Modern Management Theory Apply to You as a Market Manager of Your Own Sales Territory?

Since we noted early on that a modern salesperson must learn to think and act like a manager, let us assume that *you* are now, suddenly, a salesperson with our business firm, and start relating some management and sales/marketing theory to your specific needs and interests.

As we thus lead into specific techniques of planning your work and working your plan for your own sales territory, which will fill most of the chapters to follow, we should start thinking like and using the same vocabulary as key members of the overall management team: the president, or managing director; the vice-president, marketing, and the vice-president, sales; your sales manager; and you—the highly important local market manager.

Management at every level is concerned with seeing to it that the firm operates as efficiently and profitably as possible within the goals and objective set. This is accomplished through four generally accepted *management functions*.

- Planning
- Organizing
- Executing (or directing)
- Controlling

These are action processes essential to meeting objectives. They may occur simultaneously in different ways, at different managerial levels, at different times. Here is what each basically involves:

- *Planning* is predetermining a course of action; it starts with the establishment of goals or objectives. It is essential to all activities, is performed by all levels of management, and is a continuous, changing process. It involves, at all levels, the establishment of both long- and short-range goals and objectives and includes formulation of policies, procedures, and programs through which the desired results are to be achieved. It involves all the functional areas of business noted earlier.
- *Organizing* is the classifying and dividing into manageable units of the action necessary to meet the objectives. It involves grouping work activities into manageable units and delegating individual authority and responsibility and, like planning, is a continuous process. Staffing, or hiring the people necessary to accomplish this, falls within this process.
- *Executing (or directing)* is the carrying out of the work necessary to succeed in meeting the objectives. It is carried on simultaneously with the planning and organizing functions on a continuous basis.
- *Controlling* is the constant checking of performance results against planned objectives. It involves control procedures, such as quarterly review of costs and sales versus budget; and control systems, such as manufacturing or shipping quality control checks.

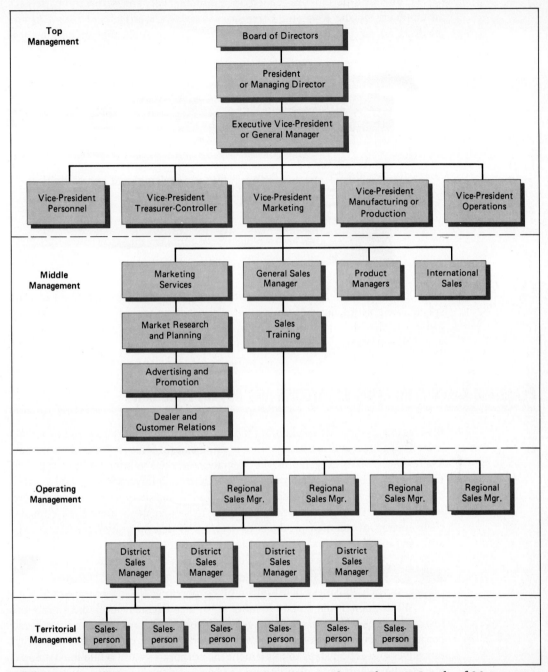

FIGURE 2.2 *Example of a Large Company Organization Chart, Showing Levels of Management Authority and Marketing and Sales Force Organization   Smaller-size Companies are Organized in Basically the Same Way, as are Non-business Organizations (to the degree applicable).*

The four functions are carried out simultaneously and with varying degrees of emphasis by the following three broad levels of management found in any medium to large business firm, and to the extent applicable in nonbusiness organizations:

- *Top management* consists of the board of directors, president, managing or executive director, group vice-presidents, secretary, and treasurer, who are concerned with overall planning, policy-setting, organizing, staffing, directing, and controlling.
- *Middle management* consists of area, regional, or divisional departmental managers, such as production, research, traffic, marketing, and sales, who are responsible for executing, supervising, and controlling.
- *Operating management* consists of foremen, supervisors, district sales managers, and you, as a sales territory manager, who execute or carry out the activities essential to successful completion of the objectives. Figure 2.2 shows how a typical large company might organize for selling in this way.

Later on, in Chapter 20, we relate these functions in greater detail to your specific role as manager of your own sales territory within a business firm, or (where applicable) as an independent salesperson managing your direct sales or party-plan territory.

PLANNING SALES/MARKETING STRATEGIES AND ACTION PROGRAMS

Business firms commence planning their sales/marketing strategies and programs around products and markets by first making careful forecasts (based upon market research) as to expected market demand and sales volume and profit potential. The end objective of planning derived from such forecasts is profitable sales.

Once they have measured or estimated their market or markets and decided what managerial organization is necessary to sell to them, they then consider their current or planned products or services to determine the overall strategy and the "marketing mix" to be employed in achieving objectives. Once this is done, the planning process begins. For most firms the end result is both a *long-range* (two to five years) and *short-term* (usually covering the next year's sales period) written "business plan" outlining corporate goals and objectives.

While some firms do all planning at top management level and simply tell lower echelons what their specific goals and objectives are, most outline broad corporate-level goals and require lower echelons to work out specific "next year" objectives and action steps to implement the corporate goals. While most companies do their short-term planning on the basis of a twelve-month calendar year, others do so on a fiscal year basis. Individual salespeople in most companies are required to carefully plan the sales management of their individual sales territory on this one-year basis.

In the forecasting stage of the above-mentioned process, determination of *market potential* (total possible sales for a given product or service in that market or market segment) and *sales potential* (the amount of expected sales that can be achieved profitably within that market or market segment) is highly important. Market potential data is usually provided by a firm's market research department. Sales potential estimates are derived from sales forecasts provided by the sales department. Overall planning for most companies usually starts with, and works back from, their sales potential estimates.

In reviewing such forecasts, company planners must pay careful attention to certain key factors that will largely determine consumer demand and trends in the future. This is necessary because such changes and trends can greatly affect planning and selling. Let us consider briefly how such planning and selling by business firms offering products and services for consumer markets may be affected by four such key factors: (1) population growth and changing age structure, (2) geographic shifts in population, (3) age mix of household composition, and (4) income distribution within market areas.

Population Growth and Changing Age Structure

The world population explosion alone poses new and difficult forecasting problems for governments and business firms alike (see Fig. 2.3). When the Christian church was established in 1 A.D., the population of the world was slightly over 250 million. It took 1600 years for this figure to double to 500 million, less than the population of India alone today. By 1850 the world population had doubled again and stood at more than one billion; by 1970, a hundred years later, the figure had more than tripled to 3.5 billion.

In 1987, the world population passed the 5 billion mark—and is expected to double to 10 billion by the year 2040 with 90 percent of this growth taking place in what we call the Third World. For a child born in 1989, this means that when he or she reaches age 51, the world will have twice as many people as in the individual's year of birth. Three billion of the world's 5 billion population will be entering their reproductive years in the early 1990s, and most of those live in poor, developing Third World countries, where birth rates are high.

On the surface such worldwide growth indicates greatly increased demand for countless goods and service. But if the many currently poor Third World countries cannot produce enough economic growth and new jobs, this population explosion may prove catastrophic.

As the World's Rich Nations Get Richer—The Poor Third World Nations—Get Children!. To bring this global demographic problem into sharper focus, consider the fact that between 1960 and 1990 (just 30 short years), the poorer Third World nations have added more people than the total populations of North America, Europe, the Soviet Union, Japan and Oceania combined. United Nations estimates are that of the 85 million new human souls born in

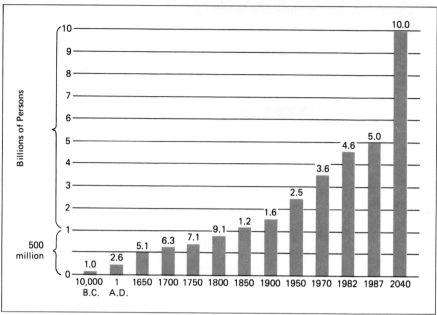

FIGURE 2.3 *World Population Growth and Future Projections* (*Source:* United Nations)

1989, 16.3 million were African, 9.6 million Latin American, and a whopping 51.7 million Asian. Nearly 665 million additional jobs will be needed in Third World developing countries by the year 2010, just for the children who are already born.

The only Third World country that is seriously trying to control its population growth is the Peoples Republic of China. That country, with its huge 1989 population of 1.1 billion, has had in place since the late 1970s a massive national family planning program with the goal of reducing the population to around 750 million by 2050—and maintaining it at that level in the future. Few western experts believe that the goal will be met.

Many western European nations, on the other hand, expect low population growth during the 1990s, with increasing median-age (aging) populations, and eventual population decline. By the year 2035, for example, West Germany's population is expected to decrease by 10 percent, from 60 million to 54 million. Sweden's population is expected to drop during that period by 6 percent, Switzerland's by 8 percent.

Japan's population of over 120 million in 1989 is also aging rapidly; by the turn of the century, demographers say, 16 percent will be 65 or older, and that proportion may rise to 23 percent or more by 2025.

The United States Faces Unique Trends. Like many western European countries and Japan, the United States also faces slower population growth and an aging one. The nation's recent population growth looks like this: 204 million in 1970, 222 million in 1980, and 246 million in 1989. If the national birthrate continues its slowdown, the population may reach only 300 million by the year 2020, then experience a decline.

Three important demographic changes facing American market forecasters in future years are (1) the changing age structure of and (2) the increased life expectancy of the population, and (3) fast-growing minority markets.

Baby Boomers. A unique American demographic trend has resulted from the "baby boomers"—that unprecented bulge of 76 million post-World War II babies born between 1946 and 1964. In the 1950s they sparked millions of sales of baby food, toys, and strollers; in the 1960s, acne medicine and Beatles records; in the 1970s, bell-bottom jeans and Volkswagen bugs.

Now stampeding into their high-earning, high spending, high-borrowing 1990s-and-beyond years, those boomers, by virtue of their sheer numbers and economic power, will determine which businesses, products, and services will succeed, and which will fail. As one forecaster put it, "Whatever the Baby Boom wants, the Baby Boom is going to get." One result will be that the free-wheeling teen-age culture that had such an important effect on American marketing during the 1970s and 1980s is being replaced by a more cautious middle-age culture that will rule for the next two decades. New buying trends will result when these baby boomers start retiring around 2011 or so.

Aging Population. Declining birthrates since the baby boom and increasing life expectancy are producing an aging American population. In 1988 the U.S. median age was 32.3; it is expected to reach 36 by the year 2000, 39 by 2010, and 42 by 2050 (Figure 2.4).

FIGURE 2.4 *The Graying of America (Source:* U.S. Census Bureau)

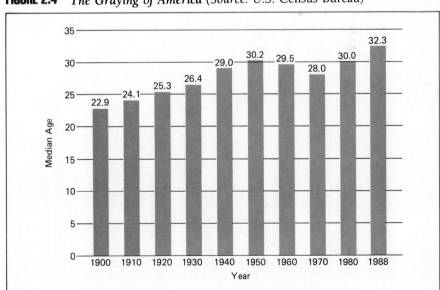

A 1988 Census Bureau study, which projects the nation's population by age, sex and race from 1988 to the year 2080, paints a statistical picture of an aging America that will have fewer young people but more than a million persons over 100 and nearly three times that number who are 95–99 years old by the year 2080.

While some people warn that this will result in a "geretocracy," a society ruled by older people, sales/marketing experts see expanding sales opportunities as a result. They realize that many of these older Americans will have a substantial disposable income to spend on such items as travel and entertainment as well as on hearing aids and denture cleaners. Figure 2.5 shows shifts in American age groups since 1970, and their projected shifts through the year 2030.

As the population ages, deaths will increase—and outstrip births every year after 2030, according to the study. By that year, there will be one million more deaths a year than there were in 1990—making the funeral business a "growth industry."

Fast-Growing Minority Markets. Another demographic change facing American forecasters is the rapid growth of minority groups. Blacks, who represented 12 percent of the population in 1988, have a higher average birthrate than whites, and the Asian population percentage is increasing steadily. But it is Hispanics who represent by far the fastest-growing minority group.

FIGURE 2.5 *Shifting Age Groups—In Percent of Total U.S. Population* (*Source:* U.S. Census Bureau)

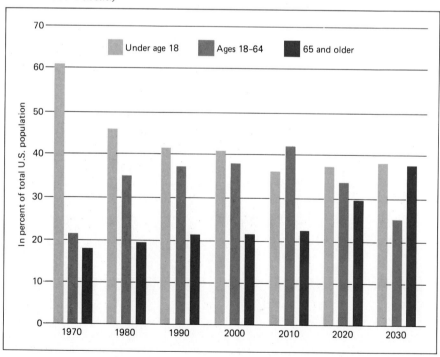

SELLING IN THE MARKETING ENVIRONMENT

According to 1988 Census Bureau estimates, the number of Hispanic U.S. residents had grown by 34.4 percent since 1980—five times as fast as the rest of the population. The Bureau put the 1988 Hispanic population at 19.4 million (8 percent of the total population), a 4.8 million increase since the 1980 census. It is the relative youth of the Hispanic community that most interests sales/marketing forecasters. Its average 25 years of age, in contrast to the 1988 U.S. median age of 31—and its continued growth through immigration and high birth rates, ensures that it will become increasingly significant in the future. By some estimates, Hispanics will overtake the number of blacks by the year 2000.

Due to these numbers and very high birthrate, the Hispanic market is one that sellers are increasingly trying to penetrate. Since Spanish is the dominant language for half this population, sales/marketing people who truly want to reach it will need to communicate in both Spanish and English.

Growth of and changing buying habits of these large minority groups interests American market forecasters greatly, since each population group has certain specific wants and buying habits.

Geographic Shifts in Population

This factor has especially influenced marketing in both the United States and Canada since the end of World War II in 1945. In 1880, 70 percent of Americans lived in rural areas. By the late 1980s 70 percent lived in urban areas, a high percentage of them having moved there from rural areas or small towns since 1946.

Within the United States people continue moving, shifting into a few broad regional areas of the country. In any average year, one American out of five moves to different living quarters. Thus, in any given five-year period the equivalent of the entire population moves to a new location. Much of this movement has been from northern and north central states to the so-called "sunbelt" southern and western states. Significant marketing changes are the result—fewer home heater sales and more air conditioner sales, for example.

Population shifts from rural to urban areas, and population concentrations in urban areas in Canada since 1946 parallels that of the United States. Today, over 80 percent of Canada's population is urban, with over 60 percent of the population concentrated in 29 major urban centers, each having a population of more than 100,000. This concentration is greatest along the Windsor-Montreal corridor. Ninety percent of Canada's total population lives within 325 kilometers (200 miles) of the Canadian-U.S. border.

Age Mix of Household Composition

Households, defined as two or more people living together who buy for the household rather than for individual consumption, are an important index of buying trends. The 18–24 age group is of special interest to forecasters, since that is the primary group for new household formation.

Although not all households represent families, since they might also include individuals not related by blood, marriage, or adoption (such as unmarried couples, or roomates), households and families are usually grouped together by market researchers as a major market target. In most advanced western countries, due to married couples preferring fewer children, and young adults putting off marriage to a later age, households continue to shrink in size.

Within the family sector, especially in the United States, the number of one-person households continues to grow at a faster rate than the conventional husband-wife unit, due to the increased willingness of unhappily married couples to separate.

In 1988, 24 percent of America's 63 million children lived with only one parent. Most single-parent households are headed by women. Bureau of the Census estimates are that only 39 percent of American children born in 1988 will live with both parents until their eighteenth birthday. Since a large number of females who head most of those households combine jobs and parenting, they represent an increasingly attractive market for convenience foods and various services, such as child care centers and health clubs, where singles can meet one another. The unit size and age mix of household units in target market areas are an area of vital concern to sales/marketing executives.

Income Distribution within Market Areas

Not only are market researchers interested in the age mix of household composition, but also in how households allocate their earnings. And they are interested in whether or not household income is going to rise or fall—an area of special

FIGURE 2.6 *The American Family's Shopping Basket* (*Source:* U.S. Department of Commerce)

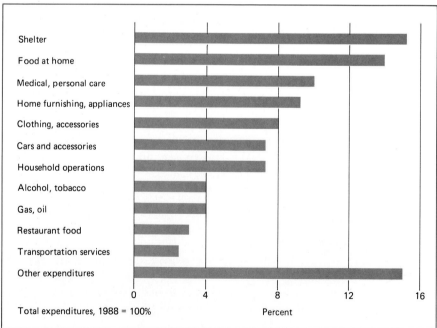

interest in the United States throughout the 1990s due to the baby boom bulge already noted. Helped along by the rapid growth of the 35–44-year-old boomers who will be nearing their career and income peaks, the 1990s will see an unusually large percentage of consumers in the high earnings groups.

Figure 2.6 shows how all American households allocated their income in 1988. By comparing how different groupings of households allocated their income in past years with future projected groupings, sales/marketing executives can obtain a good idea of how income will be allocated. This enables them to pinpoint growth markets.

PLANNING THE "MARKETING MIX" TO BE EMPLOYED IN CARRYING OUT THE STRATEGIES AND PROGRAMS

Once they have measured or estimated their market or markets and decided what managerial organization is necessary to sell to them, business firms must consider their products or services and decide upon the overall strategy and marketing mix that they will employ to achieve their desired objectives.

FIGURE 2.7 *The Overall Sales/Marketing Strategy: "Marketing Mix" and "Promotion Mix"*

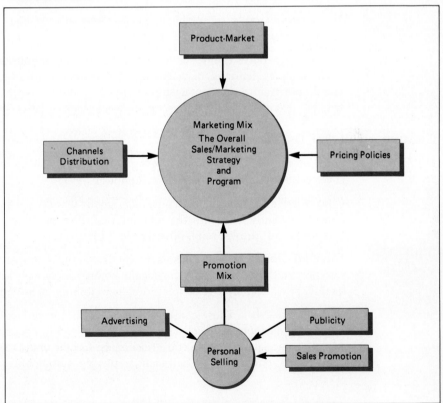

The proper *marketing mix* to be employed depends on the proper combination of four elements—the *product, channels of distribution, pricing policies,* and *promotional methods.* Since this is a book on personal selling, not marketing, we will move quickly through this complicated subject, an overview of which is illustrated by Figure 2.7. Our purpose is to provide a basic understanding of these processes, in which the salesperson plays such a vital role.

PRODUCT CLASSIFICATION

A *product,* you will recall from our earlier definition, includes physical objects, services, persons, places, organizations, ideas, and anything else of value. Marketing authorities have classified these in several ways—first, according to durability or tangibility, and then by classification into consumer goods, industrial goods, and services. The following brief overview of these classifications generally follows definitions approved by American Marketing Association.[7]

Product Classification According to Durability or Tangibility

Durable Goods.   Tangible goods that normally survive many uses (examples: television sets, shoes).

Nondurable Goods.   Tangible goods that normally are consumed in one or a few uses (examples: soft drinks, toothpaste).

Services.   Services can be activities, benefits, or satisfactions that are offered for sale (examples: haircuts, dry cleaning). Such services are essentially intangible and do not result in the ownership of anything. Product-type services are more tangible (examples: consulting services, legal services, lawn care services).

Consumer Goods Classifications

Based on the end consumers' shopping habits, the following four classifications cover goods bought for personal consumption:

Convenience Goods.   Those consumers' goods that the consumer usually purchases frequently, and with the minimum of effort in comparison and buying (examples: soft drinks, soap, lipstick).

Shopping Goods.   Those consumers' goods that the customer, in the process of selection and purchase, characteristically compares on such basis as suitability, quality, price, and style (examples: designer clothing, major appliances).

Specialty Goods.   Those consumers' goods with unique characteristics and/or brand identification for which a significant group of buyers are habitually willing to make a special purchasing effort (examples: specific brands and types of stereo components, photographic equipment, expensive automobiles).

[7] See Bennett, Ed., *Dictionary of Marketing Terms,* 1988.

Unsought Goods.   Those consumers' goods that the consumer normally does not know about nor think of buying (examples: travel accident insurance, home or automobile burglar alarms).

Industrial Goods Classifications

Industrial goods are those bought by individuals or organizations for further processing or for use in conducting a business. They are generally classified as follows, depending on how they enter the production and their cost:[8]

Materials and Parts.   Those industrial goods that enter the manufacturer's product. They fall into the following two classes:

- *Raw materials* (examples: cotton, cement)
- *Manufactured materials and parts* (examples: auto windshields and tires)

Capital Items.   Those industrial goods that enter the finished product partly. They fall into the following two classes:

- *Installations* (examples: buildings, large computer systems)
- *Accessory equipment* (examples: fork lifts, typewriters)

Supplies and Services.   These are industrial goods that do not enter the finished product in any way. They include the following:

- *Operating supplies* (examples: typing paper, erasers).
- *Maintenance and repair items* (examples: paint, light bulbs).
- *Business services* (examples: advertising agency, office machine repair service).

Classification of Services

Services can be classified in several ways. In general they can be people based (such as employing the services of a lawyer or grounds maintenance firm) or equipment based (such as vending machines in employee dining areas or limousine service). Services can also be classified according to either for-profit or not-for-profit characteristics.

Our purpose in presenting all the above classifications lies in the fact that knowledge of the degree and character of consumers' buying needs and habits has an important bearing on the sales/marketing strategy selected.

[8] See Philip Kotler and Gary Armstrong, *Marketing: An Introduction* (Englewood Cliffs, N.J.: Prentice-Hall, 1987) pp. 237–238.

Channels of Distribution

A marketing channel, or channel of distribution, is the path traced in the direct or indirect transfer of ownership to a product, as it moves from a producer to the ultimate consumers or industrial users. The chart in Figure 2.8 illustrates the most commonly employed marketing channels. Definition of the distribution institutions in the left-hand column will be found in the glossary of terms in the back of this book.

Pricing Considerations

Pricing policies play an important part in the overall marketing strategy, especially in relation to promotional policies. For example, if a firm plans to sell a product at a higher retail price than those of competing products, and offers dealers a smaller discount than competition as well, it may have to spend more on advertising, sales promotion, and personal selling than the competition to offset these pricing disadvantages, in order to achieve planned sales objectives.

The Promotion Strategy or Mix

Having defined and briefly described the four-part "promotion mix" of promotion and selling earlier in this chapter, we are aware that good promotion strategy employs all of them in combination. The proper combination or "mix" is that which will bring greatest results at least cost.

Personal selling and advertising are the two most important of the four in terms of cost and market impact. Personal selling is nearly always supported by advertising, and often by publicity and sales promotion (especially point-of-purchase (POP) displays in retail stores or at merchandise marts). Personal selling is the most effective form of promotion, because of face-to-face contact and interpersonal communication between salesperson and prospective buyers, but it is also the most costly.

FIGURE 2.8 *Marketing Channels Commonly Used in the Distribution of Industrial and Consumer Goods*

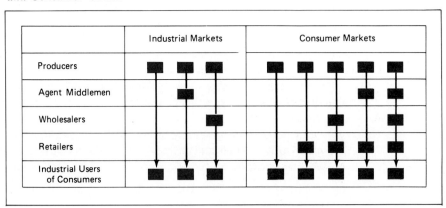

For most companies, the sales force represents the most important ingredient in the entire sales/marketing strategy and promotion mix. The individual salesperson provides an irreplaceable link between the company and its customers. To many customers the salesperson *is* the company; to the company he or she represents not only the most effective source of sales, but the best source for rapid intelligence as to the needs, wants, and problems of the often rapidly changing marketplace. Monthly, weekly, and even daily sales successes and reports represent a barometer of the entire organizational success or failure in the competitive business world.

The objectives, size, organization, and responsibilities of individual company sales forces are as broad and varied as the thousands of different types of goods and services offered. The business a firm is in, the product it sells, and the level or type of customers it sells to determine its sales/marketing strategy and the educational level, specific skills, and abilities sought in hiring its salespeople. It further determines the size and structure of the sales force, and the type of sales training offered.

Sales Force Role and Objectives

The role fulfilled by the sales force depends on such overall marketing objectives as the product markets sought, emphasis on both short- and long-range profits versus market share, and depth or degree of customer satisfaction desired. If rapid sales increases are sought, more sales call time may be needed to open new accounts. If a new product line is to be pushed, more personal sales time may have to be allocated to that line at the expense of current lines.

As well as planning how selling time will be utilized, companies plan their sales force objectives carefully in terms of overall *sales* and *budget objectives*. The overall sales-volume objective is broken down into specific goal-quotas by sales region, district, and individual salesperson. Expense budgets are broken down and assigned in the same manner. Profit objectives are made clear.

Management by Objectives for Salespeople

Let us assume, by way of example, that you are a salesperson working for a managerially modern firm that thinks in terms of *management by objectives (MBO)*. The term "management by objectives" (MBO) was first introduced in 1954, as an approach to managerial planning by Peter Drucker in his book "The Practice of Management."[9] This approach entails joint participation by you and your sales manager in the establishment of clear and definite objectives for a given period. Normally done in advance of each sales year, the idea is to discuss objectives until an agreement on clear objectives is reached that is satisfactory both to you as sales territory manager and to your superiors.

[9] Peter F. Drucker, *The Practice of Management* (New York: Harper & Brothers 1954).

Whether objectives are simply assigned, or worked out jointly MBO style, sales force objectives planning is normally concerned with *long-range goals* and *short-term objectives*. For example, both your company and you may set as a long-range goal the doubling of both sales and profits each five years. This breaks down to a 20 percent increase in sales and profits each year. Your immediate short-term objective is thus to increase sales and profits 20 percent in your specific territory next year. You can plan intermediate short-term goals within that framework simply as specific dollar and profit weekly, monthly, or quarterly objectives. You can constantly check your progress. Table 2.1 shows such a standard salesperson's annual sales, expense, and profit budget.

It is worth noting at this point that you as manager of your sales territory, in planning your territorial sales, expense, and profit objectives as illustrated in Table 2.1, are basically following the same procedure as your company president or managing director. You and he or she have a lot in common, since you are both basically thinking and planning in the same way about your respective managerial assignments.

Sales Force Size, Organization, Training, and Operations

Most business firms organize their sales-force assignments along these three traditional lines: (1) by geographic territory, (2) by industry, or (3) by product. Other, more innovative types of specialized sales-force organization used by some companies include such things as selling teams or special task forces.

A selling team assigned to a specified large account might consist of a sales engineer, a marketing expert, and other experts as needed to handle all customer requirements from selling through after-sale servicing. Special task forces are often used to introduce a new product quickly to all accounts or prospects within a given area by telephone, special presentations, or sales calls. Sometimes the entire sales force is turned into a special task force, concentrating on nothing but one product, old or new, for one day, or an even longer specified period, at a time.

TABLE 2.1 *XYZ Company, Inc. Mid-Central Territory* U.S.A. Annual Sales Representative's Budget† ($000 Omitted)*

	1st quarter	1st 6 months	1st 9 months	Total year
Sales	60.0	120.0	180.0	240.0
Commission income at 25 percent	15.0	30.0	45.0	60.0
Expenses				
Salary	5.0	10.0	15.0	20.0
Travel and entertainment	2.5	5.0	7.5	10.0
Promotion	0.6	1.2	2.0	3.0
Total expenses	8.1	16.2	24.5	33.0
Profit (before home office expenses)	6.9	13.8	20.5	27.0

* Includes states of Nebraska, Kansas, Oklahoma, Iowa, and Missouri.
† Examples of a standard salesperson's annual sales and expense budget based on a territory with planned net sales of $240,000 by a $20,000 per year salaried salesperson.

Whatever method is employed in sales force organization and assignment, the objective is that of earning profits in acceptable excess over the cost of getting the sales. The changing marketplace leads to constant reevaluation, and often to sales-force changes as the need arises.

Sales-force training, assignment, supervision, control, and performance evaluation are just some of the activities that fall under the direct responsibility of sales management. All these things, plus learning how sales management goes about planning and executing specific action programs that will enable its company to achieve planned sales and profit goals and objectives, are considered in Chapter 18, "Sales Management and Selling."

SUMMARY

The purpose of this chapter has been to provide a basic broad overview of sales/marketing—what it is, how it is carried on in the business world, and the important role played by the salesperson in the "big picture."

After describing marketing as a function of business, we discussed the customer-oriented marketing concept and the newer, emerging, societal marketing concept. Knowledge of these foundations is essential in order to understand the evolving nature and role of modern personal selling. We considered the four-part "promotion mix" of marketing, of which personal selling is, in our eyes, the most important. Tracing the history of personal selling, we concluded that modern-day salespeople are far more than mere sellers of goods and services. As fully integrated members of their firms' market/management teams, their role increasingly is that of a true consultant to their customers.

Based on these concepts, we focused attention on how business firms go about planning the "marketing mix" to be employed in carrying out their overall sales/marketing strategies, and how they basically classify consumer and industrial goods and services they offer.

We concluded with a brief look at how sales departments organize for selling, and how individual salespersons put into practice modern managerial concepts such as management by objectives, and sales, expense, and profit budgeting in managing their individual sales territories.

Questions for Analysis and Discussion

1. Define and explain the new, emerging societal marketing concept. How does it differ from the customer-oriented marketing concept of the 1950s and 1960s?

2. What four elements of the "marketing mix" do companies consider using in combination when planning their sales/marketing strategies and programs?

3. What do we mean by the term "promotion mix" as used in sales/marketing terminology? What are its four parts?

4. Name and describe the differences between the two broad types or divisions of markets.

5.	What is the difference, if any, in sales/marketing terms, between goods and products?

6.	What do we mean by the statement, "Many companies favor decentralized sales policies," and what two decisions does top management always reserve for itself, even if it employs decentralized sales policies?

7.	How would you define each of the four generally accepted functions of management? Are they carried out simultaneously or separately? Who carries them out?

8.	Suppose you formed a company to manufacture hammers.

    a.	How would you classify hammers as a product?

    b.	Through what channels of distribution would you sell them?

United States Ski Industry Schusses into Adapting to the Graying of America

A few years ago, when American ski slope operators looked out at their majestic mountains, about the only white they saw was on the slopes. But as the 1989–1990 ski season started to snowball, they saw an increasing amount of white in the hair of the skiers swooshing down those same mountains.

"It seemed just a few years ago that all our skiers were in their early 20s," said one such operator. "Now lots of them are in their late 30s and 40s," he continued, "proof that the 'baby boom' generation is rushing headlong into middle age."

At first glance, an aging national population with an average 1988 median age of 32.3 (versus 30 in 1980), a median age that the Census Bureau estimates will reach 36 by 2000 and 39 by 2010, does not seem to bode well for the multimillion-dollar U.S. ski industry. After all, the sport has traditionally drawn its base from people in the 18–30 age bracket.

Still, the ski industry hasn't started to panic! As one operator noted, "Skiing is still growing at a rate of three to four percent a year, with an estimated nearly 55 million people taking to American slopes in 1988." But the operators are concerned, because the current growth rate is far below the 10 to 15 percent growth season after season during the glory days of the 1960s.

Faced with slower growth, ski resorts are especially looking at innovative new sales/marketing programs that will attract larger crowds of older people. Their market research studies clearly show that the older a person gets, the less time he or she tends to spend actually skiing during a ski vacation. What to do about this is the Big Question for the industry. In considering new growth potential, forecasters see warm weather resorts (not other North American ski resorts) as their chief competitors in trying to lure more people of all ages in their sport. They are also eying the international market as a source of new business.

Some things are already being done—an influx of gourmet, sit-down restaurants at ski resorts, for example, as well as expanded shopping areas, hot-air balloon rides, and dog-sled rides. All that ties in with market research conclusions that aging skiers don't want to spend eight hours a day skiing. One result of this approach is the emerging "mega resort" concept of Colorado's Vail-Beaver Creek and the Summit County ski areas. These are planned communities offering varied experiences ranging from skiing to prime shopping and dining to sleigh rides.

What are other key conclusions of the market research studies? That the older, 90s yuppie crowd has more money to spend because they have better jobs, for one thing, and that they happily like to spend it, for another.

The Big Money Potential conclusion, however, is that the baby boomers of the 1950s, who were at the heart of the explosive 1960s ski growth, are now having babies! That fact calls for new and different types of services—such as nurseries, day care facilities, and ski instruction for young kids.

"The biggest sales/marketing thrust in our industry during the 1990s," said one operator, "will be to attract families. Forget movies of years past that portrayed American ski resorts as outdoor singles clubs with snow," he added, "Skiing is becoming a family sport again."

Questions for Written Reports or Class Discussion

1. Assuming that you are an American ski resort operator, what "promotional mix" will you employ to attract crowds of yuppie families with small children to spend their winter vacation at your resort?

2. Since the number of single-parent households with young children continues to grow at a faster rate in the United States than conventional husband-wife ones, what, if anything, will you do to encourage the former type of families to vacation at your ski resort?

3. What special "promotional mix," if any, will you use to attract young families of the fast-growing Hispanic U.S. population segment to vacation at your ski resort?

4. How would you go about developing sales potential estimates for next year's ski season for your ski resort?

Sales Problem 2.1	How can your commercial division reorganize its sales/marketing effort in order to increase sales, reduce costs, and increase profits?

Two years out of college, you are employed as a salesperson in the Commercial Division of Acme Office Supplies, Inc., a large manufacturer of office supplies. You and the other 45 salespeople in your division sell to the stationery and office supply trade. Two other sales divisions of Acme include (1) retail salespeople, who sell primarily to mass merchandisers and other high-volume consumer outlets, and (2) a few industrial salespeople who call on industrial supply houses. Salespeople of all these divisions call on distributors, not end-users.

Your sales manager has just told you that the division's sales are slipping in face of inflation, and that costs, especially sales force costs, are increasing rapidly. The conversation continues.

Sales manager: As you know, our division promotes from within. In order to check managerial potential, we like to see, from time to time, if key members of our sales force such as yourself can suggest solutions to business problems like this. Any suggestions about what we should do in the face of the situation I've just described?

You: Can you give me some more specific information about the sales versus profit picture as seen by top management? In other words, what seems to be the "big problem" in the "big picture"?

Sales manager: Your question is right on the mark! Our big problem is that 76 percent of our accounts are unprofitable. Any ideas how we should reorganize our sales/marketing effort in order to increase sales, reduce costs, and increase profits?

You:	Two more questions! First, is our division's sales force up to full (46 person) strength right now?
Sales manager:	I'll answer that one in a hurry—we are three below strength now, and two salespeople have given notice that they will be resigning for different personal reasons within the next 90 days.
You:	My second question is—in trying to come up with a business-like answer to the problem, shall I consider all aspects of the four-part "marketing mix" of our division's promotion and selling effort?
Sales manager:	Certainly! I don't expect you to be an expert, but you should know enough by now to give me an idea of your overall knowledge and soundness of thinking and judgment. Why don't you think it over tonight, and you can give me your ideas over coffee at that restaurant across the street tomorrow at 10 A.M. OK?
You:	I'll be there!

Question for Written Report or Class Discussion

Based on Chapter 2 material you have just studied, and your own common sense, what suggestions will you present tomorrow to your sales manager as to how the division's sales/marketing effort might be revised to increase sales, reduce costs, and increase profits?

Sales Problem 2.2

Does the world's fast-growing elderly population spell sales/marketing decline or growth?

Many of the world's business leaders now planning to tap new markets during the decade of the 1990s and beyond are keenly aware of changing population demographics that will cause many lucrative markets of the 1970s and 1980s to dwindle, and new ones to emerge.

An unprecedented rate of growth in the numbers of elderly people in many of the world's countries is giving them "prediction fits." Their problem is this: According to a 1988 U.S. Census Bureau study, the number of people worldwide aged 65 and over is growing at a rate of 2.4 percent annually, a rate much faster than the 1.7 annual growth of the global population as a whole. This means that their number will increase from the estimated 290 million of 1988 to over 410 million by the year 2000.

The question that puzzles today's market researchers is, "Does this mean that all these older people will buy less (causing a business decline), or does this trend point to new sales/marketing opportunities?"

Positive thinkers among these business leaders and market researchers argue that business should abandon its long-held, stereotyped view of the elderly as poor, feeble rejects in wigs and orthopedic shoes, and realize that most people are as intelligent and alert at 65 as they were at 40 (less than three percent are institutionalized for mental illness such as senility). Benjamin Franklin, for example, helped draft the American Declaration of Independence at 70, Verdi composed *Falstaff* at 80, and Mark Twain was on a strenuous lecture circuit at 70 plus.

They point to the fact that in many of the world's industrialized nations such as Japan, the United States, Sweden, and West Germany, millions of older people are today healthier, happier, and far more affluent than those of any previous generation. This trend, they feel, will continue well into the twenty-first century.

In order to tap into this rapidly growing population segment, some feel that answers must be sought to basic questions such as these:

- Compared to when they were younger, do people over 65 have different functional and psychological needs and wants, the identification of which could lead to the successful marketing of new products and services, as well as new ways of positioning brands?
- Are self-images of people over 65 inconsistent with how they are portrayed in today's advertising?
- Do people over 65 have specific leisure-time activities and interests that represent an untapped market?

Answers to these questions could be what California's Sutter's Mill was to American prospectors of 1848—an entree to the gold rush. Only a few of the 40,000 who stampeded to the Sacramento Valley in 1849 struck it rich. The same is true today. Only the marketer who ferrets out the true wants, needs, and feelings of people in their golden years will be successful in selling to them.

Questions for Written Reports or Class Discussion

1.   What different needs and wants do your grandparents have, compared to yours, that would affect the way a given personal care product (you name the product) for people of their age should be presented by a salesperson that would most likely result in its sale?

2.   If you owned the company offering this personal care product for sale, what "promotional mix" would you employ to achieve sales success?

3.   What age salespeople would you hire to sell this product directly (that is, face-to-face) to persons of your grandparents' age? Why?

4.   What sales appeals would you require your salespeople to employ in selling this product directly to prospects of your grandparents' age to conform to the modern customer/society-oriented sales/marketing concept?

Buyer Behavior and the Psychology of Selling: To Individual Consumers and to Organizational Buyers

After studying this chapter, you will be able to:

Explain the terms *consumer behavior, reference groups, role, status, personality, motive* (or *drive*), *needs, wants, perception,* and *learning.*

Describe the difference between emotional and rational buying motives.

Discuss how the self-concept theory of buying behavior relates to an individual's perception of his or her own self and ego.

Describe the five steps of the psychological process buyers go through in reaching their buying decisions.

Identify the three most important cultural factors, the three most important social factors, the four most important personal factors, and the four most important psychological factors that influence an individual's buying behavior.

Explain how the buying process relates to the selling process.

The subject of consumer (or buyer) behavior—how and why people buy and consume—had always been one of practical interest to traders and salespeople since the earliest days of selling and exchange. But so long as their chief concern was trying to move goods they had either produced unilaterally or obtained for resale, it was not a subject of major interest, concern, or study.

It was not until the 1960s, in response to the emerging customer-oriented marketing concept of the 1950s of understanding and satisfying consumer needs, that consumer research as a field of serious study became highly developed. Since the marketing concept focused on predetermining what goods and services consumers needed and wanted, companies had to engage in market research to find out what those needs and wants were. They soon learned that there were many different market segments, the interests and priorities of which differed dramatically.

In the face of this situation, in order to design new products, services, and sales/marketing strategies that would fulfill customer desires, they realized that they would have to study consumers and their consumption behavior in far greater depth than ever before. This rapidly led to the study of consumer behavior as a key element of marketing.

WHAT DO WE MEAN BY CONSUMER (OR BUYER) BEHAVIOR AND HOW CAN IT BE DETERMINED?

Consumer behavior has been described as the applied multidisciplinary field of study concerned with the understanding, explaining, and predicting of human actions in the consumption role. A more complete definition is this:

> *Consumer Behavior:* the behavior that consumers display in searching for, purchasing, using, evaluating, and disposing of products, services and ideas which they expect will satisfy their needs.[1]

The study includes how individuals decide to spend their money, time, and effort on consumption-related items. It is concerned with *what* consumers buy, *why* they buy it, *how* they buy it, *when* they buy it, *where* they buy it, and *how often* they buy it.

Consumer research is the methodology used to study consumer behavior. Face-to-face interviews at both outside and in-laboratory sites, telephone interviews, and written questionnaires are among the techniques used. Such research takes place at every stage of the consumption process: before the purchase, during the purchase, and after the purchase.

For example, research into an American man's end-use consumption behavior in the area of shaving cream products might include a study of why he

[1] Leon G. Schiffman and Leslie Lazar Kanuk, *Consumer Behavior*, 3rd ed. (Englewood Cliffs, N.J.: Prentice-Hall, 1987), p. 6.

BUYER BEHAVIOR AND THE PSYCHOLOGY OF SELLING

uses shaving cream (to help him shave faster and more easily), which brand of shaving cream he buys (for example, Barbasol), why he buys it (less expensive than competing brands), how he buys it (for cash), when he buys it (usually when he does food shopping), where he buys it (usually in a supermarket), and how often he buys it (once a month).

In terms of the big picture, consumer research is highly relevant to each variable in the marketing mix: product, price, distribution, and promotion. It is also quite relevant to the personal selling process, as we shall see.

WHAT DOES THE STUDY OF CONSUMER (OR BUYER) BEHAVIOR HAVE TO DO WITH PERSONAL SELLING?

While no final, perfect system for predicting buyer behavior has yet evolved, enough has been learned to greatly assist salespeople in understanding why people buy what they do when they do.

One result is the modern concept of personal selling, which holds that the selling process is actually a buying process. Because the final buying decision is made in the mind of the buyer, the function of the salesperson is to help the buyer discover his or her needs, wants, and problems, and to help fulfill or solve them through buying that salesperson's product or service.

To help the buyer in this discovery, the salesperson first asks information-gathering questions during a sales interview—around which he or she then builds selling points. Consumer research has shown that people do not buy without reason or reasons; but whatever their reasons, they are motivated or persuaded to buy basically (1) by *internal*, rational, and emotional *motivations*, and (2) by *external forces*. And whatever they finally do or decide is due to their reasons, and not those of salespeople.

In order to persuade the buyer that the product or service being offered will fulfill his or her desires, a salesperson must present advantages and benefits so that they will meet the buyer's emotional as well as rational buying motives. Here is an explanation of these terms:

- *Rational buying motives:* All costs affecting the buyer, including cost in money, cost in use, length of usage, degree of labor, and ultimate benefit.
- *Emotional buying motives:* Nonrational motives, such as impulse, habits, drive, ego, pride, and the like.

The more a salesperson knows about the internal motivations and external factors that affect a buyer's reasons for buying or not buying at a given time, the easier it will be for him or her to direct appeals to the desires and self-interest of the buyer.

To sell effectively in line with such concepts, the modern-day salesperson must keep alert to fast-moving changes affecting attitudes and buying habits within the society in which he or she lives and works. Changes such as role reversal within the family, minority group needs and interests, and the new sexual morality call for greater insight into, and emphatic understanding of, the sociological and psychological forces affecting the buying process.

To learn more about such things, let us now consider some of the major findings of consumer (buyer) behavior studies relating to both consumer and organizational buyers that affect personal selling.

WHAT INFLUENCES BUYER BEHAVIOR?

The first formal explanations of buyer behavior were advanced by economists. They considered the subject from the point of view that humans are rational buyers with price as their strongest motivation; that all things being equal they will rationally and predictably buy maximum value at lowest price. Figure 3.1 illustrates this most simple conception of buyer behavior.

The conclusion, in the eyes of economists, was that a buyer ought to do this or that rationally if manipulated or guided toward selected sets of buying alternatives. While this theory might explain, for example, why a consumer might purchase a television set from one dealer instead of another (the one offering it at lowest price), it did not explain why he or she decided to purchase an RCA brand over a Sony, or a different size, model, or color.

Emotional and Other Problems Affect Buyer Behavior

Sales/marketing people, recognizing that there were many markets, not just one homogeneous market for most products, soon concluded that consumer buying resulted not just from economic considerations, but also from other reasons.

FIGURE 3.1 *A Simple Conception of Buyer Behavior*

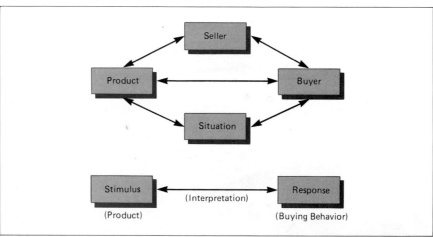

BUYER BEHAVIOR AND THE PSYCHOLOGY OF SELLING

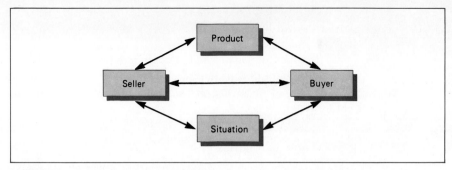

FIGURE 3.2 *Buying Behavior is Influenced by These Considerations*

Since the late 1960s, in an attempt to determine what these other reasons are, consumer research emphasis has been on more process-oriented, or comprehensive-integrated, research combining several different areas, for example, culture (cultural anthropology), reference groups (sociology), and attitudes and beliefs (psychology).

This view sees the buyer as a whole person feeling many emotions, such as love, joy, and boredom, and facing many problems, such as work and social environment, all of which ultimately involve buying decisions and consumption. Thus a consumer is not just buying toothpaste, but rather is solving the problem of oral hygiene; is not merely buying a sports car for transportation; but rather is fulfilling inner desires for status and recognition. Further, in this view, as has already been noted, while making buying decisions, buyers behave both rationally and irrationally (or emotionally).

Many Considerations and Characteristics Bear on Buying Behavior

The modern behavioral science consensus is that there are many considerations that influence an individual's buying behavior. These considerations have been classified into four major areas. As illustrated by Figure 3.2, these are associated with the *product*, with the *seller*, with the *situation*, and with the *buyer*.

Different characteristics (features, style, price) of the *product* influence buying decisions, as do different characteristics of the *seller* (reliability, friendliness, service), and various *situational* considerations (pressure of time, time of year or day, weather). While we consider these three considerations at various points throughout the balance of our text, let us first take an overview look at the four major factors that affect the buying behavior of individual and household consumers, and four major types of consumer buying behavior.

MAJOR FACTORS AFFECTING CONSUMER BEHAVIOR

We learned in Chapter 2 that there are two broad types of markets—consumer and organizational—and that the consumer market consists of all individuals and households who buy or acquire goods for personal consumption. We also learned that within the overall consumer market are many different market segments, broken down by age, income, race, educational level, and preferences of many types.

In order to plan products and services for, and to sell effectively to, all these different groups of consumers, sales/marketing people must understand different factors that affect buying behavior, and the buying decision process that buyers go through.

Studies have shown that consumer buyer behavior is affected by four major factors: (1) *cultural* (culture, subculture, and social class), (2) *social* (reference groups, family, and role and status), (3) *personal* (age and life-cycle stage, occupation and economic circumstances, life-style, and personality and self-concept), and (4) *psychological* (motivation, perception, learning, and attitudes and beliefs).

Organizational buyers (who are also human and consumers) are, of course, affected to a greater or lesser degree by many of these factors, even though they are buying for their organizations. They are also affected by business and other considerations that do *not* apply to those buying for individual or household consumption; these are treated separately later in this chapter.

CULTURAL FACTORS

The three most important cultural factors that influence buyer behavior are the culture, subculture, and social class with which the individual buyer can be identified.

Culture. The culture into which a person is born and lives exerts a strong control over his or her attitudes and actions. Basic behavior, perceptions, preferences, and values are shaped by the process of socialization involving the family and associated institutions within the culture. One born and raised within a central African tribe, for example, tends to think and act differently than does a person born and raised in Tokyo, Japan.

Subculture. Each culture contains smaller groups or subcultures that further identify its members. Easily identified subcultures include race, nationality, and religion. An Arabic-speaking, Egyptian Moslem, for example, may have attitudes toward a given need or benefit different from those of a Brooklyn-born Irish Catholic.

Social Class. Social stratification—the division of members of society into a hierarchy of distinct social classes—exists in all societies and cultures. Social class is usually defined by the amount of status that members of a specific class possess or feel in relation to members of another class. Social class membership often serves as a frame of reference (that is, reference group) in the development of buyer attitudes and behavior. A frequently used classification system consists of six classes: upper-upper, lower-upper, upper-middle, lower-middle, upper-lower, and lower-lower.

Socioeconomic differences among these classes are reflected in differences in attitudes, in leisure-time activities, and in buying habits. Upper-class people, for example, may place great value on expensive status symbols such as big homes in fashionable suburbs, even if they cannot afford them. Lower-class people may take great pride in personal maintenance of their own small, paid-for home in a less expensive neighborhood.

SOCIAL FACTORS

Nearly all individuals regularly interact with other people who directly or indirectly influence their buying behavior. Like almost all behavior, social relationships are often motivated by the expectation that they will help satisfy specific needs. For example, a person might join a social dancing class in order to find compatible new friends to satisfy social needs. Among the social factors that influence buying behavior are reference groups, family, and social roles and status.

Reference Groups

The term "reference group" is quite broad, as this definition illustrates:

"A *reference group* is any person or group of any size that serves as a point of comparison (or reference) for an individual in the formation of either general or specific values, attitudes or behavior."[2]

Traditionally, reference groups included those groups with which a person interacts on a *direct* basis, such as:

- The family
- Friendship groups (such as, close friends)
- Formal social groups (clubs, church, professional organizations)
- Shopping groups (for example, two or more people who shop together whether for food or clothing or merely to pass the time of day)
- Work groups (including all fellow workers or more informal friendship groups within the total workforce)

In recent years the meaning of *reference group* has been broadened to also include *indirect* individual or group influences with which a person does not have direct contact (for example, rock music stars, sports heroes, movie stars, or television personalities).

Reference groups such as these expose and influence the individual to possible new behaviors and life style, as illustrated by wild teenage fashion and

---

[2] Schiffman and Kanuk, *Consumer Behavior*, 3rd ed., p. 375.

taste changes that sweep the world so quickly and so frequently. And they create pressures for conformity that affect buying behavior as the individual tries to conform (that is, to "fit in") to group norms.

The Family

The family probably plays the most important single role in an individual's early attitude formation and in determining his or her lifelong buying behavior. Teenagers often rebel against their families' social values but often accept these again later. These family attitudes have a very important place in decisions on all family purchases.

In North American husband-wife households, the wife influences most of the buying and actually spends most of the family money. She usually makes the decisions on buying a home, appliances, furniture, encyclopedia sets, and clothes, and on planning vacations. The husband usually makes the decisions on buying automobiles, sporting equipment, and insurance policies. Children exert strong influence on North American family buying habits, because of sheer numbers and the fact that the family is often child-oriented. Giant food manufacturers, among others, vie on television and through packaging for the attention of the youngsters in the house.

Roles and Status

Within each group to which he or she belongs (family, clubs, work), an individual has a certain position that can be defined in terms of *role* and *status*. A *role* is a pattern of behavior expected of the individual within any given group. There may be ascribed roles or achieved roles. *Ascribed roles* are those expected of an individual over which he or she has no control (sex, family, race, and religion). *Achieved roles* are those roles that a person adopts as a result of personal attainment and growth (educational level, income, occupational or marital status).

Status relates to the relative prestige accorded to an individual or the position he or she occupies within a given group or social system. Status often results from the degree of influence the individual exerts on the attitudes and behavior of others. For example, a banker may be accorded a great deal of respect in his or her community and may influence buying behavior of others either directly (through investment advice he or she gives) or indirectly (the example he or she sets by driving a specific make of car). A person's role and status within groups to which he or she belongs influences not only general behavior but also buying behavior.

PERSONAL FACTORS

Buying decisions are also shaped by personal factors such as one's age and life-cycle stage, occupation and economic circumstances, life-style, and personality and self-concept.

Age and Life-Cycle Stage

As an individual moves through his or her family life-cycle, needs, wants, attitudes, and values change. Seven stages of the *family life-cycle* have been identified.[3] They include:

1. Bachelor stage—young single people.
2. Newly married couples—young, with no children.
3. Full nest I—young married couples with youngest child under six.
4. Full nest II—young married couples with youngest child six or over.
5. Full nest III—older married couples with dependent children.
6. Empty nest—older married couples with no children living with them.
7. Solitary survivors—older single people, either working or retired.

Buyer behavior is different at each stage. The full nest I group usually is interested in purchasing homes, television sets, baby food, furniture, and appliances. The empty nest group is more interested in recreational items, travel, and entertainment. Salespeople should be aware of changing life-cycle wants and values, and shape buying appeals accordingly.

Occupation and Economic Circumstances

An individual's occupation greatly affects his or her buying behavior. Executives are normally interested in expensive homes, cars, clothes, club memberships, and sailboats. Blue-collar workers are normally interested in lower-priced homes, fishing boats, and sports events. One's occupation also bears on his or her economic circumstances (income, savings, and assets), which in turn affect attitudes such as borrowing to spend now versus saving to buy later.

Life-Style

An individual's life-style, in terms of time (both work and leisure), values, and interests, is likely to influence decision making and buying behavior. People coming from the same subculture, social class, or occupational group may choose to lead quite different life-styles—a decision that affects their buying behavior. Many young men and women, for example, decide to marry and live a comfortable, solid, traditional life. Others elect to live the freer life of a single and often buy and consume countless expensive items with little thought to planning for the future.

Personality and Self-Concept

Each individual possesses a unique personality. *Personality* can be described as the psychological characteristics that both determine and reflect how a person responds to his or her environment. While the inner characteristics that make up

[3] William D. Wells and George Gubar, "Life Cycle Concept in Marketing Research," *Journal of Marketing Research* (November 1966), pp. 355–363.

an individual's personality are unique to that individual, many individuals tend to be similar in terms of a single personality characteristic (for example, "high" or "low" in sociability, or the degree of interest displayed in social or group activities).

Although one's personality tends to be constant and enduring, it can change abruptly in response to major life events (birth of a baby, divorce, death of a loved one), and may also change over time as part of a gradual maturing process.

Two items stemming from research into personality are of special interest to salespeople, since they relate closely to buyer behavior. They are (1) the self-concept theory of buying behavior and (2) psychographic segmentation.

- *Self-Concept Theory.* This theory of buying behavior is one of the best integrated attempts to relate buyer behavior to an individual's self-concept—the perception of one's own self and ego. It is based on the belief that buyers perceive a product they would like to own in terms of meaning to themselves and others. For example, if a young male college student sees himself as aggressive and masculine, he might buy a bright red, dual-exhaust economy sports car as an expression of how he sees himself and would like others to view him. In other words, he would see this particular car as somehow an extension of his own personality.

This theory hinges on the concept that an individual's real self and his or her ideal self are different, as seen in these four ways.

1. Self-image—how people see themselves.
2. Ideal self—how they would like to see themselves.
3. Looking-glass self—the way they think others see them.
4. Real self—the way they really are.

A person's self-image or self-concept is a basic key to any form of behavior, buying or otherwise. One's real self and ideal self are two different things, and throughout life one strives to make this self-image and ideal self coincide with the way people would like others to see them. This ideal self is the goal toward which the person strives, and concepts change frequently throughout life. The drive toward a steadily more satisfying self-concept is natural and proper from a mental health point of view.

The constant striving to match one's real with one's ideal self influences one's buying behavior, with motivation the driving force behind it.

Building on our example, to further illustrate this theory, an automobile salesperson would try, through questioning and observation, to "size up" the young potential buyer (prospect). The salesperson would mentally ask himself or herself: "How does this young man see himself? How would he like to see himself, and have others see him?" Only by ascertaining this can the salesperson most effectively present that specific bright red, economical, dual-exhaust sports car as a means of fulfilling this particular buyer's wants and desires. The emotional buying motive of ego-gratification is based on this self-concept theory of human behavior.

BUYER BEHAVIOR AND THE PSYCHOLOGY OF SELLING

- *Psychographic Segmentation.* Since the early 1970s, researchers have increasingly broadened the measurement of consumer personality variables to include related behavioral concepts such as consumer life-style, interests, attitudes, and opinions. This broadened area of research is called *psychographics*; its purpose is to provide sales/marketing people with a quantitative (measurable) rather than merely a qualitative indication of whatever psychological or sociocultural characteristics are being studied. It has proven especially useful when coupled with demographic characteristics such as age, sex, marital status, income, and occupation.

Psychographic research centers on self-administered questionnaires that most often are comprised of statements or questions concerning intangible variables, such as the respondents' needs, perceptions, beliefs, values, tastes, and problems. Analysis of this research is useful in helping to (1) segment markets, (2) position and reposition products, and (3) develop specific promotional and selling campaigns.

PSYCHOLOGICAL FACTORS

The major psychological factors that affect human behavior (including buying behavior) are motivation, perception, learning, and attitudes and beliefs. Since the field of human behavior is so large, complex, and sometimes inconsistent, we can do little more than take a brief look at each of these.

Motivation

Human behavior, including buying behavior, involves a complicated stimulus-and-response to motives.

> A *motive* (or drive) is a need or want that is so pressing that it prompts a person to seek satisfaction by acting in a certain way.

These motives may be expressed or unexpressed and are based either on deep-rooted needs or on more openly felt wants or desires. Motivation is the driving force that impels individuals to take action to satisfy them. The form this action takes—to achieve a goal that will aid in this fulfillment—is a result of the thinking process (cognition) and previous learning. In terms of sales/marketing, such goals may be *generic* (a general goal or category of goal to fulfill a certain need or want), or *product-specific* (the goal of acquiring a specific type or brand of product that the buyer sees as the means of fulfilling his need or want). Since the terms *needs* and *wants* will appear frequently throughout our book, let us examine their meaning as related to a buyer's behavior.

- *Needs,* operating just below the level of consciousness, are sometimes difficult to recognize, since they were either inherited or learned. *Innate needs,* those an individual is born with, are primarily physiological (biogenic), and include all the factors required to sustain physical life (water, food, clothing, shelter, sex). *Acquired needs*, those developed after birth, are primarily psychological (psychogenic), and include such things as love, affection, security, or safety—needs so inwardly felt that they may not even be understood by buyers themselves.

- *Wants,* on the other hand, are easier than needs to spot, since they operate closer to the conscious level and reflect positive desires (pleasure, profit, approval) or negative desires (loss, disapproval, inconvenience). Wants are more broadly defined and psychological than needs and include, from a buying point of view, consumer desires, inward motivations, personal objectives, and mental satisfaction.

When someone buys something, he or she psychologically satisfies both a need and want. As products have changed, so has the consumer, or buyer. Most buyers today in the world's advanced, industrialized nations have more money than those of earlier years and normally have already fulfilled their basic needs for food, clothing, and shelter. They can now buy what they want rather than what they simply need. They no longer have to buy a particular product; a whole host of products will satisfy their desire. The average buyer today in those countries buys a specific product because it will provide him or her with certain mental or physical satisfactions.

Theories of Motivation

Motivation is a highly complex field of study. Psychologists have been formally researching the subject for well over a century and still continue to differ on several of its basic concepts. Best known among these psychologists for their theoretical contributions are Sigmund Freud, for his "dream theory"; Victor H. Vroom, for his "expectancy theory"; David C. McCellan, for his "theory of achievement motivation"; Frederick Herzberg, for his "dual factor theory"; and Abraham H. Maslow, for his "theory of human motivation." While all these are of professional reference value to ambitious salespeople, Herzberg's theory is of special interest to sales managers, because it suggests factors that they can employ to help motivate salespeople to higher goal achievement, and Maslow's theory is most applicable overall to buyer behavior.

Maslow's "Hierarchy of Needs" Theory

Maslow believed that each human being is an organized, integrated whole, motivated by a number of basic needs that are species-wide, apparently unchanging, and genetic or instinctual in origin.[4] He categorized and ranked these into a conceptual hierarchy, based on the premises that: (1) the behavior of any person is dominated and determined by the most basic group of needs that are unfulfilled; (2) the individual will systematically satisfy his or her needs, starting with the most basic and moving up the hierarchy; (3) the more basic needs take precedence over those higher up in the hierarchy.

[4] Abraham H. Maslow, *Motivation and Personality*, 2nd ed. (New York: Harper & Row, 1970).

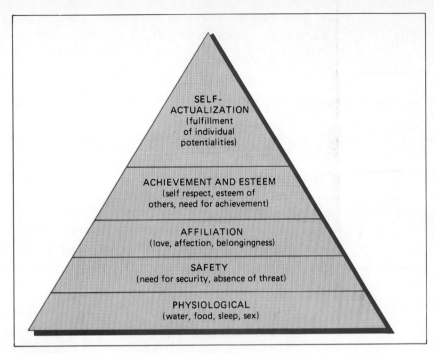

FIGURE 3.3 *Maslow's Hierarchy of Needs*

While Figure 3.3 presents Maslow's hierarchy of needs in seemingly mutually exclusive form for purposes of clarity, actually, according to his theory, there is overlap between each level, since no need is ever completely satisfied. His model suggests a state of internal motivation that incites the individual to some kind of action. The healthy person is viewed as seeking the goal of self-fulfillment, or his or her unique "self-actualization," from the beginning of life to its end. Because of the uniqueness of each person, the form or content of self-actualization is a never-ending process of finding new goals and new means of expression.

Perception

When an individual is motivated, he or she is ready to act. The decision how to act is influenced by his or her perception of the situation.

Perception is the process by which individuals select, organize, and interpret stimuli into a meaningful and coherent picture of the world.

Perception involves organizing and integrating innumerable sights, sounds, tastes, odors, and tactile impressions. Those sensory inputs are then altered by the individual's knowledge, by past experiences, by feelings and attitudes, and by his or her personality.

Most consumers tend to make buying decisions based upon what they perceive, rather than on the basis of objective reality. They usually perceive things they need or want, and mentally block out the perception of unfavorable or painful stimuli.

To take an example, consider two different people hearing separately the same words and seeing the same vehicle as an automobile salesperson points out in some detail engine capabilities and comparisons of a new model car. Although they hear and see the same thing, the two people might perceive the situation quite differently. One might consider the salesperson too pushy or boring, while the other might consider him or her extremely knowledgeable and helpful. Their individual buying decisions might rest on their differing perceptions of this one part of the overall sales presentation.

Learning

Since psychologists disagree on how individuals learn, it is difficult to come up with a generally accepted definition. The following one seems to best fit our needs:

> *Learning* is a continually evolving process resulting from acquired knowledge (gained from study, observation, or thinking) or from actual experience. Some learning is intentional; some incidental (acquired without much effort).

Here are four basic types of learning involved in the development of an individual's buying behavior: (1) basic childhood learning (which is so deeply rooted that sales appeals can seldom change it), (2) cognitive learning (that is, knowledge learned over a period of time), (3) attitudinal learning (attitudes are developed out of one's experiences, that is, they are learned), and (4) behavioral learning.

Attitudes and Beliefs

The results of motivation and perception on buying behavior is manifest in learning. Through the learning process individuals acquire their beliefs and attitudes. These in turn influence their behavior.

- A *belief* is an opinion or conviction about the truth of or existence of something not immediately susceptible to rigorous proof.
- An *attitude* is a manner, disposition, feeling, or position about a person, thing, or idea.

Ingrained beliefs and attitudes are hard to change. Success in personal selling comes most often to salespeople who fit their sales appeals into a prospect's existing attitudes and beliefs, rather than by trying to change them.

As has been noted, the process of motivation, perception, learning, and the formation of attitudes and beliefs are very complicated. Our treatment of them has been very limited. While psychologists themselves do not always agree on how these factors affect buying behavior, a salesperson should constantly be aware that these factors mediate between the product itself and the buyer's behavioral response, should attempt to assess them, and try to turn them to his or her sales advantage. This is no easy task, due in part to the fact that a person's buying decision behavior is in itself a process.

THE CONSUMER'S BUYING DECISION PROCESS

Consumer buying behavior throughout the buying process differs according to the complexity of the type of purchase being considered. Buying a tube of toothpaste, for example, is a fairly simple matter, and buyers are not likely to devote much time or thought to the purchase. When it comes to more important purchases, say for a new family car, the buying decision is much more complex and time consuming.

Whatever the type of buying decision, the decision itself is really a collection of decisions, involving need or want, product, service, price, and time. These decisions are elaborated upon in chapters to come; for now our concern is with the psychological process by which buyers make their buying decisions. As noted earlier in this chapter, consumer research in general takes place at every stage of the consumption process: before the purchase, during the purchase, and after the purchase. So too, does the consumer buying process cover a before, during and after purchase span. This is clearly illustrated in Figure 3.4, which shows the overall five stages of the consumer buying process. These are (1) need, want, or problem recognition, (2) prepurchase information search, (3) evaluation of alternatives, (4) purchase decision behavior, and (5) postpurchase behavior.

Stages 1–3: The Decision-Making Act

The *process* portion of this decision-making, or the act of making a consumer decision, is represented by stages 1–3, which we will elaborate upon as follows:

Need, Want, or Problem Recognition. The buying decision making starts when an individual recognizes a need, or want, or problem. It may be triggered by (1) sales promotion activities by the seller of a given product (such as by advertising or a salesperson's approach) or (2) by influences brought about by the buyer's

FIGURE 3.4 *The Five-Stage Consumer Buying Process*

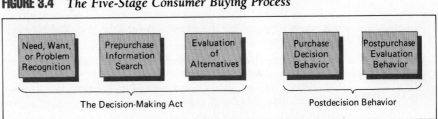

cultural/social environment (for example, a close friend has said that the product is very good).

It is important to note here that a salesperson cannot force a prospect to buy a product that he or she does not want. The salesperson can and should, however, suggest and arouse to conscious awareness a perceived need, want, or problem that the prospect might be unaware of, and encourage that individual to take action (through buying) to satisfy it.

Prepurchase Information Search.   If an aroused need or want can be gratified immediately by a purchase, a buyer is likely to do so. For example, if a person suddenly feels hungry for a hamburger, he or she is likely to buy one at the closest restaurant.

If however, the need or want involves something with which the individual has had little experience, for example, a new model or make economical, front-wheel-drive car, the individual may embark upon a lengthy information search. The search, in this case, is aimed at learning more about this particular type of car, the different makes available, the differences among these makes, and about the different dealers who sell them.

In conducting this search, the buyer relies on his or her own experience, personal sources (family, friends, business associates), commercial sources (salespeople, advertising), public sources (consumer rating publications), and experimental sources (testing the different types of cars at various dealers' show-rooms).

Evaluation of Alternatives.   Suppose our new car buyer in the above example has now found three different makes of new cars that seem to meet his basic needs, wants, and criteria gathered from his prepurchase information search. How does he finally choose among them?

The answer lies in an evaluation process involving several considerations. The prospective buyer first has to consider and at least mentally rate in order of importance his or her unique needs or wants (best mileage, exterior color of choice, immediate availability). The next step might be to evaluate these priorities between the three different brand manufacturers (Ford versus Toyota versus Volkswagen). Other considerations that might also enter into the individual's evaluation of alternatives include safety, overall appearance, durability, riding comfort, ease of handling, and eventual cost of repairs.

Stages 4–5: Postdecision Behavior

The *output* portion of the buying decision process involves the consumer's degree of satisfaction or dissatisfaction with the purchase. If happy, he or she may buy the same item again; if unhappy, probably not. Either way, the postpurchase evaluation "feeds back" as a learning experience that is likely to influence future related buying decisions. Here are some additional perspectives about stages 4–5:

Purchase Decision Behavior.   Information leads to a desire to purchase one of the items that has been evaluated (for example, a specific make of car from a certain dealer). At this point, however, other factors enter the picture. First of all, the buyer's decision may be affected by the attitude of others (a family member may object to the make of car that has been selected). Second, the buying decision has to be based on considerations such as the total cost of the car versus the benefits to be gained by buying it now. Finally, unanticipated factors may cloud the buying decision; for example, there may be a problem in negotiating mutually acceptable payment terms, or overaggressiveness on the part of the salesperson may repel the prospective buyer in the final stages of the purchase.

It is at this crucial point of the buying process (called the *close*) that a salesperson needs an emphatic understanding of various feelings and influences that may lead to the buyer's feeling a sense of risk. The salesperson should provide the emotional support and factual information that will help minimize this feeling.

Postpurchase Evaluation Behavior. The final stage of the consumer's buying process is the postpurchase evaluation behavior of the product purchased. After trying it, the purchaser will experience some level of satisfaction or dissatisfaction with what has been purchased. The degree of satisfaction felt results from a weighing of the buyer's prepurchase expectations versus the product's perceived performance.

Salespeople must pay attention to how the products or services they sell are used and evaluated by buyers. Favorable evaluation may lead in many cases to repurchases of the products. Feedback from satisfied buyers as to why they like their purchase can help develop new and better selling points around which more sales can be made. Unfavorable evaluation can pinpoint factors that can be corrected (such as poor design or unfavorable warranty).

THE ORGANIZATIONAL BUYER'S BUYING DECISION PROCESS

Organizational buyers, both profit and nonprofit, purchase products and services for consumption by the institution or organization that they represent. Manufacturers, wholesalers, hospitals, schools, agencies of government, and businesses of all types purchase and consume all sorts of items. Such purchases normally involve greater quantities, more money, and a more rational, formalized decision procedure than do those of the individual or household buyer.

While no two organizations buy in the same way, the buyers (or purchasing officers) in most types are frequently judged on their effectiveness by the profits made through resale or use of, or savings effected through a purchase. The following definition illustrates what they are concerned with:

> *Organizational buying* is "the decision-making process by which formal organizations establish the need for purchased products and services, and identify, evaluate, and choose among alternative brands and suppliers."[5]

[5] Frederick E. Webster, Jr., and Yoram Wind, *Organizational Buying Behavior* (Englewood Cliffs, N.J.: Prentice-Hall, 1972), p. 2.

Organizational Buyers Feel Dual Roles

When buying for their own individual consumption, or for their family or household, these buyers, feel, think, and act like all other consumers, and are affected in their buying decisions by all the internal motivations and external influences that we have been considering. When they go to work, although they still retain their private thoughts and feelings, they have to assume an additional role—that of representing the organization by which they are employed. This dual role can affect organizational buyers' behavior in different ways. For example, while they may be most impressed by rational considerations of cost, quality, and dependability, they also are likely to respond to salespeople who show them personal respect and consideration and who do "extra favors" for them. If a salesperson can show that it is in their own best personal interest, as well as that of their organization to buy, they tend to respond favorably.

The type of organization to which organizational buyers belong plays an important part in their buying behavior and decisions. This can be best illustrated by considering buyer behavior in the three broad types of organizations presented earlier—industrial, reseller, and government, plus separate attention to those buying certain types of largely intangible services.

INDUSTRIAL BUYERS

Representing both profit and nonprofit organizations, buyers in the industrial market purchase countless goods and services for their own use, for use in producing other goods and services, or for meeting other requirements. Most are sizable organizations that buy in large quantities through a centralized purchasing or buying department staffed by highly trained purchasing agents or buyers. These buyers make both routine reorder purchases (typical office use products) and purchases of new items ranging from small items to expensive computer systems or custom-designed plants or buildings.

Industrial buyers acquire goods and services through a buying (or procurement) process somewhat like that of consumers described earlier. A total of eight stages has been identified[6] for more important new purchases (see Fig. 3.5); fewer for less important ones.

The greater the size, cost, and risk of the proposed purchase, the greater the number of individuals involved in the purchase-decision process: the greater the alternative-information searching, and the longer the process itself. If buying an expensive new computer system, for example, many people throughout the organization get involved in the buying-decision process: users, technicians, mid-level executives of different departments, top executives who must approve the cost outlay, and the purchasing agents. In many such large-scale cases, the buying

---

[6] Patrick J. Robinson, Charles W. Faris, and Yoram Wind, *Industrial Buying and Creative Marketing* (Boston: Allyn & Bacon, 1967), p. 14.

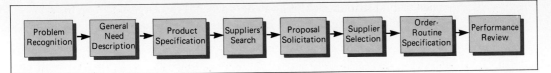

FIGURE 3.5   *The Eight-Stage Industrial Buying Process (for more Important Purchases)*

organization prefers to buy one whole integrated system, and sellers employ entire teams of highly trained technical salespeople to try to get the business.

Industrial buyers respond both to rational economic factors (such as, cost, delivery time, after-sale service) and to personal (motivational) considerations. If price between two competitor sellers is approximately equal, buyers are likely to respond favorably to other more personal influences.

BUYERS IN THE RESELLER MARKET

The reseller market consists of individuals and organizations that acquire and resell goods and services produced by others. Buying responsibilities in small jobber or wholesale firms may be handled by one or two individuals. Larger organizations have purchasing departments staffed by professionally trained buyers.

Buying is carried out in different ways by the many different types of resellers. Large retail store chains (department store, drug store, supermarket) for example, usually have specialty (by merchandise lines) buyers at corporate head-quarters, and frequently at regional headquarters as well, to review new product line offerings and see salespeople. Sometimes these buyers do the buying for all their retail outlets. In other cases they merely make recommendations to a central "buying committee," or to individual retail store managers within the chain who do their own buying.

The buying process employed by resellers is much the same as that just described for industrial buyers. Standard line items are simply reordered when stocks run low, usually from the same supplier if terms, conditions, and service remain competitive. Some or all of the eight stages of the industrial buying process shown in Fig. 3.5 are involved for new item or line purchases—the number and amount of time spent on each being determined by the cost and risk of the proposed purchase.

In selling to resellers, a salesperson must be aware that the reseller buyer's interest in the salesperson's offering depends largely on how other resellers of the buyer's product, throughout their channels of distribution, view it in terms of reselling it themselves. The first reseller is not likely to purchase the salesperson's product if its own customers are unwilling or unlikely to buy its own product.

To sell effectively in this situation, a salesperson must be aware of how his or her own product will ultimately be used to satisfy succeeding buyers in the channel of distribution. This awareness depends to a large extent on the salesperson's understanding of buyer behavior at different stages of the consumption process.

BUYERS IN THE GOVERNMENT MARKET

As noted earlier, the government market consists of governmental units at different levels (national or federal, state or provincial, and local) that purchase or rent goods or services in order to carry out functions of government. Government buying agencies or centers exist at each of these levels in many of the world's countries.

In the United States, since government is an institution of the people, by the people, and for the people, buying agencies at all levels go to great lengths to announce specifications for intended purchases and urge qualified suppliers to bid. Normally, government contracts are awarded to the lowest bidder. Since taxpayers' dollars are involved, several "watchdog" agencies of government, such as Congress and the General Accounting Office at the federal level, and many private organizations keep tabs on cost and spending efficiency. Since they are subject to so much oversight, government buying agencies follow detailed procedures that entail a great deal of paperwork and investment of bidders' time and money.

It is obvious that advertising, sales promotion, or personal selling plays a less important role where governmental units buy on an open-bid basis. Nevertheless, the sum total of government business is so huge that in the United States at least, a number of large companies have established separate, special sales/marketing departments to prepare and present such bids carefully and properly in a "sales-minded" manner.

Many Sellers or Providers of Services Face Unusual Buying Problems

While everything presented so far in relation to organizational buying of goods and services also applies, special attention must be given to those providers of services who face unusual buying considerations or problems.

The service sector of most of the world's industrialized countries is growing rapidly; in the United States it has become the dominant sector—accounting for over 70 percent of the gross national product. Services are offered by individuals and businesses seeking profit (accountants, food caterers, beauty salons), by not-for-profit organizations (museums, churches, symphony orchestras), and by governmental agencies (information services, fire departments). Services are consumed by individuals for their personal use (haircuts, laundry service) and by organizations (office cleaning services, employment agencies).

Services are largely *intangible*; unlike physical products, they cannot be touched, seen, or smelled. Services are *less standardized* than products, and because they are labor dependent the quality may be inconsistent over time. The quality of service rendered in a retail store, for example, may depend on the clerk or clerks on duty at any given time. Also, services are *perishable* and cannot be stored—a new, higher product price change, for example, will make useless yesterday's television commercial built and filmed around a lower price. Successful sellers of intangibles have to "tangibilize" and "personalize" their offerings in every way possible; ways to do this are presented in Chapter 16.

Selling to service providers offers tremendous potential to alert salespeople, but requires an emphatic understanding of motivational buying reasons, both of the provider's buyer or buyers, and of the provider's end-use buyers. The buying process is much the same for both small and large organizational sellers of intangible services as for sellers of tangible products, but their real reasons for buying may be more emotionally based.

RELATING THE BUYING PROCESS TO THE SELLING PROCESS

The purpose of devoting this chapter to buyer behavior is to help you better understand the buyer, both consumer and organizational—from the viewpoint of the salesperson. In describing the buying process through buyer's eyes, we have pointed out the different and complicated cultural, social, personal, and psychological factors and characteristics of buyers that can influence buying behavior. In so doing, we have said that the selling process is actually a buying process.

In order to accomplish his or her selling objectives, the salesperson must move a buyer through the stages of the buying process. From here on in this book, we use the term *selling process* in describing how salespeople can help move buyers through the buying process. Five major parts of the selling process we consider in some depth are (1) prospecting (Chapter 5), (2) planning (Chapter 6), (3) presentation (Chapters 8–13), (4) handling objections (Chapter 11) and the close (Chapter 12), and (5) follow-up and follow-through (Chapter 13). Figure 3.6 illustrates how these steps of the selling process relate to the steps of the consumer buying process. The same relationship exists, in a more complicated way, with the eight-stage industrial buying process presented on pages 88 and 89.

FIGURE 3.6 *Relating the Buying Process to the Selling Process*

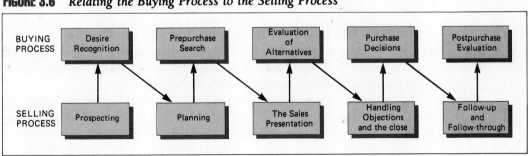

By now you have a limited but broad insight into many of the internal and external reasons that motivate buyers. As you gain sales experience you will develop an even greater insight into the psychological factors that influence buyer behavior. Your sales job is to determine, through questioning, listening, and observing, what your prospects' real motivations and wants are and to build your sales presentation around them.

Once you have determined the real reason your prospect wants to buy, you may have to consider your ethical and moral responsibilities as a salesperson. The power of persuasion, combined with psychological insight, sometimes is so great that experienced salespeople can discover the prospect's real buying motivator or reason without he or she realizing it themselves. You may inwardly feel this need to be ridiculous, but your empathy should tell you that it is a real one for that individual, no matter how unimportant it may seem to you. You have the obligation to serve him or her out of genuine respect for his or her personality. And you have the serious professional responsibility of fulfilling this need by providing something of value.

What we are referring to is the fact that an experienced salesperson, in many types of selling, often encounters less intelligent or immature prospects who may be unable to resist the salesperson's persuasion and want to buy something they should not buy. The salesperson is well aware, through his or her greater psychological insight, of this situation.

We consider in Chapter 17 the legal and ethical considerations involved in such psychologically and emotionally difficult situations. It is important now, however, to make clear that when specific sales techniques are discussed in the pages to follow, you should consider them as honest sales techniques, and not as "tricks of the trade." Good professional selling rests on solid ethical and moral foundations.

SUMMARY

The purpose of this chapter is to help salespeople better understand the internal and external factors that influence buyer behavior. We learned that people do not buy without a reason or reasons, that they are motivated to buy basically (1) by internal, rational, and emotional motivations and (2) by external forces. As a salesperson, you should remember that whatever they finally do or decide is due to their reasons and not yours. To sell effectively, salespeople must present the advantages and benefits of their product or service so that they meet the prospect's emotional as well as rational needs and wants.

After dividing buyers into two broad market groups: (1) consumer and (2) organizational, we considered the four major groups of factors that influence an individual's buying behavior. These are associated with the *product,* the *seller,* the *situation,* and the *buyer.* We then focused on the different cultural, social, personal, and psychological factors affecting the buyer that can influence buying behavior.

The three most important *cultural factors* are the culture, subculture, and social class with which the buyer can be identified. The three major *social factors* are reference groups, family, and role and status. Four major *personal factors* are one's age and life-cycle stages, occupation and economic circumstances, life-style, and personality and self-concept. Finally, the four major *psychological factors* are motivation, perception, learning, and attitudes and beliefs.

Noting that the selling process is actually a buying process, we concluded that whatever the type of buying, decision (simple or complex) the decision itself is really a collection of decisions involving need or want, product, service, price, and time. The consumer buying process consists of five stages: (1) need, want, or problem recognition, (2) prepurchase information search, (3) evaluation of alternatives, (4) purchase decision behavior, and (5) postpurchase evaluation behavior. Buyers in the industrial and other organizational markets follow a similar buying process, which for high-cost items might go through as many as eight stages.

We then noted that from here on in our text we use the term *selling process* in describing how salespeople can help move buyers through the buying process in a highly ethical, professional way.

Questions for Analysis and Discussion

1. Has a final, perfect system for predicting buyer behavior yet been developed to help salespeople sell effectively? If not, why not?

2. What motivates a person to buy anything?

3. Assume that you are about to purchase a box of breakfast cereal at a supermarket. What basic need and what emotional buying motives are you about to fulfill?

4. Explain how the purchase of an expensive bottle of perfume by a young female secretary might really be based on a deeply felt need or want, not even understood by the woman herself.

5. What is meant by the statement, "Because of the uniqueness of each person, the form or content of 'self-actualization' is a never-ending process of finding new goals and new means of expression?"

6. When an individual is motivated, he or she is ready to act. The decision how to act is influenced by his or her "perception" of the situation. In this sense, what does "perception" involve?

7. What are the five stages of the "consumer buying process," that psychological process by which buyers make their buying decisions for individual or household consumption?

8. What is the difference between "needs" and "wants" in the psychological sense as applied to personal selling?

CASE STUDY 3

The Impulse to Buy—It's Almost Like Being In Love!

The sweater was following me. I had gone to a different part of the store, but it pulled me back to the men's department where I finally bought it.
—A 38 year-old male describing an impulse purchase.

Nine people out of ten have succumbed to impulse buying, a mid-1980s study concluded, and many have lived to regret it. A large number of the more than 300 people surveyed by California marketing expert Dennis Rook portrayed themselves as the innocent victims of seductive products whose forces they felt powerless to resist.

Rook, then an assistant professor of marketing at the University of Southern California, Los Angeles, conducted the survey to learn what consumers feel when the impulse to buy comes over them, and how they cope with the compulsion. The following five distinctive features of the experience as presented in a *USC Trojan Family* (magazine) article,[7] emerged from respondents' descriptions:

- *Excitement.* Many said the sudden urge to buy is exciting, thrilling, stimulating—almost like falling in love. "The impulse can be so strong that it even produces physical symptoms, such as goosebumps, hot flashes and tingling sensations," Rook reports.
- *Conflicting feelings.* More than 40 percent of the respondents said the impulse to buy makes them feel happy, satisfied, wonderfully light,

or "high." But many of the same respondents said the impulse also triggers feelings of guilt, distress, helplessness, even panic.

"This ambivalence emphasizes the psychological complexity," says Rook. "Much of the marketing research has treated it simply as 'unplanned' purchasing, but it's not just that. Essentially, impulse buying is an irrational process in which the urge to gratify an impulse triumphs over the rational parts of the mind."

- *Intensity and force.* About a third of the respondents said the urge to buy is a powerful force, and some invested that force with quasi-mystical properties. "Some said they feel hypnotized or mesmerized during an impulse buying episode," says Rook. "They said they would find themselves moving toward a cashier, as if in a dream.

  "Others animated the objects of their desires, empowering products with motility and will. They talked about candy bars calling out to them, about shoes staring at them."

- *Synchronicity.* Some respondents reported that the sudden urge to buy is invariably accompanied by a feeling of being in the right place at the right time, of being the beneficiary of some unique fortuitous convergence of events. "Some people feel that a product is personally made or meant for them," says Rook. "This feeling is sometimes accompanied by a flash of recognition or illumination. As one 22-year-old male explained it, 'You suddenly feel compelled to buy

[7] From "The Impulse to Buy: It's Almost Like Being in Love," an article written by Diane Swanbrow, which first appeared in the May–June 1986 issue of *USC Trojan Family*, the alumni magazine of the University of Southern California.

something. It feels like getting an idea'."

- *Resistance.* Struggling with a powerful compulsion to buy, people use a wide variety of strategies to maintain, or regain, self-control. More than 70 percent of the respondents said they conduct an emergency cost/benefit analysis, on the spot, asking themselves such questions as these: Do I really want it? Can I afford it? Will I regret it? Would I get my money's worth, or would I use the product once and forget it?

  Some respondents reported trying to distance themselves—in time or space. Others try substituting a small purchase for a large, more costly (or fattening) one, imposing rationing devices on themselves, such as leaving credit cards at home and carrying only so much cash, or inviting others to shop with them, knowing they are far more likely to give in to impulse purchase when they shop alone. The problem, Rook notes, is that resistance strategies often fail. "At their strongest, impulses to consume are impossible to resist," he says. "And recent marketing innovations such as 24-hour retailing, instant credit and telemarketing make the impulse to buy even easier to gratify, without even setting foot in a shopping center."

More than 80 percent of the respondents said they had suffered negative consequences after impulse buying episodes, such as fiscal resource problems, product disappointment, and others' disapproval.

"Some people suffer a tremendous amount of guilt just for having the impulse, whether they give in to it or not," Rook reports. "On the other hand, some people said that impulse buying elevates their mood and boosts their energy. For them, giving in to the urge is a highly satisfying experience—a way to fill the emptiness of their lives, either literally or figuratively."

Questions for Written Reports or Class Discussion

1. Studies have shown that consumer buyer behavior is affected by four major factors. What are these four factors, and which one or two of them, in your opinion, influenced most of Rook's respondents when making their impulse buying decision?

2. Do you see one's real self-image coming into conflict with his or her ideal self-image in an impulse buying decision? Explain your reasoning.

3. Motivation was obviously the driving force that impelled Rook's respondents to take the action of impulse buying to satisfy their wants. Do you feel that their buying action that expressed this motivation was more generic or product-specific based?

4. What is meant, in terms of the Rook survey, by the notion that most consumers tend to make buying decisions based on what they perceive, rather than on the basis of objective reality?

What motivates people to buy hope?

"Where vanity is—there shall be cosmetics," is a statement attributed to the "man who made Revlon," one of the leading companies in the multimillion-dollar American cosmetics and beauty industry. Nearly everyone agrees that consumers don't have to buy expensive facial creams, but they do—by the millions of jars and tubes—out of hope! That's what the industry sells—hope.

Most authorities agree that the beauty industry fills no physical need for most people but does fill a psychological need. One executive of the Helena Rubenstein company insists that cosmetics provide women especially with both psychological and tangible benefits. She feels that cosmetics "help women look better, therefore feel better, and as a result do things better."

Women have used cosmetics in one form or another since the beginning of time. While the basic ingredients that go into the manufacture of cosmetics have not changed much over the years, the cost of buying hope has. It is easy to spend well over $200 for a day of treatments at New York Fifth Avenue beauty salons or well over $1500 for a week at lush beauty spas (sometimes called "fat farms"). In recent years, the industry, has seriously been selling cosmetics for men (colognes, for example, with names like "Tiger Sweat" and "Studd") to the tune of hundreds of millions of dollars per year.

Hope is offered through the numerous cosmetics and toiletries lines sold in department stores, supermarkets, and drug stores, and by direct selling. Many of these items are also available at the more than 270,000 beauty shops and an even larger number of barber shops throughout the United States.

Here is an eyewitness account of how some salespeople sell hope in one fancy and expensive salon:

> Male hairdressers, themselves gorgeously coifed, dressed in London suits, often made up and occasionally decked in false eyelashes, are the aristocrats of the salon. Then come the visagists, with their trays of color and soothing chatter. One of the latter, a young male, cooed to me, "Oh, these lashes are just absolutely aching to go on your lids." "Will they stay on in bed?" I asked. Smilingly, he replied, "Madame, it all depends on who you're with . . . !"

Questions for Written Reports or Class Discussion

1. Do you think that the role or status to which a person aspires affects his or her purchase of cosmetics products? Explain your reasons.
2. What effect do you feel a person's age and life cycle have on purchases of cosmetics products?
3. What reference group or groups with whom you have contact exert the greatest influence on your buying or not buying cosmetics products? Why is this so?
4. Assuming you are about to purchase a given cosmetics products in a drug store, how do you perceive this product in terms of the self-concept theory that was presented earlier?

How will you choose between two competing "achieved roles" in this sales situation?

You will recall that in our chapter discussion of role and status, two types of roles were presented and explained. *Ascribed roles* are those expected of an individual over which he or she has no control (for example, sex, family, race, religion). *Achieved roles* are those that a person adopts as the result of personal attainment and growth.

Assume for a moment now that you are a male commission salesperson selling a basic product with many optional accessories to your brother-in-law. You find yourself in the position of having to choose between one of these two competing achieved roles:

1. *Your role as a salesperson*—with its implicit goal of closing the largest sale possible in order to earn the highest commission possible.
2. *Your role as an in-law*—with the felt urge to give the best value for the lowest cost to your wife's brother.

Questions for Written Report or Class Discussion

1. Which of these two achieved roles will you choose?
2. On what basis did you make your decision?

PART TWO

ORGANIZING, PROSPECTING, AND PLANNING FOR PERSONAL SELLING

Part Two of our book leads us into the first half of a simple but vital secret for success in personal selling: Plan your work; work your plan. We start by applying the first two of the important four management functions (or stages) presented in Chapter 2—*planning* and *organizing*.

These will be intertwined as we first consider how salespeople learn more about their industry, markets, firm or organization, and their competition; then some techniques of prospecting for new

4 Know Your Company or Organization—Its Products, Policies, and Promotional Support—and Know your Competition

5 Prospecting and Organizing Your Prospect List

6 The Preapproach: Getting in to See the Decision Maker

7 Planning Your Presentation

potential customers.

How can a salesperson discover all possible information about a potential customer (prospect) he or she hopes to visit, and how can one get the desired interview? Those and other points will be covered in describing a sales process known as the *preapproach*. Finally, since careful preplanning of sales presentations leads to greater sales success, Part Two concludes by describing the essential steps of such planning.

Know Your Company or Organization—Its Products, Policies, and Promotional Support—and Know Your Competition

After studying this chapter, you will be able to:

Identify three major reasons why knowledge about one's company or organization and its products or services is important to salespeople.

Explain why it is so important that salespeople be able to explain and justify their business firm's pricing and discount policies to buyers.

Explain the important relationship between a business firm's credit department and its sales department.

Tell what kinds of information a salesperson should learn about his or her major competition, and how it can best be obtained.

Describe five commonly used types of advertising that support a business firm's personal selling effort, and tell which ones of these might also be employed to support nonprofit organizational marketing efforts.

Let us use our imagination for a moment and suppose that you have unexpectedly found, tucked inside a dusty old library book, a map showing the location of fifteenth-century buried pirate treasure deep in the Central American jungle. Afire with excitement over your good fortune and the prospect of great riches, you fly to a riverside town closest to the site. Across the river, in the direction you must go for over 60 kilometers (37 miles) to reach the treasure, lies a thick dark jungle—no roads, no paths, just a mass of thick dark jungle.

Now what? You have some choices to make. One is to simply cross the river, plunge into the jungle, trust to luck, and get to the treasure site as fast as possible. But—are there man-eating wild animals out there? Poisonous snakes, spiders, or plants? Could you get lost even in daylight in the jungle darkness? Will you be able to find a safe, dry place to sleep at night? What are your real chances of success in the face of so many possible obstacles? What good will the treasure be to you if, on the way to it, you become something's dinner?

Here's another choice: Ask people in the town about the obstacles and dangers you might face, check library sources if possible, see if there are jungle experts close enough at hand to visit or phone for information, and equip yourself for the trip (food, water, weapons). In other words, take the time to prepare yourself in every way possible for a successful mission before plunging into the unknown jungle. Success will be to get back safely with the treasure.

What is Your Choice? To be brave but stupid and plunge right in without any preparation, trusting to blind luck? Or to use your head before your feet and take the time to investigate probable and possible obstacles and dangers ahead and prepare yourself in every way possible to meet them—before entering the jungle. Which choice offers the best chance for success?

Why use four paragraphs to describe the above totally mythical situation?

> Because the real life world of personal selling *is a jungle*—full of resisting buyers, hidden dangers, obstacles, and countless carnivorous, around-the-clock, predatory salespeople who simply love to eat alive unprepared competitors!

Not too many years ago, when personal selling was much less sophisticated than today, newly hired salespeople were usually given a brief explanation of and a sample of their product or products, a price list, and an encouraging pat on the back as they were sent (or pushed) into the jungle to sell what they could as best they could. A minority of today's direct sales organizations still practice a refined version of that method.

Overall, however, more and more of today's business firms and not-for-profit organizations are interlocking their own research, development and/or manufacturing, and sales/marketing strategies and programs with those of the customers they serve or hope to serve.

This approach requires improved communications between buyers and sellers from start to finish, with professional salespeople acting as the vital face-to-face link between them. In fulfilling this more demanding and responsible role, these modern salespeople no longer act as mere "pitchers" or prescribers of their company's products or services. Their professional challenge is to act as a "diagnostician" (or expert) in determining the identity, cause, or nature of a customer's problem or situation and to suggest solutions.

In this chapter we will concentrate on the degree and type of knowledge that is needed about one's own company or organization—its business or industry and markets, its products or services, its policies, and the promotional support it offers its salespeople. The aim is to alert you now to the need for, and how to obtain, information necessary to help you succeed as a true professional salesperson before entering the sales/marketing jungle. In later chapters we focus on how to succeed once inside the jungle.

Our theme of presentation will continue to be built around you as a newly hired salesperson now concerned with organizing your thinking, facts, and sales tools in preparation for prospecting (the process of checking out and looking up potential new buyers), planning your sales presentation, and contacting both potential buyers and established customers for sales interview appointments.

WHY IS KNOWLEDGE OF YOUR COMPANY OR ORGANIZATION AND ITS PRODUCTS OR SERVICES IMPORTANT?

If you go to a doctor for medical advice concerning a suspected illness, you expect him or her to be well-trained, confident in manner, professional and helpful in his or her advice and possible treatment. As a modern "diagnostic" salesperson, it stands to reason that you also should appear knowledgeable, confident, and helpful to prospective buyers considering your product or service as a possible solution to needs, wants, or problems.

In a way, you face a more difficult problem than medical doctors; their patients don't often know enough to question or challenge their statements or prescribed treatment, but in most cases your customers will. Modern organizational buyers, and increasingly, individual customers are, on the whole, far more sophisticated, better educated, and more demanding than those faced by salespeople of past years. As the world's economy becomes more consumer oriented, this trend will continue.

The first major reason that knowledge of your company and its products is important is that modern buyers, especially organizational buyers, demand and expect facts. If you want to succeed in selling, you simply have to know your company and its products and policies thoroughly—from managerial policies to manufacturing to distribution—and be able to relate these to industry trends and compare them with competition.

Second is the fact that only if you are armed with such knowledge can you face buyers with confidence and assurance to begin with, or hope to gain their confidence and trust.

A third reason lies in the fact that much of modern personal selling is but the end of a sales/marketing strategy that sets many forces, especially the three other sales promotion forces, into operation long before your final salesperson-to-buyer personal approach. You must know about your organization's overall marketing and merchandising strategy and plan and understand how to build on it and use all aspects of it to your immediate personal sales advantage.

WHAT SHOULD YOU KNOW ABOUT YOUR COMPANY OR ORGANIZATION?

Some of the more obvious facts and knowledge you should have are listed below. This is only a partial list, and while it is primarily business related, the principles (as adapted) apply as well to not-for-profit organizations. Much of this information is initially taught in sales training courses; much else is gained from diligent and constant personal study, observation, and "question-asking." As in medicine, keeping up to date and thoroughly informed of all aspects of one's business is a never-ending task throughout a salesperson's professional career. Many of the items listed below are in question form, representing types of questions buyers may ask. You should have ready, intelligent, informed answers for them.

Its Standing Within the Industry and Community. Before studying your company or organization, you should research the beginning and development of the industry of which it is a part. What is the relation of the industry to other industries? What is the standing of your organization within the industry, in terms of physical size, financial strength, credit standing, past and current standing in the stock market (if listed), product line, distribution methods, and future plans? What are current trends within the industry? What current or proposed government regulations or consumer demands may affect such trends (and your organization)?

Of what industry or trade associations is it a member? What are its plans and policies within the industry as compared to those of its competition? What is its standing globally, nationally, and within its local community? Are you proud of your organization? Why?

History and Current Organization. Studying the history of your employer and learning about the people who devised its offerings and brought it sales success helps you to understand current policies better. Knowledge of the organization and its physical setup enables you to judge the quality of production, its standards of workmanship, and the efficiency and well-being of its employees; this enables you to speak authoritatively about it to others. Why and how did your firm or organization originate? What new or unusual products or services has it developed? What contribution has it made to society? How did it get its name? Has it merged with or acquired other companies or organizations along the way? Has the buyer any reason to feel pride or unusual confidence through buying from your employer?

Executives and Key Personnel. You should know something about the top executives of your organization and about those to whom they are accountable. You can then judge their success for yourself by studying past annual reports issued by them. You can also learn from such reports something about the assets, liabilities, and overall financial setup of the firm or organization. You have every right to learn everything possible about these matters and to judge the situation for yourself.

Were or are any of your employer's founders or current executives well-known internationally, nationally, or within their local community for any reason? Have any of them invented or developed any product, service, or ideas of unusual interest? Have any of them served in a leadership capacity on national government, state or provincial, or local advisory committees, or with social action, political, or community groups concerned with the welfare of society? Have any of them served as leaders in industry-related affairs?

Its Policies in General. Your knowledge concerning these is tied in with the reputation the company or organization enjoys internationally, nationally, within the industry or trade, and with end-consumers. Is it generally considered an organization of stability, integrity, and responsibility? Do its policies overall reflect a genuine interest in consumer satisfaction and the welfare of society? If so, how and in what ways? Can you give examples?

Do you understand completely, and are you able to explain clearly and accurately to buyers, all relevant warranties, guarantees, and service policies offered by your employer? Do you have any questions about information contained in your organization's advertisements or literature?

Its Products. Full knowledge is required concerning the type, quality, uses, and technical details of the product or service line or lines being offered, a topic that will be covered in greater detail shortly.

Sales/Marketing Policies and Channels of Distribution. Both overall organizational policies and specific sales/marketing policies are decided by top management, not by you, the salesperson. But you must know about such and be able to explain them. Prospects and established customers alike will often question certain policies, thus offering you an opportunity to turn them into selling points, where possible.

What market or markets does your company or organization serve, and what channels of distribution are employed to reach it or them? What are its policies concerning exclusives, marking products with jobber's brands, or price maintenance? What if it sells both direct and through retailers or other types of resellers? Is this not hurting those resellers? If your employer is a business firm that sells both to a large chain store and to small independent retailers, and the chain sells at lower prices, is this fair to the small retailers?

Those are just some of the typical questions commonly asked of business firm sellers by both individual and organizational buyers. Here are some others: How are orders fulfilled? Who receives them? How long does it take to fulfill them? When can I expect delivery and is the delivery date guaranteed? Who pays transportation costs? If the product or service is out of stock and back ordered, will I be informed in advance of its date of shipment? A billing error was made; how can it be adjusted?

Selling is only part of a salesperson's duties—a great deal of his or her time is spent servicing customers, answering questions, and solving problems such as these.

Pricing Policies. As any salesperson soon learns, his or her organization's pricing policies are an item of deep interest to buyers. An understanding of those policies and the ability to justify them are important, especially if your prices for a given item are higher than those of your competitors.

Business firms frequently, and sometimes not-for-profit organizations, follow different pricing strategies for different types of products. Pricing of new products or services, for example, is often based on a "skimming" or "penetration" price strategy. *Skimming* involves selling at a high price and then lowering the price later to attract new buyers. Many new items are initially offered at a low price in order to penetrate the market, then increased as the sought-after market share is reached. While top management sets basic pricing policies, feedback from the sales force is often an important factor in the formulation of those policies.

Price objections are constantly raised in most sales interviews and have to be handled by the salesperson; we shall discuss how in Chapter 11. A high price often has to be justified in terms of superior quality (to end-consumer), or greater profit potential (to middlemen or retailers). If the price seems low, it may have to be explained in terms of a better buy. Whatever the situation, price is a matter of serious interest to most buyers.

In discussing price, you must be familiar with pricing terminology used within your industry. These include such general terms as *list price, net price, FOB price,* and *guaranteed price;* definitions for these can be found in the glossary at the end of this book.

Discount Policies. Discounts are always of interest to customers who qualify and must be offered and explained carefully. Most business firms offer trade, quantity, and cash discounts. *Trade discounts* are those offered to wholesalers, jobbers, distributors, and retailers, with larger discounts generally going to the middlemen. Your company's discount schedules must be strictly adhered to, or legal troubles may follow. *Quantity discounts* are offered in return for purchasing in multiple units or bulk. *Cash discounts* may be offered in return for payment of a purchase before certain preset dates. Often special advertising allowances or special services, such as helping train the customer's sales force in how to sell items purchased, are offered.

In discussing discounts, you must be familiar with the three types of discounts just noted, and with other types of discount terminology common to your industry. Definitions for several such general terms can be found in the glossary at the end of this book. You must also be able to compute discounts quickly, as well as quantity prices; libraries and book stores offer many books on business mathematics from which you can learn helpful calculation shortcuts.

If you are given leeway to recommend special discounts in your sales territory, manage them carefully, keeping in mind that profitable sales are the objective of both you and your company. Greater profits often result from smaller sales and shorter discounts than from greater volume sales at excessive discounts. The salesperson who sells on cheapest price alone usually has nothing of real value to offer.

Credit and Collection Policies. Many a salesperson has learned, to his or her regret, the truth of the old axiom that a sale is not complete until it has been paid for. If products are returned by a customer due to his or her inability to pay for them, or if the sale is written off as a bad debt because of inability to collect, the "sale" is deducted from the total, and the salesperson loses sales credit.

In business firms most salespeople are required to obtain and submit full credit information on a new account before the sale is approved by the company credit department and the order is fulfilled (see Figure 4.1). In most companies the credit manager holds decision-making power over whether or not to approve credit. This is often frustrating to salespeople, who are primarily interested in the sale alone. They do not realize that the credit manager is actually their friend; the credit function and the brakes it employs along the way are designed to help, not hinder, salesperson and customer alike. Approving or rejecting credit is not a whimsical matter. Most companies' credit department policy is (1) "Know your customer" and (2) "When in doubt as to whether to approve or reject, resolve that doubt in favor of making the sale."

To salespeople, an order is a piece of gold. It represents profit to the employer, possible bonus for themselves, and an ever-expanding market for future sales. To the credit manager, at the company or organization's head office or branch, it may represent just one more piece of paper. He or she may lose sight of the fact that behind that piece of paper is a flesh-and-blood, living human being whom the salesperson has cultivated as a *customer*.

Modern, customer-oriented credit theory recognizes the importance of close cooperation between the salesperson in the field and the head office, or branch; that there should be recognition and respect for each other's problems. Such cooperation results in teamwork that promotes profitable sales and harmonious customer relations.

Today, it is more necessary than ever before for both business firms and not-for-profit organizations to maintain tight control of their money. The experience of having to "write off" $150,000 due from one bankrupt account is traumatic. It is equally traumatic to write off 150 accounts owing $1000 each. The close cooperation and continual two-way flow of information between credit and field, and field and credit, is more essential than ever before in today's business world.

Here are some practical guidelines for salespeople concerning such cooperation that are typical of those formulated by many of the world's leading business firms:

1. Compliment the credit department's effort by acting upon its communications. Copies of letters are supplied to inform the salesperson of the status of overdue accounts. Primarily these are for information only and most require no action. But if a direct memo is sent, specifically spelling out a particular problem, the salesperson should take immediate action—other-

```
                                    AS OF (DATE) _____

ACCOUNT NAME _____

ADDRESS _____

           _____

OFFICERS (IF A CORP.) _____

OWNERS (IF A PROPRIETORSHIP OR PARTNERSHIP) _____


                        B A L A N C E    S H E E T

              ASSETS                              LIABILITIES & CAPITAL

CASH                                    ACCOUNTS PAYABLE

ACCOUNTS RECEIVABLE                     NOTES PAYABLE

INVENTORY                               OTHER (LOANS, ETC.)

OTHER              _____       _____  _____

        TOTAL CURRENT                           TOTAL CURRENT

PLANT & EQUIPMENT                       LONG TERM DEBT

OTHER                                   TOTAL LIABILITIES

                   _____       NET WORTH               _____

        TOTAL ASSETS                            TOTAL LIABILITIES &
                   ══════════════               CAPITAL          ══════════════


                    O P E R A T I N G    S T A T E M E N T

        FOR PERIOD _____  THROUGH _____

SALARY

RENT                                    SALES

TAXES                                   COST OF GOODS SOLD

OTHER              _____       GROSS PROFIT

·TOTAL EXPENSES    _____       LESS EXPENSES           _____

                                        NET PROFIT              ══════════════



                        SIGNED _____
```

FIGURE 4.1 *Example of a Typical Credit Information Form*   *This type of credit information is often obtained by salespeople for their company's credit department.*

wise (in the absence of any response) the credit manager will feel that the salesperson has no interest in the case.

2. Volunteer information about special circumstances affecting an established customer—good as well as bad. For instance, a retail store customer may be planning an autograph party or a special sales campaign. Conversely, the manager of that store (or an individual customer of, say, insurance) may be having trouble with a landlord, or sickness in the family, or damage due to a flood or a fire. Keep the credit manager informed ahead of time if possible.

3. Counsel a customer who has been receiving collection letters (salespeople are normally sent copies). Advise him or her that the credit department is under constant pressure (especially in any period of difficult economic climate), but that the credit manager will be sympathetic to any special problem. Remember, though, that the credit manager is in a faraway office and won't know about any extenuating circumstances unless the customer or salesperson advises him or her.

4. It is particularly important to submit financial information promptly on new customers. A businessperson especially expects to be asked for references. It is best to report information you have gained in:

   a. *New customer information*—this may be a memo, or company-supplied form for this particular reporting. If on a business firm customer, it should include not only factual information (type of business, number of employees, and so forth), but also your personal comments. These should include your general impressions such as age and health of the principal owner and/or manager, general housekeeping, size of store (or other type of operation), whether the principal owner and/or manager is mayor of the town, president of the local library association, and the like.

   b. *Financial statement*—this is a standard business format form showing assets, liabilities, and other basic financial information (see Figure 4.1). The new business firm customer may have such a form on hand, recently prepared. If there is one, ask for it. If not, ask if the customer has filed such a statement recently with any local financial information collection firm (in the United States, Canada, and some other industrialized nations of the world, this may be Dun & Bradstreet). If neither, leave a form (most companies issue them routinely to salespeople) and ask the customer to fill out the data and mail it promptly to your organization's credit department. Attach one or both of the above reports to your initial order to speed processing.

Businesspeople are accustomed to supplying the type of financial information noted above, and normally are most cooperative in supplying it when asked for it in a straightforward manner. If reluctance is encountered, the matter can often be resolved by asking the prospect to submit the information directly to your credit manager, saying that it is your company or organization's policy not to consider extending credit until this request has been complied with. In most cases, if you arrange this properly, along with your personal estimates of the prospect's business situation, the credit manager will, if the information is favorable, be only too willing to cooperate with you by approving the sale. In most companies, the sales and credit departments work closely together to overall customer and company advantage. Most such companies need healthy middlemen and retail accounts and often go to great lengths creditwise to help them stay in business.

Credit information and follow-up on individual consumers, needed by direct salespeople, outside salespeople of small business firms, or even by churches or other nonprofit organizations who depend on donations or pledges, can be handled via the same (or abbreviated) kind of methods employed by business firms.

The best way for a salesperson to avoid possible credit problems is to put all terms of sale down on paper, explain them carefully, and obtain the buyer's signature. In cases where you are asked to help effect collections personally, an often distasteful task to salespeople, you should handle them along the lines suggested in Chapter 13 on pages 340–342.

WHAT SHOULD YOU KNOW ABOUT YOUR PRODUCTS OR SERVICES?

Product knowledge is essential to successful selling. As a "problem solver" you will have to thoroughly understand your product or products in order to show prospects how and why they stand to benefit by buying.

This task can be never-ending if your product line consists of hundreds or thousands of different items or variations of items. Your company training program, its manuals or sample range, and your own study will furnish you with the necessary initial background to start your calls. After that, it is up to you how fast you gain additional knowledge. Most people are not blessed with the power of total recall and have to absorb bits and pieces of information each day until the mind, like a computer, puts them together clearly in some flash of insight.

The best way to become an expert in product knowledge is to try to learn something new each day, building systematically on previous knowledge. Your customers will gladly help you learn; the best way to get this help is to become sincerely interested in trying to understand and solve their problems.

The following is a list of some of the more important areas of product knowledge about which you should be informed. But first, it is important to note that knowing a lot about your products or service is not enough; the main thing is that you be able to express this knowledge in terms of user benefits. If your prospect is more interested in quality than price or service, you must be able to illustrate, prove, or demonstrate convincingly the quality-features, advantages, and benefits offered by your product. How to do this is discussed in some detail in chapters to come.

Origin and History.   Does your product or service represent a new invention? If so, what led up to the invention, and how was it developed into its present form? If it is an improvement on earlier ones, what led up to the development? Try to develop an interesting (even dramatic) story about the origin and history of your offering, a story that will illustrate one or more selling points.

Research and Development. Can you build an interesting story about the initial technical research that went into the product? Was it created especially to meet specific consumer demands learned about through market research? Is it an offshoot of some exciting venture such as the space program? How long did it take to develop? Articles, charts, or tables that show depth and results of technical or market research can offer convincing proof that your offering is indeed as good as you say it is.

Manufacturing/Production. If a physical product, what is it made of? You should know both the materials and their characteristics. How is it made? Can you describe the process in an interesting way and show pictures to illustrate various stages of production? What is the quality of the workmanship? Can you show samples or illustrate or demonstrate quality features in any way?

What about its design? The engineering that went into its manufacture? What improvements does it have compared to earlier models or to the competition? What new scientific developments does it incorporate? What safety features?

The Physical Product/Operation, and Performance Data. You must be able to describe your product in every physical detail and relate key features as a means of solving needs or problems. What will the product or service do? How does it work? How long will it last? What will it cost to use or operate it; can you break these costs down into person-hours saved or other cost reductions? Knowledge of technical facts and performance is what buyers are normally seeking. Features should be translated into user benefits at every opportunity, in every sales presentation.

After-Sale Servicing. Will your company help teach buyers or their staffs how to use or utilize the product or service? Will you personally follow up to see that they are utilizing it properly and are satisfied with their purchase? Does your company have trained technical or service representatives who can be called upon for technical or professional help? What about a guarantee, if any? How will your firm back up its guarantee?

THE MORE KNOWLEDGE YOU HAVE, THE BETTER YOUR CHANCES OF SURVIVING IN THE JUNGLE

It may frustrate you as a reader to read obviously incomplete lists like the above and see so many questions without answers. We cannot, however, go much further here into specific company or product knowledge required, since we do not know what products or services you may represent. But we can stress once again the importance of knowledge. The more knowledge you have, product and otherwise, about your firm or organization and its business, the more respect you will get from your customers. This respect leads to sales and profits, because if you have knowledge and work in a professional way you will get results. Also, as you gain respect, knowledge flows back from the customers through you to your employer so that better products can be devised to fill their needs. It will pay you to enter the jungle prepared!

WHAT PROMOTIONAL SUPPORT CAN A SALESPERSON EXPECT?

In Chapter 2, we defined and briefly discussed the four-part "promotional mix" of promotion and selling. Advertising, publicity, sales promotion, and personal selling are the four parts of that mix.

Since no two sales/marketing situations are exactly the same, the proper mix depends on the objective or objectives. For business firms, the overall annual goal of the sales/marketing effort normally is to maximize profits. To accomplish this, specific activities are planned in terms of intermediate objectives, which ultimately lead to accomplishment of the overall goal.

Many business firms and other types of organizations that have marketing departments spell out their planned "promotional mix" as part of an annual written "marketing plan." For salespeople who work for such organizations, it is important to know, at least generally, what this mix entails, and specifically how they can turn key elements of it to their personal sales advantage. If not given details routinely by sales management, salespeople have every right to ask for such—and should do so!

For greater understanding, let's take a closer look at what a "marketing plan" covers, paying special attention to its advertising and sales promotion aspects.

THE MARKETING PLAN

It was pointed out in Chapter 2 that top management of both business firms and other types of organizations normally drafts both long-range and short-term written "business plans" that outline overall organizational goals and objectives. There we noted that many then require lower echelons to also prepare written plans that spell out specific "next-year" objectives and action steps to implement that echelon's (or division's) part of the overall organizational goals. Among these is the marketing department, which prepares a "marketing plan."

This usually written plan, based on careful market research and covering any agreed-upon time period, is normally drafted and presented in at least the five different sections shown in Table 4.1.

Section 5 of Table 4.1 is the basic working section, outlining within the overall marketing plan the specific tactical action programs to be implemented by the advertising, sales promotion, and public relations departments, and the sales force. The organization's marketing, sales, and advertising directors normally are all vitally involved in final formulation of the overall plan. During such formulation, the sales force is often called upon for marketing feedback or suggestions.

Once the overall marketing plan is approved by management, it must be put into action. It is the step-by-step master action plan, periodically reviewed by

TABLE 4.1 *Five Basic Sections of a "Marketing Plan"*

1. Current situation	This section answers the question "Where are we now?" by presenting data on current markets, products, distribution, and competitive standing.
2. Problems and opportunities	This section covers problems or issues that might impede growth or profitability, and evaluates all possible areas of growth opportunity.
3. Goals and objectives	The purpose here is to set clear-cut "Where do we want to go?" goals and objectives that are specific as to time (for example, month and year of achievement), quantity (percent, market share, and the like), and achievable within reasonably available resources.
4. Marketing strategy	To answer the question "How do we get there?" alternative strategies are evaluated in this section and the best, or "optimal" solutions are finalized and presented.
5. Tactical action programs	The action steps necessary to implementing the selected strategy are spelled out here in the form of who, what, when, and where "marching orders."

management to check progress on implementation and effectiveness of its various parts, flexible enough to allow for any adaptations in tactical plans required by any along-the-way changes in the marketplace.

Once this plan goes into effect, a whole series of preplanned interdependent merchandising activities take place involving the advertising program, publicity, and sales promotional activities—all designed to pave the way through information and preselling for your personal selling efforts.

Advertising: The Most Important Promotional Aid to Salespeople

Advertising and *personal selling* are by far the two most important parts of the promotional mix. They work as a team toward the same end—that of selling products and services. The role each plays is determined by the product being sold and the overall marketing plan. In cases of companies like Avon Products, Inc. (cosmetics) and Electrolux Corporation (vacuum cleaners), which concentrate on direct selling, relatively little is spent on advertising. Other companies, such as direct-mail houses, utilize advertising almost exclusively.

For most companies, a closely coordinated program of preselling by advertising (to gain interest and acceptance of the product and build goodwill), lays the groundwork for the salesperson to present final selling points around the prospect's needs or wants and close the sale.

Advertising is most effective in impersonal selling to a mass audience (such as in retail self-service stores) and encompasses all merchandising activities that take place *outside* the store. Shoppers in such retail stores make quick selections, spending little time in deliberation. Brand identification plays a vital role in their selection. The job of advertising here is to presell shoppers on the producer's brand beforehand through such means as television commercials, radio announcements, magazine ads, billboards, and the store's own ads in newspapers.

Advertising is least effective for higher-priced items such as machine tools or industrial products where buyers need explanations and demonstrations of technical features. In such cases the salesperson plays the most important role in the promotional mix.

Advertising is highly important in the selling of products such as foods, beauty aids, and soft drinks, and for services such as car rentals, insurance, and packaged travel tours. It also plays an important role in institutional and organizational-cause selling. Institutional advertising is concerned with telling about the company or industry (for example, "Commercial banks are a safe place to invest money"), rather than about a specific product. Advertising is used to sell causes like fighting drug addiction or supporting your local police, and to raise funds for various purposes.

Types of Advertising

Various forms of advertising are employed along the way from producer to buyer which normally are part of an advertising plan mix within the complete marketing plan. Among the major ones with which salespeople should become familiar are the following:

National Advertising. This is advertising by the producer aimed at the end-consumer, asking them to buy the trademarked product through retail outlets. Examples include countless well-known brands such as Lipton tea, Volkswagon automobiles, Singer sewing machines, Crest toothpaste, and Kellogg's Corn Flakes. Certain types of nonprofit organizations, such as, American Cancer Society, also employ national advertising directed at individual consumers.

Retail Advertising. This is also aimed at the end-consumer, but is done by retail chains or independent stores like department stores and supermarkets. Some of this retail advertising is for nationally advertised products (often through co-op ads where manufacturer and retailer share the cost of the advertising), but it can also be for nonnationally advertised manufacturers' brands, or for the store's own brand (often featured by chain-store organizations).

Trade (and Professional) Advertising. Advertising by the producer aimed at middlemen or retailers who will buy large quantities of the product for resale to end-consumers is called *trade advertising.* Such advertising stresses why they should buy and resell the product offered. *Professional advertising* is directed by the producer to those who can either recommend its use to end-consumers or who buy it for their use (such as pharmaceutical houses advertising specific drugs or medications to doctors).

Industrial Advertising. This advertising is addressed to manufacturers who use the offered product in the making of their own product (such as tire manufacturers advertising to Toyota or General Motors).

Direct-Response Advertising. This is advertising by the producer direct to the end-consumer in which a direct response is sought, either in the form of an order or a request for additional information by mail, or through a sales representative. Such advertising can be done by direct mail, telephone, television, or radio. Direct-response advertising seeks an immediate reply in response to the ad.

Cooperative Advertising. This widely used type of advertising is unlike all the others, because it can be used in conjunction with all the above types. Frequently used as a special managerial option, it is especially important to salespeople, because it can help get new and repeat sales. It involves working out cooperative arrangements with customers whereby the product or service is advertised in association with the dealer's name and costs are shared. In many such cases, the creative work and materials are prepared by the salesperson's company. In other cases, the customer prepares the material, which features the producer's product or service as offered by the customer's own organization. The customer then sends a copy of the ad to the salesperson (or directly to his or her company), upon receipt and approval of which a certain prearranged dollar amount is credited to the customer's account.

Advertising Works Around the Clock

Overall, advertising assists the total marketing effort of a producer in many ways. Apart from increasing sales directly, it benefits the middlemen and retailer by supplying product information that enables them to buy wisely and more economically, thus increasing their profitable turnover. In addition, it helps the retailer build store prestige and promote in-store traffic.

Advertising benefits you as salesperson by helping secure leads to potential new customers, preselling prospects and customers prior to a personal sales call, reinforcing selling points, and contacting prospects or small-volume customers you might not be able to reach or visit otherwise due to time limitations.

Above all, from your point of view, advertising is working for you twenty-four hours a day, seven days a week, throughout the year—between calls, while you sleep, when you are ill, or on vacation. Advertising and personal selling constantly supplement one another; a good mix of the two produces greater results for most firms than either could do alone.

Sales Promotion and Publicity

Basically, sales promotions are usually short-term or temporary activities designed to support advertising or sales-force activities and often involve "more for your money" or temporary price reductions. The three major types of sales promotion and types of activities within each were explained in Chapter 2. Various types of and advantages of publicity programs and events were also presented in that chapter.

In line with our theme of considering you as market manager of your sales territory, it should be noted that managers do not simply passively accept what is handed down to them. They *manage* events, within the limitations of their responsibilities and authority. Thus you should learn everything about and get to know personally all key people possible concerned with your firm's advertising, sales promotion, and publicity or public relations departments. Don't just wait for them to help you; actively seek their extra help to ensure your personal success. Far too few salespeople make any attempt to do this; the others' loss could be your gain.

WHAT SHOULD YOU KNOW ABOUT YOUR COMPETITION?

We said early in this chapter that you should learn everything possible about your industry, your company (products and policies) or organization, *and your competition,* in order to measure up to the modern concept of a problem-solving, diagnostic salesperson prepared to discuss all aspects of the business with your prospect or customer. Information should be sought in these basic areas.

Who are Your Major Competitors? Where are their head office and other major facilities located? How are they organized to do business? Approximately what percentage of the business in your industry do they receive, and why?

How are Products Within the Industry Sold and Distributed? You should seek information about the sales, cost and profit, history, and current picture of key competitors' major competitive products, and relate them to your own products. Distribution channels should be studied, and sales methods that affect sales through these channels.

Individual Competing Products Should be Studied in Comparison With Your Own. Information needed for such comparisons includes design, price, quality, sizes or models, packaging, delivery, and after-sale service, plus overall performance comparisons. You should ask yourself questions such as these: Do I know my competitor's strengths and weaknesses by product line? Do I know the features and benefits of their key products as compared to mine? Am I able to compare my selling and warranty policies against theirs?

Who Uses the Product(s)—Your Competitors' and Yours—and Why? Where possible, your end-consumers or prospective buyers should be identified and classified by age, sex, education, income level, occupation, and geographical location. What are their attitudes toward your product and service, and your major competitor's? What are their purchase habits, how do they use the product, and what trends may affect their future buying attitudes, purchase, and use habits? What are your competitors doing to capitalize on these trends?

Where Can You Get Information About Your Competitors?

Gathering all possible information about your competitors is a challenging and never-ending task. Most can be obtained from two broad source areas. First, you can learn by asking questions of experts within your own organization and from among your customers. Second, you can turn to published information available in libraries, or from published information available from other sources such as trade association journals, media advertisements of competitors, and government publications.

In the United States especially, a great deal of statistical, financial, and trade data is published by various government agencies. Various types of statistical and financial breakdowns for business and industry are made available, for example, via publications of federal agencies such as the Department of Commerce, Bureau of Internal Revenue, Federal Trade Commission, and the U.S. Department of the Treasury. The Bureau of the Census and Department of Commerce publications offer extensive historical and current trade data. Other industry/product data is available not only from some of these already mentioned agencies, but also from others such as the Department of Agriculture, the Interstate Commerce Commission, and the Bureau of Labor Statistics. Many state and local agencies of government also publish helpful data of various types.

In addition to all the various governmental sources already noted, many American brokerage firms and investment advisory services publish information by industry, as do general financial services such as Moodys and Standard & Poors. The *Fortune Directory* identifies major corporations by rank in sales, and the *Newsfront Directory* offers an even more detailed classification. Articles in business publications, such as *Fortune, Barron's, Forbes,* and *Business Week,* carry current information on both American and international business and industry. All these sources are readily available in most large American and many international public, university, and business libraries. Their trained librarians are normally pleased to assist you in tracking down the specific information you desire.

SUMMARY

We have, in this chapter, continued to develop the theme that you as a modern, customer-oriented, problem-solving salesperson must know a great deal about your industry, your company (its products, policies and promotional support) or organization, and your competition. This is essential if you are to truly become a diagnostician, able to discuss intelligently and professionally all aspects of your prospects' or customers' business, and to advise solutions to their problems in the form of your product or service, presented in terms of user benefits.

Without knowing what type of selling you are now in, or may enter, we discussed generally the type and degree of knowledge you need about your organization and its products. We then considered the promotional support it provides, or should provide, to assist you in your personal selling. This was presented first in light of the overall marketing plan, for which you might be called upon to provide suggestions, and then in terms of the advertising and sales promotion parts of the four-part promotional mix that constitutes the total, integrated sales/marketing program for any organization's product or service. All this build-up leads to your personal sales task of meeting individual buyer needs and closing the sale.

Finally, tying in both company or organization and product knowledge needed with similar knowledge about your competition, we presented various sources of information from which you can obtain data about your industry and competition other than from your own organizational sources.

Questions for Analysis and Discussion

1.   What is the meaning of the statement "A sale is not complete until it has been paid for"?

2.   Describe and explain one good system that you as a salesperson might employ at the time of making a sale to avoid future credit problems between your company and your customer.

3.   Would you consider advertising to be more effective in selling lower-priced mass-market items such as canned fruit, or higher-priced items such as data-processing systems for a business firm? Why?

4.   Before studying about your own company prior to going out to sell, what should be researched first?

5.   A great deal of a salesperson's time is spent answering questions by prospects or customers. Name four such questions that you feel might be most commonly asked, and indicate how a salesperson should prepare before hand to handle them.

6.   How might you best handle a situation where you have asked a new customer for certain necessary credit information, but the customer appears reluctant to give it to you?

7.   Describe the difference between retail advertising and trade advertising.

8.   Assuming you are an experienced typewriter salesperson, in what ways do you think you should usefully advise management in the early stages of drafting a marketing plan as to what advertising mix and sales promotion should be employed in introducing a newly developed "talking typewriter" (you talk and it types what you say) to potential business and organizational consumers?

Sales/Marketing with Lipton: Some Excerpts from their Professional Sales Training Courses

In 1871, an enterprising twenty-one-year-old opened his first provision shop in Glasgow, Scotland. He had a real talent for selling and he combined it with efforts to sell his customers nothing but the best. By the time he was thirty, he had a chain of twenty shops and was selling throughout the United Kingdom. Tea was among the items featured in his growing chain of stores, and to ensure consistent top quality he traveled to Ceylon and bought his own tea estate. By the time he was forty, he was known as "Mr. Tea" and had the commission to supply Queen Victoria with tea. He was, of course, Thomas J. Lipton.

He was the first to package tea and sell it under a name brand, so that his customers could be sure they were getting the same high quality each time they bought Lipton's tea. Lipton was also the first to advertise tea. His prices were reasonable; his quality was always the best. Sir Thomas began marketing tea in North America in the 1890s, as well as throughout other parts of the world. Today Lipton's tea is world-famous.

The growth of Thomas J. Lipton, Inc. in the United States has been rapid and innovative. Since 1938 a part of Unilever, one of the world's largest international corporations, it is today a large and highly respected member of the American food industry, with annual sales of over $1.4 billion.

The company's sales force of almost 800 offers a diversified range of brand products in addition to tea. These products include beverages under the Lipton and Wyler's names, soup under the Lipton and Cup-A-Soup names, Lipton side dishes, fruit snacks and juices under the Sunkist name, condiments under the Wishbone name, seasonings under the Lawry's and Tio Sancho names, and the tabletop sweetener Equal. In addition, ice cream products are sold with the Good Humor name. These products make up the company's two marketing divisions—Foods and Beverages.

Lipton's programmed sales training courses are among the best in the food industry. Here are some extracts (in text form) from one of their sales training manuals[1] that illustrate how Lipton American sales representatives first learn about many of the topics covered in the chapter material just presented.

WHO BUYS LIPTON PRODUCTS?

1. Lipton is a consumer goods company, which means that our products are bought and used by consumers such as yourself or your family.

2. We're not in a service business, because we sell products rather than services. We're not an industrial goods company, because our products are consumed.

3. Because our focus is on the consumer, marketing is the heart of our business. Marketing includes all the many things that fall between manufacturing and the ultimate consumer.

WHERE DO CONSUMERS BUY OUR PRODUCTS?

1. The final step in marketing is sale to the consumer. From your own experience,

---

[1] Material excerpted from Thomas J. Lipton, *Marketing with Lipton, Course 1* (Englewood Cliffs, N.J.: Thomas J. Lipton, Inc.), pp. 1–3. Reprinted by permission.

you know that this sale takes place in grocery stores.

2. More specifically, most sales take place in supermarkets. You're probably familiar with supermarkets from shopping in them, or perhaps from working in one. There are many things that characterize supermarkets—self-service, a variety of departments, check-out stands, etc. But, technically, a supermarket is a grocery store doing over $2 million in business per year. In other words, the definition is based upon the size of the store's sales.

3. Most sales of our products take place in stores doing a minimum of one-half million dollars a year, and most of these sales are by stores defined as supermarkets.

4. Supermarkets are surprisingly big businesses; they do over $228 billion a year.

5. In fact, the food industry as a whole is America's largest retail industry, and most of the industry's sales are through supermarkets.

HOW DO OUR PRODUCTS GET TO THE STORE?

1. The marketing steps between Lipton and the consumer are determined in part by the sheer numbers involved. Consider these statistics (in round numbers):

> 246,000,000 consumers
> 150,000 grocery stores and over 30,000 supermarkets
> 700+ Lipton sales representatives

2. Obviously we don't sell directly to consumers. Similarly, we don't sell directly to all those stores and supermarkets. But we do sell directly to over 1,239 selling locations of which approximately 469 are chain customers, 459 wholesale customers and 311 miscellaneous customers. These customers represent over 25,000 retail stores.

WHAT INFLUENCES BUYING?

1. Merchandising is that part of buying that most directly influences the consumer. Merchandising includes nearly everything that influences people to buy our products. (Your own personal selling is an exception, but even there, you'll often be selling merchandising plans.) One influence that applies outside the store is advertising; other merchandising activities take place in the store.

2. Two other influences that apply in the store while a consumer is shopping are sales promotion and shelf arrangement. As the terms imply, sales promotion is a means of promoting sales, and shelf arrangement is the way our products are arranged on the grocer's shelves.

3. Short-term, or temporary, activities designed to increase sales are called sales promotions. They very often, but not always, involve the offer of "more for your money," such as a temporary price reduction.

4. One example of sales promotions are displays. Displays are extra space for our products. They're temporary, and they're in addition to the regular space for our products on the shelves. They're part of sales promotion because they influence buying.

5. Shelf arrangement is the way our products are ordinarily made available for sale to the consumer—the way they're shelved, in other words. Unlike advertising, this kind of merchandising takes place inside the store. Unlike sales promotion, it's relatively permanent.

6. In some respects, shelf arrangement is the most critical merchandising activity, because it influences the vast majority of our sales. The amount of space allocated to a particular product and the condition

of the product are very strong influences on the consumers. Thus, shelf arrangement is a very strong part of merchandising.

7. So, the three main parts of Lipton's merchandising are (1) advertising, (2) sales promotion, and (3) shelf arrangement.

8. Merchandising is one part of marketing; personal selling is another. Personal selling means the kind of face-to-face selling you'll be doing when you call on the trade. Since supermarkets are self-service, the trade sells to the consumer mainly through merchandising but not through personal selling. We sell to the trade through merchandising and through personal selling.

9. In personal selling, you have a kind of double role: the grocery trade is our customer, but it's also our partner in selling to the consumer. One way of putting this is that your job is to "aid and persuade the trade." Because we sell to them, we depend upon you to persuade. Because we depend upon them to market our products effectively, we depend upon you to aid.

PLANNING FOR SELLING LIPTON PRODUCTS

1. The third major area of marketing is planning. The first two, which we have already discussed, are merchandising and personal selling.

2. Our planning is based on what is sometimes called the "marketing concept." This means that we plan all of our operations to produce a profit by meeting the needs of our customers and their customers. In other words, the single most important question to consider for each of our product is: "Will it sell?"

3. We plan all of our operations (1) to produce a profit and (2) to do so by meeting the needs of our customers and their customers. Thus, planning starts with the needs of our customers, the grocery trade, and the ultimate customers, the consumers.

4. Consumer needs are the basis for a product concept. On the basis of consumer needs, we develop a product that has certain features which will produce the benefits the consumers need or want.

5. A benefit is a need that has been met. The characteristic of the product that produces the benefit is a feature. Taken together, the characteristics and benefits form the product concept.

6. One feature of our Instant Tea is that we remove elements that would cause cloudiness when the tea is prepared by the homemaker. The benefit that results is clear, noncloudy tea.

7. "What's in it for me?" is something we all want to know before we buy. So, in selling it's more effective to stress benefits than to stress features.

8. New product planning starts with the product concept, then continues through the market research and test market phases. Then, if the product has proven itself to be a winner, it goes into the national introduction (launch) phase.

9. The first few weeks of a new product's life make it or break it. If the introduction isn't successful, the product very probably won't survive.

10. The merchandising of a new product in the store is the critical factor in the introduction. One of your most critical sales responsibilities is to ensure the successful introduction (merchandising) of new products.

11. Annual planning is the marketing planning that is done for established products. A plan is developed for each category—Soup Mix, Wishbone, Instant Tea, etc. The plan is developed each year.

12. An important part of annual planning is development of an attainable volume (sales) objective. We call this objective

proforma. Proforma is developed for each product category for the coming year. Proforma is an attainable volume objective. Or, in other words, it's a reliable projection of sales for the year.

13. Besides estimating our sales figures or proforma for the year, we also plan the profits and costs for the year. As a formula, it could be put this way, proforma = costs + profit.

14. One of the major factors in cost is the amount we invest in advertising and sales promotion. We develop these costs at the same time that we develop the figures for proforma and profit, and we actually make these investments well in advance of sales.

15. Achieving proforma requires skill in each area of marketing. Thus your responsibility is to achieve proforma through planning, personal selling, and merchandising, the three main types of sales/marketing that concern us most.

Questions for Written Reports or Class Discussion

1. Do you feel the above information tells a new salesperson enough about Thomas J. Lipton, Inc. and the American food industry? If not, what other information should be presented, so that he or she will go into the field thoroughly informed of all aspects of Lipton's business?

2. Concerning tea as one of Lipton's products, what would you, as a new Lipton salesperson, want to learn about it?

3. What three topics from the Lipton sales training course extracts would you consider to be the most helpful to you as a new Lipton salesperson? List and defend your choices in order of ranking priority.

4. From what sources could you, as a new Lipton salesperson, learn everything possible about the competition you can expect to face for each of your different product lines?

Sales Problem 4.1

Can Potterbridges' paper sacks be sold profitably to Winterbottom in Peas Pottage?

This is not a tongue-twisting riddle but a serious problem in paper-sack selling to Paul P., who represents Potterbridges' Proved Paper Products, Ltd. (fondly known throughout the trade as PPPPL in southern England) out of his home town of Newton Poppleford, Devon.

Paul, his company, and his prospect may be mythical, but paper-sack (not bag) selling is a big and very competitive business in Cornwall, Devon, Hampshire, Dorset, Somerset, and Wiltshire counties. Heaps of potatoes, fruits, vegetables, chemicals, coal, seeds, wheat, corn, and refuse all go into paper sacks in this part of England.

Our friend Paul has just spotted a potential new sales prospect. Frisky Fido Food ships its product in big paper sacks. Thinking quickly, Paul decides that there could be one dog for every 10 people in southern England and if Frisky

Fido reaches even one in 100, it could mean many extra paper-sack sales—in the hundreds of thousands over a period of time!

He notes that the manufacturer of Frisky Fido is A. Winterbottom & Sons Fertilizer Processing Co., Ltd., of Peas Pottage, Hants. Being a customer-oriented salesperson, Paul decides to scientifically study the needs of this potential customer and to prepare a sales presentation of PPPPL paper sacks that can offer Winterbottom better value for his money. Price means everything in the competitive paper-sack business, so his basic problem is to offer Winterbottom this better value at a lower price if possible and still to allow PPPPL to make its profit. If a lower price is impossible, then he will have to use "extra value" as a selling point to justify the price difference.

Here are some of the problems Paul has to solve in order to come up with an answer to Winterbottom's packaging needs.

Customer Information

(1) How big a supplier is Winterbottom? (2) How many sacks of Frisky Fido does he ship per week or month? (3) What other products does he manufacture and ship in paper sacks? (4) What other products does he ship in competitive packaging (that is, cardboard cartons, wooden crates, or plastic containers) that could be shipped in paper sacks?

Packaging Information

(1) Who manufactures the currently used Frisky Fido sack? (2) How much does the presently used sack cost Winterbottom? (3) What is the quality of the competing sack: how many layers does it have, what are the properties of each layer (for example, waterproof or extra tough), and what are the reasons for extra layers if any?

Product Information

(1) What are the properties of Frisky Fido, the product being shipped? (2) What properties are necessary in the PPPPL sack to protect the product being shipped (such as, waterproofing, oil base)? (3) What strength PPPPL sack is needed to ship Frisky Fido properly?

Paul's Overall Problem

Through knowledge of his product, the competing product, and the customer's needs, he must work out what it would cost PPPPL to produce a better sack at a lower price if possible. If a lower price is impossible, then he will have to use extra value to justify the difference.

Question for Written Reports or Class Discussion

Paul knows that in order to work out what it will cost PPPPL to produce a better sack at lower cost, he will first have to get all information possible in the following three areas. Assuming that you are Paul, list under each heading the different types of information you will need to get, and where you will obtain each.

1. Customer information
2. Product information
3. Packaging information

<table>
<tr><td>**Sales**
Problem 4.2</td><td>Do you really know as much about your company as you do about your product?</td></tr>
</table>

You are ready to go out selling. You feel confident because you've learned a great deal about a great many things. First, what you sell—for example, what it's composed of, what it will and won't do, how it stacks up against the competition. Second, your prospects—for example, their ways of operating, their needs and problems, the benefits they will desire from what you sell. Well trained in good selling techniques as you are, why wouldn't you feel confident?

But wait a moment! There may be one important area in which your knowledge may be deficient—the company or organization you represent. Have you learned all you can about it? Are you prepared to respond to a prospect or customer who asks you a question or questions such as:

1. "I know your company is about 75 years old, but was it always in its current line of business?"
2. "That new plant you people are putting up in Ridgefield is the second one you've started this year. Planning any more between now and 1997?"
3. "I read in last night's paper that your firm is adding two new directors to your Board. Does this mean anything special?"
4. "I know that your company has several manufacturing plants. In which one do you make this specific product?"
5. "I saw your organization's ad in a couple of purchasing magazines last week. Where else do you advertise?"
6. "So your sales increased 15 percent last year! How does that compare with the previous few years?"

Questions for Written Reports or Class Discussion

1. For each of the above questions: How would you respond? Should you know this information? If so, and you don't, how and where can you find out?

2. In order to test your own "managerial thinking abilities," please list six additional questions to the ones listed above that will represent knowledge areas about which you should learn more in order to sell at a higher professional skill level.

Prospecting and Organizing Your Prospect List

After studying this chapter, you will be able to:

Define the sales terms *prospect, prospecting, qualified prospect, sales lead, referral lead, cold-call canvassing,* and *bird dog.*

Identify two common steps employed in the prospecting process.

Explain why it is so important to qualify a prospect prior to a sales call and presentation, and cite the three questions that must be answered in order to ensure proper qualification.

Describe three major advantages offered by the telephone in prospecting and selling.

Identify six progressive steps involved in precall planning prior to qualifying prospects and making appointments by telephone, and explain key factors to be considered under each.

Develop a direct-mail prospecting letter that will also serve to qualify the prospect.

No matter what you sell (product, service, idea, cause, or person) or to what type of consumer (individual or organizational buyer), your search for new potential buyers or increased business (or support, financial or otherwise) from current ones will normally be constant and never-ending.

A major first step in analyzing a new sales area or territory, or in starting to work a list (such as, for charitable fund raising), is to determine which firm, organization, or individuals are or could become "buyers" of whatever you are selling.

Most established business firms provide their new salespeople with a current customer list, but from there on, for them as for the firm's longer-time salespeople, it is normally part of their sales job to increase sales by finding more customers. They need to find new ones not only from a personal point of view but also to replace the average 10 to 20 percent of customers normally lost by any business firm during the year for one reason or another. This same situation also exists, in many cases, for sales/marketing representatives of not-for-profit organizations, agencies, or groups. No matter what you are selling, you constantly have to be aware of this need.

Why do regular customers drop away and need to be replaced? Transfers, deaths, retirements, liquidations, corporate takeovers, and real or fancied grievances are but a few such reasons. Another is your competition, whose eager and aggressive salespeople like nothing better than increasing their business at your expense. You have to be competitive in spirit, and sales and service-minded enough to hang onto your current customers and to increase their business where possible. You also have to be prospect-minded, constantly alert to the fact that a steadily expanding list of qualified prospects is vitally important to the increased sales necessary for your success.

What do we mean by a prospect? A qualified prospect? What is prospecting? How does one find and qualify new prospects? These are questions we consider now.

WHAT IS A PROSPECT? A QUALIFIED PROSPECT?

There is a big difference between a mere list of possible new customers, called *leads,* and a list of *qualified prospects.* A *lead* (pronounced "lēd") in sales terminology refers to a person or organization that may be a potential prospect. Sometimes leads are referred to as "suspects" (in contrast to prospects). A *prospect* is any person or organization that may have a need or want for the seller's product or service, or who can benefit from buying it. A *qualified prospect* not only needs and can benefit from it, but also can afford it and is able to make the decision to purchase it.

WHAT IS PROSPECTING?

The process of looking up and checking out leads is called *prospecting*. It involves a *continuous* search for and qualification of individuals, firms, organizations, or groups that might be in the market for whatever it is that you are selling. Once identified, qualified prospects with apparent highest potential should be contacted first—others in descending order of potential.

While salespeople in different types of selling may encounter different problems in finding qualified prospects, the process in most cases involves these two steps: (1) checking all possible sources for leads that may become prospects and (2) qualifying these prospects as to their buying potential.

In this chapter we examine first where you can find prospects and then methods of qualifying them. Finally, we discuss the use of the telephone in carrying out both the above steps and also in making an appointment to see the prospect.

HOW YOU CAN LOCATE NEW PROSPECTS

The basic equation of selling is salesperson + prospect = sales. You as the salesperson represent one-half of this equation, but where do you find prospects, the missing part? The answer is almost anywhere and everywhere. The sources for finding prospects are all around you. You have to discover what these sources are and employ all the initiative and persistence necessary to put them to work for you.

What are some of the sources for finding prospects? Your company (or organization), your industry, your competitors, customers or clients, and even prospects who do not buy from you—these are but a few. One secret of prospecting success is to utilize each to the greatest depth possible. Here are some hints.

Leads from Your Company or Organization

These are the easiest to obtain, yet it is amazing how few salespeople use initiative enough to get maximum benefit from all possible company or organizational sources. Sources for leads exist in many different divisions and departments but are seldom available from one single source in easy-to-obtain form. You may find it worthwhile to meet various department heads and to ferret information out for yourself from among the following sources.

- *Current active customer lists* are the easiest lists to obtain and are normally handed over to you as a matter of course. But what about customer lists from other divisions of your organization? Another division may sell a different product with its own salespeople, mailing lists, and records. If there are such different divisions, check them to see if they have any additional names, apart from those on your own lists, who may be potential customers for you.

- *Credit departments* are useful for inactive accounts or for credit bureau rating reports on noncustomer accounts. You can often turn people who bought from your employer in the past once again into productive customers. Even if they cannot be resold, they can often tell you about others who may buy from you. Your credit department probably subscribes to a credit-rating service that gives information about newly formed companies, yet credit department personnel may not be sales-minded enough to even think of turning over such names to the sales department as potential leads. Can you get them for yourself?

- *Company service department records* may indicate calls to service equipment for which a new replacement may mean savings for the customer. Service personnel may or may not be trained to report such possibilities to the sales department. Perhaps such people can become "bird dogs" for you, reporting to you alone (personal gifts or a commission cut would help win them over) on all sorts of sales possibilities inside firms or homes on which they make service calls.

- *Advertising* plays an important part in every company or organizational promotion plan. It will pay to know what advertising will be going out and to what specific lists well in advance of publication and mailing. You may be able to personalize such ads to your advantage. Few sales-people take the trouble to initiate meetings with key advertising people and thus miss good opportunities. Would it not be helpful if a higher than usual percentage of customer reply cards were handed over to you personally by your friends in the advertising department?

- *Exhibits, conventions, and trade fairs* in which your company or organization participates are excellent sources of leads. Attend to all these you can, even if you are not a delegated representative, and exchange business cards with everyone you meet. Study these afterward, and ask yourself which ones may need your product or service. Then write or phone them, saying that, since meeting them, you have thought of an idea which may benefit them.

  People who attend such exhibits or conventions are usually interested in the products on display. You thus have a chance to meet prospects from areas you may have overlooked on regular calls, and certainly have an excellent opportunity to talk easily with a larger than average number of potential prospects during the day or evening.

  Since exhibit booths at such affairs are normally manned by the exhibitor's salespeople, you have an unusual opportunity to ask them questions. If they are direct competitors, and they don't know you personally, so much the better! Those who sell noncompeting products in your market may be able to supply excellent sales leads or inside or personal information about some of your customers.

  Later on, in Chapter 16, we explore techniques of turning exhibits manned by you at such affairs into both prospecting and on-the-spot sales opportunities.

- *Direct mail,* either on a systematic company basis or through your own initiative in utilizing company resources and lists, can work while you work, getting new leads for you. A well-written, direct-mail piece contains triple bait for prospects—news, benefits, and confidence—that help set the stage for your personal follow-up call. The difference between a *direct mail* mailing and a *mail order* mailing is that direct mailings consist of a single mail piece (such as a letter, flyer or foldout), while a mail order mailing may include many different mail pieces in one envelope or packet.

  Direct mail is a relatively inexpensive prospecting technique that helps qualify a prospect. Your company can send such letters out for you, or you can have it done at your own expense. Insurance companies often send out such direct-mail letters, in which, for example, a small free gift may be offered in exchange for either the prospect's birthday or that of a friend (see Figure 5.1.). If the information is returned, the name and birth date become a lead to be followed up by a qualifying phone call or even by a personal visit from the salesperson.

  Direct-mail prospecting is also employed by many nonbusiness organizations, commonly to obtain members to support a cause of one kind or another, or to solicit donations.

- *Telephone prospecting* is discussed at length later on. But we mention here that some business firms have special operators who do it on a large and systematic basis. They call home or business telephone subscribers, often offering special prices if the prospect agrees to see a salesperson at home. The lead is thus qualified, and a salesperson calls on what is considered a prospect. Individual salespeople can employ the same technique on a similar basis, either through company or personal arrangements.

- *Inquiries* from interested firms or individuals may come into various departments of your company or organization. These may be in response to advertising, referrals, or word-of-mouth information about one or more products or services. Does your employer have a system for turning these over as sales leads? If not, try to find out who receives such calls or letters and whether the potential leads from them could be turned over to you.

- *Canvassers* are employed by some companies or by some individual commission salespeople to take part of the burden of cold-call canvassing or prospecting away from the real salespeople. *Cold-call canvassing* (or *prospecting*) means to physically call on someone for the first time without any prior contact. Often called *spotters* or *bird dogs*, they most often use the telephone in prospecting, but frequently call door to door to qualify prospects and to arrange appointments for evening or other callback interviews. Firms selling such things as encyclopedias, home oil heating systems, vacuum cleaners, and automobiles often employ canvassers.

  Some commission salespeople use a modification of this system. They employ such people as elevator operators, barbers, bartenders, or waitresses to be their "bird dogs" in spotting potential customers.

INTERGLOBAL INSURANCE COMPANY
New York — London — Toronto — Tokyo — Buenos Aires

Bob Figgie
Branch Manager

60081 Eastern Avenue
Dallas, Texas

PHONE (214) 111-2345

February 16, 1990

Mr. R.V. Brinkerhoff
General Manager
Montalvo Products, Inc.
43 Tightrope Walk
Flintknoll, Arizona

Dear Sir:

Would you mind just giving me your date of birth below so that
I may furnish you complimentary data on a new executive
protection plan which, due to its low cost, is probably the
most discussed policy in the insurance world today?

A self-addressed, postage-paid return envelope is enclosed for
your convenience.

Very truly yours,

Bob Figgie

Bob Figgie
Branch Manager

- -

Name_____

Address_____ City_____

Telephone Number_____ Date of birth_____

FIGURE 5.1 *Example of a Direct-Mail Attempt to Qualify a Prospect.
The prospect's name could have been obtained from any number
of sources.*

- *Your own records* can be a profitable source of leads if kept up to date
  and properly indexed. A prospect may say, "I'm not interested now but
  may be next summer." If you feel it to be a valid lead, you should put it
  in your follow-up file and call again in the summer. The same holds true
  if you learn of future industry or prospect developments that could
  mean one or more sales at a later date. A professional salesperson takes
  note of everything of potential interest learned on each call and turns
  the files into a rich source of future leads.

Leads from Your Current Customers. These are perhaps your best single
source. A fundamental fact of selling is that it is usually easier to sell more to or
get more information from an established, current satisfied customer than from a

new one. If you have done a good sales job and your customers are pleased with your products, company, service, and you, they will be only too happy to pass the good word along. Few of them volunteer, however, they have to be asked.

> *You may say for example:* "Mr. Apostolas, do you know of any personal or business acquaintance who may benefit, as you have done from my product?"
> *If he says yes, you may then suggest:* "Do you mind my using your name as an introduction when I contact them for an interview?"

Quite often your customers, or their secretaries, or even their key employees, will be unable to think of specific people they feel may consider your product. It may therefore be useful to ask them a question in general terms such as, if you are selling insurance, "Do you know anyone who has gotten a good promotion or raise lately? If so, I wonder if you could help me meet him or her."

Called *referral leads*, these specific leads given you by a satisfied customer are generally considered the most valuable for getting you in touch with truly qualified prospects. The best kind of referral lead is a formal letter of introduction, recommending both you personally and your product. Few customers are willing to take the time to write such a letter, but if customers allow you to prepare a draft for their approval, it is very easy for them merely to turn it over to their secretaries for typing.

Perhaps the easiest system of getting customer referral leads is to have the customer dash off a brief note of introduction on the back of a business card. Such a note need only be something like the one in Figure 5.2. You can also ask that such a brief introduction be jotted down on the back of your calling card. In this case, you should ask for a full signature. Either way, this personalized card serves as a quick, valuable, attention-getting lead and should enable you to get in to see the new prospect without delay.

FIGURE 5.2 *Customer's Referral to a Business Friend, Written on the Back of the Customer's Personal Business Card*

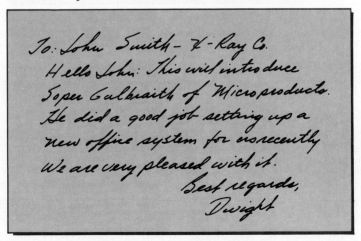

You can also obtain business-card referrals from a prospect you fail to sell! You can ask for help in recommending new prospects, providing you did a good selling job and feel the climate is right for making such a request. The prospect probably will feel a little bad about having turned you down and will therefore be glad to do you a small favor by suggesting one or more good potential prospects.

You can make the same request to a prospect to whom you have just made a sale, whether an old or new customer. You simply ask if there are friends or business associates who may have problems similar to the one for which your products or services have just provided a solution. If you have sold an encyclopedia set, for example, you may ask:

> "Mrs. de Pinzone, can you give me the names of any friends or relatives with children around the age of your own who may find such a set useful for schoolwork reference?"

Such customers may phone for you on the spot, or even write you a testimonial letter that you can show all future prospects.

If you are an industrial salesperson calling on company purchasing agents, or a fund-raiser for some charitable organization or cause, the question is basically the same. In fact, you should talk up your own business in every way possible with each regular customer or new prospect you meet. Tell them what you are doing, what you hope to accomplish, and ask for their advice and guidance in reaching new prospects. If your listeners are not in the market themselves for what you sell, they may know someone else who is or who could become interested if aware of it.

Leads from Competitors and Noncompetitors. Leads from competitors can be obtained by tracing the movement of competition products. You can learn of such activities from your own customers as well from industry journals, the newspaper, or organizations such as your local chamber of commerce.

Salespeople of noncompeting companies can be especially good sources for leads. They often have inside information on company buying policy, names of key decision makers, and dates purchases will be made. You may, for example, sell typewriters and learn from a friend in an employment agency that a given company plans to double its secretarial and clerical staff early next year. This can be a valuable lead to a quantity sale of your typewriters plus other office machines produced by your company. It pays to cultivate salespeople of noncompetitive products and to reciprocate by providing them with information when possible.

Canvassing Your Industry. Another way to obtain excellent leads is to canvass your industry. You can get lists of potential customers from trade journals, chambers of commerce, credit bureau reports, and other sources. Many of these list names of purchasing officers or key department heads. These sources also often indicate the growth potential and latest developments of the industry and of companies within the industry. If conditions are changing, then you possibly can move in with new ideas that will help individual companies retain or improve their competitive positions.

Business and financial news within the industry or associated ones is especially important. A new contract, a merger, a building permit, a new bond issue, or a dramatic increase in profits spell opportunity for you. News of promotions or new appointments can lead to sales of real estate, investments, insurance, or new automobiles. Management changes of any sort are especially important.

You can find worthwhile industry leads in the yellow pages of your telephone directory, and in city, trade, social, and professional directories. You can canvass leads obtained in this way by letter, by telephone, and through personal office calls.

Governmental departments, business libraries, and clipping services are all additional sources for leads. Many companies and many commission salespeople or individuals subscribe to clipping services, whose staffs read all journals and newspapers, both national and local. For a fee, they cut out and mail all clippings that may be of interest to the subscribers.

Social Contacts. Social contacts are an excellent source of leads. Many salespeople are not only members of but also active leaders in such organizations as toastmasters' clubs, church, golf or other sports clubs, alumni associations, fraternal organizations, service clubs (such as Lions, Rotary, Kiwanis, or Sertoma), and all kinds of other community and social organizations. The element of reciprocal selling is strong in many of these groups, but the wise salesperson keeps social contacts social. Such contacts often turn into good leads, but selling should be done during business hours. It may help a sharp young insurance salesperson to be thought of as "that terrific song leader at our club-sponsored picnic," but not as "that bore who tried to sell insurance at our club picnic."

Many aggressive and successful salespeople respect their social responsibilities and treasure their personal lives, to the extent that they refuse to sell to relatives, close friends, or even neighbors. This gives them an ease in social relationships that is denied the hard-sell character always trying to use friendship as the means to an easy sale. Salespeople who clearly separate their business and personal social life are generally admired.

Finding Leads on Your Own. Called *cold-call canvassing* (or *prospecting*) this is still the backbone of creative prospecting for most salespeople. The trick here is to know all the potential markets for your product or service and then to classify all potential buyers who have a need for it and who can easily be contacted. Since there could be hundreds of such prospects, proper organization of your prospect list is highly important. You first have to list companies, organizations, agencies, or individuals who (1) should have a basic need for the product and (2) should have the money to pay for it. Once the listing is made in order of apparent potential, you should make persistent, systematic calls on all groups or individuals listed.

Some successful salespeople organize their cold-canvassing prospect list along the lines of the yellow pages in the telephone directory. If, for example, you are selling air-conditioning equipment, you can parallel the listings in the yellow pages with a list of potential users for your product, arranged by industry with sublistings of companies or individuals.

No matter how you organize your list, the possibilities for finding leads are virtually unlimited, depending of course on the potential need for your product. Here are but a few sources for such leads.

- *Door-to-door canvassing.* This can be done house-to-house in residential areas or on an office-to-office basis in a large building complex.

- *Your own creative ideas* can provide leads. You may, for example, read about a new product being developed by a local company. Perhaps you can devise a way it can be combined with your product and thus open entirely new sales possibilities for that company—and yourself.

- *From other people with whom you do business.* If you are a home owner, you deal with many people: banker, home builder, electrician, plumber, grocer, doctor, milkman, lawyer, and retailers of many types. Any of these can either become a prospect or refer you to others.

- *Special-need groups* can provide leads for finding prospects. Does your product appeal to working adults, retired people, white-collar workers, teenagers, executives, lawyers, artists, people who sit while at work, or fishermen? If you list such special-need groups and find out how and where they can best be reached, you may be on your way to rapid sales success.

- *Newspapers* provide new potential prospect names by the scores each day if you know where to look for them. Birth, promotion, business, financial, and real estate notices or stories can, when linked to your product, lead to new prospects. It is indeed a wise salesperson who obtains a daily newspaper when heading off to work each morning and scans it for all appropriate news and for potential prospects whenever a few waiting-time moments become available throughout the day.

- *Influentials* (centers of influence), or people in your area who know many others and are known, can provide excellent leads. Newspaper editors, presidents of chambers of commerce, leading bankers, college professors, or well-known socialites can, if convinced of the merits of your product, express favorable opinions and give recommendations that make your selling job easier.

- *Your friends and acquaintances* may know people who are good prospects. Even if you do not like to sell to your friends, you should ask them for leads. If your products offer real benefit, do not be afraid to tell your friends or acquaintances in a conversational manner what you sell, what it can do, and why it is good. This is often called the "endless chain" method of prospecting.

- *Join professional organizations,* participate in their activities, and read their journals. Sales and Marketing Executives International is an important professional sales organization with national clubs in 49 countries of the Free World and with local chapters in various cities. The American Management Association, with head office in New York City, has affiliated chapters in most major American cities. Similar, internationally affiliated, national management groups exist in most countries.

These are but two examples of professional organizations you may find worthwhile joining where possible.

- *Other ways of finding leads* through personal initiative include examining (where possible) the files of trust companies and the deed recordings at municipal offices and reviewing newly issued business licenses.

HOW CAN YOU QUALIFY NEW PROSPECTS?

It costs you and your company or organization time and money to locate new prospects. This time is wasted if you make a sales presentation only to find that your prospect is unable to consider your proposal for honest reasons—including lack of money in the budget or lack of authority to make a decision.

Your initial task therefore is to qualify your prospect before getting into the sales presentation. The depth of qualification depends in part on the product you are selling. If you are proposing employee accident insurance to a firm, you must find out who (which individual or group) makes the decision, when present coverage if any expires, and when the firm will be able to make a decision. If you are selling a diaper or baby napkin home delivery service, you must find out whether there are small babies in the home and whether the family already subscribes to such a service. If you are selling an automobile, you need to find out how the prospect will use it, so you can aid in selecting the proper vehicle.

Proper qualification of prospects involves obtaining satisfactory answers to these questions:

Do They Have a Need for the Product or Service? If you determine that your product can help your prospects make money, or do a better job, or otherwise honestly benefit them, then a need exists. You still have the task of persuading them to want the product now, but at least you have qualified them as to need.

Do They Have the Authority to Buy? Getting the answer to this question is just as important when you are calling on business firms as when you are calling on individual consumers in their homes. Qualification of the authority to buy involves determining whether the prospect can make the buying decision alone, or must first consult with others. In selling to prospects in their homes, you should keep in mind that in most North American homes the wife plays the key role. Husband and wife make most expensive purchases jointly, however, although the woman may still make the final decision. Thus, in selling a children's encyclopedia set for the home, you should make your presentation to the husband and wife together.

If you are selling a computer system to a company, or seeking a fund-raising donation, you may have to see several decision makers individually or make a presentation before a group of executives.

Key questions to ask before making your presentation are

"If interested, Mrs. Cress, will you be the one who makes the decision alone, or will others be involved?"

If others are involved, you can continue by asking:

"How can I best present my product for the benefit of your entire purchasing committee?"

It often saves time to ask your prospects' advice and help in such situations.

When two or more people are involved in a buying decision, determine who the key prospect is and plan your presentation accordingly. In the case of a husband and wife, the wife may be the key prospect. In a partnership business, you may first ask to see the "partner who usually does the buying." In companies, your key prospect may be the department head whose people will be most actively using your product. You can save time and money by trying to locate the key prospect or decision maker at time of qualification.

Can the Prospect Pay for It?   Qualifications of a prospect's ability either to pay in cash or to qualify for credit terms often depends on your personal estimate of his or her surroundings, status, and occupation. He or she may appear willing to pay but really not be able to afford to do so. If a cash payment is required, it doesn't take long to find that out—your prospect either has the cash or doesn't. But if credit is involved, caution is called for. There are certain types of prospects who have no scruples about signing an agreement to purchase something on a credit basis, with little intention to pay if they can possibly avoid it. Others readily sign up either knowing then, or discovering later, that they really can't afford to meet the payments as they fall due.

Remember, no sale is complete until it has been paid for! If you are selling to home owners or individuals, you can tell a lot about prospects' financial position by the way they dress, the way they talk, the kind of car they drive, and their readiness to disclose the name of their bank or other companies with whom they do business.

When selling to firms, ask your company credit department for a credit check before spending time on a full-scale presentation. Commission sales representatives often find it worthwhile to subscribe to credit-rating services, such as Dun & Bradstreet (with offices in many of the world's countries and cities).

If you are selling abroad, the commercial attaché at your nation's embassy, or officials of your nation's trade commission (if any), or consular officers at your nation's consulates are normally glad to assist you in obtaining local country or city credit information. Chambers of commerce in host country nations may also be able to assist and advise you in such matters.

Newspaper reporters get all the facts on a potential news item by seeking answers to who, what, when, where, why, and how. Good salespeople ask themselves the same questions in order to completely qualify their prospects.

Up to 20 percent of a salesperson's selling time is often wasted in simply waiting to get in to see and talk to prospects, even if an official appointment has been made. Someone else is often in the prospect's office first, and others must wait their turn.

One secret for making more prospect calls in less time and for less money is the telephone. The law of averages normally applies here: the more prospects contacted, the more who are qualified; the more effective presentations made, the greater number of closes; the more closes, the greater the sales volume. Proper use of the telephone can often help salespeople in certain fields to greatly increase their sales volume. Some companies and not-for-profit organizations sell or solicit entirely by telephone, and telephone companies in most major cities of the world are ready to advise salespeople on proper telephone-selling techniques.

Three major advantages of telephone prospecting are these:

1. It enables you to identify yourself, your firm, and your business, and gives you a chance to quickly qualify your prospect and make a specific appointment.
2. It helps you screen prospects in advance and avoid unnecessary travel time and expense.
3. The prospect is prepared to see you when you appear for your appointment and usually waits to hear your story before making a buying decision.

There are also some disadvantages. A secretary may prevent you from talking to the prospect. If so, the secretary may remember you on personal callbacks and still not let you contact him or her. So you have to face the secretary as an in-between person who has to be sold before you can contact the key prospect. And if you do get to talk to the prospect, he or she may also turn you down before ever hearing your full story. The telephone is a cold, impersonal instrument. It is psychologically easier for a secretary or a prospect to turn you down over the telephone than to do it in person.

Certain techniques, apart from those of normal face-to-face selling, apply to successful telephone prospecting or telephone selling. You may turn your prospecting call into a presentation and a sale closed on the spot. Thus you must be knowledgeable and alert enough to manage the situation, whatever it is, to your advantage.

We will discuss basic principles and techniques of prospecting and selling by telephone in two parts: (1) qualifying prospects and making appointments, to be considered now, and (2) the complete telephone sales presentation, which we take up in Chapter 16. For a complete overview of telephone selling, both sections should be studied together.

Qualifying Prospects and Making Appointments by Telephone

Careful planning and step-by-step following of the plan will assure greatest success in using the telephone to qualify prospects and make appointments. We will consider this in two parts: (1) precall planning, and (2) the telephone call.

Precall Planning.   This planning involves thinking through and putting down on paper an outline of exactly what your objective is and the words you intend to say. This careful planning will save time and produce most successful results. Your planning should involve these six logical, progressive steps:

1. *Decide on what basis you will qualify prospects.* The basis selected will depend on the product you are selling. If you are selling power lawn mowers to homes you can phone homeowners, but you must find out if they have lawns. If selling a product or service to a business firm, you may need to know the type and size of the prospect's business, the facilities for handling, storing, or using your product, and how or if the prospect can pay for it. If you are selling heavy-duty trucks, large contracting firms would obviously be better prospects than bakeries who use light delivery vans only. If you aren't certain whether a firm to be called is a potential customer for your heavy-duty truck, you will have to frame questions to find out quickly.

    If you are seeking charitable donations, or support for special community fund-raising programs, you must plan accordingly.

2. *Draw up a list of prospects.* Again, this list depends on the type of product or service you are selling. Once you identify the type of individual, business, or organization that seems to represent market potential, then you have to draw up a list of such prospects. If you are selling electric golf carts, your logical market might be sporting goods stores, country clubs, or large department stores. You could get lists of these from such sources as telephone directory classified pages, the chamber of commerce, or local trade associations.

3. *Outline your opening statement.* It is important to know exactly what you are going to say in the first ten to fifteen seconds. The telephone is such an impersonal instrument that unless you quickly arouse the prospect's attention or interest, he or she may say no and hang up quickly. An effective opening statement should include these three essential steps:

    a. *Identify yourself, your firm, or your organization:*

    "Good afternoon, Mr. Walters, my name is Joe Burke of Anscon Products Corporation."

    b. *Quickly attempt to establish rapport,* to overcome any negative reaction to your call and warm the prospect up to listen to your sales message. This can be done in one of these ways:

    Make a friendly remark: "It is a pleasure to be speaking to such a well-known leader in community affairs."

Mention something you and the prospect have in common: "I understand you are an alumnus of City College, as I am; that makes us fellow Bears (name of the school athletic team)."

Tactfully acknowledge that he is probably busy: "I realize you are a very busy person, but . . . "

Say something to stimulate his or her pride: "I've been reading in the newspaper about the grand opening of your new store; it must make you feel proud to have helped plan it."

    c.   *Make an interest-arousing statement about your product:*

"Did you see the picture in last week's newspaper of our state's Senator Gilhooly and the President riding together on one of Anscon's new electric golf carts at the Pebble Beach Golf Course in California?"

4.   *Outline fact-finding questions to be asked.* You need to ask fact-finding questions to help determine whether or not the prospect is qualified. Open-ended who, what, when, where, and how questions are best:

"What kind of sporting goods sell best in your store?"
"Where do your golf customers buy their electric golf carts?"
"How much of your business relates to golfers?"

5.   *Outline your sales message.* In order to make an appointment, you must present enough sales points to arouse enough interest on the prospect's part that he or she will agree to see you at a specific date and time. This can be done by presenting no more than one or two *features* and *benefits* of your product. A feature is a description of the product; a benefit, the satisfaction that the prospect will receive from the feature. Each feature should be turned into a customer benefit (which represents value), since it is really benefiting that customer's buy. Both features and benefits should be described in interesting, sales-vocabulary words that help the prospect visualize it mentally over the phone.

"Our new electric golf cart that the senator and the President were riding on is an all-new, sturdy, dependable vehicle, with silent but thrusting power. It represents a real breakthrough in electric-golf-cart development. They seem to be enjoying their ride, probably because it operates so easily and is so much fun to drive."

6.   *Outline your request for an appointment.* This has to be presented in two parts, the lead-in and the request itself. The lead-in should point out how the prospect will benefit from making an appointment.

"I would like to meet with you to explain exactly how you could gain sizable extra sales volume by working with Anscon Corporation to promote sales of our electric golf cart through your stores."

The request, which follows, is the actual question you will use to get the appointment. The *wrong* way to do this is merely to ask if you can visit him sometime; this makes it easy for him to say he's too busy. The *right* (best) way to do this is to ask him to make a choice between two appointment times. If he doesn't like either, it is easy for him to suggest an alternative.

"Would 10:15 Thursday morning or Friday at 3:15 be better for you?"

The Call Itself.   In order to further illustrate, in a slightly different way, some of the principles and techniques we have just considered in our planning, let us assume that we are listening in (as sales trainees) to a telephone approach being made by our sales manager, Lyall Gleeson. Some new elements are introduced, so pay particular attention to how he handles the three people he will talk to and the qualifying techniques he will employ.

The Telephone Call	*Sales and Telephone Techniques Involved*
Lyall Gleeson sells a Young Executives' Training Course and has just dialed XYZ Company.	He has observed the first rule of good prospecting by listing companies that should have a need for his training course. He now wants to find the decision maker, qualify him or her, and make an appointment to talk in person.
Company switchboard operator: Good morning, XYZ Company *Gleeson:* Can you help me, please? Which of your corporate executives is most concerned with executive training or development? The key person? Can you give me the name please and put me through?	He does not know whom to ask for and has framed his question so that the operator will give him the name of the key decision maker. Note that he has gotten the name from the operator and not the secretary. The complete name and title!
Operator: That will be Mr. Rodney Horwitz, our personnel manager, I'm putting you through to his secretary. *Secretary:* Mr. Horwitz's office. *Gleeson:* Mr. Horwitz please. Lyall Gleeson calling. *Secretary:* From what company, please?	Gleeson is trying to visualize Horwitz as a friend and to ask for him in a casual way, smiling into the phone. Note that he does not ask if he is in and thus risk being put off by the secretary. In a high percentage of cases, Gleeson finds that prospects personally take such calls.
Gleeson: Executive Publishing Company, is he there?	His answer to the question is rapid and straightforward. If Horwitz is in, and the secretary is busy, the easy way out is to put Gleeson right through to him.

At this point many secretaries want to know what Gleeson is calling about. He usually tries to avoid that question by first cheerfully asking, "May I have your name? Are you his secretary? I'm calling to make an appointment. May I speak to him directly?" If the secretary still persists in knowing what the call is about, Gleeson explains very briefly and again asks to speak directly to Mr. Horwitz. If the secretary suggests calling someone else because Mr. Horwitz is busy, Gleeson replies, "Good, I'll be glad to talk to the other person after speaking to Mr. Horwitz. When would you suggest I call Mr. Horwitz again?" Gleeson always tries to use the confident, direct approach first in his telephone calls, and, as in this case, usually gets through.

The Telephone Call	Sales and Telephone Techniques Involved
Horwitz: Horwitz speaking. *Gleeson:* Hello Mr. Horwitz, this is Lyall Gleeson of Executive Publishing Company. We have a new junior executive training aid that could be of real value to your in-plant executive training program. Aren't you the one who supervises your company's executive training? *Horwitz:* Well, we have only an informal program with about six people in it, but I guess I am in charge. What type of training aid is it?	Gleeson identifies himself and his company and starts his qualification. If XYZ Company does not have a program, Gleeson may then try to sell Horwitz personally. If they do have such a training program but Horwitz does not supervise it, the question is framed so that he should give the name of the individual in charge. The lead has been qualified; the company does have a small program and Horwitz is in charge. And by asking, "What do you have?" he has tossed out a buying signal. Gleeson now classifies him as a qualified, live prospect.
Gleeson: Our material must be seen to be appreciated, and we tailor its use to your specific needs. May I have an appointment to show it to you at 3:15 P.M. tomorrow, or would 10:30 A.M. Wednesday morning be more convenient?	Gleeson uses a preplanned presentation involving visual aids. He wants to present his product in person. Beforehand, he will make up a card file with XYZ Company stamped on the cards, plus a sales story built around whatever else he learns about the company between now and the appointment. Note that Gleeson gives Horwitz a choice of appointment times, thus eliminating the possibility of a "next-year" answer.
Horwitz: How about making it Thursday at 2 P.M.? *Gleeson:* Thank you. I'll be at your office Thursday at 2 P.M. sharp and look forward to meeting you personally. Goodbye.	Gleeson is careful to repeat the place, date, and time. This fixes it clearly in the minds of both men. Gleeson immediately writes the appointment information down after hanging up.

Good telephone prospecting and selling techniques involve careful preparation of opening statements and of questions that will rapidly qualify your prospect. The opening sentence is especially important at each stage, as was illustrated in this example.

SUMMARY

We have discussed in this chapter the need for you as a salesperson to constantly develop new lists of prospects. Even though your company or organization may provide a current customer list, a certain percentage is lost each year for various reasons. You need to replace them and also to seek out new qualified prospects whose needs can be converted into wants and those in turn into the new sales necessary for volume increases.

Finding these prospects involves building up lists of firms or individuals who may have a need for your product and then checking them out in order to discover whether they have a need, the authority to buy, and the money with which to make the purchase. This procedure is called *prospecting;* the result is a qualified prospect to whom you can make your sales presentation.

We reviewed in some detail how to go about finding new prospects and concluded that for many products the possibilities for finding prospects are virtually unlimited. We then explained how to qualify these prospects.

Finally, we considered the specific use of the telephone as one special means, among many, of finding and qualifying prospects. We treated this method separately from direct-mail or certain other types of prospecting methods because the special techniques employed, as is the case with cold-call personal prospecting, can often lead right into a sales presentation.

Constant, systematic, persistent prospecting is an absolute necessity if you are to always have available what every top salesperson needs—an endless supply of potential customers.

Questions for Analysis and Discussion

1.   Explain the difference (in sales terminology) between a lead and a qualified prospect.

2.   What are the two main problems faced by most salespeople in prospecting, and what steps are involved in solving them?

3.   Proper qualification of a prospect involves obtaining satisfactory answers to what three important questions?

4.   What are two major advantages in using the telephone for prospecting? What is the major psychological disadvantage of using the telephone?

5.   What do we mean by the terms *junior salespeople, spotters,* and *canvassers?* How are they used in prospecting, and by what types of sales organizations or individual salespeople?

6.   What is *referral lead?* Why is it considered the most valuable type of lead for putting salespeople in touch with truly qualified prospects? What is the best single type of referral lead?

7.   Assuming that you are a real estate salesperson selling family homes and are planning to call numbers cold from the telephone book, describe two qualifying open-ended questions you expect to use.

8.   What is involved in precall planning insofar as using the telephone to qualify prospects and make appointments is concerned?

CASE STUDY 5

Singer Salespeople's "Magic" Words for Chain-Reaction Reference Leads

In the United States alone, some 50 million household sewing machines are in use, most of them Singer machines. Somewhere around 1½ million new household sewing machines are sold annually in the United States, approximately half by Singer. These machines are sold through several channels of distribution, including a network of approximately 2000 Singer-approved independent dealers by (1) outside salespeople and (2) shop demonstrator-salespeople. Traditionally, most of their leads for new prospects have come from satisfied Singer customers. Here is a summary of what one training leaflet had to say to new Singer salespeople about where and how to get good leads through customer reference.

OBTAINING REFERENCE LEADS

A sure indication of a successful Singer salesperson is the ability to develop chain-reaction reference sales. Most of our top-flight producers can point to four, five, or six sales that are direct results of proper cultivation of a single customer. People interested in home sewing usually have close friends who share their interest. They usually know other people who need a modern sewing machine. Thus you can get reference leads on home calls as well as many other places during the course of your field work. Here are some examples.

1. *In a home*, on almost any kind of call—repair, free service, new sewing machine, or rental delivery—you can obtain reference leads by using these seventeen "magic" words—memorize them: "Whom do you know who might be interested in a wonderful buy in a Singer sewing machine?"

2. *In the field,* ask on every opportunity! Even after business hours, never forget that you are a salesperson of one of the finest lines of consumer products in the world. Be sure your friends and relatives know that you are working for Singer and that you are looking for leads. Some of them may be planning to buy a new sewing machine, and you can be sure that they would rather see you get the sale than give it to a stranger. The same thing applies to the merchants in your community. You buy from them, and they will be glad to buy from you if you let them know what you are selling. By being alert to opportunities after hours—in fact, any time, any place, anywhere—you will find many people who are in the market for a new Singer sewing machine or who know someone who is! Just ask them!

ONCE YOU HAVE ASKED THE "MAGIC" WORDS

1. Keep suggestions coming from neighbors, relatives, bridge-club members, church groups, etc., by asking questions.

2. Do not start qualifying until you have obtained all possible leads—then go back for details.

3. Review each lead to find out how to locate special interests, age of children, etc.

4. On every reference sale go back immedi-

ately and personally thank your reference source—you will often find that in appreciation of your courtesy you will be given one or more additional leads.

___

Questions for Written Reports or Class Discussion

1. If you were a new Singer salesperson, would you be content with only the leads obtained from the suggestions noted above? Where else could you obtain leads that might be equally good?

2. Would you consider the name of a next-door neighbor, given by a satisfied customer to whom you have just delivered a new Singer sewing machine, to be a good lead? Why? Explain fully all your reasons.

3. Assuming that you feel the neighbor's name given by the customer noted in Question 2 to be a good lead, how would you follow it up?

4. Assuming that you follow up the lead in Question 2 and make either telephone or personal contact, how would you qualify your new prospect? What would your opening remark be?

Sales Problem 5.1

Prospecting for future honeymooners—a problem for Rita and Jerry of Four Seasons Travel Agency

Rita and Jerry, outside salespeople for Four Seasons Travel Agency, don't seem at all cheered by the brightly colored, festive travel posters that decorate the walls, desks, and front counter about them.

It is well after 6 P.M., the end of a long and busy wintertime working day, and their faces are as gloomy as the dull and fast-closing dusk outside. The reason? Only an hour earlier their boss, on the way to a meeting, had asked them to come up with a prospecting plan by tomorrow morning for finding and qualifying prospective honeymooners. Let us listen in on Rita and Jerry for a moment as they discuss their prospecting problem.

Jerry: Well, the boss is on the right track—honeymoon trips are a most lucrative and steady source of business for travel agencies like ours (as well as for the airlines, railroads, shipping lines, hotels, and resorts they represent).

Rita: Yes, but how can we find out in advance when weddings are going to take place?

Jerry: That's the big problem! If we wait until engagements or weddings are announced in the newspapers, we won't have any advantage over our competitors! We must figure out some ways to contact prospective brides and grooms—in advance.

Rita: Let's concentrate first on brides-to-be; they seem to make most of the decisions concerning wedding matters.

Jerry: What about phoning or writing local priests or ministers to see if they will tip us off in advance?

Rita: They probably wouldn't tell us, and besides, we've got to contact our prospects as early as possible.

Jerry: I've got it—let's combine with the bridal department of two or three of our leading local fashion stores, to place newspaper advertisements at regular intervals. These will announce bridal fashion shows at which a nice Four Seasons prize will be awarded through drawings.

Rita: That's a good idea! Prospective brides and their grooms can write or telephone the store in advance for invitations, and the store can send them both a formal invitation and a Four Seasons form which, when filled in completely, gives them a lottery-type chance to win a free prize.

Jerry: Our prize can be a One-Day Sightseeing Tour Plus Dinner for Two Anywhere You Go on Your Four-Seasons Honeymoon. The bridal department managers should go along with this idea, because they need names and addresses of prospective honeymooners as much as we do. We can both get the names, addresses, and other information when the couples call or write in response to the advertisement.

Rita: We must make certain that all names, obtained from the leads are quickly followed up by telephone, mail, and personal visit if necessary in order to qualify the couple as real prospects. And we must also plan to offer the prize personally to each couple.

Jerry: Okay, that's settled! Now, what other good prospecting plans for locating prospective honeymooners can we come up with?

Questions for Written Reports or Class Discussion

1.   Do you feel that the "One-Day Sightseeing Tour Plus Dinner for Two" idea will by itself work as a means of locating prospects? Explain.

2.   Can you think of any ways to make this prospecting concept even more attractive for bridal department managers, upon whose cooperation it depends?

3.   What other prospecting ideas, other than the "One-Day Sightseeing for Two" idea, do you feel might help Rita and Jerry locate more future honeymooner prospects?

Sales Problem 5.2	**Why did Mary Maloney fail to secure this appointment for a sales interview?**

Mary Maloney, of Accru-Vision, Inc., sells soft contact lenses to busy opthalmologists and optometrists, virtually every one of whom carries an inventory of competitive products. Accru-Vision is a fairly new manufacturer, not familiar to most of them.

Mary needs time for a careful sales presentation if she is to persuade any of these prospects to change their habits and try the Accru-Vision lenses. Her first task is to secure an interview appointment. We will now listen in as she rings up the office of an optometrist, Dr. Ehret, whose name she has obtained from the Optometrist listings in the telephone directory yellow pages.

Answering voice: Good morning, Dr. Ehret's office.

Mary: I am Mary Maloney of Accru-Vision, can you put me through to Dr. Ehret, please?

Voice: The doctor is busy, may I help you?

Mary: It's very important that I speak to Dr. Ehret personally. Will you ask if I may speak to him for just a moment?

Voice: He's with a patient now. I am his receptionist; what is it you wish to speak to him about?

Mary: I wish to arrange an appointment to tell him about our new and exciting line of soft contact lenses.

Voice: We carry several lines already. What are the particulars of yours?

Mary: We have a special three-month consignment program with built-in discounts that will be of great interest to him if he fits 10 or more pairs of soft lenses a month. Once he tries them he will undoubtedly find that our lenses offer better visual acuity, fit, and durability than the other lines he now carries. May I talk to him?

Voice: I can't interrupt him now. But I will tell him what you've told me. Send us some of your literature as well. Thank you for calling; I have to hang up now because my other phone is ringing (hangs up).

Mary hears the disconnecting click at the other end and sadly puts her own phone back in place. "What did I do wrong this time?" she asked herself.

Questions for Written Reports or Class Discussion:

1.   Mary failed to get past the receptionist, and failed to get her desired appointment. What caused her failure?

2.   Having failed in this attempt, what can Mary do now, since she still wants to contact Dr. Ehret personally in hopes of securing an interview appointment?

3.   Assuming that you are Mary, what will you plan to do on your next telephone prospecting call to accomplish more satisfactory results with a new and different prospect?

The Preapproach:
Getting in to See the
Decision Maker

After studying this chapter, you will be able to:

Explain the term *preapproach*.

Describe the three most common ways to get sales interview appointments, and identify the one that is used most often.

Summarize the many specific techniques for obtaining an interview through (1) trying for an appointment by telephone, letter, and other means and (2) securing it without a prior appointment on a cold call.

Explain what is meant by the statement, "No matter what approach you use in securing the appointment or interview, your objectives are to (1) sell yourself and (2) sell the interview, in that order."

Summarize the importance of the first five seconds with a prospect in terms of how he or she views the salesperson and how his or her impression can so vitally affect the rest of the interview.

In the preceding chapter we discussed prospecting, or the qualifying of a specific prospect as to need for, ability to buy, and authority to buy your product or service. In this chapter we will cover the steps in bringing you face to face with your prospect, fully prepared for a successful interview.

Called the *preapproach*, the process involves (1) finding out all you can about your prospect prior to the interview and (2) getting the specific interview, either through prior appointment or without an appointment.

WHAT ELEMENTS ARE INVOLVED IN THE PREAPPROACH?

Once you have located a qualified prospect, your first tendency may be to rush over to see him or her as soon as possible, ready to start selling.

But stop for a minute and consider these points: (1) How are you going to get in to see him or her—by appointment or cold call? And when you do get in to see your prospect, (2) do you know how to adapt your knowledge to his or her specific wants or needs? Finally, (3) are you fully prepared to adapt yourself to whatever personality he or she has?

Your aim is to be professional in your sales planning and selling, so why not consider what other professional people do at this stage of their work? Doctors carefully diagnose a patient before prescribing a cure; structural engineers thoroughly consider all factors before starting work on a costly suspension bridge; trial lawyers carefully study the jury before presenting their closing arguments. You, as a professional salesperson, should use this preapproach period to find out everything you can about each prospect you plan to see, so that you can most effectively build your presentation around his or her needs or wants.

You may feel that all these points have already been considered as part of your prospecting process. Indeed, it is often difficult to determine when prospecting ends and the preapproach starts. That point comes, however, when, in your own mind, you have qualified a prospect. But overlap occurs, since you continue to find out even more information during the preapproach process.

The preapproach period gives you an opportunity to consider different elements of the impending interview that may affect it in special ways.

Are There Any Special Local Conditions to Consider? Climate and ethnic, cultural, and religious backgrounds should be considered prior to the interview. People living in warmer climates often lead more relaxed personal and business lives than do those living in colder regions. The fast-moving sales presentation successful in New York City may not be so useful in Mobile, Alabama, or Rio de Janeiro. And a prominent Seventh-Day Adventist business person may not look favorably on a salesperson's trying for a Saturday appointment.

What Will the Interview Situation Be Like? Selling situations differ according to the product sold, the customers called upon, and how, when, and where these customers permit interviews. If you sell an intangible specialty product, you may have to be prepared for a reception at the prospect's home, where the spouse may influence the buying decision, rather than at the office.

If you generally call on wholesalers, retailers, or purchasing agents, your interview situation will normally differ from that of direct selling in the homes of individual consumers. The former groups are used to seeing salespeople and are generally friendly, while home owners may be initially suspicious or even hostile, even if you are calling per prior appointment.

Selling to industry presents other possibilities for consideration, such as the necessity for group interviews or for making presentations to several individuals before obtaining a decision.

What Will Your Prospect's Personality Be?   Since people differ in personality, you should try to anticipate in advance the personality of your prospect. If you cannot do that, then you can at least anticipate certain personality responses and know how to handle them. Here are two standard personality types and some general techniques for handling them. We cover these and other types in greater detail in later chapters.

> *The grouchy type.* He or she may not be feeling well or may be having family or business problems, or perhaps is holding a grudge against your company or product. Try to solve any problems quickly and then concentrate on your presentation, cheerfully and helpfully, and try to take his or her mind off his or her troubles.
>
> *The indecisive type.* Some prospects just can't seem to make up their minds. They need your help in doing so. Just keep asking easy questions that he or she can answer with a simple "yes."

No two selling situations are exactly alike. Much of the fun and challenge of selling lies in matching your wits in differing circumstances against different prospects. There are obstacles to be overcome in all selling situations, and the surmounting of them depends on your initiative, resourcefulness, and imagination. Your goal during the preapproach is to try to anticipate the situation as far as possible. By anticipating certain elements, you can prepare yourself to meet them and thus increase your chances of getting the interview and of closing the sale.

FINDING OUT ABOUT YOUR PROSPECT PRIOR TO THE INTERVIEW

The amount of time to be spent on preapproach information gathering and the degree of information sought depends in large part on what you are selling. If you are presenting something for personal use, you may be chiefly concerned with gathering personal background information. If your prospect is buying for a company or organization, you should seek, in addition to personal information, facts about the industry, the company, and the prospect's specific job.

The more information you have, the easier it is to uncover clues to the prospect's idiosyncrasies and personal or business problems. This preapproach investigation applies not only to new prospects but also on a continuing basis to customers on whom you make regular callbacks.

Systematic collection of this background information means deciding (1) What kind of information will be useful, (2) how to go about collecting it, and (3) how to organize it efficiently for permanent referral and rapid use.

Personal Information and Where to Get It

If you know something about the personal background of your prospects and let them know that you have gone to the trouble of seeking it out, they are normally flattered and thus interested in you. Since your first job in any interview is to sell yourself, such research efforts help you gain the immediate attention and respect of your prospect.

What personal information may be useful? Why? Here are some examples. Can you think of others?

Names. People love to see their names written and to hear them spoken correctly. Wouldn't you, if as a third-generation American, your name happens to be Wojciech Wszolczyk, Marie Subramanyam, or Emad Al-Baaj?

You must learn to spell and pronounce names correctly, since mistakes can be costly. Ask the secretary or anyone who knows your prospect to spell and pronounce his or her name for you before the interview. If you are unable to do this beforehand, ask your prospect promptly for his or her name, write it down then and there, and use if often throughout the interview. Prospects will not be offended if you do this; they will be pleased and flattered at your interest. If the name is a difficult one, jot down your own phonetic interpretation of it to help your remember its correct pronunciation. A person's name is one of the most beautiful sounds in the world to him or her.

Some new salespeople find it difficult to remember names, especially if the prospect's name is an unusually difficult one. Because it is so important to remember names in sales situations, here are some additional memory-jogging suggestions that may prove useful:

Step One. Get the name right, even if you have to ask the prospect to repeat it until you do get the proper pronunciation (and correct spelling if necessary). Mr. Wszolczyk won't mind at all!

Step Two. Observe the prospect's face carefully, and mentally associate it with his or her name.

Step Three. Make an association of the name and face. For example:

- Try to link the name to something with a similar sound that you can visualize. If a woman's name is "Terri," try to picture her "picking berries." Or break the name into a silly idea; such as associating the name "Madison" with the expression "mad at his son."
- If you can't think of an association, think and rehearse! Mentally repeat the name as soon as you've been introduced; wait a few seconds, and mentally say it again; then wait twice as long and do it again. Such

mental "wait" periods force you to sustain attention, and are more effective than simple rapid mental repetitions of the name.

- Or perhaps you can associate it with an outstanding physical feature, or associate it with someone, or something, with the same name. You may also be able to break the name down into meaningful syllables. Or you may be able to associate it with a catchy rhyme or jingle, a business, hobby, or profession; or associate it with a name that has meaning in itself. Try some of these suggestions on the honest Polish-American name Wojciech Wszolczyk—it will be good practice!

Age.   Neither older men nor older women like to be reminded of their age, but if you are younger than they, they will appreciate an appropriate air of respect for their seniority. If prospects are younger than you, they will normally respond to your recognition that they have achieved certain things (such as, number of children, nice home, important job, or community leadership position) at this stage of life.

Education.   Since many people spend years getting formal general or professional education, they like to have these achievements noticed. If a person has a Ph.D. degree or a professional title, use "Doctor" or whatever title is appropriate. Self-made people, who have achieved something without formal education, are proud of their attainments and respond favorably to your notice of them.

Family.   The response of most people is normally favorable if you know about or ask about their families. For example, what person would not be impressed by your saying that you had just read in the newspaper of his or her son's being elected captain of his college swimming team!

Place of Birth and Current Residence.   People are often quite proud of their country or area of birth and enjoy talking about it. Others are proud of their neighborhood or area of current residence, since it may reflect their social or economic status. Having this information helps you to determine a line of questioning that may appeal to your prospect along social or status lines.

Nonbusiness Associations.   It helps to know of any religious, civic, and fraternal groups to which your prospect belongs. It may develop that you are members of the same religion, were in the same branch of military service, or belong to the same social or fraternal organization.

Hobbies.   Perhaps you are fellow weekend sailplane pilots, stamp collectors, or sports fans. If you share similar feelings towards the same hobbies or if you know of his or her pet hobby and appear interested in it, it may be easy to establish a personal rapport.

Idiosyncrasies.   Does your prospect like to see salespeople only by written appointments? Does he or she have an unusually strong dislike for cigarette smokers? Many individuals have personality quirks, and if you know of them in advance, you can frequently turn them to advantage.

Where can you get the personal background information we have just mentioned? (1) Track it down from various sources and (2) ask someone who knows either the prospect or something about him or her. You can obtain personal information from telephone books, street directories, city directories, school, college, or university yearbooks, professional organizations, your company files, newspapers, and many other sources. Business associates, personal friends, neighbors, fellow social or sports club members, and other salespeople, both in and outside your company, are just some of the contacts you can ask for personal background information.

KEEPING TRACK OF CUSTOMER PERSONAL INFORMATION

Since it is impossible to mentally keep track of countless bits and pieces of personal information gathered about both established customers or potential new prospects over a period of time, some easy recording system becomes essential. While different salespeople employ different methods for doing this, their common aim is to record it quickly in some easy reference format that (it is hoped) doesn't entail having to rewrite or transfer it to some more permanent form later on. The point is to do it right the first time; the easiest way is to devise, right from the start, a simple system that works.

Some carry small pocket- or purse-size data books and jot information gathered about one person per individual page. Others carry postcard-size blank cards; still others blank memo-size pieces of paper. Most salespeople later toss these quick notes (always dated) into a special name-file (or firm or organization/name-file), which they quickly review before phoning or visiting the individual concerned. Figure 6.1 shows use of a simple running postcard-size system.

FIGURE 6.1 *Running Postcard-Size Individual Customer Personal Information Recording System*

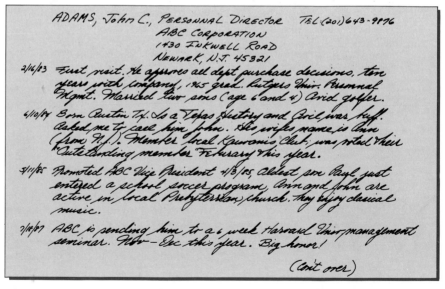

Industry Information and Where to Get It

If your prospect is a business, industrial, or nonprofit organizational prospect, you need not only personal background information such as we have discussed, but also quite specific information about his or her organization. In Chapter 4 we covered the topic of what kind of industry and company information in general might be helpful and where and how to go about getting it; we now build on that by considering what specific information might be most useful, and how to get it.

The more you know about the business your prospect is engaged in, the more you know or are able to find out through intelligent questioning about his or her business problems. Gathering such information in advance allows you to plan your presentation around benefits that will help your prospect solve those problems.

It also helps to know the language of the industry or trade in which your prospect is involved. This knowledge allows you to talk together on the same level. You do not necessarily have to be a chemist to sell industrial chemical products to a chemical engineer, but you should know something of the chemical industry and the processes used so that you can present your product intelligently.

The best way to get background information on the business or industry is to read its trade journals or other special publications. Such reading gives you a familiarity with its history, state of development, current problems, and goals.

Other sources of information include trade advertising produced by your company and competing companies, text or reference books, trade association publications and directories, and governmental publications. Another good way to get information is to talk to people engaged in the industry. People at all levels like to talk about their work and will usually be happy to explain their field to you if you express a sincere, intelligent desire to learn.

Specific Company Information and Where to Get It

Whether your prospect owns a company or is employed by one, the more you know of its operations and its standing within the industry, the better prepared you will be to help solve its specific problems. Here are some questions that you should try to answer prior to the actual interview.

Overall Company Operations

What kind of company is it—public or private?
What does it produce or offer for sale?
Who owns it, and who manages it?
What is the quality of its products and services?
What are its history and current standing in the industry?
What are its annual net sales, assets, liabilities, worth?
Is its management considered conservative or progressive?
What is its size? How many employees does it have?

What is the extent of its operations—locally, nationally, and internationally?

Is it considered a growth company? Why?

How has its stock fared in recent years? What is the current market price of its stock?

Do you know of any pending mergers or acquisitions in which this company is or may be involved?

Is its credit good?

What is its plant capacity?

What manufacturing processes are employed, if any? What kind of materials and what kind of machines and equipment are used?

What seasonal factors, if any, are involved both in production and in maintenance schedules?

Company Purchasing Practices

What purchasing systems and procedures are followed?

Does the company buy from single or multiple sources?

What lead time is involved in purchasing decisions?

What seasonal factors, if any, are involved in buying decisions?

What are the credit factors involved in doing business with this company?

Company Personnel Factors

Is buying done by individuals or on a committee basis?

Who are the heads of individual purchasing departments?

What is the specific name, job title, and buying authority of the actual purchase decision maker(s)?

What people within the purchasing department(s) may influence the buying decision?

Answering completely or partially the above questions and others help you to become informed about your prospect and his or her needs. You can obtain such specific company information from annual reports, house organs (internal company publications), advertising, your own company sales and credit files, other published sources we have mentioned, and by simply asking people, both inside and outside that company.

HOW TO GET THE INTERVIEW

We have been considering the first step in the preapproach process—finding out all you can about the prospect prior to the interview. Let us now turn our attention to how you are going to get that interview, with or without an appointment. We will assume that the qualification has been complete and that your prospect is the decision maker, with full buying authority.

Bear in mind that the prospect does not owe you an interview or anything else! You are asking for a portion of his or her valuable time, and if it is granted, you should feel professionally obliged to make the time spent worthwhile.

If you make your sales presentation and your prospect buys your product or service, feeling that it will increase profits, cut costs, or offer tangible or intangible benefits, then his or her time was profitably spent. If the prospect decides that your offering won't be useful, and does not buy, then you should at least leave the feeling that he or she has gained information of value and interest from your call. This will leave the door ajar for callbacks.

With these thoughts in proper perspective, we can now discuss some specific techniques for getting the interview by appointment.

Techniques of Making Appointments

Why make an appointment? The chief reason is so you will not waste time on a cold call to your prospect's office only to find that he or she is out of town, is in conference, is too busy to see you now, or sees salespeople only on certain other days or periods of the week.

Specific appointments not only save you hours of travel and waiting time but also make the approach phase of your interview easy, since prospects know at least your name and that of your company. It also means that they have set aside some time, optimally free from interruptions, to give you their undivided attention. Having a firm appointment also adds prestige to your call.

Appointments save you time and energy, and they can also increase your earning power. Your time is valuable, and since appointments increase your face-to-face selling time, they lead to increased sales and income.

The most common way to get appointments is by telephone or letter, either directly or through a third person. You can follow up advance advertising by a telephone or letter request for an appointment, or you can simply send your business card or a postcard in advance, saying that you will be calling at a certain time (see Figure 6.2).

You can use many other methods apart from telephone or letter to secure appointments. You can send a telegram or cablegram, contact the prospect's secretary or spouse to arrange it for you, ask other associates in the company or organization to arrange it for you, or employ more dramatic approaches. No matter which method you use, you must cover the following points, which we discussed in Chapter 5 under the topic of qualifying prospects and making appointments by telephone:

1. Introduce yourself and your company.
2. Capture your prospect's immediate attention and interest.
3. Present a brief sales message of no more than two features and benefits of your product, stressing benefits that will turn his or her interest into desire.

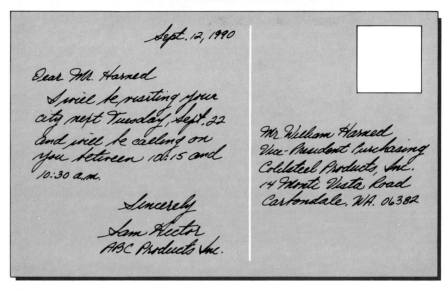

Sept. 12, 1990

Dear Mr. Harned

I will be visiting your city next Tuesday, Sept. 22 and will be calling on you between 10:15 and 10:30 a.m.

Sincerely

Sam Hector
ABC Products Inc.

Mr. William Harned,
Vice-President Purchasing
Coldsteel Products, Inc.
14 Monte Vista Road
Cartondale, WA. 06382

FIGURE 6.2 *Message Side of an Announcement Postcard*

4. Let him or her know how those desires can be fulfilled (by letting you explain the benefits more fully in person).

5. Ask for a specific appointment date and time.

Attention-Getting Approach Suggestions

The key to any type of approach is to get to talk with and quickly capture the attention and interest of the prospect. Here are some specific suggestions that, although written in the form of telephone approaches (the most common form), can easily be adapted to letters, telegram, or other methods for obtaining appointments that will be discussed shortly.

Solution Approach

Mr. Gentilini, this is Gus Jensen of Arno Office Services, Inc. Our new Zeno system has been especially designed to speed up your record keeping at less cost to you. May I call on you Wednesday at 11:30 A.M. to show you how it can be done in your office, or would 2:30 P.M. Thursday be more convenient?

Service Approach

Mr. Achenbach, this is Ric Campbell of Industrial Chemicals. Many companies have been surprised and pleased to learn that we now handle industrial service and repairs on your type of plant equipment on an annual, modest, fixed-cost basis. May I call on you to explain details Wednesday at . . . ?

After-Mailing Approach

Good morning, Mrs. Ramos. I mailed you a letter and brochure last week about our new Ajax Kitchen Helper. What did you think of it?

Follow up immediately. If she likes it, make an appointment for a demonstration; if she has any objections, try to turn them to advantages and to arouse enough interest for a demonstration appointment.

Thank-you Approach

Mr. Chapple, this is Haydee Vasquez of Columbian Coffee Exports Co. I want to thank you for your August 5 order, which we just received. At what level does this put your stock inventory? May I add a reorder to it now for delivery later, and save you some money?

Congratulations Approach

Good morning, Mrs. Iden. This is Ron Voights of City Chevrolet Co. May I congratulate you on the approaching wedding of your daughter Christina as announced in the society pages today? We have a beautiful new red convertible sports car in stock that would make a perfect wedding gift for such a well-known couple. May I show it to you this evening at 6 P.M. or tomorrow at 12 noon?

Social Approach

Good morning, Mrs. Ikeda. This is Judy Tanner of Royal Piano Company. You visited our store last month looking at pianos for your daughter but decided to wait for after-Christmas discount sales. Well, for one day only, next Tuesday, we are offering $100 off on all Rolay models, and you won't beat that anytime. Can you come in at 10 A.M. Tuesday, pick your model, and let us deliver it for Christmas Day? Or would 11:30 be more convenient?

Seeking Appointment by Letter

A carefully written letter gives you a chance to cover all your points without fear of the interruption that could affect a telephone call. Control is lost once you mail it, however, and unless it captures your prospect's attention and interest, it will not evoke a response.

Your prospect is probably a busy person, and your letter is only one of many that arrive in his or her mail each day. It comes as an uninvited guest, and if it does not stress benefits to him or her, it is not a welcome guest. Unless you secure the appointment, all your preliminary investigation and planning are to no avail, so as much care and attention should go into preparation of the appointment-request letter as into planning the presentation itself.

A good appointment letter will have the following characteristics. These are further illustrated in Figure 6.3.

```
ACME TILE MANUFACTURING COMPANY

                                                    1700 Avon Road
                                                    Martinsville, Ohio 07631

                                                    TELEPHONE (302) 761-2598

March 17, 1981



Mr. Ronald Tilly, Manager
Newtown Hardware Company
467 Main Street
Newtown, KY  32546

Dear Mr. Tilly,

     You are losing up to $1.25 every time you sell a case of porcelain
wall tile other than the brand I sell!

     I will be in Newtown Wednesday, March 28, and will be calling on
you at 10:15 a.m. to explain why, and to tell you about our delivery,
payment, and advertising support programs.

     In case you are unable to be there at that time and wish an appoint-
ment later that day, please phone me collect at the above number before
3:00 p.m. March 25.

Sincerely,


Sally Anderson
Wholesale Products Consultant
```

FIGURE 6.3 *Sample Letter Seeking an Appointment*

Personal. The prospect is basically not interested in you, your company, or your product. He or she is thinking only, "What's in this for me?" Thus, your letter should be personalized, addressed to him or her!

Positive in Approach. Both your opening and follow-up points should be positive, not negative. The letter should be forceful, interesting, and logical, built entirely on one major appeal.

Concise. A letter that is clear, concise, forceful, and well-organized will be easy to understand. Make your point near the beginning of the letter, ask for action at the end, and include all the facts. Also, use simple, specific words and short paragraphs; limit sentences to one idea each.

Interesting.   Since your prospect may receive other appointment letters or advertising at the same time, yours must obtain his or her immediate interest. Thus it should have an original, fresh approach, with clear, picture-building words that catch his or her eye and attention. Use action words to get response; words that tell the prospect to do something, such as:

> "Send back the enclosed card."
> "Pick up your phone and . . . "
> "Act now to take advantage of our special offer."

Proper Tone.   In order to be effective, a letter must be easy to understand. It must also have the proper tone. This means it should sound friendly, natural, and courteous.

Ask for Action in the Last Paragraph.   The reader should not have to go back to the beginning of the letter to find out if the next move is up to him or her. Make your request or give instructions at the end of the letter. His or her responsibility will then be uppermost in his or her mind.

Other Techniques for Appointment-Making

You are limited only by your own imagination in employing techniques other than telephone or letter to secure interview appointments. If you use dramatic means, they should be in good taste and should appeal to your particular prospect. Timing is important; you should be prepared to follow up promptly, no matter what method you employ. Here are some examples of other appointment-making techniques.

Send a Telegram or Cablegram.   They are instant attention getters and are always read immediately. Here is how you may put this technique to use.

> Arriving Chicago Wednesday August 15 stop. May I see you 10:30 A.M. or 3:15 P.M. regarding new money saving personalized estate-insurance plan stop. Cable desired appointment time collect. Bruce Weber, Equitable Insurance.

Use a Third Party to Get the Interview For You.   Many successful salespeople ask mutual friends, business associates, spouses, or secretaries to write, to telephone, or to introduce them personally in order to get appointments.

Advertise for the Appointment.   This is especially effective when combined with prospecting on a blanket basis. An insurance salesperson, for example, may send out form letters with an enclosed calling card and prepaid postcard on which the prospect asks for an appointment and lists convenient times. In a similar manner, automobile salespeople can leave such return cards under automobile windshield wipers in supermarket parking lots.

Use Radiation Methods.   For certain types of selling, one sale can be exploited to lead to other sales in the same area. If, for example, you are selling a home-landscaping and yard-maintenance service, one nicely landscaped yard you have just completed may stand out in the neighborhood. You can write, telephone, or personally call on neighbors, asking whether they have noticed the "new land-scaping of your neighbors, Mr. and Mrs. Po." This question can be a lead-in for asking them for an appointment to discuss similar landscaping for their property.

Send an Announcement Card.   Many salespeople use postcards (see Figure 6.2) as a simple, inexpensive, positive, and surprisingly effective way of obtaining appointments. A salesperson uses such an announcement most often on regular calls, when he or she or the company is known to the prospect, but it can also be useful as a cold-call appointment-getting technique. It is not so effective as an acknowledged specific appointment, but it does alert the prospect to your im-pending arrival.

Contact Good Customers at Home.   If your regular good customers are diffi-cult to reach during normal business hours because of their own out-of-office calls, you might consider telephoning them at home to arrange the appointment. If you have something of real interest to them, they probably will not object to having their privacy invaded. Normally, however, this technique is a last resort.

The methods we have described are practical examples of appointment-getting techniques used daily by salespeople all over the world. Make appoint-ments whenever and wherever possible; they assure more face-to-face selling time.

But what can be done if you do not have an appointment? Can you go directly to the prospect and stand a reasonable chance of getting an interview? The answer is yes, but you must be prepared to cope with a new set of problems, as we shall discuss.

How to Get the Interview Without an Appointment

In professional sales terminology, going to see your prospect without a prior appointment, in the expectation of getting either the interview on the spot or at least an appointment for one, is called a *cold call.* The name itself gives an inkling of the problems to be faced. Your prospect may be busy or may be impatient at or even suspicious of your unannounced approach.

In any such cold call you must be prepared to quickly sell yourself and to sell the interview. And you may have to sell these two points to others, such as a receptionist, secretary, or assistant, before getting in to see your prospect face to face. Thus you have to be prepared to face several possible types of situations and plan systematically in advance how you will meet and overcome them.

The problems you meet depend in part on what you are selling and the prospect you are calling upon. Purchasing agents are often easy to reach if they are not busy, since it is their job to see salespeople. Door-to-door selling is more difficult than calling on purchasing agents, since outright suspicion and even fear may be encountered.

The more important your business prospects, the more valuable their time; they often jealously guard against unexpected interruptions with a series of buffers designed to protect them from unannounced callers and sales representatives. Part of the function of a good executive secretary or of an assistant is to protect the boss from unnecessary demands on his or her time. Some of them may be initially neutral, negative, or even cold toward your unannounced visit. They will not necessarily be unfriendly, but they may sometimes be negative rather than positive.

It is part of the selling game, as in any other profession, to take the bad along with the good. Negative or indifferent responses on cold calls are to be expected. Success is based on mathematics; the more calls you make, the more prospects you will be able to make callback appointments with. A realistic percentage figure for an average salesperson in many types of selling might be one out of three. Since negative responses are quite common, you simply have to recognize them as sales problems to be handled. We will discuss some techniques for handling them, but first let us consider how the prospect views you!

Selling Yourself (Those Important First Five Seconds).   You have walked in unannounced, full of enthusiasm, ready to solve the prospect's problems or to bring health, wealth, happiness, or other benefits. You are ready to get on with the interview or at least to get a specific appointment.

But to the prospect's way of thinking, you are or could be an unwelcome intruder on his or her time. Some prospects may take one look and make up their minds negatively about you forever. Others are more open-minded but still remain influenced throughout your call by the first impression they formed of you.

Many professional salespeople feel that the first five seconds with a prospect are perhaps the most important of the entire call. During this short time receptionists, secretaries, and prospects, men and women alike, may decide whether or not you are a person with whom they would like to do business. The reception you get depends to a great extent on which way their decision goes.

What do they look for in these first five seconds that can so vitally affect your whole approach?

Your Appearance.   Are your dress and grooming up to the standards they expect from a professional salesperson in their business or occupation?

Your Manner.   Do you approach a prospect with confidence and a smile, secure in the knowledge that you are sincerely trying to help? Or do you appear hesitant, nervous, or worried about your reception as if you have something to apologize for? If your approach is confident and cheerful, and if you smile and look directly at the other person, chances are that his or her decision will go your way.

Selling the Interview.   Having first sold yourself as a person worth talking to, you now have to sell the interview—either to get in immediately or at least to set up a specific appointment. You may simply have to ask for an appointment, but it may be more difficult if the interview is not readily or freely granted.

Your best chance for sales success is in an interview situation in which you can sit down face to face with your prospect alone, if at all possible, and have his or her undivided attention. Your approach should be aimed at gaining such an interview. Here are some of the problems you may normally expect to encounter and some techniques for handling the situation.

Getting Past the Receptionist or Secretary. The prospect's secretary or receptionist can pose real problems on business and industrial calls. Sometimes instructed to act as a buffer between you and the boss, other times merely liking to feel important, he or she is either a potential ally or a real barrier between you and your prospect.

If the secretary likes you, you will get help in seeing the boss or in setting up a mutually convenient appointment date. If secretaries decide they do not like you, they can be most uncooperative and can cause real trouble if you try to go around them or over their heads once they have turned you away.

It is best to tackle the receptionist-secretary problem head on by trying to make friends from the start. It helps to find out his or her name beforehand if possible; if not, ask for it and use it often but not too obviously in your conversation. Your very best approach is simply to ask, "Can you help me?" If you call back regularly on the prospect, you may best gain long-term friendship by sending a friendly note of thanks for the help and assistance. A warm smile and cheerful greeting always help win people over.

During initial cold calls, a receptionist-secretary can thwart your reaching your prospect in the following ways.

1. *Trying to find out your business and then deciding whether to let you see the boss.* Your best course is the direct, positive approach, which tells secretaries as little as possible and discourages them from asking questions. Your approach may run something like this. "Good morning. Will you please tell Mr. Moore that Mr. Matheson, M-A-T-H-E-S-O-N, is here?" Then move away and try not to invite further questioning. In many cases they will assume you are expected, since you act expected, and will ring through to the prospect. The odds of being seen at that point are favorable.

   If they persist in asking what your business is, without contacting the boss, you might say, "Mr. Matheson of Southern Cross International. Will you please tell Mr. Moore that I would like to ask him a question? Is he in?" If the secretary still persists, you may have to tell a little more and ask for help.

   > It's about a possible new non-association-sponsored publishing plan for your firm. I would like to see him now if possible, but if he is busy, I could see him at 2:15 this afternoon. Will you ask him which time would be more convenient?

   The aim of these progressive steps is to create the impression that you will be received. You must be truthful, but by confident manners and actions, you can imply a lot. This throws the problem of uncertainty on the secretary, whose path of least resistance is to ring through to the boss and let him or her make the decision.

2. *Telling you that the boss is too busy to see you.* This may be a valid excuse. You can test by replying, "Would it be more convenient for me to call back in half an hour?" If sincere, he or she will probably help you by arranging a convenient appointment time. If, however, this is merely an excuse to get rid of you, then you should quietly persist by asking if you may speak to the boss on the phone for a second. If you can do this, you are at least discussing the call with the prospect.

3. *Telling you that the boss will not be interested in seeing you.* You may have to be persistent at this point, as the following example illustrates, but you must be careful in what you say and how you say it (smilingly yet confidently, so as not to personally offend him or her).

> What is your name, please? You are making a big decision that could cost your firm quite a bit of money. Don't you really think you should put me through to Mr. Moore and let him decide?"

Selling an Assistant or Subordinate. A problem is sometimes caused either by the receptionist-secretary's directing you to an official other than your decision-maker prospect or by having your prospect tell the secretary over the phone to send you to that individual first.

If you determine that you have to clear the appointment interview with this subordinate, then you have to concentrate on selling the need for the interview. In order to accomplish this goal you may have to state the essence of your proposal but without going into the details, especially concerning prices and the like, on which the final decision must be made. Your chief objective in this encounter is to sell this subordinate on the need for the decision maker to hear the full proposal and to have a specific appointment time arranged for you.

Your Cold-Call Approach on the Prospect. This approach should be the straightforward one of stating your name, company, and purpose in calling. You can use any of the techniques previously discussed in this chapter to arouse his or her interest and to create a desire to hear your whole story.

Remember, your aims are to sell yourself and to sell the interview. Since you want to control the presentation, you should try to avoid a too-hasty stand-up, or reception-room interview. You may handle the situation something like this.

> Mr. Puffinbarger, I am Loehr Rigby of Marko Products Corporation. Our new records system has helped more than twenty industrial firms in this area to cut plant overhead costs from 15 to 20 percent. I have made a tentative study of your operation and would like the opportunity to go over my checklist with you in the hope of offering you a similar saving. It will take half an hour to explain my proposal fully in connection with your specific plant problems. Your time is valuable, I realize. May we sit down together now or would 2:30 this afternoon be more convenient?

This strategy is effective in most appointment-seeking cold calls, whether they be business, industrial, retail, or door to door. Know what you are going to say and appear intelligent and sincere in talking about your prospect's needs, profits, convenience, or whatever benefits are likely to have the most immediate appeal. If you approach him or her in this straightforward manner, the odds are very much in your favor that the interview will willingly be granted.

THE HONEST, STRAIGHTFORWARD PREAPPROACH IS ALWAYS BEST

The method employed to secure the appointment interview is merely a means to an end. You can have a lot of fun in selling by constantly seeking new, interesting, and creative methods to accomplish your objectives. People like dramatic approaches if they are in good taste, and they like to have their interest and curiosity aroused. They respond to, respect, and remember your originality.

You should remember however, that while it pays to be creative and to come up with honestly conceived, ingenious ideas for securing the interview, there is no substitute for the honest and sincere approach. The easiest way to get the interview is simply to ask for it; the best way to start is to sell yourself as someone worth the prospect's time.

SUMMARY

In this chapter we have discussed the preapproach, or getting in to see your prospect by appointment or without it. We considered the need to plan this preapproach phase just as carefully as you do the presentation itself. Unless you are able to sell the interview itself, you will not be given a chance to make the presentation.

We considered the need for getting, and how to get, as much information in advance as possible about the prospect personally and, where necessary, about his or her industry, organization, and specific job function. We then discussed techniques of getting the interview: first, trying for an appointment by telephone, letter, or other means; second, securing it without a prior appointment on a cold call. We illustrated these several techniques with many specific, practical examples used successfully in the past as well as present by thousands of salespeople the world over.

Our conclusion was that techniques are only the means to an end, and while prospects respond to creative approaches and techniques if in good taste, there is no substitute for the sincere, honest approach of simply asking for the interview. No matter what approach you use in securing the appointment or interview, your professional objectives are to sell yourself and to sell the interview, in that order.

Questions for Analysis and Discussion

1.   List three advantages of making appointments prior to a sales call.

2.   What are the three most common ways to get sales appointments? Of these three, which one is used most often?

3.   Describe or outline a service approach you, as a salesperson for a home-heating fuel-oil company, might use in writing heads of households in your community for an appointment to call on them to sell your product and your home heating unit inspection and repair service.

4.   What is meant by the statement, "In order to be effective, an appointment letter should have a proper tone?"

5.   In an appointment letter, should your action request be in the first paragraph, in the middle, or in the last paragraph? Why?

6.   What types of third parties in your community could you call upon to help get appointment interviews for you? What two major action requests would you make of them?

7.   What two major objectives must a salesperson plan to accomplish in making a cold call for an appointment with any type of prospect?

8.   What is the best single approach a salesperson can make to a secretary in order to secure cooperation in helping to obtain an appointment interview with the boss?

CASE STUDY 6

Getting the Appointment Without Telling Too Much is Important to Insurance Salespeople

Getting the appointment, either by telephone or personal call, without telling the prospect exactly what is to be discussed is a serious matter to agent-salespeople of all insurance companies. They have to sit down face to face with the prospect to determine real need and to tailor an insurance plan to that need. Thus they have to handle questions and objections at this stage with only one objective in mind—to get the interview appointment without telling any more than they have to in the process.

Here, in his own words, is how one veteran northwestern United States insurance salesperson, Doug Murray, handles his problem of getting the appointment by telephone.

I work through referral leads, so I call the prospect by phone directly and ask to speak to him or her. If a secretary answers, I handle it this way (using a pleasant and authoritative tone of voice) "Mr. Hatton, please," or "Will you put me through to Mr. Hatton, please?" or "Please let Mr. Hatton know that Mr. Murray is on the telephone." (I never ask "Is Mr. Hatton in, please?") Then, when the prospect answers, I go right into my appointment presentation as follows:

Good morning, Mr. Hatton. My name is Murray, Doug Murray, and I represent Interglobal Insurance Company. We have a mutual friend (acquaintance) in Mr. Cy Nelson. I'm phoning you because I would like the opportunity of meeting you to discuss a new concept for thousands of people like ourselves who are interested in saving money. I would like to call and tell you a little more about the idea, and you could very quickly tell me whether it would be of value to you. I'm wondering if Thursday morning at 11:15 would suit you, or would you prefer Friday afternoon at about 3:45?

It may seem easier to say, "I have an appointment near your office, may I drop in?", but such a wrong statement could lose the interview. I'm trying to convey the impression that I'm going to make a special trip to see him. That makes him feel important and makes it easier for him to say yes.

HANDLING QUESTIONS OR OBJECTIONS

Once in a while I secure an appointment immediately. Most of the time, however, I encounter questions or objections that pose problems. Here are a few examples of some I get, with the more or less standard ways I have of handling them. Although I may vary my pattern, I never change one thing. My last sentence always is something to this effect. "Will Thursday morning at 11:15 suit you or would you prefer Friday afternoon at 3:45?"

Question: What is your idea about? Tell me a little more about it.

Answer: Frankly, Mr. Hatton, it's a little difficult to explain over the telephone. It would hardly be fair to you or myself to do so since it requires certain visual aids. That is why I'm suggesting I call to see you on Thursday at 11:15, or would you prefer Friday at 3:45?

Question: Is this life insurance? This is insurance, isn't it?

Answer: Well, Mr. Hatton, I did say I was with an insurance company, so naturally there is a connection; but as I told you, many people in positions similar to your own have found this particular idea of tremendous value. This is why I would like to come along and have you tell me whether you are interested. Would Thursday suit you or would you find Friday at 3:45 more convenient?

Question: I have plenty of insurance.

Answer: Mr. Hatton, that's fine. I would be most surprised to come across a person in your position who didn't own a lot of insurance. In fact, if you didn't, this idea wouldn't be of the slightest interest to you. It is designed for people with a lot of insurance, and that is why I'm suggesting that I come to tell you more about it. Would Thursday at 11:15 be all right or would you prefer Friday at 3:45?

Question: I couldn't afford any more insurance even if I wanted it.

Answer: Mr. Hatton, I couldn't possibly expect that at the precise moment that I speak to you on the telephone (or to anyone else for that matter), you would be about to take out more insurance. What I'm suggesting is that I come along to show this idea. It may well interest you and help you, if not now, then perhaps at some time in the future. Would Thursday at 11:15 be all right or would you prefer Friday at 3:45?

Question: I'm very busy, I can't spare the time to see you.

Answer: I have perhaps suggested an inconvenient time, but I promise you that it will only take a few minutes to tell me whether you are interested. Looking at my diary again, I could make it at 9:45 on Monday, or perhaps Tuesday at 1:00 would be better for you. Which time suits you, Mr. Hatton?

Please note that I have been very careful up to this point not to divulge any information to the prospect. It is vitally important that I arouse interest and attention strictly by the offer to explain a particular idea.

If the prospect keeps switching to different objections, he or she is probably stalling, and I have to determine quickly whether he or she is worth spending time on. It is better to get on to the next call than to waste time now. Sometimes the prospect asks me to send an illustration by mail. This is a brush-off, and I never agree to such requests.

Do not be impatient to put down the receiver after making the appointment. Rather, in closing the conversation, I say slowly, "That's 10:15 on Thursday, the fifth, then, Mr. Hatton; I'm entering it in my diary." (This will encourage him to do likewise.) "Thank you very much; I look forward to meeting you at that time. Good-bye."

Questions for Written Reports or Class Discussion

1.   What major advantages does Murray gain by confirming such appointments by telephone rather than visiting the prospect at his or her office or home?

2.   We noted in this chapter five basic points that should be covered when one is making an appointment by telephone or by any other means.

What are these five points? Does Murray's telephone technique cover all of them to your satisfaction? Why?

3.   Do you feel that Murray uses proper techniques in his telephone approach? Does he cover all the aims of a good telephone approach?

Could you improve on salesperson Alice Smith's methods of handing these two common receptionist put-offs?

Alice Smith sells office equipment in the large city of Sydney, Australia, concentrating on a systems approach that involves selling a complete integrated line of dictating machines and desk calculators which, if purchased as a system, offers significant cost reduction. She favors cold calls to seek interview appointments.

She often faces put-offs, or stalls, from receptionists or secretaries who are overzealous in protecting their bosses from unannounced callers. In her own words, the two most common put-offs she faces, and how she handles them in a friendly but businesslike manner, are these:

Put-off 1: "I know Mr. Westin-Colton wouldn't be interested in buying a lot of new office machines."

Alice usually handles this by pointing out that this put-off could be costly to the secretary's boss: "Mr. Westin-Colton must have plenty of confidence in you. He is letting you make a decision that could save him at least $5000 over the next two years. Why don't you just tell him I am here and let him decide whether or not he will see me?"

Put-off 2: "Mr. Westin-Colton is busy right now; he's not seeing anyone."

Alice knows that this could be true, but feels she should make certain it's a fact and not just a put-off. She tests by seemingly agreeing with the secretary's statement. "I see. I know how busy he must be. When would be a good time to call back—say about 3 P.M.?"

Alice realizes that if the secretary accepts the callback time suggestion, or suggests an alternative time, the boss really is busy right at that moment. If, however, the secretary replies that she shouldn't bother to call back any time, she knows he or she is acting independently in putting her off. If she feels it is a put-off, she then uses the same technique for handling the situation as in number 1 above.

Questions for Written Reports or Class Discussion

1. What would you do in Alice's situation if, after making the statement and asking the question noted in number 1 above, the secretary still won't announce you to his or her boss?

2. Can you suggest two different ways that Alice could handle the put-off noted in number 1 above?

3. Could Alice, or any salesperson on a similar cold call, do anything before asking if she can see the boss to make the secretary more inclined to try to help get her in?

4. Whether Alice is successful in getting past the secretary or not in such cold-call cases, how should she handle her departure so that she might call back in the future, as far as the secretary is concerned?

THE SITUATION

The charming young secretary has just told you, a young male salesperson, that her boss—and your important prospect—Mr. Robert Bartlett, is in an important conference and will be delayed half an hour in meeting you for the scheduled appointment in his office.

YOUR PROBLEM

What to do the next half hour? You have driven 112 kilometers (70 miles) to keep this appointment, your first at this very large and potentially good company account. The highway was thick with traffic, and you feel that a cup of coffee would hit the spot. The secretary is pretty, seemingly friendly, and you and she are alone in the waiting room. She is busy, but some current popular magazines and a daily newspaper are on a small table nearby, plus some industry trade catalogues, company reports, and employee bulletins. You have another important appointment scheduled in two hours, 64 kilometers (40 miles) distant, and you still have not checked the arithmetic of one of your proposals for this interview.

Questions for Written Reports or Class Discussion

What is your decision? What will you do with your time for the next 30 minutes?

CHAPTER 7

Planning Your Presentation

After studying this chapter, you will be able to:

Explain the term *sales presentation,* and the four basic types of sales presentations.

Describe the importance of planning your sales presentation in advance in terms of knowing *why* you will say or do what you plan rather than just how or when to do it, so you can *react to* rather than simply *present to* the prospect.

Explain the four basic, logical steps essential to any effective sales presentation.

Describe many of the key principles involved in effective two-way communication and understanding, such as how to be a good listener; correct word usage, proper use of words, eyes, and body; and proper use of demonstration, sales tools, and other techniques that aid communication.

Summarize through examples the importance and proper use of negative and positive facts or words in planning or making a sales presentation.

Identify the objectives and importance of presentation planning which will tie together those principles, practices, and techniques essential to sales success.

Analyze the difference between a good, properly planned, organized, and effective sales presentation and a poor one.

Once you have qualified your prospect as to his or her need for your product, and are confident that he or she has both the money and authority to buy, you are ready to plan your sales presentation, tailored to what you anticipate will be your prospect's needs, wants, or problems.

Success in selling comes most often to those salespeople who take the time to carefully prepare and present each sales presentation for maximum effect. They measure each presentation in terms of its power to inform, persuade, and convince, to avoid any and all possible misinterpretation, to close the sale, and to leave the door open for future orders. An effective presentation represents the very heart and backbone of modern personal selling. Knowing how to plan and give a dynamic, action-inciting presentation is the surest and quickest way to achieve success in selling.

FOUR BASIC TYPES OF SALES PRESENTATIONS

In order to get their sales message across most effectively, most business firms or nonprofit organizations have their salespeople use one of the following four types of sales presentations.

Canned (or Memorized) Presentation. Some require their salespeople to memorize and strictly follow a carefully tested and written *canned presentation*. These presentations are especially useful to those selling the same product all the time. They are so carefully worked out that a high percentage of closes result from methodically memorizing and presenting the *canned* wording. Such presentations are dead or listless unless the salesperson, like an actor or actress, strives to make the words come alive on each interview.

This type of presentation is most effective in the selling of nontechnical items door-to-door or by telephone, where time is short. Requiring limited training time, it offers organizations the advantage that all salespeople will deliver the same well-planned presentation. One major disadvantage is that it allows for little prospect participation; another is that since several closing attempts are usually made in a rather rapid manner, prospects may view it as high-pressure selling.

Planned (or Formula Presentation). By far the most widely used of the four types is a carefully planned, structured, yet personalized sales message called a *planned presentation*. In it, the organization provides, or the salespeople write their own, key sections, the main points of which, with their carefully chosen wording, are committed to memory. It offers the advantage of being more conversational and less formal than the canned presentation, yet the salesperson still follows a carefully prepared outline and script built around questions designed to uncover buyer needs, wants, and problems.

This type of presentation, while allowing the salesperson to maintain control of the interview, also invites constant prospect involvement and interaction. Its structured approach may follow the planned AIDA (attention, interest, desire, action) sales presentation progression, which is described shortly, or other such formula approaches.

Automated (or Audiovisual) Presentation. For this type of presentation, the salesperson chiefly relies on portable audiovisual aids to get the sales message across. This method involves use of such audiovisual devices as movies, video, slides, microfiche, computer-generated graphics, or sound film strips, and is most often employed to present products that are otherwise difficult to explain or demonstrate. At the end of the audiovisual presentation, the salesperson handles questions or objections and moves to close the sale.

Automated audiovisual presentations are widely used at trade shows, consumer shows, and free-standing exhibits. Many offer a continuous play mode. Some units are portable enough to be taken to customer locations for showroom, office, or store presentations. While audiovisuals can be an effective way to communicate, salespeople must be carefully trained in their use.

Survey-Proposal (or Problem-Solution) Presentation. This type, used frequently in systems selling or in the selling of highly complex technical products or services, normally involves a two-step sales approach.

The first step involves selling the prospect on the idea of allowing the salesperson (or an entire selling team) to make an in-depth study of possible problems or needs concerning which the seller might be able to propose a solution. Normally this survey is done free of charge.

Once such a study has been made (often taking many days or hours) and the seller and prospect have agreed that real problems or needs have been pinpointed, the second step takes place. This normally involves an oral sales presentation based upon a carefully written proposal, performed either by an individual salesperson or a selling team before a group of prospect-organization executives.

HOW TO START PLANNING THE PRESENTATION

Regardless of which of the just noted four basic types of presentations you will use (and that depends on the specific situation to be faced), the best way to start preparing for a sales presentation is to sit back for a moment and imagine that you are the prospect (individual or organization). For simplicity's sake, we will assume that you are planning for presentation to an individual prospect. That being the case, let us start by your putting yourself in your prospect's shoes; on his or her side of the fence!

This act forces you to start thinking as he or she might think—an important first step, for you can then assume that your prospect will have these questions in mind:

Do I have a need? Or a problem?
Would this product fill that need? Or solve my problem?
Is the price right?

Is this the right company for me to deal with?
Is this the salesperson I want to do business with?
Should I buy now? Is the time right?

The most important of these, the questions always at the back of your prospect's mind, are "What's in it for me?" "Why change?" and "Why should I buy this product now?"

A good way to start planning how to answer these questions is from a problem-solving point of view. Here are the basic problems you face, and the order in which you should approach them in developing your presentation:

1. How can I best approach prospects so as to gain their attention and interest so that they will willingly bear me out?
2. How can I most quickly discover any needs, wants, or problems, and get prospects to admit to them?
3. How can I best develop the prospect's continued interest in what I am offering?
4. How can I best fit my presentation around my offering that will best satisfy the prospect's needs or wants, or help the prospects solve their problems?
5. How can I most convincingly demonstrate that the benefits of my particular offering can bring prospects the greatest satisfaction?
6. How can I plan now to shape any anticipated questions, complaints, or objections that the prospect might raise into reasons for buying now?
7. How can I best close the sale?
8. What after-sale follow-up or follow-through steps can I anticipate and plan for now—whether or not I close the sale during this coming presentation?

We discuss these points in this chapter and in Chapters 8–13, where we will elaborate upon and extend our concepts of principles and techniques of a complete and effective sales presentation.

IMPORTANCE OF KNOWING WHY AS WELL AS HOW IN THE TOTAL SELLING PROCESS

We are now ready to consider the basic structure and steps involved in planning and making the sales presentation. But first we must stress that the presentation to come will be a dynamic process with constant action, reaction, and interaction between you and the prospect. The word *presentation* has an unfortunate connotation, since it denotes the act of presenting or delivering *to* someone; actually, the kind of sales presentation we will discuss involves a total communications interaction *between* prospect and salesperson.

The strategy and concepts—the why of what you are planning and will do during the physical presentation—are more important than the how-to tactics you will employ. In presenting the anatomy and structure of a planned, organized, logical-sequence sales presentation, we will provide a basic framework of principles, practices, and many specific techniques around which you can build any presentation of your own (business, cause, or personal). But you should constantly be aware that understanding *why* something is done is more important than just knowing *how* or *when* to do it. Knowing how and when to *react* to your prospect will close more sales for you than just knowing how to *present* to him or her step by step.

Your planning, therefore, is basically to set the strategy you will follow in the presentation: to plan, analyze, and set objectives around which you will adapt, react, and move your prospect to the close during the dynamic interplay of the face-to-face total selling process.

BASIC ANATOMY OF THE SALES PRESENTATION

The amount of time and effort to be spent in planning the sales presentation depends on the particular type of selling one is engaged in. A salesperson who sells one impulse-type product, such as a vacuum cleaner, repeatedly to individual consumers can use the same preplanned sales presentation over and over. An industrial salesperson, on the other hand, who sells complex technical products, may have to spend a great deal of time in planning and developing a presentation adapted to the special situation of each individual prospect.

Assuming that you may face competition from other sellers of similar products or services, in all but the simplest cases (such as repeat selling of a single item), you should organize your presentation systematically to fit each individual prospect. Your abbreviated outline may follow this sequence:

1. Identify your prospect's business or other objectives.
2. Collect information about both your prospect's business and objectives, and about the offerings of your competitors.
3. Through evaluation of the above information, develop *selling points* around the benefits of your offerings in terms of how they might best meet the particular needs, wants, and problems of your prospect. A *selling point* (or sales point) is made when a *benefit* is presented that should be of interest or value to the prospect (for example, "Use of my product will cut your operating costs by 50 percent next year").
4. Systematically plan how you will accomplish the four basic progressive psychological steps or requirements of any organized presentation. Described in the section to follow, they can be summarized as (1) *attention,* (2) *interest,* (3) *desire,* (4) *action.*

Four Basic Requirements of Any Sales-Boosting Presentation

Every good presentation is a smooth sales communication that leads logically and convincingly from the opening sentence to the last. No matter what it is designed to sell, it must meet these four basic requirements if it is to sell successfully.

- It must catch your prospect's instant and undivided *attention* by aiming at his or her self-interest.
- It must arouse your prospect's *interest* by describing benefits and pointing out their advantage to him or her.
- It must stimulate *desire* for the benefits and their advantage by offering factual proof.
- It must motivate your prospect to take *action* by agreeing to buy.

Not all presentations require in-depth concentration on each of these steps. It is possible in some cases, such as selling a simple impulse item like a new type of flashlight, to simply arouse attention by showing it with a quick demonstration and asking promptly for the order. Example: "See how this new flashlight works? Would you like to own one?" In most cases, however, these four steps have to be covered in logical progression.

Some salespeople find it easy to remember this progression by recalling the key letters A.I.D.A., in connection with the famous opera *Aida* by Verdi. Such memory-recalling word associations are called *mnemonic devices*. A simplified "sales handle" (or formula) such as this often helps nervous sales trainees or new salespeople recall the sequence.

Do not underrate the simplicity of these four basic steps, since they can be expanded in countless and often highly sophisticated ways, depending on experience, type of product or service being sold, or company or organizational training or policy. Case Study 7.1, at the end of this chapter, shows how the A.I.D.A. concept was utilized by the Singer Company to outline, develop, and put into words a highly effective presentation to sell its vacuum cleaners. In chapters to follow, we develop these and other steps of the presentation in considerable detail. For now, it serves our purpose to take a brief look at each of the four steps as a guide to developing the key points of a planned presentation.

1. *Arouse and hold the prospect's immediate attention.* The first few seconds of your sales presentation are all-important. Your aim is to focus your prospect's attention immediately on you and what you have to say. It isn't always easy to win attention—his or her thoughts may be on other things, or he or she may simply be indifferent.

   Whether your prospect actually asks it or not, there is always that overriding thought in his or her mind: "What's in it for me?" You must answer this question from the start, and keep on answering it throughout your presentation. From the beginning, your presentation must be aimed at what your prospect wants—greater profits, more customers, less pilferage, and so on.

   The best way to quickly gain a prospect's attention is to carefully plan beforehand some key opening sentences that relate his or her probable needs or problems to your offering. Here are two examples:

   "Mr. Prospect, did you know that one out of every two firms in your industry uses our XYZ Product in its shipping department?"

   "Mrs. Prospect, would you like to know how you can cut employee pilferage in your department store by as much as 40 percent?"

2. *Create and hold interest.* Once you catch your prospect's attention, you must quickly convert it into favorable interest, and hold that interest while you help him or her discover and clarify any needs, wants, or problems, to admit them, and to indicate a willingness to consider your proposal as a solution.

    The best way to do this is to carefully plan (and write down, at least in outline form) key selling points or statements built around benefits. In order to do this effectively, you must know your product thoroughly, know how it works or what it will do for your prospect, be able to clearly explain its benefits, and be prepared to offer proof if asked. Commonly called the Feature–Advantage–Benefit sales approach, it can be outlined like this:

    > *Feature*—a characteristic or fact about a product or service that produces a benefit.
    > *Advantage*—how the feature works or what it will do.
    > *Benefit*—advantage offered to the prospect by the feature; backed up wherever possible by evidence or confirmation to back up your statement.

    There are basically two types of benefits: plus benefits and minus benefits. Plus benefits are those the prospect stands to gain, such as mental peace, increased profits, emotional satisfaction. Minus benefits are risks or losses that he or she wishes to avoid, such as financial loss, loss of prestige, loss of health.

    Which benefits will appeal most to your prospect? Here's the best way for you to answer this question.

    - Find out *why* your prospect does *what* he or she does now. What it is he or she wants most?
    - Relate what you are selling to those desires or wants.
    - Select the benefits offered by your product or service which seem to interest your prospect most, and start building appeals around them.

3. *Arouse desire and secure conviction.* As you link your benefits to your prospect's interests and desires, he or she will be thinking: "What you are offering sounds good, but how do I know you are telling the truth?" "Why should I believe you?" Your planning for this point in the presentation is to help your prospect realize that what you are offering will provide the solutions or answers that will satisfy him or her, and then, through proof and demonstration (where possible), to convince him or her that your offering is the best possible means to that end. The best way to do this is to be prepared to how facts, such as:

    - Specifications—facts about materials, design, workmanship: the "nuts and bolts" of what you are selling.
    - Expert evidence—in the form of reports of authorities, results of tests, and the like; the bigger the name of the authority, the bigger the proof.

- Guarantee (or warranty)—if at all possible, plan to have one to show. It always helps to be able to tell your prospect that what you are selling is so good it carries an unqualified guarantee or warranty.

It is at this point that you invite any as-yet-unexpressed questions or objections so that you can promptly answer or handle them to your prospect's satisfaction. Chapter 11 describes both common and less common types of questions or objections that may arise here; you must think out your answers beforehand as you plan for the presentation, and be prepared to handle them easily.

4. *Motivate action to buy—which means closing the sale.* Closing the sale, or getting the order, is the purpose of most sales presentations. You must plan carefully in advance how you will take the initiative and ask your prospect to buy. Seldom will a prospect tell you outright that he or she wants to buy, but if you have convincingly aroused interest and stimulated a desire for what you are offering, he or she will flash "buying signals" that you must be prepared to recognize and act upon by attempting a "trial close." Although we must await Chapter 12 for a full discussion of these two terms, and the term *close* itself as used in selling, since they will come up occasionally beforehand, we will briefly introduce them here as follows:

- *Close.* In selling, the term means getting the prospects' verbal or signed agreement to buy the sellers' offering.
- *Trial close.* To ask for the order at different times throughout the presentation, especially whenever the prospect flashes a "buying signal."
- *Buying signal.* Signs given by a prospect (such as spoken words, facial expressions, and physical actions) at any time during the presentation which might reflect interest in buying. For example, halfway through your presentation your prospect, who has been verbally noncommittal so far, suddenly shows interest by picking up the on-hand sample of your product and asks its cost. This is definitely a signal for you to stop talking and ask for the order.

HOW TO COMMUNICATE EFFECTIVELY WITH PROSPECTS

Important to both planning and making an effective presentation is communication, or two-way understanding. You have to understand what your prospect is saying and thinking, and vice versa, or the time spent may be wasted. And it is your responsibility to communicate with your prospect in his or her own language, level of interest, and comprehension. The opening of such lines of understandable communication requires that you think, write, or speak clearly enough for your prospect to understand what your are communicating.

Clear Thinking Involves Mentally Outlining Your Presentation

In addition to converging all basic steps just noted when developing your presentation, here are three other elements that should be considered:

1. Decide on the length of your presentation.
2. Plan how to be a good listener and thus absorb feedback, so that you will be better prepared to interact with your prospect.
3. Plan ways to sharpen emphasis of your key selling points through techniques that will aid your prospect's understanding.

How Long Should Your Presentation Last? The length of your presentation depends in large part on what you are selling. You can effectively present some products, both tangibles and intangibles, in two or three minutes. Such brief presentations consist of perhaps 200 to 300 carefully chosen words. The average sales presentation lasts from ten to fifteen minutes, but others, especially those of a more technical nature, last longer. Many salespeople feel that under no circumstances should any interview last more than 30 to 40 minutes.

The presentation itself should be carefully prepared to be delivered with maximum effectiveness within the shortest time and to ensure full understanding by the prospect. The length of the remainder of the interview then depends on the interest of the prospect as evidenced by the questions asked. Most experienced salespeople try to close the interview as soon as possible so as not to waste any of the prospect's valuable time. Their advice is: Give your presentation, get the order, and then leave—all in the shortest time possible.

Learn to be a Good Listener. The best way to discover needs or problems is to ask intelligent questions; in following chapters we go into considerable detail about effective questioning techniques. And, when you ask questions, listen carefully to the answers. One of the parts of being a good conversationalist, or a good communicator, is to be a good listener. Show your prospect that you are sincerely interested in what he or she is saying, and your job of persuasion will usually be easy.

Why discuss intelligent questioning and the art of being a good listener as part of planning your presentation? The answer lies in the fact that your first interview task is to quickly get your prospect interested in you, your product, and your firm or organization, in that order. The best way to get someone interested in *you* is to ask questions that will get your prospect telling you about his or her life, job, and problems.

True professional selling usually involves more careful listening than talking. Countless salespeople have talked themselves right out of a sale, simply by not knowing when to start listening. In some sales situations, especially where tangibles are concerned, the actual sales talk is most effective when it is used merely to explain what it is the prospect is hearing, seeing, feeling, smelling, or tasting.

Sharpen the Emphasis of Your Key Points Through Techniques That Aid Understanding. Unless you are an expert, your prospect will not be particularly interested in your personal opinion or advice. The best sales presentation, especially with sophisticated buyers, is one that is simple, frank, direct, and factual. To be most effective it should be built around (1) demonstrations, (2) sales aids, and (3) an oral sales presentation built around benefits, positive facts, and convincing proof.

Clear Writing Involves Putting Your Presentation into Words

In order to gain the attention of your prospect and to hold it throughout the interview, your presentation has to be well organized and smooth-flowing from start to finish. You should tailor it to the prospect's needs and point of view, fill it with facts that can be proven or dramatized, and present it effectively through well-chosen thought patterns and vivid, persuasive language. For planning purposes, as we have indicated, the best way to approach this is to put your thoughts down in writing. In putting your thoughts on paper, aim to include one or all of the following items:

1. A simple or detailed outline in either chart or graph form.
2. Specific written proposals, which can be submitted either prior to or during the interview.
3. A planned presentation—a detailed outline with selected key points carefully written out for later word-for-word presentation.
4. A canned presentation, in which the entire presentation is carefully written out and memorized in its entirety for later word-for-word presentation.

You have only a limited time in which to make a complete presentation in terms of your prospect's values (which may differ from your own) and level of understanding. Thus, your presentation must be clear, convincing, interesting, brief, factual, and to the point.

Words Make Images. Basic to any effective written or oral communication is the fact that words create images. Advertising copywriters take great pains in constructing the product advertisements in magazines and other media. They test, polish, and revise each word until it glitters with meaning. A good salesperson does the same thing in committing thoughts to paper when developing a presentation. His or her words have impact and are persuasive upon delivery.

You can make your presentation effective by using image-packed key words that give your prospect a mental picture of your sales points and of how your product will benefit him or her. A good dictionary or thesaurus is a rich source for vital, description selling words, or picture-building words. Here are some examples of vivid words which, when contrasted with weak ones, better describe the sales points of an ordinary fluorescent desk lamp.

Weak Descriptive Words	Strong, Image-Building Descriptive Words
200-watt light	An easy-on-the-eyes, soft but bright, 200-watt fluorescent light.
Good shade on top	The adjustable shade cuts glare and prevents eyestrain.
Two-button light control	These two conveniently placed buttons assure instantaneous fingertip light control.
Heavy base	This sturdy, graceful-looking base will not scratch your desk.

Correct Word Usage. Know the meanings of words and how to use and pronounce them correctly. This knowledge is essential for using words in general and also for using the technical words of the industries or businesses to which you sell. If, for example, you are selling insurance and introduce "statistical facts shown by these actuarial tables," you should know the correct pronunciation, usage, and meaning of word *actuarial.* Many salespeople like to have others go over their written presentation to check the clarity and effectiveness of the wording and to catch any grammatical or technical errors.

Why Discuss Clear Writing in Presentation Preparation? Because clear writing is a logical and vitally important extension of clear thinking about the approaching interview, putting your thoughts down on paper enables you to do the following things:

1. Decide what you are going to say and how and when you will say it.
2. Organize key selling points logically so they can be easily remembered and presented more effectively.
3. Use vivid, picture-building words that will enable the prospect to understand your key points and to visualize how your product will benefit him or her.
4. Speak convincingly, with good grammar, logical organization, and understanding and correct usage of technical language.

Clear Speaking Involves Words, Eyes, Face, and Body

No matter how carefully you prepare and deliver your presentation, your prospect may understand or absorb only part of what you say. Oral communication is only about 30 percent effective in conveying an idea accurately. The problem is that both you and the prospect are communicating with words, and words have meaning only in terms of how one or the other of you uses or reacts to them. Meaning does not exist in a word as such; it exists in the significance each of you assigns to it in terms of your own experiences, attitudes, and beliefs.

It takes two people to communicate an idea, one to send it and one to receive it. If you and your prospect fail to understand each other, your message won't get across. Such understanding is a two-way street. The prospect must understand what you are saying, and you must not only understand what he or she is saying but also try to understand what he or she is thinking.

The burden of establishing this important level of understanding falls upon you, the salesperson. You have to consider the motives, prejudices, and other things the prospect may have on his or her mind. If you aren't careful, he or she may miss your point and either be embarrassed to admit a lack of understanding or too proud to admit that he or she didn't get your full meaning.

There are two basic ways you can make certain your prospect understands your message, not an interpretation of it. The first is to communicate clearly and carefully yourself; the second is to have the message repeated in his or her own words, and to *listen* carefully to what is said. If he or she gives back the same picture you tried to send, you can be fairly certain you have been broadcasting on the right wavelength.

In broadcasting your message, use all these "languages" to help insure that your communication gets across—words, voice, eyes, face, and body.

Words. Words make images, as we have already said. Use action words to get response: "*What* do you feel about that?" "*How* do you like the feature I have just demonstrated?" Spice up your verbal presentation with words and illustrations that are truly arresting and imaginative. Use short sentences; use selling adjectives and action verbs. Key words or phrases, such as *bargain* or *close-out*, should be emphasized.

Voice. Speak clearly and with enthusiasm at a steady, not-too-slow and not-too-fast pace that is understandable to your listener. Avoid mumbling, unnecessary expressions such as "like" or "you know" to bridge phrases, droning, stridency, or listlessness in your presentation. Try to vary the pitch, tone, and speed of your voice; project warmth, vigor, vitality. Talk *with* your prospect, not simply at him or her.

Eyes. Try to maintain eye contact with your prospect as much as possible. Use your eyes to transmit enthusiasm, alertness, and sincerity. Use them to indicate that you are receiving his or her communication in return—interest, approval, alertness. When selling to two or more people, let your eyes sweep from person to person while transmitting and receiving communication.

Face. Let your face register happiness, confidence, warmth, and conviction. Smile often.

Body. Sit or stand upright and alertly; don't slouch or hang your head listlessly. Gesture only if it comes naturally to you. Your body stance should convey your confidence and interest.

Although we touch on some of these points again in pages to follow, they are mentioned now in the planning stage because once you have planned and organized your presentation, you should rehearse it, aloud, on your feet, two or three times, before trying it on a live prospect. You should tape it on a recorder and play it back to edit and polish any irrelevant or rough spots. If friends, family, or fellow salespeople can hear your rehearsal and offer you helpful tips on improvement, so much the better.

Demonstrations and Sales Tools Aid Communication and Help Offer Proof of Claims

To be most effective your presentation should be built around (1) demonstrations, (2) sales aids, and (3) negative and positive facts built into your oral presentation; back up these in turn by the just-considered effective nonverbal communications tools such as "body language"—use of hands, arms, eyes, and expressions.

Demonstrations. These should be made whenever possible. Your prospect does not believe what you say nearly so much as he or she believes what can be seen. A physical demonstration of the point you are trying to make is always the most effective, interesting, and believable sales technique.

A physical demonstration so effectively dramatizes a sales presentation that it should be used whenever and wherever possible. If you cannot demonstrate the actual product, then try to demonstrate a reasonable imitation of it, all or in part, tangible or intangible. Table 7.1 gives some examples.

Sales Aids. These can also be used to effectively dramatize your verbal sales presentation. Good sales aids can offer illustrations that enable your prospect to see as well as to hear what you are saying. Keep in mind that selling aids (such as color brochures) merely illustrate your presentation. When the prospect starts giving a reason why he or she should buy, quickly put the aid aside, even though you may be only halfway through showing it. You are there to write an order, not to deliver a lecture.

Here are some examples of selling aids that can be used along with your oral presentation and some tips on how to use them most effectively:

Presentation (or Sales) Manual. Such a manual, either provided by your firm or organization, or compiled by you, represents a highly effective sales aid or tool. It should include such things as descriptive brochures, price lists, photos or drawings, advertising materials, testimonial letters from satisfied customers, competitive comparisons, and anything else that will help present your product and its benefits. It should always be neat and tidy in appearance; nothing is so unprofessional as a tattered, messy sales or presentation manual.

Be aware that *you must control use of the manual* during your presentation; practice using it during your planning stage to illustrate sales points as you come to them. Plan not to ever let your prospect take it away from you; to do so may lead to loss of control of the interview.

Sales Kit. Whereas presentation (or sales) manuals are usually made up in formal three-ring binders, sales kits are more informal, possibly consisting only of loose materials inside a file folder. The materials might consist of current bro-

TABLE 7.1

Your Verbal Lead-in	Demonstration (Let Your Prospect . . .)	Appeals to Prospect's Sense of:
"Notice how quietly the motor runs."	Listen to it.	Hearing
"You can drop this shockproof watch and it still keeps running."	Drop it.	Seeing
"Feel how soft this strong new carpeting is."	Feel it.	Feeling
"Doesn't this new food product taste good?"	Taste it.	Tasting
"Your wife will like the scent of this new after-shave lotion."	Smell it.	Smelling

chures, copies of advertising, descriptive bulletins, and price lists. Again, you should practice using this material as part of your presentation before the interview so that you do not fumble or lose or drop anything in the prospect's presence. Above all, you should keep the kit neat and presentable, replacing literature or samples as soon as they become tattered, torn, or smudged.

Catalogues and Price Lists. You must know how to find things quickly and accurately in your catalogues or price lists yourself before trying to locate items in front of your prospect. As with the sales manual, control it (or them) yourself and do not let your prospect have it until you are ready to turn it over. Use only new, fresh copies if possible.

Samples. These should be clean and in good condition. Whenever possible, you should attach information that will help the buyer order by number, size, cost, and so forth. Try to show only those samples issued to a prospect's needs, not necessarily the whole range.

Charts and Graphs. Tell your prospect what these illustrations mean before you show them, so that he or she will understand them correctly. Use them in a dramatic way by holding them up so that they can easily be seen, and control their use as with the sales manual. Practice using them before your presentation.

Testimonials. These can include letters from satisfied customers, photographs of your product in use, lists of prominent firms or individuals who use the item, or case histories. For best results they should come from an individual or firm whose opinion the buyer respects and preferably from someone in the same business and industry.

Audiovisual Equipment. If you plan to use such equipment, make certain beforehand that you know exactly how to use it (practice makes perfect) and that it is in good operating order. Many an AV-based sale has been lost due to unexpected equipment malfunction; prior testing can help keep this from happening to you.

Order Form. Many salespeople use their order forms as effective sales tools by having them in sight but out of the prospect's reach at all times during the presentation. If you use them in this way, make certain that you plan in advance how to display and explain them. Information or specifications can often be written onto the openly displayed order form as a matter of course during the presentation, and then effectively used to close the sale in this way:

> "Mr. Vanderhoef, I've been listing on this form all the specifications we have discussed. Will you look them over, and if satisfied just OK it by signing here on the signature line?"

Get Your Prospects Involved

In order to keep their interest, plan ahead to involve the prospects in the presentation as much as possible by giving them a job to do and by making them look and feel good as they do it. For example, if selling an automobile, ask prospects to sit behind the wheel and test the automatic gearshift, lights, and windshield wiper for themselves. You can make them feel good by a comment such as, "Your neighbors and business associates couldn't help but be impressed at seeing you drive up in an economical but beautiful new automobile like this, could they?"

Use of Negative and Positive Facts or Words in Planning and Making the Sales Presentation

Since many buyers are often reluctant to bring themselves to the point of saying yes in a buying situation, part of the art of selling is recognizing their hesitancy and helping them make the decision. You can help manage this situation by planning how to use key negative and positive facts or words.

Negative. Emphasis on negative facts or words often proves effective when introduced early in the presentation. If your prospects are considering changing to something new, they are probably already basically dissatisfied with the old. You will not offend prospects by building into your presentation early on negative facts such as these:

> Doesn't your current cumbersome system waste a lot more employee time than would be the case if you were using our modern product?
> Aren't your operating costs much higher now than they would be with our new product?

Here are some examples of negative words which, when coupled with facts, paint powerful verbal images:

- Inconvenient
- Old-fashioned
- Inefficient

- Unsafe
- Inadequate
- Wasteful

Positive. When speaking of a new product or service, present only positive facts, illustrated and dramatized with positive words. The following examples show the use of positive facts.

> Our brand-new, space-age system will save you over 40 person-hours a day more than your existing less modern system does.
> Our new product will cut your current operating costs 50 percent and should increase your profit by at least 10 percent.

Here are some other examples of positive words that help dramatize facts:

- Convenient
- Up-to-date
- More affordable

- Completely safe
- Highly efficient
- Cost efficient

SUMMARIZING OBJECTIVES OF PRESENTATION PLANNING

Let us now tie together the several principles, practices, and techniques we have discussed through the following illustration of notes for a planned presentation made by a salesperson of a new electronic office machine. Coupled with the Singer illustration (see Case Study 7), it should offer you good indication of the type of careful planning that is essential to greatest sales success.

1. Briefly outline the topic (proposition) to be covered and the conclusions to be reached:

> "Mr. Evans, I would like to demonstrate how this new machine works in order to show how it can cut your costs by allowing the operator to process twice as much information in the same amount of time the machine you are currently using takes."

2. Simplify the complex by a step-by-step demonstration and explanation:

> "Step one, Mr. Evans, involves a single key-setting like this (demonstration). Your current machine requires three similar procedures. Step two involves one movement of this other key. Try it (which prospect does). Isn't that easier than the two comparable steps on your current machine?"

3. Present new, important information in small doses:

> "Technically speaking, Mr. Evans, this machine is better than others on the market in three basic ways:
> a. (Brief description). Any questions?
> b. (Brief description). Don't you agree that this is an important feature?
> c. (Brief description). Please feel free to ask any questions."

4. Relate explanations to his needs and problems:

> "Mr. Evans, now that I've shown you how this new machine works, what specific problems can you see it handling more efficiently for your office?"

5. Use any devices or techniques that illustrate the point:
   a. Use of interesting stories that illustrate benefits others have gained from using the new machine. Such stories can put prospects' imaginations to work and can help them see solutions to their own problems through visualizing how someone in a similar situation was helped.
   b. Appeals to any of the five senses.
      (1) *Hearing*. "Notice how little noise the machine makes when turned on."

      (2)   *Seeing.* "The designers did a good job on this machine. Isn't it modern-looking?"

      (3)   *Touching.* "If you rest your hand on top here, you will notice the complete lack of vibration."

      (4)   *Tasting.* (Not applicable with this machine).

      (5)   *Smelling.* "Since this machine doesn't heat up as your current one does, the operators can't complain of any odor from the ink."

   c.   Example and comparisons that may help clarify the statement:

> "Mr. Evans, I've just demonstrated how this machine can enable an operator to do twice as much work just as easily in the same amount of time. For example, it would enable you to get your monthly statements out several days earlier. Couldn't you use that time saved for other things?"

   d.   Use of any appropriate, available visual aids such as brochures, catalogues, samples, testimonials, charts or graphs, filmstrips, presentation kits, or photographs.

6.   Check and recheck constantly through the question technique to make sure each step is fully understood:

- "Do you have any questions, Mr. Evans, about the operational steps I've just demonstrated?"
- "Mr. Evans, how could the process I've just outlined apply to your own monthly statement problem?"

7.   Summarize the original topic (proposition), the key illustrative points (proof), and the conclusions (benefits):

> "Mr. Evans, I have tried to demonstrate how this new machine can cut your costs by allowing your operators to process twice as much information just as easily in the same amount of time as with the machine you are now using. We discussed three ways in which this could be done. Briefly, they were step 1 and step 2. Do you agree with me that its chief benefit to you would be the considerable time and costs it would save by enabling your office to process monthly statements five working days sooner than they do with the machine you are currently using?"

SUMMARY

One of the most important keys to sales success is planning, especially of the presentation itself, which consists of four basic elements: (1) the approach (gaining attention), (2) creating interest, (3) arousing desire, securing conviction, and handling any questions or objections, and (4) closing the sale (getting the prospect to take action). You have to persuade most prospects that a need exists, that your product will fulfill that need, and that they should take action to fulfill that need through buying your product.

Since two-way communication is so important to understanding during the presentation, prior planning of it involves thinking points through carefully and putting your thoughts into words that will persuade and motivate. The first step in planning an orderly presentation around benefits that will arouse interest, create conviction, and motivate action is preparing a structured outline of the presentation. You can then develop this outline into a more or less detailed planned presentation or into a highly detailed, word-for-word, canned presentation.

In this chapter we have considered most of the aspects and techniques involved in planning a presentation. These are elaborated upon, and other concepts considered, in Chapters 8–13. These chapters should be reviewed before you sit down to plan your presentation. The concepts covered here were illustrated by way of overview in the detailed presentation planning notes of our electronic office-machine salesperson.

Questions for Analysis and Discussion

1.   What are the four basic steps of planning and making any sales presentation?

2.   What key factor does communication involve in the sales process? What three points have to be considered in planning a presentation to ensure good communication?

3.   Of what value is the phrase *words make images* to a salesperson planning or making a sales presentation?

4.   How long should a sales presentation last? What determines its time length?

5.   What are the two basic ways described in this chapter that a salesperson can make certain that the prospect's own interpretation of it is correct?

6.   What particular type of demonstration of a sales point is always the most believable, interesting, and effective? To what senses can it appeal?

7.   Halfway through your page-by-page sales presentation, using a presentation manual with illustrations, charts, and graphs, your prospect says he or she thinks it would be nice to own the product being shown. Do you continue leafing through to the complete end of your visual/oral presentation, or do you stop then and there? Explain the reasons for your decision.

8.   Assuming that you are a retail bookstore salesperson selling this book to an interested customer, how will you involve him or her in your presentation through use of the book itself as a demonstration aid?

CASE STUDY 7

How the Singer Company Outlined, Developed, and Put Into Words a Highly Effective Presentation to Sell its Vacuum Cleaners

The Singer Sewing Company, formerly the Singer Company, has long been known as the American firm that introduced the sewing machine to the world. Few Americans are aware, however, that among other consumer items Singer marketed in the United States were vacuum cleaners, which it has manufactured since the 1920s. A few years ago Singer decided to try to triple its share of the upright-cleaner market and to double its share of the canister-cleaner market within a year in the following way.

1. Selling two cleaners to every prospect who did not have a good upright or canister cleaner.
2. Selling an upright cleaner to every prospect who already had a new canister but not an up-to-date upright.

MARKET RESEARCH INDICATED POTENTIAL AND NEED

This program represented positive sales thinking at its best, but Singer also knew that the market was huge at that time (over 5 million vacuum cleaners sold annually in the United States to an average of one in ten homes, at an average unit price of $88.36) and realized that the need or want for clean homes is always present. In addition, Singer market research indicated (1) that the average life of a vacuum cleaner is seven to ten years, (2) that a high percentage of women buyers want to take advantage of new and improved model changes, and (3) that vacuum cleaners are impulse sale items.

A COMBINATION PRODUCT OFFERED QUALITY AND VALUE

In order to reach its goals, Singer devised a unique plan for presenting and selling not one, but two vacuum cleaners (an upright and a canister model) for $99.90—only about $11 more than the then average, industry-wide price of $88.36 for one upright cleaner with attachments. The only way Singer could profit at those prices was through volume sales. In short, Singer had to sell and to keep selling if it was to reach its first annual sales and profit goals.

PLANNING THE SINGER PRESENTATION

In planning the presentation for this *impulse item,* Singer had the advantage of having hundreds of retail stores throughout most cities of the United States with well-trained in-store sales personnel. Trained outside salespeople also operated out of most of the retail centers. In addition, the Singer brand name was well established and highly respected.

The presentation had to cover the basic elements essential to any sales effort.

Get prospect's attention (the approach).
Arouse interest.
Create desire (and secure conviction).
Close the sale (action).

It also had to be built around a demonstration of the vacuum cleaners themselves. Here, then, is the basic presentation (in brief) as developed around the above four sales steps and communicated successfully by hundreds of Singer salespeople. We will assume that the presentation is being made in a Singer retail shop with models on display for demonstration purposes.

DEVELOPMENT OF THE SINGER PRESENTATION: QUESTIONS, OUTLINE, WORDS

The Approach (and Qualification of Prospect)

Q: Should you demonstrate vacuum cleaners to everybody?

A: No. When selling vacuum cleaners, find out who the really interested prospects are by asking three key questions. This questioning will lead you very quickly to those people who are prospects and who, because they are interested, can be closed quickly. In this way you use your time most efficiently, because you do not demonstrate vacs to cold prospects. After all, time is your most precious tool. When you use it efficiently, following a sales plan, you have a good chance of success.

Q: Why do you ask everybody the three key questions?

A: A person may be in the market for a new cleaner but may not be thinking about it at the time. The questions make people think about it.

Q: What is the first question?

A: What kind of cleaner are you using now?

Q: What is the second question and what does it tell us?

A: How long have you had it? This question tells whether it is worth continuing; the cleaner may be too new to replace.

Q: What is the third question? What does it tell us?

A: Have you ever thought of making a change? This question tells whether this person is a prospect.

Q: What is the key sign he or she may give you in answer to the third question?

A: If he or she hesitates and does not immediately say no, this is a prospect worthy of your very best effort, and you should demonstrate the vacuum cleaner.

Q: Is there an ideal location in the shop for asking the three questions?

A: Not really. Ask wherever the customer is. If he or she happens to be near the vac area, that is fine. If the prospect has expressed interest and has given the right answers, you can easily ask him or her to step over to the vac area.

Q: Where else, besides the shop, can we ask the three questions?

A: Wherever we are with people we know— in our own homes, or in friends' homes, on service calls, and in many other places.

Q: After you have received the right answers to these questions, you have to decide whether to demonstrate an upright or a canister. What do you ask that helps you decide?

A: Won't you step over to the vacuum cleaners, please? As you can see, we have both upright and canister models. And, as you know, we generally recommend an upright when a home has extensive carpeting, and a canister when most of the cleaning is of bare floors and is above the floor. What kind of cleaning do you find most important in your home? That is, which type would best suit your needs?

Q: The canister demonstration differs from the upright in one important way. Why do you demonstrate the powerful suction of the canister cleaner before going into the other features? How do you demonstrate the powerful suction?

A: To get customers into the demonstration quickly and to get agreement that the canister is a powerful cleaner. You establish the fact by inviting the prospect to hold a hand up to the end of the hose and to feel the powerful suction.

Create Desire (and Secure Conviction)

This is the heart of the presentation and involves pointing out, describing, and demonstrating the various features of the cleaner being presented. Throughout, the prospect is invited to touch, to hold, or to try some of the operations of the cleaner. A key prop of the presentation is a demonstration rug, use of which is explained as follows.

To sell vacuum cleaners, you have to be prepared to sell them. The vacuum-cleaner display area must be in shape and ready for selling. For an effective demonstration, we need a quantity of each of the materials that, when spread on the demonstration rug just before the demonstration, represents the three kinds of dirt commonly found in the home today. The materials are

1. Baking soda, which represents light surface dust.
2. Kapoc, which represents stubborn, clinging lint and litter.
3. Sand, which represents embedded grit.

Features of the Singer vacuum cleaner as presented in planned order include positions the cleaner can work in, different power settings, tool storage, and use of furniture nozzle and dusting brush. The salesperson cleans the different types of simulated dirt on the rug through demonstration of nozzle and brush and of the most efficient cleaning strokes.

Q: How many steps are there in the demonstration? What are they?

A: (1) Show the suction; (2) show the features; (3) show and explain nozzle construction; (4) make parallel stroke test.

The salesperson can forestall two possible major objections, or reasons for not buying, at this point by anticipating them as questions and by asking and answering them.

Q: Now you may ask, Mrs. Barnes, why should a person interested only in an upright with attachments buy our "Two for $99.90 Combination?"

A: Because it costs only about $11 more to have two separate cleaners instead of one upright with attachments.

Q: You may also wonder whether there are any advantages to owning two cleaners in your home. May I suggest at least five such reasons. (1) The upright cleans better on carpeting. (2) The canister cleans bare floors and everything above the floor better than an upright cleaner with attachments. (3) The motors last much longer because they share the load. (4) Two people can clean the house at the same time. (5) If one cleaner needs repair, the other can do the cleaning job.

The Close

At this point, or even earlier in the demonstration, if the prospect acts or looks interested, the Singer salesperson goes into a trial close. Here are some of the questions he or she asks in order to effect a rapid close.

Mrs. Barnes, if your present six-year-old vacuum cleaner had all these modern features, you would make good use of them, wouldn't you?

Wouldn't it be a pleasure for you to own two such easy-to-use vacuum cleaners at such a low combination price?

You've thought that some day you'd like to have both an upright and a canister vacuum cleaner like these, haven't you?

How long have you been wanting a vacuum cleaner like this?

You can readily see that you have a need for these two vacuum cleaners, and you will use them to full advantage, won't you?

Once a yes, a nod, or an affirmative gesture or look is noted to trial-close questions such as these, the salesperson can start talking about delivery date, credit arrangements, or other formal closes (which are discussed in Chapter 14).

SINGER PRESENTATION SUMMARY

A Singer summary of planning and remembering the above steps in this successful presentation may run something like this.

Q: What are the four logical steps to a sale that we should remember when planning a sales presentation?

A: (1) Attention, (2) interest, (3) desire, (4) action (close).

Q: What can we do to help us remember these four steps to a sale?

A: Remember the key letters A.I.D.A. by thinking of the famous opera by Verdi.

Q: Name five secrets of successful creative selling employed in selling our "Two for $99.90 Combination."

A: (1) Acquiring a thorough knowledge of the product being sold and preparing a definite sales talk and demonstration. (2) Getting our prospect to talk by asking questions and then listening! (3) Building desire by giving a complete, dramatic, enthusiastic, and convincing demonstration. (4) Stressing quality and customer benefits that relate to the prospect's interest. (5) Using trial-close questions that get yes answers and buying decisions.

Q: What is the practical formula for sales success in presenting this combination offer?

A: (1) Ask everyone the three questions. (2) Sell the two-in-one concept. (3) Give a short demonstration to many people. (4) Try for a fast close. Do not overdemonstrate to a difficult prospect. Save your time for the next prospect—he or she may be much easier. It is not how long but how often we demonstrate that counts.

Questions for Written Reports or Class Discussion

1.   Would you describe this carefully laid-out Singer sales message as a canned or a planned presentation? Explain?

2.   The Singer presentation features built-in answers to two possible major objections, or reasons for not buying, by anticipating them as questions, and by asking and answering them. Can you think of two more such possible objections that could also be handled in the same way? How, and at what point, would you build them into the presentation?

3.   The Singer presentation stresses practical benefits (such as, it cleans better) of owning their product. Should some plus benefits of the emotional satisfaction to be gained by ownership also be introduced? If so, how and at what stage of the presentation?

4.   No mention was made during the Singer presentation of a written guarantee concerning their vacuum cleaners, yet we can assume that they did have one at the time. Would it have been helpful to present it as part of the presentation? Why? If so, how could it be most effectively introduced, and at what point in the presentation?

What kind of presentation can you develop to sell the new "Trav-L-File"?

You are an independent manufacturer's salesperson who has just secured an exclusive franchise for the American state of Maryland for a new product called "Trav-L-File." This is a rugged $7\frac{1}{2}$ lb 18 in. × 12 in. × 11 in. plastic container with movable inserts that can be divided into partitions for hanging file folders. It has been designed specifically for use in the trunk or back seat of a car.

Since several large companies in other parts of the country have bought quantities of it and issued it to members of their sales force, you too plan to sell it, initially at least, to sales managers of firms in your area. The manufacturer has told you that salespeople-customers like the containers for three main reasons: (1) they help them keep files, catalogues, price lists, and the like orderly, (2) are handy to reach in their cars, and (3) are so well constructed and durable that they will last for years. Before getting the Trav-L-File most of these customers apparently used cardboard or wooden boxes or heavy metal trays.

The Trav-L-File is made of the same tough plastic used in American-style football helmets. A special feature is a see-through corner with easy access to the inside. Your price schedule is

1–9	$21.95 apiece
10–24	20.95 apiece
25–49	18.95 apiece
50 or more	16.96 apiece

An 18 in. × 15 in. × 11 in. version, for legal-size material, is available for the same price. Customers can order the files in any of four colors (gray, brown, blue, or red). A customer's logo/message will be imprinted free on each file for orders over 50 or for a $50.00 fee for orders less than 50.

Questions for Written Reports or Class Discussion

1.   What type of presentation would you develop to sell this product face-to-face to sales managers: canned, planned, automated, or survey-proposal? Explain.

2.   How do you plan to answer these three questions that you know will be in the back of any prospect's mind: "What's in it for me?" "Why change?" "Why should I buy your product now?"

3.   How can you most convincingly demonstrate the benefits a salesperson will gain by owning a Trav-L-File?

4.   List four positive "picture-building" words that you would use to illustrate and dramatize Trav-L-File features and benefits. At what point in the presentation could they be used most effectively?

How can Barry Cummings prevent another misunderstanding of the spoken word "production" from spoiling tomorrow's sale?

Barry Cummings is unhappy! He sells expensive machine tools and lost a sale last week that hurt. He had tried hard to show that his Z-Type machine would cost less to operate for the same production than his prospect's currently used machine. But his prospect had kept insisting that he was getting all the production he wanted out of his machine, and didn't see any need or reason to buy a new one.

Barry has an appointment with another prospect tomorrow and expects to face the same problem. As he goes over the key points of his upcoming planned presentation, he suddenly thinks to himself: "I wonder if I lost that sale last week because the prospect and I each attached different meanings to the word *production*? Actually, what I meant was that my machine offers equal *production* (total machine output) to his, and better *productivity* (output by the machine by person-hour and other costs). We both kept saying only production!"

"At what point of my presentation shall I anticipate this probable question or objection," Barry now asks himself, "and how can I make it verbally clearer than I did last week?"

Question for Class Discussion or Written Report

What would you advise Barry to say during tomorrow's interview to avoid last week's semantic misunderstanding, and at what point during the presentation should he say it?

PART THREE

Working the Plan: Steps in the Selling Process

Part Three of our book takes us through the second half of that simple but vital secret for success in personal selling, "Plan your work—work your plan." Our concentration is on the second two of the important four management functions (or stages) presented in Chapter 2—*executing* and *controlling*.

These are intertwined as we focus our attention on how to go about making a face-to-face sales presentation with a prospect. Our aim is to present the logical, progressive steps of a well-organized, basic planned presentation that will

lead to maximum sales success in all types of selling.

Along the way we consider the strategies, tactics, continuity, and controls necessary to achieve success. And we offer a wide range of principles, practices, and techniques which you can easily adapt to your own individual selling needs.

We start by looking over the shoulder of salesperson Bob Collins as he plans and executes a "real-life" complete sales presentation. Then we break that overview down into parts as represented by these chapter headings:

EXAMPLE OF A COMPLETE SALES PRESENTATION
How Bob Collins Sold a Cash Register to Mr. Alexander

Bob Collins is a successful young cash register salesperson for XYZ Company in a southern U.S. metropolitan area. His methods are based on an understanding of proven sales techniques developed by several big American office-machine companies which he has adapted to his specific product and local market needs. He has developed a planned sales presentation, following an A.I.D.A.-type sequence, based on persuasive logical and emotional key selling points built around the features, advantages, and benefits of his new-type cash register. In his planning, he has anticipated questions and objections he is likely to encounter, and is prepared to handle them easily while constantly working to a strong close that will motivate his prospect to buy.

Let us look over Bob's shoulder as he makes a cold call on Mr. Alexander, owner/manager of a prosperous, medium-sized fruit and vegetable market. As we follow him through the steps of a successful sales presentation, we will pay attention not only to how he goes about it, but also to why he does what he does at various stages.

PROSPECTING AND PREAPPROACH

In his sales territory Bob has some 1200 retail business concerns that use cash registers. They range from movie theaters to department stores to butcher shops. He normally plans his day's routing to work four blocks at a time methodically, making a cold-call approach to anyone he feels may use a cash register.

His normal weekly scheduling calls for making these approaches between 9 and 12 A.M. Monday through Thursday. Friday is for callbacks. He seldom makes calls between 12 and 2 P.M., since that is the busiest period of the day for retail businesses. He uses that time to scour his territory, prepare for presentations, and write reports. Late afternoons are reserved for callbacks by appointment.

Today, we find him approaching a fruit and vegetable business he has never called upon before. He stands just inside the front entrance for a moment—surveying the situation. Since no customers are at the check-out counter, he approaches a middle-aged man standing there inserting a new roll of paper into the cash register. Bob quickly notes that the register is a twenty-year-old XYZ machine no longer manufactured by his company.

APPROACH

Whether an XYZ machine or a competitor's cash register is currently being used, Bob likes to open with a service approach and talk about business systems rather than about cash registers. Since an XYZ machine is in use, he makes this approach:

Bob:	Good morning, sir. Are you the manager?
Prospect:	Yes, I own the place. Can I help you?
Bob:	I'm Bob Collins from XYZ Company. What is your name, sir?
Prospect:	Alexander is the name. What can I do for you?
Bob:	I see that you are using an XYZ machine. I'd like to ask you how it's working and if you are satisfied with the system and the service our company provides.
Mr. Alexander:	It works OK, so I hope you aren't going to try to sell me a new one!

Bob expected a stock reply such as this. He smiles, nods, and proceeds to get immediately into a common conversational ground with his prospect. His aim is to quickly get Mr. Alexander talking about his problems with himself as a sympathetic listener, while he guides and controls the interview.

He starts by asking a question of general interest. "How are the prices of tomatoes today?" Since Bob keeps up to date on general business conditions by reading various newspaper and market reports each evening after work, they are soon engaged in friendly chat about tomato prices and prices of one or two other visible items. Mr. Alexander relaxes, realizing that Bob is sincerely interested in and quite knowledgeable about such matters.

Bob quickly raises a key question to switch the conversation onto cash registers.

> Mr. Alexander, I've been able to help several businesses like yours to get better control over stock and money than they had before. If there were a system that could give you this control and if it were a good buy, would you want to know about it?

Bob realizes that his prospect may (1) say no at this point, but he does not plan to take no for an answer, (2) offer positive objections (which will represent difficulties to be overcome), or (3) advance negative objections (which probably will not represent real objections).

Mr. Alexander:	I suppose you want to try to sell me a new XYZ machine! What would it cost me—several thousand dollars?

Bob feels this retort is a trap, and he does not intend at this point to talk either about XYZ cash register or price. He answers instead:

> Well, I don't know whether you do need a new one, because I don't know anything about your business or the way you handle money. May we take half an hour now or later at your convenience to talk about how you handle your stock and your money (the two greatest problems of any retail business)?

Securing agreement to carry out this survey will, in Bob's mind, qualify Mr. Alexander as a live prospect. He needs half an hour to do the survey properly and so will be happy to make an appointment to call back and do it at the prospect's leisure if he is too busy to do it at this time.

Mr. Alexander: Well, I'm not too busy right now. What is it that you would like to know?

Bob's unobtrusive survey questioning begins with this lead-in:

Mr. Alexander, I'm going to ask confidential questions as a doctor does, but I assure you that whatever you say will go no further.

Bob then asks a series of indirect questions about how Mr. Alexander handles his stock and money, after asking permission to take a few notes along the way. Once his survey is completed, he asks his prospect if he can think it over carefully and put it in the form of a letter proposal to be presented at another meeting the next afternoon. Having nothing to lose at this point, and sensing that Bob is sincere about trying to help him, Mr. Alexander agrees to their meeting the following day at 2:15 P.M. Bob departs.

That evening, Bob studies the problem and then writes a letter to Mr. Alexander, stressing possible losses that could be suffered now or later as a result of the outdated system currently being used. The psychological theme he builds around is fear of loss. The weaknesses and probable loss points built into the letter are based on facts and figures obtained or shown during the survey.

As a conclusion to this letter, in order to arouse interest, Bob writes:

XYZ would be pleased to demonstrate to you a system that will overcome the weaknesses in your present system as described in this letter. We feel this system will place you in the position of knowing whether you are getting all the money possible for the goods and services you sell.

CREATING INTEREST

The following day, at the appointed time, Bob again meets with Mr. Alexander. He reads his letter point by point to secure his prospect's agreement that these weaknesses exist in his present system. Bob secures agreement by asking, after reading each point, a question such as: "Do you agree that this is a real weakness that could cause loss?"

Bob realizes that his prospect will not agree to every point and is quite prepared to concede that some points are not real problems. He is most interested—as he watches his prospect's facial expression and movements and listens to his words—in which point or points seem to the prospect to be his real or imagined weaknesses or fears. Bob knows that what he thinks is unimportant; what the prospect thinks or feels is what counts.

Bob's plan is to try to sell the highest-priced system he feels will be best for the prospect; he will work down to a less expensive one only if he has to. Since both XYZ Company and Bob personally are highly ethical in their customer problem-solving sales approach, they do not believe in either overselling or underselling. Bob sincerely wants to demonstrate the best system for his prospect's needs. He knows that in some cases he may be able to oversell but that the truth—that the system is too much and too expensive for the prospect's needs—will sooner or later emerge. Even if the prospect never knows, Bob will. And since he is a salesperson of high personal integrity, doing the right thing for his customer is important to him.

AROUSING DESIRE AND SECURING CONVICTION

Having read the letter aloud, including the final paragraph noted earlier, Bob then asks, and secures agreement to his question:

> I have a new XYZ cash register in my car. May I bring it right in now and demonstrate its features to you?

After bringing the machine in and setting it up for operation on the checkout counter, Bob goes into a planned-presentation demonstration of the machine itself. For this demonstration, he has carefully studied all the important technical features of the machine and has mentally keyed important features to demonstrations on or with the machine.

He does not cover every point—only those which seem of greatest interest to his prospect. Since he has studied this part of his demonstration carefully, he does not have any trouble integrating just those features of greatest interest into his smooth-flowing presentation. He also knows the advantages offered by his machine versus its leading competitor, and is prepared to point these out if Mr. Alexander raises the issue. In this case, since his prospect has been using an XYZ machine for years, Bob does not raise the issue himself.

Throughout his demonstration, he urges Mr. Alexander to use the machine himself where applicable at key points. After each, he asks a "yes-building" question such as "Isn't that a handy feature?" "Isn't that step easier than doing it on your present machine?" By stressing benefits, Bob continues to hold his prospect's interest. As he responds favorably to these minor-point, easy-to-answer questions (which don't commit him to buy), Mr. Alexander's interest begins to turn from interest to desire, to conviction. Halfway through this demonstration, Mr. Alexander suddenly asks: "Over what period of time could I pay for this machine, in case I decide to buy it?"

At any point throughout the interview Bob realizes that a statement of interest, a look, or a gesture may represent a "buying-signal" which indicates that his prospect may be ready to buy.

CLOSING THE SALE

Bob immediately recognizes this question as a buying-signal, and goes immediately into a trial close by saying: "Assuming I can set payments up to your satisfaction, I could install it next Monday, or Thursday. Which day would be most convenient for you?" (a closing technique built around a minor point of "which day," rather than asking outright if he wants to buy). Mr. Alexander's reply is this, "Well, the sooner the better—Monday is OK. But first, let's hear what it costs, and over how many months can I stretch payments!" Bob, realizing that the sale is basically closed, now, for the first time, places the XYZ Company formal printed purchase agreement and guarantee on the checkout counter. Ballpoint pen in hand, he goes over it point by point (but quickly) with Mr. Alexander, and answers his questions. He points out that while the cost is $2000, he can offer a special 10 percent allowance if full payment is made within 90 days. Mr. Alexander looks interested, so Bob hands him his pen, points to an X-marked signature line on the agreement, and says, "If that saving appeals to you, Mr. Alexander, just jot your name down here on this line, and I'll get to work arranging Monday's installation for you." Mr. Alexander signs the purchase agreement. Bob thanks him warmly for his order and departs shortly after promising to personally make this installation.

FOLLOW-UP AND FOLLOW-THROUGH

The following Monday, after personally installing the new machine, Bob once again fully demonstrates use of the machine to Mr. Alexander and to another employee who frequently relieves him at the checkout counter. Then, for the next four days, at the end of his own day's work, Bob calls by to answer any questions and to help Mr. Alexander do the daily summary record. In this way, he makes certain that the new register is operating properly and that Mr. Alexander is fully satisfied with his new purchase.

On the last of these four follow-up calls, realizing Mr. Alexander is quite pleased with his new purchase, Bob asks him if he has any other business-owner friends who might be interested in a similar system. Mr. Alexander willingly gives him the name and phone number of a cousin of his who owns a nearby restaurant. He also readily agrees that Bob is free to use his name as an introduction (an excellent referral lead).

We will leave Bob now, knowing that he also plans to continue calling back on Mr. Alexander once a week for ten to fifteen minutes over the next three weeks just to see how the system is working and to let his new customer know of his appreciation for and continued interest in the sale. There is an incentive for Bob to make these callbacks. The XYZ purchase agreement calls for a 10 percent deposit, with the balance within 90 days of delivery. Since Bob is on a draw-against-commission compensation agreement, any commission paid out against such a sale can be charged back if the customer becomes dissatisfied and refuses to pay within the 90-day period. He will also lose quota points for additional commission if the customer pays after the 90 days. Thus he plans his follow-up calls to ensure customer satisfaction and prompt payment.

The Approach: The Important First Few Minutes of the Presentation Interview

After studying this chapter, you will be able to:

Describe the purpose of the approach phase of the sales presentation interview, and give its three component parts.

Explain how much time is normally devoted to the approach phase and cite what two subphases it is broken into with regard to objectives and time.

Identify the two basic structured approach methods presented.

Summarize four basic points to be covered in any type of approach.

Describe 20 basic approaches suitable for use in a wide range of sales situations.

Summarize some basic principles and practical techniques of overcoming any fear or tension new salespeople might feel.

Describe six different personality types a salesperson might meet on any given day, and some practical, psychologically sound methods for warming up and relaxing each type.

You are now face-to-face with your prospect—ready for the opening words of the presentation interview. Hours (or perhaps days or weeks) of careful research, organization, and planning have led up to this moment. Even if the presentation interview is a cold call that may be concluded within a few minutes, every action and spoken word is the result of cumulative planning, preparation, and experience.

You may spend the next 15 minutes—the average interview time in many types of selling—or longer with your prospect, depending on the situation, what you are presenting, and his or her interest in what you are proposing. The amount of time you spend is relatively unimportant; what you accomplish counts.

For many salespeople, especially those selling a single product or service house to house or office to office, the presentation is an all-or-nothing process. They close the sale or do not. They apparently don't believe in the value of, or feel they can afford the time for, a callback or second try.

Some products or services do not lend themselves to a close on the first presentation call. The product may be left for a trial period, or further study may be necessary before an intelligent purchasing decision can be made. In some cases you may not effect a final close or even expect it until the third or fourth callback. Some salespeople do not even try for a close on the first call and tell the prospect in the beginning that they are not trying to sell anything. They use this technique to disarm the prospect, to gain his or her confidence, and to develop their sales story before making a final close.

Regardless of whether you try to close the sale at this interview or merely sell the first stage in a planned multi-interview sequence, a sale of some sort is made. Either the prospect sells you on the idea that he or she is not interested or will not buy now or later, or you sell him or her on buying now or allowing you a follow-up opportunity.

The way the interview goes depends largely on what you do and say during the first few seconds and minutes. This important first part of the presentation is called in sales terminology the *approach phase*. Before we discuss it however, let us consider what the ideal sales interview is like.

THE IDEAL SALES INTERVIEW

In the ideal presentation interview you and your prospect sit down face to face for an uninterrupted, relaxed, informal, conversational discussion. You immediately like and respect each other; the prospect is interested in your proposal and senses that you are trying to solve one or more of his or her problems or to offer a benefit.

Through questioning, you find out what those problems or wants are and persuasively explain verbally and with demonstration and proof (if possible) how your product or service will accomplish what he or she wants or needs. You answer your prospect's questions, handle objections, and ask for the order. The whole procedure is relaxed and easy, and you spend more time listening attentively than talking. Once the sale is made, you each have a warm feeling: your prospect is pleased with the benefits you have brought, and you are pleased not only with the sale, but also with being able to help.

Many sales are made just that easily. Many professional salespeople, in fact, say that their biggest sales are often their easiest. Most sales situations, however, are more involved, uncertain, and difficult than is the ideal one we have described. While your professional aim should be to work toward this ideal in every sales interview, you should realize that only careful study, planning, and practice will make it an easy process for you.

WHAT IS THE APPROACH PHASE OF THE SALES INTERVIEW?

The complete sales presentation, as outlined in Chapter 6, is a smooth-flowing, integrated, four-step process. More or less time may be spent on the individual steps, depending on how the interview goes, but all the steps are included.

The approach phase, aimed at gaining and holding attention, is the first of these steps. It has three parts:

1. Introduce yourself so that prospects feel it will be worth their valuable time to talk to you.
2. Sell yourself, your product, and your company or organization, in that order.
3. Get and hold prospects' attention and interest so that they will willingly give you information. From it you can determine their needs, wants, or problems, around which you later present advantages of your product or service in terms of benefits.

Many salespeople consider the approach phase the most important part of the interview. For new salespeople this opening step is often as difficult as closing the sale. It involves making a sale within the sale—selling yourself and the interview! Unless you accomplish this presale successfully, your prospect may brush you off before hearing your full story.

How Long Does the Approach Phase Last?

The approach phase covers the first few (usually less than five) minutes of the presentation interview. You should know exactly what you are going to do and say during this period. Plan and rehearse your opening remarks so that you can deliver them positively and confidently without thinking.

Your aims are to get down to essentials quickly, but not abruptly, and to control the interview from the start. The approach divides into these two phases.

1. *The first five seconds of the interview.* During this time your prospects decide that they will see you and will hear your story.

2. *The balance of approach time necessary to obtain your objectives.* During this time you establish rapport, briefly introduce yourself, your company, your product or service; ask questions and get the prospects to tell you their problems or needs.

What Do Prospects See?

What prospects see during this entire period, especially during the first five seconds, when they size you up, may be equally as important as what they hear. Most salespeople take a minute to consider, just prior to the interview, how they will look to prospects from their side of the desk as well as what they will say in their opening remarks.

Many individuals pride themselves on being able to size other people up within a few seconds of meeting them. Most experienced salespeople realize you cannot intelligently judge another person that quickly, but your prospect may not realize it. You have to assume that they may make their minds up about you in the first five seconds.

We touched on this first five-second problem in the preceding chapter by discussing its importance in initial meetings with receptionists, secretaries, assistants, or subordinates, as well as with the prospect. We concluded that they chiefly observe your appearance and your manner (that is, air of confidence and sincerity). Let us now add mannerisms to these other two characteristics and give some further consideration to what positive or negative impressions your prospects may have as they observe you throughout the interview and especially in the beginning. We can do this most easily by considering some dos and dont's suggested by professional salespeople (see Table 8.1). These comments come from many sources, and many, we suspect, were learned the hard way!

Many of these points are so self-evident that they hardly seem worth mentioning, yet salespeople who fail to heed them lose sales daily. In order to command respect and attention, you have to deserve it. If you do not look the part of a successful businessperson, you will not be able to command the respect of successful businesspersons. Gear your grooming to the prospect being called upon; what he or she considers appropriate counts.

But careful grooming alone will not impress a prospect; you have to be mentally and physically fit as well if you expect a favorable reaction to your approach. If you have a heavy cold or a hangover or if your entrance is a shuffling gait and your handshake limp, you are bound to give an unfavorable impression that will spoil your chances of success.

Many sales are also lost because the prospect becomes annoyed at some irritating mannerism of the salesperson. Most of these, such as slouching when seated, failing to look the prospect in the eye, and ear-pulling or chin-rubbing, are due to nervousness. Because you cannot see yourself as other people do, you may be unaware that you have these mannerisms. The best way to check is to have a friend, spouse, or fellow salesperson listen to a demonstration presentation and tell you of any such irritating mannerisms. Once you become aware of them, you can usually easily overcome them.

TABLE 8.1

Do's	Don'ts
Appearance	
Take your cue from the type of prospects you call upon. Wear the kind of clothing they wear and you will look right to them.	Avoid colors or patterns that clash.
Manner	
Be enthusiastic; look your prospect in the eye.	Avoid appearing overfriendly or unbusinesslike.
Bear yourself with dignity and composure.	Avoid showing impatience, even if you feel impatient.
Appear relaxed, poised, at ease, and confident.	Do not interrupt, contradict, or argue with your prospect.
Be an attentive listener.	Do not speak disrespectfully of your employer or of friends or business acquaintances of the prospect.
Mannerisms	
Develop the habit of repeating the prospect's name often.	Avoid both bone-crushing and wishy-washy handshakes.
Show, by your words and actions, appreciation for his or her time.	Do not smoke without your prospect's permission, or nod continuously.
Show genuine warmth in your smile.	Do not rub your chin, tap your toes, or toy with watch, chin, fingers, etc.
Stand and sit up straight; be businesslike.	Do not slouch or give the appearance of timidity or uncertainty.

Your Approach Must Gain and Hold Attention

Some professional salespeople feel that the first sentence uttered in the prospect's presence is the most important of the entire presentation. A good idea, expressed in those opening words, can capture the prospect's imagination, interest, and attention.

These opening words are vitally important because your immediate task is to sell the interview itself. If you accomplish this initial sale within a sale, then the prospect is ready to hear your full presentation.

Ways to create interest are to smile, because it eases tension, and to use your voice in a pleasant, conversational manner that sounds positive and impressive. An inexperienced salesperson often talks nervously and rapidly in initial approaches. This mistake creates a bad impression.

Introducing Yourself, Your Product, and Your Company

You should spend time devising a proper approach, carefully designed for the specific prospect and interview situation. It is an insult to open with such phrases as "I was just passing by" or "I apologize for taking your time." Each call must be a planned occasion.

Plan your approach to accomplish these objectives:

Be different.
Gain your prospect's undivided attention.
Avoid a "No, thank you, not today."

To accomplish these goals, you can structure your approach in one or two basic ways: (1) a natural introduction, followed by one of several basic approaches fitted to the particular call; or (2) a lead-in, attention-getting opening sentence, followed by the introduction of yourself, your product, and your company. The following examples help illustrate their differences; 20 practical variations of these basic approaches are outlined shortly.

Example 1

> Good morning, Mr. Halvorsen. I am Arch Layman from Arco Products Corporation, here to inquire whether you have seen a demonstration of our new AK model office duplicator. X-Ray Products Corp., just down the road from you, has found it cuts their duplicating costs 25 percent. Would you be interested in effecting such savings?

Example 2

> Mr. Halvorsen, your friend Pierrette Laverdure, purchasing officer at X-Ray Products Corp., down the road, suggested I ask whether you would like to see a demonstration of our new AK model office duplicator. It cut their duplicating costs 25 percent. I am Arch Layman from Arco Products Corp. May I have the opportunity to demonstrate how our machine may effect similar savings for your company?

The introduction of yourself and your company normally comes first. You should stand erect, speak clearly and confidently, and smile with warmth while looking your prospect in the eye. Do not shake hands unless he or she extends a hand first. Do not be seated until asked to do so; although if he or she does not do so shortly, as a means of controlling the interview you may suggest, "Do you mind if we sit down so that I can answer any questions with visual material from my presentation kit?"

Normally, you also state the purpose of your visit, mentioning briefly your product or service. In some cases, especially in specialty selling, it is desirable to avoid mentioning the product as long as possible. This technique is not trickery; the purpose is to prove that a need exists, and then to show how your proposal can satisfy that need. In most sales situations, however, the honest, sincere, straightforward approach—a complete introduction and a brief explanation of the purpose of your call—brings best results.

The introduction should be a cheerful, natural one, based on your positive mental assumption that you are glad to meet the prospect and have something of value to offer. You are, in effect, a guest in a place of business or home and want to get down to matters of specific interest as soon as possible.

When to Present the Business Card

When to present the business card is a problem that may come up during the approach phase of the interview. Salespeople are divided as to when it should be presented. Most of them, unless it has been sent in ahead through a secretary during a business call, tend to present it at the time of the introduction. Others however, prefer to present it only at the close of the interview.

For many, the problem is solved prior to the interview since they have presented their business card when requesting the interview appointment, either by letter or in person. When to present the business card may depend to a large extent on the type of selling you do, the individual interview situation, your company or organization's policy, or personal choice. Some salespeople even present their business cards twice at each interview—one at the beginning, another as they prepare to depart. Their hope is that perhaps their prospect will pass the second one along to an associate or personal friend who might in turn develop into a prospect.

Twenty Useful, Basic Approaches

Here are 20 basic approaches that may be useful to you. Explained and illustrated by example, they are attention-getting, interest-arousing techniques adaptable to a wide range of sales situations. They can easily be adapted to fit any of the following common buying motives that account for most sales:

- Ease and convenience
- Profit and thrift
- Safety and protection
- Sex and romance

- Adventure and Excitement
- Play and relaxation
- Pride and prestige
- Love and affection

Any good approach should contain (1) a positive opening, (2) a benefit for the prospect, (3) something to arouse curiosity, and (4) assurance that you are not wasting the prospect's time. For example:

> Good morning, Mr. Kim! I've got a proposal that can double your profit on every item that you sell. However, I know you're a busy person, so if I'm here over ten minutes it will be because you insist.

Use of dramatic devices or showmanship to show as well as tell can be highly effective when used in combination with the verbal approach, as some of the following approach examples illustrate.

1. *Benefit approach.* You can open the interview with a statement or a question that focuses the prospect's thoughts directly on the benefits your proposal offers. When using this approach, you must make sure that you are stating a real benefit and not just a smash opener that can easily be punctured. A benefit, when used as an approach, should meet the following requirements.

a. It should be one the prospect wants.

b. It should be thoroughly substantiated in the rest of the presentation.

c. It must be something that you can deliver in full.

d. It should be specific. A dollars-and-cents offer is more effective than a sweeping generality to get attention.

You may phrase the benefit as a question: "Mr. Ruiz, would a 15 percent saving on your present shipping costs interest you?" or as a statement: "Mr. Ruiz, I want to tell you about a new type of shipping service that will save you up to 15 percent on your present shipping costs."

2. *Curiosity approach.* An unexpected approach immediately arouses a prospect's interest and curiosity. Use of a question or a gadget, honestly and not as a trick, can often lead quickly to a warm reception.

Here is how one coffee vending-machine salesperson approaches his busy prospects—normally owners or managers of small offices or businesses: "Mrs. Melendes, how would you like an extra branch office that could earn you $69 a week without any extra work on your part?" He then explains that his vending company completely services the machine once a week and that its representative turns over a percentage of the coins collected at the time of servicing.

3. *Dramatic (or theatrical) approach.* Everyone loves a show, and an eye-opening, dramatic approach always arouses interest. It works best when you can get the prospect into the act, as this example shows!

> Dr. Boardman, our new shatterproof water tumblers may be just the thing for your church's kitchen and social hall. They won't break when dropped. Here, try it for yourself! Just hold it up over your head and drop it here on the hardest part of the floor. You see, it didn't break!

4. *Factual approach.* You can turn an interesting fact connected with the product or service you are offering into an opening appetizer sentence. The facts must be true and the sentence brief. Such an approach is usually followed by the introduction.

> Mrs. Steiner, did you know that over fifty companies in this state alone increased plant efficiency 20 percent within the past twelve months without adding new staff? They have done it, as this report shows, by instituting the new system of Rablaco Corp., which I represent.

5. *Idea approach.* Every businessperson is looking for helpful new ideas. If you can open with a good one, they will listen.

> I came up with an excellent new profit-making idea for you yesterday, Mr. Kashani; one that you could easily put to good use. Since it costs you nothing to listen, will you let me tell you about it?

6. *I-am-here-to-help-you-approach.* Few people can resist a confident, direct, enthusiastic offer to help. This approach can be quite effective if you follow the opening sentence with facts that prove your proposal can help them.

Mr. Chang, I am here to honestly see if I can help you cut your plant operating costs 30 percent with only a small initial investment on your part. In these days of mounting costs, that's an interesting offer, isn't it?

7. *Introductory approach.* This approach usually features a letter, card of introduction, or testimonial from a friend, customer, or business associate of the prospect. It can be used as a lead-in to the presentation, as follows:

Mr. Dupree, I am here at the suggestion of your friend Randy Woods of Maxwell Products, Inc. He felt you would be interested in our new E-Zee conveyor system, which cut his plant operating costs 20 percent the first month. Here is a note he sent you through me. He said it would serve as his introduction and endorsement.

8. *Mystery approach.* In the right circumstances, nothing earns attention quite like the dangling statement that leaves the listener eager to know more.

Here's a new development that will interest you. Ms. Rykowski; one that can help you in three different ways.

Once you've made such a statement, and caught the prospect's interest, you must, of course, be able to deliver—to tell about a *truly* new development and how it can help.

9. *News approach.* Newspaper stores or trade-journal articles often provide personalized information about your prospect or his or her situation. You can use this information to lead into a specific presentation. An insurance salesperson may use this approach.

Mr. Mustelier, I've just read some more bad news about Bigtown Department Store, which burned down yesterday. The insurance covered only three-fourths of the damage. It's a warning to us all. May I go over your firm's present coverage with you, just to make sure you are protected 100 percent?

10. *Opinion approach.* This disarmingly effective yet simple approach immediately focuses attention on your product and makes the prospect a participant in your presentation. The idea is simply to show your product, give an example of what it can do, or just provide an illustration of it, and ask, "Mr. Hudson, what is your honest opinion of this?" or "Mrs. Calissi, I would like your honest opinion as to whether this would be of benefit to you." If the prospect hesitates, you may suggest moving over to see it under better light or may hold it up at another angle for better display.

11. *Premium (or gift-giving) approach.* Because everyone likes to get something for nothing, few prospects turn down a free gift or sample. By accepting it, they usually feel obliged to hear your presentation. The more interesting or unusual the gift, the warmer the atmosphere for the interview. The gift itself should tie in with what you are selling. For example:

Mr. Szvetics, here is a little complimentary present for you. It is intended merely as a goodwill gesture and a way of saying thank you for the time and courtesy you are extending in seeing me today.

12. *Problem-solving approach.* Most prospects are interested in ideas that help them solve their problems. The more you know about specific problems the better, but you can also aim the approach at solving common problems, as this example points out.

> Mr. Ristoli, your company, like others in your industry, can cut carton-banding labor time 50 percent and costs 15 percent by using our new tape-binding process instead of your older wire-banding machine. Would you like to know how it can be done?

13. *Praise (or compliment) approach.* Honest praise or compliments are usually very well received. False praise or flattery is not. If you notice something on the prospect's office wall or desk or home that may be a source of pride, you can often use it as part of your approach.

> Mr. Tarasenko, may I ask what kind of sailboat that is in the picture on the wall behind you? Are you a sailing enthusiast?
>
> Ms. Rodgers, do you mind if I compliment you on the orderly appearance of your desk? I know how busy you are, so it must mean that you have an unusual ability to manage your time and paperwork.

14. *Product (or exhibit) approach.* Many small and eye-catching items sell themselves. People like to see, feel, hear, taste, and smell things for themselves. This approach simply involves handing the item to the prospect and asking such questions as these: "Did you ever see anything more beautifully designed than this?" "Did you ever see a wristwatch with a built-in alarm system like this?"

15. *Question (or probing) approach.* This approach normally consists of giving an interesting fact about what you are offering, framed as a question. The question should be simple and noncontroversial and should call for a reply to stimulate the prospect's participation in the sales presentation to follow.

    This approach is more flexible than most, since there are four basic types of questions that can be used. These include: (1) direct, (2) nondirective, (3) rephrasing, and (4) redirect questions—as illustrated by the following explanations and examples:

    - *Direct questions* should be phrased so as to elicit either a "yes" response or specific, positive short answers from a prospect, such as: "Would you like to cut your operating costs 20 percent next year, Mr. Watson?" "If I can show you a way to cut your next year's company phone bill 20 percent, how many dollars would that save you?"
    - *Nondirective (or open-ended) questions,* starting with words like who, what, when, where, and how help gets prospects talking about themselves and their needs, as these examples illustrate: "How many times a week could you use this item?" "Who else in your office could use this product?"
    - *Rephrasing questions* help clarify statements by the prospect and better determine the prospect's needs or interest. They can be used

in this way: "Are you saying that if we can deliver to you by June 1, you are ready to consider our proposal?"

- ■ *Redirect (to direct again) questions* are helpful in moving conflicting views between salesperson and prospect to a more mutually agreeable positive or neutral level of communication. For example, if your prospect says, "I am sorry, but we don't plan to change suppliers now," you as salesperson might use this redirective question to keep the conversation open: "Right, but can we agree that if another supplier can offer you equal service at lower cost it makes good business sense to make comparisons?"

16. *Referral (or third party) approach.* If you've been referred to the prospect by someone he or she knows, mention the name of that person right away.

> Michael Galloway, over at White Brothers, thought you might be interested in this new item of ours, Mr. Jackson.

17. *Service approach.* Who can resist the appeal of having someone else do some of their work for them or relieve them of responsibility or worry? Offers that promise these services, especially at lower or similar cost, have wide appeal, as the two following examples illustrate.

> Dr. Comer, wouldn't you and your wife like to be completely free of fuel or unit-breakdown heating worries this winter? My firm keeps your oil tank full and guarantees free emergency unit-breakdown repairs day or night. All we ask is that you buy your fuel from us at normal rates. Can you beat a service offer like that?
>
> Mrs. Cancio, our laundry van will call at your door every Tuesday morning whether you have anything to send out or not. Anything picked up will be delivered the following afternoon. Our charges are reasonable, as this list shows. All we ask is that you agree to sign up as one of our regular customers.

18. *Shock approach.* A mild form of shock can be effectively used in many types of selling. Insurance salespeople and memorial park counselors often employ a form that runs like this:

> Mr. and Mrs. Kuhnert, as we sit here together talking seriously about that one fact of life from which there is no escape, do you realize that in nine cases out of ten the American husband passes away before his wife? Are you prepared for such a tragic possibility in your family? Don't you agree that now is the time to think about it—to lay rational plans—while you are both here together in good health?

19. *Startling-statement approach.* This rarely fails to attract attention—and puts you well on the road to the sale if you can back it up.

> Mr. Lorinzo, I've discovered you've been losing up to 20 percent sales volume. Fortunately, I can suggest a way to help you recoup.

20. *Survey approach.* This approach can be used in several ways. Survey approaches, for example, are commonly used in business and industrial selling when study of a complex internal system or operation is necessary before an intelligent sales proposal can be made. Executives know that solving their problems involves study, and they normally pay attention to the salesperson who takes the time to survey in advance and to plan a specific presentation tailored to their needs. This is problem-solving selling at its best.

Another approach involves the presentation by a salesperson of public-record industry or governmental survey or statistical information that might apply to a prospect's given situation. For example:

> A recent government study shows that our XYZ product ranks first in long-term reliability. Would you like to see the report?"

Some unscrupulous salespeople, especially those in direct sales, have used surveys as pretexts to get in to see prospects. People naturally resent such trickery. The direct "I am making a survey" approach works best as a legitimate activity for qualifying prospects and as a basis for making an appointment to call back later to give the presentation.

A door-to-door encyclopedia salesperson, for example, may use an honest survey approach in this fashion when making cold calls in a neighborhood: "Good morning, madam. I represent XYZ Encyclopedia Company, and I'm making a personal survey of your neighborhood to find out how many families have an up-to-date reference encyclopedia in their homes for their children. Do you have one?" The reply may be, "No, we don't have an encyclopedia, since our children are not yet in school," or "Yes, we have a set, but it's not very up-to-date." Whatever the answer, the salesperson has qualified the prospect and can try for a callback appointment if it seems worthwhile. When one is making this type of approach, care must be taken that it is legally correct. Legal and ethical issues involved in such approaches are discussed in Chapter 16.

OVERCOMING SALES APPROACH FEAR AND TENSION

It is easy to write about how to make a proper approach and what to say in your opening remarks. It is much more difficult to write about how to reduce the tension and even fear that new salespeople often experience when knocking on strange doors, meeting people in unaccustomed surroundings, confronting different personality types, and always facing the unexpected. Many experienced salespeople, like actors and actresses, are still tense as they go into important interviews. This problem is a common one, worth more attention than most of the sales literature pays it.

A certain element of tension is normally present when salesperson and prospect meet each other for the first time. You as a salesperson are facing the unknown; the prospect may be on the defensive against salespeople in general, and you are each sizing one another up.

The burden is on you to be confident in appearance, manner, speech, attitude, and bearing in order to reduce the tension and to sell yourself and the interview. This task is not easy if you feel apprehensive. Just remember that thousands of salespeople face this same fear daily and steel themselves to overcome it.

Are You Afraid To Make This Sales Call?

One of the greatest single reasons for failure in selling is the salesperson's thinking, "I just can't get up the nerve to make the next call." It is easy to make excuses—to feel sick, to decide to have a cup of coffee instead, to postpone the call if at all possible. Many potentially excellent salespeople quit the selling game before they master this fear of the approach.

Do not be alarmed if you have this feeling of timidity, apprehension, or fear. Modern selling requires a perceptive, sensitive person. If you feel bashful and timid, it may be a good sign, because you can understand and sense that your prospect may have similar fears.

Once you face this problem, it is best to tackle it head on. Turn on your will power and tell yourself that you will do it! Then switch your thoughts to your prospect, imagining that he or she has your fears and that your tasks are to relax him or her and to communicate that you sincerely want to like and help.

Practical Ways to Overcome Fear and Tension

Practical ways to overcome fear include making practice calls in which you work only on the approach and do not even try to sell anything. You may give away a few samples or small gifts that tie in with what you are selling. Just make the call saying, "Good morning, here is a small complimentary gift. It is a goodwill gesture from my company. My name is Russ Elfvin, the new salesperson for XYZ Company in your area." The point is not to sell anything. You can answer questions and even take orders, but do not try to sell. After a few such calls you should be able to meet future prospects without hesitation.

Another useful technique for overcoming fear is especially valuable, even for an experienced salesperson apprehensive about facing a tough buyer or a technical buyer whose questions he or she feels inadequate to answer. Pick the toughest, most difficult prospect in your territory and go after him or her. Lay siege to this prospect if necessary; think up and try every sales technique or device imaginable to sell him or her. Ask the help of your sales manager or a fellow salesperson in winning this person over.

Keep after this prospect until you succeed, remembering always that if he or she really needs or wants what you are offering, he or she has to buy it from someone. Why not you? You may fail in your initial attempts to sell such tough prospects, but once you succeed, your new feeling of confidence will enable you to enter all future interviews with assurance.

The way you look to yourself and to others can play an important part in reducing fear and tension. If you wear good, appropriate, successful-looking clothing, you tend to feel good and to be success-minded. If you look and feel good, you think positively and act with confidence. Your prospects see and feel this; their fear is eased; and they tend to accept you readily.

ESTABLISHING RAPPORT AND GETTING DOWN TO BUSINESS

Once you have made your opening remarks and the prospect has accepted you by indicating a desire to hear more, here is your next task:

1. Establish rapport quickly so as to get the interview on as relaxed a basis as possible.
2. Get the prospect to willingly give you information that will help you determine any needs, wants, or problems.

While a certain amount of small talk may be necessary to ease tension and give you and your prospect a chance to relax, neither of you is there to visit. Your job is to get down to business, to get the prospect talking about his or her problems, and, as you listen carefully to what is being said, to try to determine his or her personality type.

The best way to get prospects talking is to ask a question that will also elicit some valuable information for you. Most planned sales approaches include at least one question within the first two minutes of the interview. Your questions and comments should also secure their agreement with what you are saying because you are trying to get them, from the start, in a "yes" frame of mind. Your "yes-building" introductory comments and questions may run something like these:

> *You:* Ms. Comerford, you certainly have a nice office; the view outside the window overlooking the pond is very relaxing.
>
> *Prospect:* Yes, it is a nice view.
>
> *You:* But I am sure that a busy person like you doesn't have much time to sit around enjoying it.
>
> *Prospect:* Yes, you are certainly right there.
>
> *You:* It would be nice of some magic machine could do all your paperwork in half the time, wouldn't it?
>
> *Prospect:* Yes, but I'm afraid I'll be out of this world before they ever invent magic machines.
>
> *You:* Well, Ms. Comerford, it may surprise you to know that a wonderful new recording and memory-storing device can help busy people like

you cut their routine paperwork in half. Are you interested in a time-saver like that?

Prospect: Yes.

Continue in this manner throughout the interview, changing the pace, but yes-building all the time.

BUILDING AN ATMOSPHERE OF WARMTH AND CONFIDENCE

In order to get your prospects talking about themselves and their problems, you must hasten to create an atmosphere of warmth and confidence. As has been noted, along with hearing your opening words, they are visually sizing you up. Just as they are sizing you up, so too are you sizing them up—to find out what type of people they are so you can quickly lead in creating the necessary atmosphere of warmth and easy communication.

What if you suddenly discover that the stranger-prospect you are facing is *not* the warm, friendly, happy-to-hear-you-out "ideal type" we have more or less pictured up to now in our approach-phase discussion? What if he or she appears indifferent, cold, or even somewhat hostile? How can one quickly establish a bond of warmth and confidence with perfect strangers of different personality types?

People study is a fascinating hobby and a never-ending source of enjoyment for a good salesperson. Unless you sincerely like people, you probably would not have considered selling as a career. But merely liking your fellow human beings does not necessarily lead to sales success. Simply knowing different types of sales approaches, such as those just considered, is not enough. You must develop the flexibility to approach each prospect according to his or her individual personality and feelings of the moment, and quickly employ the type of approach you sense best fits the situation. This ability comes with practice.

We will discuss different individual prospect temperaments and how to handle them at some length in subsequent chapters, especially in Chapter 9. For now, as conclusion to our study of the approach phase of the presentation interview, let us introduce the subject by considering briefly six different personality types that you may encounter during any given day.

Warm, But Will Not be Pinned Down.   The person sincerely enjoys your visit as a break in routine. He or she would rather chat about weather, local sensational news items, or the international situation than about business problems. Unless you are careful, his or her interview time will run out before you get around to your presentation.

Cold.   This person listens to your story without warmth or emotion and gives you a cold, but polite, "I don't think I am interested."

Indifferent.   This person's attention may wander; he or she may ask completely irrelevant questions, may turn to work on the desk when talking, or may make phone calls in your presence.

Warm.   A friendly, warm reception that encourages your presentation and usually leads to a sale.

Hard.   This prospect may want what you are offering but may challenge or bait you all the way, often leaving you mentally and emotionally exhausted whether you make the sale or not.

Unpleasant.   Possibly even rude, this person could not care less about you or your product. He or she just is not interested in hearing you out.

The first practical step you can take to face these different personality types is to realize that you and every other salesperson has to take the bitter with the sweet. Then you can relax and start planning how you can meet and win over whatever personality type is next thrown in your path.

If you accept warming prospects up and winning them over as a challenge, you can continue to face even a series of hard prospects cheerfully. Just do not take the hard encounters personally. Try to make a game out of winning over all the different personality types; relax and enjoy it.

Here are some laws of human nature—of getting along with or handling people—that will help you rise to the challenge. Some have already been considered; all are powerful psychological weapons for you if used sincerely.

- Smile warmly and often.
- Call the person by name.
- Show genuine interest.
- Be a good listener.

- Sympathize with problems.
- Show respect.
- Make the prospect feel important.
- Use often those magic words: thank you and please.

Your basic aim during the approach phase has been to quickly gain and hold your prospect's attention and interest so that he or she will willingly give you information. From this you will determine needs and wants, around which you will present your product in terms of benefits to your prospect. From here we move, in our next chapter, into a consideration of how to further create and hold the interest you have aroused during these opening seconds and minutes of the interview.

SUMMARY

In this chapter we have concentrated on the proper approach to use in calling on a new prospect. In many types of selling the job is not complete until after the third or fourth call, but such follow-up calls are built on the results obtained in the initial call.

The purpose of the approach is to gain and hold attention. It should be carefully planned and executed, because successful accomplishment of this sale within a sale is often as difficult for new salespeople as is the final close. Lasting from the first two to five minutes of the interview, the approach phase breaks down into (1) the first five seconds and (2) the balance of approach time necessary to gain your objectives. These objectives are to sell yourself, your product or service, and your firm or organization, in that order—and to avoid being brushed off.

We discussed the importance of creating a good first impression and of encouraging prospects to accept you with confidence so that they will tell you their problems, wants, or needs and hear you out. We stressed that your appearance and manner are equally as important as what you say.

We covered many specific approaches and approach techniques. We discussed the fear and tension commonly felt by new and sometimes even by experienced salespeople and how to overcome them. And we noted practical ways through which the prospect can also be relaxed and encouraged to talk and by which a warm interview situation can be quickly established.

Questions For Analysis and Discussion

1.   How long does the approach phase of the sales presentation interview last, and into what two subdivisions is it broken?

2.   What do prospects inwardly see and judge a salesperson on during the first five seconds of the interview?

3.   What three purposes does one seek to achieve by using a planned, proper approach?

4.   Why are the opening words of the approach so important? In what two ways should they be structured?

5.   How would you describe two of the four requirements of a benefit as used in a benefit approach?

6.   How can you most easily determine if you unconsciously project some personal mannerisms, such as nervous finger drubbing, that a prospect might quickly notice and find irritating?

7.   In what two ways can you best structure a planned sales approach?

8.   What is generally considered the most effective technique for quickly getting prospects to start talking about themselves and their interests or problems during the approach phase of a sales interview?

You Are Asked to Head a Local Charitable Fund-Raising Drive—What's Your Best Approach?

Sooner or later during your lifetime, if active in most types of collegiate, charitable, community, sporting, or religious organizations, you will likely be asked to help raise money for some worthy project or cause. Especially if you are a business or organizational executive, or a successful salesperson, you may be asked to serve as chairperson or head of the group's next fund-raising drive. The aim of this case study is to help you approach that task properly.

Achieving success as an organizational fund raiser is no easy job, as anyone who has done it will tell you. Whether the amount you need to raise is $5000 or $5 million, most of the sales techniques employed, whether by letter, telephone, or one-on-one verbal presentations, will involve principles, practices, and techniques presented in this book. In order to help relate what you are studying to real-world applications, here are some tried-and-true fund raising methods as researched and presented by internationally acclaimed *Changing Times*, the Kiplinger Magazine.[1]

PLANNING AND ORGANIZATION—TWIN KEYS TO SUCCESS

Successful fund-raising drives, like military campaigns, begin with good planning and with well-trained people (volunteer or paid) who are thoroughly versed in the needs of the organization and convinced of the worthiness of its cause. Before making the first call or sending out the first letter, say the experts,

---

[1] This case study is based in large part on the article, "The Fine Art of Fund-Raising," *Changing Times*, The Kiplinger Magazine © 1988, The Kiplinger Washington Editors, Inc., August 1988. Used with permission.

make sure that the organizing committee follows these guidelines:

- *Set specific monetary (dollar) goals.* Fund-raising targets should honestly reflect how much the organization needs for on-going plans and special projects and the monetary amount that can realistically be raised. The best campaigns are run as a "continuing program" not as one-time or on-again, off-again affairs.

- *Provide your people with adequate information about how the donated money will be used.* Potential donors will ask about this, and every one of your fund-raisers must know the answers in order to be totally convincing.

- *Develop training and backup material for your fund-raisers.* Whether volunteers or paid staff, your people must be trained and shown how to make effective presentations that will produce contributions. They must be adequately informed about the donors they are to contact either in person or by phone. And they need to know the different kinds of donations you are after—cash, "in-kind" gifts of equipment or services, seed money, or challenge grants.

- *Draw up a campaign blueprint and timetable.* Outline the methods to be used—from personal solicitations to special events, such as a testimonial dinner or a golf tournament. Break jobs down to bite size and assign enough people to each. Establish dates for progress reports, follow-ups to actually collect the contributions, and a final tally. Devise ways to praise and reward your workers for their efforts.

- *Set aside seed money.* It takes money to raise money—at the very least for printing brochures, mailing letters, giving appreciation certificates (to volunteers), and paying hired staffers or researchers. For most types of fund-raising organizations, as a rule of thumb, costs may absorb around one-third of the fund goal in an ongoing campaign, possibly even more the first year or two. Only the largest and smallest of operations are usually able to keep costs below ten percent.

WHAT ARE YOUR BEST SOURCES (PROSPECTS) FOR CONTRIBUTIONS?

Prior and continuous ongoing research is necessary to uncover the most probable sources of charitable contributions. This is where they are usually found:

- Your organization's own members normally represent a secure, long-term source of financial support through dues, special gifts, bequests, and the like.
- In North America, contributions from business firms are the fastest-growing source of charitable or philanthropic contributions. In addition to cash, businesses may donate equipment and services, such as printing or office space, make low-or-no-interest loans, and encourage their employees to pariticipate in your organization's fund-raising campaign. Get names of businesses you might want to approach from local directories, chambers of commerce, and trade associations.
- Affinity groups, special interest groups, and family and corporate foundations often are interested in aiding specific kinds of causes. The latter usually have a set procedure by which your organization can apply for grants. In North America, check public libraries for *The Foundation Directory*, published each year.

WAYS TO RAISE THE DOUGH!

The most effective way to raise money, say the experts, is usually to ask for it one-on-one. But to assure greatest success, they add, it is necessary to prepare the groundwork carefully before the final presentation. As an example, the fund-raising director for United Way in a medium-size American city began her annual drive by first surveying the top 25 employers in the community to determine what fund-raising goals for their companies were realistic.

This strategy enabled her to get to know the chief executive officers of these major employers—and, equally important, their secretaries, before actually drafting her campaign plan. Once the drive began, it received enthusiastic support from these CEOs and their assistants who were duly credited publically for the fund drive's success.

Another way to raise big amounts is to hold or sponsor special events in which donors get something for their contributions—a rock concert, a tote bag, or simply a good time. Art shows, golf tournaments, testimonial dinners, marathons, car washes, or raffles for cars, TV sets, or bicycles are also popular fund-raisers. Direct mail solicitations can also be effective, especially for organizations with a broad base of potential supporters. But for best results, direct mail programs require professional advice, test runs, and a considerable up-front investment in printing, postage, and list rental.

Bookstores and public libraries worldwide offer many publications about fund-raising methods. Among them are these two books: Ted D. Bayley, *The Fund Raiser's Guide to Successful Campaigns* (McGraw-Hill), and Thomas G. Dunn, *How to Shake the New Money Tree* (Penguin Books).

Questions for Written Reports and Class Discussion

1. Why did the above-noted fund-raising director for United Way consider it as important to meet the secretaries to the chief executive officers of the 25 major employers in her community as to meet the CEOs themselves?

2. What two methods can a person, calling on a prospective contributor as a fund-raiser, employ to create interest without showing or demonstrating any physical objects?

3. Why, in your opinion, do fund-raising experts say that usually the most effective way to raise money is to ask for it on a one-to-one basis?

4. Describe five types of special events, other than those noted in the case study, that you feel could successfully serve as a community fund-raisers.

Sales Problem 8.1

What words can insurance salesperson Shirley Richardson write down for these two sales approaches?

Shirley Richardson has just completed her first month in the field as a life insurance agent following her initial training at her firm's head office. She is having trouble getting enough leads for new prospects to call upon, and is now discussing her problem with her area sales manager. Let us listen in on the following portion of their conversation.

>*Shirley:* I've gotten referral leads from most of the current policyholders of our firm here in my local area, and from personal acquaintances, but that's not enough. I need many more, but am not quite sure how to get them.

>*Sales Manager:* Well, Shirley, one good way is to ask anyone and everyone you meet each day for help.

>*Shirley:* So far I've hesitated to ask strangers for this kind of help, basically, I suppose, because I don't really know how to approach them.

>*Sales Manager:* Most people like to be asked for help, Shirley, but you've got to know how to approach them. You've spent a lot of time developing your planned sales presentation, memorized the key words and phrases, practiced its delivery, and developed and practiced your answers to questions or objectives that may come up. Why don't you do the same for verbal cold-start, referral lead approaches?

>*Shirley:* That sounds like a good idea, but where do I start?

Sales Manager:	One good way is to frame your approach words in terms of offering something that will be in the "best interest" of or "benefit to" the people they know. Here's an example. (He writes down the following words) "Mr. Stranger, most insurance agents spend 80 percent of their time looking for people to work with and only 20 percent of their time actually servicing their clients. I am looking for clients who would benefit from working with an agent who wants to reverse those percentages. Can you give me any names of people you know who might be interested in such benefits?"
Shirley:	That's a very good approach! I get your point.
Sales Manager:	Let's see if you do, Shirley. Why don't you write down the approach words you might use based on these other two approaches:

1. From the "asking for help" perspective.
2. From the "looking for prospects in specific fields; such as electrical engineers" perspective.

Question for Written Report or Class Discussion

Assuming you are Shirley, what opening words will you now write down in response to your sales manager's two suggested approaches?

Sales Problem 8.2

How can one use "make happen questions" to arouse the attention and interest of industrial buyers.

Jim Green sells expensive technical equipment to industrial buyers, most of whom schedule appointments for different salespeople one after the other at certain hours three times a week. These buyers are there to see salespeople who have products to sell. But since they see so many salespeople, they are often so busy and brusque in manner that unless Jim quickly captures their attention and interest during the first few seconds of his approach, he may be cut short with a cold "no interest today" and dismissed before he can make his presentation.

To overcome this problem, Jim has worked up a series of what he calls "make happen questions" to quickly arouse the attention and interest of these buyer prospects. The idea behind it is to translate opening statements *he wants to make* into statements he feels *his prospect wants to hear!*

Prior to each call, Jim briefly lists statements he wants to open with based on the product he wants to present to his prospect, alongside which he jots down questions he will quickly ask to make the prospect interested in what he wants to say. He does it in the simple, yet highly effective way shown in the following table.

Statements I Want to Make to My Prospect	Questions I can ask Which Will Quickly Arouse Interest in What I Have to Say
By using our machine you have to stock fewer parts. Our price is competitive.	How many different kinds of spare parts do you now have to stock for your present machine? How much is your present equipment closing you to maintain each month? How much of a saving would please you?

Question for Written Reports or Class Discussion

Assuming you are Jim, what questions would you ask concerning each of the following statements?

Statements I Want to Make to My Prospect	Questions I can ask Which Will Quickly Arouse Interest in What I Have to Say
1. We offer a lifetime guarantee with our new X-Machine. 2. Our equipment will cut down materially on your handling costs. 3. I need to know the specs you require for a new proposal we wish to make.	

The Presentation, Part I: Creating and Holding Interest

After studying this chapter, you will be able to:

Summarize the strategic objectives to be followed in the body of the presentation—Part I (creating and holding interest).

Identify five decisions a prospect has to make in his or her own mind before agreeing to buy.

Describe various principles and techniques in arousing and holding a prospect's attention and interest.

Summarize the importance of questioning and listing, and explain some specific principles and techniques of such that salespeople should be aware of.

Cite eleven prospect personality types a salesperson can expect to encounter, and how to identify and handle each type.

Describe how to handle various types of interruptions that might be encountered during a sales presentation.

Having achieved success in the approach phase of gaining the attention of your prospect, you are now ready to continue with your presentation. While it will be a smooth-flowing, integrated process throughout (from approach to close), since there is much to be considered, we shall discuss the body of the presentation in two parts. Part I (creating and holding interest) is the focus of this chapter. Part II (arousing desire and securing conviction) is the focus of Chapter 10.

PARTS I AND II: YOUR STRATEGIC OBJECTIVES—AN OVERVIEW

To start, let us consider for a moment the strategy to be followed throughout Parts I and II as you persuasively lead your prospects from interest to desire to conviction to action.

Your objectives during Part I (creating and holding interest) are to help your prospects to discover and to clarify their needs, wants, and problems, to admit and to discuss them, and to indicate willingness to seek a solution. At this point you have already aroused your prospects' interest by establishing rapport and have made a few tantalizing suggestions as to how your product or service may benefit them. Now you are in a position to start finding out their *real* wants or needs or *major* problems.

Your objectives during Part II (arousing desire and securing conviction) are first, to help your prospects realize that your product or service will provide solutions or answers to it or them. Then, through proof and demonstration where possible, you seek to convince them that your offering will be the best possible way of fulfilling their desires.

As we go through these steps, keep in mind that at any point your prospect may flash "buying signals" that call for an immediate "trial close." These terms, briefly introduced in Chapter 7, are far more fully discussed in Chapter 12.

In order to carry out all these strategic objectives successfully, you must keep in mind the five decisions your prospects must make before agreeing to buy. Briefly mentioned earlier in Chapter 6, they are important enough to warrant the following more detailed explanation.

FIVE DECISIONS YOUR PROSPECTS MAKE BEFORE BUYING

All prospects have to make the five decisions listed below before agreeing to buy. Some or all may be expressed as questions or objections, or may not be expressed. Realizing this, you should build answers to all into your presentation—backed up by facts upon which they can base their decisions. This will help forestall your prospects' raising them as objections, which may be more difficult to handle.

1. *Need.* No prospect buys until he or she recognizes a need, want, or problem. His or her first step in this direction is to feel dissatisfied with the present situation. Desire for your offering is aroused by pointing out the advantages of having it (desire for gain) and the disadvantages of not having it (fear of loss). Stressing the benefits now being missed which would be gained and enjoyed by owning or using your product intensifies desire.

2. *Product.* Your prospect, before buying, has to be convinced that your product (a) will do what is claimed for it, (b) is the best available for his or her special needs or situation, and (c) will be the best for some time to come (in order to justify the cost).

3. *Service.* Your prospect has to agree that your company or organization offers guarantees or other backing of the purchase and that it can deliver as promised. He or she must have confidence in the reliability of the source and of after-sale service if necessary.

4. *Price.* The prospect has to decide first whether he or she can afford to buy and then whether the benefits will offset the cost. He or she also has to make a value decision: Does the product or service offer more value than that of the competition?

5. *Time.* Your prospect has to decide whether he or she wants to enjoy the benefits enough to buy now or whether time of purchase is of little importance. He or she also has to take into consideration any promised delivery date.

HOW TO CREATE AND HOLD INTEREST

Having aroused your prospect's attention and interest through your approach, you must hold on to it before you lose it. To do this, you must *continue* to arouse and hold that interest.

Arousing and holding interest can best be accomplished by doing something yourself while you talk to your prospect. Depending on what it is you are selling, you should, if possible, use visual aids, show your product, or demonstrate it as you tell what it can do and how it can benefit the prospect. The more you show and tell, the better you sell. The only real interest you can arouse is interest in something that is directed to your prospect personally—his or her own self-interest.

We have a great deal more to say about effective showing and demonstrating techniques in our next chapter, where we discuss them in connection with Part II (arousing desire and securing conviction). For now, we are chiefly concerned with the basic strategy to be followed in arousing and holding interest (see Table 9.1).

To illustrate this strategy, let us first focus our attention on some key principles and techniques of proper questioning and listening. Following that, we go into greater detail about how to arouse and hold the interest of different personality types, and then focus on how to handle interruptions during your presentation.

TABLE 9.1 *How to Create and Hold Interest*

Center Attention	*Through These Techniques*
by Discussing the prospect's needs, wants, or problems	Reduce Tension: by asking opinion, leading off with a story or "news," or by praising him or her.
and helping him or her discover, clarify, and admit them;	Win Undivided Attention: by catching his or her eye and ear and promising a benefit of value.
then *Hold Attention and Interest* to the point where he or she indicates a willingness to consider your proposal as a solution to them.	Discover Key Buying Motives: through proper questioning. (Listen and watch for buying signals all the time.)

QUESTIONING AND LISTENING AS TECHNIQUES TO AID PROSPECTS IN THE DISCOVERY PROCESS

Before moving on, we must first switch our thoughts back to that most important material presented in Chapter 3 concerning why and how consumers buy. You should not only reread that chapter in its entirety before proceeding here, but should *study* it carefully. This is because the techniques to be presented in this chapter and those to follow, in order to be most effective, must be based on the psychological principles and concepts presented in those pages.

To get started now, you will recall that the selling process is actually a buying process and that your goal at this stage of the presentation is to help your prospect discover and acknowledge any needs, wants, or problems. No matter whether these are openly acknowledged or subconscious, you have to help your prospect discover, clarify, and intensify them.

You can most easily accomplish this task *by asking questions* about likes, dislikes, hopes, fears, and problems and *by listening* carefully for answers that give you clues to their strongest desires or greatest fears.

As you question, guide your prospects toward a favorable image of and positive response to your product or service as a means of fulfilling their desires or solving their problems. By narrowing the questions down to the most basic or important interests, you help clarify in their minds as well as in yours their areas of greatest concern.

You can intensify this concern by continuing to frame questions that require "yes-building" answers to the desirability of their obtaining the benefits you are offering. We discuss this yes-building question technique in detail shortly, and again in Chapter 12, where it is presented as a highly effective closing technique. For now, we concentrate on the general principles of, and some specific techniques concerning, effective questioning and listening.

The Importance of Questioning

You want to help your prospects solve their problems, but how can you talk about their specific problems and interests if you are not familiar with them? Fortunately for salespeople, most people like to talk—especially about themselves. Thus, the best way to discover your prospects' problems or interests is to ask questions. Get them to tell you their opinions, experiences, needs, and difficulties before you start to sell. Chances are, if they talk enough, they will show you exactly what you have to do in order to convince them that what you are offering is just what they want or need.

By getting them to talk, you also make them think. Perhaps they do not even know they have a need or problem. If so, your first step is to help make them aware of such. Unless they recognize a need or problem and appreciate its importance, you will not be able to hold their attention or interest for long.

You gain other advantages by getting them to talk: It makes them feel important and flattered, and they warm up to you as someone sincerely interested in them. When you show that you respect their opinion, they are likely to respect yours. And continuing to ask questions throughout your presentation helps uncover the key issue around which you can close the sale.

What kind of questions should you ask? The best are those that challenge them to think and to answer as a matter of personal pride.

- *Who, what, when, where, why, and how questions* open discussion, create interest, provoke thought, help develop a subject, discover buying motives, and uncover hidden objections.
- *Short, specific questions,* especially ones requiring simple yes or no answers, help define points readily.

Here are some more helpful principles and techniques of good questioning:

Ask Questions Directed at the Prospect's Specific Situation.   If selling in the prospect's home or office, relate questions to that environment and situation. For example, "Ms. Bernstein, wouldn't this color rug (showing swatch) look nice here in this living room with all your beautiful antiques?"

Ask Questions Aimed at Specific Major Buying Motives.   Through questioning you can determine what is most likely to motivate the prospect to buy and then can further direct your questions to that major motive (convenience, profit, prestige, and the like).

Ask Questions to Make Sure You are Being Understood.   Stop after each point to ask the prospect if there are any questions. For example, "Do you have any questions about what I've just demonstrated, Mr. Schulte?"

Ask Questions That Require the Prospect to Observe What Is Happening. For example, "Mr. Eberhardt, how do you think the motor is going to sound when I push this button?"

Ask Thought-Provoking Questions to Gain Attention. For example, "Ms. Fernandez, can you really afford not to have this labor-saving device in your plant?"

Ask "Why" Questions—the Hardest of all for a Wavering Prospect to Answer. You can ask this simple question over and over again to pinpoint specific objections, and to get a prospect to answer his or her own objections. For example, "Why do you believe it costs too much?" "Why don't you like the push button instead of the older dial system?"

You can ask simple, direct questions in many ways and for many reasons: to open and control the interview, to draw out silent or hesitant prospects, to discover buying motives, to find hidden objections, and to help make the final close. One highly effective method of questioning is the "yes-building" question technique noted earlier, which is worth additional consideration.

How to Get Information Through the "Yes-Building" Question Techniques

One secret for readily discovering needs, wants, and problems is to forget yourself and what you want for the moment. Try to put yourself in your prospect's shoes and think from their points of view. The yes-building question technique offers a highly effective way to most quickly find out what they know and feel about your company, product, or service. The aim is to direct your questions step by step toward what you are offering and toward securing their agreement on various points along the way.

Through questioning, you attempt to determine their problems or needs to find out what product they are currently using, and to break items down into characteristic components to find out what they like about your product or service, what they dislike about it, and what it can do for them (benefits).

It is easier to illustrate this technique than to discuss it. Since many people use typewriters or are prospects for one, we can put ourselves in the place of a male typewriter salesperson and see how he may approach a business prospect to sell a new electric portable model.

Let us assume that this prospect has replied to a mailed questionnaire. He is a typewriter owner or user and a prospect. In this example, the sales message is relatively unimportant; we are interested basically in the salesperson's approach—how he arouses interest and employs the yes-building question technique to ferret out problems, objections, and wants or needs.

Technique	Dialogue
Uses question approach. Has friendly smile. Introduces company and product.	*Salesperson:* Mr. Lawson, do you realize that you are a 1-in-500 person? According to a mail survey recently made

Technique	Dialogue
	by my company, Regal Typewriter Corp., to which you responded, one out of 500 people in this city owns or uses a typewriter. Yet only 15 percent have heard of our new, low-cost, portable, electric Stylerite model.
Makes personal introduction. Proposes a free offer with no effort involved on part of prospect and no obligation to buy. Assures prospect he will not have to make a decision now. Makes trial close.	My name is Sergi Volkov, and I am here to ask you personally whether you would like a free, ten-day trial of it in your office. There is no obligation on your part, of course. Are you interested?
	Prospect: Not particularly, my present machine is adequate.
Ignores negative answer and asks specific factual question. Uses his name.	*Salesperson:* Is it a big, standard, manual machine, or a portable, Mr. Lawson?
	Prospect: Well, it's a standard manual, but I'm not interested in a new typewriter.
Gathers more valuable information.	*Salesperson:* How old is it?
	Prospect: Eight years or so, I suppose.
Asks for a noncontroversial yes-getting response, acknowledging reliability of firm and product.	*Salesperson:* May I ask you a question? Are you familiar with Regal Typewriter Corp., and its national reputation of standing behind its products?
	Prospect: Oh yes, everyone has heard of your company.
Still appears not to sell; just asks personal information in a friendly inquiring manner. Finds out other users besides prospect and determines objections.	*Salesperson:* Just out of curiosity, may I ask what kind of work you do on your machine and whether anyone else in your office uses it?
	Prospect: My secretary and I both use it, mainly for correspondence and reports. But look here, I am busy and am not interested in a new typewriter.
Apparently agrees with prospect, but asks another personal, inoffensive question in an interested manner. Uses his name.	*Salesperson:* Good! But Mr. Lawson, may I ask, does your work require a lot of carbon copies?
	Prospect: Yes.
Breaks objections into components. Finds out what he likes best!	*Salesperson:* For my own information, what do you like best about your older manual machine.
	Prospect: I am used to it, and it does the job for me.
Finds out what he likes least!	*Salesperson:* What do you like least about it, again for my personal information. And how does your secretary feel?
Gains valuable, specific information around which benefits of new machine can be built.	*Prospect:* Well, my secretary says that she gets tired after using it a while and that is pretty slow compared to the new models.
Secures agreement.	*Salesperson:* Would you agree, Mr. Lawson, that she has a good point?
	Prospect: Yes, I guess so.

This salesperson has now completed Part I (creating and holding interest). Through use of the yes-building question technique, he has helped the prospect uncover and admit certain wants and problems, and to indirectly indicate willingness to seek a solution.

Can we leave our salesperson at this point without learning how the presentation turned out? Since the presentation is a complete process from approach to close, let us continue by noting briefly how the salesperson completes Part II (arousing desire and securing conviction) by proving his claims and successfully closes the sale.

Technique	Dialogue
Offers proof.	*Salesperson:* If I can prove to you that our modern, lightweight, Stylerite electric portable could do your work and your secretary's easier and in half the time, would you be interested in a trade-in arrangement?
A buying signal! The prospect is interested.	*Prospect:* What would it cost me?
Avoids price if possible (but will disclose it if customer persists). Stresses benefits of saving time and of reliability. Closes on minor point of trial demonstration. Makes it easy for prospect to agree, since he is not being forced to make buying decision now.	*Salesperson:* The cost is very low compared to a 50 percent saving of your valuable time. My company is interested only in having you try it in your office for ten days without obligation. We feel our marvelous new Stylerite has to sell itself. May I bring one in for you tomorrow at 10:30 A.M., or would 2:30 P.M., be more convenient?
Knows sale after trial is almost assured if Stylerite accomplishes benefits claimed.	*Prospect:* Yes, I guess so, I've got nothing to lose by trying it out, and it sounds interesting. Make it 10:30.

Learn to Be a Good Listener

It is one thing to be able to ask questions in such an interested, forthright manner that your prospects want to tell you about their problems and needs. It is quite another thing to be an intelligent enough listener to turn what they say into sales points that help you guide them toward a favorable buying decision.

Being an intelligent listener may not be enough, however. You should not only give them a chance to talk and encourage them to do so from time to time by asking questions, but also *try to understand their feelings* as well as their words. Once again, your empathy becomes important—your ability to understand how someone else feels. You don't have to agree with all their opinions or conclusions, but you should let them know that you appreciate, respect, and understand them.

It is to your advantage to be a good listener for four major, basic reasons.

1. *You can win prospects' attention, interest, and confidence by being a good audience.* People in general like to hear themselves talk and to be listened to. If you show sincere interest in their thoughts and opinions, they will like you and will be strongly motivated to repay you with an order.

2. *You can determine their real interests and needs only by paying careful attention to what they say.* Your prospects must have a chance to talk, to ask questions, and to state their feelings and opinions. Through careful listening you can discover their interests and reasons for buying. Many prospects do not know what they want, and the only way you can find out is to listen carefully and to frame new questions to draw them out.

3. *You can check prospects' understanding or comprehension only through feedback.* People as a rule do not like to admit that they do not know or understand something. You can test your prospects' comprehension step by step by asking them to restate in their own words what you have said. This is called "feedback." Their answers to your questions reveal whether they are still with you or whether they have failed to get your message. If they miss your point, you may lose the sale.

4. *You can realize when they are ready to say yes.* Far too many sales are lost daily by salespeople so interested in talking themselves that they miss buying signals or verbal expressions of interest that may indicate that the prospect is ready to buy. Salespeople have the reputation of being glib talkers, and many do, in fact, talk themselves out of sales. We noted earlier that many professional salespeople feel that a good presentation involves only 25 percent talking on their part and 75 percent listening. If this is true, if listening is that important, how does one know (a) when to stop talking and start listening and (b) how to be a good listener?

Here are some tips! You should stop talking and start listening when your prospect sends you signals such as these:

1. *If he or she interrupts you.* If he or she wants to get a word in, let it happen as long as you still maintain control of the interview. Listen attentively, for this may be a way of saying yes.

2. *If he or she starts to agree with you.* This may indicate a readiness to buy. You can encourage the prospect to continue expressing why he or she agrees. The prospect may further the sale with his or her own words.

3. *If he or she says you have given him or her an idea.* If this happens, let the prospect talk; he or she may give you pointers around which you can frame your selling points.

4. *If he or she expresses a liking for what your product or service will do.* This means he or she is ready to buy; it is time for you to stop bringing up new points and to go into a trial close.

You can develop the art of good listening by observing the following do's and don'ts:

Do's	Don'ts
Give your full attention to what is being said.	Do not pretend to listen when your thoughts are elsewhere.
Listen for key facts rather than for overall ideas.	Do not get annoyed by phrases or words you find objectionable.
Look and act interested in what is being said.	Do not allow yourself to be distracted by outside sounds, sights, or activities.
Mentally attempt to anticipate what the prospect is trying to get at, what the point will be.	Do not try to take notes of what is being said.
	Do not interrupt at any time.
Mentally, summarize what has been said to be sure you get the point.	Do not mentally criticize his or her looks, manners, tone of voice, or ideas.
Try to learn something from his or her words, manner, actions, tone, and looks.	Do not try to rebut every minor negative idea expressed.

Listening is an art that requires concentration and energy. You may become mentally tired after listening actively to several prospects during the day, but you will have to be prepared to give your fresh, complete attention to the next one. You cannot hope to win and hold attention and interest unless you can first project the feeling that you are sincerely interested.

Two-way communication requires an interchange of ideas, and a salesperson has to give the prospect a chance to talk. Since, according to psychologists, you can think about four times faster than a person can talk, you have time to plan your strategy around the prospect's comments. You can best do this by listening attentively for expressions that may indicate needs, expressed or hidden objections, and reasons for buying. If you are alert to buying signals, you can base your closing efforts around favorable comments.

At the same time, however, you should listen with more than your ears. People give out nonverbal signals as they talk, as lovers do when they look into each other's eyes. The look on a prospect's face, the stance, gestures, pauses, and hesitations may tell you more about his or her real feelings than the words that are being said. By carefully observing your prospect's "body language" you stand a better chance of learning how he or she really feels.

How Can You Make Sure Your Prospect is Listening? What can you do if you suspect that his or her mind is wandering and that you are not holding the undivided attention and interest? How can you tell whether he or she is paying attention to what you are saying? If a person seems too relaxed, just sits back and listens without offering either objections or positive comments, you probably are not holding his or her interest.

You can check this situation and force him or her to fresh attention by getting your prospect to participate in the discussion: ask a question, invite him or her to read something or to check figures, or show something and ask a question about it.

How Can You Let Your Prospect Know You Are Listening? One of the best ways of being empathic is to be a good listener. If your prospect senses that you are sincerely interested, he or she will open up and tell you more. How can you communicate that you are listening attentively to what is being said?

The best way is to briefly summarize what he or she has been saying. For example, "If I understand you correctly, Mr. Lombardo, you are most interested in the problem of preventive maintenance for your machine tools. Is this true?" Frame such summary questions so that the prospect will give you a yes answer, around which you can build the next point in your presentation. As you proceed, you continue to hold interest, because you have demonstrated that you are a good listener and truly interested in his or her feelings and opinions.

AROUSING AND HOLDING THE INTEREST OF DIFFERENT PERSONALITY TYPES

Part of the excitement and challenge of face-to-face personal selling lies in the fact that each prospect faced represents a unique individual with differing interests, prejudices, likes, and dislikes. Once you have aroused your prospects' attention and interest, you face the problem of holding that interest, whatever the personality type. What kind of a person is he or she? How do you meet the challenge of his or her personality, likes, and dislikes? How can you get through to that unique individual? The place to start is with an analysis of your own attitudes and manner.

Are You Mentally Prepared to Meet Any Situation? It was near the end of Chapter 8, you will recall, that we introduced the subject of different individual prospect types a salesperson might encounter on any given day. To expand on that important topic, it must be emphasized that you, as a salesperson, constantly have to be mentally prepared to handle any one of a number of generally recognized personality types on their terms and on their home ground.

The first step is to adjust your own manner, words, and actions to those of your prospects'. The second step is to judge them as rationally as possible before typing them. It is risky to make snap judgments—the most unlikely prospect may be the biggest buyer.

You can read about handling various personality types, but only you can train yourself to be sincerely interested, flexible, adaptable, and even-tempered. Start by refusing to accept your prospects' initial behavior at face value. Perhaps one is not feeling well, or perhaps an attitude or response is merely a defense employed against or to test all salespeople. Whatever the case, you should try to find the real nature—what the inner person is like. Do not worry about whether he or she likes you or is impressed with you; just act as though you like him or her and find him or her a reasonable and intelligent person, and control your own actions.

Can You Remain Cheerful, Even-Tempered, and Calm Regardless of the Situation? You have to face whatever personality type you encounter cheerfully and with equanimity. If a prospect is rude and unpleasant, you cannot afford to take it as a personal affront and let it ruin your day. Just accept this reaction as part of your work and refuse to let a rebuff get under your skin.

People in different positions and jobs think and act differently. Busy executives may be brusque and intent only on getting to the practical point immediately. Some business and home buyers are swayed by emotion rather than by reason. Technical-minded people may be slow and analytical in considering your proposal. The personality of each may change throughout the day because of work pressure, worry, fatigue, or even indigestion.

In order to arouse and hold the interest of your prospect, you should be constantly alert to signals that indicate mood and be prepared to handle it successfully. Although it is frequently difficult to type some persons specifically, sales professionals via sales literature have made some general breakdowns of personality types and have offered suggestions for handling them that may be useful to you.

It is easy to get carried away with typing prospects and planning sales techniques to hold their attention and interest. Common sense is the best rule to follow in meeting different people, along with recall of these tested suggestions for handling different personality types:

TABLE 9.2 *Typical Prospect Personality Types—How to Identify and Handle Them*

How to Identify Them	How to Handle Them
Glad-Hander Prospects They are glad to see you and happy to talk about anything, to listen to your proposal, and to hear your story, but they are not interested in buying. If you are not careful, they thank you graciously and send you away empty-handed.	They may not be the real decision makers. Ask questions they find difficult to answer: How could they use your product or service? When would they consider buying it? Can they refer you to anyone who may be interested in buying now? If you cannot get them seriously interested, then do not waste your time.
Talkative Prospects They are so cheerful and talkative that they wander from the subject. If you are not careful, they sidetrack you, and time runs out without your getting down to the business of closing the sale.	Give them a reasonable amount of time to talk themselves out but use every opportunity to steer them to your proposal. Agree with a comment they make and tie it in with your next one. Keep your own points in mind and guide the discussion your way.
Impulsive Prospects They appear impatient and interrupt you often. They may agree to buy, then change their minds. They may try to stall or delay you. They may get bored easily.	You have to try to deal quickly with them, stressing benefits and making trial closes. Offer proof if they want it but keep pressing them in a friendly and businesslike way for an affirmative decision. If they seem bored, forget details; outline major benefits, and try for a close.
Vascillating Prospects They probably hate to make decisions; they appear nervous, uncertain, and undecided in words, manner, and actions.	You can best help by focusing attention on a single course of action. Offering them a choice only makes them think they have to make the decision. Offer them authoritative proof and logical reasons for taking a specific course of action. Be firm.

TABLE 9.2 *(continued)*

How to Identify Them	*How to Handle Them*
Deliberate Prospects They appear calm, serious, and unhurried in speech, manner, or actions. They listen carefully, ask detailed questions, and consider every point of your proposal thoroughly.	Be sure you know your product or service carefully as compared to that of the competition. Offer plenty of proof as you stress the value of the benefits they will gain. Try to give all the proof they want, since they are seriously considering your proposal.
Silent Prospects They may just sit there listening, saying nothing, without offering any clue by manner or facial expression to their inner thoughts.	They will be impressed most by facts. Offer proof of the benefits and value they will gain by accepting your proposal. Treat them with dignity and respect. You should ask questions in an effort to get them to talk, remaining silent yourself after each one and outlasting them.
Closed-Mind Prospects They are firmly satisfied with the status quo and with current suppliers' products and service and see no reason to change.	Question them in detail about why they like the present situation, and watch for clues that may indicate any dissatisfaction. Then try to find out what could be improved in the present situation and build your points around how you can offer greater value.
Shopper Prospects They listen to your story, get all price quotes and literature, and put you off with a "I'll let you know later." You suspect that they will go elsewhere and try for a better deal. This type often plays one salesperson off against another, trying for special discounts or prices.	Try to create a sense of urgency in buying from you now. Stress the benefits, such as faster delivery or lower price, they will gain by taking action. You must try to prove that it is in their best interests to decide now.
Procrastinating Prospects They listen to you but just will not or cannot make up their minds. They ask for more time in which to reach a decision.	Check the reasons for delay by asking such "why" questions as, "Why can't you make your final decision now?" Get them to outline affirmative and negative reasons and build your close around the affirmatives. Show testimonials from satisfied users. Show them that they will save time by deciding now.
Grudge-Holding Prospects They see you but promptly attack your company or product for real or imagined lapses in past performance, for poor service, for credit troubles, or for any other unsatisfactory experience. Their complaints may not even be specifically against your company but against industry policies in general.	Your first job is to find out whether they have a real problem that you can help with. If so, meet it head on and do everything possible to solve it promptly. Then switch to a personal basis by saying, "I can't help the mistakes made in the past, Mr. Drake, but I can avoid them in the future. Will you give me a chance to prove that by considering my proposal today?"
Opinionated Prospects They are forceful and positive, real or imagined know-it-all decision-makers. They intend to make their own decisions, and they may be brusque or even rude in language and manner.	Compliment and flatter this type; praise whatever you can about them or their businesses. Appear to respect their success, intelligence, and opinions. And, once they warm up to you, ask their opinions about your proposal!

As follow-up to the very practical, helpful tips concerning handling of different prospect personality types just considered, here are two additional time-tested suggestions:

1. Do control yourself, relax, ask questions about what your prospect likes and dislikes, wants or does not want; agree whenever possible; remain alert, cheerful, and interested.

2. Do not lose control, get angry or argue, appear nervous or jittery, offend him or her in any way, or talk too much yourself.

HANDLING INTERRUPTIONS DURING YOUR PRESENTATION

Relatively few presentations have no interruptions. The phone may ring, a secretary may appear with an urgent question, or a visitor may intrude. Whatever the case, the communication bond between you and your prospect has been broken. How do you pick up the threads again?

If the interruption is a long one or requires urgent attention or action on your prospects' part, you may do better to make a new appointment to continue at a more favorable time. If you are not sure of the situation, it is best to ask.

> Mr. Esposo, it is to your advantage that we spend at least another quiet ten to fifteen minutes together discussing this proposal. May we take that time now, or would this same time tomorrow be more convenient?

Most interruptions are short, unfortunately just long enough to break the attention bond. The telephone is the greatest cause of such interruptions on business or industrial sales calls. If your prospect is a key executive, you may even have to put up with a succession of such interruptions during the interview. Here are some techniques for quickly focusing prospect Mr. Esposo's attention back to the subject.

1. Just sit quietly until he has a chance to switch his thoughts back to you and your proposal.

2. Repeat the last point under discussion before the interruption:

> Mr. Esposo, you were saying just before the phone rang that you were interested in the cost-cutting features of our service. In what way does this most interest you?

3. Briefly restate points covered prior to the interruption.

> Just prior to the phone call, Mr. Esposo, we had covered the key features of our service and were relating them to your specific interest in cost-cutting applications. In what way does this most interest you?

4. Hand him a brochure or catalogue to create interest as you verbally reengage his attention.

> Mr. Esposo, here in one of our advertising brochures is a photograph that illustrates the point you were making about cost-cutting. Is this illustrated situation similar to yours? If not, in what way does our cost-cutting feature most interest you?

5. Jot down some figures or make a rough sketch and hand it to him while asking a question similar to that in 4 above.
6. Ease back into the presentation by first talking for a moment about a subject of mutual interest.

> Mr. Esposo, it amazes me how busy people like you can accomplish so much with constant telephone interruptions. How can you keep track of things? For example, we were just discussing cost-cutting. In what way does it most interest you?

During telephone interruptions you may feel uncomfortable listening to what may be a confidential or personal discussion. The best way to handle this situation is to offer by voice, look, or gesture to leave the room. Your prospect will appreciate your consideration and will indicate his or her desires. Even if it is unnecessary to leave the room, you should keep busy reading sales material, taking notes, or doing some other quiet activity that avoids any impression that you are eavesdropping.

SUMMARY

We have focused our attention in this chapter on creating interest and holding the continued attention and interest of your prospect. Your objectives during this phase of the interview are to help the prospect to discover and to clarify needs, wants, or problems, to admit them, and to indicate a willingness to consider your proposal as a solution.

We considered five decisions your prospect has to make before deciding to buy: (1) need, (2) product, (3) service, (4) price, and (5) time. Arousing and holding interest can best be accomplished by doing something while talking. Real interest is achieved by stressing benefits in terms of your prospect's own self-interest. The strategy of how to create and hold interest was discussed and presented visually, and various techniques to implement them were considered.

We discussed many principles and techniques of good questioning and careful listening and expanded on the earlier introduced topic of how to arouse and hold the interest of different personality types. We also discussed how to handle interruptions that may occur during the interview.

Questions For Analysis and Discussion

1.   What is the basic objective during Part I (creating and holding interest) of the integrated body of the sales presentation?

2.   How can a salesperson make certain that a prospect understands or is even listening?

3.   What central question must be answered to the prospect's satisfaction in every sales presentation? At what point in the presentation should a salesperson start to answer this question?

4.   How can a salesperson most easily help a prospect recognize and admit any conscious or unconscious needs, wants, or problems?

5.   What is the aim of the yes-building question technique? Why is it such an effective sales technique?

6.   Many salespeople feel that the best way to check a prospect's understanding or comprehension of what the salesperson has been saying or doing is through feedback. What is meant by the term *feedback*, and how can it best be employed during a sales presentation?

7.   What is the hardest of all sales techniques for a wavering prospect to answer?

8.   How would you as salesperson handle a prospect who just sits there listening, saying nothing, not offering any clue by manner or facial expression to his or her inner thoughts? How should you treat this prospect? What will impress him or her most?

A Former Fuller Brush Dealer Describes His Rapid-Fire Approach To Creating and Holding Interest

George Frim was for many years a Fuller Brush dealer (salesperson to us) in a medium-sized New Jersey city. Now retired from selling, he still speaks with pride of his former company and of the scores of former customers who continue to speak highly of the cheerful service he gave them over many years.

Ever since farm boy Alfred C. Fuller started making his famous boar-bristle brushes in his sister's basement around 1906, the Fuller Brush Company has been known as "that grand old company of door to door sales." Over the years the company's direct sales line has expanded to make its motto— "45 brushes, 69 uses, head to foot, cellar to attic"—obsolete. Today, Fuller makes and sells cotton mops and dusters, brooms, personal care products, household and industrial cleaning products, and even those little plastic eggs that house L'eggs pantyhose.

When George first started, most of his 25,000 or so fellow Fuller Brush dealers in the United States were men. Today, due to a declining customer base since the 1960s (as more women have entered the work force) the company's direct sales force numbers around 13,000, 80 percent of whom are women.

To prevent the company from ending up as a corporate Willy Loman, Fuller has been seeking new markets. In early 1987 it published its first nationally distributed mail-order catalogue, and later that year opened its first two retail stores. If the latter are successful, it plans to open more retail outlets. Company executives feel that the catalogue and retail stores will actually help increase direct sales, since they will introduce the company's products to a wider clientele.

Many of Fuller's pioneering sales techniques, which George employed so successfully, are of interest to today's salespeople. One of the most interesting of these is what he likes to call his "rapid-fire approach" to creating and holding interest and closing all possible sales within a very short period of time. Let us recall with George a typical interview and see how to put the famed Fuller sales technique into action, as he knocks at the door of a home in a typical middle-class surburban neighborhood.

Although he could have worked by appointment only (as many Fuller Brush dealers do), since homes in his neighborhoods were close together, he preferred cold-call, house-to-house (or door-to-door) selling. He worked on the law of averages, knowing that if he knocked on enough doors he would hit his planned sales goals. Working on an average $33\frac{1}{3}$ percent commission, he established his gross sales goals by week and day. For example, if his weekly net sales goal was $500, he knew that he must sell $300 gross daily during his regular Monday through Friday work week.

In order to reach his goal, he had to knock daily on approximately 75 doors. He averaged 30 to 35 presentations daily, closing 15 to 20 of them for an average $20 or $15 gross sale. He kept a weekly call and sales record showing street and house address.

THE FOLLOW-UP AND FOLLOW-THROUGH

His follow-up was a personal delivery of the items a week after closing the sale. On such follow-up calls he did not try to sell but usually mentioned an item he knew would be on sale in the future. For example, "May I mention on a new item, suntan lotion, which will be a future special? May I bring a bottle on my next visit?"

COVERAGE

George covered his city territory of 7500 homes each six to eight weeks and started over again. If the homemaker did not buy on one visit, he called again seven or eight weeks later. He always tried to satisfy promptly any customer complaints and aimed overall to establish a list of repeat customers on whom he called at least four times each year.

Here is the way he went about his selling:

Comments	The Presentation
The Approach	
He knocks; when someone answers he takes one step backward (so as not to alarm people by the sight of a stranger) and says:	*George:* Good morning, I'm George Frim, your local Fuller Brush man. Here is a free sample for you.
This famed Fuller approach technique involves giving a small but useful gift, such as a wash-and-dry towel or small brush, absolutely free, without obligation.	*Homemaker:* Well, thank you very much. (Accepts the gift with a surprise, pleased smile.)
Having accepted the gift, most homemakers invite him in.	*George:* I am pleased to offer you this free gift in order to introduce you to Fuller Brush Company. May I step inside and show you our items that are on sale? (He is smiling, relaxed.) *George:* (once inside) Your name is _____ ? *Homemaker:* Mrs. Williamson.
After obtaining the name during brief small talk, he gets them seated.	*George:* Your home is certainly nice (looking around the living room)! May we sit down a moment so I can show you the illustrations in my catalogue? *Homemaker:* Yes, certainly. Won't you sit here?
The Presentation	
Then without delay he produces his sales catalogue and order pad and goes into his rapid-fire presentation.	*George:* Do you need anything? Are you short of anything around the house, such as cleaning materials, toilet articles, or brushes?
If the answer is yes, George first fulfills the need, although nine out of ten his customers reply, "No, I don't need anything." If the answer is no, after he has fulfilled the request, he then continues.	*Homemaker:* No, I think I have nearly everything I need right now.
He writes the order in his order book (if the answer had been no, he would have said "fine") and continues to the next item (pointing it out in his sales catelogue).	*George:* Fine, Mrs. Williamson, but may I mention our Fuller special offers of the day? For example (pointing to an item in the four-color catalogue), we are offering two cans of spray insecticide for use both indoors or out at only $4.98. The regular price is $5.78. Are you interested? *Homemaker:* Oh, yes. I can use that! *George:* Thank you very much. I'll just make a note of it in my order book. Here is a handsome club brush-and-comb set with stand mirror for only $12.89 as compared to our regular price of $14.74. It makes a perfect gift for a teenage boy. Can you use one?

Comments	The Presentation

He notes this interest in his notebook for a future pre-Christmas callback.

The Close

George continues in this way to point out his no more than five or six specials, trying for a close after each, jotting the order down immediately if the answer is yes. He never tries to rebut a no.

He calls this close indirect or low-pressure selling, or soft-selling. He feels a hard-sell close such as, "I'll put you down for two sets," is a mistake because he hopes to make each homemaker a repeat customer.

The Departure

Homemaker: No, thank you: I'll save that for a later date, perhaps before Christmas.

George: (Next item) Would you like this?
Homemaker: No, thank you.
George: (Next item) Does this interest you?
Homemaker: Yes, I'll take that, it's nice (etc.).

George: Well, thank you very much for your order, Mrs. Williamson (puts away his catalogue and order form, arises, and slowly moves toward the door, smiling). I will personally deliver these items to you Saturday morning to make certain you are completely satisfied with your purchase.
Homemaker: Thank you for coming, Mr. Frim.

Proof of the success of this sales approach to George is the fact that as a Fuller Brush dealer for many years in this area, he was always warmly welcomed by his hundreds of satisfied, steady, repeat customers. "Direct selling of this type has been a most satisfying experience to me, all these years," says George.

Questions for Written Reports or Class Discussion

1. Does George's rapid-fire presentation indicate his interest in the homemaker's problems and not merely his own desire to make a sale? Explain.

2. How does George make certain that his prospect is paying attention during his presentation?

3. What are the two basic principles of arousing and holding the interest of a prospect? How does George specifically employ these principles in his Fuller presentation?

Sales Problem 9.1

Two ways to present the palm-sized flashlight that lasts forever! Which one will you use?

As a student of selling, you are aware that even the simplest sales presentation must quickly capture attention and interest, and lead the prospect through desire and conviction until a successful close is reached.

Here are two short, but quite different, presentations that might be used by a salesperson to sell a new type of pocket-sized flashlight.

PRESENTATION A

This little flashlight (holding it up) is built into a good, black plastic cover. Instead of batteries, it runs on a built-in small generator that will keep it operating for many years. It's very modern, and is an outstanding value at $5.95.

PRESENTATION B

Have you seen the amazing new palm-sized flashlight that is guaranteed to last forever? Here, hold it (hands it to the prospect), push the button on top forward, and squeeze the handle on the bottom! Note that as long as you squeeze it keeps on shining. Isn't that a strong steady beam of light? You'll laugh at blackouts with this pocket-sized beauty! It will never disappoint you—next week—next year— even 25 years from now. Since it doesn't use batteries, there is nothing to put in or plug in or replace. Its secret is a built-in miniature generator that runs when you squeeze. We are offering it today for only $12.95. Isn't that a small price to pay for a lifetime of light you can rely upon?

Question for Written Report or Class Discussion

Which of these two sales presentations would best grab and hold your attention and interest? Explain why.

Sales Problem 9.2	How can Don Lence use "value analysis" to quickly arouse the interest of a tough industrial purchasing department buyer?

Don Lence sells wire-bound cardboard shipping cartons to industrial firms. He has just arranged an appointment to call on Ted Rawlings, the quiet but tough-minded buyer in charge of BeeMar Manufacturing Company's purchasing department. Twice before he failed to sell Rawlings on the benefits BeeMar could gain by shipping their line of small but sturdy electric motors in his cartons rather than the heavier wooden ones they have been using for some time.

On the first call Don had concentrated on the superior strength of his carton to arouse his prospect's interest; the second time he had concentrated on how convenient they were to use—and how economical they were. Each time he had failed to arouse any real interest, and Rawlings had quickly cut the interview short by saying that he had to attend an urgent intercompany meeting.

Don is determined to succeed this time! He has a fresh approach to build on, a question raised by his prospect during the last call. Rawlings had asked, "How will your cartons increase our net earnings—and by how much over a year's time?" Don couldn't answer that question to the buyer's satisfaction then, but he is ready this time.

He has devised a new sales presentation for the interview, built around "value analysis"—a concept that places emphasis on how much the product will save the buyer, not how little it costs. Don has all his key points worked out, as well as the dollars and cents figures, but he still hasn't figured out how to handle this problem:

> What can I say, do, or show early on in the presentation about a concept like "value analysis" that will really arouse and hold Ted Rawlings' interest to the point where he will give me enough time to present my provable and persuasive facts and figures?

Question for Written Report or Class Discussion

What can you recommend as a solution to Don's problem?

The Presentation, Part II: Arousing Desire and Securing Conviction

After studying this chapter, you will be able to:

Identify the six essential points to be covered in any effective sales presentation.

Describe key factors involved in these three methods of getting and holding continued attention and interest: (1) discussion (talking), (2) demonstration (showing), and (3) participation (doing).

Explain what is meant by the statement: "Interest changes to desire when advantages and benefits so dominate the prospect's mind that he or she is ready to take action to gain them."

Cite two important factors necessary to secure conviction, and show how to incorporate them into a sales presentation.

Identify key factors involved in these three techniques of indirect suggestion: (1) narrative, (2) dramatic parallel, and (3) analogy.

Describe the "feature-advantage-benefit" technique of arousing and building desire and securing conviction, for key points of a sales presentation.

Summarize the importance of securing agreement after each sales point, so that the prospect recognizes and accepts the value of the noted benefits.

Describe what is meant by the term *suggestive selling*, and how techniques of both direct and indirect suggestion can be employed in a sales presentation.

Having aroused the attention and interest of your prospect as described in the preceding chapter, you are now proceeding in a smooth-flowing manner into the next important part of your presentation. Your strategic objective now is first to help the prospect realize that your product or service will provide solutions or answers to his or her needs, wants, or problems. Then, through proof and demonstration where possible, you seek to convince him or her that your offering will be the best possible way of fulfilling those desires.

Priority now centers on product presentation. It is at this stage that your sale will basically be won or lost. As we shall discuss, many things have to be anticipated now and built into your presentation along the way. In considering how to go about this, we will focus first on six essential points that must be covered, and then on the process of how to explain and show exactly what your product or service is, and what it will do for your prospect. We will then show how you can help your prospect convince himself or herself by employing certain motivational techniques of suggestion and logical reasoning that lead to desire, conviction, and action.

SIX ESSENTIALS OF A GOOD PRESENTATION

In building toward desire, conviction, and action (buying), there are certain points that, if anticipated and built into your presentation along the way, will help eliminate many questions or objections.

- First, you have to broadly, yet clearly and carefully, explain in a convincing manner what you are proposing as well as its benefits.
- Second, you have to establish the fact that what you are proposing will satisfy one or more buying motives and will answer to your prospects' satisfaction any questions or objections raised.
- Finally, you have to arouse such a desire in your prospect's mind for the benefits your proposal offers that he or she wants to buy it.

While these broad steps may sound like a mere restatement of items already discussed, your success now depends on how closely your presentation follows this outline. Success also depends on how well you relate them to your prospect's personality and responses.

Successful accomplishment of these progressive steps are far more likely if you keep in mind the following six essential points that should be covered in any effective sales presentation.

1. Your presentation must be complete.
2. It should eliminate competition.
3. Questions should be anticipated and built into the presentation.
4. Your presentation must be clear.

5. The question of price must be handled.
6. Logical and emotional selling points should be developed around needs and key buying motives so that they arouse desire and secure conviction.

Your Presentation Must Be Complete. You should tell the whole story so that your prospect knows exactly what it is you are proposing. Completeness does not necessarily mean giving details about everything, but it does involve covering all the elements of the presentation: attention, interest, desire, conviction, and the close. Within this framework, you have to cover in logical sequence all the important points of your sales story.

It Should Eliminate Competition. From your point of view it is best not only to anticipate competition as a factor in your sales situation but also to plan to meet it. Building it into your presentation from the start renders it as harmless as possible or may even eliminate it completely in advance as a possible objection.

Your prospect may be a satisfied customer of a competitor or may be aware of competing products against which to compare claims made for your product or service. You can handle either situation by first studying the products, advertising claims, or performance claims of your competition and then being prepared to point out specific superior points of yours.

Prior planning enables you to acknowledge competition while stressing the advantages your own proposal offers. These advantages may be

- Better technical performance
- New and unusual features
- Lower price

If you cannot offer these advantages, you may have to emphasize such things as:

- Faster delivery
- Better personal service
- More efficient follow-through servicing

Careful questioning as to what your prospect both likes and dislikes about competition presents ideas around which you can frame positive sales points.

Should you mention competition, either organization or product, by name? The answer is "Not unless it is absolutely necessary," and then only briefly. Never criticize your competitors; it will only demean you and often has a way of getting back to them. If you make any comparisons or statements concerning the competition, be sure you can back them up with facts.

Even in the face of unfair competition, always be fair yourself and say only good things about a competitor or its products. This course will gain respect and will give your prospect confidence in both you and your claims.

Here are two useful techniques you can employ in bringing up and eliminating competition.

1.   *Acknowledge competition, praise it, and pass on.*

> Mrs. Deeks, you are as aware as I of the several excellent competing products on the market. We think ours offers you greater value for your money. For example, . . .

2.   *Meet competition head on, armed with facts.*

> Mr. Pellacani, our low-priced, American automobile delivers only 30 miles per gallon compared to 37 for its chief competition, the well-known Brand X foreign import. But ours offers 136 horsepower compared to its 65, can seat six adults comfortably compared to four in theirs, offers more luggage space, and you can get service and parts readily in every city and town of the United States. Wouldn't you prefer all these benefits since the price is approximately the same?

Anticipate Questions and Build Them Into Your Presentation.   Your prospect wants to know and has every right to ask what your proposal will do, how it works, what is its price, and perhaps even how its technical details compare with those of competing products. You are asking someone to spend his or her money, so it is only natural to want these questions answered. You too probably take all factors into account when you consider a major personal or home purchase.

You can help avoid questions' becoming possible objections by anticipating them in advance. In the planning stage of your presentation, list every possible question you feel the prospect may ask. You can then work out planned answers to these questions and include them automatically as part of your presentation.

Another way of approaching the problem is to list all the key features, positive facts, or other advantages of both your product and your company. You can then rephrase these advantages in terms of benefit statements when planning your presentation. During your presentation, you can include them in your logical development of points, thus in effect answering your prospect's questions even before they are asked.

The most effective sales presentation is one that anticipates and answers as a matter of course and logical development every question that the prospect may want answered. Upon completion, the story is so thoroughly convincing that your basic job is merely asking, "When do you want it delivered?"

Your Presentation Must be Clear.   Your prospect must understand exactly what your product or service is, how it works, and what it can do. As shall be discussed in some detail shortly, this requires an integrated, progressive presentation involving discussion (talking), demonstration (showing), and participating (doing).

The Question of Price Must be Handled.   Since the question of price comes up sooner or later in nearly every sales presentation, you must be prepared to handle it positively and with confidence at the proper time and place. You may want to introduce it early in the presentation and then justify it in terms of value, or you may elect to postpone it until you have stressed benefits and clearly demonstrated value. There is no rule as to when to introduce price; it depends in part on what you are selling and the prospect you face. You may even want to refer to it several times throughout your presentation.

In Chapter 11 we discuss many techniques for handling specific questions, challenges, or objections concerning price. For now, here are two helpful suggestions for quoting and minimizing price if you introduce it yourself, and a technique for postponing price quotes until you are ready to give them.

Quoting Price With Confidence. Unless your price is without question the lowest, you should dwell on benefits and value and try to avoid a situation in which price becomes the point around which success or failure revolves. You may want to avoid it as long as possible without giving the impression of stalling.

When you do quote price, do so with confidence and in a straightforward manner. If your product or service does offer value, price may be of secondary importance. You should know the reasons why the price is as quoted and convey the feeling that you believe it to be fair for the quality offered. If you are in a position to offer a range of prices, it is normally best (except in retail selling, as we discuss in Chapter 15) to start with the highest ones first. You can always work down the scale from a higher price, but it is difficult to open with a lower price and try to work up.

Although price is nearly always an important factor in a sale, it more often than not is not the only or even the major factor. Your job during the product presentation stage of the presentation is to offer proof of value, and to stress the differences that make your offering worth the price asked for it, in a positive, confident manner.

Minimizing Price. This can be accomplished by breaking it down into smaller units (such as operating costs per day instead of per month) or by using key words that tend to minimize price. For example, "Mr. Ohgaki, it will cost less than $2 a day for you to own this reasonably priced item."

You can also minimize price by suggesting higher prices for similar products or services or by emphasizing cost-cutting or other savings that could be effected. For example, "Ms. Joseph, wouldn't you expect a cost-cutting item like this to be worth $1000 or at least $800? Well, I can offer it to you today for a mere $500."

Postponing Price Questions Until You are Ready to Quote. Prospects often ask the price before you have had a chance to discuss benefits or value. In order to avoid a quick objection based on price alone, you may want to acknowledge but pass over a direct quote. Here are two practical suggestions for accomplishing this.

- May I answer your price question in a moment, Mr. Ellis? I would like to show you this brochure first. What do you think of this specific illustration?
- The final price depends on the style selected and the delivery date, Mrs. Chu. May I first show you these illustrations of various models and styles? What do you think, for example, of this particular one?

Sometimes the prospect insists on knowing the price and refuses to let you pass it off. In such cases quote it promptly and then continue with your presentation.

Logical and Emotional Selling Points Should be Developed Around Needs and Key Buying Motives so That They Arouse Desire and Secure Conviction. Along with being complete and clear, your presentation should develop logically and emotionally around key selling points and benefits so that the prospect moves from desire to conviction and action (buying). We shall shortly, in this chapter, discuss how you can best accomplish this.

HOW TO EXPLAIN AND SHOW YOUR PRODUCT TO ITS BEST ADVANTAGE

Explaining to a prospect exactly what your product and service is, how it works, and what it can do for him or her, to his or her complete understanding, involves (1) discussion (talking), (2) demonstration (showing), and (3) participation (doing). These can be integrated in such a way that key points are presented and developed in terms of the prospect's interests or point of view in this sequence:

1. Briefly describe the topic to be covered and conclusions to be reached.
2. Break it into more readily understandable parts; present a step-by-step development of points reinforced by explanation and demonstration.
3. Illustrate it as dramatically as possible with appeals to any or all of the five senses.
4. Check and recheck constantly through the question technique to ensure full understanding.
5. Invite participation by letting the prospect do something. This technique provides constant attention, interest, and involvement.
6. Summarize the topic and points in terms of benefits and value to the prospect.

One highly effective way to develop sales points along this line is through use of the features-advantages-benefits technique.

Features-Advantages-Benefits Technique

This highly effective way to arouse and build desire and secure conviction was first presented in Chapter 7 and then illustrated in Case Study 7. We can further illustrate how it works by noting that it involves developing each key sales point in this order:

1. *Feature.* Tell or show exactly what your product or service is, how it works, and what it can do.
2. *Advantage.* Point out or demonstrate by examples how it will meet his or her needs or solve his or her problems.

3.   *Benefit.* Point out benefits to be obtained by having it (desire for gain) or lost by not having it (fear of loss), backing claims with confirmation or proof wherever possible.

What is the difference between a feature and a benefit? Let us go over it again.

A *feature* is a description of a product or service.
A *benefit* is the satisfaction your prospect will receive from the feature.

For example, if you tell your prospect, "This coffee pot is automatically controlled," you are pointing out a feature. On the other hand, if you say, "All you have to do is plug it in and forget it—it's automatic," you are explaining a benefit.

Features themselves have no impact. You as a salesperson have to give each feature a value (that is what benefits are), since *benefits are what prospects will really buy.* Benefits give them a reason for buying; your sales points should be based on benefits rather than features. We can define and illustrate in greater depth features, advantages, and benefits as follows:

A *feature* is a part of or a characteristic of your product or service. There may be many features to your specific product or service, each relating to a specific need, problem, or interest. Combined, they represent the total features. For example, (1) is portable, (2) can operate either on batteries or plugged into a light socket, and (3) is instantly convertible to either 110 or 220 voltage.

You normally present each feature separately so that you answer these two questions:

1.   *What is it?* You can answer this by telling prospects the name of the feature and pointing it out.
2.   *What does it do?* You can explain and briefly demonstrate, adding further interest and conviction by letting them do it.

For example:

I gather from what you have told me, Mr. O'Carroll, that you travel both here and abroad and need a lightweight, portable tape recorder you can use easily anywhere in the world.

A key feature of our machine is its light weight. Here, won't you hold it for a second? Wouldn't you agree that it is almost as light as a small camera? And it is easy to carry, too, don't you think?

A second feature of interest to you is that it can operate either on batteries (pointing them out) or plugged into any home, office, or hotel wall socket.

Advantages of the feature are how it helps solve problems or fulfills desires. Pointing out the advantages of the feature in terms of your prospects' interests and to their full understanding is highly important if you expect to arouse desire and secure conviction. Lead from the feature into the advantages through verbal phrases such as, "This is important to you because . . ." "Others have found this useful because . . ." "This will help solve your problem because . . ." For example, "The light weight and portability of this tape recorder are important to you, Mr. O'Carroll, since you do so much traveling."

Benefits are the advantages your prospects obtain through ownership (desire for gain) or disadvantages they may suffer by not having it (fear of loss).

Here is an appeal to gain:

> Based on what you've told me, Mr. O'Carroll, it appears that this lightweight, easy-to-carry, portable tape recorder will be convenient to use and will save you time on your frequent business trips. Such convenience includes the ability to plug it into either a 110 or 220 light socket anywhere in the world or to operate it on batteries at any time, day or night.

Here is an appeal to loss:

> Owning this machine will free you from the inconvenience and loss of time involved in not being able to record whenever or wherever you want, day or night, anywhere in the world.

When using this technique, it is important that you secure agreement *after each point,* that your prospect recognizes and accepts the value of the *benefits* pointed out. You can secure agreement after each point by asking yes-building questions such as: "Don't you agree that this will help you?" or "It is indeed easy to operate, isn't it?"

If the prospect doesn't agree, then ask why, in an effort to find out what real or imagined objection he or she might have, and handle it via the several techniques we describe in Chapter 11.

Role-Playing Helps

As we learned in Chapter 3, prospects are motivated to buy largely because the ideas presented seem to be consistent with ideas, values, and beliefs they already hold.

It is your responsibility as salesperson to try to understand their self-images, or the way they see themselves or would like to see themselves, and shape your presentation accordingly.

To do this, you can role play, or act as necessary to make yourself understood, in order to establish good communication, rapport, and possibly complete empathy. Good role-playing is one of the most important psychological techniques of a superior presentation. Through it you tell your story so completely in accord with what prospects say, think, and believe, that they feel it is directed to them alone.

As you size up your prospects and try to assume the role that will help them better understand you and accept your ideas, you strive to get and hold their undivided attention and interest. Among the concepts introduced to help accomplish this in Chapter 7 (in connection with presentation planning) were discussion, demonstration, and participation. Since each assumes new importance at this stage of your presentation, here are additional thoughts on how you can utilize them to accomplish your purpose.

Discussion (Talking)

Psychologists have shown that people remember only about 10 percent of what they hear. Since you are engaged in talking and discussion throughout the interview, you want to maintain your prospects' level of attention and interest at the highest level possible. A high level of attention improves chances for understanding and remembering. Here are some practical suggestions for making your speaking more interesting through the use of contrast.

Change the Pitch or Tone of Your Voice. Nervous people often speak rapidly in a high-pitched voice; less nervous ones may speak more slowly in a deep, yet flat, monotone. Each can become monotonous and uninteresting if continued for any length of time. Your prospects are likely to remain interested in what you are saying if you change your pitch or tone of voice frequently. You may, for example, drop from a higher pitch to a lower, more deliberate tone when emphasizing an important fact or conclusion.

Change the Pace of Your Delivery. If, for example, you are speaking rapidly at a high pitch, you can not only lower the pitch when stressing an important fact or conclusion but also slow down your pace of delivery.

Add a Pause for Suspense. A continuous flow of words, regardless of change of pitch, can become confusing. A brief pause, either before or after you say something important, helps make the point stand out in your prospects' minds.

Phrase or Paragraph to Make Your Points Stand Out. By presenting one fact or conclusion at a time, you avoid an overlapping of ideas that may confuse your prospects. Your planning of the presentation should provide individual units of thoughts, and you should make them effective through your verbal emphasis.

Give a Cheerful, Positive, Confident Delivery to Create Interest. A ready smile at the proper moment helps relax and reassure your prospects. A positive, flowing delivery helps create confidence, whereas a faltering one betrays anxiety and worry. If you believe in what you are selling and mentally picture the benefits you are proposing, you tend to speak with the confidence that enables your prospects to buy with confidence.

Speak Clearly and Distinctly. If you talk too rapidly and mumble words, your prospects may have to ask you to stop and repeat yourself. Practice your presentation so that you speak clearly and distinctly enough to avoid any possibility of misunderstanding.

Use Proper Body Actions to Add Contrast to Your Speech. Spoken words can be emphasized by certain bodily actions made at the proper moment. You can change position, stand up, walk over beside your prospects, sit down, raise an eyebrow, nod your head, or use gestures. Practice makes them appear natural and relaxed.

Repeat to Enhance Understanding.   Psychologists and educators tell us that we learn many things rapidly through repetition. Some prospects are more intelligent than others and can grasp even complex ideas quickly. Others may not understand until the point has been repeated a second or third time.

A prospect may be reluctant to say that he or she does not understand; you can make sure by repeating the point two or three times during the presentation if you are in doubt. You can also describe the point in a different way, such as through a story, and thus repeat what you have already said in an inoffensive way.

Use Comparisons, Such as Similies, Metaphors, and Analogies, to Add Clarity and Meaning.

- A *simile* is a comparison often made by using the words *as* or *like*. For example, "This new plastic tubing is as strong as iron."
- A *metaphor* is like a simile except the words *as* or *like* are omitted. For example, "He is a bear of a man."
- An *analogy* is a comparison between two situations, which though dissimilar have certain points in common. For example, "Having this fire extinguisher in your home is much like having a life jacket handy on overseas air flights. You don't expect to use it, but you feel more comfortable knowing it's close at hand."

Demonstration (Showing)

Your prospects probably have rather short attention spans and have many thoughts and problems on their minds. Unless you arouse their interest and get their thought focused completely on your presentation, their minds are likely to wander. Mere words may soon bore them; thus you somehow have to add showmanship, drama, and sparkle to your presentation through demonstration.

You have to bring your presentation to life and make it so intriguing and interesting that they cannot help but give you undivided attention. Fortunately, many techniques and tools at your disposal help picture what your product or service will do. These tools illustrate far better than words alone the benefits and value.

"Seeing is believing," "A picture is worth a thousand words," and "Everybody loves a show" are common expressions that illustrate what psychologists tell us about the importance of seeing as well as hearing. We noted previously that people remember about 10 percent of what they hear.

Psychologists also tell us that what people see attracts their attention almost nine times more than what they experience through the other four senses combined. Furthermore, they remember approximately 35 percent of what they see. Thus, if you can demonstrate or show what you are proposing, as well as talk or tell about it, you stand a far greater chance of creating and holding interest and of assuring remembrance.

It is important to keep in mind two important principles concerning the use of visual demonstrations.

1. The objective of any visual demonstration is to show what the product can do rather than how it does it.
2. Demonstrating or showing is always accompanied by telling or explaining in terms of the prospect's needs.

An interesting demonstration is not an end in itself; it is a technique to enhance the point you are making by arousing and holding interest through appeals to basic psychological instincts or motives.

Since sight plays such an important part in arousing attention and holding interest, you should use demonstrations and visual aids whenever and wherever possible. Shown in the box are but some of the sales tools and devices that can be employed. We described others in Chapter 7.

Pencil and Paper.   A moving pencil holds attention and enables you to sketch your own visual aids as you go along.

The Product Itself.   If you sell an item too big to carry, perhaps you can use a smaller, working, demonstration model. If your product is small, get a bigger model for demonstration purposes. Tell the prospect what you intend to show before demonstrating.

Photocopies of Orders or Repeat Orders.   These copies of orders and especially of reorders from satisfied customers offer convincing testimony to your claims.

Charts, Graphs, Tabulations.   Such items reflect the experiences of individuals or groups of customers and make especially good demonstration aids. They can depict economies resulting from use, performance features, or increased production or sales.

A Telephone Call.   This can be showmanship at its best. What better confidence can you display in your product than to call a current user from the prospect's own phone and to let a satisfied customer help you close the sale?

Demonstration aids or visual sales tools not only attract and hold attention but also help your prospect remember product or service facts and information. If used properly, they can offer dramatic proof of your claims and thus save time and discussion. They not only make your presentation more interesting but also reveal uses, features, and benefits better than explanation alone does. They help focus your prospect's attention, often offer him or her an opportunity to participate in the demonstration, usually are pleasing, and seldom are irritating. You can greatly increase your own selling power by using showmanship techniques in dramatizing benefits through the use of demonstrations.

Demonstrations are most effective when presented in the prospect's home, office, or plant—in the physical location where they will be used. You should avoid being overtechnical, explain in advance what you are going to show, keep

SOME DIFFERENT TYPES OF DEMONSTRATION AIDS

Photographs	Flip charts
Sound filmstrips	Flash cards
Movies	Maps
Overhead projectors	Scrapbooks
Visuals	Exhibits or displays
Slides	Mock-ups
Presentation books	Blackboards
Sales portfolios	Flannel boards

the demonstration short, and ask questions before starting and as you demonstrate to keep the prospect thinking and to ensure complete understanding. Whenever possible, you should get him or her to take an active part in the proceedings.

Participation (Doing)

We can best indicate the importance of seeing, hearing, and doing by noting conclusions of psychologists that people remember up to 65 percent of what they see and hear and up to 90 percent of what they see, hear, and participate in. Thus, you can best arouse and sustain interest by showmanship sales techniques that bring your prospect into the act. As one veteran salesperson put it, "Stage a show with the prospect as the star." You can accomplish this by letting prospects operate, clean, use, work, or experience your product or service. This participation should involve as many of the senses as possible.

> If you are selling an automobile, let them drive it!
> If you are selling a house, let them walk through it!
> If you are selling textiles, let them feel the fabric!

This participation is intrinsically interesting if you relate new information about your product or service to something your prospect is already familiar with.

All the areas we have just covered—discussion, demonstration, and participation—revolve around selling the prospect on the idea that your product or service meets his or her needs. You sought information about these needs from the start and continue to seek it through questioning and listening. You can now extend these thoughts into the areas of logic and emotion, as you continue to frame yes-building points around the key buying motives that arouse desire and secure conviction.

Up to this point in your presentation you have aroused and held the interest of your prospects, but now you must make them desire the product or service you have been explaining. Interest is largely a mental reaction, but want or desire involves the emotions. *Interest changes to desire when advantages and benefits so dominate the prospect's mind that he or she is ready to take action to gain them.*

As you have questioned your prospect, you have been seeking clues to points around those buying motives that bring the most favorable responses. In essence, you have been judging the degree of logic or emotion to be used in your appeals both to his or her needs and emotional buying motives.

Your prospect may be a very shrewd buyer, one who buys strictly on the basis of logical reasoning. Many purchasing agents may make a decision based on 90 percent logic and 10 percent emotion. He or she may be a comparison shopper, looking for either the best value or the best deal for home or business. The decision probably will still be based on 50 percent emotion. Or perhaps this is one of the majority of buyers who often make a decision based on 10 percent logic and 90 percent emotion. Whatever the case, thinking is influenced by background—cultural, social, psychological, and environmental. He or she tends to believe or accept what authorities, advertising, business associates, or friends have reported. Perhaps more importantly, he or she tends to believe, rationally or irrationally, what he or she wants to believe.

Bearing all this in mind, you should adjust your presentation to the prospect's beliefs or point of view so that he or she starts to accept your ideas. Once there is recognition that a need exists and that what you are proposing is desirable, you should concentrate on that fact and personalize it in every way possible.

A prospect will start desiring your product or service when convinced. Thus desire and conviction are intertwined, although we will, for clarity, now discuss them separately.

AROUSING DESIRE

Interest changes into desire when these events take place:

1. Your prospect accepts the fact that a need or want exists.
2. The benefits to be gained from fulfilling that need satisfy his or her emotional buying motives.
3. The advantages of the benefits (value) dominate his or her mind.

It is easy to state the principles, but getting the prospect through these psychological steps requires all the art and skill of persuasive, convincing personal selling that you can command.

Basically, most prospects prefer to put off the buying decision. They are afraid of being high-pressured into something they do not want. Thus, if you bluntly ask them to buy your product or service, without leading them up to the buying decision properly, it is like taking them to the top of a tall diving tower at an unknown swimming pool and asking them to jump in. A better way to get prospects into the deep end of the pool is to start at the shallow end and to let them wade in, to feel their way into the unknown deep end. And so it is in selling. Avoid a possibly frightening big decision by developing the yes-building little decisions, each leading on to the next.

Establishing a need or want is, of course, your first sales goal. One way to accomplish this is to turn it into a little rather than big decision. Getting them to agree that your product or service would be useful and that they would like to have it is a little decision—they are not saying that they will buy it. Yet this decision is vitally important to you, for unless you can get them to decide that the product or service would be useful (would fulfill a need or want) and that they would like its benefits, you probably will not make the sale.

Showing how emotional buying motives can be fulfilled is your second goal. If they like the product or service, you have to show them that your specific offering will do the best job of fulfilling their needs and that its value justifies the cost. Then you have to prove that they can afford it and show how they can obtain it. You can create desire for your specific product or service by showing or demonstrating how it will do a better job for them than any other. By stressing, from their point of view, the exclusive or special features of your proposal, you can dramatize even minor points into desirable advantages.

> See how easily this fingernail-sized battery slips into the camera. Other cameras also have small batteries like this, but ours is guaranteed to last twice as long as theirs. This means you will have to replace it only once every two years instead of once a year. That's a definite advantage, don't you agree?

Once they accept the fact that they would like to have your specific item (a little decision that still does not require them to say whether they will buy it), you can start talking about color, style, and delivery dates. You thus assume that they will buy and switch them onto easy-to-answer secondary questions. This assumption technique frees them from the burden of facing directly the big decision of "Yes, I'll buy," or "No, I won't buy." Many prospects are relieved when the presentation develops this way and the decision is, in effect, made for them.

> Since we have only this one camera of this model in stock now, may I gift-wrap it for you now?

You can create further desire at this stage by helping prospects justify their personal enthusiasm by pointing out that their feelings are a reflection of sound business or personal judgment.

Dramatizing the advantages of the benefits (value) to the point that they dominate prospects' minds continues to involve devising little yes-building decisions that increase desire. If they agree that they would like to have what you are proposing, that its value is worth the cost, and that they can afford it (or cannot afford not to have it), then you are well along the route to closing the sale.

You can now increase desire by personalizing or glamorizing your appeals and by showing how desirable the benefits are in terms of their needs and interests. Here are some illustrations of points around which such special appeals can be directed to various categories of prospects.

- With retailers or wholesalers—talk profits, fast turnover, satisfied customers.
- With individual consumers—talk economy, beauty, utility, prestige.
- With industrial buyers—talk performance, savings, efficiency.

Once you have aroused desire to the point where the benefits (value) start dominating their minds, you promptly strive to secure conviction so that they can justify action to fulfill those strong desires.

Securing Conviction. Your prospects may have developed strong logical or emotional desires but may want to be further convinced that your proposal is sound or at least to have their inner convictions reinforced. Your entire presentation up to this point should have been planned and delivered around the idea of building up and securing conviction. This may be the time to reemphasize points made earlier, however, or to summarize evidence that your proposal is a sound one. Whatever the case, consider the two important factors that secure conviction in prospects' minds.

1. Their acceptance of, and belief in, you.
2. Proof that your product or service will furnish the benefits claimed.

Your attitude and manner go a long way toward securing conviction that your proposal is a sound one. If your attitude is that of the sincere, straightforward, customer/society-oriented, problem-solving, professional salesperson we have depicted in the preceding pages, then your prospects will accept you with confidence. If you do not project that positive attitude and are merely out for a quick sale, your prospects will probably see through you and immediately lose confidence in your proposal. Here are some positive and negative mannerisms that influence their degree of conviction.

Conviction Builders	Conviction Destroyers
Being enthusiastic, yet realistic	Being excitable and unbusinesslike
Being calm, serious, deliberate	Being emotional
Speaking clearly and forcefully	Gushing or speaking falteringly
Explaining points carefully so that they are clearly understood	Giving superficial explanations and answers to questions
Being cheerful, eager to please, and straightforward	Appearing more anxious to close a sale than to render a service
Showing loyalty to your company and product	Disparaging your or competing companies' products
Making only those promises you can keep	Making wildly extravagant promises or claims
Showing that you are thinking of customer satisfaction	Appearing self-centered and know-it-all

Proof or evidence to substantiate your claims is also necessary to secure conviction. Whether they are spending company money or hard-earned personal cash, they want and expect facts that clearly show the value they will get for the expenditure. They also want facts that will make them proud to recommend, use, or own the product or service—facts they can tell superiors or business associates or family, friends, or neighbors.

You can suggest believable facts or evidence, but the most effective proof is facts or evidence that prospects can see as well as hear about. Psychologists estimate that people receive over 85 percent of all impressions through their eyes and not their ears. Thus your actions, such as being confident in manner and willing to show visual evidence or proof of your claims, weigh far more heavily in securing conviction in their minds than do mere verbal statements.

PERSUASION AND MOTIVATION ARE THE KEYS TO DESIRE, CONVICTION, AND BUYING ACTION

Early in Chapter 1 the point was made that persuasion is central to selling. Every sales presentation, easy or difficult, involves persuasion from approach to close. You must persuade all prospects, before they decide to buy, that a need or want exists and then motivate them to take action to fulfill it (through buying). Persuasion is aimed at inducing (motivating) another to believe or do something (take action) differently. Persuasion is thus at the core of the selling process.

Two generally accepted methods of persuasion induce (motivate) another person to believe or do something (take action) differently. The first is by logical reasoning; the second, and of greater importance to selling, is by suggestion.

Motivation by Logic (Selling Through Logical Reasoning)

Logic or logical reasoning appeals to rational buying motives by presenting sales points that lend themselves to comparison. Logical reasoning is more likely to appeal to technical or to professional buyers, who tend to buy on rational grounds, than to the average prospect.

It is most effectively used when selling complicated proposals involving detailed cost comparisons or when the price is so great that prospects must weigh every fact carefully before reaching a decision. It is also effectively used when presenting a radically new item. The selling or leasing of an expensive new computer installation requiring a different programming language from the one being used is an example of a sales situation in which logical, comparative sales points are highly effective.

Logical reasoning is built around syllogisms, arguments (or sales claims) based on major premises, minor premises, and conclusions. Here is an example.

Major Premise.   This computer will save more executive time than any other.

Minor Premise.   You are a busy executive.

Conclusion.   Therefore, you should have this computer to save your time.

This argument is logical enough, but a great many people do not react positively to such reasoning. Instead, they tend to react for emotional reasons (their reasons), and they often resent being convinced against their will.

Thus, in most cases, it is best to employ abbreviated syllogisms, which allow prospects to draw their own conclusions from the premise. Here are three common techniques for accomplishing this aim.

1. *Offering alternatives* allows prospects to draw a rational conclusion from two or more alternatives. The computer salesperson may say, "If you agree that our computer is the best and will save you time, let us examine what you may gain and lose by waiting until next year to buy and examine what you will gain and lose by buying now."

2. *Suggesting a comparison of similarities* invites an examination of two possible situations and a noting of the similarities. Our computer salesperson may give a reason such as this one.

    > Addo Company down the road faced a dilema similar to yours six months ago, when they were deciding whether to install this computer now or to wait a year. They elected to wait and just last month lost a large account because they were unable to process its orders rapidly enough.

    The present customer can picture his or her company in the same situation and can draw the logical conclusion—that he or she should buy now rather than run the risk of losing potential new accounts.

3. *Employing the if-then technique* involves stating an assumed (if) premise followed by reasons based on it. For example, a salesperson may say, "*If* you wait a year before deciding to buy this computer and prices keep going up the way they have the past three years, *then* it will cost you more."

    Almost all prospective buyers want to be, or at least to appear to be, rational in arriving at their decisions to buy. But frequently this rational idea seems impossible to achieve—as when two similar products, equally priced, offer equal and similar benefits. How shall the buyer decide? What can you as a salesperson do? In such situations, the more difficult it is for a prospect to make a rational decision, the bigger the opportunity you have to use suggestive selling.

Motivation by Suggestion (Suggestive Selling)

Suggestion is a far more widely used key to motivation in selling than is logical reasoning. Psychologists agree that people respond more often to suggestion, involving their emotional buying motives, than to logical reasoning, directed at rational buying motives. They tend to react favorably to or to accept suggestions, ideas, or conclusions unless they have a strong reason to object. They react to suggestion on the basis of habit, instinct, imitation, and personal bias, and because it is the easiest thing to do.

To suggest is to put into your prospect's mind the thought of something, or the desire for something. You as salesperson can employ it as a powerful motivational selling technique via a combination of emotional appeals. By way of illustration, here's how you might employ suggestion in selling an exclusive new product to a retail chain buyer.

> Mr. Adams, you are losing money every day by not carrying this new product (fear of losing money). Your competitor over on Main Street is outselling you overall in this product-line area because he does carry our product (rivalry), and that location is no better than yours (rivalry, imitation). Certainly that buyer is no better a businessperson than you—and certainly not as experienced (pride), but that store is certainly making more money now than it did before it started carrying our product (rivalry, gain of money). You would like to increase sales and profits, wouldn't you (desire for gain)? Why not start by taking on this new product right now (desire for gain)?

The power of suggestion, as the above illustration shows, is a stimulus to a prospect's imagination; when it is strong enough, it takes a strong grip on the prospect. Suggestion is always at work in our lives. You greet a friend, and he or she extends a hand; automatically you extend yours for a handshake. Someone smiles at you, and you find yourself smiling back. The restaurant waitress cheerfully offers to refill your coffee cup, and you smilingly nod assent, to find later that 50 cents has probably been added to your bill.

Psychological suggestion to motivate people to take action falls into three major classifications:

1. *Ideomotor suggestions* are statements that suggest that the prospect do something, such as "If you will just OK this agreement with your signature, I'll have the item delivered to your home tomorrow by 2 P.M."
2. *Autosuggestion* involves setting the stage so that the prospect's own thoughts suggest action. An example is showing a colored sales-kit brochure picturing a young man sitting in a new sports car surrounded by beautiful and admiring women. Any young man considering a new car can easily identify with such a pictorial autosuggestion and decide that he may also gain feminine admiration by buying a similar car.
3. *Prestige suggestions* offer a prospect the same benefits as those enjoyed by movie stars or other such personalities.

SUGGESTIVE TECHNIQUES THAT CAN HELP PROSPECTS CONVINCE THEMSELVES

Here are a few persuasive types of suggestion that will help your prospects sell themselves.

Direct Suggestion. "Since you like the article and it's on sale today—three for the price of two—why don't you take six and save money?"

Indirect Suggestion. "I appreciate your reasons for delaying a decision, but neither of us knows what it may cost six months from now, with prices going up all the time the way they are."

Most professional salespeople generally prefer indirect suggestion over direct suggestion; they employ indirect suggestion through techniques such as these:

Narrative involves telling a story about someone else (in a position similar to that your prospect) who made the purchase and was very pleased afterward. Your prospects subconsciously put themselves in the position of the other person and deduce that they will also experience profit or pleasure from the purchase.

Dramatic parallel consists of asking a leading question that poses a challenge to your prospect. Here's an example:

Question: Is it your company's policy to keep equipment until it wears out even if it cost money?

Answer: No, our company doesn't have a policy like that.

Question: In that case, the facts I've presented as to how our new machine can cut costs should go over well with your divisional vice-president if you decide to take advantage of our offer.

Analogy is a comparison between two situations which, though dissimilar, have certain points in common. You can apply it as a sales technique by describing a situation in another field and through inference suggesting that results would also be applicable in relation to your own proposal.

Suggestion Through Action. "Here, try it for yourself! Isn't it light and easy to move around?"

Positive Suggestion. "You do like this article, don't you?"

Negative Suggestion. "You wouldn't like to be without such a convenience for long, would you?"

Whether you employ suggestion directly or indirectly, it is an easy-to-use technique that will work on seven out of ten prospects in most types of selling. Suggestion works best, of course, when directed at the subconscious (emotional and instinctual) mind rather than at the conscious (reasoning) mind via implanting an idea in prospects' minds so that they accept it uncritically without further proof or evidence.

Rational reasons to support suggestions should always be on tap. While more buying decisions are based on emotional than on rational motives, a salesperson must always be prepared to help buyers justify their emotional decision. Thus, if a couple has just decided to buy a more expensive home than the one they had planned on, the salesperson can reassure them that they will never regret the purchase because of the higher resale potential or their increased status in the eyes of their friends and acquaintances.

Suggestion as a psychological sales tool is also most valuable in preventing argument. For example, if you make the statement, "Ours is the best industrial chemical on the market today," your prospect might disagree in an argumentative way. This possibility can be avoided by employing suggestive wording such as this:

Let's assume that you want to get maximum efficiency at lowest cost. Ten out of twelve firms in this area have switched to our chemical because it offers just that. As a result, most of their buyers say that ours is the best industrial chemical on the market today.

SUMMARY

We discussed in this chapter the principles and techniques of arousing desire and securing conviction. We started from the point at which prospects had admitted needs or wants, had discussed their desires or problems, and were willing to consider a solution.

Six essential points that must be built into the presentation were explained. These are: (1) The presentation must be complete. (2) It should eliminate competition. (3) Questions should be anticipated and built into the presentation. (4) The presentation must be clear. (5) The question of price must be handled. (6) Logical and emotional selling points should be developed around needs and key buying motives so that they arouse desire and secure conviction.

We continued by outlining progressive steps, involving discussion (talking), demonstrating (showing), and participation (doing), showing prospects what the product or service is, how it works, and what it can do. We suggested use of a feature-advantage-benefit sequence for each key point developed. A major goal at this stage of the presentation is to help prospects recognize that your specific proposal offers the best fulfillment of their desires. Once they recognize this fact their interest starts changing into desire and desire into conviction. We concluded that interest changes into desire when advantages and benefits so dominate your prospects' mind that they are ready to take action.

Although arousing desire and securing conviction are intertwined as part of the developing presentation, we discussed them separately for clarity. We pointed out that conviction is secured chiefly through the prospect's acceptance of and belief in you personally and proof or evidence that the proposal being offered will furnish the benefits claimed. Your manner and attitude are chiefly responsible for prospect acceptance of you personally, and visual evidence is the best form of proof.

We concluded with an explanation of how both direct and indirect suggestions can be employed as a powerful emotional and logical motivational technique to help prospects sell themselves.

Questions for Analysis and Discussion

1.   What is your first sales task now that your prospects have admitted their needs or wants, have discussed their desires and problems, and have indicated a willingness to consider your solution to them? How do you accomplish this task?

2.   What is your second sales task, following completion of the above task, recognizing that the two are actually intertwined?

3.   At what stage does interest change to desire in the above process?

4.   What are the two important factors that secure conviction in your prospects' minds?

5.   Why is it important to change the pitch or tone of your voice or change the pace of your delivery during a sales presentation?

6.   What two important principles concerning the use of visual demonstrations during a presentation should a salesperson always keep in mind?

7.   Why do most professional salespeople agree that in many types of selling the most effective appeals are to the emotions rather than to the mind?

8.   What are the differences between using indirect versus direct suggestion as motivational techniques in personal selling?

CASE STUDY 10

Convincing Proof Through Demonstration Wins the Sale of Electronic Jet-Engine Component

Bob Reid is the energetic owner-president of a small but highly regarded manufacturers' representative firm in the state of New Jersey. He and his sales team have successfully competed against some of the largest electronic manufacturers in the world in supplying vital components to the engineering, aviation, and space-technology industries in the eastern United States.

His engineer prospects have always been glad to see any salesperson who can offer them new and easy solutions to their difficult problems. They are very objective, however, and since Bob and the group of small manufacturers he represents are often relatively unknown, he has to sell hard to prove the value of his components. Product knowledge is essential to his sales presentations, for unless his prospects feel that he knows exactly what he is talking about, he probably will not get their business.

Bob feels that proof through demonstration is the most effective way to arouse and hold their interest and to secure their conviction that his product provides the best solution to their problems. Thus he goes to great lengths, in time and effort, to demonstrate the claims for his products. Here, in his own words, is how he put his product knowledge and sales techniques into action to successfully close one unusually large and important sale.

The company I was calling on is a large manufacturer of electronic jet-engine ignitions. In this ignition they use a high-voltage rectifier, which I was trying to sell them. My competitor had the business, so I had to prove beyond doubt that it would be to this company's advantage to modify it specifications to require my rectifier.

I knew that jet-engine parts are subjected to high levels of vibration and that my rectifier, although higher in price, would withstand higher level of vibration than would my competitor's. To demonstrate this I had one of my rectifiers, which is of solid encapsulated construction, ground down so that is was effectively sectioned in half and the internal construction could be seen. My competitor's rectifier was a glass tube with the parts inside held in contact with each other by a spring. I purchased a competitor's rectifier from a distributor, broke it open, and placed all the pieces in a lucite box.

I called on key individuals in the engineering department, demonstrated the superior construction of my rectifier, and showed that the occasional intermittent contact they were experiencing was caused by the spring in the competitor's part, which would flex with sufficient vibration in the right plane. I demonstrated how this flexing could not happen with our part.

I also emphasized that this problem with intermittent contacts was costing them a lot more than the small extra cost of my rectifier. I persuaded them to issue an amendment to their purchase-part drawing, specifying that rectifiers with springs could not be supplied. When the requirements went to the purchasing department, the amended drawing put me in a sole-source position, and I was able to obtain the business at a higher price.

Questions for Written Reports or Class Discussion

1. Bob knew from the start that he faced both a specific competitor and a lower price. How did he plan correctly in advance to handle competition and price during his presentation?

2. This sale was won by demonstrated technical superiority. Suppose the rectifier had been just as good as but not superior to the competition. What three reasons could Bob have advanced as to why the company should have let him supply the rectifiers anyway?

3. We do not know exactly when Bob introduced price into his presentation. Had you been in his place, at what point in the presentation would you have introduced it? What is the general rule for introducing price, if there is such a rule?

4. What are the two most important factors that secure conviction in the mind of any prospect? How did Bob work these factors into his presentation?

Sales Problem 10.1

Can visual sales aids really make a difference in arousing a buyer's desire and conviction?

Molly Corrigan calls on American retail store buyers in the states of Illinois and Wisconsin, selling "The Active Young Women" line of women's sportswear coordinates (so called because they are merchandised together), including skirts, blouses, and vests. Since it's a new line in a highly competitive field, her sales task is not an easy one. Let's look over Molly's shoulder to see how she handles this selling situation where Ms. Howell, the buyer, has indicated initial but only lukewarm interest. Molly is now directing appeals that she hopes will change Ms. Howell's interest to desire, to conviction, and first-time sale.

> *Molly:* Ms. Howell, if I can show you how you can increase sales and profit by taking on our "The Active Young Women" line, would you be interested?
>
> *Ms. Howell:* Naturally, but you'll have to be very convincing, because I don't see that your line is really different from those offered by other companies.
>
> *Molly:* We help you sell more of our line and make buying easier and more risk-free! We do this in three ways. First, we have a big national advertising campaign underway featuring positive comments by popular movie stars Nancy Natale and Gloria Morgan. Here (showing) are our ads that are appearing in this month's issue of *Glamour, Cosmopolitan, Seventeen, Teen,* and *Co-Ed* magazines. Aren't they terrific?
>
> *Ms. Howell:* Yes, they are indeed excellent.
>
> *Molly:* Second, we have a product-mix of 75 percent regular and 25 percent promotional merchandise. That means you won't have to hunt

around to pick up residue merchandise for standard sales days like the day after Christmas or national holidays when your store is open. We are a one-source supplier! Won't that make life easier for a busy buyer like you? (Molly shows announcements of "special sales event" separate items and promotional ad-prices featuring them.)

Ms. Howell: I like the idea of being able to buy special sales day items from a regular item supplier.

Molly: Third, and best of all—since we are the only manufacturer to do so—we will furnish you, assuming you place an order, with this (holding it up) helpful six-month planning guide, or flow chart. It shows you (pointing to the chart) what specific product groups, colors, and delivery dates you can expect from our company over the coming period. Don't you agree (handing the chart over) that it will really help both your buying and budgeting?

Ms. Howell: Why, I've never seen anything like this before from any company in the industry. It's exactly the sort of guide I've wanted.

Molly: To save you time now, Ms. Howell, will you let me write up a $5000 trial order for delivery next week?

Ms. Howell: Make it $3000, and if your line does well, I will order more on your next call.

Questions for Written Reports or Class Discussion

1.   At what point in Molly's presentation do you feel that Ms. Howell's interest turned into an intermixing of desire and conviction?

2.   If Molly had not shown visual aids to back up her three-point benefit appeals, do you think she would still have closed the sale? Explain.

3.   What other types of verbal or physical evidence do you feel Molly could have presented to make her three-point benefit appeals even more convincing?

Sales Problem 10.2

What was the real interest factor in this technical reference book "component-cost comparison" sales technique?

Tom MacElwee has just commenced his presentation of an expensive and highly specialized reference-book set to Alfiero Palestroni, a leading East Coast building contractor in the United States.

The appointment was set after Tom had called, saying that Mr. Palestroni was one of a few selected executives whose opinion he would like to ask regarding the value for office reference use of this new set, which had been published recently for firms in the building and contracting industry.

Seated behind his office desk, Mr. Palestroni has listened carefully as Tom told him about the set, showed him a sample book and colored brochures, and pointed out all the easy-to-use features, illustrations, quick calculation tables, and special reference service advantages and benefits of the set. Tom now pauses, listening and watching carefully for his prospect's response.

Mr. Palestroni:	Well, the set looks OK, but it probably costs too much to really interest me.
Tom:	Mr. Palestroni, you have several reference books in your office already, and you know how much they cost you individually. But you bought them not because they were books, but for information, didn't you?
Mr. Palestroni:	I'll have to say yes to that one!
Tom:	Well then, let me just hold up this sample book, one of thirty in the set. It has over 600 pages, is full of color illustrations and technical charts, is beautifully bound, and has an index designed for a busy executive like you. How much do you think it would cost you by itself outside?
Mr. Palestroni:	Well, technical books are expensive, so I guess a single book of this quality would cost around $65 to $75.
Tom:	Well then, Mr Palestroni, if you bought thirty books of the same identical quality at $75 each, how much would you be up for?
Mr. Palestroni:	$2250, of course.
Tom:	(handing Mr. Palestroni a piece of paper and a pencil) Would you mind writing that figure down here? (Mr. Palestroni—out of curiosity—does as requested.)
Tom:	I can tell, Mr. Palestroni, that as a successful executive in the highly competitive building industry, you appreciate value. Am I right?
Mr. Palestroni:	I can't disagree with that.
Tom:	If you could obtain this $2250 value today for only $995, would you be interested?

As Mr. Palestroni said later that day to his secretary in describing the sales presentation:

I was interested, and soon found myself signing an order form. I feel I got a good buy on a very useful professional reference set. More than that, however, I am still impressed with the way that salesperson came up with the best possible way to break down my price resistance. He broke his proposal up into thirty components and had me assign my estimate of value to each. He then got me to add it up and physically write the price down. When he finally presented his price, it looked very reasonable indeed compared to mine. Since the set did offer benefits to me and the value looked excellent, I felt I could not afford to pass up the opportunity.

Questions for Written Reports or Class Discussion

1.   What was the real interest factor in this sales approach to Mr. Palestroni?

2.   What other methods, apart from the component-cost comparison, did Tom use to back up the image of value in the eyes of his prospect?

3.   What excellent method did Tom use in relating value to something specific in his prospect's mind?

Principles and Techniques of Handling Objections

After studying this chapter, you will be able to:

Explain why objections are raised, why they are to be expected, and what the attitude of a salesperson should be toward them.

Cite two common honest objections of a business nature and four sincere objections of a personal nature that are frequently encountered during sales presentations.

Describe techniques for handling these frequently encountered five types of standard or common objections: (1) price, (2) no interest or need, (3) product, (4) company, organization, or source or supply, and (5) stalling or procrastination.

Identify six principles involved in how a salesperson should react to any type of objection.

Summarize five strategic principles that can help turn objections of any type into sales.

Discuss six basic techniques for handling objections.

The two greatest problems faced by both new and experienced salespeople are (1) how to handle objections, and (2) how to close the sale. In the case of a new or inexperienced salesperson, fear is often part of the problem— fear that he or she will be unable to handle objections and will thus lose the sale. This fear is justified because, with only rare exceptions, you cannot close a sale as long as the prospect has any major objection or objections. Thus you have to understand the principles and techniques of handling objections before attempting to master closing techniques.

Objections or doubts are present in nearly every sales interview. They may be real or valid ones, hidden ones, or mere excuses to put you off. Once you learn how to anticipate, recognize, and handle them, your fear will vanish and the problem of facing them will diminish. True professional salespeople not only welcome but also seek out objections so that they can answer them to the prospect's satisfaction at the earliest strategic moment.

Your prospect's objections, properly answered, can help you make a sale— but if you encounter strong resistance in presentation after presentation, it may be a signal that it's time to review your presentation. Does it still sound fresh? Are you putting into it the same enthusiasm you once did? Are you really tailoring it to individual prospects? Are you yourself sold on what you sell, and does that come through in your presentation?

If your presentation is carefully prepared and carefully delivered, with sensitivity to your prospect's problems, objections in most cases will be relatively few, and temporary. Since objections and doubts are present in nearly every sales interview, however, you must be prepared to recognize and handle them, and to turn them to your advantage. The purpose of this chapter is to show you how to do this.

Once a salesperson has answered a question or objection, a favorable response to the answer by the prospect can often be turned immediately into an excuse for a trial close (trying to get a quick decision). In some cases, even the first objection is a signal that the prospect is ready to buy. In those cases, rare though they may be, the salesperson can close within a few minutes. With such possibilities always present, the salesperson who knows how to handle objections quickly becomes a better closer.

WHY ARE OBJECTIONS RAISED?

Since all salespeople have to deal with objections day after day, interview after interview, it may help to give some thought to why they are raised. Some objections are honest ones; others are mere stalls for time, and others are intended as bids for information. Many people object to the idea of being sold; others just do not like to part with their money and thus try to avoid a decision as long as possible.

Honest objections of a *business nature* may involve the following points.

1. A desire to know all facts of your proposal as they affect the buyer's firm or organization. Since the buyer is paid to handle the money of his or her organization carefully, he or she has every right to voice objections or doubts until each if fully satisfied.
2. A search for proof that your product or service will fulfill a need, will increase profits or cut costs, and will perform exactly as you claim.

Sincere objections of a *personal nature* may involve the following points:

1. A desire to feel that he or she (the buyer) is making the decision and is not being sold anything.
2. A desire to know all the facts so as to be reassured in his or her own mind that the purchase will be of value.
3. A need to be a participant or partner in the sale—to have his or her opinion listened to with respect.
4. A basic fear of making a decision, which indicates that he or she is not yet convinced in spite of apparent agreement with the salesperson.

A salesperson may encounter objections of both a business and a personal nature when selling to the buyer of a firm or organization. As we learned in Chapter 3, while such buyers strive to effectively represent their organizations through a rational decision-making process, they are also influenced by personal feelings and emotions.

Many objections, especially some of the standard ones such as "It costs too much," "I can't make a decision at this time," or "I'll have to think about it" are mere smoke screens and do not represent the real objection at all. Thus you cannot afford to take all such objections at their face value; you have to find the real objection and answer it. But this real objection may be so deeply rooted in preconceived ideas or prejudice that prospects themselves are not specifically aware of the inner reasons for their negative responses. We will discuss methods for discovering the real or hidden reasons shortly. First, however, we consider your personal attitudes toward objections in general.

WHAT SHOULD YOUR ATTITUDE TOWARD OBJECTIONS BE?

Your attitude should basically be that of welcoming objections and answering them positively rather than evading, ignoring, or resenting them. As we shall soon discuss, timing and controlling the handling of them may vary, but you must finally acknowledge all objections to the prospect's satisfaction in order to close the sale.

Questions designed to uncover hidden objections must be phrased carefully, however, in order not to accidentally trigger a flat "no" response. Once prospects have said "no," they have a position to defend, and your job of persuading them to say "yes" becomes much more difficult. Thus, yes-building questions are desirable, and it is best not to try for a decision until you are fairly confident that it will be a favorable one.

Major closing problems come more often from procrastinators, who cannot make up their minds, than from prospects who have solid reasons for not buying. In either case, you should not consider a "no" or "not interested now" as final but merely as an invitation to continue selling harder.

Most objections are standard ones, common to all fields of selling, and salespeople have devised many persuasive techniques to cope with them. Other objections require special handling and considerable knowledge, empathy, and flexibility on your part. Your attitude in all cases should be on of securing agreement rather than securing mere submission from your prospect.

You should welcome an objection because it offers a clue to what your prospect thinks or feels. It pinpoints an area on which you should concentrate and offers insight into his or her wants and buying motives.

PRIOR PLANNING CAN ANTICIPATE OR FORESTALL MANY OBJECTIONS

What kind of objections may be encountered, and how can they be forestalled within the presentation? Here is a brief list of some common (or standard) objections plus a few less common ones. We will present techniques of handling these and others shortly.

Some Common Objections	Some Less Common Objections
Your price is too high.	Your product is too new.
I cannot afford it.	Your credit terms are not favorable enough.
I am not interested at this time.	We have a better offer from your competitor.
I am satisfied with what I am currently using.	I have heard that some other company had trouble with your product.

Such objections can be forestalled by incorporating into the presentation certain points that counter the objection before it is voiced. This forestalling can be accomplished without your having to ever state the objection yourself. For example, if your product or service is higher priced than that of a competitor, you can openly acknowledge the fact, then proceed quickly to stress value, benefits, quality, performance, satisfaction, or any key features other than price.

Mr. Carruthers, ours is a quality product priced not to be the cheapest item available but to give you the high standards and long-lasting dependability you require. Its high quality will save you a great deal in the long run.

You can anticipate some of the less common objections, and, as in the case of the "your-product-is-too-new" objection, you can forestall them during the presentation in much the same manner as you can the price objections. Knowledge of what is going on in your industry and of what your competition is offering prepares you to handle promptly other less common objections.

A carefully planned interview, presented in a logical, clear, understandable, convincing manner, can effectively eliminate all or most basic objections. Nevertheless, prospects raise some objections in nearly every interview, so you have to understand the strategy, psychology, and techniques of dealing with them.

BASIC STRATEGY AND PSYCHOLOGY FOR HANDLING OBJECTIONS

During an average sales interview you may have to handle from two to five objections. Your first problem is to determine whether they are real objections or mere excuses or stalls. Your second problem is to decide on the strategy and tactics of handling them in order to retain control of the interview.

Your standard reaction to all objections should involve these principles:

Welcome the Objection. Do not resent it or attempt to argue. The prospect may be offering you a point around which the sale can be rapidly closed.

Listen Carefully to It. Keep quiet, smile, and concentrate on what your prospect is saying. You may think the matter is trivial, but to him or her it may be very important. Allow the prospect adequate time for full expression—to finish speaking. Do not make the mistake of cutting him or her off in mid-thought even if you do recognize the objection and are eager to acknowledge it.

Rephrase and Repeat the Objection. By taking the time to rephrase and repeat the objection, you accomplish three major goals:

1. You demonstrate that you have understood and respect the objection and thus please him or her with your interest.
2. You gain time to think for a moment how best to handle it.
3. You can soften the objection by rephrasing it into a question, which is easier to handle than an objection, and you put yourself in the position of helping answer it.

For example, if the complaint is that your product is too expensive, he or she may really be wondering if a cheaper one would not be just as practical. You can test this objection by rephrasing it into a question, such as, "Mr. Kobayashi, aren't you really wondering whether the expense for this item can be justified?"

Do not guess at the reasons behind objections. Your aim is to try rapidly to pin down the real issue. Sometimes the problem bothering the prospect is not clear even in his or her own mind. You have to find the right question if you expect to handle the objection. You then have to give facts that will influence him or her to answer the question favorably rather than unfavorably. Rephrasing and repeating the objection help clarify the issue for both of you.

Agree at Least in Part.   By agreeing with the prospect's right to object and by agreeing that he or she has raised an important point, you avoid contradiction and take him or her off the defensive. You lose nothing by agreeing that the complaint is reasonable, logical, and worth thinking about. You can then supply additional facts that may help to show the situation differently and may turn the objection to your own advantage by making it a positive sales point.

Uncover Hidden Objections.   The process of rephrasing and restating objections into questions helps determine whether the objections are valid ones or mere excuses or stalls. If your prospect offers more than five objections during the interview, you can assume that he or she is probably stalling. Most likely he or she is hiding the real objection, and your problem is to bring it out into the open.

How can you uncover hidden doubts or objections? The best technique is to ask questions that bring them into the open. You have to watch as well as listen for clues, since some prospects mask their real emotions or feelings. Keep searching for the real reason. Here are some question techniques that may be of practical value to you in uncovering hidden objections.

Mr. Smythe-Jones, I feel that there may be some reason that's bothering you other than the ones discussed. What is your real objection?

I feel that you may be holding something back. Would you mind telling me what it is?

You can be frank with me. What is your real objection to this proposal? Does it have to do with payments?

Let's forget that I am a salesperson and assume that we are two businesspeople discussing a problem that offers a great deal to each of us. What is your real feeling about this proposal?

Ask What and Why Questions.   Asking questions prefixed by *what* or *why* helps uncover primary buying motives, clues to real or imagined objections, and countless other vital bits of information. *What* and *why* are perhaps the two most valuable tools in your sales word kit, and you can use them as effective aids in your sales strategy and tactics as well as techniques. Here are but a few examples of how what and why questions can help you control and manage the interview.

What is your real purpose in considering purchasing what I am offering?
If you decide to purchase it, what do you hope it will do for you?
Why do you feel that way about it?
Why don't you purchase it now and start realizing its benefits immediately?

Make Tact Part of Your Overall Strategy.   Because you are interested in asking opinions and encouraging questions, you have to avoid being delayed by irrelevant objections. You are interested only in valid objections concerning your specific proposal. Many salespeople make the mistake of getting involved in irrelevant discussions concerning politics, religion, local issues, or personalities.

The danger here is that the prospect may sense your basic disagreement no matter how carefully you try to hide it. Thus you can lose a sale because of a totally minor and irrelevant point not at all connected with the proposal.

Good sales strategy and common sense dictate against allowing yourself to get trapped into such a situation. If caught, try to remove the "objection" from the prospect's mind without being offensive. Here are a few statements that may help you get out of such a situation quickly without giving offense.

> I respect your thinking on that matter, but may I ask you something specifically concerned with my proposal?
>
> Your point is well taken, but perhaps you feel that way because I did not state the facts clearly. For example, ...
>
> Others have expressed the same thoughts to me, but perhaps this new factor could have some bearing on the situation. For example, ...

HOW TO TURN OBJECTIONS INTO SALES

Underlying the strategy of handling objections, which we have just discussed, and the specific techniques, which we cover in subsequent pages, are a few general principles that help turn objections into sales.

1. *Place Yourself, from the Start, in the Role of a Question Answerer Rather Than of an Objection Handler*

    Invite the prospect to raise questions freely at any time, since it is your duty to answer them. The psychological theory behind this technique is that prospects do not feel they have to defend questions as they may feel they have to defend objections. By placing yourself in the position of a question answerer rather than of an objection handler, you probably will be in rapport rather than at odds with prospects. Here is an example of how you may initiate such rapport.

    > Mrs. Engstrom, as we discuss this proposal, please feel free to ask questions at any time. It's my pleasure and my obligation to assist you by answering any question at any time. You are entitled to expect this of me; don't you agree?

2. *Employ the Buffer Technique as a Further Means of Putting Your Prospects at Ease*

    Best articulated by real estate sales authority Chester H. McCall, Sr., this device is the starting point for handling all objections. This buffer technique is a refinement of the rephrase-and-repeat-the-objection and agree-at-least-in-part techniques discussed earlier; here is what this authority has to say about it.

    > The "buffer" is a statement made by the salesperson before he or she starts to answer the prospect's objection. This shows that the salesperson has respect for the objection and that it deserves proper consideration. It is an

indirect agreement with the prospect, without necessarily agreeing that the objection is true, valid, or proper.[1]

Here is an example of how the buffer works in practice.

> *Prospect:* I think the price of your item is way out of line.
>
> *Your Buffer:* I'm sure you have some very definite reasons for feeling the way you do, Mr. Kuruvila, and I think we should discuss them thoroughly.

3. *Deal with the Objection Initially as a Mere Excuse and Evade It Where Possible.*

As a follow-up to the rephrasing, restating, partial-agreement buffer, many sales authorities suggest the perfectly ethical tactic of evading the objection if at all possible. There is no use in wasting time handling an objection unless it is a real or valid one. If the objection is not an important one, you may be able to pass over it and continue with the presentation. But always keep one fundamental rule in mind: *If the objection is truly important to your prospect, in most cases you should deal with it promptly and fully.*

Making exceptions to this rule is necessary (1) when a price objection is raised before you have had a chance to explain fully all the features and benefits and thus to establish value and (2) when the objection can be answered more fully later on in the orderly development of your presentation. In such cases, you can acknowledge it as valid and request permission to come back to it in this way:

> Mrs. Gobel, you have raised a very important question, which I will answer to your complete satisfaction in a moment. May I first point out these features by way of leading up to it?

Nothing is lost by evading the objection until you are certain that it is a truly important one. If it is a mere excuse, this tactic may avoid your devoting time to acknowledging it in depth. If it is a valid objection, one that your prospect raises again, then you must handle it promptly.

4. *Ferret out Any Hidden Objections*

We have already discussed how to accomplish this, but we reemphasize its importance here as a means of turning objections into sales. Unless you bring all important objections into the open, the sale can be lost. Thus, a good salesperson constantly probes for any such hidden objections.

5. *Close Immediately on Any Buying Signals*

Although we discuss closing techniques in detail in Chapter 12, throughout the interview the possibility always exists to turn an objection into an immediate close. Your prospect may make a statement in the form of an objection that is actually a buying signal. For example, "Your proposal sounds good, but I suppose I should think it over before finally deciding." "I

---

[1] Chester H. McCall, Sr., *Complete Guide to Turning Objections into Real Estate Sales* (Englewood Cliffs, N.J.: Prentice-Hall, Inc., 1968), p. 1.

suppose" indicates a decision to buy. If he or she has not yet decided, he or she probably will say, "I will think it over." Facial expressions and general attitude as well as "maybe I will" or "perhaps I should" all represent buying signals. When you detect such signals, as stated previously, you should immediately stop selling and go into a trial close.

SIX TECHNIQUES FOR HANDLING OBJECTIONS

Once an objection has been raised, you can handle the situation in several ways. Sales authorities and trainers have refined many rather standardized techniques, of which these are the six most basic.

1. Yes–but (indirect-denial) technique
2. Question (interrogation) technique
3. Boomerang (capitalization) technique
4. Offset (compensation or superior-point/fact) technique
5. Direct-denial (contradiction) technique
6. Pass-over (pass-by) technique

Yes–But (Indirect-Denial) Technique

This technique is perhaps the most widely used of the six. It is a tactful way of denying the validity of the objection without offending the prospect. No one likes to be flatly contradicted—to be told that his or her beliefs are wrong or that facts are inaccurate. This technique enables you to dull the force of the objection, to flank it, and often to turn it to your advantage.

Suppose your prospect makes a flat statement such as, "I don't think your product is as good as you claim it to be." How can you use this technique to handle the objection? An incorrect way would be to say, "You are dead wrong, Mr. Abushaban; you don't understand what I've been telling you." Such a statement would be in poor taste, would cost you the sale, and would probably cause the prospect to throw you out of the home or office.

You do not have to agree with the statement, but the yes–but technique can help you handle the situation correctly: "Yes, Mr. Abushaban, but aren't you impressed with this feature? May I show you how it works? See this red button. . . ." Or you can use words of indirect denial other than yes–but, such as: "I can understand, Mr. Abushaban, that you may feel that way and for that reason I would like to stress the superiority of our special feature. See this red button. . . ."

Question (Interrogation) Technique

If used sincerely, this technique not only can get the prospect to talk but also, if pursued, can help clarify his or her own thinking. In many cases the use of a question to counter an objection causes the prospect to answer his or her own objection.

We noted earlier the importance of initially getting the prospect thinking in terms of questions rather than of objections. The same point applies to you; if you start thinking of every objection as a question, it will train you to quickly frame questions in employing this technique.

Basically, this technique involves agreeing that the prospect has raised a good question and inviting agreement that the objection is a question. We can use the previous objection for illustration.

Prospect: I don't think your product is as good as you claim it to be.

Salesperson: (using question technique) You have raised a good question, but aren't you really asking whether it will do a superior job for you, in your special situation?

The prospect may agree that it is a question but still persist in his or her claim. Your task is to break the general statement down to find out what the real (hidden) objection is. In a continuation of the above interview situation, you may find the word *why* of great assistance.

Prospect: Well, yes, I guess that's the situation, but I just don't think your product is as good as you say it is.

Salesperson: Why do you feel that way?

Prospect: It doesn't seem sturdy enough.

Salesperson: Aren't you really saying that it may not stand up to your specifications? If so, that's a fair question, and here are some facts to help you decide.

Boomerang (Capitalization) Technique

This strong technique involves turning objections back on your prospect as reasons to buy. Normally you should employ it only once during the interview and ideally should reserve it for handling the final objection that seems to be blocking the sale, because proper use of this technique involves going immediately into a close. The combination of boomerang and proper closing techniques is commonly referred to in sales terminology as "closing on resistance."

This technique is most effective when used by skilled salespeople, and since it is a strong technique, it should be softened by a smile and friendly look. It is especially effective in meeting objections not strongly backed by facts or reasons.

Here are some examples of how you may employ the boomerang technique. In effect, and through different wording, you are telling the prospect that the objection raised is the reason to buy.

Prospect: I can't afford it now.

Salesperson: (using boomerang responses) Mrs. Khoury, it is only natural that you should feel that way. But in this period of rising prices, can you really afford not to consider buying now?

Mr. Logan, you say you can't afford it now, but that may be the very reason why you should consider buying now.

Offset (Compensation or Superior-Point/Fact) Technique

This technique gives some validity to the objection but detracts attention from it by pointing out features that offset or compensate for the deficiency.

Very few products are perfect in all characteristics. Many of them embody, for a reason, design limitations to which a prospect may honestly object. Your job as a salesperson in such a situation is, through use of this technique, to persuade the prospect that the advantages outweigh the disadvantages.

> *Prospect:* I was looking for a new home with a fireplace in the living room, but this doesn't have one.
>
> *Salesperson:* (using offset technique) A fireplace would be nice, Mrs. Armstrong, but have you really ever seen a home within this price range with more extra features, such as. . . .
>
> Our architect thought of including a fireplace, Mrs. Armstrong, but since they cost so much to install, she decided to put that money into other features that would give you more house for your money. As an example, . . .

Direct-Denial (Contradiction) Technique

This technique must be used carefully, because it flatly contradicts the prospect's objection and says that he or she is wrong. Use it only in those rare cases when he or she voices incorrect objections or attacks your company or organization or its product or service with a derogatory comment.

In such unusual cases, a direct denial may be the only way to meet the situation. However, use the yes–but technique first if at all possible. If offered with a smile and in a sincere manner, the direct denial may impress your prospect with your sincerity and belief in the quality of your company or proposal.

The danger of employing this technique, especially for new or inexperienced salespeople, is that unless very carefully handled it can offend the prospect. It should never be employed against egocentric individuals and is better suited to answering those objections voiced as questions rather than as statements of fact.

Here is an example of how it can be used in practice, assuming that it is the only effective way to handle the situation at the moment.

> *Prospect:* Why can't your firm ever do anything right? Your shipping department must be the worst managed in the entire industry.
>
> *Salesperson:* (employing with sincerity the direct-denial technique) Mr. Vega, you and I both know that your statement can't be true. All my other customers tell me our shipping department offers generally the best service in the industry. Can you give me a specific example of recent poor service to you so I can take care of it now if possible?

Some buyers are chronic complainers. They complain to every salesperson in exactly the same manner. By putting them immediately on the spot with a request for specifics, you can often put a stop to this kind of illogical objection at once. If they do have a specific complaint, try to settle it to their satisfaction immediately.

The Pass-Over (Pass-By) Technique

This technique is generally used only in the face of trivial or flimsy objections. If the objection is too unimportant to waste time on, you can simply gloss over or ignore it if at all possible. In practice, the technique can be employed in this way.

Prospect: Your last statement sounds pretty farfetched to me.

Salesperson: (using the pass-over technique) Well, Ms. Conroy, we try to point out everything of possible interest. You did seem interested in our other feature. If you will note this red button again. . . .

POINTS TO CONSIDER IN HANDLING OBJECTIONS

As we enter a discussion of how to handle certain specific objections common to most types of selling, keep in mind the law of averages. You will not handle every objection successfully, and you will not close every sale. But if you work hard, consistently, and intelligently, the law of averages will be in your favor. Ten failures in a row are discouraging if you make only ten sales presentations and then give up in disgust. But if you make 30 presentations, ten failures, even in a row, are just part of the game. The average for many types of selling is one close for every three presentations.

The more professional you become at handling objections, the greater your number of closes. Many salespeople become so adept at handling objections raised by even the most difficult prospects that they regularly close one out of every two presentations. This sales-close ratio depends, of course, on the type of selling in which you are engaged.

We now consider the handling of objections in these two parts:

1.   Standard or common objections you may encounter
2.   Some less common objections you might encounter

Each of these objections should be evaluated in light of the following criteria:

Is It a Valid Objection?   If your prospect voices an objection relating to design, performance, construction, or other factual details, you have to consider whether it is a valid or genuine objection. A valid objection to one prospect may not be a real or important one to another.

Is It a Stall, or Put-off, Objection? Whatever the objection, you have to determine whether it is genuine or merely an alibi, stall, or procrastination. Since some prospects are simply afraid to make a decision on the spot, they try to stall or otherwise avoid making it. The common objection "I have to discuss it with other associates" (or my husband, my wife, my partner, etc.) may be genuine in some cases and may be a common stall or delaying tactic in others.

Is It a Prejudiced or Trivial Objection? Many objections may seem trivial or unimportant on the surface yet reflect prejudices which can spoil chances of a sale unless handled carefully. These objections may be based on deeply felt personal, social, religious, or business attitudes or prejudices. They may or may not be valid and may be based only on something the prospect has heard or feels instinctively.

Is it an Impossible Objection? Valid reasons for an objection by one prospect may not apply to the next. If there is not enough money in the current budget to buy this year or if all allocated funds have already been spent, then the objection may be valid and impossible to overcome. On the other hand, such an excuse may not be the impasse it seems. Creative thinking on your part may help find ways of overcoming such a problem (for example, delayed billing).

In dealing with the standard or common objection, then, you first have to determine its depth and validity. Second, you have to determine whether it is the only or real objection in his or her mind. We have already discussed how to do this.

STANDARD OR COMMON OBJECTIONS YOU MAY ENCOUNTER

No matter what type of selling they are engaged in, all salespeople encounter certain standard or common objections. Classifying them as follows, we will discuss them in detail in subsequent pages.

1. Price objections
2. No-interest-or-need objections
3. Product objections
4. Company or source-of-supply objections
5. Stalling or procrastination objections

PRICE OBJECTIONS

Price objections are generally the most common and the most difficult questions to handle. Countering such objections is and will continue to be perhaps the most frustrating part of the job for a high percentage of both new and experienced salespeople as they face statements such as these:

Your price is out of line.
Your price is too high.
I can't afford to buy it at that price.
The cost is far over our budget allowance.

No matter how carefully salespeople plan their presentations or frame their answers, more sales are lost because of their inability to handle questions of price like these than for any other single reason.

What can you do to handle these serious and frustrating price objections, which you are bound to face so often? Successful salespeople who have found their own answers to this problem have written thousands of words and have advanced hundreds of solutions. Basically, however, these three general rules for handling most price objections sum up their findings.

1. *Since price is bound to come up in almost every presentation, anticipate and control its introduction to the greatest extent possible.* In some cases this means deliberately introducing price early in your planned presentation. If the prospect brings it up early, you may elect to ignore, evade, or pass over it, for the time being. If so, you should secure agreement to do so, come back to it when you are ready, and answer it to his or her full satisfaction. Or you may elect to meet it head-on immediately and deal with it at once, turning it into an immediate trial close.

2. *Do not attempt to answer or handle a price objection until you learn why it has been raised and for what reason.* Use the question, or why, technique to find out whether it is a real excuse or a relatively unimportant question. Perhaps the prospect is really asking for more facts or is basing the objection on misconceptions.

3. *Handle the objection by making other considerations so overwhelmingly important in the prospect's judgment that the value and benefits of the product or service outweigh the cost.* Price is relative; people buy what they want even ahead of what they need. If you talk only price, you probably will lose the sale, because someone can nearly always beat you on price alone. Your aim is to convince the prospect that he or she can afford what you are offering by showing why he or she needs or wants it. Thus you stress value, quality, efficiency, ease of use, satisfaction, turnover, profit, economy, prestige, or whatever else appears to have the greatest appeal.

Successful handling of price objections must start in your own mind. You cannot dodge the issue; the prospect will raise it, and you must handle it. In many types of selling a salesperson seldom makes a call without being told that the price is too high. In many cases the prospect simply hates the idea of parting with a sizable amount of money. In others, especially in industrial selling, the best price for value offered is the key issue for the professional buyer.

If you believe in your product and feel that it does offer value and benefits to your prospect, then you have no reason to fear the question. By eliminating fear of the question from your mind, you can concentrate completely on answering price questions in a positive, confident manner.

The prospect determines whether value outweighs price. Just as you like to feel you are getting value for your money in any purchase, so do home, store, office, and industrial buyers. Proper and continued use of the question technique should bring out the buyer's feelings on the subject. Your detailed knowledge of your industry, your product or service, and what your competition has to offer helps give reassurance of your claims.

Benefits That Help Justify Price

Profit (Savings). Business buyers are always interested in ideas that increase their profits or save them money. Industrial buyers are generally interested in such items as savings in operating costs, reduction of upkeep or maintenance costs, or labor- or time-saving features. Home, business, and industrial buyers are usually interested in proof that your offering may in time pay for itself through lower operating costs or other economic advantages.

Quality. The long-range value of quality often outweighs price in the mind of your prospect. Price objections can often be handled easily by proving or demonstrating that the quality of your product or service offers more and costs less in the long run than does the inferior quality of a cheaper product or service.

Satisfaction. Higher price usually means quality, and quality adds up to fewer complaints and greater satisfaction with the purchase. Satisfaction can also come from the pride of owning a prestige product in quality or design.

Prestige. Higher-priced items offer prestige to individuals and businesspeople alike. To the latter, they also offer higher profits. Higher price is often due to national advertising, which helps build the image of prestige, quality, and desirability.

Performance. People often happily pay more for superior performance. They normally respond to claims that your product reduces maintenance costs, saves time, has a long, trouble-free life, and performs with efficiency and precision.

Service. Talk service instead of price whenever possible. Tell your prospect about each service or extra offered by your company or organization, and stress any personal follow-up service you are prepared to offer.

Long-Term Value. Many industrial buyers in particular consider price as only one factor. They seldom buy costly plant machinery, for example, on price alone. The long-term value offered by your product or service interests most purchasing agents and other rational buyers.

Techniques That Help Prove Value and Justify Price

Break Price Down into Small Units. A high-priced item, especially if it is to be used over a long period of time, can be attractive if the cost is broken down into small units. A $1200 office machine sounds expensive compared to an $800 one, but when the cost is broken down a different picture emerges, as this comparison indicates.

> The extra cost per week, Mr. Kanuk, is only about $7.50 per day, during a five-day work week, only $1.50 extra; and for each hour of the eight-hour day it is less than 19 cents. Wouldn't it be worth 19 cents extra per hour to have all the extra features that add up to faster production and thus greater profit?

Use Price-Is-Relative Claims. You can often prove that your higher-priced item will be less expensive in the long run than a competitor's initially cheaper product by comparing the economy of better quality, troublefree service, and longer life.

Stress Exclusive Features or Differences. Since very few products are built exactly alike, it is usually easy to find, stress, prove, or demonstrate exclusive or different features of your product or service. By talking about differences you avoid making comparisons from which your prospect may conclude that he or she can get a product just like yours at less cost somewhere else. The more differences you can stress or prove, the less important relative price comparisons are.

> Mr. Heisbourg, our storage tank is of standard size and looks on the surface like any one of its four competitors. But it costs one-third more. It costs more because we've made it rustfree and guarantee it to last ten years. The others can't claim that, and not one offers a guarantee beyond five years. Don't you agree then that in the end ours will cost less and offer you longer guaranteed satisfaction than the others?

Offer Proof That the Prospect Will Receive More Than He or She Gives. Your higher-priced item may look something like a less expensive one but may offer far greater value. Facts, figures, testimonial letters, written guarantees, or service contracts offer proof of that value. You can often demonstrate such proof with creative showmanship.

> Here, Mrs. Jones, is proof of what I've been saying about confidence in our product. Will you look at the specific guarantees in this warranty? Have you ever seen such a comprehensive guarantee covering a two-year period?

Dramatize Possible Loss From Not Having Your Product or Service. Price often becomes secondary when your prospect is dramatically shown how much there is to lose by not having what you have proposed.

> The superior quality and craftmanship of our machine tool will free you from worrying about the costly breakdowns you may face by continuing to use your old machine.
> Your neighbor, Mr. Naron, didn't think he could afford extra life insurance this year either, and now that he has just been operated on for cancer, he is uninsurable for the next ten years, even if he recovers completely.

Turn High Price Into an Asset Rather Than a Liability. You can often turn high price into the good news that, for slightly extra cost, many extra benefits can be acquired. High quality is a major benefit that often outweighs price because it brings satisfaction, prestige, profit, economy, or long, troublefree service.

Admit High Price and Sell Anyway. If your product is high-priced, you can openly admit it and immediately start proving or demonstrating the special qualities that justify the difference. Rolls Royce automobile or Tiffany jewelry salespeople do not worry about price; they talk instead about the craftsmanship, quality, long-term value, and prestige that accompany the purchase.

Standard Replies to Common Specific Price Objections

Your Price is Too High. Do not even try to compete on price alone. Talk to the prospect only about value, quality, satisfaction, profit, prestige, or service.

> Yes, Mr. Krasner, our product is higher-priced, but since we sell thousands each year around the world, it must offer value to offset the difference. Here are some reasons why it will be worth the difference to you.
> Your point is well taken, Mrs. Meilinger. I make no claim to offering a cheap product. What I do offer is value for your money, and here are some reasons why.

I Can't Afford to Buy it at That Price. If you qualified the prospect properly as to ability to buy, this objection simply means that you have not made him or her want or desire your product or service. Your tasks are to show why he or she wants it and how it can be obtained most easily.

> Is that the only problem standing in the way of an affirmative decision, Ms. Abeyta? I appreciate your feelings, but perhaps you can't afford not to buy it now. By installing it now you will save money in the long run and enjoy the pride of immediate ownership for the following reasons.
> I am glad you said that, Dr. Ottander, because it gives me a chance to explain how our exclusive features enable the service to pay its own way and, in the end, to save you money.

Your Price is Out of Line; I Can Buy Something Like it for Less Money. Very few products are exactly the same. Your tasks are to avoid argument and to concentrate on differences that avoid direct comparisons.

> I don't doubt your statement, Mr. Perrot, but let me ask you a question. Would you rather have a major operation performed by the best surgeon possible or shop around for the cheapest doctor? You will be happy and satisfied with our product because of the superior craftsmanship and quality materials that go into its manufacture. Here are some specific reasons why it will offer you satisfaction.
> Probably you can, Mr. Winsaki, but I know the craftsmanship and the quality of the materials that go into our product. That knowledge gives me the confidence to say to you that our product offers you greater value for your money than does anything else on the market. It is a better buy because. . . .

The Cost is Far Over Our Budget Allowance.   Show the buyer through facts and figures how your product will increase profits or cut costs and how much it could cost not to have it.

> Budgets are a problem, Mr. Zamil, but let me show you with facts and figures how a modest expenditure for our product now can increase profits for you within this budget year. Will you check these comparison figures with me to make sure I've estimated your costs accurately?
>
> Two of your three local competitors have installed our service within the past year, Mr. Zamil. I have some comparison facts and figures here that may convince you that even a month's delay may put your firm at a competitive disadvantage because of that fact. Will you go over them with me now?

NO-INTEREST-OR-NEED OBJECTIONS

Second to price in order of difficulty for many new or inexperienced salespeople is a series of objections that can be brought together in the "not-interested" or "I-don't-really-need-it-now" categories. Inability to handle these objections successfully over a period of time can become most frustrating, because such inability signals failure on the part of the salesperson to create interest or to present convincing reasons why the prospect should buy now.

Here are some examples of such standard or common objections:

No Interest	*No Need*
"I'm not interested."	"I'm all stocked up at present."
"I want to look around some more before making a final decision."	"The equipment I have is still good."
"I'm just shopping or looking around."	"I'm satisfied with my present product and don't see any need to change."
"Your product doesn't appeal to me."	"I don't have any need (or room) for your line at this time."

Why is the Prospect Not Interested?

If your prospect admits to a need, takes the time to listen to your proposal, and then voices some of the not-interested objections noted above, you have most likely failed to arouse interest. Some prospects do shop before buying, however, and do not like the idea of rushing into a buying situation, even though they may not admit it. Others merely use the objection as a defense mechanism against salespeople, viewing them in general as high-pressure types out for a quick sale and nothing else.

The important thing for you is not to get discouraged at hearing such objections. Such prospects do not always mean what they say, and you can turn so many such objections into sales that it pays to keep trying as long as any chance for success exists.

You can often avoid this objection by asking during the qualifying part of the interview such questions as "Are you considering this for yourself or someone else?" "Are you considering this item for immediate purchase?" or "If we offer you exactly what you want at the lowest possible price, are you prepared to make an immediate decision?"

Your first step in the face of such objections is to try to find out the reason for the prospect's lack of interest and to determine whether that reason is a valid one or a mere excuse. One technique is to appear to give up, to ask, purely as a matter of interest, why your proposal really failed to arouse him or her. Then be prepared to keep selling if the objections turns out to be a mere excuse.

> Well, Mr. Khayat, I just want you to know how much I have appreciated the opportunity to tell you about my product. Since you aren't interested in buying now, would you mind telling me as a matter of personal interest the real reason why you aren't interested (or why you want to look around some more, or what you really object to about our proposal)?

If, after this question or succeeding why questions, you decide that he or she is just a shopper and probably had no intention to buy in the first place, close the interview as quickly as possible and depart. If the objection really means that he or she is not interested now but will be later on, try to arrange for a future delivery (thus a sale) or at least a future appointment for another try. If a genuine objection is uncovered that can be handled on the spot, go back into a presentation of the benefits to be obtained by making an immediate, affirmative buying decision.

Why Do They Not Need the Product or Service?

We have stressed that objections are useful sales tools and should be welcomed as such. If prospects say they do not need or have room for your product, you can cheerfully use that objection to point out why they do need it or should make room for it.

"I'm satisfied with what I have; why change?" is a commonly held attitude and standard objection. Too many salespeople give up in the face of such statements, unaware that there are many valid and convincing answers. Why are they so satisfied with what they have? Maybe it is because they do not know enough about the differences in similar products or services to even be able to compare them intelligently.

Your approach to this objection, no matter what product or service is involved, may be (1) to point out constructive reasons why the current situation may not be completely satisfactory and (2) to show something new or different so that they are able to visualize contrasts, make comparisons, and have the basis for making an intelligent choice.

A simplified example is this approach by a propane gas-heater salesperson to a rural rancher prospect who says he is happy with his 20-year-old wood and coal-burning home heating unit.

Apart from the possible problem of dirty smoke, Mr. Elivin, do you know how much money you could save by using a cleaner-burning propane gas heater over a year? May I show you these cost comparisons between older wood- and coal-burning units such as yours and our modern energy-saving propane gas heater? They will help you visualize how our heater can pay for itself in only three years.

If a store owner objects that she does not have room to carry your product, you can point out that your line moves better than other lines and could thus mean faster turnover and greater profits for her. You can dramatize by selecting a specific window, shelf, or counter and comparing the turnover and profit advantages if your product or line were on display there. When making this comparison, forget the competition and concentrate on the benefits offered by your proposal.

PRODUCT OBJECTIONS

Prospects can voice objections to your product or service in many different ways, as these examples illustrate:

Your product is too new (or untried).
Your product does not fit into our normal range of stock.
Your product has been on the market too long.
Your product is not well-known.
There is no demand (or call) for your product.
I have heard reports of customers' having trouble with your product (or of dealers' having trouble selling it).
Your product would cause too many servicing problems.
It's too complicated for my people to operate.
I doubt that it will do the job for me (or what is claimed for it).

In general, if this type of objections is voiced early in the interview, it very likely is nothing more than an excuse and can be handled by the pass-over (or pass-by) technique.

If voiced again during or after your presentation, it is a serious objection that may indicate a directly competitive situation. What prospects may be asking for is proof or justification of the benefits you are offering. In other words, they may want to be reassured that they will be making the right decision. Testimonials from satisfied users, orders from other companies, and other visual evidence offer more convincing proof than words alone.

Here are some practical suggestions for handling certain categories of objections relating to products.

Too New or Not Well-Known. Every product was too new when it was first placed on the market. You can tell about and show proof of the market surveys and pretesting that went into preparing your product. Why would your company spend money developing and marketing it unless it expected it to gain customer acceptance? Show the advertising that will help make it well-known, demonstrate it if possible, and stress benefits, value, quality, and performance.

Has Been on the Market Too Long; No Demand for It. Knowledge of your own and of competing products is essential in handling this objection. If your product sells well elsewhere, then back this fact up with evidence from your sales kit and proof in the form of statistics or testimonials. Perhaps the prospect needs advice or help in marketing it properly. If so, you should be creative and resourceful in offering practical suggestions as to how to increase profitable turnover. Your own enthusiasm can rebuild the prospect's.

Not in Our Line. Diversification of merchandise in a few large outlets has been one of the most striking changes in modern retailing history. This trend has been especially strong in the United States and is rapidly extending all over the world. Major retail buyers have to keep abreast of new product lines or lose out to competition. Independent small store owners in particular face great competitive problems. A new line can help attract new customers and enable old customers to buy more than they did before when visiting the store.

Rumors of Trouble or Dissatisfaction with It. Your first step is to find out whether the dissatisfaction is a fact or merely a rumor. If a fact, try to solve the problem or let prospects know that the trouble was handled promptly and that all is well now. You can then secure agreement that misunderstandings can always occur but do not necessarily affect the validity of the proposal. Once they become open-minded, continue stressing benefits, especially the guarantees or follow-up servicing offered by both your company and you.

Doubts That It Will Offer What is Claimed for It. Make every effort to pin down specific objections and to discover whether they are valid doubts or mere excuses. Find out specifically why prospects have such doubts; do not accept generalities. Once you uncover their specific reasons, convince them with proof that your product performs exactly as you claim. Compare it with competing products; show testimonial letters or other visual proof; offer to telephone satisfied users and let prospects talk to them.

Too Complicated. Show them once again how easy your product is to operate once the procedure is mastered. Let prospects and also those who may be working with it in the future operate it themselves. Offer to help train operators as time permits, and stress the benefits it offers. Product knowledge, confidence, enthusiasm, and showmanship should easily dispel this problem.

COMPANY OR SOURCE-OF-SUPPLY OBJECTIONS

Many specific objections belong in this category. Some have to do with past problems in dealing with your company or former salespeople in the area. Others concern convenient competitive warehouse facilities, which may offer fast delivery or follow-up servicing, or the size of your company. Other objections center around the fact that the prospect is currently buying somewhere else and for a variety of reasons is reluctant to change.

Perhaps the best way to illustrate these objections and to consider how to handle them is to break them down as is done below. In general, they are best handled during the interview with attentive consideration. If expressed initially they may be mere excuses; if voiced once more or later on, they deserve serious attention.

ABC Company Can Give Me Better and Faster Service, Because Its Warehouse is Close By. Close proximity of central warehousing does not necessarily lead to fast or good service. But you have to present both solid reasons and factual evidence to justify claims that your company can offer comparable or better service. Testimonials from customers in the same or equally distant areas, written guarantees, or dated invoices and delivery dockets offer convincing proof that your service can and will meet requirements.

We Have Bought From ABC Company for Years and are Satisfied with Its Service. Your prospects will never know whether they can get better service until they give you a chance to prove it. One excellent appeal is to suggest that two satisfactory sources of supply are better than one and that they can only benefit from having two firms in friendly competition for their business. You can also point out that it is good business to make the wisest buying decision and to get the best products and prices from any source possible. Ask outright for an initial order to give you a chance to prove your claims.

I Buy From ABC Company Because I Have a Close Friend (or Relative) Who Works for Them. Prospects' first duty to themselves or to their organization is to get the best value and benefits money will buy. Apart from the value of the product itself, guarantees or assurances of efficient follow-up service should outweigh personal friendship. Loyalty to one's friends or relatives is an admirable trait, but surely friends do not expect prospects to continue buying from them if it is to their personal disadvantage or to that of their companies. Your task is to show how it is advantageous to give you at least part of the business and thus a chance to prove your claims of superiority.

We Have More or Less Promised to Buy From Some Other Salesperson. No order is firm until it has been officially placed by the buyer and accepted by the seller. The buyer's first duty to self or organization is to make the best buy possible. If your product is new, is inexpensive, is suited to the need, or offers other immediate benefits, it is only to the buyer's advantage to act now.

I Prefer to Buy From a Big (or Small) Company. You should treat the size of your company as an asset. Smaller companies can often render better personal service than large companies can, and they may be more specialized. Larger companies offer other advantages. In general, however, the size of the company does not count so much as the quality and reliability of the product and the reputation and service behind it.

Your Company (or Former Salesperson in the Area) Caused Me a Lot of Problems in the Past, and I Don't Want to Deal with You. Your immediate task is to find out exactly what the past problems were and to correct them immediately if still pending. Beyond that, your best rebuttal is to ask the buyer to forgive and forget and to let you try to make up for past problems by superior future service and special personal attention to needs.

STALLING OR PROCRASTINATION OBJECTIONS

Few things are more frustrating in selling than to make an enthusiastic presentation to an apparently interested prospect who, when asked for the order, makes one of the following replies.

> I'll have to think it over.
> I'm too busy to make a decision now.
> I must discuss it first with my wife (or husband or business associates).
> Leave your card and I'll get in touch with you.

This situation is frustrating because you apparently have not lost the sale, but you have not landed it either. The prospect usually does not need the extra time to make a decision. The objection may signify that he or she has not been completely convinced or still has some hidden objection or some personal misgivings that have not been brought to light.

Since he or she has not said, "No, I won't buy," you should not accept the statement at face value but should try for an immediate decision. In most cases, the prospect is just trying to postpone a decision that ought to be made now. If you let him or her postpone it, he or she probably will never get around to it and will finally forget it.

Such objections are usually mere stalls or procrastinations. You should view them as buying signals requiring a prompt, strong close. Here are some specific suggestions for handling such stalling objections.

I'll Have to Think It Over. Your first task is to find out the reason for delaying the decision; your most effective word tool is a simple why: "Why do you have to think it over?" If it is a mere excuse, the prospect may not be able to think of a good answer and may agree that there is no valid reason for delay. In such a case, ask for the order again. A valid reason is an objection that has to be handled. If it appears to be the only objection blocking the sale, then use of the powerful boomerang technique may be most effective.

Prospect: I'll have to think it over because of the cost involved.

Salesperson: It is only natural that you should feel that way, but in this period of rising prices, can you really afford not to consider buying now?

Another effective retort is this one.

Prospect: I'll have to think it over because of the cost involved.

Salesperson: Aren't there really two things to think over: (1) Do you need and want it and (2) can you afford it?

Prospect: Yes, I guess so.

Salesperson: You know just as well today as you will next month that you need and can use it, don't you?

Prospect: Yes.

Salesperson: And don't you know today as well as you will a month from now whether you can afford to enjoy its benefits?

Prospect: Yes.

Unless a valid objection is advanced, the prospect's problem is probably the psychological one of hating to make the decision. Thus you may have to help him or her over the psychological decision-making barrier. Here are some suggestions.

1. *Appreciate his or her caution.* Agree that is is never wise to rush into things but reemphasize the benefits that can be had immediately if he or she decides now.

2. *Offer special inducements for an immediate decision.* Perhaps you can throw in a bonus for an immediate decision in the form of merchandise, extended credit terms, or use of the buyer's name or name of his or her organization in a forthcoming advertising or promotional campaign.

3. *Offer protection against risk.* Since the purchase decision may have to be justified to others, you can stress again the guarantees offered by your company plus your personal involvement in protecting his or her interests and making sure that follow-up matters are handled in a satisfactory manner.

4. *Make the prospects feel obligated to you.* This involves doing something for them or getting something of value into their possession so that they may feel obligated to you, even in a very small way. You may act very eager to help or agree to send things anyway until they can make a decision. In effect, you are acting as though they have already inwardly made an affirmative decision.

5. *Stress the satisfaction that comes from having made a sound decision.* People who dislike making decisions usually feel quite relieved and happy once they have done so. By pointing out the pleasure and satisfaction that follow a sound purchasing decision, you help prospects to think positively beyond the immediate decision, which then becomes a minor or secondary consideration.

I'm Too Busy to Make a Decision Now.   If they had time to listen to your presentation, this objection is usually a mere excuse or stall. Again use the word *why*—"Why can't you take the time to decide now?" Use the technique noted in the "I'll-think-it-over" section noted previously and press for an immediate decision.

If it is a valid objection, do not waste their time, but fix a definite later appointment: "May I call back tomorrow at 10:20 A.M. to settle details, or would 2:30 P.M. be more convenient?" If they agree, they have probably decided in your favor, and you should talk and act from then on under that assumption.

I Must Discuss It with Someone Else.   If you qualified prospects properly and know they have the authority to buy, this objection may be a stall. It frequently means that your prospects are basically sold; they are just avoiding an immediate decision. You must immediately seek to find out why they have to talk to someone else and exactly who this person (or group) is. Suggest that the other person be brought in immediately so that you can talk to him or her or that you be allowed to go to see the other person at once.

If another discussion has to take place—between husband and wife or buyer and other business associates—make every effort to be present yourself. If this is not allowed, then go over the key points of your proposal once again with your prospect to make sure he or she understand them well enough to present them convincingly to someone else. Then try to set a specific time limit: "May I call back at 10:30 A.M. tomorrow for your final decision, or would 2:45 in the afternoon be more convenient?"

Leave Your Card, and I'll Get in Touch with You.   This is a polite way of brushing you off. You have failed to sell the prospect. It does not help to ask, "When will you call?" or to try to pressure him or her with "our special-offer-won't last" tactics. Just accept the fact that you have failed to hold his or her interest or pinpoint needs, and make a fresh start.

One technique for handling this situation is that useful one of apparently giving up, engaging in conversation only, and then going back into your presentation.

> Fine, Mr. Penkus, but before I go, for my own information, what point in my proposal appealed to you most? And what did you find most objectionable? Your comments may enable me to help someone else with problems similar to yours. Will you help me out by giving me the benefit of your honest opinion?

SOME LESS COMMON OBJECTIONS YOU MAY ENCOUNTER

Many less common objections can spoil a sale. Some are mere excuses; some reflect prejudice or misunderstanding; others result from previous, unfavorable experiences with your or some other firm or organization.

Some typical less common objections you may encounter involve credit terms or other company policy questions, legal questions, trade-in considerations, or technical performance questions. Your prospect may want to stock items on consignment to test resale rather than on outright initial purchase or may object even to your trying to close the sale or to other sales tactics. Proper handling of some of these questions may require assistance from the head office of your company, assistance from outside sources, or rapid creative thinking on your part.

A few such objections that may confront you are listed below. In general, you should strive to get your prospect to answer them before you do. Ask your prospect why he or she considers it a problem. Their talking about it may disclose hidden objections and suggest an easy solution for you.

Credit Problems. Such objections, which are usually mere excuses, may have to do with past credit or payment problems or with the fact that your credit terms are considered too difficult to meet. Usually, they are the standard gripes your prospects voice to competitive salespeople as well. They are merely trying to get the best bargain or the best terms. From their point of view, they have a lot to gain and nothing to lose by objecting to terms that you may be able to improve to their advantage if you want their business badly enough.

If they have a current problem with your company, try to resolve it immediately. If they have been refused credit before, assure them that the judgment was impersonal and that your company has to adhere to good business policies just as they do if in business or would do if they were in business. Try to get the facts, absolve yourself of personal blame, and let them know exactly what the credit conditions and terms of your company are.

You can point out justifications for such policies and help them see the reasonableness of them from your point of view. If you are honest and constructive in your approach, they will respect your loyalty to your company. In such cases, successful selling of your company usually leads to a sale of its specific product or service as well.

Legal Department Review. If prospects object that their legal departments or attorneys must review the purchase agreement first, (1) be sure no other objections are involved, and (2) write up the agreement and get a signature, based on a brief written-in contingency clause that the agreement is not to take effect until it has been approved by legal advisors. In many cases this procedure will satisfy prospects, and they will tell you to go ahead and fill the order as it stands, confident that you will stand behind the claims made.

Consignment. Selling on consignment is generally a bad practice simply because a customer does not have any incentive to push your product. Normally, if a businessperson stocks two items, one on consignment and one that must be paid for, he or she is inclined to push the one that he or she is obligated to pay for. This reason for not selling on consignment may make good business sense to prospects and causes them to drop the objection. You may be able to offer extended credit or returns concessions that reduce the element of risk from their point of view just as well as outright consignment does. Stand firm on your policy, and sell benefits; this objection is just an excuse.

Secondhand One Is Cheaper. Buyers get what they pay for. New products usually offer guaranteed performance and a known, high trade-in. Secondhand items often cost more in the long run, and are frequently turned in or offered for resale because they proved unsatisfactory. You can best prove cost differences by using facts and figures based on your prospects' cost or operating figures.

Trade-Ins. Trade-ins are often an important factor in many sales, especially those of durable goods such as automobiles, machine tools, or larger household appliances. Many suggested list prices, such as those in the automobile field, have built-in, sliding trade-in allowances.

Most sales authorities concerned with this problem suggest the following techniques for handling trade-ins, recognizing that prospects normally place a higher value on the older article than what it is worth.

1. Sell the new item first; avoid handling the trade-in until the prospect has been completely sold on the desirability and benefits of the new item.
2. Have the prospect place a value on the item before it is sent out for appraisal (hoping that it will be low).
3. Have the appraising done by a third or outside party when possible and outside the presence of the prospect (to avoid argument).
4. Try to make the final close on value and benefits of the new item, with the trade-in handled as a secondary, or minor, consideration.

If the prospect then strongly objects to the trade-in valuation, you simply have to persuade through facts, figures, and comparisons that the valuation is realistic.

SUMMARY

In this chapter, we first discussed the strategies, tactics, psychology, and techniques involved in handling objections. Handling objections and closing the sale are the two greatest problems in selling for both new and experienced salespeople.

Our discussion covered why objections are raised, what your attitude should be toward them, and how prior planning can help anticipate or forestall them. We covered both the broad strategy and the six basic techniques for handling objections, concluding with a number of observations that should enable you, with practice, to handle them successfully.

We then extended the discussion to consider in detail techniques for handling specific objections, standard as well as less common ones. We elected to call objections questions wherever possible and pointed out five major classifications of standard or common objections: (1) price, (2) no interest or need, (3) product, (4) company or source of supply, and (5) stalling or procrastination.

The point was made that an objection often provides an opportunity to go into a trial close. Thus we have already touched upon closing the sale—a subject that is covered in depth next chapter.

Before moving into that chapter, however, we should recall part of our opening statement in this chapter, since it relates so importantly to what we have been covering and what we will cover regarding objections and closing.

With only rare exceptions, you cannot close a sale as long as the prospect has any major objection or objections. Thus you have to understand the principles and techniques of handling objections before attempting to master closing techniques.

Questions for Analysis and Discussion

1.   What should your attitude be toward objections raised by your prospect?

2.   Why are objections so important to salespeople?

3.   What should be the standard reaction of any salesperson to an objection?

4.   If an objection appears truly important to your prospect, how should it be handled?

5.   What objections, commonly raised, are for most salespeople the most difficult to handle?

6.   Why is it so vitally important for a salesperson to understand the principles and techniques of handling objections?

7.   What is role-playing, and why is it especially useful in connection with handling objections?

8.   Since price is bound to come up in almost every presentation, what is the first thing you should do about handling it?

CASE STUDY 11

Over and Over, the Same Two Objections: "I'm Too Busy to See You Now:" "Your Prices are Too High!" Just Part of a Day's Work for Sales Engineer Tom Pih

"Although I hear these same two objections several times each normal working day," said Tom, signaling the waitress to refill his coffee cup, "they don't get to me because both to my regular customers and new prospects they usually are valid objections!

"You see," he continued, "I call on plumbing, heating and ventilation, and mechanical contractors, some running large companies, others much smaller operations—all of whom really are very busy! It doesn't help that most of my visits are, of necessity, cold calls. Fortunately, 80 percent of my calls are on regular customers who have known me for years, and our relationship is good. So good in fact, that my pet "counter" to these "I'm too busy to see you now" objections works to get me on-the-spot interviews nearly half the time."

Curious, Tom's lunch-table companion asks the logical question: "What is this magic 'counter' of yours?"

"Let me build up to my answer a bit," comes the reply. "First off, my 20-employee company, Warden & Sons, is a very well-known and highly regarded American manufacturer's representative and stocking distributor. In business since 1923, it represents 20 different manufacturers throughout southern California, southern Arizona, and all of Nevada. Some of these manufacturers, especially the very highly regarded three companies of the Armstrong group, we represent on an exclusive basis; the others on a nonexclusive basis.

"We have our own large warehouse in the Los Angeles area in which we stock hundreds of items such as steam traps, vents and drainers; steam and liquid coils, boiler blow-down separators, sight flow indicators, electric valve actuators and so on! Not very sexy stuff I guess—but all are essential items to our contractor customers.

"In order to sell those items, I, along with our company's seven other outside sales engineers, have to know (1) our customer's business thoroughly, (2) how each of our products work and how they fit into our customer's projects, and (3) how our products compare to competing products.

"Now, finally, back to my 'counter!' With my college engineering degree, 15 years experience in this field, and both my personal and my company's reputation on the line, I simply ask, 'Do you have any type of problem that I might be able to help you with so long as I am here?' Since nearly all of my customers bid on projects for others, such as designing and installing a custom steam-heating system for a new office building, they nearly always face problems of one type or another.

"Since my offer to help now is free, most reason, why not put me to work for them?—and they invite me in! As we discuss their problem, I naturally ease the conversation toward one or more of our products that might help solve it. If a competitor's product will do the job better, I frequently point out that fact—something that enhances my personal integrity and reputation in their eyes over the long run. A key element here is the fact that by inviting me in to discuss their problem they have mentally raised me from a petitioning salesperson to fellow professional level."

"That's good selling," said Tom's table companion, admiringly. "But you also mentioned another constant objection you face—that of 'Your price is too high.' What's the story on that one?"

"Unfortunately, that too is usually a valid objection," grinned Tom. "First, because they have to try to bid lower than their competitors to get a job, my contractor customers are always looking for the lowest price possible on a given product. And our products, especially our high-quality Armstrong ones, are seldom the least expensive to be found. Also, since our company must maintain its profit margin to remain a healthy business, stock our large inventory, and maintain our highly efficient customer service, we are seldom able to negotiate lower prices with our end-customers. Thus I hear over and over, day after day, the objection—Your prices are too high! I keep cool by remembering that my customers consider it an honest objection."

"Well, how do you handle it?" said Tom's companion, pushing his by now cold half-full second cup of coffee aside.

"Once again, the problem-solving approach works best for me," came the reply. "I always ask to look at the drawings done for my customers by their internal or outside engineers in order to compare how certain of my products conform to the intent of the presented specifications. If the specifications call for a competing product, I try to show how my product will do a better job. If experience allows me to pinpoint anything that may not work as well as they expect, they are respectful and pleased. But then that price question usually rears its ugly head!

"Once again, with my personal experience, sincere desire to help solve their problems regardless of immediate sale prospects, and personal and company reputation on the line, I counter-close by simply asking, 'Will you use my product and let me prove that I'll back you up with truly fast, reliable personal service?' Since both Warden & Sons and Tom Pih personally are in this business for the long run and have proven their after-sale reliability over many years, it's a powerful counter and close to the objection 'Your price is too high.' Best of all, its one that works to my advantage more often than not."

"Well," said Tom, as the waitress moved in to clear the table, "this chat has been fun, but it's now time to make my afternoon calls. Can you guess what two objections I will hear most often?" He laughed cheerfully as he strode briskly toward the restaurant cashier's counter.

Questions for Written Reports or Class Discussion

1. Would you consider the two objections faced so often by sales engineer Tom Pih to be honest objections of a business nature, or more along the lines of a personal nature? Explain your reasoning.

2. Putting yourself in Tom's shoes for a moment, and knowing that you are likely to face the honest objection, "Your price is too high," outline some ways that you can build counters to it into your presentation, to be employed before the objection is verbally raised during future sales calls.

3. What types of proof might you offer during a sales presentation, assuming that you are Tom, that may justify the higher cost of one of your products—one that you feel is best for your prospect.

4. Based on information contained in this case study, present two additional ways that might enable Tom to handle his commonly encountered valid objection, "I'm too busy to see you now."

Planning how to handle objections that may be raised in a bid for provincial government business in western Canada

Bill Bradley, technical sales representative for Southwestern Pipe Manufacturing Co. of Tulsa, Oklahoma U.S.A. is sitting in his hotel room this evening in Edmonton, Canada. Tomorrow morning he has an appointment with James Pike, Chief Engineer for the western province of Alberta, of which Edmonton is the capital.

Bill's sales objective is to persuade Mr. Pike to at least approve Southwestern's culvert pipe for trial use in provincial culverts. Right now he is writing on a sheet of paper some objections Mr. Pike is likely to raise, thinking out his best possible answers, and jotting them down alongside each objection. He will later build these into his planned presentation.

Realizing that Mr. Pike, like all prospects, will probably have a variety of reasons for raising objections, Bill also knows that any objections raised will most likely fall into one of these three categories:

1. Those raised very early in the interview, in the event Mr. Pike decides quickly he isn't interested in spending much time with Bill.
2. Those intended to avoid the necessity of Mr. Pike's giving in to Bill's logical presentation because he isn't ready or willing to make a decision then or there.
3. Those that are really valid.

Bill has divided his planning sheet into these three parts. His aim is to briefly acknowledge category 1 objections and carry right on with his presentation, unless he senses that his prospect really means what he says. He plans to handle the category 2 objections, which may be raised at any point in his continuing presentation, in a "yes, but" style. Since the category 3 objections will be serious and important ones, he wants to handle them immediately to Mr. Pike's satisfaction.

Here is what he has written down so far:

Possible Objections	Planned Response
Category 1	
a. I have only a few minutes to spend with you today.	That's fine. My time is limited, too. If I haven't got exactly what you need, it will be obvious in a few minutes, and we can both take care of more important matters.
b. I'm not buying anything today.	
Category 2	
a. Your culvert pipe may be acceptable. Why don't you leave your descriptive brochure and price schedule, and I'll let you know our decision later.	

Possible Objections	Planned Response

b. Sounds interesting, but I've already
   exhausted my current open-to-buy.
   I'll drop you a note when I have
   more money available.
c. I'll think about it.

Category 3
a. We have only limited warehouse
   space and can't make room for your
   pipe at this time.
b. I am satisfied with the pipe we are
   now using.
c. I am not certain that your pipe can
   meet our provincial requirements/
   specs.

Question for Written Report or Class Discussion

Assuming that you are Bill, what planned responses will you write in the blank spaces alongside the as-yet-unanswered objections?

<table>
<tr><td>**Sales
Problem 11.2**</td><td>**Time is running out—how can salesperson Chuck Nelson handle this objection? "I tried a similar line before and it didn't turn over"**</td></tr>
</table>

Salesperson Chuck Nelson has just finished presenting his line of plastic-packaged small hand tools to Mr. Edwards, manager of a large hardware store. The presentation has gone smoothly, and Chuck feels confident of success as he moves into this close.

> *Chuck:* Would you like to start with our 2500-lot order, which includes a free display case, or a smaller one without it?

> *Mr. Edwards:* I don't believe your line will sell here. I tried a similar line once before and it just didn't turn over.

The phone on Mr. Edward's desk rings, and he turns to answer it. As he does so, Chuck's mind is racing as he seeks a way to handle this difficult, surprise opinion objection.

"I've already pointed out the extra profit potential of my really superior line," Chuck thinks to himself. "And I've also pointed out that our suggested display case arrangement will help increase sales of other noncompeting items."

Chuck wonders what he will say when Mr. Edwards hangs up the phone and faces him once again. "I'd better not repeat my sales story point again that our line will be a good seller, because it's Mr. Edward's opinion that it won't, and that could start an argument between us."

Time is fast running out. Mr. Edwards is saying goodbye to the caller and will hang up any second now.

"What *can* I do or say to change his opinion?" Chuck mentally asks himself.

Question for Written Report or Class Discussion

Assuming you are Chuck, how will you handle this objection and turn it into a sale?

CHAPTER 12

How to Close the Sale

After studying this chapter, you will be able to:

Explain, from a business point of view, the chief justification for the existence of a salesperson.

Describe what is meant by the statement, "A successful close starts in the salesperson's mind and manner."

Identify three actions or "buying signals" on the part of the prospect that indicate that it is time to try for a close.

Cite three points of the theory of multiple-close, or trial-close, technique.

Summarize what is meant by the statement, "Selling starts when the prospect says no."

Describe how and when to use fourteen closing techniques.

We are now ready to tackle our moment of truth—the close! To *close* is to end or terminate something one has set out to do. From a sales point of view, closing means getting the prospect's verbal or signed agreement to buy the product or service offered.

All your planning and hard work and your careful presentation have had one purpose—to secure your prospect's agreement or "Yes, I'll buy." Your buildup to this single objective involves the use of logic, reason, emotion, persuasion, and impulse. During one or several moments during the interview the prospect may be ready to buy. Even the most experienced salespeople feel a thrill of excitement at the approach of these moments.

What can you do at such times to help your prospects over the hump—to change their possible wavering indecision into either a direct or an indirect "Yes, I'll buy"? Answering this question is the objective of this chapter.

CLOSING THE SALE IS THE CHIEF OBJECTIVE FOR A SALESPERSON

Asked to list their major job duties, most salespeople could give a pretty good and quick answer. They'd mention such things as finding prospects, researching their operations, making appointments, tailoring their presentations for each one. Surprisingly, however, a good percentage of them would not think to mention their single most important duty: closing the sale.

You might ask, "Don't all real salespeople know that their main purpose when face to face with a prospect is to *sell*?" The answer to that is yes—but sometimes they get so involved in concepts such as "solving prospects' problems" and "helping them do their jobs" that they forget these concepts are not ends in themselves, but merely tools to facilitate making the sale. Frequently, in fact, all too many salespeople don't even *ask* for the order—and are surprised when this is pointed out by their sales managers (or in some embarrassing cases, by prospects themselves).

To succeed in selling, you must always keep in mind that the multitude of duties you perform has one major, overriding purpose—to enable you to close sales. Important though all these duties are, none constitutes a valid test of your ability as a salesperson. If, for example, you are the best salesperson in your sales force at prospecting, that gives you a good head start, but in itself it doesn't earn you a single sale. There is only one test of your selling ability: How good are you at closing?

Let's make it clear! Closing the sale or getting the order is the justification for your existence as a *real salesperson*. Getting the signed order is your job; it is what you are paid to do!

If you seriously aspire to sales success or aspire to reach management ranks through selling, you have to accept and act upon the assumption that, unless you close sales, you will not be successful.

Very few prospects volunteer orders; they have to be asked for their business. Mere asking is not enough, however; you, as a salesperson, have to ask in such a way that you get a "Yes, I'll buy now," instead of a "no," a stall, or a put-off. This problem poses one of the greatest challenges to both new and experienced salespeople. It involves knowing when to close and how to close.

A SUCCESSFUL CLOSE STARTS IN YOUR MIND AND MANNER

When considering the mental attitude of your prospects in a closing situation, put yourself in their shoes for a moment; try to see things as they see them. They are comparing the advantages of buying now with the disadvantages. Unless the advantages offer great appeal, their initial reactions are generally those of caution—to either refuse or postpone the decision.

From your point of view, you are there (1) to help prospects make up their minds, (2) to convince them that they do need or want your product or service, and (3) to persuade them to take action now to acquire it. If you feel confident that your product offers value and are enthusiastic in your presentation of the benefits, you tend to act with confidence and enthusiasm. They sense your confident attitude, which has a positive effect on them. Conversely, any negative attitudes, any wavering, hesitation, or lack of force in your verbal expression, attitude, or manner have a negative effect. Thus you have a good chance of closing if you can create the proper psychological climate by being positive in attitude and speech and confident in manner.

This positive attitude on your part together with knowledge of the proper strategy, tactics, and techniques of closing will help overcome any fear of asking for the order—a fear quite common among new salespeople especially.

WHEN DO YOU TRY TO CLOSE (BUYING SIGNALS)?

In the early days of sales analysis and training, much was made of the so-called single psychological moment during a presentation when the sale would either be made or be irrevocably lost. This older single-moment theory has long been discredited.

The modern concept of personal selling holds that there are many situations or psychological moments during a sales interview when prospects may be prepared to buy. The "yes" may come following any plausible, believable, compelling reason to buy now. Such a compelling reason may come after the approach, after any one of the selling points in your presentation, or after you have successfully handled an objection. Your prospects may also feel compelled to buy after your complete presentation.

Many salespeople make the mistake of not trying to close until they have completed their entire presentation and thus miss earlier opportunities. How do you know when to try for a close? The answer to that question has been presented several times up to this point in our text—whenever you sense that your prospect is sending out "buying signals" such as:

- *Spoken words.* The prospect may ask the price, or ask that you repeat details, or ask about delivery time, or give other verbal indications of interest to you or to a third party who may be present.
- *Facial expressions.* A raised eyebrow, a nod, an interested look in your prospect's eyes may indicate a positive interest and readiness to say yes.
- *Physical actions.* He or she may examine details of your demonstration model closely, or may pick up your agreement form and start reading it carefully.

These actions, among others, are signals that indicate or express prospect interest. Whenever you notice them, you should stop talking and attempt a trial close.

In Chapter 11, it was noted that certain types of objections might actually represent buying signals worth an immediate trial close. Unfortunately, far too many salespeople fail to recognize the difference between a buying signal and an objection. They too often handle it as an objection and keep selling—to the point where they lose the sale. The problem in such cases is, how can you tell the difference between a buying signal and an objection? There is no hard and fast answer to this problem. Your best solution is to "work with" the objection, and attempt a trial close after any point that appears to interest your prospect.

Finally, of course, you should go into a close at the conclusion of your presentation.

THEORY OF MULTIPLE-CLOSE, OR TRIAL-CLOSE, TECHNIQUE

The modern approach involves trying to close at every possible opportunity or at least testing the prospect's readiness through multiple, or trial closes, sometimes called experimental or test closes. You thus make several attempts to close throughout the interview. You may not succeed on any one try, but you have lost nothing and can continue with the next point in your presentation.

Key points of this dynamic theory are (1) it is never too early to try for a close; (2) try for a close after each strong point; (3) a negative reply to a trial close is never to be regarded as final but just as an invitation to continue selling.

PRACTICAL SUGGESTIONS FOR CLOSING

Avoid Atmosphere of Pressure or Tension

Some prospects have an illogical, emotional fear of making a buying decision. This can cause trouble in closing situations unless possible problems are anticipated and avoided. Some prospects are so nervous about being sold something that they resent any attitudes, words, or actions that to them might indicate high-pressure tactics.

In such cases you may have to help your prospects make their decisions. You try to help them by giving reasons why they should buy. This should be done carefully, so as not to increase the emotional tension they feel or ruffle them. Do this by stating specific facts or benefits as reasons for buying, and base your closing attempt on them rather than on any emotional pressure. Thus we can reemphasize that before closing you should know what the prospect wants to accomplish or what his or her desires are and should direct your presentation and closing remarks to satisfying those needs or desires.

For example, in selling a new automobile to a woman who seemingly has agreed to all the points but who now just can't emotionally make up her mind to buy, using price as a reason for hesitation, you can ask quietly, "Is price your only reason for not buying?" If she agrees, then show savings she can expect in maintenance and fuel cost. Such a review of benefits will show the price to be reasonable. Then try to close again by saying, "Wouldn't you like to own this truly economical new automobile?" Make it easy for her to say yes.

Another way to handle this emotional situation is to say, "Take your time in thinking it over, I don't want you to buy this car if you are not really convinced that it is both reasonably priced and the type you want. Suppose you think it over tonight, and I'll hold it for you until noon tomorrow. May I telephone you at 10:00 A.M., or would 11:30 tomorrow morning be better?" Not only have you relieved her anxiety, but if she agrees to your hold and call, it means the sale is in effect closed.

Handling the Order Form or Agreement

Since the order form or agreement, if suddenly produced for the first time during a closing attempt, frightens some prospects many salespeople (as was noted in Chapter 7) lay it out at the start of the presentation so a prospect can get used to it. When laid out from the start like this, the salesperson can often write on it during the interview without offending the prospect. If the salesperson takes it out early and finds that it does offend the prospect, he or she can put it back in with other sales material so that it is readily available at the proper time. When to make the order form or agreement visible, and how to handle it during a sales presentation may be a matter of personal salesperson choice or a matter of employer policy. Some salespeople table them only after making a successful verbal close.

Positioning Seating for Control

A practical suggestion is to try to seat yourself to the left of your prospects so that visual materials, calculations, or the order form or agreement is in their line of vision. This position also enables you to control the presentation steps, the closing situation, and the signing of agreement or any other forms.

SELLING STARTS WHEN YOUR PROSPECTS SAY NO

Very few prospects are ready to buy when called upon—they have to be persuaded to do so. Their initial reluctance to buy is therefore natural and to be expected, and their negative replies to trial closings are nothing to become unduly alarmed about. It is easier for prospects to say no than to say yes because it is a safer position.

Selling really begins when prospects say no. As has been noted previously, what they often really mean is "Maybe," "Tell me more," or "I'm not exactly sure I know what you mean." General Dwight Eisenhower said no many times before agreeing to run for President of the United States in 1952, and most big American automobile manufacturers initially said no to the idea of producing compact cars to compete against the Volkswagen and other small European and Japanese automobiles. In other words, a no does not necessarily mean what it says: your prospects can always change their minds. You as a salesperson must be a mind changer; it is your job to turn negative doubts into positive desires.

HOW TO CLOSE THE SALE: FOURTEEN TESTED TECHNIQUES

The literature of selling contains more discussion about closing sales than about any other single topic. Many complete books have been written on the subject, especially on specific closing techniques.

Perhaps the best-known author of such books is Charles B. Roth, an American sales consultant. Here are his four basic closing secrets.

1. Start your presentation on a closing action, continue it on a closing action, and end it on a closing action. In other words, close, close, close, all the time.
2. Make it easier for the buyer to say "yes" than "no."
3. Have at least one closing action in reserve to use when everything else has failed.
4. Try once more. Even when it seems impossible to make a sale, go back for one more try.[1]

Most of the books and articles on closing name and describe from six to fifteen specific techniques. These have been researched, redefined, and, with new material added, regrouped into the following fourteen tested closing techniques. As you study these various techniques and put them into practice, you will find that some are easier to use and bring better results than others. You can never hope to close every sale, but mastery of these techniques is essential to continued sales success.

[1] Charles B. Roth, *My Lifetime Treasury of Selling Secrets* (Englewood Cliffs, N.J.: Prentice-Hall, 1957), p. 110.

1. *Ask-for-the-Order (Direct-Question) Close*

    This is the simplest and often the most effective closing technique—a logical conclusion to the rational presentation in which no unusual objections are encountered. This technique is based on the assumption that your prospect will buy. After the facts have been presented, what could be more natural than to ask for the order in a straightforward manner: "How would you like me to handle your order?" or "Can you give me your purchase order number now?"

    Many salespeople, amazingly enough, do not frankly ask for the order because of a hidden fear that, after the presentation has gone so well, the prospect will suddenly say no. However, you will never know until you ask for the order. Simply asking for it under favorable circumstances can often settle the question quickly and easily.

    Although this direct-question technique is normally employed only in the simple and easy situation just described, you can use it in some unusual situations. For example, if competitive products and prices are about the same and you feel that the prospect likes you as a person, you can simply ask: "Since all things are equal, Mr. Giannoni, will you give me the chance to handle this order for you?"

2. *Assumptive (Presumption or Assumption or Possessive) Close*

    This simple yet highly effective technique is based on your assumption that the prospect is going to buy and that only the details need to be worked out. You make a statement that presupposes buying, and if he or she agrees with it, the sale is closed.

    You can accomplish this close by words alone, as this example shows.

Salesperson: Don't you really feel, Mr. Gonzales, that this offer is a good buy?

Prospect: Yes, I do think it's worth the money.

Salesperson: (using assumptive close) I am certain you will be satisfied with it. I'll mark it down for immediate delivery if that is all right.

Or you can accomplish it by a physical action.

Prospect: Yes, I do think it's worth the money.

Salesperson: (simply hands the prospect a pen and points to the X beside the signature line on the agreement form, indicating, without saying a word, that he or she is to sign).

Or you can use a combination of words and physical action.

Prospect: Yes, I do think it's worth the money.

Salesperson: (handing the pen and pointing to the order form) If you will just OK this agreement by the X here, I'll mark you down for immediate delivery.

The psychology behind this close is that it is easier to get tacit approval than to get a specific yes. With this technique a nod, a grunt, or even silence signifies agreement. In effect, you are asking the prospect to stop or to deny your positive, confident action—a smooth-flowing, logical development of your yes-building steps of the presentation. If he or she does not stop you, then you have approval, and the sale is made.

You do not offend your prospects if you go smoothly into this close following a positive statement. Do not use it after a strong objection or a not-interested comment until that has been properly handled and positive agreement reached. They know you are there to try to close a sale, and if you smoothly conclude it in this way, they are in agreement with your words or actions.

If they object they will tell you so, and you can back off and start on another selling point for which you seek agreement. Then try this closing technique again or one similar to it, such as the minor-point technique, or a totally different one.

When the order form is introduced from the start and the salesperson writes upon it throughout the interview as a record, this assumption technique is, of course, being used powerfully.

You can soften this closing technique by using a few cushion words that further reduce chances of your prospects' getting the feeling that they are being nudged into a close. For example, the salesperson in our illustration might have said, "Assuming that you want me to mark you down for immediate delivery, may I have your OK by the X here on the agreement?"

This assumptive close is one of the easiest and most effective of all closing techniques if used at the proper time—following agreement to a positive statement or even following an affirmative silence after such a settlement. It suits all types of selling and all sales personalities.

3. *Minor-Point (Alternative or Choice-Technique or Minor-Issue or Double-Question) Close*

This technique is especially suited to vacillating prospects or to those who honestly fear making a final decision. It involves passing over the big decision and asking them to make a choice between two minor issues. Making that easier decision implies an affirmative decision. For example, "I assume you like this time, Mrs. Tolbert; would you prefer to save 2 percent by paying cash, or would convenient, extended payment terms suit you better?" The attention of prospects is drawn to a decision between cash or charge—a much easier decision to make than one on the object itself. The cushion "I assume" helps soften the effect. A harder but acceptable lead-in may also be "Do you want to pay cash and save 2 percent, or charge it?"

The minor-point close is a modification of the assumptive close discussed previously in that it too involves an assumption on your part that prospects are going to buy. Your aims are to secure their agreement to a positive sales point or statement, to assume they are going to buy, and then to offer them a choice between two minor alternatives, such as guarantees, dates of delivery, models, or color.

> Would you prefer one-year payment terms or twenty-four months?
> Would you like the agreement shown in your name or jointly with your spouse?
> Would you like shipment made here or to your overseas branch office?

Whichever choice prospects make, the sale is closed. If they refuse to make the choice, then you merely continue with the presentation.

4. *Continued-Affirmative (Yes-Building Stimulus-Response, or Continuous-Yes) Close*

Some prospects apparently agree with all the major points of your presentation, yet do not give final approval. They can often be closed with a rapid, enthusiastic, logical, yes-building summary of major issues from their point of view. The psychology of this approach is that a series of yes answers leads to a final, easy yes answer that brings the sale to a close.

Salesperson:	If I am correct, you are most impressed with the quality and durability it offers in view of the reasonable price, is that true?
Prospect:	Yes, I believe it does.
Salesperson:	And don't you agree that our payment terms are reasonable?
Prospect:	Yes, they seem to be.
Salesperson:	Would you like to have delivery next Tuesday if it can be arranged?
Prospect:	Yes, that will be satisfactory.

5. *Narrowing-the-Choice Close*

In many types of selling prospects face such a bewildering array of choices that they find it difficult to make a decision. Consider this problem in a retail situation: a puzzled man trying to select a necktie from a wide assortment of colors and fabrics; or a perplexed woman seated before the store mirror, trying on one new hat after another from the nearby large collection of bright colors and styles. The situation in many American and Canadian automobile showrooms is somewhat the same: Selecting the brand (Ford, Chevrolet, Plymouth) is only a start; then come the various styles, models, price ranges, accessories, and color choices.

The salesperson can often bring about a rapid close in such cases by helping narrow the choices and by putting the items rejected, insofar as possible, out of sight and out of mind as decisions are made. Here are some examples:

Do you prefer bright or dark colors?
Would your spouse like this color best or that?
Any of these three would suit you. Am I right?
Don't you really like this one best?

This same situation can often occur as well with intangibles, such as life insurance or mutual-investment funds, when a wide variety of programs or plans is offered. The salesperson can help narrow the choice in such situations by offering a specific plan for the protection or investments desired or by determining the size of yearly or monthly premiums or payments. Proper use of this technique, especially in such technical areas as insurance or securities, not only helps close the sale but also offers guidance and service to prospects. And, when prospects have made their final choice, they have, in effect, given approval to your proposal.

6.   *Narrative (Report-Technique) Closing*

You can often restate closing points most convincingly in the form of a narrative or story that points to a situation similar to that of your prospect. Since we all like to profit or learn from the mistakes of others, this seemingly neutral approach can often be more effective than your personal sales summation.

The purpose of the story is to tactfully drive home the point that your prospect would be unwise to delay a decision. By pointing out the benefit gained by another who bought in similar circumstances or the loss suffered by one who failed to buy, you help your prospect get the message.

Such narratives should sound plausible and not made up, yet it is unnecessary to give names. Not using names often makes it easy for your prospects to picture themselves in the described situation.

Here is how an insurance salesperson might employ the narrative closing technique.

Prospect: Your protection plan sounds good; but I'll have to think it over.

Salesperson: I respect your thoughtful attitude, Mr. Wilkins, but sometimes it pays to act now. Just last month, for example, a gentleman in nearby Oakdale considered a $200,000 life insurance plan similar to this. He didn't have a lot of ready cash, but I helped him work out a convenient payment plan. One week later, just seven days exactly, he was killed in an automobile accident. He had paid only $100 into the plan.

The $200,000 from the policy he had just taken out one week, seven days to the day, earlier will enable his wife and two children to get along without her having to work. Don't you owe it to your family to act now and to give them the same immediate protection?

7.   *Follow-the-Leader (Testimonial or Bandwagon) Close*

Nothing succeeds like success, and this simple yet effective closing technique basically follows that line of reasoning. By looking over the biggest list possible of recent (and, through proof or implication, satisfied) buyers, your prospects, not wanting to miss out on a good thing, gain the confidence or conviction to go along with the others.

When using this technique, cite by name those buyers who by sheer size or importance rate highly in your prospects' minds. Apart from a list of these important trend-setting buyers, a lengthy list of recent buyers can often impress them. Showing copies of orders from your own order books is convincing proof of your claims. Testimonial letters from recent buyers, citing impressive resales or performance results, offer further persuasive proof.

8. *Summary (Balance-Sheet or Tip-the-Scale or T-Account or Build-Up) Close*

This technique can either be the simple one of holding up a finger for each major point or reason for buying, along with a verbal summary, or writing them down briefly in front of prospects. Like a lawyer summing up the logical point of proof in a courtroom case, yet much more informally, you strive to build up a convincing list of reasons why prospects should act now to obtain the benefits offered. This rapid summary or resumé of points in which they seem most interested, when presented in logical and enthusiastic manner, should build up in importance to the point that has the greatest appeal. You can tie in this build-up summary with any one of the other closing techniques to secure final assent.

The simple T-account of the sort show in Table 12.1 appeals especially to the rational-minded business or industrial buyer accustomed to balance-sheet, asset-and-liability, profit-and-loss thinking. Needless to say, your list of reasons to act should be far longer and more impressive than the list of reasons not to act! A suggested close is "In view of these impressive facts, Mr. Parr, is there any reason not to act now?"

9. *Question (Why-Not or Doubt-Eliminating) Close*

The purpose of this technique is to uncover any doubt that may be holding up a final affirmative decision. Acting as if and assuming that prospects are going to buy, you ask in a straightforward manner what reasons, if any, they have for not acting now. Your question may be, "What have I failed to make clear that keeps you from acting now?" or "You seem to be hesitating, Ms. Easter; what is the reason?" The reply determines your course of action. You may elect to use the objection as the reason for buying now through employment of the trap, or boomerang technique, or you may use any one of the other closing techniques.

10. *Surprise (New-Angle or Hat-Trick or Conquer-by-Yielding) Close*

We noted earlier the importance of keeping at least one strong sales point up your sleeve for emergency use. The necessity of having that reserve ammunition becomes apparent as we consider this last-resort closing technique, to be employed only after all others have failed.

Some tough or sophisticated prospects refuse to be swayed by logical or emotional arguments. They do not offer any objections but just try to put

TABLE 12.1 *Example of a Simple T-Account Summary, Often Drawn up in Front of a Prospect as a Closing Technique*

Reasons Not to Act	Reasons to Act
1. Budget problems	1. Will save $1000 per year operating costs
2. Must consult with others	2. Will do the job better and faster
	3. Is easier for unskilled employee to operate
	4. Can get immediate delivery if ordered now
	5. Can save $300 by buying at special introductory price until the end of this month

you off with an "I'll have to think it over." They may really want to buy but for some reason do not want to give in to you.

In order to avoid a personal or emotional situation in which they may say no because of your insistence on bringing the issue to a close, you can appear to quit trying. As illustrated by earlier examples of this technique in action, in the face of your apparent giving up, or quitting, they relax their guard. Also, they feel the emotional satisfaction of thinking they have won a minor victory over you. This satisfaction switches their thoughts from resistance to the true picture of your proposal and its benefits to them.

Words such as, "Well, thank you for your time and attention, Mr. Lambert" or actions such as picking up your papers or even standing up indicate that you have given up trying to close the sale and are ready to depart; the prospect, sensing that you have quit trying to sell, relaxes.

Salesperson: (speaking casually) By the way, Mr. Lambert, before I leave, may I make one more brief point?

Prospect: (relaxed and happy to oblige) Why, certainly, go right ahead.

Salesperson: (bringing up an entirely new sales point) I almost overlooked a very important point in our guarantee. It provides free inspection and minor repair service for a whole year. Here is how it saves you up to $250 per year. (Goes back into this new sales point, around which he or she attempts another closing.)

The defenses of your prospects are down because they thought you were departing; their poise and self-assurance are shaken as you go after them with a new sales point. If it is a strong and convincing one, it can swing the put-off into a reason for action now.

11. *Emotional (Appeal-to-Pride, or Fear) Close*

If you sense that a prospect's final decision to buy is likely to be based largely on impulse or emotion rather than logic or reason, this close may bring quick results. It is a closing technique that appeals specifically to emotions such as pride, thrift, or prestige. Normally used in a positive manner ("Wouldn't it feel good to be seen driving this powerful new car?"), it can also be used in a negative sense in some types of selling. An insurance salesperson, for example, may appeal to fear ("Have you considered your spouse's situation if you pass away without any insurance protection?"). It is normally employed after a careful build-up to help certain slow-moving prospects make their final decisions.

The emotional close works most effectively with certain prospects—some women home buyers, for example—and in some types of selling, such as insurance, or fund-giving for specialized types of causes (for example, help for African famine victims). It is not an effective technique for selling machine tools to industrial buyers. Our previously mentioned man looking at new ties or woman looking at new spring hats may not need or even want one. But they can be moved to an impulse buying decision by a salesperson's emotional appeals, such as "It will make you feel good to wear it," "You will be in step with fashion," or "The color suits you."

A dramatic, emotional story to illustrate a closing point can be a powerful psychological weapon for an experienced salesperson facing certain susceptible prospects. As such, it should be used with care and with the highest ethical considerations. Especially when built around fear, these closes are last-resort techniques. They should ethically be used only when prospects need the benefits, can afford them, and have no real or valid objections.

12. *Boomerang (Trap or Closing-on-the-Objection or Closing-on-Resistance) Close*
   As discussed earlier, this technique involves turning prospects' major objections for not buying into reasons why they should buy now. It is normally reserved as the most powerful last-resort technique for handling the final objection that seems to be blocking the sale. It is especially effective in meeting objections not strongly backed by facts or reasons. Ideally you should soften it by smiling and looking friendly.

   Prospect: I can't afford it now.

   Salesperson: You really can't afford not to buy now at this special, low introductory price. If I can offer acceptable payment terms, is there any reason not to act now?

13. *Inducement (or Concession) Close*
   In some cases an extra push is necessary to secure final agreement. You may be able to offer a special concession as inducement for an immediate affirmative decision. This closing technique is effective in final appeals to the two major factors that move prospects to action: (1) the desire for gain—"If you'll take it now, as a favor I'll phone our shipping department to deliver it tomorrow. Would you like that?" or (2) the fear of loss—"Unless you decide now, I can't guarantee delivery for 90 days at least."

   Many inducements urge the prospect to buy now: special extended credit terms, advertising allowances, seasonal packaging, an extra bonus, cash discounts (ethical, legal, and industry codes permitting), or other offers.

   Usually you should hold this easy-to-use technique in reserve. A danger in using it is that a sharp trader may sense eagerness on your part and hold out for additional concessions.

14. *Standing Room Only (or Last Chance) Close*
   This close involves an honest statement by the salesperson as to why prospects should buy now, assuming that the item being sold may not be available later. Real estate salespeople often use this technique if homes in a new development are nearly sold out (for example, "We have only a few models available for sale at these prices. Prices in the next section to be developed will be higher due to inflation."). This technique must only be used ethically.

Nearly all prospects, whatever the product or service they are considering, tend to have this in common: they would prefer to put off the buying decision. Your closing task as a salesperson is to overcome this tendency—to persuade prospects to buy now, today.

What prospects dislike most is a high-pressure salesperson or sales presentation—it frightens them. It is always wrong for a salesperson who finds a prospect unimpressed to try to strengthen a weak and unconvincing sales story by applying pressure of any sort. If prospects sense this is happening, they are likely to feel insulted, decide they dislike the salesperson personally, and become disinclined to buy then or ever.

Conversely, the salesperson who carefully prepares a presentation, who meets questions or objections calmly as they are raised, and who can carry prospects along step by step as he or she outlines the benefits prospects will reap from buying will impress and retain the confidence of prospects. Work this way, look for and quickly act on opportunities for closing, and the order will most likely follow.

As conclusion to our chapter on closing, here are three special opportunity signs that, in addition to others already discussed, represent signals to *start closing*.

The Prospect Indicates Interest in Making a Greater Profit

If this opportunity sign rises, move quickly to turn a profit urge into a reason for buying now. Try to dramatize, with figures, how much it will cost to delay the decision. For example, perhaps your product offers a small per-unit cost advantage over what is being used now. Suppose the prospect needs 1000 of them. For every month delayed, it is costing 1000 × the per-unit savings of your product versus the competition's.

Does the Prospect Fear or Envy a Competitor?

If the purchase of what you sell is not confidential or proprietary, why not mention to the prospect that competitor X Company seems to be on the verge of making a decision, or has just made one? Competition is the life blood of business. Stimulating or capitalizing on rivalry can often lead to a quick close.

Does the Prospect Indicate Interest in a Bargain?

If so, hit this bargain nerve by moving right into a trial close. Say, if it's so, "This is the last week we can accept your order on this basis," or "I'm sure you realize that prices are rising, and that this price may not be available again." State your proposition to highlight any bargain aspect you can offer.

We have covered in this chapter the basic strategy, tactics, and techniques of closing the sale. Closing, or getting a verbal or signed agreement to buy, is the basic objective of every real salesperson and the chief justification for his or her existence from a business viewpoint. We noted that the psychological climate for a successful close starts in the mind (having a positive attitude) and manner (being confident) of the salesperson.

We posed the question of when to try to close. The answer was basically close early, close often, close late. We discussed buying signals as clues to when to close; they involve spoken words, facial expressions, and physical action. Trial closes are part of the multiple-close theory of trying to close often throughout the interview. We offered several practical suggestions for creating the physical and emotional settings conducive to successful closing.

We agreed that selling starts when the prospect says, "No" or "Not interested now." Such negative expressions not only should be expected but also should be considered as invitations to continue selling. In conclusion, we presented fourteen tested closing methods or techniques.

Questions for Analysis and Discussion

1.   From a business point of view, what is the chief justification for the existence of a salesperson?
2.   What does modern sales theory have to say about the so-called single psychological moment for the close during a sales presentation?
3.   At what point during a presentation should a salesperson try to close?
4.   Why was the statement made in this chapter that closing techniques should be built around yes-building questions?
5.   In cases where a prospect apparently wants to buy but emotionally cannot manage to say yes, what can an empathic salesperson do to help him or her decide?
6.   What do we mean by the statement, "Selling starts when your prospect says no?"
7.   What is the simplest and most often effective closing technique any salesperson can use?
8.   The minor-point closing technique is especially suited to the vacillating prospect or to the one who honestly fears making a final decision. What does it involve?

Volkswagen Stresses the Gentle-But-Firm Approach to a Satisfactory Buying Decision

Rising up from the rubble of their bombed-out Wolfsburg, Germany factory in 1945, Volkswagen executives started manufacturing and selling both at home and abroad their strange looking little "peoples' car," which soon fondly became known as the "VW Beetle." By the mid-1970s, with over 22 million sold in some 130 countries, the "Beetle" represented one of the world's greatest sales success stories.

How was it that such a small and different-looking foreign car arose from nowhere to challenge even the mighty American auto manufacturers of Detroit right in their United States home market? And how did the company continue to expand its market share both in the United States and worldwide with subsequent newer automobiles such as the Golf, Jetta, and Sirocco?

Volkswagen of America, Inc. with over 1015 authorized dealers and over 9000 employees (including dealership personnel) has some answers. They say success is due to fine products, a unique marketing and service concept, and an enthusiastic team of customer-oriented salespeople committed to Volkswagen's famed *low-pressure philosophy of selling*. As described in the company's salesperson training materials:

> VW low-pressure selling is active selling—aggressive yet thoughtful and imaginative. Salespeople are trained to use a planned sales presentation built around specific prospect interests and reactions. Sales success comes not from pushing prospects to buy, but from leading or helping them, gently but firmly, to a satisfactory buying decision based on their best needs."

Two steps advanced by VW to use in leading up to this closing situation are (1) gauging the prospect's readiness to buy and (2) properly timing the closing. Let us examine in detail what VW means by these statements.

Gauging the prospect's readiness to buy means that you continue to qualify his or her interest by questions or statements, such as these, that help measure it:

1. Ask open-end questions, such as "How do you like the car, so far?" or "Why do you want to wait until June to buy?" Such questions do not allow a yes or no answer. Instead, they encourage prospects to reveal their true feelings.

2. Paraphrase or summarize their remarks, carrying them a little beyond what they intended—as illustrated by this example:

> *Prospect:* Since there are only three of us in my family, I guess the sedan is big enough.
>
> *Salesperson:* I see, then you feel that space is really no problem for your family?
>
> *Prospect:* (explaining further) Well, I didn't exactly mean it was no problem. We plan on having another child someday, and then, too, we usually take my mother-in-law for a ride on Sundays.

By paraphrasing the prospect's statement and stretching it a little, you have gained valid information and uncovered a true objection hidden from you in the first statement.

3. Ask "if" questions instead of direct ones, such as, "If you buy a VW, you will save money, won't you?" Prospects feel comfortable answering, since they can respond without committing themselves. Their responses are thus usually free and candid.

Proper timing of the closing involves both careful listening and skill in employment. You want to lead prospects gently but firmly into a close but do not want them to feel you are interested only in making the sale and not in helping them. Careful listening involves catching key phrases that represent green lights or go-ahead signals for the close. These include:

1. Questions, such as "What color interior is available with a blue car?" "How much would payments be?" "If I buy, when could I get delivery?" "How much could I get in trade-in on my old car?"

2. Statements of agreement, such as "It's a nice car." "The VW is more economical than a big car." "It's easier to drive than I

thought!" "It probably would be a good second car!" "Yes, I can see the quality!"

Skill in employing closing techniques depends in part on the type of close used, which depends on the circumstances. One such technique (among many) is to use a question similar to an "if" question. For example: (1) "Mr. Lyon, you seem to like the blue and the beige sedans; which would you want?" (2) "We've looked at the sedan and the sun-roof models; which one would you want?" The conditional "would you want" is less direct that "do you want" and allows the prospect more freedom to answer. A trial close using this phrase may not always evoke a positive response, but it is often successful and does not cause the prospect to feel pinned down.

Another very subtle technique is for the salesperson to express a response to the prospect's words or actions in such a way that the prospect takes mental ownership of the car of his (or her) choice. For example, having completed a demonstration drive of the car of the prospect's choice, the salesperson says, "Just park your car over here," or "Bring your key and we'll open the trunk." This trial close, if employed properly, is very subtle, quite effective, and remains very low key—low pressure.

Questions for Written Reports or Class Discussion

1. What is the major purpose behind the VW gentle-but-firm lead-up to the closing situation?

2. From a sales point of view, what three major aims are behind all the VW salesperson's words and actions as he or she leads into the closing situation?

3. In the above VW statement, attention was given to listening for and acting upon certain words

that are go-ahead or buying signals. What two other types of buying signals should the VW salesperson be alert to?

4. The last paragraph of the VW suggestions mentioned a trial close. What is a trial close, and when can or should it be employed during a sales presentation?

How to lose a sale—How to close a sale: selling a man nylon stockings for his wife

In these two separate retail store presentations, we have a young female salesperson approaching a middle-aged male customer who is looking in a slightly perplexed fashion at a counter display of women's nylon stockings.

SCENE NUMBER 1

Salesperson: (yawning) Are you being waited on?

Customer: My wife needs some nylon stockings. Can I look at some?

Salesperson: Sure, what size does she take?

Customer: I really don't know.

Salesperson: Is her foot as big as yours?

Customer: No, only about two-thirds.

Salesperson: Then she will take size 10. Here's a neat pair for $5.00.

Customer: Haven't you anything cheaper?

Salesperson: Sure, here's some for $3.50.

Customer: What's the difference?

Salesperson: A dollar and a half.

Customer: Well, give me the $3.50 pair.

Salesperson: Why not be generous and buy her two pairs?

Customer: Nope, just one, hurry.

Salesperson: But my sales book is low today and I need some sales!

Customer: (walking away in disgust) I'll come back some other time.

SCENE NUMBER 2

Salesperson: (smiling and alert) Good morning.

Customer: Good morning. (looks at stockings on counter)

Salesperson: They are lovely stockings, aren't they?

Customer: Yes, my wife asked me to buy her a pair.

Salesperson: What size does your wife wear, sir?

Customer:	Oh! She forgot to tell me.
Salesperson:	Then I'll give you size 10; that's the average size. Here is a very nice pair.
Customer:	How much are they?
Salesperson:	They are $5.00.
Customer:	Hm, do you have anything cheaper?
Salesperson:	Yes, sir, these are $3.50.
Customer:	What's the difference between the $3.50 and $5.00 stockings?
Salesperson:	The $5.00 pair will give your wife more miles of service!
Customer:	More miles of service! Well, that's what she needs; she's always walking them out. I'll take a pair.
Salesperson:	Is one of your wife's stockings likely to rip before the other?
Customer:	Indeed it does. She's always tearing one and throwing the other away.
Salesperson:	Wouldn't it be a good idea to buy two pairs of the same color, so she can make a new pair if one of them rips?
Customer:	Say, that's a good idea! I'll take two pairs.
Salesperson:	By the way, we have a special on this week for the $5.00 stockings—three pairs for $12.45. That means that you get the third pair for only $2.45. You save $2.55; with today's inflation, every little bit helps.
Customer:	I'll take three pairs—anything to save money (Departs thinking, "Nice salespeople in this store. They are really helpful.")

Questions for Written Reports or Class Discussion

What is your opinion of the personal selling techniques involved on the part of these two salespeople? What principles and techniques of selling and closing are illustrated that apply to any sales presentation situation?

Sales Problem 12.2

How a prospect's objection became the springboard for quick closing of a machine-tool sale

Will Wagner is an industrial salesperson for the American Hercules Machine Tool Manufacturing Company of Denver, Colorado, USA. He has just concluded the features-advantages-benefits part of his sales presentation for a new cutting and turning machine based on a colored sales brochure and small replica model. His prospect, Mr. Modeer, owner of a medium-sized Madison, Wisconsin, wood-working shop, has asked a number of questions, but Will senses that some hidden doubt or objection still remains. Here's how Will handles the situation and moves into a quick close.

Will: Based on the benefits just noted, don't you agree that our new cutting and turning machine will do a better job for you?

Mr. Modeer: Well, I like the machine—especially the extra sharp blades, but I'm afraid they might be a little too sharp. If they can cut hard wood that quickly, I am afraid that they could just as quickly cut off the operator's fingertips!

Will: Your concern for your operator's safety is quite understandable, Mr. Modeer, and we at Hercules feel the same way you do. That's why I am happy to point out that the blades on our new machine won't start cutting until the cover is securely closed (demonstrates on the replica model). That means that your operator's fingers simply won't be close enough to the turning blades for that to happen.

Mr. Modeer: (says nothing, but nods slightly)

Will: And, in addition, Mr. Modeer, as soon as the cover is reopened even one-hundredth of an inch, the blades are immediately covered by this plastic shield (pointing to it on the model) and stop rotating. It is one hundred percent accident proof! No other machine of this type on the market today provides a greater combination of safety and practical uses than ours.

Mr. Modeer: (continues to remain silent, but again nods slightly)

Will: Are you going to pay cash and get the 10 percent discount, Mr. Modeer, or is it to be billed at full price with payment due in 120 days?

Mr. Modeer: I prefer equal payments over a six-month period; is that possible?

Will: Yes, I can arrange that for you. Just sign here (pointing to the signature line on the purchase agreement form, which has been lying with the color brochure), and I'll set it up as you request.

Questions for Written Reports or Class Discussion

1.   Mr. Modeer objected to the sharp blades and was also concerned with safety. Which was the real objection, and how did Will turn it into a strong buyer benefit?

2.   If Mr. Modeer had not objected to sharp blades, and Will had simply pointed out the safety features of the machine during the course of the presentation, would the benefit have come across as effectively as it did? Explain.

3. Something Mr. Modeer said in the above words became such an extremely strong selling point that Will immediately went into a close after satisfying the objection. What words signalled this importance so clearly to Will? Why did he consider them to be so important?

4. There are many other "quick-closing sentences" Will could have used other than the one he did. Can you list three other such sentences that might have worked equally as well for him?

CHAPTER 13

The After-Sale Follow-Up and Follow-Through

After studying this chapter, you will be able to:

Tell how to properly depart from the customer after closing the sale, or from the prospect after failing to close.

Describe proper follow-up or follow-through steps to take following: (1) a closed sale, and (2) one you failed to close.

Identify self-analysis questions to ask yourself after trying hard but failing to close a sale, in order to uncover clues that might help you succeed on future calls.

Summarize three major reasons why it is normally to a salesperson's advantage to ensure a customer's continued satisfaction with his or her purchase by after-sale follow-through.

The final close has been made; the sale has been either won or lost. What do you do now? How do you manage a proper departure, whatever the decision? Can you take any action now that will increase the effectiveness of a successful close? If the sale was lost, can you take any steps now to set the stage for a callback during which you can make a sale?

A professional salesperson never quits selling, so this is no time to relax. Whatever the decision, you now have to face these questions and to take whatever action is necessary to turn the situation to your present or future advantage if at all possible.

IS THE JUST-CONCLUDED PRESENTATION ALL THERE IS?

In some types of selling, especially in the direct or specialty fields, you may never see the customer or prospect again. If the one-shot sale is made, your only task is to get on as quickly as possible to the next prospect once you have seen that delivery is made and payment is collected. If you failed to make the sale in such areas of selling, you merely make a quick and friendly exit and do not attempt a follow-up. Statistics show that the percentage of sales that may be closed on callbacks is very small compared to the much higher sales-close possibilities from calling on new, or first-time, prospects. If you are engaged in such selling areas, the experience, training, and policies of your company dictate your decisions at this time.

In most types of selling, however, you can often turn even a lost sale to future advantage or repeat business. And, if you have closed the sale, you can use these final moments to set the stage for referral leads and possible reorders. We will address our thinking during the remainder of this chapter to this common sales situation, as we consider the following points.

1. How to depart after the close—win or lose.
2. Proper follow-up after landing the order.
3. Proper follow-up after losing the sale.
4. Follow-through for repeat business following a successful close.
5. Follow-through that may turn lost sales into future business.
6. Practical steps for efficient follow-through.
7. Special problems with follow-up and follow-through.

HOW TO DEPART AFTER THE CLOSE—WIN OR LOSE

Proper Departure after a Successful Close

For many inexperienced salespeople, the period immediately following the signing of the order can be awkward. Some feel the inward exhilaration of victory. Others fear that their new customer may suddenly change his or her mind, and they want only to get away from the scene as quickly as possible so that cannot happen. Still others feel merely a sense of relief and are eager to go on to their next call without delay.

Professional salespeople, however, use this opportunity to sincerely and naturally thank the customer for his or her time and business. Their words and attitudes, as expressed in actions and manner, can do much to assure that the sale stays closed and to set the stage for reorders.

Since time is valuable to both you and your customer, (1) express thanks for the order, (2) settle any last-minute questions regarding delivery and follow-up service, and (3) assure him or her of your availability for answering questions and following up if necessary. By so doing you give reassurance that he or she has made a wide decision.

You should do this naturally in a relaxed manner and then depart as quickly as possible. Do not make the mistake of staying for a chat and thus prolonging the interview unless your customer indicates that he or she would like you to do so. It is up to you to rise or to make other moves toward prompt yet relaxed and friendly departure.

Proper Departure after Failing to Close

The same procedure holds if you fail to get the order. Your aim is to thank the prospect for his or her time, to lay the groundwork for callbacks if you feel they would be worthwhile, and to depart promptly without appearing to rush.

Certainly, loss of a sale should not lead to any feeling of defeat or sour grapes on your part. On the contrary, failure to get the order imposes some professional obligations. You should leave the prospect with the impression that his or her time has not been wasted by giving one or more good ideas that will be valuable to him or her or at least by leaving the prospect better informed.

You should also use this opportunity to leave a favorable image of you, your company, and salespersons in general. And you should ask for names of any friends or business acquaintances who he or she feels may be interested in your proposal. Perhaps your prospect will write an introduction for you or even call them on the spot.

What do you do if the prospect refuses to even give you a hearing? In this situation, it is important that you maintain an attitude of equality, of friendliness, of courtesy. However abrupt the turndown, make clear to the prospect, secretary, or receptionist that you are not disconcerted. Leave with an air of self-respect and self-confidence. Often, the last impression you make with any or all of these people is what will win success for you the next time.

In effect, your words and actions at the point of departure, whether you close the sale or not, are the first steps of the follow-up and follow-through process.

Follow-up or follow-through is pursuing an initial effort through supplementary action. Proper follow-up is especially important after making the sale since it is your obligation to ensure prompt delivery, to see that any initial installation and operation is satisfactory, and to ascertain that the customer is completely satisfied in every possible way.

To a true salesperson, a sale does not end when the order is signed; the ultimate aim is to have a satisfied customer or user. Achieving this goal involves giving follow-up service to make certain that he or she is satisfied and is secure in the knowledge that the salesperson is trying to take care of him or her and has the customer's best interests at heart.

What kind of follow-up steps can you take after the order is signed to provide proper service and customer satisfaction? What will you each gain as a result of the time and effort spent in ensuring complete satisfaction? Here are a few concrete suggestions.

Give a Warm and Sincere Thank-You.   This involves not only the immediate thank-you after the successful closing of the sale but also follow-up expressions of appreciation. A handwritten postcard or letter, a phone call, or a formal thank-you letter from your office a day or so after the sale makes your appreciation stand out.

Check Delivery.   The best way to do this is through a phone call; the best time to do it, the day of delivery. Such follow-up action not only assures you that delivery was made in a satisfactory manner but also shows the customer that you care. If any damage occurred in shipment or if other problems have arisen, your phone call assures that you will take prompt, personal action to correct the situation.

Check Installation.   A personal visit immediately following delivery to supervise or check installation allows you to take action toward solving any problems. If there are no problems, your words and presence show the customer that this is the kind of service your company and you always give your customers.

Check Operation and Training of Operators.   You can forestall many potential complaints about a newly installed product or service by helping employees of the buying company or organization learn to operate or use properly. Your presence at such introductory training sessions not only proves your interest to the customer but also impresses the trainees. You also have a chance to get feedback from them as to performance and possibly even ideas as to how your product rates against competition.

Order Adjustment.   Prompt follow-up after delivery can often lead to additional on-the-spot orders if the customer decides he or she wants more features or tie-in items, larger quantities, or additional supplies.

Ask For Referrals.   Both the customer and the operator or user-employees, if any, often feel even more pleased with the new purchase at the time of delivery or installation than they did before. If you are there to check delivery and to solve any problems, you can often get them to express their satisfaction in the form of referral leads.

Set the Stage for a Long-Term Relationship.   This initial follow-up, by telephone, letter, or personal call, can cement relations between you and your customer for the future. Your continued post-sale interest offers proof of the reliability of your firm or organization and may lead to future business. You may find this period the best time to get on a friendly basis with the customers, and the relationship will be enhanced by the pleasant, mutually profitable sale just concluded.

PROPER FOLLOW-UP AFTER FAILING TO CLOSE THE SALE

Use This Defeat to Set the Stage for Future Sales

To a professional salesperson, a lost sale often spells opportunity to set the stage for callbacks that could lead to sales. A warm thank-you for the time and courtesy extended during the just-concluded presentation proves your sincere interest. People like to deal with salespeople and firms with an interest in their business or personal affairs, and they remember how well you took defeat.

If you feel that your prospect should be using your product or service, then you have to try again later. Persistence does pay off in many areas of selling. Even if prospects are satisfied with their present situation, they may become dissatisfied later; if you get in touch with them again at one of those moments, their business may be yours.

Many salespeople, after receiving a definite no, disappear for several months, assuming that the buyer will not change his or her mind. Don't make this mistake; let prospects know now and later that you are interested in them and their organization and want to build a continuing business relationship.

Proper follow-up after losing a sale to such prospects is a sincere thank-you by telephone or letter a day or so later. This thank-you leads to sustained, long-term follow-through, which we shall discuss shortly. Proper, initial follow-up steps taken now can lead to success later.

Find Out Why You Lost the Sale—the Real Reasons!

Use this follow-up period to find out the reasons you failed. If you take defeat well and honestly ask your prospects their real reasons for not buying now, they may give you interesting and helpful insights. As well as asking them, you should immediately analyze your failure by reviewing each stage of the interview and asking yourself, "What went wrong with my presentation?"

Ask Your Prospects Their Real Reasons for Not Buying.   Did you lose out because of price, delivery date, credit terms? What other advantages may have outweighed these factors in prospects' minds had you suggested them or been authorized to offer them? This feedback may help both you and your company to devise ways of overcoming such stumbling blocks in the future. Ask these or any other questions about your specific proposal; you may find they are very glad to help you.

> Ms. Rittenberg, you have been most generous in listening to my proposal. I appreciate your reasons for not buying now but somehow I feel I may have failed in making my proposal sound convincing. I am sincere in wanting to improve my sales approach and wonder if you could help me.
>
> Since you have seen many other salespeople, can you offer any concrete suggestions as to how I could have improved my presentation just now? Could I have been better prepared? How could my actual verbal description or demonstration be improved? Is there anything I can do to improve my appearance, actions, or manner that would help me become a more professional salesperson?

Honest, sincere questions like these are very likely to bring honest answers. You may learn something, and the prospect will remember you for a long time. It is an easy way to set the stage for a callback.

Make a Personal Review and Analysis of What Went Wrong with the Presentation.   You tried hard but failed to close the sale. What went wrong? Careful critical analysis of your just-concluded interview may uncover clues that will help you get the order on your next call.

Just as airline pilots run through a standard printed cockpit instrument checklist prior to takeoff in order not to forget anything, so should salespeople (especially during their first year of selling) run through a prepared checklist following failure to close.

The best way to analyze your handling of that presentation is to ask yourself any or all the following questions, or any others that seem applicable. By making up such a list, tailored to what you are selling, making photocopy sets, and answering the questions honestly in writing for yourself, you will help train yourself to better plan and execute your next sales presentation.

My Failed Presentation Self-Evaluation Checklist

Yes	No	Questions	How Could I Improve On My Next Call?
My Preparation			
_____	_____	Did I carefully review beforehand all the material I had gathered on this prospect's operation or circumstances?	_____
_____	_____	Did I anticipate trouble by figuring out which objections were likely to be raised and planning the most effective ways to answer them?	_____

My Failed Presentation Self-Evaluation Checklist *(Continued)*

Yes	No	Questions	How Could I Improve On My Next Call?
————	————	Did I pick out a few sales aids to use and decide when to use them?	————————
————	————	Did I preplan the most effective way to demonstrate my product or service?	————————
————	————	Did I select my approach carefully enough beforehand?	————————
————	————	Did I preplan several trial closes and figure out when to use them?	————————
————	————	Did I prepare for this interview as carefully as possible, without skipping a single step to save time or effort?	————————

My Approach

Yes	No	Questions	How Could I Improve On My Next Call?
————	————	Was I awkward in approaching and greeting the prospect?	————————
————	————	Did I greet him or her pleasantly and go right into my planned approach?	————————
————	————	Was I inwardly proud of being a salesperson and of my company and product?	————————
————	————	Was I businesslike in my approach?	————————
————	————	Did I feel nervous and timid?	————————
————	————	Did my opening remarks arouse interest and make the prospect want to give me some of his or her time?	————————
————	————	Did I find that the elements of a sale were really there: the need, the ability, and the authority to buy?	————————

Creating and Holding Interest

Yes	No	Questions	How Could I Improve On My Next Call?
————	————	Did I quickly arouse and hold my prospect's attention and interest?	————————
————	————	Did I encourage him or her to talk and then did I listen attentively?	————————
————	————	Did I create the impression that I was sincerely trying to help him or her?	————————
————	————	Did I get the prospect to ask questions? Did I answer them to his or her satisfaction?	————————

Arousing Desire and Securing Conviction

Yes	No	Questions	How Could I Improve On My Next Call?
————	————	Did I make my whole presentation, or at least all the key points?	————————
————	————	Did I refuse to let questions, objections, or interruptions throw me off the track?	————————
————	————	Did my product or service really meet the prospect's needs and offer true benefits?	————————
————	————	Did I cover all the benefits of my product?	————————
————	————	Did I establish the need for at least two of those benefits?	————————
————	————	Were the benefits I stressed the ones of greatest interest to the prospect?	————————

My Failed Presentation Self-Evaluation Checklist *(Continued)*

Yes	No	Questions	How Could I Improve On My Next Call?
_____	_____	Did I bring out the strong points of my proposal?	_____
_____	_____	Was I enthusiastic enough about the benefits?	_____
_____	_____	Was I convinced that he or she would benefit from my proposal?	_____
_____	_____	Did I get point-by-point agreement on the value of the benefits?	_____
_____	_____	Did I prove the value of my proposal?	_____
_____	_____	Were my statements consistently positive and not negative?	_____
_____	_____	Did I win his or her confidence?	_____
_____	_____	Did I secure conviction that my product could fill his or her needs?	_____
_____	_____	Did I recognize buying signals and try to turn them into trial closes?	_____

My Demonstration

Yes	No	Questions	How Could I Improve On My Next Call?
_____	_____	Did I use all my sales aids effectively?	_____
_____	_____	Did I fumble or have trouble finding and using my sales-kit aids?	_____
_____	_____	Did I show all my samples or demonstrate my product to show its value?	_____
_____	_____	Did I show too many samples or sales aids and thus confuse the prospect in any way?	_____
_____	_____	Was my demonstration disjointed and thus unclear?	_____
_____	_____	Was I able to get the prospect to participate in my demonstration?	_____
_____	_____	Did he or she fully understand all the points of my demonstration?	_____

Heading Objections

Yes	No	Questions	How Could I Improve On My Next Call?
_____	_____	Was I successful in getting the prospect to voice all his or her objections?	_____
_____	_____	Was I able to restate those objections in the form of questions, and to handle them as questions that I was happy to answer?	_____
_____	_____	Was I able to get him or her to explain the basis of these objections?	_____
_____	_____	Did I show any irritation with any objections, questions, or negative responses?	_____
_____	_____	Did any objections or questions rattle me and throw me off track?	_____
_____	_____	Was I able to turn objections into yes-building questions?	_____
_____	_____	Was I able to answer all questions effectively?	_____
_____	_____	Did I attempt to turn any objections into a trial close?	_____
_____	_____	Did I misrepresent my product or service in any way?	_____
_____	_____	Did he or she raise any questions that I disregarded?	_____

My Failed Presentation Self-Evaluation Checklist *(Continued)*

Yes	No	Questions	How Could I Improve On My Next Call?
———	———	Was I well enough informed about my product and company policies to answer all questions?	———————
———	———	Did I avoid or fail to answer any valid objections?	———————
———	———	Did I lack conviction, pep, or enthusiasm in answering objections or questions?	———————
———	———	Did I listen carefully to his or her answers, after restating objections or questions, and then handle them?	———————
———	———	Was I able to uncover all hidden objections?	———————
———	———	Did I uncover the real objection?	———————
———	———	Was I able to handle his or her complaint or objection promptly, properly, and to his or her satisfaction?	———————

My Close

———	———	Did I use the trial closes I had prepared?	———————
———	———	Did I fail to recognize any buying signals or critical items to close during my presentation, prior to the summary?	———————
———	———	Did I secure the prospect's agreement to each point of my summary?	———————
———	———	Did I ever have the prospect ready to say yes and then lose the sale by overselling or simply talking too much?	———————
———	———	Did I inwardly give up the first time he or she said, "I'm not interested?"	———————
———	———	Could he or she have sensed my discouragement at any time?	———————
———	———	Did I uncover all the reasons he or she would not buy?	———————
———	———	Did I ask for the order?	———————
———	———	Did I fail to suggest action now?	———————
———	———	Did I have only one closing argument?	———————
———	———	Did I keep a final, new, and strong reason to buy in reserve as a last resort?	———————
———	———	Did I know when and how to close?	———————
———	———	Did I let him or her sell me on the fact that he or she was not interested or ready to buy now?	———————

My Personal Attitude, Appearance, and Manner

———	———	Did I have a proper, positive, will-to-win attitude throughout?	———————
———	———	Was I confident and cheerful?	———————
———	———	Was my personal appearance satisfactory—was I dressed appropriately and well groomed?	———————
———	———	In general, did I feel, look, and act in a professional and businesslike manner?	———————
———	———	Was I proud and enthusiastic about my company and product or service?	———————

My Failed Presentation Self-Evaluation Checklist (Continued)

Yes	No	Questions	How Could I Improve On My Next Call?
_____	_____	Did the prospect seem annoyed at some mannerism of mine?	_____
_____	_____	Did I knock a competitor?	_____
_____	_____	Did we get into an argument?	_____
_____	_____	Did I talk too rapidly or too much?	_____
_____	_____	Was I awkward and unsure of myself at any stage of the interview?	_____
_____	_____	Did I willingly discuss every important point he or she mentioned?	_____
_____	_____	Did I talk at the prospect's level in terms he or she understood?	_____
_____	_____	Did I avoid looking him or her in the eye or fail to smile often?	_____
_____	_____	Did I use too many I's and not enough we's or you's?	_____
_____	_____	Did I leave the interview pleasantly?	_____
_____	_____	Will I be welcome there on a callback?	_____

The preceding series of self-evaluation questions covers fairly completely all the stages of the sales presentation. Answers to most of the problems such a review poses are in the preceding chapters of this book. All salespeople will profit from seriously and honestly asking themselves the above questions upon failing to close after a full presentation.

The art/science/skill of personal selling is a never-ending process of self-evaluation, study, and practice. You cannot hope to close every sale, but you can, through intelligent application of basic principles and techniques, increase your percentage of closes. And, as we have said, closing, or getting a verbal or signed agreement to buy, is your basic objective and the chief justification for your existence as a real salesperson.

FOLLOW-THROUGH FOR REPEAT BUSINESS AFTER A SUCCESSFUL CLOSE

As stated earlier in this chapter, the ultimate aim of a professional salesperson is to have satisfied customers (or users). You can make sure they are and remain satisfied, with you, the product or service you have sold, and your company or organization, by providing effective and efficient follow-through service.

For many good reasons, in most types of selling, you should spend all the time and effort necessary to ensure customer's continued satisfaction. Here are three major reasons:

1. It is easier in most cases to sell satisfied users more or something new than to find and sell entirely new prospects.

2. Satisfied users are the best source, through referral leads, for locating and gaining access to potential new customers.

3. Callbacks or user calls on satisfied customers give you an opportunity to see your product or service in operation. Through discussions with staff supervisors and line users or operators, you can often discover new advantages or ideas for its use that can be applied elsewhere.

There are no hard and fast rules for when or how often you should make such follow-through callbacks or user calls. Because time represents money to both you and your company or organization, the time thus spent has to ultimately result in profitable sales. Thus you have to ask yourself first, will callbacks on this customer pay for themselves, and second, how can they be made to pay for themselves? Deciding factors are the nature of your selling, the nature and situation of your customer, and your own experience, based on your records.

What you can gain from time spent on callbacks? And what can your customer gain? These are the two major questions you should keep in mind as we delve into the three major reasons, noted above, that justify sustained follow-through callbacks.

It is Easier to Sell Satisfied Customers More or Something New Than to Find and Sell Entirely New Prospects

Let us first consider this point from your view as a customer of all sorts of goods and services yourself. Do you not prefer to buy gasoline or petrol from the service station where the attendants greet you cheerfully by name, know your automobile through constant, repeat servicing, and give advice and have experience you trust? And do you not like to patronize the banks or department stores whose owners or employees recognize you and help you on a personal basis with your needs and problems?

Just as you like to deal with people, companies, and institutions you can trust to give efficient, personal, cheerful attention, so do your customers. In fact, a major problem for many business and industrial buyers is to find salespeople willing to give them such service, since they are now buying increasingly on the basis of overall service rather than on price alone. Also, customers in general are not only expecting but also demanding more efficient follow-through service from salespeople. In spite of new marketing approaches that tend to bypass the salesperson, your personal touch—your personal interaction with your customers on a face-to-face basis—continues to make the difference between volume sales and mere distribution or initial sales.

If your customers like and trust you, most often on the basis of the follow-through service you render, they tend to give you their repeat business. Such business is easier to get than entirely new business, since you eliminate all the time-consuming steps—prospecting, making the appointment, making the approach, and making that hardest sale of all, the initial one.

Keep in mind the useful advice passed along by veteran salespeople through the years: "Never forget a customer; never let a customer forget you." We discuss how to put this motto into practice in the next few pages.

Satisfied Customers Are the Best Source for Referral Leads

Noted earlier has been the fact that satisfied users are the best source for referral leads. If they respect your follow-up interest and service, the easiest way for them to repay you is to give you names of others who may also be interested in the product benefits and superior follow-through service offered by you and your organization.

Callbacks on satisfied business or organizational users especially give you the relaxed opportunity and time to get to know the decision maker or other executives on a personal basis as well as the line supervisors and operators or clerks who may be able to give you specific referral leads. These can often be turned into immediate and profitable telephone or letter introductions or written testimonial letters. Because they are the best, you should follow up such referral leads promptly—immediately if at all possible. No better proof of the claims of your proposal can be offered than the testimony or recommendation of a satisfied current user, whether it be household, business, or organizational.

Callbacks on Satisfied Users Can Give You New Ideas for Profitable Sales

For continued sales success, your product must serve the purpose for which it was sold. It is one thing to offer a product designed to produce specific results. What happens after is has been sold and put into use, however, may be quite another thing. The only way you or your organization can actually know how well your product performs is to see for yourself! And because problems often multiply faster than profits, good follow-through service can pinpoint new ways your product can cut costs, increase sales, or boost efficiency.

Peter F. Drucker, leading American management consultant and author, pointed out this problem most tellingly in his book *The Effective Executive* when he said, "Failure to go out and look is the typical reason for persisting in a course of action long after it ceases to be appropriate or even rational."[1]

Times change, markets change, and customer needs change constantly. If you as a salesperson and market manager are to keep up with these changes and are to provide necessary feedback and recommendations to your employer, you have to get out and see the situation for yourself. User calls are the easiest, fastest, and most reliable way to keep up to date; they provide new ideas for future profitable sales.

Such calls are especially useful in uncovering creative new sales ideas when competing products all seem alike to the customer. For example, successful selling of basic products such as matches and salt depends largely on new sales ideas or packaging or better follow-through servicing in areas such as shipping and in-store promotions.

[1] Peter F. Drucker, *The Effective Executive* (New York: Harper & Row, 1967), p. 142.

Should you spend time calling back on a prospect after failing to close the sale? The answer depends largely on your careful evaluation of why you lost the sale and on whether you have enough interest or potential to make it worth your time to try once more.

You must decide whether your prospect had a need that your proposal could fill. If so and if he or she had the money and authority to buy, then he or she still remains a prospect. If that is the case, why did you fail to sell? Did he or she have a valid reason for not buying now, such as no money for new expenditures during the remaining budget period? If it was a valid reason and if he or she appeared interested, then a callback or several callbacks may be in order. If the excuses for not buying were merely stalls or put-offs, you failed to sell him or her. Since you have already fired most of your sales ammunition on the initial presentation, will you be more successful next time?

How Much Time Should Be Allocated to Such Callbacks?

The amount of time to spend on callbacks to customers you failed to sell depends to a great extent on what you are selling and on the sales-call ratio in your industry. In many types of selling, sales are seldom made until the third or fourth callback. And sales of some sophisticated equipment or systems may not be made until after many callbacks and perhaps after detailed bids or proposals. Your own sales records or those of other salespeople in your organization or industry may offer helpful guidelines.

Some business or industrial buyers follow a policy of refusing to buy on any salesperson's first visit because too many salespeople in the past promised but did not deliver on after-purchase service and follow-through. These buyers are often more interested in service than in price and want to see how regular and persistent you are in your follow-through efforts to get their business.

Keeping all these factors in mind, you have to consider whether you have a chance of making a sale if you do call back. If the prospect understands your proposal, if you are making progress, and if he or she either requested or is not opposed to a callback, then it may be worth your time.

What New Approaches Are Necessary in Such Callbacks?

If you do plan a callback, you should present new and additional information and reasons for buying. You should find out the best time to call again by appointment and confirm that appointment by telephone shortly before the call. When you do see the prospect, your best approach is to briefly review major points covered during your initial presentation and to offer the new information or ideas you have developed since then.

If the business is worth having, many persistent callbacks following failure to close initially may be well worth the time and effort. Offer on each call new facts about your proposal, new ideas or industry information, and let the prospect know that you are sincerely interested in helping solve his or her problems. Seek even an initial small order that will enable to get your foot in the door and thus give you a chance to show how you can give superior service. It is hard for any buyer with a need to keep from saying "yes" to a friendly, sincerely interested, helpful, persistent salesperson.

PRACTICAL STEPS FOR EFFICIENT FOLLOW-THROUGH

Here are some practical suggestions you may employ in your own sales area to provide the efficient, systematic follow-through servicing required by today's increasingly sophisticated buyers.

Practical Suggestions for Good Follow-Through

1. Develop a systematic schedule for checking on the performance of products you've sold through regular telephone or letter contact. And use this opportunity to present any new ideas on how customers may get even more use or benefit from them.

2. Meet and maintain regular personal contact with key management and purchasing agents who can influence the buying decisions of their firms or organizations.

3. Provide time for periodic telephone or personal calls on, or letters to, users or potential prospects not sold initially to maintain regular contact.

4. Make every effort to immediately handle personally or to follow up on your organization's handling of any customer problems.

5. Try to make yourself always available to the customer. You can telephone at regular intervals or send postcards to let him or her know you are thinking of him or her. You can even leave your evening or weekend home or emergency telephone number. Customers seldom use the latter but are impressed that you are always available if they need you.

6. Relay promptly to all customers any new ideas developed elsewhere for your product or service that may increase their sales and profits, cut their costs, or increase their efficiency.

7. Put all your contacts to work for your customers. You may know of a capable executive who desires a change and of a position available in another organization, or you may learn of an organization planning to purchase something sold by your customer. You lose nothing by putting them in touch with one another. If they get together for mutual profit, each will thank you. If they make contact but fail to reach agreement, they will thank you anyway. In either case they appreciate your thinking enough about their problems to try to help find a solution.

Practical Follow-Through Steps Through Your Company or Organization

1. Make sure any complaints, problems, or requests for information from your customer to your company or organization are handled promptly and efficiently. Your head office should handle these by phone or wire if necessary

and keep you informed at all times so that you can take whatever action is necessary.

2. Keep your organizational customer, his or purchasing department, and key line supervisors on your company mailing list for new announcements brochures, or other helpful information. Such advertising works for you in between your personal calls.

3. See to it that any promotional or advertising material developed by your company is promptly called to the attention of your customers and is made available to them. You save time by arranging for your head office to do this directly.

These are but a few of the many practical ideas you and your company or organization can employ as systematic follow-through steps to let your customers know you are constantly thinking of them. Your customers want and need all the ideas and assistance you can furnish them and will usually reward your efforts with increased sales volume.

SPECIAL PROBLEMS WITH FOLLOW-UP AND FOLLOW-THROUGH

Some problems with follow-up or follow-through require special attention and handling. We will touch on four of these in a general way: promises broken for reasons beyond your control, cancellations, specific complaints, and the dissatisfied customer.

Handling Broken Promises

At times circumstances beyond the control of you and your company or organization lead to failure in providing the rapid delivery or prompt follow-up service you promised at the time you closed the sale. If your customer schedules costly operations based on delivery of your product at a certain time, he or she is bound to be unhappy if it does not arrive as promised.

Your proper follow-up in such cases is to notify him or her at once of the situation and to state the reasons openly and honestly. Break the news in terms of your keen personal sympathy and your understanding of the problems the delay is causing. You can then let him or her know that both you and your employer are going to do everything possible immediately to help solve these problems. State specifically what you can do to help and what you cannot do.

Finally, suggest the best solution possible for this predicament, even if that means asking a competitor to give him or her immediate delivery. You may lose the order by such drastic action but may gain goodwill that can set the stage for future orders. Your first task is to help solve his or her problems.

Handling Cancellations

Customer cancellation of orders occurs from time to time. Some of these result from legitimate reasons such as sudden financial reverses, illness, or loss of key personnel or staff.

Others, however, result from the failure of the salesperson to sell his or her customer completely enough on the benefits to be derived from the purchase. For example, you may have closed a given sale more because of your warm personality than because of benefits and value. Then, after your departure, the customer becomes worried, talks it over with someone else, and suddenly phones in a cancellation directly to your company. In such cases, it is often difficult or impossible to resell him or her.

When a cancellation occurs, your proper follow-up is to contact your customer quickly to ask the reasons for the cancellation. This should be done in a friendly way, such as your expressing concern that whatever the problem is, you feel it is your personal responsibility to help in any way possible. If you can save the sale at this point, so much the better, although chances probably are against that happening. If the cancellation holds, for whatever reason, then use this opportunity to set the stage for future callbacks and future sales.

The best way to handle cancellations is to avoid them in the first place. If you make certain that the prospect fully understands what he or she is buying, take the time to answer any last-minute questions, and reinforce his or her confidence in having made a wise buying decision, cancellations should not become a real problem.

Handling Specific Complaints

Customers often make specific complaints that your product simply is not doing the job they thought it would at the time of purchase. This and other specific complaints are, for purposes of our discussion here, beyond the control of you or your employer. Your product may be good, but their unique requirements may make it unsuited to their needs.

The temptation arises, in such case, to hold the customer to the signed agreement and to let the problem remain his or hers alone. But if you accept the proper viewpoint of serving your customer rather than exploiting him or her, you should make every effort to adjust the situation to his or her satisfaction. Sometimes technical or other experts from your company or organization can solve the problem through adjustments or new techniques. You should make every effort to handle such specific legitimate requests in this way.

If all efforts fail, you should advise your employer to take the long-range view and to help the customer out of the predicament in any way possible. This may entail cancellation of the order, payment adjustments, or other solutions. By making the situation right, you gain his or her goodwill and future business. The proper approach in such matters is to help if you can and to turn the situation to your future advantage in every way possible.

Handling the Dissatisfied Customer

Sometimes the customer makes no specific complaint but is just generally dissatisfied with the product or your personal—or organization's follow-through service. Often such a dissatisfied customer may be emotionally upset and may require special understanding and handling on your part.

Your first task is to approach him or her in a friendly manner that indicates your sincere desire to get to the bottom of the dissatisfaction and to help if you can. A good way to start is to talk it over after taking the complainer to lunch or even for just a cup of coffee. Your second task is to hear him or her out and to try to find the real reasons for the dissatisfaction. Giving complaining individuals the chance to let off steam may go a long way toward placating them.

Once you get to the root of the problem, you have to decide what, if anything, can be done about it. Courteous, straightforward discussion can often lead to understanding if not complete agreement. Even when your employer's policy decisions are involved, convey the impression that you consider it a personal responsibility to handle it yourself as best you can.

You may have to tell your customer in a straightforward manner that, although you are sorry, you are unable to help in any concrete way. Then you have to sell him or her on the fact that the decision is the only realistic one you can make on behalf of your company. If you can make any adjustment by way of minor concessions, it may help overcome the harshness, in your customer's opinion, of your big "no." In any case, your prompt, honest, and undivided attention to this expression of dissatisfaction may mollify him or her to some extent and allow you to retain his or her goodwill and a possible chance of future business.

SUMMARY

We have considered in this chapter the proper follow-up and follow-through steps for both a closed sale and one you failed to close. Your ultimate professional aim as a salesperson is to have satisfied customers or users. Planned, sustained, efficient follow-up and follow-through service is the best way to assure utmost satisfaction. Since many sales are not effected until after repeated callbacks, you should also extend such follow-through service to initial nonbuyers, providing you feel that possibilities exist to make a sale commensurate with the time expended.

We considered proper departure methods following both a successful and an unsuccessful sales presentation and offered a comprehensive self-evaluation checklist against which you should check reasons for failing to close your sale.

We then presented reasons for after-presentation follow-through, win or lose, as well as specific practical procedures. In conclusion, we considered how you can handle specific complaints, or after-sale problems such as cancellations, other complaints, and the dissatisfied customer.

Questions for Analysis and Discussion

1.   What do we mean by the statement, "To a true salesperson the sale does not end when the order is signed?"
2.   What is the proper attitude for a salesperson to take after failing to close a sale?

3.   When does a professional salesperson quit selling?

4.   Why is proper follow-up after closing a sale important?

5.   If a salesperson fails to close a sale and doesn't really understand why, what can be done to find out before leaving the prospect?

6.   Name and explain two reasons why it is so important for a salesperson to have satisfied customers (or users).

7.   Are new sales approaches necessary on sales callbacks? Explain.

8.   If your company or organization cannot deliver an item sold on the date of the sale, what should the salesperson do about it—in terms of the customer?

CASE STUDY 13

After-Sale Follow-Through—A Major Reason for the Outstanding Worldwide Sales Success of Coca-Cola

The business of The Coca-Cola Company is one of the greatest sales/marketing operations the world has ever known. Developing Coke in 1886, the creator of the formula, Dr. John S. Pemberton, thought of it primarily as a sweet syrup mix for the bitter prescription compounds made to order for physicians to give their patients. However, it has never been advertised as a medicine, and no medicinal claims have ever been made. On the contrary, it was first advertised as a delicious and refreshing soft drink in the *Atlanta Journal* for May 29, 1886. By 1988, more than 100 years later, over 400 million drinks of Coke a day were being consumed in approximately 160 countries, more countries than are members of the United Nations.

Coca-Cola is sold as a wholesome family drink for all occasions. Who really wants or needs Coke? Probably even the top company executives cannot say for sure, but they continue selling it the world over in ever-increasing quantities. They claim there is no market saturation point. Enjoy a drink of Coke, and 30 minutes later, you are theoretically ready for another. According to the company, no one in the world between the ages of 13 and 50 is too poor to buy a drink of Coke a week. In the United States, the average consumption of Coca-Cola is about 290 drinks per person per year.

COCA-COLA DRIVER-SALESPEOPLE "SOFTEN THEM UP WITH A COLD COKE" SALES APPROACH SCORES WORLDWIDE

Much has been written about the successful advertising programs for Coca-Cola, but little about the day-to-day sales activities of thousands of route managers and the average of five driver-salespeople they each supervise in so many of the world's countries where Coca-Cola is entering new markets outside of the United States.

The driver-salespeople of these largely decentralized sales operations generally follow the same pattern in making an initial approach to prospective dealers. Analysis pinpoints geographical market areas, and such areas are assigned to one or more route managers. The route manager's list may be one of current soft-drink outlets, or he or she may seek his or her own. Any place where people gather—schools, food markets, factory canteens, or cafes—is a potential marketplace for Coca-Cola. An advertising campaign usually precedes personal sales calls in a newly opened territory or country, and potential dealer-prospects usually know that Coke is being introduced in their communities before being called upon.

The route managers, or their driver-salespeople, have a secret weapon in the back of their delivery trucks—some ice-cold bottles of Coke. They take one or more bottles of Coca-Cola with them on their calls on prospective dealers; they ask for glasses, pour a glass of cold Coke for everyone, and only then do they talk business—while the prospect is enjoying a glass of cold Coke!

The general lead question, depending on the outlet situation, runs something like this: "How many cases of soft drink do you sell a week?" Taking a percentage of that, the salesperson then suggests, "Perhaps you should start with X (number of) cases per week" (citing a conservative figure).

The aim of this first call is to get even a few cases of Coke into a dealer outlet. From then on, the goal is to help the dealer sell the Coke he or she has purchased through all possible sales/marketing means.

AFTER-SALE FOLLOW-THROUGH—HELPING DEALERS SELL THE COKE THEY HAVE PURCHASED (SO THEY WILL KEEP REORDERING)

Executives of Coca-Cola claim this after-sale follow-through to be the key to the phenomenal success of the Coca-Cola business. How do they do it? After the first sale, the route manager and his or her driver-salespeople have three major objectives: to create demand, to create new consumers, and to create situations in which customers can consume Coke. Their aim is to get increasingly more customers to ask for Coke so that the dealer gets interested enough to promote and stock it actively.

Aiming for a bandwagon effect, they employ all sorts of sales and promotional techniques to push Coke as the drink suitable for all ages in any family or social gathering. They give free samples at picnics, supermarket openings, or sports/or group meetings. They sponsor essay-writing and other contests through schools and clubs, show educational films, and erect Coca-Cola signs and billboards, which are often so numerous they appear to be part of the local scenery. All these activities stress the wholesome approach with Coke—the "happy" drink, always where the action is.

Selling Coke merely on the basis of an advertising slogan is not enough for these energetic salespeople. They picture Coke being consumed at meals, reasoning that if a consumer drinks anything with his lunch, why not Coca-Cola? And to carry this vision even farther, why not drink it at dinner as well? As far as social groups are concerned, the aim is to create the impression that wherever there is a gathering of people, Coke is or should be there.

This sales follow-through for Coca-Cola, through sheer ubiquity and untiring repetition, has made Coke a familiar trademark around the world. Thus, selling to dealers who want to get on the bandwagon is easier today than in the past. But a major sales problem for the route manager is to keep dealers interested and sales-minded.

A major after-sale follow-up and follow-through effort is directed toward the dealers as well as the consumers. The route manager and driver-salespeople sell the dealer on the need (1) to provide advertising both inside and outside so that customers know Coke is there and (2) to keep Coke cold at all times. This latter point is important because if the first bottle sold is not a cold one, all chance for a second sale is lost. Dealers are warned that if they serve warm bottles of Coke, their customers will go elsewhere next time. Each route manager tries to call on each dealer covered by all the five driver-salespeople at least once every two months. This sustained follow-up and follow-through sales effort puts into daily practice the feeling that good merchandising and personal selling are "helping the dealer sell what we sell him."

Questions for Written Reports or Class Discussion

1. List three follow-up and follow-through after-sale steps, other than the three mentioned above, that driver-salespeople for Coca-Cola may find effective in opening new markets. How would each work in practice?

2. What three basic things should a driver-salesperson do to assure that a just-concluded sale stays closed and to set the stage for reorders of Coca-Cola?

3. A prospect has just said to a Coca-Cola driver-salesperson, "Thanks, but I don't care to order any Coca-Cola right at this time." Since the prospect's business seems a logical outlet for Coca-Cola, yet has never carried it, what do you feel the driver-salesperson should do or say at this point that might set the stage for a future trial order?

In Sales Problem 4.1, we left Paul P., our British PPPPL salesperson, wrestling with the problem of devising a paper sack in which prospect Winterbottom could package his Frisky Fido dog food. He made the sale for an initial 100,000 sacks a month, with prospects of larger reorders, and knew, because he had phoned to check, that the shipment had reached his customer safely and on time.

Today, two weeks later, on a personal follow-up call, Paul finds both Winterbottom and his sons furious at both PPPPL and him. They had good reason to be angry, as we shall see.

Winterbottom: (angrily) You have some nerve, to show your face around here!

Paul: (surprised) What's wrong, Mr. Winterbottom?

Winterbottom: Nearly 30 percent of your flaming PPPPL bags split open before we can even truck them out of our shipping yard to customers! That's what's wrong!

Paul: Our sacks have never done that before. May I take a look?

Winterbottom: Yes, you take a look—over here—before I have my sons toss you out of here! And then (sputtering with anger) I'm going to sue your company for damages!

Paul: (keeping calm as he surveys a big pile of split PPPPL sacks) Well, they're split all right! And you have every reason to be angry about the situation. But before you do anything drastic (smiling, relaxed), will you let me check your packaging and handling operation to see the situation first hand so I can make prompt recommendations for adjustment to my company?

Winterbottom: (cooling off a bit) Well, we have nothing to lose now—the damage has already been done. Go ahead and take a look.

Knowing his product is good, better in fact than the previously used paper sacks, Paul felt there must be some unusual reason for the problem. He knew the sacks were tearing but had to find out why. He went through each step of the entire packaging and handling process, from machine-loading to transport out, and soon found the reason. The handling equipment that moved the filled sacks from the storeroom to the lorries (trucks) was a chain-and-fork affair, a loose section of which was making a very small tear in roughly one out of two sacks. When thrown by workmen into the lorry for stacking, many of the sacks split open.

Paul: (motioning Winterbottom to join him at the conveyor belt) Mr. Winterbottom, I think I've found the cause of the problem! This loose section in your chain-and-fork handling equipment seems to be making a tear in every second or third sack. The sacks then split when being hand-tossed into the lorry.

Winterbottom:	(after calling his sons over) You are absolutely right; this is the cause of the problem, not your sacks.
Paul:	Why don't you install a leather-covered chain? Won't it solve the problem quickly, and at small cost?
Winterbottom:	You are jolly well right, old chap! Thanks awfully for noticing that our faulty conveyor belt system was causing the cuts. Neither my sons nor I ever noticed that. Actually, we had experienced the same problem with your competitor's sacks that we used before ordering yours. We had hopes that your sacks would solve the problem.
Paul:	Well, I am glad the problem is solved. I have to go now to catch another appointment. Give me a ring at PPPPL if I can help in any other way. (Paul departs).

Questions for Written Reports or Class Discussion

1.   Paul demonstrated how a customer's complaint can be turned to one's own sales advantage. But there is one final thing he failed to do to turn this situation to even greater advantage. What else should he have done at this time?

2.   What three after-sale follow-up or follow-through steps do you feel Paul should now plan to take in order to keep Winterbottom as a satisfied, regular customer?

3.   What two major advantages do you feel Paul will gain by future regular callbacks on satisfied customer Winterbottom?

Sales Problem 13.2

How can you as a salesperson get your old customers to think of you when they have a problem?

Far too many salespeople settle for a comfortable order size or volume of business from old customers when they could be getting more. Without becoming overly aggressive, it is possible in a high percentage of such cases to sell these old customers on the idea that it may be to their advantage to buy more, or to buy from you a better (higher-priced) line than the one they have been using.

Let us assume you are one of these salespeople, and you want old customers to think of *you* when they have a question or problem concerning any phase of their operation with which you or your company or organization might be able to offer advice or assistance.

Question for Written Report or Class Discussion

List and describe three things you could systematically employ to get your old customers to think of you when they have a question or problem.

PART FOUR

SPECIAL TOPICS IN MODERN SELLING

Having now completed our study of the basic principles and techniques of a complete one-on-one personal sales presentation, we will now focus on some more advanced applications of what has been learned.

Part IV of our book takes us into more difficult, technical areas of personal selling as we consider first how to sell to organizational buyers in the industrial, reseller, government, and services markets. From there, we move into a two-chapter review of retail (to end-consumer) selling. One chapter focuses on in-store retail selling; the other on nonstore retail selling by telemarketing, direct selling, and service providers. This latter chapter also presents important material on trade show, sales seminar, and exhibition selling.

Since salespeople have always to be concerned with legal implications of their actions, as well as ethical considerations, an entire chapter is devoted to social, legal, and ethical issues in selling. Finally, attention is centered on sales managers: what they do, and how they go about doing it, in fulfilling their important managerial and leadership role.

Selling to Organizational Buyers

After studying this chapter, you will be able to:

Describe at least six characteristics common to the buying of goods and services by organizations in the industrial, reseller, government, and services markets.

Summarize what is meant by the term, commonly used in selling to organizations in the industrial market, *systems buying and selling.*

Explain the difference between the terms *consultative selling* and *relationship selling* to organizations in the industrial market.

Tell what a salesperson, in making a presentation before a group, should do to make all present feel included while at the same time deferring to the formal leader of the group.

Identify the first rule in selling to a buyer or buyers of large organizations or institutions in the industrial market.

Discuss how and why organizational buyers of the industrial and reseller markets differ in their approach to the buying process.

Explain how good billing and collection procedures can serve to help ease a consumer's unhappiness or resentment due to his or her inability to recognize the degree of quality of a given counseling service.

Early in Chapter 2 it was made clear that the world of sales/marketing centers around two broad, basic types or divisions of markets: (1) consumer and (2) organizational. In defining both, we noted that the *organizational market* is composed of both for-profit and nonprofit organizations that buy both products and services for their own use, use in further production, resale, or redistribution. Also in Chapter 2 three major types of organizational customer markets were described (industrial, reseller, and government), as were major classifications of products and services sold to them, as defined by the American Marketing Association.

Based on the concept that the type of organization to which organizational buyers belong plays an important part in their buying behavior and decisions, much of Chapter 3 was devoted to organizational buyer behavior and the psychology of selling to them. There we considered separately buyers within the above-noted industrial, reseller, and government markets, plus those in the services market. The point was made that some differences in approach are necessary for effective selling to these four markets, differences that are explored in this chapter.

The above brief review lead-in highlights the fact that key parts of Chapters 2 and 3 relate directly to our focus in this chapter on applied sales techniques, and must be carefully restudied in conjunction with this chapter.

ORGANIZATIONAL BUYING IN THESE FOUR MARKETS SHARES COMMON CHARACTERISTICS

Before going into some of the differences between organizational buying in the industrial, reseller, government, and services markets, let us first consider the following characteristics generally common to them:

- Organizational buyers are fewer in numbers and usually buy in much larger quantities and over a longer period than individual consumers. Also, the organizations they represent (for example, manufacturing or government) tend to be more geographically concentrated than consumer markets. Some sales to large organizations can take up to two years to conclude and run into millions of dollars.

- Larger organizations normally employ full-time professional purchasing agents, trained to buy rationally (where they can think the selling proposal over carefully and analyze, measure, evaluate, and discuss it over a long period of time). Others in those organizations besides the purchasing agents may have to be involved in the purchase decision, including formal committees composed of several people.

- They often buy on a basis of specifications that are put out for bid. Performance, quality, delivery date, or other special features may outweigh price as a key factor in their buying decision.

- They may seek, or even be required to seek, alternative sources of suppliers for various needs.
- Since suppliers frequently have to customize their offerings to meet customer needs, a close relationship often develops between buyer and seller and may continue over a long period of time.
- Three important factors relating to demand affect a great many organizational buying decisions. First is the fact that the demand for most organizational goods and services, called *derived demand,* is linked to end-consumer demands. An auto manufacturer, for example, will only buy tires and batteries from suppliers for the number of cars it expects to sell.

  Second, the demand for many organizational products is *inelastic,* in that it is not basically affected by price changes. Since production is planned, our auto manufacturer is not going to rush to buy a lot of extra new batteries in case the price goes up or down a few dollars per battery.

  Finally, often there is the problem of *fluctuating demand* caused by a volatile marketplace. A modest increase in end-consumer demand, for example, might require a much larger percentage increase in production capability.

Due to the common characteristics just noted, most selling to organizations in our four market areas is direct between producer and user, although various types of middlemen also sell to these buyers. Independent sales groups (such as, manufacturers or factory representatives) or divisions of companies that sell to such organizations (a process traditionally described as industrial selling) are normally much smaller in numbers than consumer sales organizations which sell directly to individual or household consumers. Also, these fewer salespeople, many of them engineering-, science-, or management-trained college or university graduates, often undergo training programs that can last up to two years.

WORKING THROUGH THE "SELLING PROCESS" WITH ORGANIZATIONAL BUYERS—AN OVERVIEW

Careful attention was paid in Chapter 3 to the overall organizational buyer's buying decision process, one that may involve as many as eight separate stages or steps. It was there that we settled on using the term "selling process" to describe how salespeople can help move organizational buyers through this buying process. Before discussing some specific individual market applications, it will help to take a broad look at how selling to organizations has changed since the 1950s, and get acquainted with some important terminology and related concepts.

The Changing Nature of Selling to Organizations

Prior to the 1950s most of the world's highly trained salespeople calling on organizational markets (traditionally called industrial salespersons) were more product-oriented than customer-oriented in their selling. Product knowledge was considered more important than any other sales or knowledge attributes. Starting in the 1950s, however, as industries began increasingly to consolidate and larger companies kept taking over smaller ones (trends that continue today), economic and other factors forced changes in sales/marketing as well as in other areas of business.

Costs of plant and equipment skyrocketed, for example; product technology became more complex, and the computer revolution created new, competing industries and changed traditional ones. Manufacturers and other types of organizations responded by taking a longer-range look at their goals and objectives, and a fresh look at all aspects of their overall operations. This led to a decrease in item-by-item, or current requirement-by-requirement buying, and to an increase in the *systems (or overall) approach to buying and selling,* pricing for which is frequently subject to lengthy *sales negotiation.*

Purchasing agents, who are the officially appointed buyers for large companies or organizations, are far better trained today than in the past. Most are skillful, technically oriented individuals, often with an engineering or production background. Most large globally oriented companies, such as America's General Electric and IBM, conduct lengthy training programs to teach purchasing agents how to buy. These people are interested in value as well as price, and insist on superior quality and service. They respond favorably to salespeople who can sell in terms of *value analysis, cost analysis, assured quality,* and *assured supply.*

Increasingly, in recent years, purchasing agents have become only the first level in organizational buying decisions. Due to growing cost-consciousness, top organizational management and senior technical people have become ever more involved in what are frequently committee or group buying decisions. This in turn has led salespeople to get involved in *consultative selling* or *relationship selling,* and has required them to become proficient in *group selling.*

These changes have led to an increase in the team-selling approach, whereby different experts of the selling firm call on their counterparts in the prospects' buying organization. In some cases it takes a salesperson or a selling team up to a year or more to get to know all the key people, study the operation, and identify the problems of just one large account, and the stakes can be enormous.

Getting to Know You—Some Important Organizational Selling Buzz-Word Phrases and Strategies Explained

In order to sell creatively in today's fast-changing world of organizational selling, a salesperson must be proficient not only in product knowledge and the psychology of selling, but also in understanding the buyers' values. And, to compete successfully in the "high stakes" game of large-scale organizational selling especially, he or she must understand and be able to apply the following concepts and strategies, terminology for which was introduced (but not explained) in the preceding section.

Systems Buying and Selling

Traditionally, sellers sold their individual products or services to fit into a buyer's existing system. During the late 1930s, however, as war clouds gathered in Europe and the Far East, various governments started asking their armaments manufacturers to develop and assemble complete weapons and communications systems. That trend has accelerated into today's civilian as well as governmental world—to the extent that in many areas (such as, complete telephone or computer systems) the supplier not only designs, builds, and installs the system, but also enjoys a long-term contract to maintain and service it.

Systems buying and selling is big business worldwide today, for some small- as well as many large-scale industrial organizations. In the United States, both government agencies and civilian organizations of all types either publicly announce bids for entire systems, or are open to new system proposals by alert American as well as foreign sellers.

Sales Negotiation

It was stated early in our book that *persuasion* is at the core of selling and personal selling. *Negotiation* differs from persuasion. In a business sense it involves mutual discussion and arrangement of the terms of a transaction or agreement. In a sales sense it implies collaboration, cooperation, and coordination between seller and buyer.

Negotiating skills are especially important to salespeople selling to organizations where variables can affect price, scheduling, quality of product or service, current and follow-up service, business risks, and uncontrollable external factors. Such skills can be very important at time of sale, and as later problems arise.

Another word for negotiating is "bargaining"; the number and types of situations where it may take place, and the number of different parties that might be involved is virtually unlimited. Good negotiation skills can help *you* determine the price and terms at which you buy and sell, persuade others to work with and not against you, help work out a problem with someone important to you, and help break or avoid a serious interpersonal or business impasse.

Due to its specialized nature, there are many good books available on the subject. Most of them stress prenegotiation strategic planning, followed by specific negotiation tactics under topic headings such as: "avoid making the first major concession," "applying authority tactics," "don't give a concession away for nothing," and "nibbles that add up." Two such applied books, written by professional negotiators, that can help any salesperson improve the outcome of his or her future sales negotiations are (1) Homer B. Smith, *Selling Through Negotiation* (Marketing Education Association, 4004 Rosemary St., Chevy Chase, Md. 20815), 1987, and (2) Chester L. Karrass, *The Negotiating Game* (Negotiating Books, 84 Lone Oak Path, Smithtown, N.Y. 11787), 1970.

Value Analysis and Cost Analysis

These two terms are dear to the hearts of organizational purchasing officers, technical experts, and cost-conscious top executives. From a sales point of view "cost" is relative, should be presented (and judged) only in terms of "value" and "results," and should not even be discussed (if possible) before true value is determined. Rather than restating sales applications described in earlier chapters, the following examples will illustrate how these terms can be put to good use in selling to organizations.

Let us assume that a young man we know, Steve Popovich, is an industrial salesperson for a plastics container company, calling on two manufacturing companies in his territory. He elects to approach Company A with a sales presentation built around *value analysis*. His presentation to Company B will be built around *cost analysis*. Let us see how he goes about each, and with what success.

Company A (A Presentation Built Around Value Analysis)

The Plan.   Steve knows that *value analysis* is a modern, cost-cutting technique built around three simple questions: (1) What does it do? (2) What does it cost? (3) What would do the job cheaper? He decides that if he can come up with the right answers, he's got a sale.

Results.   Steve asked permission to study their manufacturing and shipping operation in which items were packaged in plastic containers. He got all specifications and cost figures for their operation and found that his firm could provide equally acceptable containers of a slightly different type for half the price of the competitor's container they were currently using. Since they spent over $100,000 a year on their containers and affiliated operations, and since Steve proved he could save them $18,000 a year by answering the three *value analysis* questions, he got the order.

Company B (A Presentation Built Around Cost Analysis)

The Plan.   Steve knows that the most important processes for his account are manufacturing and marketing; they are the principal areas of major costs. He decides that they are also the most attractive targets for cost reduction and builds his approach around proving how his products can (1) reduce the company's manufacturing cost, and (2) increase salability of their products. Company B is a manufacturer of household products.

Results.   Steve's approach was to ask, "May I make a two-day study of your operations to see if I can help you cut costs?" The company had nothing to lose, so they gave him permission. After studying their manufacturing, shipping, and sales/marketing, Steve came up with the following:

Manufacturing.   He found a way to repackage two of Company B's products in equally acceptable but slightly lower-cost containers; he suggested an idea that eliminated one stage in the manufacture of one of their products; by suggesting round-edged square containers rather than the round ones they had been using, he reduced their shipping costs 10 percent. Overall cost savings per year resulting from all this was estimated at $35,000.

Sales/Marketing.   Steve came up with new design ideas for his containers that so improved the packaging appearance of the two repackaged products that Company B's sales manager estimated it would not only be worth an extra 10 percent increase in market share at retail-store point-of-sale, but should gain that even by decreasing the retail price 5 percent. Overall extra profit at no extra cost was estimated at $20,000 over the next year.

Steve's twin-pronged *cost analysis* sales strategy and final presentation were gratefully received. He closed by offering to imprint the new design at no extra cost provided Company B gave him a two-year rather than the normal one-year contract. They said yes—and Steve thus in effect doubled the size of the order.

Assured Quality and Assured Supply

Here are two more terms dear to the hearts of purchasing agents and other organizational buying decision-makers. They can be valuable "picture building" words for salespeople who learn how and when to use them in their sales presentations. The word "quality" ties in with "value" in the minds of those buyers who realize the importance of buying products or services that will unfailingly do the job they are being asked to do. Salespeople who can promise and deliver "assured quality" items are on their way to long-term sales success.

Along with assured quality items, organizational buyers need guaranteed, "assured supply" of ordered items—they must arrive on time, as promised, every time. Imagine the dismay and anger of our earlier-mentioned auto manufacturer if his tire supplier is unexpectedly unable to fulfill a scheduled delivery of 4000 tires as new cars sell off the assembly line at the rate of 200 per day!

Consultative Selling

An important buzz-word phrase in organizational selling today is *consultative selling*. As a theory, it goes beyond the traditional personal selling topics of precall planning, handling objections, and postcall follow-up by centering on the goal of profit improvement for both the salesperson personally and his or her key accounts.

In terms of strategy, it first involves the salesperson's gaining such an understanding of an account's business that he or she is able to relate closely and confidentially with its key people over a long period. As this close relationship grows, the salesperson strives to embed his or her products or services into the long-term business plans of the account, always toward the end-goal result of profit improvement. Many detailed practical suggestions on how to implement such strategies are contained in a splendid little book entitled *Consultative Selling*.[1]

---

[1] Mack Hanan, James Cribbin, and Herman Heiser, *Consultative Selling,* 3rd ed. (New York, AMACOM), 1985.

In line with this concept, it's not surprising that a great deal of sales training by large corporations today centers on gaining a detailed understanding of the needs and major developments in key customers' industries. During the 1980s especially, this new emphasis led to changes in many corporate sales training programs, as well as in their selling tactics. The creation of large key account (or national account) management is one example, where one salesperson is given full-time responsibility for servicing one lone customer, or just a few, to keep key accounts satisfied. This "account manager" can call in other company sales or technical experts as needed, and strives at all times to act as a "true consultant" to accounts served. Here is an example of "Big League" consultative selling in action:

THE SALE THAT TURNED GE ON

"We at GE would like to become partners with GM on your major projects," was the message delivered by General Electric's Vice Chairman, when, along with a team of corporate vice-presidents, he called on General Motors Chairman of the Board one day in 1986.

Following the GM chairman's suggestion to contact executives of the planned mammoth GM Saturn "car of the future" factory in Spring Hill, Tennessee, GE put together a 40-person sales team committed to landing a major, sole-supplier contract to totally electrify the huge plant.

Not only did this sales team include top executives from several different GE divisions, but a deliberate effort was made to match ages and personalities with the counterpart GM Saturn team. This even included some hotshot young engineer counterparts in their early 30s.

By the time they closed the sale in 1987, GE's team members had escorted their GM counterparts on tours of GE plants, participated in GM's front-end product planning, jointly worked out a multitude of specifications, and carefully negotiated pricing.

General Electric won its sought-after multimillion-dollar "single electrical supplier" contract for the Saturn plant—the grand prize for a superior team consultative effort. Due to the success of this sales approach, new GE sales teams are today working closely with other major American accounts toward similar goals.

Relationship Selling

Relationship selling is one of the newest buzz-word terms in the lexicon of sales/marketing. On the surface it appears to be almost the same as consultative selling, but, in practice, is more broad-based, higher-level, and interpersonal in nature.

Like consultative selling, it involves the seller's executives and salespeople working closely with a relatively few important (to the seller) major accounts on the complete spectrum of business issues. Often these exchanges go far beyond sales/marketing. The seller's engineers might advise customers or potential customers on upgrading their manufacturing processes. Their human resource people might suggest ideas on manpower planning and training of personnel, and their financial specialists might help with profit analysis. The aim is for the customer to start viewing the seller as a total partner.

It is on the "getting to know you" social personal level however, that relationship selling really moves beyond consultative selling. No businesspeople in the world practice interpersonal relationship selling to the degree of, or more successfully than, the Japanese. Evening after evening, week after week, year after year, the Japanese executive and key-employee workday extends far into the night, "socializing" with customers or potential customers. North American and European businesspeople, who don't always go along with such long hours, are frequently criticized by their Japanese counterparts as "not trying to sell hard enough!"

SELLING TO A GROUP

Salespeople working in our four organizational markets, as well as those in most other types of selling, frequently have to make both formal and informal presentations before groups of people.

Often a large company or government or private organization publicly announces that bids will be accepted for certain items for certain purposes at a stated place and time. Usually certain specifications are announced at the time. In such cases, the buyer brings together a group of purchasing officers, technicians, and executives to hear a formal sales presentation by a salesperson or a sales team from different producers. In some cases the groups will tour factory locations, observe special showings, or see the item in operation at some location, along with the presentation. Direct "party-plan" salespeople make such presentations before groups constantly, in private homes, at places of work, or other locations.

Assuming that you have been asked as a salesperson to formally present your product or service before a group, here are some techniques that will help you succeed:

Planning for Group Selling

Prior to such formal gathering, you as salesperson or sales-team leader should try to meet, or at least find out all you can about, each individual member of the group. Your purpose is to try to discover each one's rational and emotional likes and dislikes, both about your product and competing products. Armed with this information, you can then carefully prepare your formal presentation and assemble all necessary samples, charts, statistics, testimonials, and visual aids necessary to demonstrate and dramatize them most effectively. Whether you are given a specified length of time for the presentation or the time limit is self-established, you should practice and polish your delivery and demonstrations step by step beforehand.

The Presentation Before a Group

Once a formal presentation gets underway, you will normally present your case point by point, asking for and accepting limited questions from time to time to keep the group involved, but always maintaining control of the situation. While progressing, you try to determine from attention, facial expressions, or body motions or positions, the degree of acceptance, indifference, or opposition to your points. While deferring to the formal leader of the group, you must try to include each member—by looking at each one individually from time to time, or through question and discussion breaks.

Interestingly enough, in most such situations one or more of the group will probably take your side. Once this becomes evident, you can often work through this person, especially if differences of opinion break out among various group members. Also, in such groups one or two people (often not the leader) turn out to be the real "influentials," selling others of the group on their point of view. A major purpose in trying to meet each member privately prior to the formal meeting is to try to anticipate who such influentials might be. If one is very much in favor of your proposal, you can play off him or her by asking his or her opinion concerning a point you have just made. Conversely, a prior knowledge of possible opposition and the reasons for it may enable you to build any negative points into your presentation and handle them before they are vocally raised as objections before the group.

Most questions are reserved for a question and discussion period following your presentation; lengthy or off-the-point queries should be discouraged during the presentation. This can be done merely by acknowledging and asking consent to return to it later.

A close, as practiced in face-to-face selling to one person, is seldom applied in such formal group presentations, although in some situations it can be done. Circumstances will dictate your closing action or end-of-presentation statement. Sometimes the group will hear presentations by several competing salespeople, one after the other, at an all-day sitting. Normally they advise you beforehand in such formal presentation situations when the decisions will be announced.

While the above discussion centered on a situation where you as salesperson had been called upon for a presentation at a stated time and place (such as a bid situation), the same principles apply when you, on your own initiative, organize a group of two or more people for a formal presentation. In this case, you can more easily attempt to close on the spot.

PERSONAL SELLING TO DIFFERENT ORGANIZATIONAL MARKETS REQUIRES DIFFERENT SALES APPROACHES

In addition to the material on organizational buying presented in Chapters 2 and 3, many applied examples of how to sell to organizational buyers were presented throughout Chapters 8 through 14 (steps in the selling process) of our book. Based on them, and on what we have learned so far in this chapter, we will conclude our special focus on this topic by considering some differences in sales approach required for effective personal selling to our four organizational markets.

Selling to Buyers in the Industrial (and Institutional) Market

Construction, manufacturing, banking, communications, agriculture, and public utilities are but a few of the many huge industries that comprise the industrial market. While relatively small individual sales are constantly being made to subunits within each industry, other individual sales can run into millions of dollars.

Since the stakes can be very high, the first rule in selling to such organizational buyers is to prepare thoroughly prior to the approach. As one successful salesperson put it, "In 'Big League' industrial selling, the salesperson who gathers the most information in advance about the buying organization and its decision-makers is really in the winning position." If selling abroad, this includes researching the culture, politics, and ideology of the prospect's country, as well as the target organization and its top people.

In order to carefully prepare for such a sales approach and presentation a salesperson seeks all possible information in getting answers to these two basic questions: (1) What and on what basis does this industrial organization buy? (2) Who makes the buying decisions, and how are these decisions made?

What and on What Basis do Industrial Organizations Buy?

We know that industrial organizations buy all sorts of products and services, both for their own use and to use in producing their own products or services, which they sell or lease to others. Some products become part of another product: raw materials such as steel or cotton, for example, or off-the-shelf, standard-item components such as nuts and bolts. In each case the product to be purchased is needed, and provided it meets acceptable quality standards, the only real issues to be decided between buyer and seller are price and delivery terms.

Some products needed as parts for another product have to be specially designed and manufactured. Called *subassemblies,* they have to meet firm buyer specifications. Sellers of subassemblies must show proof that they can fully meet these specifications, as well as agreed-upon price and delivery terms.

Other products purchased by industrial organizations are those that facilitate production. These include not only products such as lubricants, paint, and countless other minor but important items used in the organization's manufacturing or production process, but scores of operational (for example, office supplies) and housekeeping (for example, janitorial supplies) items as well. In making purchases of "facilitating" items like these, normally done on a repeat basis, buyers tend to be more concerned with efficient (frequently local) service than price, and if they find a reliable supplier, to stay with it on a long-term basis.

Many types of services may be purchased by industrial organizations—legal, security, accounting, trucking, employment agency, insurance, consulting, to name but a few. In all these areas experience, reliability, and service are often more important concerns to the buyer than lowest price.

Who Makes the Buying Decisions, and How Are These Decisions Made?

In small owner-managed operations, one person may make all purchasing decisions; in larger industrial organizations, the key contact for salespeople is the purchasing agent (PA) or buyer. Small organizations may have only one such person; larger ones are likely to have a "buying center (or department)" full of them. Typically, these PAs see salespeople, one after the other, all day long on a prearranged appointment basis. Others have "open days" with no appointment required. As professionals, they respond most favorably to a "professional" salesperson. Double-cross, lie to, or try to end-run a PA, and you are "finished"; help them solve a problem or do a better job for which they receive recognition, and you may have won a long-term friend at court.

Most routine new or reorder off-the-shelf purchases (called a *straight rebuy*) are made by PAs alone. In cases where the buyer wants to modify product specifications, or price or delivery terms, or to change to a new supplier (called *a modified rebuy*), other people within the organization may be involved in the buying decision. And even more people, including key technical and top executive level individuals may be involved in important, first-time, new product or service purchasing decisions (called a *new-task buy*).

Many industrial purchases are made on a "bid" and "to specifications" basis. In some such cases a salesperson may be able to see the person or persons who drew up the specifications and work up a mutually satisfactory bid together. In other cases the organization may let the salesperson study the situation or problem so he or she can draw up a proposal. It is usually to the buyer's advantage to cooperate with knowledgeable salespeople so as to "put them to work for us." Where detailed, written proposals are required, every effort must be made to find out what the buyer needs, wants, and expects—and give it to them.

Industrial buyers work within strict budget guidelines. If their budget is exhausted, they simply cannot buy now. If they have unspent funds available near the end of the budget year, that might mean an easy on-the-spot sale for the alert salesperson who discovers the situation.

Selling to Institutions (Private and Government)

Selling to private hospitals, nursing homes, schools, prisons, and other such profit or not-for-profit institutions that buy countless end-use products and services is essentially the same as selling to other buyers in the industrial market. Selling to government-owned ones, as to other agencies of government, usually follows a different process, which will be explained shortly.

Some institutional organizations are small, and are likely to have only one or two people concerned with purchasing. In a small private hospital, for example, the food services manager may buy food, and an administrator, all other supplies and medications. Larger organizations, say city school systems, are likely to have a buying center staffed by professional buyers. For each, the buying process is similar to other types of industrial organizations.

SELLING TO BUYERS IN THE RESELLER MARKET

The reseller market consists of those individuals and wholesale and retail organizations that buy products and services both for their own use and to sell or lease to others. As in the industrial market, small operations may have only one or two people concerned with purchasing, while larger ones (such as a supermarket chain or a large automotive parts distributor) are likely to have national and/or regional buying centers staffed by professional buyers.

A major difference between industrial and reseller buyers is that since the latter are buying for their customers, they have to think like and for those customers. A buyer for an American retail women's clothing chain, for example, has to judge whether the new, fashionable-in-New-York-City, fall line of dresses will sell in the chain's Great Falls, Montana store. In many cases, the buyers or "buying committee" can only make recommendations, with individual store managers having final buying authority.

Other considerations, apart from expected consumer acceptance, influence reseller buying decisions. These include merchandising and promotional assistance, special discounts, and help in training retail salespersons. Salespeople who are authorized to offer exclusive distribution rights, consignment or special extended-term payment plans, special promotional allowances, or point-of-sale merchandising displays are especially favored by reseller buyers. Above all, when dealing with such buyers, salespeople have to keep in mind the fast-changing needs of the resellers' customers, and come up with new ideas and service to help them meet those needs.

SELLING TO BUYERS IN THE GOVERNMENT MARKET

In nearly all the world's countries, government in its many forms and at different levels buys an amazing array of goods and services, ranging from jet fighter planes, to buildings, to janitorial supplies, to school books. In most countries, agencies of the federal or national government are the biggest buyers, servicing both the military and civilian sectors.

The United States government is the largest single purchaser of goods and services in the world. Although its various agencies do business in their own often complicated way, since they usually try to minimize taxpayer cost, their buyers normally favor lowest-cost bidders who can meet stated specifications. Additionally, they go out of their way to assist small American businesses who want to sell to them, and both at home and abroad frequently encourage foreign suppliers to submit bids in equal competition with domestic ones.

Since nearly every supplier then has a fair chance at some American federal government business, how does one go about such selling? Answers to that question, which follow, also suggest guidelines for selling to lower levels of government in the United States, as well as in most other countries of the world. We tackle how to successfully sell to Uncle Sam via these three "keys to success" headings: (1) First, Study the Market and How to Sell to It, (2) Develop Your Sales Strategy and Action Plans, and (3) Don't Get Discouraged—Stay With It.

First, Study the Market and How to Sell to It

Especially to first-time, would-be sellers, selling to agencies of the American federal government can be a frustrating experience due to the large number of buying agencies and the complexities of their differing purchasing procedures. To successful, experienced sellers, however, as with any other large, complicated, big-money customer, the trick is to learn how to do business the government's way, and through hard work and discipline, sell that way. Establishment of separate departments, or simply appointing government account executives who specialize in selling to the government can make the task easier. Here's how you, as one of the latter, might go about, for the first time, researching the American government market as a prospect for your small business firm's products, and how to effectively sell there:

- *Find buying agencies and buying offices that match your firm's sales goals and its best-chance products.* Start by checking your direct competitors; are they selling to government agencies? If so, get the facts about their current pricing and services, most of which is public information that can be gathered from the agency or agencies they sell to, simply by asking. The next step is to check with U.S. government agencies involved in advising suppliers about what and how to sell to government agencies. Both the Small Business Administration and the General Services Administration operate business service centers in many major American cities, with trained staff on hand to guide and advise you. In smaller cities the Chamber of Commerce can often help. Overseas, the commercial attache at American embassies or United States Information Agency (USIA) center librarians can help.

  There are also many types of publications available to help you, most of which are government publications. Among these are (1) *Commerce Business Daily* (Department of Commerce), a daily listing of both proposals and new contracts for federal government business, (2) *Federal Executive Directory* (Carroll Publishing Co.), a semimonthly listing of up to 85,000 entries including federal departments, agencies, and offices and their key executives by name, and (3) *U.S. Government Purchasing and Sales Directory* (Government Printing Office), an annually updated publication designed specifically to tell small businesses what products and services are purchased by what specific government agencies and offices. These are only a few of the excellent published sources available to you. The reference librarian at any good American university, college, or public library can quickly direct you to others.

- *Find out how and when your selected target agencies or offices buy.* It is vitally important to make certain that you meet the quite specific federal purchasing requirements. The government has different procedures for purchases under $25,000 and for those over that amount. Purchasing procedures for amounts under $25,000 are less formal and favor small business suppliers. The Small Business Administration (SBA), while it cannot help you land a specific contract, can offer helpful information and guidance about how to apply for such.

Purchases over $25,000 are determined by formal bidding procedures, which fall into two types: the *open bid* and the *negotiated bid*. Under open-bid buying, bids for carefully described items are invited from "qualified" buyers. Under most circumstances the contract goes to the lowest bidder. Negotiated bids are those negotiated directly between the agency and one or more companies which involve specific (usually large-scale) projects and terms. In either case, since the supplier must be "qualified" (that is, be financially and operationally capable of fulfilling the contract it is bidding for), it is important for the seller to perform two tasks very carefully. These are (1) first get on the buying agency's approved buyer list, and then (2) prepare and submit the bid exactly per required specifications.

Develop Your Sales Strategy and Action Plans

"The best strategy to follow in selling to government agencies," advises one highly successful sales executive, "is constant, careful study of your selected, target agencies. Get to know their programs, their needs, their procedures, their time constraints, and their key people."

Ways to do this include study of published information sources such as *Congressional Quarterly* for news of pending legislation, and of agency activities and their key personnel changes. Other government publications offer clues as to what projects are likely to be authorized and funded—and when.

Since specific action plans are most effective when based on hard, accurate information, it pays to make sales calls on, and get to know personally to the fullest extent possible, key officials of the agency or agencies you hope to serve. Most are eager to provide information on their procurement needs and procedures. Membership in associated professional organizations can aid in making and improving such contacts.

It will further pay to keep those officials being cultivated up to date on your company and its products via mailings, visits to your display centers, samples, notices of your firm's ability to modify its offerings to meet specifications, and any new, special sales terms and conditions that meet their agency's normal needs and procedures. Finally, make certain that they are provided with up-to-date names, addresses, and phone numbers of your firm's key sales and technical people, and are informed that these people are fully accessible to them.

Don't Get Discouraged—Stay With It!

Persistence does pay off in seeking government business at any level. Especially for small business suppliers, it pays to keep submitting proposals to agencies even in cases where winning the contract seems unlikely. There are two major reasons for this: first, you learn more about the system in general, and the specific agency and its procedures and key officials each time you submit a bid, and second, the agency officials get to know your firm and you (the salesperson) better each time. When you lose out on a bid, you have a reason to ask agency officials why you lost; by doing this they eventually get to know you and become aware of your sincere interest in serving them.

SELLING TO THE SERVICES MARKET

As was noted in our Chapter 3 discussion concerning the marketing of services, this sector of the industrialized world's economy is marked both by its rapid growth since the 1950s and its variety. There it was pointed out that in so many areas, the intangibility of the service or services offered can pose special emotional buying decision considerations for end-consumer and service-provider organizational buyers alike.

For salespeople charged with selling to organizational buyers in the services (or service provider) market, this means that buying decisions by these people may be more emotionally based than those of buyers in the industrial, reseller, and government markets. This isn't the case, of course, for routine operational purchases such as office suppliers or housekeeping items, but may very well be the case for services either to be resold to end-consumers, or provided free to end-use consumers or clients.

Here, to help guide our thinking, are four major groupings of service providers, and a few of the many types of services, offered by individuals, firms, or organizations within each.

Private Business	Professional Business	Nonprofit Orgs.	Government Orgs.
Airlines	Accounting	Colleges	Military
Banks	Legal	Universities	Police and fire
Hotels	Consulting	Museums	Courts
Insurance companies	Medical	Symphonies	Schools
Real estate firms	Advertising	Hospitals	Libraries
Retailers	Counseling	Nursing homes	Social security

What Special Types of Marketing Problems Do Such Service Providers Encounter that Can Affect Purchasing Decisions by Their Organizational Buyers?

In considering the above question it will help to recall that a service can be any type of activity, benefit, or satisfaction either given free or offered for sale; is essentially intangible, and may or may not be tied to a physical product. Also, the quality of many types of services (for example, restaurant, nursing care) can vary greatly depending on the people on duty at a given time. With so many variables, which can cause end-consumer prepurchase doubts and postpurchase unhappiness, it is no wonder that emotional factors frequently weigh heavily in services buying decisions of both end-consumers and organizational buyers.

Listed below, as examples, are a few of the special types of sales/marketing problems faced by service providers trying to serve end-consumers. Your own customers may face the same type of problems, or quite different ones. The only way to find out is to ask them.

- Many people are reluctant consumers to begin with, to the point that even the best of service fails to please them. Examples include mass transit riders, telephone company patrons, users of certain government social services, prison inmates, and those required to buy expensive medicines.

- Consumers who are buying because they have to, not because they want to, are often fearful or hostile. Examples include those forced to seek expensive medical or legal assistance, to pay taxes for perceived un-needed or unwanted government services, or to buy required unwanted insurance.

- Consumers commonly resent being referred to a specific service provider, without the opportunity of choice. Examples include being referred to an expensive unknown medical specialist or to a distant hospital with specialized treatment facilities, or a ticket-holding airline passenger forced by deliberate overbooking to take a later, less convenient flight on another airline.

- Individual consumers often feel unhappiness or resentment due to their inability to recognize the degree of quality of a given service, or the fairness of the cost of the service rendered. Examples of such consumer reaction are common in service areas such as construction or repair, hospitalization, travel, interior design, trade level education, advertising, and consulting of all types.

HOW CAN SALESPEOPLE HELP SERVICE-PROVIDER ORGANIZATIONAL BUYERS ANTICIPATE, AVOID, OR COPE WITH SUCH PROBLEMS?

As a "problem-solving" salesperson, you may find that the following suggestions on how to anticipate, avoid, or cope with some of the above problems can be adapted and turned to your personal direct or indirect sales advantage. Most of these suggest ways to "tangiblize" and "personalize" the services offered, a topic that is further addressed in Chapter 16.

- *First—ask, listen! Seek out the real problems.* Most mass service providers (such as, government agencies, mass transit, banks) can involve consumers via formal and informal surveys, and arrange personal interviews and focus group meetings. Smaller organizational (law firms, beauty parlors) or individual service providers can do the same on a more informal basis. As in all types of selling, the objective is to gain consumer attention, interest, and it is to be hoped understanding, advice, and cooperation.

- *Then—communicate with consumers.* Communication is the key to developing satisfied consumers, clients, or patients. Mass service providers can use statement stuffers, radio, television, newspapers, billboards, and telephone calls to alert patrons to problems or disruptions (and how they will be handled), the likelihood of service improvement, and what options exist for payment. Most professional and many business providers can make certain that buyers have realistic expectations of services to be provided by preparing detailed written estimates or quotes in advance. Phone calls can keep consumers informed about services that take time, and medical or dental patients happy during periods of at home recuperation.

- *Make consumers, patients, and/or clients feel welcome.* Visitor welcome signs in institutional and large business parking lots and inside buildings, plus a manned information booth just inside the main building entrance make people feel good. Waiting locations inside buildings should reflect a warm atmosphere. A good training program will help maintain uniform quality and standards of employee service; complaints of poor service should be handled quickly.

- *Proper billing and collection procedures are important.* Billings should be quite detailed, so as to avoid buyer questions or perceptions; try to turn them to public relations advantage! Since an unpaid bill may reflect customer dissatisfaction with the provided service, a phone call to ask reasons for delayed payment (before ever tougher form collection letters) may save a customer's goodwill and future business.

- *Finally, follow up and through properly.* For organizational service providers, as for sellers of products, proper after-sale follow-up and service are a major key to continued success.

SUMMARY

Building on earlier Chapter 2 descriptive and Chapter 3 behavioral aspects of organizational buying, this chapter focused on applications of personal selling to the industrial, reseller, government, and services markets.

First presented were characteristics generally common to these four markets, such as their frequent use of professional purchasing agents and the fact that they often buy on the basis of specifications put out for bid. After noting how personal selling to these has changed since the 1950s, a number of important buzz-word phrases and strategies affecting today's selling there were explained. Systems buying and selling, sales negotiation, value analysis, cost analysis, consultive selling, relationship selling, and selling to a group were among those phrases and strategies.

Some differences in sales approach necessary for effective personal selling to each of those four organizational markets were then presented. After noting the need for careful advance preparation (in all four markets) prior to the approach, some practical tips on how to sell raw materials, off-the-shelf standard components, and made-to-specification subassemblies to buyers of industrial organizations were given. Then came suggestions how to sell successfully to buyers of reseller organizations who, unlike buyers in the other three markets, since they are buying for their customers, have to think like and for those customers when purchasing.

The discussion of selling to the federal government market that followed centered on finding the right agency or buying office, how to handle purchasing in amounts under $25,000 and over that amount, and how to get to know key agency decision-makers. Our concluding section addressed some of the special problems encountered by organizational buyers in the services market whose customers may resent or fear having to buy the provider's service.

Questions for Analysis and Discussion

1.   Explain how the term *negotiation* differs from persuasion as it applies to personal selling.

2.   What is meant by the term *national account management,* and how does it tie in with consultative selling and relationship selling principles and techniques?

3.   Assuming that while making a sales presentation before a group of ten people, you sense that all but two are apparently opposed to or indifferent to your proposal. How will you try to turn this situation to your advantage?

4.   What is meant by the term *subassemblies* as used in industrial selling, and what must sellers show proof of in connection with it?

5.   What is the difference, in terms of selling to organizational market buyers, between a *straight rebuy* and a *modified rebuy?*

6.   How would you, as a salesperson, go about finding which federal government agency or office in your country, out of many, might be the best single one to try to sell your company's products to for the first time?

7.   If your company loses out on a bid made to a government agency, what, if anything, is there to be gained by your spending time to visit that agency to inquire why it lost out?

8.   Why are new task buys by buyers of large service-provider organizations, intended for resale, apt to be more heavily based on emotional considerations than same-type purchases by buyers in the industrial market?

CASE STUDY 14

Unisys Implements "Line of Business" Sales Strategy by Reorganizing its Sales Force Around Six Commercial and Governmental Clusters[2]

The year was 1985; and as two major American corporations, Burroughs and Sperry were completing their merger to form the giant Blue Bell, Pennsylvania-based Unisys Corp., their basic information systems market suddenly hit a saturation point. Market growth which had averaged about 20 percent over the past 20 years suddenly dropped to about 10 percent. Resulting computer price declines of close to 21 percent had a dramatic impact on the new firm—it suddenly found its revenue growth cut in half!

A few months later, in 1986, the newly merged, nearly $10 billion computer company set out to streamline and reorganize its sales/ marketing operations. The first step was to carefully analyze trends affecting the marketplace.

A major new trend uncovered was the shift in decision making for computer purchases. Historically, corporate managers of information systems had decided what hardware and software their companies would buy. But now, in the mid-1980s, analysis showed that managers in departments that actually used the computer were increasingly influencing purchases. This shift in decision making posed unexpected new problems for the Unisys sales force. Not only were they faced with selling systems and products to the Management Information Systems (MIS) people, but now they had to learn to understand their customers' businesses well enough to also sell front-line operational managers on their products.

[2] This case study developed by permission from "UNISYS: Lining Up Business Targets" by Kate Bertrand, *Business Marketing* (October 1988), pp. 41, 44, and 46.

Action Taken—Sales Force Reorganized around Segmented Market Clusters

A new Unisys sales strategy evolved; one aimed at discovering what changes were driving the business of each of their several different market segments, what each end-user customer really needed, and why each bought what they did, when they did.

To implement this strategy, the company reorganized its sales force around six commercial and governmental clusters: (1) the industrial and commercial markets, (2) financial services, (3) the communications and airlines markets, (4) the public sector, (5) the federal government, and (6) the defense market.

Each of these clusters in turn were further segmented according to the kind of products they purchased. For example, the public sector market was divided into four groups: state and local agencies, health care providers, educational institutions, and utility companies. And yet another segmentation cut split each of these four: the health care group, for instance, was further broken down into smaller market segments (hospitals, health maintenance organizations, and private practices).

By 1988, Unisys had completed reorganization of its 2200 sales reps around the six primary industry clusters. Training of in-place sales managers and salespeople focused on their viewing customers as belonging to vertical markets first, and geographic locations second. Salespeople and service specialists were assigned to accounts by "line of business" rather than by geographic locations. Efforts were made to hire new salespeople from the industries they were slated to serve.

Unisys executives agree that while segmented reseller programs, sales and service training, and advertising expenses are costly, they are crucial to the success of their corporate "line of business," segment-based sales/ marketing strategy. "Great strategies poorly implemented can become disasters," said one. "Quality execution is the key to success." Today, as Fortune 500 Unisys moves into the twenty-first century, sales and profit figures seem to show that their sales strategy is working.

Questions for Written Reports or Class Discussion

1. If you were national sales manager for any single given Unisys sales division, and felt that appointment of a few "key account" managers might further add to existing "line of business" selling to accounts, what would be your criteria for making such appointments?

2. If you, as a Unisys salesperson, specializing by "line of business" in selling to banks and savings and loan organizations in a single major city, wanted to develop "relationship selling" with your key accounts, how would you go about it?

3. Assuming that you have been asked to make a first-ever sales presentation on behalf of your Unisys sales division to a group of eight to ten purchasing officers and MIS people in a large federal government agency, what two basic questions relating to that agency will you try to find answers to beforehand?

4. What are the major advantages and the major disadvantages, in your mind, of Unisys's striving to recruit and hire new salespeople from the specific industries they will be trained to serve as Unisys sales reps?

Sales Problem 14.1

Can you help me reduce energy costs and still get the needed light in my stores?

Mr. Edward Levinson, vice-president and part owner of a 20-store Michigan, U.S.A. menswear chain has just asked a question of Tom Kubiak, industrial sales representative for a large manufacturer of lighting fixtures. Let us see how Tom answers this question, and how the discussion continues.

Tom: Do you have a specific problem, Mr. Levinson?

Levinson: Yes! We started a month ago to try to reduce the electric bill in one of our stores by removing half the lamps. We thought it might be a fine energy-and-cost-saving technique, one that, if it worked in this test store, could be expanded to the other stores in our chain. The trouble is, the idea didn't work.

Tom: What happened?

Levinson: It made the stores too dark. The merchandise didn't show up properly, and customers complained that a dark store is not the ideal place to stay and shop. Pulling out half our lamps in each fixture had a decided negative effect on impulse buying, and sales really dropped.

Tom: So where do you stand now? How can I help you?

Levinson: We are looking for another way to reduce energy costs and still get the needed light. Got any ideas?

Tom: I believe that we may be able to solve your problem by replacing your original number of currently used 75-watt fluorescent lamps with our new 60-watt "Watt-Miser" fluorescent lamps, and save 60 watts per fixture. That's about $24 annual savings for each fixture at a 10-cents-per-kwh power rate. With 400 to 600 fixtures in each store, savings can add up quickly.

Levinson: I agree. Your idea is worth considering. What will it cost me to replace all my current lamps with your "Watt-Misers," and what will I save in operating costs? What's the bottom-line figure?

Tom: If I can get some necessary technical information from you or from your staff this morning, I can give you a firm answer in writing at this same time next week. I have a lot of work to do between now and then to come up with the figures.

Levinson: OK, I'll answer your questions now, and will plan to see you here at 10 A.M. one week from today.

Question for Written Reports or Class Discussion

Assuming that you are Tom, what information-gathering questions will you now ask Mr. Levinson, and what will you do between now and next week in order to come up with the answers to his questions?

| Sales Problem 14.2 | Suddenly, industrial sales rep Ray Lewis doesn't have enough steel to sell to his good customers—what should he do in the face of this situation? |

TO: All Sales Representatives
FROM: L. R. Bennington,
V.P. National Sales Division
Due to worldwide raw material shortages which have suddenly and seriously curtailed steel production of both domestic and foreign producers, all Armco sales representatives will immediately inform their customers that we will be able to supply only 75 percent of any new orders. No new account orders will be accepted. This situation will exist for at least six months—possibly much longer!

Ray Lewis, a young industrial sales representative for Armco Steel Co., based in Houston, Texas, U.S.A. has just read this company memo in stunned disbelief. Since joining Armco upon graduation from college five years ago he has, through hard work and effective personal selling, registered sizable sales increases each year. He has increased business consistently from the established accounts he inherited in his south Texas and Louisiana sales territory, and has added important new accounts.

Armco produces steel in various forms which Ray sells to companies that manufacture storage tanks, oil rigs, and electric utility poles. From the start, Ray has had plenty to sell; now, for the first time, he finds himself in the position of having to ration steel to his customers.

Ray's mind races as he considers some of the problems that lie ahead and steps he must start taking now to handle them. This new allocation program, which allows no provision for new accounts, is especially frustrating, since he naturally would like to see his sales increase. However, since it is an equitable program he realizes that it will be easy to explain to his anxious purchasing-agent customers. Thinking positively, he wonders how this allocation system, which will deny steel to customers now, can be turned to his advantage as a valuable tool for building future sales.

He mentally asks himself, "Since this new situation calls for an immediate revamping of my sales plans and schedules for the next six months at least, what new goals and objectives should I set? What specific action steps should I take immediately, and what follow-through steps? I'd better start putting a new sales plan together right now, so I can present it tomorrow to my sales manager—he will appreciate my managerial thinking if I can get it to him before he asks me for it, as he most certainly will."

Ray pulls a piece of yellow scratch paper from his briefcase, and sits down to start putting his new, positive objectives and action plans down on paper.

Questions for Written Reports or Class Discussion

1.   What immediate action steps should Ray take so far as his customers are concerned?

2.   How can Ray turn the new allocation system, which denies steel to good customers now, into a valuable tool for building future sales?

3.   Assuming that Ray will have time to contact new prospects in the six months ahead, as he has in the past, should he call on any? If so, what can he say to them?

4.   Since he can't supply additional steel, what *can* Ray do to help keep his good customers as fully supplied as possible during this period of temporary shortage?

CHAPTER 15

In-Store Retail Selling

After studying this chapter, you will be able to:

Discuss major trends and developments in North American retailing over the past three decades, and how these may affect consumers, retail selling, and retail salespeople worldwide in the 1990s.

Explain the basic difference between in-store retail selling and nonstore (outside) retail selling.

Summarize sales techniques involved in handling two common retail objections: (1) excuses or stalls, and (2) indecision.

Identify techniques that will help an in-store retail salesperson solve these four special retail sales problems: (1) the shopper, (2) two customers at once, (3) a group of shoppers, and (4) the complaining or irate customer.

Summarize basic sales techniques for handling these four common retail merchandise sales problems: (1) selling specials, (2) making second sales, (3) trading up for bigger sales, and (4) selling substitute items.

Describe proper follow-up or follow-through steps to take concerning these special retail sales problems areas: (1) promises broken for reasons beyond your control, (2) cancellations, (3) specific complaints, and (4) the dissatisfied customer.

I t was noted early in Chapter 1 that the largest percentage by far of the world's salespeople are and will continue to be engaged in retail selling. Now we stop dead in our tracks to pose the question: "What do we mean by retail selling?" The wide-ranging answer may surprise you! We start by defining retailing.

> *Retailing* includes all the activities involved in selling products and services directly to final consumers for their personal or nonbusiness use.

Any individual, business firm or nonprofit organization that does this type of selling is engaged in retailing; no matter *how* the products are sold (by salesperson, telephone, or mail) or *where* they are sold (in a store, in a consumer's home, or at a trade show). Products and services sold to end consumers for their personal, nonbusiness use range from food products to ocean cruises to legal and accounting services. Management consultants selling their services, postal clerks selling stamps, colleges and universities soliciting new student applicants, hospitals publicly offering their birthing facilities to expectant mothers, and salespersons in every type of store are all engaged in retailing.

THE BROAD FIELD OF RETAILING AND RETAIL SELLING

The field of retailing and retail selling is so broad that marketing authorities have broken it down into two separate areas: *in-store (inside)* and *nonstore (outside)*. The major difference between these two classifications is that in-store retail salespeople work inside stores, where customers come to them, whereas nonstore retail salespeople call on prospects and customers outside of stores.

Following this breakdown, we will cover retail selling in two chapters. Here, in this chapter, we focus on personal selling activities that take place in a retail store setting. In Chapter 16 we focus on nonstore retail personal selling via direct marketing (for example, telemarketing), direct selling (such as, house-to-house, or party plan), and by service providers, and we touch on nonpersonal selling methods such as direct mail, automatic vending machines, and buying services. In both chapters our attention centers on North American retailing trends and developments which continue to lead the world in pace and variety of change.

THE CHANGING RETAIL SCENE

Retailing as we know it today evolved from the eighteenth century trading post and the nineteenth century general store. The general store has become the department and chain stores, and they in turn have continued to evolve in many innovative ways, as we shall see.

Prior to the 1930s, retailing in North America was concentrated in the hands of operators who owned their own stores. That pattern began to change in the early 1930s with the development of the department store concept, which usually featured a central city store and several satellite stores. Their salespeople enjoyed a new, higher status and, since many were paid on a commission basis, rising affluence in their communities.

As unions pressed their organizing efforts during the late 1930s, they found department store employees relatively easy to organize. This was due in part to union approval of commission remuneration as a just form of employee participation in retailers' profits. By the 1950s, however, union influence had declined as retailing began to be concentrated, especially in the United States, in the hands of large holding companies like Federated Department Stores and general merchandise chains like Sears, Roebuck and Co. As these retailers grew more powerful and their salespeople more transient and part time, management began to pay less-costly-to-administer salaries rather than commissions.

1950–1980 Suburban Shopping Malls, Credit Cards, Big Chain Stores, and Mushrooming New Forms of Retailing

Following the end of World War II in 1945, as millions of Americans and Canadians moved from inner cities and towns into rapidly expanding new suburban housing developments, they were followed by new suburban shopping centers and malls. Along with the great North American love affair with the automobile came mobility for consumers to shop quickly at different locations. Credit cards were introduced, and as their use became widespread, shopping became easier. Fast-food chains such as McDonald's and Burger King swiftly opened new outlets everywhere—a new and major revolution in restaurant retailing.

The 1970s especially was an era when people thronged shopping malls and seemed to have more time. During these years the general merchandise department stores and big retail chains, especially Sears, J. C. Penney Co., Inc., and Montgomery Ward & Co., dominated the American retailing scene. At their height, stores of these three chains alone, each selling goods under their own label, numbered in the thousands. Where they had no branches, consumers could buy from catalogues. In Canada, chains like Sears Canada, Zaton's, and Hudson's Bay Company enjoyed the same status. While Mom and Pop retail stores and larger independent stores also thrived, the period was marked by increased growth of large chain operations in all areas of retailing.

These years were also marked by the introduction, testing, and in some cases rapid start-up expansion of many new and innovative types of store retailing. Here are some of the more important types:

- *Specialty Stores.* These usually offer, on a self-service basis, wide assortments of specific products (food, jewelry, shoes, sporting goods, children's toys). Targeting their customers by age and income, they can respond quickly to changing trends and offer a certain type of image. Well-known American specialty chains include The Limited, Benetton,

The Gap, and Toys Я Us; in Canada, the huge Dylex chain of ten different-named subchains dominates the malls specialty shop scene.

- *Supermarkets.* These are high-volume, low-cost, self-service operations (both independents and chains) normally specializing in food items and household products. There are nearly 35,000 of this type in North America, accounting for nearly 75 percent of American and Canadian grocery sales. There are also specialist drug, toy, and other types of so-called "supermarkets."

- *Convenience Stores.* Usually small in size, these stores sell high-turnover food and other consumer items at convenient business and residential area locations. Most are open 24 hours a day, seven days a week. Seven-Elevens, besides being perhaps the best-known American convenience stores, are also well-known across Canada. Other Canadian convenience store chains are Becker's and Mae's Milk.

- *Mass Merchandisers.* Stores such as those operated by the Woolworth chain offer a wide range of mainly lower-end of the market general merchandise plus the convenience of one-stop shopping.

- *Discount Stores.* These offer a variety of merchandise categories, including national brands at low prices. In addition to well-known general merchandise chains such as K-Mart, Wal-Mart, and Target, there are scores of other discount stores and chains in the United States that specialize in specific types of products such as electronics (Radio Shack) and books (Walden Books). The three largest Canadian discount store chains are K-Mart, Woolco, and Zellers.

- *Manufacturers' Outlet Stores.* Usually found clustered together in specially built outlet shopping centers (or malls) in far off the beaten path countryside locations, these outlets offer brand-name merchandise at discounted prices averaging 40 percent. Unlike off-price chain stores such as T.J. Maxx and Marshall's, which sell discounted goods from many different manufacturers, most of these stores are owned by and offer merchandise from one designer or manufacturer only.

  One of the fastest growing segments of the retail industry during the 1980s, these often huge in size outlet centers grew in number from 28 in 1982 to over 200 by 1990. In spite of their deliberate out-of-the-way locations, the manufacturer-owners of these outlet stores face the problem of how to keep their regular full-price urban retailer customers happy, while continuing to enjoy these booming outlet discount sales.

- *Warehouse Stores/Wholesale Clubs.* These are large, limited-service, no-frills general merchandise operations aiming for high volume at low prices. Some operate as clubs, offering membership only to select consumer groups, such as government employees. Examples include Wal-Mart's Super Saver Warehouse Club stores and its nearly 70 Sam's Wholesale Club outlets.

- *Hypermarkets.* These huge stores strive to exceed $100 million in annual sales while giving consumers lower prices and the convenience of one-stop shopping. Such operations as Biggs, Hypermarket U.S.A., and Wal-Mart's new hypermarkets planned for the 1990s do and will offer the same general merchandise as discount stores plus a full-line supermarket. Many retailing analysts believe that hypermarkets will be the major retailing development trend of the 1990s.

- ■ *Other Types.* There are also other new types of retailers, many being mutations of those just noted. Among them are catalogue showrooms, factory outlet stores, superspecialty stores, off-price centers, hypermarches, supercenters, superstores, combination stores, and destination stores. And there is the very new integrated retail center concept, where two or more well-known noncompeting retailers locate together at one location to share promotion and other costs and draw on each other's customer base. An example of this latter concept is Montgomery Ward, which in 1987–1988 leased excess space in some of its stores to Toys Я Us.

The 1980s—Speciality Retailers Cut and Slash the Big Department Store and General Merchandise Chains

Big changes hit the North American retail scene in the 1980s. First recognized by only a few astute retailers and market researchers was the fact that by the late 1970s working women in both the United States and Canada were starting to spend less time shopping. By the early 1980s this trend had become a groundswell. When these women needed an item, they tended to go directly to the store where they were most likely to find it. Increasingly they turned to the speciality retailers.

Both department stores and the huge general merchandisers were hit hard. From 1982 to 1985, to give an example, American speciality store sales grew 60 percent faster than department store sales. Some entire well-known American department store chains, such as Ohrbach's and Gimbel's, closed their doors. Those remaining rushed to streamline their operations and start a "comeback war" by installing jazzy new in-store speciality boutiques, or by greatly improving customer service.

Among the American general merchandise giants, Penney was the first to change. In 1983 the company began to move toward speciality retailing by focusing on its clothing lines. It discontinued hardware and automotive items and closed unprofitable stores. By the late 1980s its profitability had increased dramatically.

Sears moved much more slowly, but in 1987 it too began a push into specialty selling, especially into consumer-oriented financial services through its in-store and outside Coldwell Bankers real estate, Allstate insurance, and Dean Witter Reynolds investment sales operations. Then, in face of continued fierce competition from specialty chains and discount chains such as Wal-Mart, Sears, in February, 1989, suddenly changed its pricing policy to one called "everyday low prices." Aimed at remaking its image, in just two days the chain's 820 American stores rolled back prices on 75 percent of Sears own brands and on 1,000 other brand names it then carried. It was a bold new strategic move for Sears—aimed first at holding its market share, and second at attracting new customers.

Size and financial power still count, however, and as they entered the 1990s the four largest American retailers in decreasing order of size were Sears Roebuck, K-Mart, Wal-Mart, and J.C. Penney; in Canada, Sears Canada, Eaton's, and Hudson's Bay Company topped the list in decreasing order. In the United States, the decade of the 1980s ended with Wal-Mart Stores, Inc. waging a major offensive to conquer the nation's retail market. Its goal—to surpass both K-Mart and Sears and become the nation's and the world's largest retail chain.

What Will Retailing be Like in the 1990s?

The trends of the 1980s will continue and accelerate in the 1990s, but with definitely less wear and tear on the consumer, say retail industry leaders, who foresee these changes and innovations:

- Electronic devices for filling prescriptions.
- Completely automated food shopping in nearly unattended food stores. Shoppers will use computer cards and no carts. (This system is already in successful operation in western Europe today.)
- Shopping centers in the sky, where tall inner-city buildings will feature high-level floors devoted to shopping facilities.
- Drive-in food stores and vending machines that accept credit cards.
- Shopping from home by closed circuit television and telephone.
- New methods of presenting merchandise and ideas. Changes in grouping merchandise.
- Show-business techniques.
- Fads and fashion will change overnight. Shoes will become clogs, then shoes again. Dress lengths will ride up and down like an elevator. Hats, out now, will suddenly be in—then out again. Life-styles and the things that accompany them will change rapidly.
- Today's credit card, although not always an economic success, is a marketing success (consumers like it). Over the next decade credit card and transfer systems will be wedded to electronic point-of-sale terminals in many new types of retail outlets.
- International point-of-sale transactions, now in the planning stage, will permit retailers to derive the full benefit of electronic transactions from across national borders, especially between the United States and Canada, between whom a Free Trade Agreement went into effect January 1, 1989. This agreement calls for elimination of all tariffs between the two countries over a 10 year period. The result will be a two-country free trade market with a combined population of over 275 million.

  The same should occur between the 12 member nations of the European Economic Community, who are working toward full economic integration by as early as 1992. If all the community's trade barriers then fall as planned, Belgium, Britain, Denmark, France, West Germany, Greece, Ireland, Italy, Luxembourg, The Netherlands, Portugal, and Spain will become one huge market of 322 million people.

How Will These Changes Affect Consumers?

While these changes may save the consumer wear and tear, certain of these trends indicate a serious imbalance against the customer. Automatic payments, for example, benefit banks more than they do consumers.

Bankers or retailers who assume, "What's good for the product is also good for the consumer" may find themselves in trouble. Systems that reduce paper burdens and man-hours, or improve bank accuracy, may *not* offer comparable consumer values.

If retail selling is to keep in favor with the changing consumer market we studied in Chapter 2, it must pay careful attention to consumer advantages and benefits—for the 1990s will be increasingly consumer controlled.

How Will These Changes Affect Retail Sales Opportunities and Compensation for Salespeople?

"All the just presented trends and developments in retailing and retail selling are interesting," you might say, "but what do they really mean to me?" The answer is simple! Truly outstanding, high-paying career opportunities will continue to exist in many areas of retailing, in case you are interested, but you must consider the various types of retailing and independent or chain store operations within each carefully, since there are deep differences in salesperson compensation and promotional opportunities among them.

Taking the down side first, management in many of today's large retailers, those who offer mainly limited and programmed sales jobs, regard those jobs merely as "revolving doors" that offer employees short-term extra money and give management interchangeable bodies to fill a slot. Nearly anyone can learn these jobs in a short time. As one such manager put it, "We offer just a job—a way for people to earn some extra money. It's not a career."

Today, most older stores or chains are likely to offer total or partial commission remuneration, and newer ones are more likely to pay on a salary-only basis. There are also segments of the retail industry that tend to pay excellent commissions. One such segment is shoe stores. Another is the selling of more difficult to sell high-priced merchandise. Generally speaking, the highest-paying positions for salespeople lie in those stores where the personal sales job is considered essential, where the individual's knowledge of product, changing customer preferences, and buyer psychology help make the store successful.

Rating high among American retailers for its outstanding concern for both employee and customer satisfaction is the large and highly successful Wal-Mart chain. It calls its employees "associates," and all of them participate in generous profit-sharing and stock purchase plans. Another is the well-known Seattle-based, family-owned and managed Nordstrom, Inc. chain of specialty department stores, where all executive promotions are from within, and where 90 percent of the salespeople work on a generous straight commission plan.

No matter whether you elect to enter retail selling on a straight salary, salary plus commission, or straight commission basis, it will pay you to check out your prospective employer carefully. Chapter 19 tells you how.

Traditionally, most retail salespeople have been poorly trained. Even today in some of North America's largest department stores, for example, a typical newly hired salesperson is put through an initial training program that may last as little as two days or 16 hours. The trainees in such programs are merely taught how to operate a cash register, how to handle various types of transactions (such as charge sales, refunds, and merchandise exchanges), given a tour of the store, and told about company policies and who to call in case of an emergency. Few if any selling skills are taught, and little about product knowledge or product displays; this is left to trial and error on-the-job learning.

Many other department stores, however, offer far better training programs that not only impart product knowledge and selling skills but also aid employee self-motivation through special compensation and promotional opportunities. These stores view their salespeople as true problem solvers for their customers, and realize that knowledgeable, highly motivated salespeople, who enjoy their work and are proud of their store, can be extremely productive.

How One Customer-Oriented Department Store Trains, Rewards, and Motivates Its Salespeople

Job Titles. The title of sales associate (SA) (rather than salesperson) is promptly bestowed on each newly hired trainee. After 90 days, if performance is satisfactory, the SA is promoted to professional sales assistant (PSA) and given a modest salary increase. One year later, if performance is satisfactory, the PSA is again promoted to the position of certified sales assistant (CSA). With this latter promotion comes a gold recognition badge, increased floor responsibilities, and a nice salary increase. The steps in this career ladder are clear-cut and open to all whose performance is deemed satisfactory to management.

Initial Indoctrination and Training. This may last a week to ten days, and is followed up by an ongoing advanced education program with frequent set, short meeting periods. In these programs, video cassettes (tapes and films) and slides are employed frequently to present subjects such as colorization of the merchandise and other display techniques, and as aids to learning selling skills. Films on shoplifting are usually shown to help make trainees aware of this tremendous retail store problem, and how to help contain it.

Such training is increasingly concerned with understanding customer attitudes and motivations and developing communication skills (especially listening), as well as the steps involved in making a sale. Sales service is stressed in such programs as well, since modern retailing is increasingly concerned with providing complete sales service, with emphasis on this aspect of the inside salesperson's job.

Special Opportunities and Recognition. These are offered in several ways. For example, to help get salespeople at all levels involved in the overall decision-making process, some ten employees representing a cross section of the store's salespeople are invited to attend the regular Monday morning managers' conference. The managers use these special attendees as sounding boards for new ideas and urge them to make their own suggestions (acting on them whenever possible). Special responsibility for daily tasks such as bank drops and making sure that registers are ready and opened for business daily is allocated on a rotating weekly basis. Quotas are assigned for number of sales, increases of sales volume, and opening of new charge accounts over a given period; sales awards and recognition are given those who exceed such quotas. Special recognition and often rewards are given to salespeople who report shoplifters who are apprehended.

Special Compensation. Special commissions are frequently awarded on "big ticket" items such as appliances, men's suits, and stereo sets. End-of-sales-period bonuses are often awarded to individual salespeople, or departmental employees as a whole, for above-quota sales and profits.

Having considered these trends, we now turn our thoughts to you in terms of your possible current full- or part-time work as a retail salesperson, or your career interest in this challenging field of selling.

ALL FUNDAMENTALS OF SELLING APPLY TO RETAIL SELLING

The fundamentals of modern personal selling apply to all fields of selling. In each, there must be advanced preparation and planning, a proper approach, and a customer-oriented, problem-solving sales presentation based on offering benefits and value that will satisfy the customer's needs or wants. Proper handling of questions or objections and the all-important close, without which there is no sale, are also essential.

The fundamentals of human relations—knowledge of self and knowledge of other people—also apply to all fields of selling. If you are to be successful in retail selling, you should have a proper attitude toward life and work and toward your employer and customers. You should be sincere, courteous, tactful, and willing to work hard. In addition you must have or strive to develop a pleasing manner, appearance, and voice.

YOUR BASIC PURPOSE IS TO SELL

In spite of self-service developments in chain stores and discount houses, if you hope to earn more income and promotions, you must always keep in mind that your basic purpose is to sell. The degree of sales persuasion you may be allowed to employ varies from store to store, frequently depending on the type of customer catered to. The basic purpose of any retail business is to sell its goods at a profit, however, and it employs you as a salesperson to help do just that.

If you are really ambitious, you may wish to take a look at retail areas such as clothing, furniture, and home furnishings, which generally offer better than average opportunities. For successful, experienced salespeople, the clothing and textile industries offer top earnings potential. A rapid route to success in these fields is to begin at retail salesperson level and to advance to store buyer or to specialty commission selling. Manufacturers tend to hire their often highly paid specialty salespeople from among men and women with such a successful retail sales background.

A RETAIL SALESPERSON IS A HOST

We have already noted that the basic difference between in-store (inside) selling and nonstore (outside) selling is that the prospect or customer comes to you in in-store selling. A further difference is that the prospect approaching you very likely has some idea of what he or she is looking for. The nonstore salesperson, on the other hand, often has to devote time to selling interest or to bringing the prospect to this point of awareness.

Since the customer has come to you, you are freed from problems of prospecting or the preapproach and are now ready to move into these two phases:

1. The approach (and qualification).
2. The sales presentation, consisting of creating and holding interest, arousing desire and securing conviction, handling questions and objections, and closing the sale.

As we move into a brief review of some specific problems, approaches, and sales techniques involved in the retail situation, keep in mind that you as an in-store salesperson are somewhat in the position of a host receiving a guest; your first aim is to make your approaching customer feel welcome and at ease.

GREETING THE CUSTOMER (OR THE APPROACH)

In greeting the customer what counts is not so much what you say but how you say it. He or she may be looking for a specific item, may have only a vague idea of what he or she is looking for, or may only be browsing or looking around. Whatever the case, your task is to recognize that he or she has or may have a problem that you can help solve, but that he or she may be afraid to express it because of a hidden fear of being sold something he or she does not want—the fear of making a mistake.

Your first job is to sell yourself—to create the impression that you are a friendly, nice, sincere person who would like to help. The warmth of your smile, the friendly, relaxed, personal look in your eyes, and your attentive manner all help get over any initial psychological barrier as you open the conversation with words like "good morning" or "good afternoon."

This cheerful greeting can be said warmly, yet with a question in your eyes. The idea is to show that you welcome and understand the customer. This gives the customer greater confidence to ask you for something.

Do *not* greet a customer with negative phrases such as "May I help you," "What can I do for you?" or "Something for you?" To each of these, it is easy to say, "No, thank you." which not only places a barrier between you, but may actually induce him or her not to buy anything.

If he or she doesn't ask for anything, but you sense through empathy that an approach may be in order, go right into any one of the 20 useful basic approaches listed in Chapter 8. A good one might be a *benefit approach* such as this: "Have you seen our advertised specials feature for today? They are on that counter (pointing)." Your empathy plays an important role here. Some shoppers appreciate being noticed and helped promptly; others resent being bothered in store after store. So, while you should judge whether or not they will be receptive to an approach, don't hesitate to say something that might tempt customers to consider buying something. After all, everyone who enters is a potential buyer, and all the store's advertising, window and in-store point-of-purchase displays, attractive merchandise displays, and you the salesperson are there to tempt them into buying.

Your next task is to establish a rapport that further convinces them of your sincere interest. You are trying to win their acceptance of you as a friend and to show that you want to like and understand them. This rapport is called empathy; the best way to communicate empathy is by asking questions and listening.

Ask Relaxing Questions

To overcome customers' possible inner fears of being sold something they do not want, reassure them that you do want to be of assistance and do not just want to try to sell something. Since many shoppers do not know what they are looking for and do not like to be bothered by persistent salespeople, you can normally overcome initial resistance or even hostility by a statement such as, "Please feel free to browse; I am Mrs. Fowski and will be glad to answer any questions. Is there anything I can help you with now at this counter?"

If customers indicate a desire to browse further on their own, do not bother them again unless they stop at and appear interested in a specific item. Then you can casually walk over and ask a trial-close question that may reveal buying signals. For example, "Would you care to see the same item in other colors? I have some I can show you." If customers do not have an immediate interest and seem willing to continue the conversation rather than browse, you may try to arouse interest in a specific item. For example, "Have you had a chance to notice our special at the end of the counter? They offer splendid value at only $6.99, don't you think?"

The purpose of this kind of approach statement or question is to get customers to relax by talking about themselves or by giving opinions that to them are apparently not related to a buying decision.

Once your customers have asked to see or have expressed interest in a certain item, you are ready to enter a sales presentation. Since this presentation can involve showing many unnecessary items, it is best to ask a few more questions, particularly opinion questions, that help both you and your customers discover and clarify their problems and wants.

Many retail customers do not know what they are looking for, and you obviously cannot help them solve a problem or fulfill a need or want until you know what it is. Thus you have to get prospects to reveal their problems or wants and what is important to them before you can help persuade them to solve their problems now. You can get them to reveal their problems through questions such as these:

Are you looking for yourself or another?
What do you think of this grade or quality?
Do you like this style?
Would this be comfortable?

Creating and Holding Interest

Once you have uncovered what you feel is the customer's problem or want, your aim is to move quickly to find the solution or fulfillment to it by a process of elimination, as the above questions illustrate. Here are two techniques that can help you find rapidly the price, item, style, and quality that seem to offer most appeal.

1. *Use interest-building sentences and words.* The more carefully thought out the words and phrases you have at your command, the more quickly you create and hold interest. Vivid, picture-building words ("season's newest fabric," "the very latest fashion"), well-known brand names, and manufacturer's claims ("won't rub off," "will cut your shaving time in half") are useful selling aids that can make your job easier.
2. *Demonstrate whenever possible.* Seeing is believing, so when customers express interest in or ask for an item, present it quickly if at all possible. As you show it, briefly outline the major features and through well-chosen words help them visualize the benefits they will enjoy after purchasing it.

Your aim at this stage of the presentation is to find the product solution or fulfillment to your customer's problems or wants. If you have asked the right questions and have narrowed the choice, your task now is to help them desire your product—a desire based on the conviction that it is the best possible answer to their needs.

Arousing Desire and Securing Conviction

The next stage of the presentation, based on securing desire and conviction, is aimed at accomplishing three goals.

1. Help customers understand exactly what the product is, how it works, and what it does.
2. Convince them that it is the best solution to their problems or fulfullment of their wants.
3. Reassure them that the product will bring the satisfaction they desire.

Let us suppose that your customer is a young secretary highly interested in a newly introduced knit dress for cool weather. In order to arouse desire and secure conviction, you need to explain and demonstrate these points.

1. Feature (special characteristics of the product)
2. Advantages (of those features)
3. Benefits (she will gain by having it or lose by not having it)

Your presentation may run like this one.

You (as Salesperson):	Based upon what you have told me, one of these (laying out two styles, one red and one blue) new Dacron-wool knits appears most suitable for you during the autumn months to come.
(Feature):	Both these dresses, just coming into fashion, offer color and style and are suitable for smart workday attire or for evenings in town.
(Advantage):	This is important because you would be stylishly yet comfortably and warmly dressed for almost any occasion; don't you agree?
Customer:	Yes, that's true.
You (Benefit to gain):	Wouldn't it also feel good to know you are dressed properly for an evening out right after work?
(Benefit by avoidance):	Knowing you were dressed suitably for any occasion would also help you avoid the worry of possibly not being properly dressed for an after-work event, wouldn't it? (Use one or the other of these).
Customer:	Yes, it's certainly something to consider.

You can do many other things to point out and demonstrate other features, advantages, and benefits (such as quality, price, and value) to be gained by owning one of the knit dresses. Many suggestions have been covered in previous chapters. Your yes-building questions bring out the customer's needs or wants, which indicate the points you should stress.

Basically, you have been selling the satisfaction the dress will give, so after briefly pointing out each major feature, illustrate or demonstrate it by using the garment itself. Hold it up for her to see or let her feel it or try it on. While demonstrating you can help her visualize the nice appearance she will have after making the purchase. Whenever you use the garment (or other item) in a demonstration, handle it with care and pride.

By using the words *when* and *your* during this part of your presentation, you help give the customer a feeling of ownership. For example, you could continue the presentation by saying, "When you wear one of these warm, colored knits, you will always have the feeling of being appropriately dressed."

Handling Questions, Objections, Excuses, and Indecision

In Chapter 11 on handling objections, the point was made that a good salesperson should always frame objections into questions which he or she is then only too happy to answer. We covered in that chapter various techniques for handling standard objections such as "It costs too much," or "I can't afford it now," plus some unusual types. Since those techniques apply to retail selling as well as to specialty selling, there is no need to repeat them here. We can, however, devote attention to handling excuses and indecision.

Excuses or Stalls. These, rather than real objections, are often more of a problem for inside retail salespeople than for outside salespeople. Many store shoppers may want to buy but can think of any number of excuses to put off the decision. The listing on page 388 notes some standard excuses for not buying now and some suggestions for handling them.

Indecision. Another problem more commonly faced by inside retail salespeople than by outside ones is indecision. An example is a shopper who simply and illogically cannot make up his or her mind whether to buy. You do not want to force a decision and run the risk of losing a future customer, but you should try to help him or her decide to buy if you feel he or she wants the item.

Here are some suggestions on helping shoppers who cannot make up their minds to buy.

Present Favorable Alternatives. Ask which of two presented items they prefer rather than whether they like either. Then they have a choice between two things rather than between something and nothing.

Mention Testimonials. Whenever they are available, mention testimonials. For example, you may say, "It's featured in the leading fashion magazines," or "Margret Bidlingmaier, the television star, has one." You can also mention favorable comments of your own satisfied customers and can stress store or manufacturer's guarantees. Customers may like the item but be uncertain of its quality. Your explanation of the guarantee may provide a lead-in to a trial close.

Stress the Timeliness of the Item. Since people want fashionable items while they are still exclusive, you may say, "This style will be the height of fashion this season. If you get it now you'll be one of the first to wear it."

Excuse	One Way of Handling It
"I'll have to think it over."	"Why do you have to think it over?"
"I'll come back and buy it later on."	"I appreciate your feelings, but it may be sold before you return. May I put it aside for you now?"
"I think I'll look around before deciding."	"Fine, but before you go, may I ask what feature appealed to you most?" Appear to give up, get the customer relaxed and chatting, and then go back into a close based on the feature with the greatest appeal to the customer.
"I would like my spouse to see it first."	This may be a valid reason or a mere excuse. If the former, try to set a specific time for them to call back together, saying you will hold the item until then. If you feel it is just an excuse, try to close immediately.

Stress Limited Quantity. If the item is in short supply, explain that they probably will not be able to get it later. You must be honest in your use of such a statement, however, since customers are wary of such warnings. Be sure the supply is limited!

Once you have handled a question or objection or turned the excuse or indecision into positive interest, you can briefly restate the features, advantages, and benefits each customer appears most interested in.

Closing the Sale

When you sense that your customers are interested at any stage in the above process, you should stop showing the merchandise and go immediately into a trial close. We outlined in previous chapters the buying signals that may indicate interest and the several specific techniques you may employ in closing the sale.

HANDLING SPECIAL PROBLEMS IN RETAIL SELLING

As we lead into a review of how you as an in-store salesperson may handle certain special problems often encountered in retail selling, we should note once again the difference between improper high-pressure selling and good customer/society-oriented, problem-solving selling. The basic difference is customers' acceptance in the latter case of the fact that you are sincerely trying to help them buy wisely and are not just selling them anything for the sake of a sale.

If you are trying to help, then your suggestion of higher-priced items, substitute items, or specials should not normally offend customers. Thus your attitude and manner are basically more important than the specific words or techniques you employ in handling some of the special retail problems involving customer situations and merchandise (or products), which we now consider.

Special Customer Situations

The Shopper. A common problem faced by inside retail salespeople is how to get the shopper or browser interested in something you could turn into a sale. Far too many salespeople do nothing when, in response to an unwise and poor "Good morning, may I help you?" greeting, the customer replies, "No, thank you, I am just looking (or shopping)."

We considered a few pages back how, once you have greeted customers properly and gained their attention and interest, you may try to call their attention to certain items. Our suggestion in general was that you try to guide them at least to the proper section for the merchandise they may be interested in and to let them know of any specials. A second suggestion was to encourage them to continue looking around, not to bother them while they are looking, but to give your name and let them know you are available to answer questions. If you keep them in mind and are alert to move over to help if they do appear to find something of interest, you at least stand some chance of turning a "just looking" into a sale.

Our chief reason for bringing this common problem up again is to encourage you to think and try to do something about the situation. Your degree of success in turning shoppers into buyers can spell the difference between being a mere order taker and being a professional salesperson.

Two Customers at Once. Suppose you are waiting on one customer and another obviously interested one comes along. How do you as a salesperson handle the situation? Here are three suggestions?

1. If another salesperson is available, call him or her over to help the second customer.
2. Continue to assist your first customer but give a nod of recognition to the second to indicate that you are aware of his or her presence. If he or she is nearby you may even say, "Good morning. Someone will help you shortly."
3. If the first customer is just looking, excuse yourself for a moment to at least welcome the second and to get him or her started looking at a specific item. Before doing this, you should let the first know that you will be back to continue helping him or her.

Because most stores require that you assist the first customer before spending any time with the second, the issue presents problems. If the first just looks and the second appears highly interested, you may have to use your judgment, excuse yourself by telling the first you will be back shortly, and complete the sale with the second.

Group of Shoppers.   A group of shoppers can pose problems to you as a retail salesperson. A common example is that of a friend's trying to dominate the buying decision of the customer. You may have to sell the friend in this case, but should pay primary attention to the wants and desires of the customer. If the friend is an annoyance, you may even signal another salesperson to engage him or her in conversation and allow you to concentrate on helping the customer. Some further suggestions for handling group selling situations are in Chapter 14.

Complaining or Irate Customer.   Exchanges of merchandise, normal complaints (such as, "The toaster won't work," or "It won't do what was claimed for it"), and angry or irate customers often pose problems for retail salespersons. Even though the store may have an adjustment department, customers usually first go back to the original salesperson or department where the purchase was made with their complaints.

Although the fault may be that of some other department such as advertising, delivery, or accounting, such complaints are basically sales problems. Because the success of both you and your store lies in having satisfied, repeat customers, your basic sales tasks are (1) sincerely trying to help solve problems to customers' satisfaction if possible and (2) trying to turn complaints into new current or future sales. Never argue with a complaining or irate customer. Here are some of the steps you should promptly take to handle the situation.

1.   Acknowledge both the right to complain and the specific complaint at once.
2.   Ask for full details, listening carefully without interruption until he or she finishes.
3.   Repeat the complaint to the customer to clarify both the problem and all details to your full understanding.
4.   If the customer is right, admit the error and take steps to correct it. If he or she is wrong, do not try to prove it, but instead ask for his or her help and suggestions in trying to find an answer to the problem.
5.   Call your manager or other store experts or executives for assistance if you are not able to resolve the problem to the customer's satisfaction.

Know Your Merchandise and How to Handle Special Problems in Selling It

Having information about the merchandise you sell is vital to your success as a retail salesperson. You must be able to intelligently point out features, advantages, and benefits of an item to customers constantly asking themselves, "What benefits will I gain by buying it? What benefits may I lose by not buying it?"

The best way to become aware of the benefits of a specific item of merchandise is to understand what general types of benefits it may offer. As you study each item you sell in order to increase your product knowledge, look for these three types of benefits.

1. *Obvious benefits* are ones anyone can see, such as beauty, durability, or the purpose for which the item is made.
2. *Exclusive benefits* are advantages or features of an item that its competitors do not possess.
3. *Hidden benefits* are ones not readily seen or understood without explanation. For example, in the knit-dress sales situation discussed earlier, you as a salesperson were selling appearance and attractiveness for any workday or evening social occasion.

How Do You Find Out about Merchandise Benefits?   Constant interest in and study of the items you sell brings product or merchandise knowledge. Here are some questions you may ask yourself about any item in order to discover what benefits it offers customers.

1. *What is the item to be used for?* How can it be used? Is it easy and convenient to use? Is it durable?
2. *What does it look like?* Is it attractive, unusual, colorful, novel? Does it have good style?
3. *How does it compare in price?* What is its price? How does that price compare with that of similar items? If less expensive, does it offer real value? If more expensive, does it offer compensating value?
4. *How do you care for the product?* Is there any feature such as ease of maintenance that you can point out to your customers?
5. *Can it be serviced easily?* Are replacement parts readily available? Does it have a guarantee?
6. *Are any testimonials available to back up claims?* What do the various independent consumer reports have to say about it? Does the manufacturer supply any performance data measuring it against competition?

The more you know about each item of merchandise you sell, the easier it will be for you to meet and handle the following special problems.

Presenting Merchandise Specials.   Most retail stores advertise specials to attract customers to their place of business. Nothing is more discouraging to a shopper than to enter a store in response to such an advertisement only to find that the salespeople know little or nothing of either the ad or the item.

You should read your store ads daily not only to know what specials are being offered but also to know the price and other features so that you can make an effective sales presentation. Even if your customers do not know about or ask for such specials, your telling them about them presents an excellent chance to make new or second sales.

Making Second Sales (sometimes referred to as "add-ons").   The above-mentioned specials offer just one way to turn a just-completed sale into a new or second sale. If a male customer, for example, has just purchased some new shirts, you can call his attention to a range of new ties and suggest that the styles and colors go well with the shirts. If you have just sold a new steam iron, you can suggest a new ironing-board cover. In such cases show the second item if at all possible.

When customers buy anything they are in a buying mood, and if you know your merchandise and features that tie in with the initial purchase, second sales are often easy to make.

Trading Up for Bigger Sales. When customers ask to see certain merchandise, start by asking qualifying questions regarding size, style, color, or the use to which it may be put. You should not ask what price they want to pay.

After asking a few but not too many such questions, begin your presentation by showing your medium-price range. This gives you a chance to discuss quality and a chance, if they do not indicate price resistance, to introduce a higher-priced item by way of comparison. You can then demonstrate that far greater value can be realized at only slightly higher price. You can also talk quantity at this point, especially where specials are concerned.

If customers want a low-cost item, they will tell you. If they do not mention price, a fundamental rule of good in-store retail selling is to start in the middle price range and trade up, that is, show higher-quality or higher-priced items.

Selling Substitute Items. When customers ask for a certain item by brand name or price range and you have it in stock, you may have the opportunity through substitution to trade up. If you do not have it, you either have to present an acceptable substitute or lose the sale.

Since many customers object to your mentioning substitutes if the item asked for is in stock, you must handle your introduction of a possible substitute carefully. Show the item asked for, and then introduce the second item casually.

> Here is the item you mentioned, and it is indeed good. But may I, by way of comparison, also show you a newer and slightly more expensive item should you desire to compare difference in quality?

The words *should you* provide a reason for the suggestion and eliminate the overt impression that you are trying to sell something other than what was asked for. If your customers are interested in a comparison, you may be doing them a favor by presenting greater quality at only slightly higher price. Your product knowledge and skill of presentation can thus often lead to a substitute trade-up sale that helps both you and customers.

If the item asked for is not in stock, you can explain that you do not have that specific item and politely inquire about the customers' needs and wants. You can then show them a comparable or even better item from your stock. Your product knowledge comes in handy as you compare the features of your item point by point with those of the item originally asked for. The best way to arouse and sustain interest is to get your substitute item into customers' hands as quickly as possible after admitting that you do not have the one asked for and to explain its features positively and with confidence.

To most customers, and this includes you as a customer in your outside-of-work life, a store, business, or company is the people who sell and provide service in it. Thus to your customers you, the salesperson, are the store.

Just as you expect prompt, cheerful, willing service from the salespeople from whom you buy, so do your customers expect, appreciate, and remember the same kind of reception from you. No matter how good the merchandise or how beautiful the displays, your store will not enjoy a good reputation or attract satisfied, repeat customers unless you play your part in making it a pleasant place in which to shop and buy.

You as a retail salesperson have a heavy responsibility—as an official host—to ensure that your customers are always met and treated in the courteous, pleasant way in which you would expect to be received at their places of business or in their homes.

As customers depart, take a moment to smile at them and say, "Thank you for shopping with us."

SUMMARY

The field of retail selling is so broad that marketing authorities have broken it down into two separate parts: *in-store (inside)* and *nonstore (outside)*. The major difference between these two types is that in-store retail salespeople work inside stores, where customers come to them, whereas nonstore retail salespeople call on prospects and customers outside of stores. In this chapter our focus was on inside retail selling. Nonstore retail selling is covered in Chapter 16.

After reviewing retailing trends and developments in North America since the end of World War II in 1945, we noted that future career potential in retail sales is excellent. We then concentrated attention on some special applications of personal selling to the field of retail selling.

While all the fundamentals of personal selling studied so far apply in large part to retail selling, we concluded that some differences in techniques and applications are of special interest to in-store retail salespeople. Since customers come to the retail salesperson, he or she is in effect acting as a host in meeting them. The degree of persuasion salespeople are authorized to employ is determined by the store, which has to keep in mind its customers and trade.

After reviewing the steps of the sales presentation within the retail store setting, we discussed the problems of handling excuses and indecision, noting that detailed procedures for handling objections and closing the sale had been covered in earlier chapters. We then went into the handling of special sales problems, including the shopper, two customers at once, a group of shoppers, and the complaining or irate customer.

We then emphasized the importance of knowing one's merchandise and gave suggestions for developing such knowledge for handling merchandise sales problems such as selling specials, making second (or add-on) sales, trading up for bigger sales, and selling substitute items. We concluded with the thought that, to the customer, you as a salesperson represent the store and thus have a heavy responsibility as an official store host.

Questions for Analysis and Discussion

1.   As a store salesperson, how could you help customers overcome a possible inner fear of being sold something they do not want?

2.   What are three things you as an in-store retail salesperson may do to help shoppers who for no apparent reason cannot seem to make up their minds to buy?

3.   What is the first selling job a retail person has when greeting a customer in a store?

4.   What is the basic selling difference between retail (inside) selling and specialty (outside) selling?

5.   What are the best kind of questions a salsperson can ask a customer or shopper? Why are they the best kind?

6.   What is it, basically, that a retail salesperson is selling when showing new fashions in clothing to customers?

7.   What is the best single way to handle objections or questions in an in-store retail situation?

8.   If a customer comes to you with a complaint about an item, and you are the retail salesperson who sold it to him or her, what two sales tasks should you immediately try to accomplish?

CASE STUDY 15

For You, It's Only . . . Some Tips on the Ancient Practice of One-On-One Bazaar-Style Retail Buying and Selling

Can up to an hour's "negotiations" save you 40 to 60 percent of the purchase price on jewelry, silks, camera equipment, or the like? Not in the world's "fixed-price" retail department stores and shops, but in countless other stores, shops, stalls, bazaars, and outdoor market-places around the globe—the answer is yes!

In Hong Kong especially, to travelers' great delight, the ancient practice of "negotiating," "bargaining," "haggling"—call it what you will—is very much alive! Not every shop owner there still bargains, of course—the Western practice of fixing prices is slowly spreading there as elsewhere in the Orient and Middle East. But bargaining in Hong Kong is such an honored and respected tradition, practiced so artfully and skillfully, that students of personal selling can learn much by both observing and participating in the fun.

To make such learning easier on the buyer's wallet however, here are some tips on the "rules of the game" as published in *Travel-Holiday* magazine![1]

Rule 1. Both Parties Should Part on Amicable Terms at the End of the Negotiations. Keeping this goal in mind will help set the tone of the negotiations. From the moment you enter a shop to the time you depart, your every nuance and statement should be geared towards creating a pleasant encounter.

Rule 2. Never Show Too Much Interest in a Particular Item. Even if you know exactly what you want, don't let on. Say, for example, you're shopping for wristwatches in a jewelry store. When the salesperson approaches and

asks if you need help, be noncommittal. Answer, "I'm just looking at your beautiful selection of watches." Don't tell the shopkeeper that you've already got your heart set on that watch with the diamond-studded face.

Browse. Drop clues. For instance, say, "I usually prefer Seikos, with leather bands. They're more comfortable than metallic ones, don't you think?"

Now it's time to sit back and watch the fun begin. The salesperson will display the wares, giving a running commentary on the desirability of each watch and what a buy it is. Maintain a polite but dubious expression. Do agree, though, that the watches shown are attractive.

Remain courteously disinterested even if the salesperson applies pressure for you to purchase. Then, in halfhearted curiosity, request to see two watches—the one you've got your eye on and one significantly less expensive.

If price tags are attached, don't look at them. Instead ask the salesperson what each watch costs. This gives him or her the opportunity to say, "For you, because you are a visitor in my country," or, "Because you are a very nice person (salespeople in Hong Kong are very generous with their compliments), it's only X dollars."

As you can see, bargaining requires finesse, the skill of an actor and the poker face of a card player. But that, of course, is what makes it fun.

Rule 3. Attitude is Everything. Appear to be as Interested in Staying as You are in Leaving—Whether or Not You've Made a Purchase. Whatever price is quoted, never show pleasure or shock. Move both watches closer. Examine them. Try them on. Ignore

[1] Based on an article by Laura M. Carter, "For You It's Only . . . ," *Travel/Holiday* (magazine), New York, N.Y. (September 1988), pp. 43–45. Reprinted with permission of Travel Publications, Inc., 28 W. 23rd St., New York, N.Y. 10010.

any pressure to purchase. If the price hasn't started to lower significantly, explain to the owner that you don't wish to spend that much money. Offer a price that's less than you actually hope to pay.

At this point, the owner will probably pull out a calculator to estimate how much the price can be reduced and still be profitable. Retaliate by producing a calculator of your own. Spend a minute figuring out your budget and translating Hong Kong dollars to U.S. dollars or whatever other currency you may be using.

In your calculations, remember that paying with a credit card can often cut down on your bargain. Store owners generally have to pay a five to seven percent handling fee to credit card companies, so you'll probably get a better deal by paying cash.

Rule 4. Any Time an Offer is Accepted, the Bargaining Ends. The shopkeeper may reject all of your offers, saying, "At that price, I'd lose money. It doesn't even cover my cost."

Politely answer, "I don't want that to occur. After all, I'd like to visit your shop again in the future."

In Hong Kong, an established customer is very important, not only for future purchases, but for referrals, too. Keep silent and wait to see whether the shopkeeper makes another offer. And don't forget to use your calculator whenever necessary.

If the price is right, accept and thank the shopkeeper. More importantly, ask for two or three business cards. Explain that you want to tell your friends about the marvelous shop. The shopkeeper's face will wreathe into a smile.

If the price is not acceptable, politely prepare to leave. At this point, one of three things will occur; you'll hear a final offer, a disgruntled silence, or an abrupt good-bye. Whatever happens, remember Rule 1.

Of course, not every negotiation will proceed according to formula. Sometimes, for instance, negotiations will break off right in the middle and tea or a soft drink will be served. This gives you the opportunity to learn more about the person you are facing, local customs, and interesting facts about other items being sold. And it adds to the fun and pleasure of this different method of one-on-one retail buying and selling.

Questions for Written Reports or Class Discussion

1. Two interesting and slightly unusual ways used by some Hong Kong shop salespeople to sell themselves and their shop or store were noted in the case study. Describe these, and state your opinion as to how well they might work in a North American or European fixed-price store sales situation.

2. Describe three interest-building sentences, employing vivid, picture-building words, that you, as Hong Kong shop salesperson, might use effectively to sell a new model Seiko lady's wristwatch.

3. Describe two different methods a Hong Kong shop salesperson might use to try to help a woman tourist make up her mind to buy, when her problem seems to be that of simple, illogical indecision.

4. As a Hong Kong shop salesperson, you sense that the European tourist couple to whom you have been showing new cameras are seriously interested in one specific model. Should you offer them a soft drink or tea now, in order to relax and talk more about that and other cameras, or should you go immediately into a trial close? Explain your reasoning.

How will you help this man select a present for his wife?

A male customer approaches a lingerie counter in a fashionable women's apparel shop. You, the female salesperson on duty, move to greet him and observe that he appears ill at ease because two or three women shoppers are browsing at the counter. You greet him smilingly with these words:

You: Good morning. Have you seen our advertised specials for the day? They are at this end of the counter.

Customer: Yes, well, they look interesting. (He looks nervously at his watch, and at the nearby women browsers.)

You: Are you looking for something special?

Customer: Well, I am looking for a nice birthday gift for my wife—something very personal and feminine. (He looks up and down the counter, apparently not knowing what he wants, and again looks nervously at his watch.)

Questions for Written Report or Class Discussion

1. What psychological factors should you as the salesperson recognize in this situation?

2. What sales approach will you now use?

3. How can you best move to close a sale in this situation?

Could this retail salesperson have handled this credit card problem at point-of-sale better?

A basic fact in selling is that a sale is not complete until it is paid for. Many retail establishments accept credit cards when customers make a purchase; either their own special cards or internationally recognized ones such as Visa or Mastercard. In this situation, a salesperson at a large department store is verifying the validity of a customer's card via the department's computerized register as prelude to completing the sale. The register flashes a signal that the sale is voided. Let us follow the situation to see what problems arose, and what the salesperson did to handle the situation.

Salesperson: I am sorry, but there appears to be some problem. I will have to make a quick phone call to our Authorization Department. It won't take but a moment.

Customer: (instantly apprehensive) What's the problem? I don't have much time!

The Authorization Department tells the salesperson that the sale is voided and that the customer should visit the Customer Service Department to clarify the matter.

Salesperson: I am sorry, but this sale cannot be completed here. Our Authorization Department asks that you go to the Customer Service Area on the fourth floor, where they will discuss your account with you.

Customer: (angrily) Why do I have to do that? I've been a good customer of your store for years!

Salesperson: I will be happy to hold your merchandise for you until you return from the fourth floor.

Customer: (angrily persisting) Why do I have to go to the fourth floor? I am in a hurry. Don't you want my business?

Salesperson: They would like to discuss your account with you in person. Only the Authorization Department has the necessary information.

The customer starts loudly berating the salesperson about the latter's unwillingness to be of on-the-spot help, and about the store's sales policies in general. Other customers are beginning to notice the complaining customer. The salesperson feels that the situation is getting out of control.

Questions for Written Reports or Class Discussion

1. Do you feel that the salesperson has handled the situation properly up to this point? If not, how could he or she have handled it better?

2. What would you do now if you were in the salesperson's shoes?

Nonstore Retail Selling by Telemarketing, Direct Selling, and Service Providers; Trade Show, Sales Seminar, and Exhibition Selling

After studying this chapter, you will be able to:

Relate differences between these methods of nonstore (outside) retail selling: *mail order, direct mail, buying services,* and *electronic shopping.*

Describe what is meant by the term *telephone itinerary* and how to properly prepare beforehand for selling by telephone.

List ten steps involved in a complete telephone sales presentation.

Discuss the special importance of voice and word usage in telephone selling, and give some techniques for proper use of each.

Explain what is meant by the term, commonly used by direct salespeople, *"party-plan" selling.*

Identify the four primary ways that direct-sales companies market their products.

Tell how service providers can "tangibilize" and "personalize" their offerings to individual end-use consumers.

Summarize how to plan and organize for trade show or exhibition selling, and how to personally sell at such shows.

E arly on in Chapter 15, it was noted that the field of retailing and retail selling is so broad that marketing authorities have broken it down into two separate areas: *in-store* (*inside*) and *nonstore* (*outside*). The balance of that chapter centered on personal selling activities by salespeople in a retail store selling where customers come to them.

In this chapter focus will largely center on the selling of products or services directly to final (or end) consumers for their personal or nonbusiness use—outside of a retail store setting. Although in-store sales are far greater, nonstore outside retailing, which by 1990 accounted for close to 15 percent of all North American retail sales, is growing worldwide at a much faster rate. While outside retail selling is done in many different ways, both personal and nonpersonal, our emphasis is on use by salespersons of telemarketing and direct selling methods. We also consider some special sales problems faced by service providers in selling to end-consumers, and review the large and important area of trade show, sales seminar, and exhibition selling, which concerns all types of salespeople.

THE WIDE-RANGING FIELD OF NONSTORE RETAIL SELLING

Among the many forms of nonstore retail selling, apart from telemarketing and direct selling, which will be considered separately, are mail order, direct mail, automatic vending machines, buying services, electronic shopping, and television marketing. Since these forms are basically impersonal in that they do not normally involve salespeople interacting one on one with prospects or customers, we note them only briefly.

- *Mail Order.* Mass merchandise chains like Sears, Roebuck and Co., specialty department stores, and countless other types of retailers, large and small, mail either multi-item general merchandise catalogues or packets of several different ad sheets or folders to millions of North Americans each year. These are sent both to customers by name or simply to "Current Resident" of the printed mailing address. Consumers order what they wish by phone or mail.
- *Direct Mail.* In contrast to mail order, a direct mail solicitation normally features a single-item product or service sales letter and/or ad piece sent to carefully selected "by name" market segment mailing lists. Items offered range from luggage to jewelry to books to insurance. Consumers order what they wish by phone or mail.
- *Automatic Vending Machines.* These 24-hour, self-service, coin-operated machines, found in all sorts of locations, offer a wide variety of on-the-spot merchandise ranging from soft drinks to perfume to electronic computer games to condoms. While convenient, they are expensive to maintain and as a result products offered usually cost 15 to 20 percent more than comparable ones in retail stores.

- *Buying Services.* These organizations serve large specific groups of consumer members, such as employees of a given large company or school or hospital system, by offering them special discounts from selected retailers who have signed up as member retailers of the service.
- *Electronic Shopping.* This form of shopping may increasingly represent the wave of the future as ever more consumers install certain types of personal computers or Videotext cable TV systems in their homes. In different electronic ways, these allow consumers to place orders for products or services advertised on their television screens or radios from the comfort of their living rooms.
- *Television Marketing.* Many retailers sponsor product promotions via 30- or 60-second television commercials. These normally show both a toll-free number for phone-in orders, and an address for mail-in orders. Many types of products (for example, music records and cassettes) and services (such as, legal, chiropractic, travel) are sold this way.

  Television auctions represent yet another form of TV marketing; as each item offered for sale is displayed and explained by studio salespersons, viewers can phone in their bids. More common than television auctions are the increasing number of television programs devoted entirely to selling various types of products. These feature salespersons delivering sales pitches about demonstrated items—one after another, in sometimes "high pressure" fashion.
- *Other Forms.* Newspaper and magazine ads, radio commercials, public auctions, and "flea markets" are just some of the many other different methods employed by individual or organizational retailers to sell their wares directly to end-consumers outside of a store setting.

TELEMARKETING

Shrewd North American sales managers long ago recognized the value of the telephone as an effective sales tool. They used it then, as they increasingly continue to do today, to make appointments, close sales, and free salespeople to concentrate on key accounts that demand in-person service. They, along with countless individual salespeople, have recognized that while telephone selling cannot replace face-to-face personal selling, it can—and does—help them increase sales, reduce selling costs, and increase productivity.

Starting in the 1960s, with the introduction in North America of cost-effective inward and outward Wide Area Telephone Service (WATS), use of the telephone expanded so quickly as a multiuse direct marketing tool that the term *telemarketing* was coined, a term that can be defined as follows:

Telemarketing: A marketing communications system employing telecommunication technology and trained personnel to conduct planned, measurable marketing activities directed at targeted groups of consumers.

WATS offers enormous advantages to both sellers and consumers. With OUT WATS, American and Canadian sellers can easily phone both end-consumers or business or industrial buyers to generate or qualify sales leads, close sales, and provide rapid after-sale follow-up and service. IN WATS offers toll-free 800 numbers between the two countries, and within each, to sellers that consumers can phone to place orders, request information, or register complaints.

The development of direct marketing in Europe, especially telemarketing, has lagged behind that in North America. Prior to 1990, for example, facilities (like WATS) for carrying out cross-border marketing between the various European countries was virtually nonexistent. As members of the 12-nation European Community (EC) move toward complete economic integration, however, telemarketing, combined with direct mail, appears to offer the quickest, most cost-effective way to target new customers, and sell products and services between those nations throughout the 1990s.

Telemarketing Used for Both End-Consumer and Business-to-Business Sales/Marketing

Telemarketing is a far bigger business worldwide than most people realize. Still relatively rare in 1980, telemarketing in 1988 accounted for over $100 billion in sales in the United States alone. For retailers selling to end-consumers it has become an extremely popular way to contact numerous potential customers quickly, easily, and relatively inexpensively in an effort to sell a variety of products and services. One, very irritating to consumers, method used is that of automated random or sequential dialing where prerecorded messages are voiced and no live human caller is involved. Boats, banking services, home improvements, office supplies, insurance policies, jewelry, and newspaper and magazine subscriptions are but a few of the hundreds of tangible and intangible items being sold today by telephone throughout North America and elsewhere in the world.

Every major North American city now has anywhere from 10 to 50 or more highly organized phone rooms worked by full-time or part-time professional telephone selling staffs. Telephone companies work closely with these professional groups and with business firms, nonprofit organizations, agencies of government, or individuals in helping them get set up for telemarketing and for training telephone salespeople.

Nonprofit organizations such as museums and zoos, political parties, churches and other types of religious organizations, and charitable groups constantly employ telemarketing for fund-raising and other purposes.

Business-to-Business Calls—The Mainstream of Telemarketing

While the mass of today's telemarketing contact is between retail sellers and end-user consumers, the mainstream dollar volume applications lie in business-to-business sales/marketing. While most firms and organizations employ telemarketing as a supplement to other sales efforts, others employ it as the primary means of dealing with selected market segments. Still others employ it as part of their "promotional mix" of advertising, direct mail, and sales-force effort. The rapid growth of telemarketing has been influenced in large part by the steadily increasing cost of contacting prospects and customers by regular field sales and service forces.

Here are some frequently used ways in which business firms and individual salespeople (independent contractors and company employees alike) use, or can use, telemarketing to sales advantage:

Communicating Company, Product, and Servicing Information to Customers.   Sparked largely by company advertising of their toll-free IN WATS numbers, inbound calls from customer-users, working women, and rising numbers of senior citizens have made such communications widespread. In the United States, for example, $35.2 billion General Electric's telemarketing staff of 7,000 employees, sitting at consoles in 45 different telemarketing centers with access to comprehensive data bases, made or handled over three million calls during 1989 alone—to prospects and from customers. The GE telemarketers sold by phone literally everything made by their company, from $1.98 medical accessories to hi-tech systems.

Teleprospecting.   The telephone is especially useful as a rapid means of building a base of new sales leads for sales force or promotional mailing use, and for further screening and qualifying of such leads.

The Price Increase.   If a product or service is scheduled for a price increase, phone present customers—giving them a chance to buy while the lower price is still in effect.

Introduction of a New Line.   Your company will soon introduce an entirely new line of goods. Who deserves the first crack at them? Good customers, of course—and the telephone offers a chance to reach them all, cheaply and quickly.

Inventory Clean-Out.   Here is a situation where the cost of certain company products is being reduced. These are the same products that good customers have been buying all along, so why not quickly let them know about the situation? Again, the telephone is the quickest way to contact each one.

The Pending Event.   From time to time, a pending event will increase the demand for a product. For example, when a new law is about to be passed that affects the operation of a business, it often opens opportunities to get in under a deadline. This is a key selling time, and the telephone increases many times over the amount of people that can be contacted in a short time.

Encourage Customers to Phone in Regular Orders.   Inbound WATS toll-free services designed to encourage phone-in orders are used by many companies, such as American Hospital Supply and Inland Steel, with successful results. Many of these companies have enlarged their customer service departments with inside salespeople especially trained to handle inquiries and write sales orders.

For Follow-Up and Follow-Through.   Use by salespeople of the telephone rather than trips or personal calls can save time, cut costs, and is often equally or even more effective.

Special "Telesell" Campaigns.   More important than "handling" current accounts is generating new orders by telephone. A good example is Bell and Howell's highly effective "telesell" campaigns where the company pulls its entire U.S.A. consumer product sales force off the road two or three times a year so that the salespeople can "telesell" key dealers from their homes. This is done on the last day before a price increase, to help the dealers get their orders in under the wire. Similarly, the salespeople get on the telephone at the end of a promotion period, to help the dealers take advantage of the promotion's benefits by anticipating future needs.

Sales Diagnostics.   One way to determine customer or prospect needs, wants, or interests is to arrange a several-person telephone conference among company sales and production executives and a mix of customers and prospects.

FRAUDULENT TELEMARKETERS: A THREAT TO BOTH BUSINESS AND INDIVIDUAL CONSUMERS

Along with the rise in popularity of telemarketing as a legitimate way of selling, has come its use as a means of defrauding the public. Some schemes are aimed specifically at businesses while others prey on individual consumers, including the elderly. Operating out of "boiler rooms" usually stocked with nothing more than desks, phones, and scripts, able to move within hours to a new location, fraudulent telemarketers cheat American consumers alone out of up to $20 billion a year.

Con artists are nothing new, of course. Historically, worldwide they have always been a thorn in the side of legitimate sellers. But the rapid growth of telemarketing, especially in the United States during the late 1980s, has spawned an even greater percentage of imaginative telemarketing scams. One such, called "the motorboat (or motorcycle) scam" features home phone calls to consumers who, often under the guise of participating in "market research" to test the product, are offered motorboats (or motorcycles) "free" or at substantial discounts. These consumers, however, are first asked to send the company redemption fees or shipping and handling charges, which usually turn out to be much higher than the worth of the product. Such motorboats and cycles are most often worth far less than represented by these promoters. For example, the motorboat turns out to be a small, cheap rubber raft with a small battery-powered motor so weak it can barely propel the raft.

Other dishonest telemarketers, among their other scams, frequently attempt to sell substandard office equipment and supplies to businesses by claiming to represent a supplier that is being forced to liquidate its stock at "distress prices." The items supplied are usually vastly inferior to brand-name items, are far overpriced considering their inferior quality, and in some cases cause damage when used in conjunction with other office equipment.

These fraudulent telemarketers thrive because they, like their legitimate counterparts, have learned that consumers who quickly toss out junk mail or refuse to see direct salespersons will pick up a ringing phone. The anonymity of the telephone allows smooth-talking con artists to conjure up images of reputable callers.

In spite of several federal and state laws that attempt to prevent "telefraud," and enforcement by the Federal Trade Commission (FTC) and various state agencies, bogus American telemarketers have to date been adept at exploiting legal loopholes. Worldwide, government agencies, industry associations, and public interest groups are seeking ways to contain and limit this vexing problem.

ORGANIZING FOR EFFECTIVE PERSONAL TELEMARKETING

While telemarketing (especially for telephone selling) is a most helpful and widely used supplementary personal selling tool, it is a special form of selling that requires careful preplanning, organizing, and special sales techniques in order to achieve desired results. Here are some important guidelines to consider that are useful not only to nonstore retail salespeople, but to *all types of salespeople*:

Develop a "Telephone Itinerary." One should plan in advance exactly which accounts will be called, and with what frequency. Most professional full-time telephone selling in North America is aimed at the residential or home market. Where there are plenty of prospects, calls can profitably be made from 9:00 A.M. to 9:00 P.M. Best-results periods are normally in the morning, and in the evening from 7:30 to 9:00 P.M.

Calls to commercial or industrial accounts can normally be made at any time during the business day. The best times to call retailers are the half-hour before the store opens, the hour from 11:00 to 12:00 A.M., and during the afternoon from 2:00 to 3:30 P.M. During the rest of the day, retailers are generally too busy with customers of their own to be receptive to telephone sales calls.

As in any form of selling, the more people called, the better the results. Telephone selling can be productive at almost any time; timing of calls at certain times on specific types of prospects or customers simply produces better results. In general, Friday afternoon or evening is the poorest time to call; Saturday is often the most productive day. Telemarketing should never be attempted on Sundays or holidays.

Set Telephone Sales Objectives. Each call, as well as the entire telephone effort, should have a specific sales objective. Since time is so limited, these objectives and one's opening statements should be carefully set down on paper beforehand. It is best to stress no more than one or two major features, advantages, and benefits.

Prepare Sales Tools Beforehand. Sales aids or tools should be specifically designed for telephone use; do not try to make field-sales tools do double duty. Aids should consist of factual and statistical information—laid out for immediate reference, ready for use in conversation with prospects.

Study, Develop, and Rehearse Beforehand Proper Telephone Techniques.
These techniques are discussed shortly.

Plan to Save Call Time.   The more calls made, the better your results will be.
These practical guidelines to save time should be followed:

- Know exactly why you are calling—and what you want to say—before lifting the phone. This makes calls as brief and efficient as possible.
- Make as many calls as you can at one time—say, between 9:00 A.M. and 10:00 A.M. You "get in the groove" and don't have to interrupt yourself later in the day.
- Don't hang on the line while a long-distance operator tries to reach your party. Tell the operator to call you back when he or she gets your prospect on the line.
- Say what you want to say clearly, concisely, and quickly. Beating around the bush and discussing unimportant details will cost you time. But be sure you include all essential facts relating to the discussion, or you may end up making another call later.
- Hang up when the purpose of the call is completed. Don't get involved in any unnecessary extra conversation.
- Use a three-minute egg timer, if necessary, to help force yourself to complete calls within the time limit. Set the timer at the beginning of the call.

Evaluate Results and Redirect Efforts and Techniques As Needed.   It is
necessary to evaluate results in terms of orders written, or in any other type of
specific, preset objectives; do not evaluate in terms of goodwill achieved.

Plan Direct Mail Follow-Up.   A systematic program of mailings—even if it is
only handwritten postcards—should follow telephone calls to confirm what was
agreed to. It is desirable to develop special after-call mailing pamphlets and
folders summarizing the sales presentation for (1) repeat customers and (2) hard-
to-sell prospects.

ANATOMY OF A TELEPHONE SALES PRESENTATION

In Chapter 5 we presented in detail the basic steps to follow in using the telephone for prospecting and making appointments. We will not repeat all the
basics presented there; study that section again in connection with this information. Our purpose now is to outline, illustrate, and explain use of the telephone in
making a complete sales presentation. It is done in this sequence:

1. Identify yourself and your firm or organization.
2. Establish rapport with the prospect.
3. Make an interest-creating comment.
4. Ask fact-finding questions.

WHILE YOU WERE WAITING TO MAKE THAT SALES VISIT, YOUR COMPETITOR MADE A PHONE CALL. AND GOT THE SALE.

Since 1975, the cost of the average industrial sales visit has gone up three times faster than the annual rate of inflation.

Which means that your business telephone has just taken on new importance.

Prudent use of the telephone can cut down dramatically the time and money you and your sales people spend on the road. And put to more productive use those long hours wasted sitting around in reception rooms.

You can use the phone to close a sale. Call on prospects. Submit plans and proposals. Follow up on inquiries.

Or keep in touch with customers and suppliers. With a well-planned conference call, you can conduct an entire meeting on the phone. (Just dial "0" and ask for a conference operator.)

So don't think of your telephone as just a business expense. Think of it as a way to increase business. Because that's exactly what it is.

PHONING. SOMETIMES IT'S BETTER THAN BEING THERE.

 New Jersey Bell

5. Deliver your sales message.
6. Ask for the order.
7. Handle questions or objections.
8. Close the sale.
9. Confirm details of the order.
10. Express your thanks.

To illustrate these steps, let us assume that you are selling subscriptions to a fictitious well-known national magazine called *Business and Industry Weekly* to businesspeople connected in any way with nationally known advertisers in the magazine. Let us further assume that Ford Motor Company is one of those advertisers, and that you are now working your way through the list of Ford dealers in your area as listed in telephone book yellow (classified) pages, and that you have previously obtained the name of this particular dealer whom you are now calling, who has just picked up the phone.

Table 16.1 shows the proper sequence of steps and words that will lead to the greatest chance for a successful close. This complete presentation sequence has been adapted in large part from a classic, highly successful midwestern United States telephone presentation used several years ago to promote *Life* magazine subscription offers to businesspeople. A subsequent published analysis of its effectiveness shows that one out of every two prospects (those who were not already getting *Life*) said "yes" after the initial 30-second presentation (lines 1 to 10 in our presentation), and three out of every four prospects said "yes" after the second 30-second part (lines 11 to 19 in our presentation), where it was used.[1]

Very little time was spent in handling objections in the *Life* promotion; due to the effectiveness of the presentation, it was easier to sell a new prospect than to try to convert a turndown. The wrapping-up part (with a repeat of the price and terms) of the *Life* presentation took another 30 seconds (illustrated by lines 20 to 28 in our presentation). Total presentation time, depending on questions or objections, averaged only one and one-half to three minutes.

Three out of four closes on a short but effective sales presentation such as this is, of course, very good. This high close rate was the result of a thoroughly planned, professional telephone sales promotion. The example clearly illustrates how an effective similar promotion can easily be devised by any type of business firm, by fund-raising or other types of nonprofit organizations, or by you as a salesperson on an individual basis.

Analysis of the Presentation

Let us now analyze some of the reasons why this presentation was so effective. By relating it to our ten-step sequence at the beginning of this section, we will recognize why certain key words or phrases were used:

Step 1. This was accomplished in lines 1 to 4. The salesperson puts himself or herself on a first-name basis while maintaining a respectful "Mr." or "Ms." address

---

[1] Adapted in part from Alfred Griffin, *How to Get the Most out of Promotional Telephoning* (Englewood Cliffs, N.J.: Prentice-Hall, 1966), pp. 15–22.

TABLE 16.1 *Example of a Telephone Sales Presentation in Which the Salesperson is Attempting to Sell an Annual Subscription to* Business and Industry Weekly *to a Ford Motor Company Local-Area Dealer*

(Time Length, Approximately 1½ Minutes)

Salesperson:	1. "Good morning, Mr. Puckett, my name is Gonzalez, . . . 2. Tony Gonzalez. I'm with the business office of *Business* 3. *and Industry Weekly,* and the reason I'm calling 4. is because of the money we are getting out of your organization. 5. As you probably know, Ford Motor Company pays us 6. $87,000 a *page* to advertise in *Business and Industry Weekly.* 7. To go along with that, starting May 15 we are mailing *Business* 8. *and Industry Weekly* to every Ford dealer we can reach at a 9. special rate of 98¢ a copy and I'm simply calling to ask 10. if you want yours mailed to the showroom or to your home. *Salesperson waits for an answer.* If answer is affirmative, he will complete the sale, using steps 9 and 10. If "no," he *continues as if no reply was heard.*
Mr. Puckett:	"That may not be a bad offer! How does it work?"
Salesperson:	11. "There's only one catch to it, Mr. Puckett, and that's the 12. fact that you can't get it indefinitely at that rate. 13. With over 8000 Ford dealers in the country, we can't send 14. it free, so the 98¢ covers the cost of postage and 15. bookkeeping. We can send it to you at that guaranteed low cost for as long 16. as you want up to, but not exceeding, 150 weeks. 17. That's almost three years, and that's sticking our necks 18. out plenty if postage rates go up again. Are you 19. willing to go along on that? *Salesperson waits for answer.* If "yes," he will complete the sale, using steps 9 and 10. If "no," he has the choice of either closing the call with a thank-you or asking, "Do you have any questions?" in an attempt to draw out questions or objections, which he can then handle before trying once again to close.
Mr. Puckett:	"OK—sign me up."
Salesperson:	20. "Thank you, Mr. Puckett. I shall enter your subscription 21. to *Business and Industry Weekly* for 150 weeks at 22. a cost of 98¢ per copy including postage. I'll mail you 23. a brochure outlining this special offer this evening; 24. my business office will bill you within a few 25. days. Thank you for joining so many other 26. Ford dealers in taking advantage of this special 27. offer. *Business and Industry Weekly* appreciates 28. working with Ford.
Mr. Puckett:	"OK—thanks for calling."

of the prospect. The call is treated as a business call by the prospect because the salesperson mentioned business. The salesperson gives the prospect a reason for the call before the prospect can decide for himself or herself what the reason is.

Step 2. Lines 4 to 6 establish a rapid, subtle rapport, suggesting that both the salesperson and the prospect share overall Ford interest. Line 5 flatters the prospect ("as you know") by giving credit for knowing more than he or she does.

Steps 3 through 5. Lines 7 to 10 are the key presentation-offer words. Specific figures and dates are given to reinforce credibility. The word "if" on line 10 leads the prospect to feel that this is really a soft-sell offer rather than a sales presentation (which it is). Repetition of word "mail" successfully plants the idea that the entire transaction is handled without any signing of contracts or personal follow-up calls. These three steps are combined in this presentation; the only question being asked is whether the prospect wants it mailed to the showroom or home. This is actually a combination assumptive/minor/point close; the salesperson assumes that prospect will approve, passes over the big decision, and asks the prospect merely to choose between showroom or home. Making that decision implies an affirmative decision.

Step 6. The basic purpose of lines 7 to 10 (heart of the presentation) is to get the prospect to agree, through acceptance of one of the two offered places, to mail the magazine to one of them.

Step 7. Anticipating a possible objection, and sensing that the prospect is probably thinking, "What's the catch?" the salesperson quickly puts the prospect off balance by saying (line 11) "There's only one catch to it." The prospect's reaction is to think subconsciously that if this limitation is the worst news, the good news is that he or she could get this offer indefinitely.

Use of "over 8000 Ford dealers" (line 13) implies, but does not say, that these dealers are going to get the magazine and appeals to the prospect's desire for conformity. The word "free" (line 14) is one of the most powerful words in selling; by using it the salesperson plants the idea even while denying it. Use of "98¢ covers the cost of postage and bookkeeping" after "free" further implies that it is a very good offer.

Lines 15 to 18, especially the words "for as long as you want" and "that's sticking our necks out if postage costs go up" again implies a soft-sell offer and adds conviction that it is a good, safe offer to accept.

Step 8. "Are you willing to go along with that?" (lines 18 and 19) represent the second closing attempt—by asking easily for a "yes" answer.

Steps 9 and 10. Since there are no visual means to hold attention in telephone selling, it is necessary to restate what has been offered or agreed to, repeating price, terms, and other necessary details. This and the concluding expression of thanks for the order are combined in lines 20 to 28.

Some Observations on Proper Telephone Sales Techniques

There are certain psychological factors to consider and plan for before making a telephone sales call. Since the telephone is a very impersonal instrument, unless you have your questions and presentation framed carefully, it is very easy for people on the other end to tell you they are not interested and cut you off. It is always wise to write an outline beforehand of what you plan to cover in the conversation. In face-to-face conversations, expressions, gestures, and posture help add meaning to words, but words alone have to communicate by telephone, so you should frame them carefully beforehand so as to be certain your message gets across as desired. Even though you have outlined your presentation beforehand, you should say it in such a way that it does not appear to be merely a "canned" outline that you are reading to the other person.

Your *voice* is the major thing you have going for you over the telephone. The warmth of your voice, the inflections you use, and the specific words used are all very significant. It is important to try to project yourself over the phone, especially your warmth and interest. One way to do this is to smile when you are talking, to imagine that you are face to face with your prospects and trying to project your personality to them.

When talking, it is important to try and involve prospects as much as possible, avoiding a monologue. One good way to do this is to ask involving questions from time to time. If your prospects voice questions or objections, you can establish better rapport by indicating that you are listening carefully to what they are saying. This can be done by using words like "yes," "that's right," and "I agree with what you are saying." When the prospects say something of obvious importance to them, use the technique of repeating the substance of the remark, so that they know you heard it.

The telephone can be a valuable, time-conserving, money-making sales aid in prospecting, selling, and after-sale follow-up if used properly. This is the age of the tape recorder; use it to practice your telephone calls before you make them, so you will know in advance how your voice and words will sound to others.

DIRECT-TO-CONSUMER RETAIL MARKETING VIA DIRECT SALESPEOPLE

We got our first insight into the world of direct selling, a widely practiced form of nonstore (outside) retail selling, back in Chapter 1, where it was noted that worldwide over seven million salespeople on six continents annually account for $35 billion in retail sales.

Direct sales men and women are most often independent contractors who, in effect, run their own businesses. Supported by, and selling products and services of, the companies they represent, they seek out and develop retail sales prospects, to whom they make sales presentations on a person-to-person, group, or in-home party-plan basis.

Of the approximately 3.6 million independent, full- or part-time direct salespeople at work in the United States in 1988,[2] nearly 80 percent were females. Other figures indicate that out of this total some 15 percent were minorities, approximately five percent were over the age of 65, and nearly ten percent had some form of physical disability—temporary or permanent. According to the

---

[2] This and certain other factual data in this section have been extracted from 1988 published material provided by Direct Selling Association, 1776 K Street, N.W., Suite 600, Washington, D.C. 20006.

Direct Selling Association, 75 percent of U.S. households are contacted by these salespeople each year, and half of all households make a purchase.

Direct Selling and the Changing Marketplace

In the early 1980s, as more and more women went to work and had little time or desire for "at home" sales parties or individual sales presentations, house-to-house sales in the United States and Canada generally fell out of fashion. A result was that from 1982 to 1985 North America saw a sharp decline in direct sales and profits, and in the number of salespeople employed in the industry.

In more recent years, direct sales have once again climbed as direct sellers have switched marketing emphasis from home to workplace. Since so many of

TABLE 16.2 *Some Better-Known Direct Sales Companies and Some of the Countries in Which They Sell*[3]

Company	Type of Products Sold	USA	Canada	Australia	United Kingdom	Japan	France	Malaysia	Mexico
Amway Corporation	Household, personal/home care, nutrition, catalogue sales	X	X	X	X	X	X	X	X
Avon Products, Inc.	Cosmetics and jewelry	X	X	X	X	X	X	X	X
Encyclopedia Britannica, Inc.	Educational publications, films	X		X	X	X	X		X
Grolier Inc.	Educational publications	X	X					X	
Mary Kay Cosmetics, Inc.	Cosmetics	X	X	X		X			
Shaklee Corporation	Food supplements, food, personal care products	X	X			X			
Tupperware Home Parties	Plastic food storage containers, cookware, children's toys	X		X		X	X		X
World Book, Inc.	Educational publications	X	X	X	X				

[3] *Source:* Direct Selling Association.

the 3.6 million American direct salespeople, for example, are women who hold other jobs, they find that their prospective customers are apt to be at the desks or on the production lines around them. In 1986, Avon, America's largest direct seller, began training its over 400,000 salespeople to operate in the workplace. Some Avon tips: Sell only during coffee and lunch breaks; be a walking Avon advertisement (that is, wear Avon perfume and lipstick).

Realizing that it may not pay to sell too aggressively in the workplace, direct sales companies like Avon, Tupperware, and Mary Kay Cosmetics tend to urge their salespeople to take it easy, lest employers put a stop to the practice. Dunhill of London is one direct seller, though, who doesn't worry about the boss objecting. Since late 1988 Dunhill has targeted busy executives as prospects (called "clients") for tailored suits that can cost up to $3000 each. With phone appointments, Dunhill tailors come to the bosses' offices with hundreds of fabric swatches. Once a sale is made, they return for two in-office fittings.

Among the scores of direct sales companies around the world, many operate internationally. Table 16.2 lists some of these better-known companies, the type of products they carry, and some of the world's major countries in which they sell.

DIRECT SELLING PRODUCTS ARE MARKETED IN FOUR PRIMARY WAYS

Products offered by direct selling companies, in addition to those listed in Table 16.2, sold in the home or workplace or at other locations, include clothing, decorative accessories, vitamins, and personal and home security products. Their products are marketed in these four primary ways.

- *Repetitive person-to-person.* Here salespeople visit homes, usually on a fairly regular basis, and sell products or services that are purchased frequently. They also sell in offices, factories, and other workplaces, where the salesperson may well be a company or organizational employee supplementing his or her income at lunchtime and when on coffee or tea breaks.
- *Nonrepetitive person-to-person, or to groups.* This involves occasional visits by salespeople to homes, places of work, or other locations where they sell products or services that are purchased infrequently. Their sales presentations, while usually made on a person-to-person basis, are also made before groups of people by appointment at locations such as schools or churches.
- *Party Plan.* Tupperware Home Parties has long made in-home, or in-office "party plan" selling the cornerstone of its direct marketing program. As was more fully described in Case Study I, the company's dealers (sales reps) prospect for men or women who will agree to host a party in their homes, place of work, or other locations, to which they invite relatives, friends, and acquaintances. The Tupperware dealers put on a demonstration (sales presentation) of the company's products.

The host or hostess earns free Tupperware or certain other products based on attendance and sales.

- *Temporary Fixed Locations.* This involves salespeople setting up a short-term booth at shopping malls, county, state, or provincial fairs, theme parks, or other crowded public locations where they both serve customers on the spot and obtain prospect names for future sales follow-up.

Prospecting and sales techniques employed in all four of these methods basically include a mix of all those presented in preceding chapters for one-on-one selling. How and where these methods are employed, and by whom, are illustrated in Table 16.3. Principles and techniques of selling to groups by direct salespeople generally follow those explained in Chapter 14.

Brief descriptions of how three of the world's best-known direct sales companies organize for their respective types of selling, train and compensate their salespeople, and go about selling their products to end-consumers were presented in Case Study 1.

Now it is time to turn our attention to some special sales problems faced by providers of largely intangible services.

TABLE 16.3 *1987 Direct Selling Industry Survey for the United States*[4]

Total Retail Sales: $8,789,415,000

Percentage of Sales by Major Product Groups

Personal care products	38.00%
Home/family care products	43.95%
Leisure/educational products	10.99%
Services/other	7.06%

Sales Approach
(method used to generate sales reported as a percent of sales dollars)

One-on-One Contact	80.24%
Group Sales/Party Plan	19.76%

Locus of Sales

In the Home	In a Workplace	At a Public Event*	Over the Phone	Other
77.02%	11.80	2.53%	6.87%	1.78%

Total Salespeople: 3,614,038

Demographics of Salespeople

Independent	98.58%
Employed	1.42%
Full-time (30+ hours per week)	11.65%
Part-time	88.35%
Male	21.97%
Female	78.03%

* Such as at a fair, exhibition, shopping mall, theme park, and the like.

[4] *Source:* Direct Selling Association (9/15/88).

SPECIAL SALES PROBLEMS FACED BY SERVICE PROVIDERS MARKETING TO END-CUSTOMERS

Back in Chapter 3 we learned that services are marketed both to individual consumers for their personal or nonbusiness use and to organizations by (1) individuals and business seeking profit, (2) not-for-profit organizations, and (3) governmental agencies. And we learned there the difference between products and services.

While our focus here centers on nonstore outside retail selling applications to end-consumers, since most service providers serving them *also sell* (like retail stores) *in-house or in-office,* many of the sales techniques studied in Chapter 15 apply. Keep them in mind, for they will not be repeated here. Some special problems faced by salespeople selling to buyers of organizational service providers were discussed in Chapter 14.

Hundreds of different kinds of services aimed at end-consumers are offered by individuals and businesses seeking a profit: haircuts, restaurant food, dog grooming, legal and accounting services, laundry, and travel services, to name but a few. Not-for-profit organizations such as charitable groups, museums, and zoos also offer services in return for the monetary fees, contributions, or donations needed to keep them operating. And many agencies of government offer services for which they charge fees—overnight campsites in public parks, for example, or certain types of public information services. Since such services are more intangible than physical products, both the selling and buying of them present some special sales problems.

PSYCHOLOGICAL PROBLEMS AS WELL AS THOSE OF UNDERSTANDING CONFRONT BOTH CONSUMER AND PROVIDER

Services in general are less standardized than physical products and more intangible, and their quality frequently varies between individual providers, and at different times. It's fairly easy for a consumer to focus on a specific, tangible product, such as a new automobile, offering several clear-cut choices (such as, make, model, color). Selecting a provider of largely intangible services, especially complex professional ones such as medical, legal, and accounting services, is much more difficult. Not only do the quality and level of service differ between providers, but one cannot "sample" the service in advance and may not fully comprehend or appreciate its technical implications once accepted. Additionally, the professional who provides the service also markets it—a fact that may raise implications of trust and confidence.

Especially when seeking a professional or higher-level type of service, consumers (or clients) tend to focus less on the product (the service) and more on the provider (individual or organization) and its staff, if any. He or she searches for subtle clues to help answer inward questions such as "Should I go to this particular provider now?" or "Should I wait and try to find a better one?" "Will they treat me with respect?" "Will they really try to help me?" "Will they bill me fairly?"

Many service providers, especially professionals, are also likely to face inward questions and problems—some subtle, some not so subtle. The service a doctor sells, for example, is the practice of medicine. He or she may feel that every minute taken away from it for "marketing" is a costly waste of time, if not beneath one's "dignity." And all too often they simply do not know how to go about marketing their services. Medical schools, like those of most of the professions, don't offer courses in sales/marketing. At the very least, few professionals feel comfortable in the dual role of both providing and marketing their services.

Sellers of all types of intangible services, faced with their different levels and degrees of these special sales problems, have to "tangibilize" and "personalize" their offerings in every way possible, if they hope to market them successfully.

HOW CAN SERVICE PROVIDERS "TANGIBILIZE" AND "PERSONALIZE" THEIR OFFERINGS TO INDIVIDUAL CONSUMERS?

While there are great differences between different types and levels of those service providers who serve end-consumers, enough has been learned by sales professionals over the years to suggest what does or should work best for all of them. The first step is to undertake a "marketing survey" that first considers the *views of the seller* (service provider) *and staff* (if any) about the service offered and its consumer public, and then considers *views of consumers* about the seller and staff (if any) and the quality of service provided. From that survey, a specific "marketing plan" can be developed to first "tangibilize" and "personalize" the product (service) and then "market" it. Greatest sales success, as in all other areas of sales/marketing, will come from "working the plan."

To illustrate this process, let's consider a mythical accounting firm in a medium-sized city that wants to target small business owners as clients. The firm consists of six partners, all of whom are certified public accountants (two of whom are also lawyers), and a clerical staff of eight. The firm's survey indicates that small business owners are (surprisingly to the partners) far more interested in reasonably priced professional guidance in running their business, and help in solving week-to-week problems, than they are in the specific accounting services that the firm has been promoting.

To discuss these findings, and to develop a new sales/marketing program, a weekend retreat, including all partners and clerical staff, was held at a nice resort hotel. Here is an outline of the later highly successful program they came up with, and how they "personalized" and "tangibilized" their intangible professional accounting services:

1. Established the theme: "Accountants You Can Trust—At a Price You Can Afford."

2. Set target-market goal: Long-term small-business-owner clients who want to have their financial planning, business problems and accounting needs handled by one firm, with one specific professional assigned to each client on a permanent basis.

3. Offer to put each client's program on computer, and help them prepare business plans, financial projections, budgets, and to offer "business problems" advice on an ongoing, reasonable, "set-fee" basis.

4. Each partner to visit each assigned client at the client's office at least once every six months.

5. Promotion of the new personalized service program included:

   a. A weekly half-hour radio program discussion about small-business problems featuring a different partner and two of the firm's clients each time.

   b. Radio and newspaper ads and publicity brochures offering weekday evening and Saturday service with at least one of the partners available.

   c. A monthly newsletter for clients built around point 3 above.

   d. A by-invitation, Saturday noon, buffet luncheon "open house" at firm's office, six times a year, with all possible partners and clerical staff on hand.

   e. Offering partners as a "free speakers' bureau" to local area business organizations, service clubs, and church management committees.

   f. Each partner and each staff member to join and participate actively in at least one community-related club or group, with membership fees paid by the firm.

   g. Hold an advertised, scheduled, free, "open to the public" series of seminars at a local hotel conference room built around specific small-business-related problems.

Central point of the above review is for the service provider to learn to observe its service through the eyes and ears of the end-customer it serves, not just from its own perspective, and to better serve those consumers' needs, wants, and problems.

TRADE SHOW, SALES SEMINAR, AND EXHIBITION SELLING

A trade show is a public exhibition or showing, usually of specific types of products, offered by sellers to prospective buyers. Over 10,000 trade shows and countless large and small special exhibitions or sales seminars at which salespeople represent their firms or organizations are held each year in North America. Many thousands more are held in other countries of the world. Costs of participation are often very high; for some companies such exhibitions are worthless in terms of specific sales, yet necessary from a sales promotion point of view. Other companies write almost a third of their annual business at such events.

How important is participation in such events to business firms or not-for-profit organizations? For most, participation is an extension of their overall sales/

marketing program, and a way of bringing people together less expensively than by other means. More specifically, participation helps generate qualified sales leads, is a good way to introduce new products, and increases firm and product name recognition.

One major advantage of trade shows and exhibitions is that buyers come to the seller rather than the other way around. Still, such events have to be kept in perspective, for they are not a panacea. Most experts agree that they fit somewhere in the middle of sales/marketing tools, based on cost and effectiveness. As one sales manager put it, "We calculate that it costs us $215 to send one of our industrial sales reps out on a call, and $110 per individual contact via a sales seminar; a trade show sales contact averages $60, a direct mail contact will cost us $25, and our advertising contacts run around $5 each."

Sales Seminars. One major disadvantage of trade shows and exhibitions is that it is difficult to control the quality or quantity of visitors to the booth of a specific exhibitor. For that reason, many companies and organizations are veering more to holding their own specialized sales seminars, sometimes at quiet locations adjacent to ongoing trade shows. These are more costly than booths at shows, but are more controllable and tend to produce better results. A variation of this is to attend more less-crowded, specialized trade shows such as those produced by individual manufacturers, where it is frequently easier to hold sales seminars at exhibit booth locations.

Whatever form of selling you engage in, chances are you will be involved in planning, organizing, attending, and later following up sales leads obtained at one or more such shows a year. Your participation may range from being part of a company sales team to that of organizing your own one-person show. Your efforts may be highly productive or a waste of time and effort, determined in large part by how well you and your firm or organization plan, organize, execute, and follow up before, during, and after the event.

Careful Planning Is Essential to Success

In order to obtain maximum results, preshow planning from a managerial point of view should include (1) carefully developing clear-cut written exhibit goals and specific objectives; (2) discussing these goals and objectives thoroughly in advance with your firm's advertising, sales, sales promotion, and public relations staff; (3) planning and coordinating strategy with all these people and with your exhibit designer if you are using one; and (4) communicating the goals, objectives, and working plan to all salespeople and support people who will attend.

The importance of goal and objective setting cannot be overemphasized. Objectives should be specific, with targets set realistically high for each individual participant. They should be discussed in detail with all participants prior to the start of the show, reviewed daily during the show, and evaluated upon its conclusion. Truly successful exhibition or trade show selling is, in nearly every case, the result of a carefully planned, integrated team effort.

Organizing the Show

A trade show or exhibition, as already noted, is one of the few places where the prospect comes to the salesperson. It offers opportunity to write orders on the spot without having to waste time in a waiting room or fighting for a busy buyer's time. But such shows often attract large numbers of visitors—up to many thousands over a three-day period in some cases. Some are just lookers, some are real prospects, and others are valuable established customers. With so little time and so many people crowding around, asking questions and interested in possible detailed explanations or demonstrations, how can you as salesperson-on-the-spot sort, qualify, handle, and sell selectively? The answer lies in careful planning, preparation, and organization; here are some of the major factors to consider.

The Physical Exhibit.   What is it about the exhibition that is likely to attract prospects of interest to you? What will attract and hold prospects to your particular exhibit (which may be only one of many)? Answers to those two questions are essential in planning the physical layout of your exhibit, the effectiveness of which in turn depends on what emphasis you desire to place on selected products or product features. One key to success is to develop the exhibit booth within the context of the preplanned goals and objectives; let your exhibit designer (if any) know your objectives so you will be working together.

Proper booth location in large exhibition halls often plays an important role in attracting and holding visitors. If possible, you should study the floor plan and overall exhibit-booth layout beforehand, and select the specific space location best suited to your activity and desired traffic flow. Your firm's sales promotions staff, or other experienced individuals, can offer you guidance concerning product display, demonstration, space, catalogue displays, and proper use of lighting, audiovisual equipment, and other matters.

Ample catalogues or other giveaway literature must be made available, and plans must be made for its effective distribution. If products are to be demonstrated or audiovisual equipment used, you should know exactly how it works and practice beforehand to make certain you do.

Preshow Buildup.   This takes two forms: (1) to obtain maximum publicity so as to attract potential new buyers, and (2) to make certain key prospects and important established customers are individually invited in advance to visit your exhibit.

Proper coordination with your firm's advertising department will help ensure effective pre- and postshow advertising in journals and magazines to promote your exhibit. A special "invitation to attend" might be included in any regular advertising mailing scheduled before the exhibition date. Similar coordination with the public relations and sales promotion departments might suggest prior coverage or other attention-getting ideas to attract prospects to your exhibit, both in advance and during the exhibition.

Your sales department should know beforehand which customer companies or organizations are likely to send representatives. Preshow promotion, through advertising and the field sales force, can alert them and invite them to attend your exhibit booth.

Above all, you should make a special effort to personally invite *your personal customers* to attend and meet with you. Some you will want to write or telephone, in order to arrange specific appointment times. Others you will merely want to invite to contact you upon their arrival, so you can then arrange a mutually convenient specific meeting time at the booth or elsewhere. One highly effective way to do this is to mail two postcards in an envelope to each of the key people you want to see (potential prospects or regular customers) two weeks before the show. One is a postpaid, self-addressed reply card addressed to you. An example of the other card is shown in Figure 16.1.

Selling at the Show. A carefully designed exhibit and good preshow promotion may draw initial attention to your exhibit, but they don't sell your products. You and your fellow salespeople (if any) do that. Your overall sales problem is somewhat like managing your sales territory. In most cases, your aim is profitable sales; to make enough sales to pay all costs of the show (salaries, promotion, and the like) and show a profit. As in your territory, the more qualified prospects or customers you contact at the exhibit, the greater your chance of success. As a guideline, you should aim to make as many effective sales contacts in one day of exhibit selling as in one week of field selling.

This may sound like a lot, but exhibitions normally run day and evening, and salespeople manning booths normally put in twelve-hour days, with good prospects possibly visiting at the rate of up to six or eight an hour. Your problem, especially during peak visitor hours, is to separate prospects and buyers from other visitors and handle all of them properly. Overall, you are in effect your company's host at the show, acting both as salesperson and public relations specialist. Buyers won't waste time standing around waiting for long, so you have

FIGURE 16.1 *Example of Pre-Trade Show or Exhibit Invitation. This is written two weeks in advance by a salesperson to a key prospect or customer he or she specifically wants to meet at the show.*

```
Hello, Mr. Jones,
    Hope to see you at our X-Company exhibit booth at the
National Y Exposition to be held May 18-20 at the Plaza Hotel,
San Francisco.
    Won't you let me know where you will be staying, or can be
contacted, on the enclosed postpaid card?
    We have something interesting to show you-it could save
you quite a bit of money.
    I'll be staying at the nearby Oceanside Hotel myself, but
will normally be at our booth from 9 A.M. to 9 P.M. daily.


                                            Sincerely,
```

to greet and be considerate to all visitors. And you have to be prepared to employ far more rapid-fire selling techniques, due to the short time available, than the normal, more relaxed kind of selling done in a prospect's office or home. Here are a few basic guidelines for working effectively in a crowded exhibit-booth situation.

- Greet everyone individually if possible, saying something like:

  > Hello, I'm Laura Massaro. As you can see, I'm going to be tied up for a few minutes. Won't you please look around, and I'll join you in a moment.

- Qualify each quickly as to their degree of interest—if they appear to be real prospects but you don't have time to handle them then and there, either make an appointment for another meeting at the booth or away from it later during the show, or for the after-show follow-up.
- Since you won't be able to remember every visitor, ask those showing any degree of interest to either fill in a card with their name, title, business address, telephone, and area of interest, or log it quickly yourself in your own exhibit logbook. Such exhibition prospecting is an excellent way to develop new sales leads.
- As visitors depart, try to thank each one for visiting your booth and give them all available literature concerning their area of interest to take with them.
- Rapid sales-presentation techniques common to exhibition selling, where time may be very short, are similar to those we covered in selling by telephone. For example, it is best to stress no more than one or two major features, advantages, and benefits of your product; arrange a later appointment or after-show call if a longer time is necessary to explain or answer questions.

After-Show Follow-Up. It is important to hold a final after-show sales meeting for all attending participants to review all preplanned goals and objectives in terms of results. This review will help pinpoint the strengths and weaknesses of every aspect of the show, and help all concerned plan better for future shows.

All sales contacts, specific leads, or later appointments made during the show should be followed up as soon as possible by telephone, mail, or personal calls. The after-show sales meeting is the time and place to set specific sales follow-up schedules for each concerned salesperson.

SUMMARY

The field of retailing and retail selling is so broad that we have devoted two chapters to it. In Chapter 15 the focus centered on selling activities by salespeople in a retail store situation, where customers came to them. In this chapter we concentrated largely on how salespeople sell products and services to end-consumers outside of a retail store setting.

After brief reviews of several of the more impersonal forms of outside retail selling such as mail order, direct mail, and electronic shopping, we turned our attention to the fast-growing area of telemarketing. There we followed up our Chapter 5 discussion of prospecting and getting the appointment by telephone with an analysis of how to make the complete telephone sales presentation. Illustrations and specific techniques presented should enable any company, non-profit or government organization, retailer, or individual salesperson to use the telephone as an effective sales tool immediately.

The important field of direct selling was then discussed and the four primary ways in which direct sales firms market their products were presented. Following that, certain psychological problems facing both sellers and buyers of intangible services were considered, and ideas presented to help service providers "tangibilize" and "personalize" their offerings to end-consumers.

Our chapter concluded with an overview of important trade show, sales seminar, and exhibition selling, including principles, practices, and several useful how-to-do-it techniques applicable to any such business or nonbusiness event.

Questions for Analysis and Discussion

1. If you were asked to define the term *telemarketing,* what would be your answer? Is it more widely used as a method of contact between retail sellers and end-user consumers, or as a business-to-business contact?

2. You are a retailer, planning to have your sales staff make a reduced-price color TV set offer by telephone this week during slack business hours. What prospects would you have them call? Where would you get their phone numbers? What times would be best for the majority of your preselected prospects to favorably respond to such telephone sales calls?

3. Assuming you are a salesperson for a firm whose $1600 product X is scheduled for a 10 percent price increase in one week, outline a 45-second telephone sales presentation you would like to make concerning the increase to your regular list of 100 customers. Be prepared to present it in a classroom role-playing situation.

4. What is meant by the term, commonly used by direct salespeople, *nonrepetitive person-to-person selling?*

5. What could be some of the practical and psychological problems faced by end-user consumers in selecting the professional services of a lawyer to defend them in a serious automobile accident claim case?

6. What is it about a trade show or exhibition that makes the selling situation for a salesperson so different from normal field-selling activities? Describe and explain your answer or answers.

7. Pretrade-show buildup was described in this chapter as taking two forms. What are they? Why are they important?

8. Name the major advantage of a firm's participating in a major big-city trade show, and the major disadvantage.

Holland America Line and Your Local Travel Agent Invite You—To a Fun Filled "Cruise Night" Social

If this personalized invitation came to you in today's mail, would it arouse your attention and interest?

> (Your Local) *Travel Agency*
> *requests the pleasure of your company*
> *at a gala "CRUISE NIGHT" Social*
> *featuring a November Caribbean cruise*
> *aboard Holland America Line's beautiful*
> M.S. NOORDAM
> *Please join us for complimentary wine, cheese,*
> *door prizes, and a colorful, informative film*
> *Tuesday Evening, April XX*
> *5:30–7:30 p.m.*
> (Travel Agency Office Address)
>
> RSVP

Luxury ocean cruising, once enjoyed mainly by the very rich, has since the early 1970s become a truly big-time, fast-growing industry! In 1978, for example, some 500,000 Americans took a cruise; in 1988 three million did so—to the tune of 5 billion dollars. Forty new cruise ships made their debuts between 1980 and 1989; one-fourth of them in 1988. And this is just the start; experts predict that cruising will be a 20-billion-dollar industry by 1995. Many beautiful new and ever larger ships are now being built to meet this expected demand.

Two of these new luxury cruise liners, each with a 2114 passenger capacity, will be the largest in Holland America Line's fleet when they join it in the early 1990s. World-famous Holland America Line, owned since its founding in 1873 by Dutch interests, became in late 1988 the "top-of-the-line" division (under its own name) of American-owned Carnival Cruises. Together they comprise the world's largest cruise/land tour organization.

To keep the cabins full on its current Caribbean, west coasts of Mexico, United States, and Canada, and Alaska cruise ships, and on their future ones, Holland America Line Westours Inc. (the company's full, official name) keeps its North American field sales staff of 34 busy. These men and women, most with prior travel agency, air or cruise line experience, called DSMs (for district sales managers) each attend one or two large trade shows and two or three smaller, regional ones monthly. Most of the larger ones are sponsored by leading travel magazines or ASTA (American Society of Travel Agents), the smaller ones usually by independent companies such as Travel Marketplace that specialize in organizing travel trade shows and exhibitions. They also attend one national and two regional company sales meetings annually.

When not attending trade shows, exhibitions, or sales meetings, these DSMs spend most of their time working with travel agents throughout their individual sales regions, promoting Holland America Line ocean cruises, Westours rail, bus and day cruise trips in Alaska, and the company's 18 hotels in Alaska. Proud of the fact that 99 percent of all their bookings are placed through travel agents (compared to only 60 percent for the airlines industry), these DSMs are indeed specialists at selling to buyers in the reseller organizational market.

Most popular among Holland America's different types of promotions are their "Cruise Night" (or "Cruise Afternoon") socials. Sponsored by local travel agencies, either in their offices, at other local sites such as churches, or on the premises of business firms, these gatherings are backed by heavy DSM-assisted promotional support. Such cruise (or tour) events are social forms of sales promotion that allow the travel agency to gather potential group members (prospects) together. The fun-filled social setting allows selling the program to them in an informal, enjoyable way that uses the benefits of group peer pressure to gain additional interest and sales.

Among the many promotional aids available from Holland America Line for these socials are brochures, displays, banners, counter cards, fact sheets, cruise night aids, 16-mm films, and VHS video tapes. Many are supplied free of charge, others at a modest cost. Whenever possible, the DSM attends in person. If the DSM is unable to attend, a complete "planned presentation" for the entire program is provided free of charge.

A major sales objective of "Cruise Night" socials is to try to organize bookings of so-called *affinity groups*: groups of 10 full-fare passengers who have enough of a special relationship among themselves to separate them from the general public. Holland America Line's DSMs and their travel agency buyer partners have found that concentration on affinity group selling leads more quickly to mutual sales success than single-prospect selling.

Questions for Written Reports or Class Discussion

1. Do you feel that the personalized invitation approach to attend a "Cruise Night" social is a good prospecting tool? Why? Can you describe two other different types of approaches that might work as well or better?

2. If you are asked to organize and man alone the Holland America Line exhibit booth at a trade show for both travel agents and the general public in a city of half a million population, what promotional theme will you use, and who will be your target prospects?

4. What three approaches can a Holland America Line DSM best use to contact possible affinity group individual "influentials"?

5. Draft a one-page direct mail sales letter, promoting a November cruise on the MS Noordam, to be sent to alumni of a local college or university, on behalf of a local travel agency. You are free to use your imagination!

| Sales Problem 16.1 | Would you like to adopt a baby hippo? |

Open year around, the beautifully sited Cheyenne Mountain Zoo in Colorado Springs, Colorado, U.S.A. houses an ever-changing array of more than 600 permanent animals, including giraffes, elephants, and orangutans. In addition, as reported by the area's leading newspaper, the *Gazette Telegraph,* it usually has on display other exotic animals, like Ramar, a magnificent male white tiger, on loan from zoos in other American cities, or from abroad.

"Unlike other places, things always change at the zoo, with new babies and animals coming and going constantly," says Karen Torgerson, the zoo's director of marketing and development. She has the job of "selling" benefits of the zoo to the 400,000 or so residents of the city and surrounding area, whose financial donations she depends on to support the nonprofit zoo organization. Although the zoo was created and donated to the people of Colorado Springs back in 1926 by animal lover Spencer Penrose, it is not supported financially by the city or state.

How does one "sell" a zoo? Let's see if we can help Karen come up with some ideas. To start, let's consider the zoo's basic market. One thing is for sure: animals aren't the only things that come and go at the zoo. In a typical year the animals get to enjoy watching about 320,000 interesting human visitors, 45 percent of whom are out-of-state tourists, and over 30,000 of whom are school children on educational field trip visits as part of their school curriculum.

These latter educational tours, any one of which may have as many as 300 students, are conducted by docents, a 120-member volunteer group. They have developed three basic tours for school children: a general mammal tour for third-graders, an ecology tour for fifth-graders, and an endangered species tour for junior-high and high-school students. The overall theme for each is the kinship between humans and animals in the world we share together.

One of the zoo's most successful promotions to get people to donate is through its "Adopt an Animal" program, in which people select an animal and adopt it for a year by paying for food and maintenance with a tax-deductible donation. Donations range from $15 for a small animal such as a salamander to $1500 for a large one, such as a tiger.

In return, adopters receive such items as an adoption certificate, two free visits to the zoo, and a window decal, and their name (or names) appear as "parent" at the permanent Zoo Parents Display, along with the name of their adopted animal.

Donations from the public are becoming increasingly important as the zoo gets older, more animals are added, and operational costs keep increasing. Karen, like so many other sales/marketing directors of not-for-profit organizations, faces a constantly challenging task in "selling" the zoo's benefits to the public, and soliciting badly needed financial donations.

Questions for Written Reports or Class Discussion

1.   List all other possible advantages and benefits to the general public offered by the zoo, not mentioned above, that you can think of.

2.   Based on your advantages and benefit list, outline at least six good sales/marketing suggestions other than those noted, that Karen might quickly put into effect at low cost in her "benefits/donations" sales/marketing program.

3.   Prepare a written two-minute telemarketing canned sales presentation to (1) sell the zoo's benefits and (2) ask a prospect to "Adopt an Animal" that volunteer docents could use to promote the zoo's program by telephone.

Sales Problem 16.2	What advice would you give to "miserable in la-la land"?

Not only were the many positive advantages and uses of telemarketing pointed out in our chapter, but also the vexing problem of telemarketing fraud, which cheats American consumers alone out of nearly $20 billion a year. While we noted how the many telemarketing scams hurt both legitimate businesses and end-consumers alike, nothing was said about "caught in the middle" honest salespeople.

Here is a poignant letter from just such an individual, written to nationally known and respected columnist Ann Landers. It appeared as part of her column in newspapers throughout the United States during November, 1988.[5]

> Dear Ann Landers: I've just moved to Los Angeles from the Midwest. I needed to work immediately, so I took a part-time telemarketing job right away. I started yesterday and hate it already.
>
> This must be an illegal or borderline operation, for sure. We are instructed to call businesses and inform them that their annual preventive maintenance checkup is due. We ask for the model number of their photocopier. Then we tell them that they should buy hundreds of dollars' worth of chemicals from the servicemen even though they may already have a supply of chemicals on hand because we have a *great* special on the stuff.
>
> We aren't supposed to give them the company name unless they ask for it, and then we give them a false one. We also aren't allowed to call government agencies, K-Mart, Sears and various other businesses. (No reason was given.) All this sounds fishy to me.
>
> I'm desperately looking for another job because this one is making me physically ill. Do you know anything about this type of business? What should I do?
>
> Miserable in La La Land

Ann Landers offered her excellent advice to the writer of that letter in her column, but rather than include it here, let's see how you answer the following questions that may have crossed her mind at the time of drafting her reply.

Questions for Written Reports or Class Discussion

1. What advice would you give "Miserable" in replying to his or her letter?

2. What advice would you give individual or household end-consumers to help alert them to and protect them from fraudulent telemarketers? How would you disseminate such information to them in your local area?

3. What advice would you give owners or managers of small businesses to help alert them to and protect them from fraudulent telemarketers? How would you disseminate such information to them in your local area?

---

[5] Reprinted by permission.

CHAPTER
17

Social, Legal, and Ethical Issues in Selling

After studying this chapter, you will be able to:

Explain the terms *consumerism, ethics, business ethics, morals,* and *business* or *commercial law.*

Describe why a knowledge of their nation's basic business or commercial law is important to salespeople the world over.

Identify the differences between constitutional, statutory, and common law as they relate to business law in the United States.

Identify four major federal antitrust acts and some of the major consumer legislation that affects how selling is conducted in the United States.

Relate the importance to American salespeople of the Federal Trade Commission (FTC) and the Consumer Product Safety Commission (CPSC), which have broad regulatory and enforcement powers that affect sales/marketing.

Summarize the major responsibilities salespeople worldwide face toward their companies, toward customers and society, and toward themselves.

owhere is the fact that we are living in a fast-moving world more evident
N than in the rapidly changing social, legal, and ethical issues faced by
businesspeople in most of the world's noncommunist industrialized nations, especially those working in the area of sales/marketing.

In this chapter we focus our attention on some of the more important of these issues, the challenges they pose, and how salespeople should view and respond to them. Due to the complexity of these issues, we can only highlight some of the more important worldwide challenges posed by consumerism plus the relationship of business ethics and social responsibility, and personal ethics and morals. In considering specific effects and examples of government and the law on selling, our focus centers on federal, state, and local laws of the United States that affect American salespeople.

CONSUMERIST MOVEMENT CRITICISMS OF BUSINESS

Since the 1960s, politicians and social activists in North America and Western Europe especially, have been quicker than businesspeople to recognize that a growing mass of consumers is vocally questioning traditional materialistic values and expressing interest in the social aspects of consumption. This has led to increased social and political action and overall concern via the so-called consumerist movement, especially since the late 1980s in the face of increased worldwide pollution of air and water, and discovery of expanding openings in the earth's protective ozone layer in space.

By way of definition, to *consume* means to destroy or expend by use—to use up. A *consumer* is one who consumes. *Consumerism* is the interaction of consumers, politicians, consumer advocates, business, and industry toward the achievement of consumer rights. Social action to achieve consumerism is called the *consumerist movement*.

Some of the major consumerist criticisms are listed below. They have been gleaned from many sources and are listed in no particular order of importance. They serve to identify some of the specific issues of consumerism with which modern-day salespeople should be familiar.

1. The production and selling of many products and services often wastes resources, is built on trivial differences, and is often in conflict with overall social welfare.
2. Many forms of advertising and selling persuade people to buy products they do not need; many are actually deceptive.
3. Too many products damage the environment (such as, nonbiodegradable disposable plastic packaging, or fluorocarbons from aerosol spray containers) or blight the landscape (for example, outdoor commercial advertising billboards).
4. Products are often unsafe, poorly built, not durable enough, and difficult and costly to repair.

5.   Business in general has failed to raise living standards of the poor, the elderly, certain minorities, and other disadvantaged segments of society; often-deceptive sales/marketing practices frequently hurt these groups most.

How Should Salespeople Respond to Such Criticism?

How should salespeople, proud of their sales/marketing profession, which has contributed so much toward the high standards of living enjoyed by so many of the world's people, respond to such criticism? Here are two suggestions. First, they should recognize that such consumer problems are problems of friction within a basically sound system. Second, they should welcome such criticism, just as in selling they welcome "questions or objections" from prospects and customers, because it offers clues as to what the questioners or critics really think and feel. Some of today's criticism is called for, and salespeople should take the lead in bringing about the required changes; other criticism is rooted in unreasonable prejudice or bias, and must be recognized for what it is.

Salespeople will, throughout the 1990s, increasingly find themselves personally on the firing line and in the middle of many of these complex issues. Salespeople are paid to sell their company's products or services, yet they are also consumers and members of society. What can and should each do personally to further fulfillment of the modern customer/society-oriented sales/marketing concept? Finding answers starts with an understanding of business ethics and social responsibility, and the personal ethics and morals that should guide a salesperson in his or her selling.

BUSINESS ETHICS AND SOCIAL RESPONSIBILITY

Most of the noncommunist world's people live in what are more or less business-oriented societies. In many countries, such as the United States, Japan, Italy, and Singapore, business is the major force—with society organized so that business values can be efficiently pursued. The success symbols of business power—status, high income, and fringe benefits such as the expense account—are admired, envied, and sought after by a significant number of the world's people who define and pursue their lives' goals in terms of business careers and values.

The right for a firm to make a profit by providing goods and services to others in a free and competitive marketplace has always been considered legitimate. The American capitalistic, free-enterprise system in particular has given most Americans one of the world's highest standards of living along with maximum individual freedom.

In the past, under the owner-entrepreneur business system, these rights were seldom questioned. But as large corporations have developed in size and power, their economic responsibility has in some cases come into conflict with their social responsibility. People everywhere are now questioning whether business has placed too much emphasis on the profit motive and too little on society-welfare values. Since there are often some business practices not in direct violation of specific laws, but not necessarily in harmony with them either, ethics becomes involved.

The term *ethics*, as derived from a Greek word meaning "custom," can be defined as the body of moral principles or values governing or distinctive of a particular culture or group.

Ethics within a given society pertains to commonly accepted standards of right and wrong behavior. *Business ethics* are the socially accepted rules of con-

FIGURE 17.1

Creative Code of the American Association of Advertising Agencies

ADOPTED APRIL 26, 1962

The members of the American Association of Advertising Agencies recognize:

1. That advertising bears a dual responsibility in the American economic system and way of life.

To the public it is a primary way of knowing about the goods and services that are the products of American free enterprise—goods and services that can be freely chosen to suit the desires and needs of the individual. The public is entitled to expect that advertising will be reliable in content and honest in presentation.

To the advertiser it is a primary way of persuading people to buy his goods or services, within the framework of a highly competitive economic system. He is entitled to regard advertising as a dynamic means of building his business and his profits.

2. That advertising enjoys a particularly intimate relationship to the American family.

It enters the home as an integral part of television and radio programs, to speak to the individual and often to the entire family. It shares the pages of favorite newspapers and magazines. It presents itself to travelers and to readers of the daily mails. In all these forms, it bears a special responsibility to respect the tastes and self-interest of the public.

3. That advertising is directed to sizable groups or to the public at large, which is made up of many interests and many tastes.

As is the case with all public enterprises, ranging from sports to education and even to religion, it is almost impossible to speak without finding someone in disagreement. Nonetheless, advertising people recognize their obligation to operate within the traditional American limitations: to serve the interests of the majority and to respect the rights of the minority.

Therefore we, the members of the American Association of Advertising Agencies, in addition to supporting and obeying the laws and legal regulations pertaining to advertising, undertake to extend and broaden the application of high ethical standards. Specifically, we will not knowingly produce advertising that contains:

    a. False or misleading statements or exaggerations, visual or verbal.

    b. Testimonials that do not reflect the real choice of a competent witness.

    c. Price claims that are misleading.

    d. Comparisons that unfairly disparage a competitive product or service.

    e. Claims insufficiently supported, or which distort the true meaning or practicable application of statements made by professional or scientific authority.

    f. Statements, suggestions, or pictures offensive to public decency.

We recognize that there are areas subject to honestly different interpretations and judgment. Taste is subjective and may even vary from time to time as well as from individual to individual. Frequency of seeing or hearing advertising messages will necessarily vary greatly from person to person.

However, we agree not to recommend to an advertiser and to discourage the use of advertising that is in poor or questionable taste or is deliberately irritating through content, presentation, or excessive repetition.

Clear and willful violations of this Code shall be referred to the Board of Directors of the American Association of Advertising Agencies for appropriate action, including possible annulment of membership as provided in Article IV, Section 5, of the Constitution and By-Laws.

Conscientious adherence to the letter and the spirit of this Code will strengthen advertising and the free enterprise system of which it is a part.

duct that influence businesspeople to be honest or fair in their dealings with others. Laws are specific, but ethics are based on consideration of individual or group conscience, the probability of receiving treatment in kind from others, and public opinion.

FIGURE 17.2

Avon Products, Inc.

a member of the
Direct Selling Association

and a subscriber to its nationally recognized
Code of Ethics, is proud to endorse and
support these standards that ethical
independent salespeople should follow

President
Avon Products, Inc.

President
Direct Selling Association

The Standards
That Ethical
Independent Salespeople
Should Follow

Offers should be clear, so that consumers may know exactly what is being offered and the extent of the commitment they are considering.

A description of the goods and quantity purchased, and the price and terms of payment, should be clearly stated on the order form, together with any additional charges.

Contracts or receipts used should conform to applicable laws or regulations.

Any guarantee or warranty stated by the sales representative should be consistent with, and at least as protective as, that of the manufacturer or supplier of the product sold.

Any description of after-sale service should be accurate and clear.

Any receipt or contract copy should show the name of the sales representative, and his or her address or the name, address and telephone number of the firm whose product is sold.

All salespersons should immediately identify themselves to a prospective customer and should truthfully indicate the purpose of their approach to the consumer, identifying the company or product brands represented.

Salespersons should not create confusion in the mind of the consumer, abuse the trust of the consumer, or exploit the lack of experience or knowledge of the consumer.

A salesperson should not imply that a prospective customer has been "specially selected" to receive some reputed benefit or that any offer is special or limited as to time when such is not the case.

Salespersons should respect the privacy of consumers by making every effort to make calls at a time that will suit their convenience and wishes. Selling contacts should not be intrusive and the right of the consumer to terminate a sales interview should be scrupulously respected.

All references to testimonials and endorsements should be truthful, currently applicable and authorized by the person or organization giving same.

If product comparisons are made, they should be fair and based on facts which have been substantiated.

A salesperson should refrain from disparagement of other products or firms.

A salesperson should not attempt to induce the consumer to cancel a contract he has made with another salesperson.

Society has the right to expect business and businesspeople to be ethical. And to help ensure it, in many of the world's countries, trade associations, professional groups, and individual companies have drawn up codes of ethics to guide the behavior of their members. Examples are shown in Figures 17.1 and 17.2.

In the United States, the American Management Association makes available over 400 examples of corporation codes of ethics. The Better Business Bureaus in scores of American cities, which receive financial support from member companies in their local communities, seek to promote codes of ethics for various business groups, and act as clearinghouses for complaints against local firms.

Today, due to the immense size of corporations and competitive pressures that can result in unethical practices harmful to society, more and more attention worldwide is being paid by governments, private consumer groups, and concerned individuals to the question of how business and society can exist in a way that benefits both at the cost of neither.

PERSONAL ETHICS AND MORALS

Since individuals have to make decisions, especially in business, that might affect others harmfully, personal standards of ethics and morals are important. *Morals,* defined as principles or habits with respect to right or wrong conduct, are usually identified with religion. The biblical Golden Rule, "Do unto others as you would have them do unto you," is basic to the moral codes of many.

Personal standards of ethics and morals may vary between individuals or among different groups in a society. Some people believe that another's standards need not apply to them; some businesspeople have one set of ethical standards for their personal lives and a less restricted set for use in business. In politically free societies such as Great Britain, Australia, Costa Rica, Sweden, and the United States, the question arises, "Whose ethics should prevail?" Legal rules governing conformity remain the major arbitrator, and they are constantly evolving as public opinion brings about changes in society's standards of ethical behavior.

Although every individual's behavior is influenced by law, personal morality, and group and social sanctions of right or wrong, ultimately it is the individual who chooses how he or she will behave. One's conscience will help guide one's decisions and behavior. For a salesperson, the desire to sell something of value and benefit to his or her customers, something that will bring them lasting satisfaction and/or contribute toward the welfare of society, is at the heart of the ethical and professional standards toward which he or she aspires.

While one's personal and ethical standards of what is right and wrong offer overall sound guidelines for good selling, they may not always be accurate in certain specific sales situations. Thus it is necessary for a salesperson to know about his or her responsibilities under the law.

ALL SOCIETIES ARE BASED ON LEGAL FOUNDATIONS

William Pitt, first Earl of Chatham, the famous English statesman, once said, "Where law ends, tyranny begins." All societies have devised laws to provide the rules and the methods of enforcing them to maintain order among their people, provide individual and group protection, and serve as a final recourse in settling disputes.

Law itself may be defined as principles and regulations established by a government and applicable to a people, whether in the form of legislation or of custom and policies recognized and enforced by judicial decision. Western civilization has developed under two legal systems. Noncommunist European countries and most of the world's countries formerly colonized by them live under Roman or civil law, which was founded in the Roman Empire. Most English-speaking countries, including the United States, live under the English or common law system.

Salespersons, wherever they live in the world, thus have to be aware of the laws of the nation in which they live that affect their selling activities. Since space is limited, we will consider as examples laws of the United States that affect American salespeople. Laws in certain other countries go even further to protect consumers than do American laws. In Norway, for example, laws prevent sellers from employing certain types of sales promotions (for example, contests or premiums) that are quite common in the United States. And in Thailand food processors selling brand-name food items nationally are also required to offer lower-priced "economy brands" of those same items.

LEGAL SOURCES OF AMERICAN LAW

Constitutional law is the highest source of law in the United States, followed by statutory law and common law, in that order. *Statutory law* is written law resulting from legislation of federal, state, and local levels of government, or by government agencies. Federal and state constitutions, congressional and state legislative statutes, municipal ordinances, and rules and standards of federal regulatory agencies acting under the authority of statutes comprise statutory law. *Common law* is based largely on custom and legal precedents that become established under common law; they are often incorporated into written or statutory law. Only those specific powers delegated to the federal government are exercised at the federal level; the rest remain with the individual states.

Business or commercial law is concerned with statutory and common law applied to common business transactions. Nearly every business decision or action has legal implications; disputes often arise between parties and have to be settled by due process of law. Organizations such as corporations, partnerships, and trusts, as well as other fields of business activity, are subject to statutory law; common law is the source of most laws pertaining to contracts, property, and agency.

Uniform Commercial Code

Because state laws in the past often lacked conformity, the National Commission of Uniform State Laws, working with the American Law Institute, drafted in 1957, a *Uniform Commercial Code* to standardize commercial transactions. "The Code," or UCC, as it is commonly called, regulates, among other things, general sales, negotiable instruments, implied warranties, warehouse receipts, trust receipts, bills of lading, stock transfer, and certificates of deposit. Specific interpretations of the code are to be found in court decisions concerning the code, rather than in the code itself.

Business or Commercial Law as it Affects Salespeople

A salesperson is often involved when differences or disputes arise in business, especially in matters of contracts, sales, and agent-principal relationships. While he or she is not expected to be an expert in legal interpretation and procedures, ignorance is no defense if he or she is implicated personally in a conflict.

Not only should every salesperson have some familiarity with basic business or commercial laws, especially those concerning contracts, property, agency, negotiable instruments, and sales, but also with other laws and regulations aimed at regulating activities of business in the marketplace and protecting the consumer. We shall now consider some of these laws, the agencies that enforce them, and some of the more important issues connected with them that are of special importance and interest to American salespeople.

BASIC LAWS REGULATING AMERICAN BUSINESS

Until the late 1800s there were relatively few legal constraints on American business, but by then it had become apparent that many business firms had little respect for unwritten common law, and the federal government began to enact antitrust laws aimed at maintaining a competitive marketing environment. Over the past 60 years in particular, as corporations have grown in size and power, both the federal government and many states have placed increasing restraints on business in the form of laws affecting price and competition, labor, protection of the environment, and regulation of many industries such as communications, public utilities, and transportation. And, in more recent years, numerous laws have been passed to protect consumers by regulating sales/marketing activities.

The principal statutory laws of concern to most salespeople can be found under the headings of major antitrust laws and major consumer legislation. There is also a variety of other laws and ordinances of concern to special groups of salespeople—for example, the so-called Green River ordinances. Here are highlights of some of these different types of laws, and how they are enforced.

Major Federal Antitrust Laws

There are four federal antitrust acts that are of special concern to most American sales/marketing people.

1. *The Sherman Antitrust Act (1890).* This was the nation's first major legislation aimed at prohibiting monopolies and certain types of restraint of trade. It declares illegal every contract, combination, and conspiracy in restraint of trade or commerce that crosses state boundaries. Here are but two of the many items it covers:

   - *Resale restrictions* set by a company to the effect that its customers can resell its products or services to a specific clientele have generally been held by the courts as illegal under this act when competition is proved to have been substantially lessened.

   - *Conspiracy.* It is illegal, under this act, regardless of the effect on competition, for competitors to conspire or make an agreement to set prices, terms, or conditions of sale, or to divide up or assign territories. The granting of exclusive territories, for example, by a buyer to a seller is circumscribed by this act, and such arrangements are increasingly being viewed by the courts as per se or outright violations of the law.

2. *The Clayton Act (1914).* This act clarified and strengthened the Sherman Antitrust Act by prohibiting specific monopolistic practices such as:

   - *Price discrimination* that favors one customer over a competitor (as well as inducements of such favoritism) where the effect would be anticompetitive.

   - *Tying contracts* in which a customer has to buy a product he or she does not want or need to get a product he or she does want or need.

   - *Merger of corporations* where the probable effect would be to lessen competition or to tend to monopolize.

   - *Interlocking directorates* of competing corporations, where the probable effect would be anticompetitive.

3. *The Federal Trade Commission Act (1941).* This act prohibits unfair methods of competition and unfair or deceptive practices, such as:

   - *Reciprocity,* or the requirement by a buyer that those from whom he or she purchases must also be buyers of his or her products, is prohibited under this act when a substantial amount of commerce is involved and where reciprocity is prevalent and systematized.

   - *Commercial bribery,* the offering of bribes by a seller to a buyer in order to induce the buyer to purchase the seller's products, is viewed as an unfair practice under this act.

   - *Delivered pricing policies* also fall under this act if their effect is construed as similar to that of price collusion between sellers. Delivered pricing concerns the quotation of prices by a seller so that all customers within a given area pay the same price for a given product regardless of differences in shipping costs from the seller to his or her customers.

4. *The Robinson-Patman Act (1936).* This amended the Clayton Act by placing further restrictions on discriminatory prices, prohibiting fictitious broker-

age allowances, and placing more control on the use of promotional allowances. This act can affect policies such as:

- *Price discrimination by buyers:* the requirement by a buyer that a seller offer him or her a price lower than that offered or available to his or her competitors. Such policies are directly circumscribed by this act.
- *Refusal to deal:* the right of the seller to choose his or her own customers or to stop serving a customer if they are so employed as to substantially lessen competition.
- *The offering of special incentives for seller's employees,* while generally permitted, is limited by this act, and by Federal Trade Commission (FTC) rules, if they can be shown to injure competition substantially, as are certain types of *functional discounts.*

The Robinson-Patman Act also created the Federal Trade Commission (FTC) to enforce the Clayton Act by giving it the power to define, investigate, and prosecute unfair methods of competition. We shall have more to say about the FTC shortly.

Major Consumer Legislation

The list of federal laws to protect the American consumer is so lengthy and varied that we can only briefly mention a very few of them. Some of the acts noted are considered as both antitrust and consumer legislation. One of the first such laws was the *Federal Food and Drug Act (1906),* which forbade the manufacture, sale, or transport of adulterated or fraudulently labeled foods and drugs in interstate commerce. *The Flammable Fabrics Act (1953)* prohibited the interstate shipment of any wearing apparel or interior furnishings (rugs, carpets, upholstery, and so on) that can be ignited easily. The *Federal Cigarette Labeling and Advertising Act (1966)* required cigarette manufacturers to print the words "Caution: Cigarette Smoking May Be Hazardous to Your Health" on cigarette packages.

The important *Truth-in-Lending Act (1968)* requires full disclosure of annual interest rates and other finance charges on consumer loans and credit purchases (including revolving charge accounts), protects consumers against unauthorized use of their credit cards, and regulates the advertising of credit terms. The *Public Health Cigarette Smoking Act (1971)* restricts cigarette advertising on radio and television and amends the 1966 Cigarette Labeling Act by changing the required printed caution on cigarette packages to read: "Warning: The Surgeon General Has Determined that Cigarette Smoking is Dangerous to Your Health."

The *Consumer Product Safety Act (1972)* established the Consumer Product Safety Commission and authorized it to set and enforce safety standards for consumer products. The *Magnuson-Moss Warranty Act* (1975), while it does not make warranties mandatory, does require that all warranties offered must be complete and written in simple language; it also sets forth procedures to help consumers resolve complaints.

Others include the *Privacy Act* (1975), which gives individuals the right of access to information on file about them and the right to have inaccurate data corrected, and the *Toy Safety Act* (1984), which gives the federal government the power to quickly recall dangerous toys from the marketplace.

If this listing of just some of the major antitrust laws and consumer legislation seems mind-boggling just to scan, it can become downright scary to sales and other business managers when they consider the alphabet-soup host of federal and state agencies that exist to enforce these and other such laws.

FEDERAL ENFORCEMENT AGENCIES THAT BACK UP ANTITRUST LAWS AND CONSUMER LEGISLATION

There is a sizable array of federal agencies that, collectively, have broad legal responsibilities and powers affecting sales/marketing in the United States. Most of these agencies are a result of the flood of federal regulatory laws enacted since the mid-1960s.

Among the other more important federal organizations empowered to move against business firms suspected of deceptive sales/marketing practices are the Federal Trade Commission (FTC), the Consumer Product Safety Commission (CPSC), the Environmental Protection Agency (EPA), the Department of Health and Human Services (HHS), the Federal Communications Commission (FCC), the Interstate Commerce Commission (ICC), the Occupational Safety and Health Administration (OSHA), the Federal Reserve System, and the Department of Agriculture. This is only a partial listing—there are many more!

Among these, two are of special importance to salespeople: the Federal Trade Commission (FTC) and the Consumer Product Safety Commission (CPSC).

The Federal Trade Commission (FTC)

First created under the Federal Trade Commission Act (1914) primarily as a supplemental antitrust agency, FTC has broad powers in two areas that greatly affect American sales/marketing—(1) antitrust and (2) consumer protection. Over the years Congress kept giving it ever more oversight powers, including (in 1938) explicit power to protect consumers from "unfair and deceptive" practices. Since that time, FTC has had a number of other consumer protection laws specifically assigned to it.

Today, the FTC is an independent administrative agency with such broad power to oversee specific sections of the economy and to initiate action on a nationwide basis that, in spite of the fact that its action can be vetoed by Congress, many Americans have proposed limits on its powers.

In its efforts to keep competitors competing fairly, the FTC has increasingly named specific companies and specific company officers as liable and responsible for deceptive selling, advertising, or other practices.

To see how its actions may affect salespeople, let us see what the FTC may consider grounds for prosecution in the antitrust and consumer protection areas.

Antitrust. The basic and most important of several laws relating to antitrust administered by the FTC is the Federal Trade Commission Act of 1914. Here are but a few business practices the FTC has found to be unfair under the broad antitrust wording of the FTC Act (that is, "Unfair methods of competition in or affecting interstate commerce are hereby declared illegal"):

- *Price fixing and division of markets.* Agreements among competitors to (1) raise or otherwise control prices; (2) tamper with the price structure; (3) divide up sales territories; or (4) curtail sources of supply, thus allowing market forces to drive up the prices bid for a product.
- *Exclusive dealing.* Keeping a customer by one means or another from buying from competitors.
- *Boycotts.* Refusing to buy from sellers in an attempt to force them to give preferential treatment to the buyer either individually or in combination with other buyers.
- *Breach of contract.* Inducing breach of contract between competitors and their customers (that is, taking away sales already contracted for by a competitor).
- *Bribery.* Secret bribery of buyers or other employees of customers to increase sales to those customers.

Consumer Protection. Section 5 of the FTC Act, as amended by the Magnuson-Moss FTC Improvement Act of 1974, offers an intentionally broad law to give the FTC the flexibility needed to deal with the myriad ways a consumer can be deceived. Over the years the commission has refined the meaning of "unfair and deceptive practices" to cover many misleading forms of advertising and sales practices. Here are just some of the many practices that the FTC considers illegal and grounds for prosecution, or has rules about:

- *"You have been specially selected . . ."* This appeal to vanity has produced substantial profits to many a vendor. A salesperson approaches the prospect and announces that a new product is being introduced (or an established product is being given a promotional sales campaign), and that it is to the company's advantage to have the first customers be people of prestige in their locality. These "favored" few will get a reduction in price. Under the glow of flattery, the prospect signs a sales contract for the product at the same price any other buyer with enough money to make a down payment could buy it for.
- *"You can earn up to $$$ a week . . ."* False representations as to earnings accounts for a sizable number of FTC actions each year. These so-called opportunities cost the buyer not only money but also time and effort. Typically, the schemes involve gross exaggeration of potential earnings and hollow assurances of help in obtaining a market when, in fact, the sole motive is to sell the product or vending equipment to those being promised rich earnings. Often victims are the elderly who, in seeking to augment their slender retirement incomes, end up making expenditures they can ill afford.

- *Guarantees.* A common form of deception is advertising of guarantees without disclosure of their limitations. The FTC has issued a general guide on the whole subject of guarantees and their advertising. Among other things, the guide prohibits the use of the word "guaranteed" in an advertisement unless the limitations are disclosed.

- *"Bait and switch."* Here the scheme is to advertise a popular article at a low price simply for the purpose of luring customers to consider buying. The fraud becomes apparent when the bargain bait cannot be purchased, for one pretext or another, and salespeople, after disparaging it, attempt to switch the customer to higher-priced substitutes. This scheme has been under steady attack from FTC.

- *The fictitious bargain.* This common form of deception employs many devices to lure buyers into erroneously believing they are getting unusual value for their money. Prices may be advertised as "greatly reduced," "cut in half," "formerly sold for," or otherwise touted as exceptional bargains when in truth the merchandise is being sold at the seller's regular price. The FTC has no quarrel with legitimate bargain claims, but insists that the "former" or "regular" price (from which the reduction is claimed) must be the usual price for the product and not a fictitious one. In the FTC's eyes a former price must have been maintained for a reasonable period of time before the reduction claims are made (that is, you can't raise the price on Sunday and offer a reduction as a bargain on Monday).

- *The signing of sales contracts (or agreements).* Once a buyer and a seller sign an agreement requiring the seller to perform a service or deliver a product, they both have entered into a contract. A contract is a legal document. Some contracts are very formal and "official looking"; others are handwritten on a sheet of paper. A contract describes the exact obligation of the signers one to another, and once in force, it generally cannot be changed or broken unless both parties agree in writing. An important FTC rule provides a three-day cooling-off period that allows consumers three business days to cancel any contract over $25.00 in value signed as a result of a direct (house or office) sales call. At time of sale, the salesperson is required to give the customer a cancellation form that explains this right and how to handle it. If the buyer cancels within that time frame, and returns the purchased item, the seller must return any money or trade-in merchandise that was taken in at the time of sale.

The Consumer Product Safety Commission (CPSC)

Created in May 1973 as a result of the Consumer Product Safety Act (1972), the CPSC has far-reaching options to impose new and stringent legal actions against individuals for consumer products (not services) their company has made, supplied parts for, distributed, or sold that are found to be unsafe by the commission. While top executives of offending companies are in the gravest jeopardy, any other individual (including sales managers and salespeople) bearing responsibility for any part of production, distribution, advertising, or sales connected with any product deemed unsafe may also be affected.

This powerful regulatory agency has jurisdiction over many thousands of consumer products and is of concern to countless manufacturers, distributors, importers, and retailers who deal with consumer products under CPSC's jurisdiction. It has the power to require businesses to give a refund for repairing or replacing a product containing a "substantial product hazard." It places the onus on producers to be responsible for and liable for any products they produce and sell.

The CPSC works in positive as well as punitive ways, such as by helping various industries develop voluntary standards; when an industry complies with voluntary standards, the CPSC often decides that it is not necessary to set mandatory standards. While many Congressional panels and consumer groups criticize the commission for not having issued enough product safety standards quickly enough, and industry and trade groups criticize it frequently for overreacting, it appears that its actions to protect the public from unsafe products will continue to expand.

STATE CONSUMER PROTECTION LAWS AND ENFORCEMENT AGENCIES

In addition to the many federal laws and regulatory agencies we have noted, many states have also been active in areas of environmental and consumer legislation and in taking legal action to protect consumers. For example, some states have cooling-off laws similar to the FTC rule just noted but covering additional circumstances.

Also, many states have their own enforcement agencies—such as the Office of Consumer Protection of the New Jersey Division of Consumer Affairs. This law-enforcement agency (civil violations only, not criminal) investigates and handles complaints concerning deceptive or fraudulent advertising and selling practices (such as "pyramiding schemes") by retailers (not manufacturers) and other sellers.

LOCAL ORDINANCES REGULATE SELLING ACTIVITIES

In addition to federal and state laws, many local ordinances also exist to regulate both in-store retail and direct selling activities. Frequent consumer complaints over the years have led to creation of local ordinances regulating direct selling especially. The invasion of the privacy of the home and the irritation or nuisance of unsolicited calls have been the basis for the establishment of such regulations.

Many local ordinances are called "Green River ordinances" because Green River, Wyoming was involved in a test case that went to the United States Supreme Court. This court upheld the Green River ordinances, which state:

The practice of going in and upon private residences . . . not having been requested or invited so to do by the owner or owners, occupant or occupants of such private residences, for the purpose of soliciting orders for the sale of goods, wares and merchandise . . . is hereby declared to be a nuisance, and punishable as such nuisance as a misdemeanor.

Some Green River ordinances provide that uninvited commercial solicitation in person or by telephone is allowed only during certain hours of the day, and is prohibited altogether on most holidays such as Thanksgiving and Christmas. Other ordinances prohibit salespeople from soliciting when homes are posted with "No Soliciting" signs. It pays salespeople to carefully check the local ordinances of any city or municipality in which they plan to sell.

PERSONAL RESPONSIBILITIES

The modern salesperson, wherever he or she lives and works, as the face-to-face link between producer and customer, is in the very eye of the swirling storm of social, legal, and ethical issues and problems we have been considering.

These issues and problems will continue to simmer and grow throughout the rest of this century and into the next as society seeks the goal of a proper balance between the rights of the producer, the distributor, and the end consumer which will produce an orderly and efficient sales/marketing structure. Salespeople, individually and collectively, should do what they can to help attain this worthwhile goal.

"But what can I, as an individual, do?" you might ask. Obeying the law in spirit as well as deed is, of course, part of the answer. But beyond that, the answer depends on the personal ethics and standards set by individual salespeople toward company, customer, and society, and toward themselves. Let us briefly examine some of the responsibilities you might face in these areas as a salesperson.

Toward Your Company

When you join a company or organization, we can assume in this day of enlightened business that it has extended to you many important rights, benefits, and privileges. But since any relationship is a two-way street, it is fair to examine the responsibilities toward your company you are expected to assume in return for your salary or commission.

To begin, if your employer has entrusted you with outside sales work, its executives are not likely to know if you goof off or spend an afternoon a week at the movies. You are ambitious and naturally will not do that, but it is fair enough to state that your employer expects an honest day's work for wages paid.

Your company is something to be proud of. Some salespeople think it is smart or clever to knock their company. This is an immature attitude, of course, and customers wonder what such a person may say about them to others. If you are willing to accept company pay, you owe it a certain loyalty or should get off the bandwagon.

Management expects you to get paperwork in promptly, just as you expect it to get you a paycheck on time. Your bosses also expect you, as their ambassador in your territory, to keep them fully informed of all major developments there that have any bearing on your work or its potential. They should not have to constantly ask for it; you should train yourself to think as a manager does and to provide it beforehand.

A final personal responsibility is your attitude toward the spending of company money. You should always think of spending it wisely, as if it were your own, and make sure you get a good return on each dollar spent. When deciding whether to spend company money for something (such as entertainment), be practical; for a moment pretend you are in business for yourself. Then ask yourself, "If this were coming out of my own business pocket, would I spend it?" Remember, there are basically only two ways for your company to make profits: by keeping sales up and costs down. It judges you as a salesperson on both counts.

Toward Your Customers and Society

A sale should offer benefit to both buyer and seller. Before you can sell a product or service successfully, you as a salesperson have to first "sell yourself" as an individual whom the prospect can trust. This implies an obligation on your part to present features, advantages, and benefits truthfully—to avoid misrepresentation in any way. Personal integrity is an important factor here—full information should be given, not withheld; excuses should not be given, or false information or data.

Confidences must be respected. If the customer discloses (or you yourself learn) trade or business secrets or plans, you should keep this information to yourself. You should never seek to bribe your way to a sale by offering under-the-table money, gifts, or any form of kickback, and you should politely refuse any attempts on the customer's part to bribe you. If conflicts of interest arise, be guided by industry guidelines, company policy, and your own conscience in resolving them fairly.

Professional sales ethics require that you do not take advantage of prospect or customer ignorance, lack of experience, or inability to resist a psychologically persuasive sales approach; your guideline is to offer something of value that will bring real satisfaction. In presenting your proposal, treat competing products or services fairly if you have to make direct comparison, and never knock competition. Once you've made the sale, follow up and through as time and circumstances permit to make certain the customer is satisfied with his or her purchase.

In all these matters, your goals and guidelines are those of creative, responsible selling; at the heart of this is service and mutual gain, with consumer and society welfare enhanced as a result of the exchange between buyer and seller.

Toward Yourself

In the final analysis, it is up to you as an individual to set and live by your own ethical and moral standards, both personally and in business. If you are honest with yourself, accept full responsibility for your thoughts and behavior, and treat prospects and customers as you would like to be treated in their place, then you will be known as an honest, respectable, trustworthy salesperson. The ethical way is the best way to success in selling or in any other career.

SUMMARY

Over the last quarter-century politicians and social activists worldwide have been quicker than businesspeople to recognize the ever-growing consumerist movement, which challenges certain traditional and business values. This consumer mass movement continues to effectively criticize specific abuses of business such as demand manipulation, cultural and environmental pollution, and the sheer power of large national and multinational corporations which increasingly control our lives.

To answer the question, "How should salespeople respond to such criticism?" it was suggested that salespeople should welcome such criticism, just as in selling they welcome questions or objections and, as consumers themselves, try to help change things for the better. To do this, they first need to gain an understanding of good business ethics and social responsibility, and second, a sense of the personal ethics and morals that should guide a salesperson in his or her selling.

While knowledge of the latter two points offers overall sound guidelines for good personal selling, it may not always prove accurate in certain sales situations. Thus it is necessary for a salesperson to know about his or her responsibilities under the law. After noting that all societies are based on legal foundations, and that salespeople in different countries should know the laws of their country, our focus centered, as examples, on federal, state, and local laws in the United States as they affect American salespeople.

In conclusion, it was noted that salespeople worldwide, as the face-to-face link between producer and customer, will continue to be in the center of swirling social, legal, and ethical issues and problems as they continue to simmer and boil for the balance of this century and into the next. To help them cope, we considered some of the personal responsibilities that can serve as guidelines toward one's company or organization, toward one's customers and to society in general, and to one's self.

Questions for Analysis and Discussion

1.   If someone asks you, "What lies at the heart of ethical, responsible personal selling?" what will your answer be?

2. What is the difference between "laws" and "ethics" as they apply to selling?

3. Do you agree or disagree with the statement, "Consumer problems (and criticism) in the free-enterprise countries of the world are problems of friction within a basically sound system?" Explain your position.

4. What is meant by the term *consumerist movement?* Describe two examples of consumerist movement activities you have observed or heard about recently in your local community. Do you agree with their aims and methods? Explain why you feel the way you do about them.

5. As a consumer yourself, can you describe any recent advertising seen or purchase made which you feel to be deceptive and not in the best interests of other consumers or society? To what extent do you feel the companies concerned who manufactured, advertised, and sold the item should be held accountable? To what extent should the salespeople of those companies be held accountable?

6. As a salesperson, you have a chance to close a big sale that will mean a lot to you and your company. As an "implied condition" of giving you the order, however, the buyer, who is purchasing agent for his or her company, has hinted that he or she would not be opposed to accepting a free gift of a three-day, all-expense-paid trip to an expensive resort area during a major upcoming national holiday long weekend. What will you do?

7. Why should every salesperson have some familiarity with basic business and commercial laws of his or her country, and also with other national laws and regulations aimed at regulating activities of business in the marketplace and protecting consumers?

8. In order to sell a product or service most successfully, you as a salesperson first have to "sell yourself" as an individual whom the prospect can trust. What obligations are implied by the term *sell yourself?*

CASE STUDY 17

CPSC—A Powerful U.S. Government Agency Watches Business and Industry (and their salespeople)

The Consumer Product Safety Act was signed into American law in October, 1972. In May 1973, the Consumer Product Safety Commission, created by the Act, went into business. Today, there is hardly a manufacturer or businessperson in the United States who is not aware of the CPSC or its far-reaching options to impose new and stringent legal actions against individuals for any consumer product their company has made, supplied parts for, distributed, or sold that is found by the commission to be unsafe.

While top executives of offending companies are in the gravest jeopardy, any other individual bearing responsibility for any consumer product found to be unsafe may also be affected.

The Act calls for both civil and criminal penalties. The most usual procedure is to notify the company or companies involved that a product is not considered safe by commission standards and ask that it be recalled, repaired, or refunded. Should that method not succeed in removing the offending product from the marketplace, then the commission has a number of alternatives open to it. These include both civil penalties (fines) and criminal penalties (which can involve both fines and jail sentences) for knowing and willful violation of the act.

HOW CPSC PINPOINTS VIOLATORS

One of the CPSC's most active pipelines of information is the scores of selected hospital emergency rooms throughout the United States and its territories who monitor each emergency handled. If a consumer product was in any way involved, that information is funneled into NEISS (the National Electronic Injury Surveillance System) and it feeds the data to the CPSC. The system is operational 365 days a year. Injure yourself with an electric shaver this morning, and by ten o'clock tonight Washington can know about it.

Other sources of injury reports include consumer complaints, newspaper accounts, and reports from a selected group of medical examiners and coroners, and governmental agencies outside the commission. In addition to all this, consumers nationwide are publicly urged to phone in complaints about product safety directly to the commission via this toll-free number: 800-638-2772.

The CPSC, after putting all this information together, makes up from time to time a list of products that have caused injuries and even deaths among consumers. This list is public information, available from the CPSC. As each of the products on the list is investigated, and its potential dangers are researched, the commission will decide what steps, if any, are necessary to protect the public.

WHAT HAPPENS TO VIOLATORS

Before issuing any product recalls, CPSC contacts the manufacturer and tries to work out voluntary corrective or recall actions. As one example, Radio Shack (a nationwide chain of retail electronic stores) agreed in 1988 to recall outlet adaptors, sold since 1987 for use in operating electrical appliances overseas, because the adaptors may pose a shock hazard. The adaptors allow a voltage convertor to be

Case Study 17   **445**

plugged into foreign electrical outlets, allowing the use of American appliances on foreign electrical systems.

If voluntary action isn't taken as agreed, offending companies may face the following regulatory actions:

- Safety standards that set product requirements for composition, design, or packaging.
- Requirements for warnings or instructions on products.
- Orders that could involve recalls, repairs, or refunds.
- Product bans.
- Court orders declaring a product an "imminent hazard" and giving the CPSC the power to seize it.

Much publicity has been given to the commission's recalls of products from the marketplace and from consumers who had already purchased items before the hazards were apparent. When these recalls go out, a product is named, a manufacturer is named, and frequently labelers, retailers, and advertisers are named. The long list of products already recalled continues to grow; here are but a few of them:

1. Imported hand brakes on bicycles were recalled and repaired when it was found they might fail.
2. The users of 7000 color television sets were found to be in danger of electrocution, and the sets were recalled.
3. A small TV antenna booster has been found to be a shock hazard. Its retailers

have been publicly criticized for carrying the product, and its advertising has been turned over to the FTC for investigation as misleading and possibly fraudulent.
4. Metal tipped lawn darts, part of a target game, were banned following several serious injuries to children.

ACCOUNTABILITY AND A SALESPERSON'S RESPONSIBILITY

There are very few consumable products that do not come into the purview of the CPSC. Those that do not, as clearly specified by law, include such things as food, drugs, guns and ammunition, tobacco, aircraft, boats, and cosmetics. Anything else not specified in law falls within CPSC jurisdiction.

Enforcement comes down to accountability, which the commission sees as extending down into every area of every company where there is a man or woman with any defined responsibility related to a consumer product or product line. This includes salespeople!

Salespeople have the obligation to help make the CPSC work effectively on behalf of all consumers. A critical eye can save your company or organization a fortune in time, effort, and most of all money, for recalls, bans, or court penalties. Whatever your bailiwick, if you see a possible hazard, have reason to question it, and, keeping CPSC in mind, you don't like it . . . *tell somebody!* You might be able to blow the whistle that stops the train before it runs into the CPSC. That's a move that would have to be appreciated in the long run.

Questions for Written Reports or Class Discussion

1. Under which of the two main sources of law in the United States (common law or statutory law) do you feel the Consumer Product Safety Act falls, and why?

2. Good personal ethics require salespeople to sell products honestly, avoiding any real or implied misrepresentation. But do you feel it is fair for them to face possible personal civil or criminal penalties .

in selling when they know a product may be unsafe, if their company requires them to sell it? Explain.

3. If, as a salesperson, you discover that the product you are selling may be unsafe, what would you do about it first—call it to the attention of your sales manager or report it to the Consumer Product Safety Commission? Would you do this verbally or in writing? Why?

4. Do you agree more with certain consumer groups who criticize the CPSC for not having issued enough product safety standards quickly enough, or with those industry and trade groups who frequently criticize it for overreacting? Why?

Sales Problem 17.1 How would you handle customer complaints in this land-sale situation?

As a commission salesperson for Wide Horizons, Inc., you sell undeveloped land in a forest and lake area to buyers who plan to build recreational homes on the lots they purchase. You sell this land, often sight unseen, at dinner parties and during visits to consumers' homes.

Your own selling has been highly ethical, but two dissatisfied purchasers who bought through different salespeople five years ago have just contacted you through friends to complain that your fellow salespeople had misrepresented facts during their sales presentation. These customers say they were told that the land was a good investment, that the lots would appreciate in value 200 percent per year and could be resold in a short time, probably even being repurchased by Wide Horizons, Inc. Furthermore, they had been told that Wide Horizons would develop the property by providing utilities, shopping centers, and recreational facilities.

Since no such facilities have been built over the past five years as promised, since Wide Horizons management has refused to buy back their land, and since they have been unable to sell their land on the open market at even half the original price, the two customers feel they were misled by the salespeople who sold them their land. They say that the salespeople used deceptive, high-pressure sales tactics to make their sales.

They have come to you to ask what help or advice you can extend to assist them in redressing their grievances, and to prevent other prospective customers from being deceived in the same way.

Questions for Written Reports or Class Discussion

1. What assistance or advice can you offer these two dissatisfied customers?

2. Should you report this matter verbally or in writing to the Wide Horizon, Inc., sales manager?

3. If the company's sales practices are ethical, and it wishes to avoid such problems in the future, what steps do you feel the company should take from now on to make certain consumers have all the facts before completing a final purchase agreement?

4. If your complaint to your sales manager is brushed off, and you begin to feel that the company's sales policies are basically unethical, what can you do about it?

How can you make certain that warranties are available to consumers before they buy?

You are a salesperson for a company that sells motor homes, campers, and travel trailers. Display vehicles are parked on an open lot for consumers to examine. All purchase transactions are completed in a small office, where crowded conditions and the problem of handling questions from prospects other than the one you are dealing with sometimes prevent full and careful explanation of detailed warranty provisions. You and your sales manager are discussing how to handle this situation so as to comply with the law concerning this required presale disclosure.

Sales Manager: We've got to be certain we make full warranty provisions available to prospects before they sign the purchase agreement. In some cases we aren't doing this, and it could get us into legal trouble if we don't.

You: Why all the fuss? It takes time to do that. Why can't we just give them a copy of our warranty, and they can read it later at home?

Sales Manager: Because a regulation issued under the Magnusson-Moss Warranty Act—known as the "Presale Rule"—says we've got to make warranty provisions known to them before they buy, not afterward.

You: Well, if we've got to, we've got to, but how can we do so if time simply doesn't permit?

Sales Manager: That's the problem. Do you have any suggestions on how we can do it without taking too much time at the point of writing up the order?

Question for Written Report or Class Discussion

What three suggestions can you make to your sales manager that will solve this problem?

CHAPTER 18

Sales Management and Selling

After studying this chapter, you will be able to:

Explain what is meant by the term *sales management*, and describe the major duties and responsibilities of sales managers at different levels.

Identify different types of job titles to which the term *sales management* applies.

Describe the three basic factors upon which top management bases overall goal setting for which sales managers have the responsibilities to set specific sales force accomplishment objectives.

Summarize the three levels of sales training and development programs most often employed by organizations and explain how they differ in content and degree.

Identify the two major keys to both overall business and sales management success.

Discuss how sales quotas are commonly employed, stated, and broken down as a way to increase sales force effectiveness and productivity.

Describe the three most commonly found sales force organizational structures and identify the two most often found.

No matter what type of selling they have entered, newly hired salespeople quickly become aware of the important role that sales managers of various types and levels play in their lives. From their first day of employment, they each are directly supervised by a sales manager to whom they report. This individual assigns, controls, and evaluates their work and makes periodic evaluation reports that are reviewed by higher levels of sales management.

"What is sales management?" these salespeople ask. "What specific duties and responsibilities do my sales managers fulfill in our organization's sales/marketing program? What do they expect of me; how can I best please them?"

Then, as these new salespeople gain experience, they become aware of the personal promotion opportunities available through sales management. It is not at all uncommon for successful new salespeople to be appointed as sales supervisors themselves after a year or so in the field; this is the first step up the sales management ladder.

In this chapter we answer the question, "What is sales management?" and describe the duties and responsibilities of sales managers, both those of an administrative nature (such as, recruitment, training, supervising, and evaluating) and those relating to other tasks and responsibilities of a far broader nature. Also, we explore the leadership role faced by sales managers. Later, in Chapter 21, we pose the question, "Do you personally have what is takes to be a successful sales manager?" and offer guidelines on how to plan your own career toward sales management, if you so desire.

WHAT IS SALES MANAGEMENT?

In preceding chapters we learned that there are many different ways in which business firms and nonprofit organizations can organize and employ salespeople to personally contact prospects or customers. While each involves different approaches, the basic principles of sales management are common to all. The selling effort in all cases is managed by sales managers who, at different levels of responsibility and under different job titles, plan and implement the strategies, tactics, and action plans necessary for success. This process is called *sales management.*

A widely accepted abbreviated definition of sales management holds that it is "the planning, direction, and control of the personal selling activities of a business unit, including recruiting, selecting, equipping, assigning, routing, supervising, paying, and motivating as those tasks apply to the personal sales force."[1]

This definition makes clear that the primary mission and responsibility of sales management is to effectively and efficiently manage the personal selling effort of the sales force within the overall sales/marketing program. But it does not paint a clear picture of the many other responsibilities that sales managers are concerned with. The modern sales manager is concerned not only with adminis-

---

[1] Bennett, Ed., *Dictionary of Marketing Terms*, 1988, p. 178.

tering and managing the personal selling activity, but is also a key member of his or her firm's overall executive group that makes sales/marketing decisions of many types.

Before explaining further the duties, responsibilities, and activities sales managers engage in, let us note that in carrying out the sales management mission, different types of sales managers are required. The term *sales manager* may be applied to any or all of the following:

- The highest ranking sales/marketing executive (vice-president, sales).
- The head of the sales force (national sales manager, international sales manager)
- Geographic area sales managers (sales manager, Africa).
- Divisional sales managers (responsible for two or more regions).
- Regional sales managers (responsible for two or more sales districts).
- District sales manager (responsible for two or more sales areas).
- Sales supervisors (responsible for one or more sales territories or salespeople).
- Any other ranking for outside or inside selling of any type in which the individual is responsible for managing the personal selling effort of others in an assigned activity (national accounts manager; technical sales manager; manager, inside sales; manager of telemarketing).

WHAT DO SALES MANAGERS DO?

Sales managers, along with other types of organizational managers, get things done by working with people and other resources. In this sense, management can be described as the process of planning, organizing, directing, and controlling organizational resources of Manpower, Money, Materials, Methods, and Machines (the so-called 5Ms of resource management that any organized activity works with) to achieve state organizational goals and objectives. This description builds on the definition of management presented earlier in Chapter 2.

Sales managers manage by planning, organizing (including staffing), directing, and controlling the personal selling effort to meet planned goals and objectives established by their organization's top management.

Top management of a business firm bases its overall goal setting on three basic factors: (1) sales growth, (2) return on sales, and (3) return on investment. Other long-range nonquantitative factors, such as being the industry leader, can be involved, of course, but these factors are the most important. They can be illustrated as follows:

Factor	Desired Goal
Sales growth	Annual 10 percent sales increase
Return on sales	Annual pretax return on sales of 20 percent
Return on investment	Annual pretax return on investment of 25 percent

Having set these broad business goals, top management of a business firm then assigns to sales management specific sales volume and profit objectives to accomplish these goals. Individual sales managers at various levels are judged upon their success or failure in meeting their respective assigned share of these objectives. Management of nonprofit organizations functions in much the same way.

Success most often comes to those sales managers who follow this broad two-part overall strategy and order of priority:

1.   Develop a written sales plan, or blueprint, to manage sales volume, costs, and profits for maximum profit contribution to the firm or organization.
2.   Organize, train, lead, motivate, and manage members of the sales force to successfully accomplish the sales plan.

Building on the managerial concepts introduced in Chapter 2, let us continue to explore what "real-life" sales managers at their different levels really do.

PLANNING SALES FORCE GOALS, STRATEGIES, PLANS, AND BUDGETS

It is no accident that nearly every management authority emphasizes planning and control as the two major keys to business success. *Planning* is the basic process by which management decides what its goals and objectives will be. Planning is an analytical and decision-making process that ends with the development of specific action plans.

Control is the process of making sure that performance conforms with plans. Control cannot effectively take place unless a plan or plans exist. For sales managers, as well as for other types of organizational managers, the most common link between planning and control is through a budget; a second important linkage in many companies is through "bottom up" sales force participation in planning (such as Management by Objectives (MBO) described on pages 63–64).

The type of planning done by sales managers depends on their level in the sales organization (top, middle, or operating) and the size of the organization. Top management, for example, is more concerned with broad-based goals and strategies and what policies will guide it in the pursuit of these. Lower-level managers, such as regional and district sales managers, are more concerned with tactical planning, which is directed toward the implementation of strategy through achieving short-term (annual, quarterly, or monthly) objectives.

Plans at any level may be formalized in written form, or take the form of budgets, charts, or networks. *Sales force goals and objectives*, based on sales forecasts, may be established for sales divisions, product lines, single products or services, and individual salespersons.

Sales budgets especially, as standards against which performance is measured, help control sales volume, selling expenses, and net profit. A sales budget can be defined as a realistic estimate of the expected volume of dollar and unit sales, and the expense of getting them. They represent statements of the financial resources set aside to carry out specified activities.

Most organizational budgets fall into one of three types: (1) capital, (2) financial, and (3) operational. Operational budgets are of special importance to sales managers in areas of planning, motivation, and evaluation. While different business firms may require their sales departments to prepare different types of operational budgets, three common types are (1) sales budgets (relating to sales volume), (2) expense budgets, and (3) profit budgets.

Sales managers at all levels are called upon to implement budgets and in many cases are heavily involved in their planning on an annual basis, and in their quarterly or monthly revision where necessary.

TO LEASE AN INDEPENDENT AGENT SALES FORCE OR DESIGN AND ORGANIZE YOUR OWN—THAT MAY BE THE QUESTION

Many small businesses start out with one or two bright individuals inventing or developing a product or service that they wish to market themselves. Frequently, lack of start up money is not their major problem; two bigger problems (requiring outside expert assistance) are likely to be (1) how to develop a good business plan and (2) how to go about marketing their "baby". A common solution to the latter problem is to lease or hire an independent agent sales force (sometimes called independent manufacturers representatives) to do the selling for them.

It is not unusual for small businesses to have their own staff Vice President of Sales and Marketing who personally calls on key accounts, supervises a show-room and a "Gal Friday" (who handles clerical duties and assists in the show-room), and works with the firm's outside, independent sales agent organization. The agent's salesforce is comprised of independent manufacturer's or agent sales reps who work under contract as exclusive agents for the producer's products in an assigned geographical area.

Nearly all such independent agent sales organizations have their own offices and showrooms, and represent several manufacturer/producers, some of them perhaps with directly competing products. Normally working on a commission-only basis, the job of these reps is strictly to sell. Orders taken by them are usually sent directly to the manufacturer/producer for fulfillment, and the after-sale handling of any customer questions or problems.

Advantages and Disadvantages of Using Independent Agent Sales Organizations

Small companies who engage outside, independent sales agent organizations to do their selling for them, while enjoying certain advantages, face at the same time some major sales/marketing disadvantages. Advantages are that it's less expensive to lease a sales force than to maintain a company one, selling expenses are tied to productivity (thus enabling pricing to be more accurate and competitive), and the agent is responsible for his own medical, disability, and unemployment insurance coverages. Also, some customers prefer to see sales agents who both represent several competing lines and, as sales specialists, have good overall product knowledge.

A major disadvantage in using outside sales agents is the lack of direct sales/ marketing control by the manufacturer/producer. The agents, as independents, manage their sales territories as they see fit and, since they normally represent several product lines, decide themselves how and when to push a specific product or needed promotional followups. They tend to concentrate selling time where it will produce greatest immediate personal profit, and spend little if any time on preparation of sales forecasts or sales reports for the clients they represent. Use of sales agents limits a producer's aggressiveness and responsiveness to needs of the marketplace, and may retard rapid company growth.

Most small business managers prefer to have their own sales force rather than to use sales agents. Their major reason is the desire to better control their sales effort in order to maximize growth and profit potential. As soon as they can afford it, most growing business firms proceed to design and organize their own sales force.

DESIGNING AND ORGANIZING THE SALES FORCE

The overall goals, objectives, and strategies of a business firm or nonprofit organization, based on the needs and wants of the market or markets to be served, form the basis for the design or structure of its sales force.

While there is no "one best way" to design and organize a sales force, three key concepts that underlie planning for such are (1) define objectives, (2) group activities (rather than people), and (3) fix individual job position, authority, and responsibility. These concepts represent a general yet basic three-step procedure to be followed, in either developing a sales organization from scratch, or in revamping and improving an existing one.

Three Basic Sales Force Organizational Structures

In an effort to coordinate all the different elements of the sales organization into an effective and efficient unified whole some sort of formal structure is necessary. This is usually reflected in a formal *organization chart*, which is a diagram of the functions, departments, or job positions of the organization and how they are related.

While such charts do not reflect the actual degree of responsibility and authority at each managerial level, nor the informal relationships and channels of communication that are so important to a smoothly functioning organization, they do help define managerial authority, responsibility, and accountability.

While there can be many variations of structures, most sales organizations are organized along the lines of one of the following three basic types: (1) line organization, (2) line and staff organization, and (3) functional organization, the first two of these types being most widely used. These can be briefly explained and illustrated as follows:

Line Organization.   This type is most often used by small to medium-sized organizations where it is desirable to have a high degree of centralized control. As illustrated by Figure 18.1, its chain of command runs from the chief executive downward with each level responsible only to one manager at the next higher level.

Line and Staff Organization.   This type is used in some form by a majority of the world's large and medium-sized business firms. As illustrated by Figure 18.2, it combines the best features of the line form of organization, which provides direct control and rapid communication upward and downward along the chain of authority, with the added advantage of providing staff specialists to assist line managers.

Functional Type of Sales Organization.   Under this form of organization, the principle of specialization is employed to the fullest extent by assigning duties, authority, and responsibility according to functions. Whereas under the line and staff-type specialist executives such as the advertising manager normally have only *advisory authority*, under the functional type, as illustrated by Figure 18.3, they have full *line authority* over their function wherever it appears throughout the organization. While this can speed program implementation and aid follow-through and control, confusion is all too likely to arise when lower-level sales managers or salespersons receive orders from more than one person.

FIGURE 18.1   *Line Organization in a Sales Department*

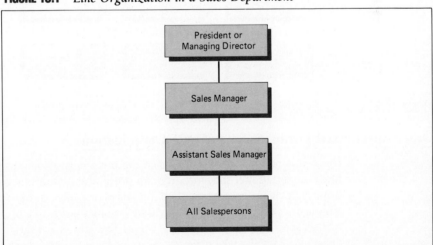

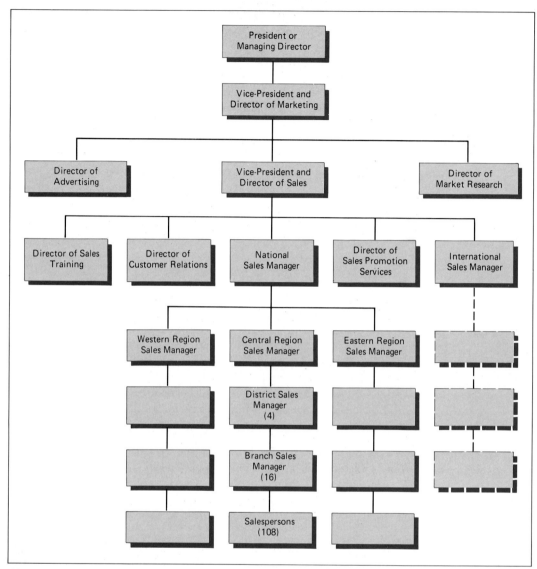

FIGURE 18.2 *Line and Staff Sales Organization*

Other Specialized Forms of Sales Force Organization

Up to this point we have considered the three most widely used forms of sales force organizational structure from an overall basis with line authority deriving from the chief sales executive. As the sales force increases in size, however, the administrative burden on this executive becomes more difficult, and the need for further specialized organization becomes evident. As a result, new groupings or divisions of activity take place, each headed by executives charged with managing specialized areas of operations, each reporting to the chief sales executive.

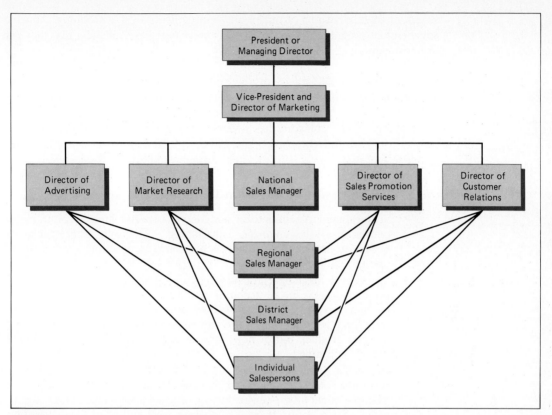

FIGURE 18.3 *Functional Type Sales Organization*

Normally this regrouping involves subdividing the field sales force along some form of sales specialization, such as by (1) geographic area, (2) by customer type (classed by industry, size, or channels of distribution), (3) product, (4) a combination of these three, or (5) along more innovative lines, such as by selling teams, special task forces, national account sales forces, or technical sales groups. Here are some examples:

By Geographic Area. Organization of sales territories by geographic area, depending on actual or potential sales volume, may vary, say in the United States, from one city block in New York City, to a single state, to a region, such as six or more southeastern states. In establishing such territories, the number and clustering of current customers and prospects for efficient coverage (in both time and expense) is an important consideration, second only to profit-potential of the territory.

By Customer Type. While assignment of a salesperson to certain customers, classed say by industry, may also fall within specific geographic areas, the idea is that he or she will sell only to a specified industry, such as to automobile repair shops, or to subdivisions of this or any other allied industry grouping. A major advantage of assigning salespeople by customer type lies in the fact that they get to know that customer type thoroughly.

By Product. Assignment by product line can also be made within a specific geographic area. The chief advantage of this form of assignment lies in the fact that the salesperson soon develops in-depth knowledge about the products. A disadvantage, if the company has several product lines, is that different salespeople from the same company might call on the same prospect, and cause him or her to feel that time is being wasted through duplication of sales effort.

Other More Innovative Types of Organization Include:

- *Selling Teams.* A selling team, assigned to a specific large account, might consist of a sales engineer, a marketing expert, and other specialists needed to handle all customer requirements from selling through after-sale servicing.
- *Special task force.* Special task forces are often used to introduce a new product quickly to all accounts or prospects within a given area by telephone, special presentations, or sales calls. Sometimes the entire sales force is turned into a special task force, concentrating on nothing but one product, old or new, for one day, or an even longer specified period, at a time.
- *National account (or key account) specialists.* Frequently a few very large accounts constitute a large percentage of an organization's sales. An example might be the central buying office of a large chain store organization. Such accounts require special, frequently full-time, attention provided by highly trained salespeople or even sales executives. Many firms set up separate sales divisions or teams to handle these major accounts. Such firms might also set up another separate sales division or team to sell only to federal, state, or provincial buying centers.

Whatever method is employed in sales force design, organization, and assignment, the objective is that of earning profits in acceptable excess over the cost of getting the sales. The changing marketplace leads to constant reevaluation, and often to sales-force changes as the need arises.

STAFFING, TRAINING, DIRECTING, AND MOTIVATING THE SALES FORCE

In carrying out the second part of the broad two-part strategy for success noted on page 452, sales managers face a wide range of tasks and responsibilities. Intertwined with the ongoing mix of planning, organizing, directing, and controlling are many specific administrative tasks traditional to management of the sales force, as well as those of a far broader nature. Let us consider some of the more important of these.

Among the most important sales management activities are those of (1) determining sales-force requirements, (2) recruiting well-qualified applicants, (3) selecting from among applicants the most desirable ones, and (4) hiring the ones selected.

The stakes are high throughout this process for the following reasons. Hiring of poorly qualified or inadequately motivated sales force personnel can cost an organization dearly in terms both of possible loss of future sales and profits and of time and money spent in training them. Able people who become dissatisfied and leave represent not only the time, effort, and money lost in training, but also the productivity, enterprise, and leadership they could have contributed over the years as they gained experience and moved up in managerial ranks.

Every inexperienced salesperson hired represents a gamble, since it may be some time before the sales he or she brings in begin to exceed the costs accumulated in recruiting, training, and compensating him or her. The time needed for inexperienced salespeople to begin paying their own way varies from six months to a year for many types of selling, up to from two to five years in some highly specialized or technical areas of selling. Due to these reasons careful planning and follow-through of staffing is essential to success.

Specific responsibility for sales-force recruitment, depending on a firm's policy, may be assigned to the personnel department or to sales management, or may be shared jointly. In most cases the personnel department is responsible for recruiting and preliminary screening, with sales management making the final selection. In all cases, the personnel department and sales management work in close cooperation, due in part to the many national laws, and in some countries, state or provincial laws as well, that must be strictly adhered to. In the United States, for example, there are federal laws pertaining to equal employment opportunities and equal job rights that are of major concern to American personnel and sales managers in the area of recruitment and selection.

Most of the world's countries have laws that affect the hiring, working conditions, dismissal, and retirement of nationals within the country by domestic or foreign firms or organizations. In many European countries, such as the United Kingdom or Denmark, for example, while it is easy to hire salespeople, dismissing them for whatever reason is far more complicated and difficult than in say the United States or Canada—due to stronger national worker-protection laws.

Determining Sales Force Requirements

Sales force requirements are based on sales management's analysis of the organization's internal environment, external considerations, and a forecast of specific needs over a set time period. From this forecast is developed a *sales job analysis*, which in turn involves development of written *job descriptions* (what each job entails) and *job specifications* (what kind of people should be hired) for each job. It is upon this that the recruiting and selection process is based.

Sales Force Recruitment

Once the numbers and type of needed new sales force personnel has been determined, management faces the task of recruiting well-qualified applicants. Most larger business firms have ongoing recruiting programs aimed at developing more applicants than are needed to fill current or anticipated job openings in order to select the better ones. Many of these larger companies have full-time recruiters, who actively recruit at universities, colleges, and other types of educational institutions, deal extensively with employment agencies, and work closely with their firms' personnel departments in recruiting via other sources.

Many smaller firms assign recruiting as a field sales management responsibility, often utilizing employment agencies for initial recruiting and screening of applicants. Most business firms, whatever their size, look for sales force recruits both from within the company and from sources outside the company.

Sources from Within the Company. Many companies follow a policy of promotion from within wherever possible, and often offer employees from departments other than the sales organization first chance to apply for sales force openings. This offers sales management the advantage of considering applicants who already have some knowledge of the firm's products, policies, methods of operation, and possibly even its customers. Also, since such applicants have a track record of performance within the firm, the risk of failure may be less than hiring an unknown applicant, providing that they have the necessary sales ability.

Inside telemarketing sales representatives or customer service representatives are good examples of employees who may prove successful in outside selling. Selection from within the firm is especially favored by industrial sellers for whom technical knowledge of their firms' products is essential.

Sources from Outside the Company. Such sources include educational institutions, employment agencies, employees of other companies, advertising, placement services of trade associations and professional organizations, and various other sources. Primary sources utilized depend to a large extent on the educational level, technical ability, and experience sought by a given firm for its sales-force applicants.

Selection and Hiring

The all-important starting point for successful sales force development is to select and hire the "right person" for a given sales position. Unless good people are hired, all the training and development time, effort, and expense to follow are likely to be largely irrelevant.

While specific selection criteria for sales-force applicants depends, of course, on specific company or organizational needs, the emphasis generally is on seeking the best talent available—especially those self-motivated achievers who are already bent on personal and sales accomplishment. Identifying real sales achievers lies at the heart of the selection process. It is a matter of utmost importance to sales managers who are responsible for developing and leading successful sales organizations. The selection process in its entirely generally follows a seven-step sequence, which is outlined in Chapter 19.

Once an applicant has successfully completed all the selection steps and indicates a desire for employment, the company is ready to take the final step of making a firm job offer, based on mutual agreement as to financial compensation.

TRAINING AND DEVELOPMENT

The overall objective of an organization's sales training and development program is to help increase sales revenues and reduce costs through maximizing sales force effectiveness and efficiency. The first step in developing the program is to analyze both its business and sales-force needs in terms of its sales/marketing goals and objectives. Such needs can best be determined by questioning key members of the firm's top management, field sales managers and salespeople, and key customers in order to develop a list of such needs arranged in descending order of priority to determine broad training objectives. Once these broad objectives are defined, the priorities can be translated into specific programs, the type of learning required, and the specific training time and methods to be employed.

Training and development in most business firms is normally carried out at these three levels: (1) initial indoctrination and training, (2) advanced continuing training, and (3) management development training. The amount of time spent and the money allocated in developing programs for each of these levels depends on the nature of the firm's business, its specific training needs, and company policy. Trainers for the individual programs, in whole or in part, may be drawn from one of four sources: (1) line sales management, (2) staff training personnel, (3) the ranks of experienced salespeople, or (4) outside specialists. The training itself may take place at both inside company locations or in the field, or at outside-the-company locations such as local colleges or universities. When and where training takes place depends on whether the training is basically centralized or decentralized, and on the firm's policy concerning the type of sales training offered.

While program content differs between companies, there are certain similarities as to what is normally offered at each of three levels. *Initial indoctrination and training programs* normally cover: (1) knowledge of the company, its products, policies, and promotional support; (2) knowledge of the marketing environment and the competition; (3) fundamental selling skills; and (4) principles of time and territory management. *Advanced continuing training programs* normally provide refresher training in the four areas noted in connection with the initial training program, but also training, which is more sophisticated, personalized, and problem-centered. At this level, selling skill development is more concerned with strategies and skills in consultive selling, systems selling, and sales negotiation, than with the traditional fundamentals. *Management development training programs* center on perfecting selling skills, developing teaching and coaching skills, changing attitudes to bridge the transition in thinking and acting between that of a salesperson and a manager, and developing administrative, decision-making, and leadership skills.

At each level, many different training techniques can be used (1) *to impart knowledge*—self-instruction, lectures, sales meetings, sales conferences, role-playing, audiovisual methods, case studies or problems, or group discussion; (2) *to develop skills*—on-the-job methods include coaching (or understudy), job rotation, and special assignment training; off-the-job methods include role-playing, behaviorally experienced training, and classroom-type training; and (3) *to change attitudes*—special techniques such as sensitivity (or T-group) training methods.

If the overall training program is to achieve management's objectives, a theory of follow-up and practical methods for its implementation should be built in from the beginning. After-program follow-up techniques include such things as memos or newsletters, refresher sales meetings, and field coaching sessions (the most important follow-up method) by field sales supervisors or managers.

SETTING UP COMPENSATION PLANS

A firm's compensation policies, referred to as its " compensation plan," play a crucial role during the recruitment and selection process, and throughout a salesperson's career with the firm in terms of (1) attracting top-quality sales-people (2) motivating them, and (3) holding them. The three most widely used types of compensation plans were presented in Chapter 1. Travel and entertainment (T & E) reimbursement is normally considered as part of an overall compensation plan, as are fringe benefits (for example, medical plans, profit sharing, personal use of company car) and other incentives (such as, management training programs and sales contests of various kinds) which offer opportunity to earn extra cash, merchandise, or expense-paid vacation trips.

ESTABLISHING QUOTAS

Sales quotas, along with sales budgets, are important links between planning and control.

Sales quotas are a popular, although sometimes controversial, way to increase sales force effectiveness and productivity. Commonly employed to set specific sales volume goals and objectives, they can be stated in terms of *dollars, units,* or *products,* and can be broken down by *area, product line,* or *time.* While there are many ways to set and use quotas as a tool for sales/marketing planning and control, usage generally falls into one of four categories: (1) to raise sales volume and profits, (2) as a basis for sales-force compensation, (3) as an aid in managing sales-force activities, and (4) to help control other aspects of the sales/marketing process.

Just to give one example of quota setting, let us consider the problem faced by the national sales manager of a company whose single sales-force sells a large number of products produced by different manufacturing divisions of the company. He or she may face problems if the salespeople concentrate on selling "big ticket" items from one division, at the expense of products of other divisions, in order to increase sales. To avoid that situation, and to encourage across-the-board selling of all divisions' products, the sales manager may set up a quota percentage (expressed in either dollars, units, or products) for the product line of each division, and pay a bonus to salespeople as they reach different percentage sales levels above quota in each product line.

SALES TERRITORY ASSIGNMENT, ROUTING, AND SCHEDULING

Most of the world's business firm sales managers throughout the 1990s are likely to face, as they did during the 1980s, a business world of higher costs, lower profits, and new types of constraints. As the average cost of a sales call nearly doubled during the 1980s, the amount of time a typical salesperson spent in face-to-face selling remained consistently less than one-third. In addition, during this period, selling costs increased nearly twice as fast as average sales volume per salesperson.

Editors of Sales & Marketing Management (S&MM) magazine explained why in these words: "even though the individual salesperson has become more productive over the past 10 years, the productivity of the overall (United States) sales force has decreased. The key to this phenomenon involves an increase in the amount of time the average salesperson spends 'not selling', but rather on administrative tasks, internal meetings and travel."[2]

Table 18.1 shows the average cost-per-sales-call increases in Consumer, Industrial and Service industry catagories during the 1986-1988 period. These figures, reported by S&MM editors,[3] are based on three basic pieces of survey information: compensation data, Travel and Expense (T & E) data, and figures showing the number of sales calls made over the course of a year.

As a result of this, ever more sales management attention is being focused on problems such as how to help increase sales force face-to-face selling time, to better manage time and territories for maximum sales, to invest more time in the right accounts, and to reduce selling costs—in order to achieve the major objective of maximizing profit. One of the best and most comprehensive sources of sales-related statistics (collected from many sources) to help sales managers solve budgetary problems and control sales costs is S&MM's annual "Survey of Selling Costs" issue, normally published each February.

Business planning and control can be made more effective by breaking a market down into more manageable units. A *sales territory* is the smallest such unit from a sales management point of view, and the key element in overall sales

---

[2] *Sales & Marketing Management* (December, 1988), p. 33.
[3] *Sales & Marketing Management* (February 20, 1989), p. 8.

TABLE 18.1 *Average and Median Cost Per Sales Call, 1986–1988*

	Three Industry Average	Consumer Goods	Industrial Goods	Services
1986	$153.06	$118.46	$178.96	$161.76
1987	183.97	151.51	207.21	193.18
1988	196.79	171.57	217.92	200.87

Source: Sales & Marketing Management 1989 Survey of Selling Costs

force design, organization, and management. While the customer/prospect *sales potential* is the key determinate for allocating sales territories, these two additional criteria also have to be considered: (1) accessibility of customers and prospects and (2) the level of customer service desired. Sales territories may be based on location, product, customer size or type, or any other characteristics that enable selling effort to be matched effectively with sales potential.

Territorial Assignment Involves Geographical and Profit Potential Considerations

Commonly, territorial assignment is expressed in terms of geography, ranging from a few blocks within a major metropolitan area to several counties, or one or more states, provinces, or regions. Geographic considerations alone, however, can produce problems, for unless sales potential is the first consideration, territories might be assigned that are greatly different in the number and size of accounts and their potential. For example, in the United States, a territory in the heavily populated, industrialized state of New Jersey versus one in the less industrialized, more sparsely populated state of New Mexico would be widely different, both in potential and in work load. Work load includes travel factors, and even if the sales potential were equal in the two states, the work load involved in covering the New Mexico territory would be greater due to the increased travel requirements necessary to cover that geographically larger state.

Since maximization of profit potential is normally the prime business objective, costs involved in territory coverage have to be considered as well as sales potential. Since profitability often relates to call frequency, it is easy to understand that coverage of the larger New Mexico territory could involve more costly travel time (apart from work load considerations) than would coverage of the geographically smaller New Jersey territory. From management's point of view, the best territorial breakdown is that which maximizes profit objectives based on a grouping by customer potential, not geographic location.

While organizing a sales structure on a territorial basis is often done from scratch, such as developing one overall for a new company or one for a new and different sales force to handle a new product or product line separate from another already existing sales force or forces, in most cases sales managers are more involved in adjusting current territorial alignments in order to keep up with market, product, or staff changes. Since such changes can occur frequently, consideration of territorial assignments is, for many firms, a constantly ongoing process.

One final factor that has to be considered in assigning salespeople to sales territories is the degree of ability and experience of each salesperson. A new salesperson, for example, might be given a smaller sales territory until enough experience is gained to produce favorable results in a larger territory. More experienced salespeople, on the other hand, might be given a larger sales territory due to their proven ability and experience.

Once a sales territory is set and assigned, sales management must see to it that it is covered as effectively and efficiently as possible by the assigned "territory manager" salesperson. This involves sales forecasting and developing a composite inventory of the territory, and programming and scheduling the work to be done—matters that we discuss in Chapter 20.

MORALE, MOTIVATION, AND COMMUNICATION

One of the most important tasks faced by sales managers is that of maintaining morale of their sales force, and that of motivating both the sales force as a whole and that of each individual salesperson to produce as close as possible to potential and ability. These are never-ending and often frustrating tasks due to the fact that many salespeople work alone so much of the time under often trying circumstances and in some cases may not be in physical contact with even their immediate sales manager for weeks at a time.

Morale often depends on the satisfaction people obtain from their work; if sales are going well, for example, morale is usually high; if sales are poor, morale may go down. At the same time, on an individual basis, morale can be affected by factors outside the work environment, such as illness, family problems, and financial problems. Sales managers spend a great deal of time, at sales meetings and on a one-to-one basis with individuals, in trying to maintain a high esprit de corps of the sales force as a whole, and of raising the morale of individuals who appear to be in a slump.

Motivation is a more difficult problem than morale because motivation is based on complicated psychological factors within each individual. A sales manager, except under rare circumstances, cannot alone motivate his or her salespeople; they must motivate themselves. Sales managers not only have to be acquainted with the theories advanced by leading behavioral psychologists as to what motivates people (we touched on the topic of motivation in Chapter 3), but also must understand how to put these theories to work in a practical way.

Factors that affect motivation can be found within three levels of the organizational environment: (1) those unique to the individual salesperson such as specific needs, interests, abilities, and attitudes; (2) those relating to the sales job itself, such as the degree of authority to make decisions or the level of responsibility; and (3) those involved within the organizational environment itself, such as opportunities for advancement, peer relationships, or managerial practices.

Each of these three factors pose different problems for sales management. Adequate compensation, praise, recognition, and rewards of various kinds, offered within an open, positive, and participative environment, are just some of the many techniques that can be employed to enhance motivation.

Good up and down communication between sales management and members of the sales force is essential to maintaining high morale and positive motivation. One-to-one consultations, sales meetings and sales contests, frequent telephone calls, newsletters, and memos are among the many techniques that sales managers employ to keep the lines of communication open.

PLANNING AND CONDUCTING SALES MEETINGS AND CONTESTS

Workshops and sales meetings play an important role in maintaining good morale and motivation throughout a sales organization, and are a highly effective aid to up and down communication. In many local area sales organizations, sales meetings are held on a weekly basis. In large national sales organizations a salesperson may attend, during a given year, two district level meetings, one regional meeting, and one national sales meeting. At such meetings new product information and new selling skills are imparted, discussed, and practiced via role-playing and other techniques. Mutual sales problems are discussed, and salespeople and sales managers get to know one another better on an informal, social basis.

Due to the importance of such meetings, and the cost involved in bringing salespeople in from the field to attend them, sales managers devote a great deal of time to planning, organizing, and conducting sales meetings.

Sales contests of various types are often announced at such meetings and awards are presented to winners of previous contests. When such contests are used to stimulate competition and interest among sales districts or among individual salespeople, considerable sales management attention has to be devoted to them.

SUPERVISION, CONTROL, AND PERFORMANCE EVALUATION

As has been noted, planning and control are the two major keys to business success. There is little point in setting company and individual goals and objectives unless these are checked against overall and individual performance. For sales managers, as with other types of managers, control and performance evaluation for both the total selling function and individual salespeople involves four basic steps.

1. *Establishing standards and methods for measuring performance.* For the individual salesperson, such standards can be expressed in *monetary terms* ("Your sales quota for June is $40,000"), in terms of *activities* ("Your call average quota for June will be eight current customers and two new pros-

pects daily"), in terms of *time* (To reach your June quota of $40,000, your daily objective will be $2000, your weekly objective $10,000"), and in many other ways. Some standards of performance are *quantitative* (that is, measurable); others can be expressed in *qualitative* terms (such as, sell more top-of-the-line items); and still others can be related to the completion of *projects* (for example, if a salesperson is directed to develop a sales forecast for his or her territory, the standard of performance is the forecast itself).

2. *Measuring actual performance.* This is an ongoing task for sales managers, with the frequency of checks dependent on the types of activity being measured. Such checks can range from personal observation during field work with individual salespeople to more formal written control comparisons (such as, sales or budget comparisons).

3. *Comparing performance against standards and identifying any deviations or variances.* If performance checks against preset standards, this is simply "good news." Inadequate performance, however, calls for prompt analysis to find out *why* performance is not up to par. Perhaps the cause is due to some temporary circumstance (such as a strike or adverse weather that affects sales for a short period) and not to the basic plan itself. If the cause is more serious, then the real cause must be determined. Is it an overall problem, such as low sales-force morale? Or is it an individual problem due to personal, marital, or financial problems?

4. *Taking corrective action* (if necessary). For example, let's say that an overall sales decline has been noted. If the cause is a temporary one, all that may be required is a short-term extra sales effort, such as aiming to sell 10 percent more per week until sales are back on target. If the cause is more serious, a revamping of the sales force may be required in order to concentrate salesperson effort on greatest potential areas even if this means temporary or longer-duration territorial reassignment.

This entire control and performance evaluation process is a most important task of sales management, one requiring constant attention and supervision. Sales and profit performance criteria for individual salespeople may include all or most of these areas: total forecasted net sales versus actual net sales, sales per customer, average order size, percentage of market share, average of sales per call, percentage of sales versus quota, expenses as a percentage of sales, gross margin as a percentage of sales, and profit as a percentage of sales.

The overall planning and control process often works best when sales management employs a Management by Objectives (MBO) system, where planning and performance evaluation between sales manager and salesperson is on a formalized, yet one-to-one, basis.

SALES MANAGEMENT TASKS OF A BROADER NATURE

Apart from the administrative tasks just noted, sales managers of business firms especially are involved in many other tasks that relate to organizing, managing, and controlling the sales effort. These occur both within and outside the firm.

Within the firm, they must establish effective up and down lines of communication both formal and informal, not only within the sales organization itself, but also with other departments or areas of the firm (accounting, credit, advertising, personnel, manufacturing, shipping). Externally, they must establish effective lines of communication with distributors, customers, and the public at large.

While the topic has already been considered, the depth to which sales managers are involved in planning on a broad basis must be highlighted. For most sales managers, planning involves constant ongoing market analysis, sales forecasting, budget formulation, establishment of specific target objectives and action plans to reach them, and performance and evaluation criteria.

Other tasks involve participation with top management—to an extent that varies within different firms—in helping make sales/marketing decisions concerning product, pricing, advertising, sales promotion, and channels of distribution. They must face and handle competition and often rapidly changing market shifts.

All these tasks, administrative and others of a broader nature, are conducted within an environment of constant change where the business goal of profit maximization has to fit into the broader context of changing societal issues such as ecology, environment, and ethics.

THE "REAL LIFE" ACTIVITIES OF SALES MANAGERS

As you may have guessed by now, sales managers at all levels lead very busy, challenging, and often exciting lives. In general, they have far less time for "reflective managing" than do other types of managers within a business firm. This is due in part to the fact that the sales-force activities are largely external (away from a central office) and involve working with individual salespeople at many different locations. This means that sales managers spend a great deal of time acting as "problem solvers" or, to put it another way, as "fire fighters" in handling innumerable problems on a daily basis as they arise. Most sales managers spend a great deal of time out in the field conducting sales meetings or workshops, and working on a one-to-one basis with individual salespeople.

The "real-life" activities of sales managers have been described in many different ways. McGill University's Professor Henry Mintzberg, for example, after observing scores of sales managers at work, has concluded that they can best be described as people on the move, with activities characterized by brevity, variety, and discontinuity. He found that they are more oriented to action than to reflection, and spend nearly three-fourths of their time in oral communication (over the phone, in meetings, and face to face) with others.

Another description is this:

> In most organizations the most unpopular person is the sales manager. He is supposed to be out selling, but is seems the guy always has his nose into other things.
>
> He is concerned with quality control. He gets his fat fingers into production and shipping schedules. He interferes in billing procedures and credit. You'd think

he was a design engineer, the way he demands product changes. As a matter of course he is involved with the advertising and promotion, naming publications where he thinks advertisements should appear, and generally making the advertising manager's job a more demanding one. You'll also find him trying to influence pricing structures, and he becomes concerned with accounting procedures—especially cost accounting. Overall he is critical of personnel in every department when the job isn't being done to his standards.

In sum, he is a pain to everyone because he inserts himself into everyone's sacred territory.

Come to think of it, though, if he didn't do these things, and only tried to sell the products given him at the prices set at Headquarters, and didn't see to it that the product quality is high and deliveries made as promised, he would surely fail.

So would his company.[4]

WHAT DO SALES MANAGERS EARN?

Many successful salespeople are attracted to sales management as a full-time career not only because of the action-oriented nature of the job, but also because of the excellent compensation it offers.

The amount of annual compensation earned by sales managers varies widely, and can be measured in two ways: (1) direct monetary earnings and (2) indirect monetary or other rewards (such as, bonuses or profit sharing). Differences in educational level, job title, geographic location, industry type, individual company size, type of compensation plan, and type of selling activity account for the wide differences in earnings between Manager A's compensation and Manager B's—even when both do substantially the same thing.

Just to give an idea of this spread in earning range, during the late 1980s, a high percentage of American district sales managers earned a gross annual total remuneration of between $30,000 and $40,000, and a high percentage of national sales managers earned between $50,000 and $100,000. Many top sales executives earned between $100,000 and $200,000, and some earned well over $200,000.

Wherever they live, whatever area of selling they are engaged in, sales managers at all levels worldwide earn better-than-average executive incomes. In the United States especially, earnings by sales managers, as well as for outside salespeople on the whole, have kept well ahead of inflation since the mid-1970s.

THE SALES MANAGER AS A LEADER

We cannot conclude our review of sales management without touching on the topic of leadership. Leadership is the "process of getting things done through others." A sales manager is an effective leader only to the extent that he or she is

[4] John M. Klock, "The Most Unpopular Person" (Hazel Park, Michigan: Klock Advertising, 1978). Reprinted by permission. Klock is a former professor of business administration at the University of Windsor, Canada. He is now president of his own advertising agency.

able to influence the behavior of the salespeople being led toward attaining mutually desired goals.

A sales manager's leadership stems from two sources: (1) the formal authority derived from the job title he or she holds (positional authority) and (2) the respect and cooperation he or she commands by virtue of certain personality characteristics and social skills (personal authority).

Different successful sales managers may exhibit quite different leadership styles. Some may be autocratic, making all decisions and extending rewards and punishment based on compliance. Others depend on persuasion to secure compliance with their wishes. Some may like to consult first with their salespeople but make final decisions themselves. Others prefer the democratic approach and strive to base decisions on sales-force consensus whenever possible.

There is considerable overlap between these examples of different types of leadership, and no single pattern may work favorably at all times. To lead effectively, a sales manager must be sensitive to the changing needs both of the group being led and to those of the organization to which they all belong. Securing cooperation is the key to "getting things done through others"; the key to cooperation is leadership. The degree to which a sales manager can inspire confidence is a measure of how well the sales manager is leading.

SUMMARY

We learned in this chapter that the primary mission and responsibility of sales management is to plan, organize, direct, and control sales force activities in order to achieve the sales growth, volume, profit, and other goals and objectives set by its organization's top management.

After defining the term sales management, a listing of the many types of sales managers was presented. Emphasis was then placed on planning and control as the two major keys to overall business and sales management success with sales budgets and sales quotas as key links between them.

The three most widely used forms of sales force organization (line, line and staff, and functional) were briefly explained and illustrated, and some other more innovative types (such as, selling teams, special task force, and national—or key—account specialists) noted.

Focus was then directed on several of the more important administrative functions traditional to sales management. These included recruitment, selection, and hiring; training and development; sales territory assignment, routing, and scheduling; motivation and communication, and planning and conducting sales meetings and contests. Sales force supervision, control, and performance evaluation rated special attention, after which we considered sales management tasks of a broader nature both within and outside the firm.

Following a description of the "real life" activities of sales managers, we took a brief look at what sales managers earn, and at the sales manager as a leader. Along the way, we noted that in Chapter 21 we consider the question, "Do you personally have what it takes to be a successful sales manager?" and offer guidelines on how to plan your own career for sales management, if you so desire.

Questions for Analysis and Discussion

1. What two-part strategy and order of priority is most likely to ensure success for sales managers of all types and levels?

2. What is most often taught in initial indoctrination and training sales training programs? How long do such programs usually last?

3. Why is "quota setting" such an important task for most sales managers? How are quotas expressed?

4. Assuming that you are a sales manager, how often throughout the year would you plan to concern yourself with "performance evaluation" of each of the salespeople you supervise?

5. Why is it so important for sales managers to hire only well qualified, highly motivated applicants for sales positions?

6. What do you consider to be the overall objective of a firm's sales training and development program?

7. In what ways are sales budgets especially useful as standards against which performance can be measured?

8. From a sales management point of view, why is the sales territory considered the key element in overall sales force design, organization, and management?

"Hell Camp" For Sales Managers—Japanese Style

From their earliest days Japanese boys are taught never to shout. As they grow up they repeatedly hear that old Japanese saying, "The first man to raise his voice has lost the argument." The pressure is always there—keeping people quiet, keeping them down! Conform to the group!

So at Japan's most famous business management school, Kanrisha Yosei Gakko, where selected executives are sent to become "samurai of salesmanship," the first bit of hell is to unplug the old lifetime emotional cork! From day one of their 13-day course, busloads of the 250-student classes are driven into town to publicly shout-sing the "Sales Crow Song" at the top of their voices near the entrance to the local railway station. As always, there they are graded—loud, loud shouting is pass; anything less is fail. Here are the words of the "Sales Crow Song," as blasted out by these loyal birds of business.

> What you make with the sweat of your brow,
> You must sell with the sweat of your brow.
> What you make with tears, you must sell with tears.
> Don't be discouraged, Sales Crow, look bravely down the street
> Encourage yourself, Sales Crow,
> And fight like a warrior!

Are these corporate commandos, mid-level managers in their 30s, 40s, and even 50s from companies of all sizes, including large ones like Nissan and Honda, "volunteers" training to wrestle tigers in Asian jungles? No, they are not volunteers! They are ordered there by their companies (at a $2000 tuition fee per head) to break conceptions of themselves, and to rededicate themselves to their companies and, through their companies' profits, to Japan. And it's not tigers they are training to challenge, but American "business giants" like IBM and GE, and their European corporate counterparts.

Doesn't all this sound more like war than business? The students call it "Hell Camp"; their instructors call it "paradise." "But if it's paradise," reported the CBS News "60 Minutes" staff that filmed and twice aired a television special on the school in 1987, "the angels better bring some earplugs!"[5] Back to shouting! Everybody at Hell Camp shouts—"From the diaphragm," bellow the instructors, "like admirals!" Could these trainees really be training for "kamikaze attacks" on their unsuspecting American and European global business rivals? Some western observers feel that the school really is organized and run along the lines of Japan's wartime, kamikaze military schools.

Oh, You Harassed North American, European, or Latin American Salespersons, Can't You Happily Picture Your Immediate Sales Supervisor or Manager Here?

Typical day for Hell Camp students! Up at 4:15 A.M., then sunrise calesthenics with a towel (an old samurai ritual designed to toughen the skin), followed by fish and rice soup. March out in squads, form two facing lines, face to face, inches apart—scream several ear-splitting "good mornings." Then pin

---

[5] This case study was developed, with permission, from a transcript of "60 Minutes" television program of July 19, 1987 (New York, CBS News), "How to Succeed in Business," Volume XIX, No. 44, pp. 6–8.

onto one's chest the day's "ribbons of shame." Each recruit starts with 14 such ribbons, each listing a personal inadequacy. When he conquers a weakness and passes a test, an instructor allows him to take off a ribbon. All ribbons must be gone to graduate.

What kind of tests? Memorizing the 10 commandments of aggressive salesmanship. There are telephone tests designed to make one commanding and quick when selling by phone. There are "sales presentations" and "questions and objection handling" sessions where it's okay for one's statements to be wrong—as long as they are loud and fast. There are letters to write to your boss, promising to improve your work and show loyalty to your company. And, all throughout the long, long day, students are required to be loudly assertive, especially when proclaiming personal limitations. Collapse into bed—10 P.M.!

Graduation Day, and a Happy "Banzai" from the Survivors

Graduation day at Hell Camp is one of moving experiences—a day of great pride and satisfaction for those who pass; a day of deep personal humiliation for the up to 50 percent of each class who fail to pass. The individuals who fail will not only face their boss and family in shame, but for most their future as a manager is probably finished.

To many Westerners, Hell Camp reflects the single-mindedness and strength of the Japanese people that have enabled Japan to become such a global economic power since the early 1950s. Rather than being something sinister, they feel, the "samurai of salesmanship" concept is exciting—good for the group, good for Japan—and certainly a challenge to salespeople and sales managers of other countries.

Questions for Written Reports or Class Discussion

1. Do you feel that Hell Camp training of the type described above would work as well for sales executives of your country as it apparently does for Japanese executives? Explain your reasons.

2. What is your feeling about the constant shouting as practiced in the Japanese Hell Camp program, as a means toward improving "assertiveness" on the part of salespeople or sales managers in your country?

3. Do you feel that the deep psychological highs and lows of graduation day at Japan's Kanrisha Yosei Gakko are really good, or necessary for their Japanese executive students? Or for salespeople or sales executives of your country?

4. Do you think that a national-goal type of sales motivation program like Japan's Hell Camp might help your country better sell its products globally? Explain your reasoning.

Sales Problem 18.1   Can Wishco, Inc., make its sales-training costs self-liquidating?

Wishco Inc.'s national sales manager (NSM), Eastern regional sales manager (ERSM), and Western regional sales manager (WRSM) are in conference trying to develop a new sales training plan that will reduce the cost of sales training to zero, or as close to zero as possible. The company employs 80 independent sales agents nationally, compensated 100 percent on commission. Wishco's product is the advertising space on vinyl covers of telephone directories, which is sold largely to regional and local retail merchants. As we listen in, their discussion is moving along as follows:

NSM: Our training costs per new trainee this past year averaged $10,000, higher than the previous year. These increased costs are really eating into profits, and we've got to cut way down on them, eliminating them to zero if possible. Any suggestions on how we can do this?

WRSM: Well, one problem is certainly our high turnover within the first six months of employment. That averaged 50 percent last year. If we could keep all the new trainees for at least a year, and they all produced even our current average sales, that in itself would represent a tremendous cost saving.

NSM: You are on the right track all right, but how can we reduce the new agent turnover?

ERSM: All agents recruited are experienced salespeople, so we shouldn't have such a high turnover. Maybe we aren't screening out carefully enough those who aren't serious about staying with Wishco on a long-term basis.

NSM: You've got a point there. Currently they are hired before training starts. Maybe they don't realize at that point how tough our eight-week training program is. After all, our classes run from 9 A.M. to 6 P.M. Monday through Friday, with assignments that require an average of four hours more each night. And we have classes Saturday morning as well. Half the trainees who left last year did so before the end of the training program.

WRSM: Why don't we turn our tough training program to our advantage when recruiting by stressing that its only purpose is to ensure their sales success? By making a point of its toughness, maybe those who aren't serious will drop out before hiring, and we will have to stand the expense of training only the really serious ones.

NSM: Good idea! But let's go a step further by making the final selection and hiring dependent on their successful completion of our training program. If they don't show us during training that they are good enough to succeed at our type of selling, we can eliminate them ourselves at any point along the way.

ERSM: Right. They will enter training only on a probationary status. If they don't measure up, they will be dropped. We can have them sign a probationary training agreement.

NSM: OK, let's do it. It will greatly improve our selection and final hiring process and will make training intensively competitive. By finally hiring only serious, capable agents, we will drastically reduce turnover. Since the trainee graduates should become immediate producers, their added sales (versus our current loss from high turnover) should in effect reduce training costs to zero, or as near to that as possible.

Questions for Written Reports or Class Discussion

1. Do you think the new selection and hiring process agreed to by Wishco's national sales manager will reduce training costs to zero, or near it? Explain your reasons.

2. What essentials of successful selling do you feel should be taught in Wishco's training courses?

3. In addition to selling skills, what other knowledge and skills do you feel should be taught in the training course?

4. After completing training, do you feel that Wishco's commission sales agents should be left alone, or do you feel they should continue to be closely supervised and retrained from time to time? Explain your reasons.

Sales Problem 18.2

Could a change in focus of its recruiting interviews further help Wishco, Inc. decrease its high sales-force turnover?

Wishco's ERSM and WRSM have departed following the meeting described above; you are alone with the national sales manager (NSM). You have a feeling that perhaps part of their high turnover problem may be due to their initial recruiting, but you wish to find out more about how they do it before offering any suggestions.

You: How do you go about recruiting your new sales agents?

NSM: Well, we recruit mainly through newspaper ads. We screen replies and the ERSM and WRSM personally interview likely candidates, depending on the part of the country where they live.

You: Where do these personal interviews take place, and how are they conducted?

NSM: It's a two-stage process. Step one is a telephone interview in which we ask about their prior sales experiences. Those that seem to have the type of experience we are looking for are invited in for a personal interview with the regional sales manager. There we again closely check their sales experience and performance record, and tell them about the Wishco position.

You: Both these interviews then focus on the applicant's sales experience, right?

NSM: Right.

You: I have a suggestion that might help you better screen applicants at each stage to help avoid any misunderstanding about the type of salesperson you are looking for. If it works, it would help reduce turnover right from the start.

NSM: I am always open to new ideas—let's hear it!

Question for Written Report or Class Discussion

What suggestion will you make?

PART FIVE

How to Reach Your Personal Sales or Management Objectives

This concluding part of our book, while basically directed to the reader who is interested in a sales career, also has much to offer those readers considering how to enter and succeed in nonsales careers.

We start with a very helpful, practical chapter (19) that shows you how to go about selling yourself for the sales (or any other) position of your choice. If you are already working, the material may challenge you to go after an even better position!

Based on the assumption that you have been recently hired as a salesperson, the next chapter (20) discusses how to best set up a sales plan for your sales territory—and how to manage and work that plan most effectively and efficiently.

Chapter 21, our concluding chapter, presents sound self-motivational and applied techniques of great value to readers who strongly desire to reach high income brackets in personal selling, or to advance to sales management or top management via the sales route.

How to Sell Yourself for the Sales Position of Your Choice

After studying this chapter, you will be able to:

Describe how to go about getting a desirable sales position: where to look for such positions, and how to contact firms or organizations that may offer positions of interest.

Summarize how to contact companies or organizations you might be interested in joining, either through an employment agency or on your own.

Develop a proper, attention-getting sales job application letter and experience resume.

Describe three common steps in the employment process, and tell what to expect and how to handle each.

Identify several basic personal traits and characteristics a prospective employer looks for when considering an applicant for a sales position.

By now you have learned a great deal about selling in general and personal selling in particular; how business firms and other types of organizations plan and organize for selling—and how salespeople sell. You know enough about the theory, principles, practices, and "how to" techniques of personal selling to quickly arouse the attention and interest of any potential employer. It is now time to think about "cashing in" on your newly acquired knowledge and skills.

If you have by now decided that you wish to enter upon a sales career, you will find the contents of this chapter most helpful, for its purpose is to show you how best to select and obtain a suitable sales position of *your choice*. Other readers, not interested in a sales career, will discover that the principles and techniques discussed will also help them secure a desirable position in their career field of interest.

In presenting this important topic we first explore how to go about finding and selecting a desirable sales position. Then we review the various steps in the employment process used by most of the world's business firms and other types of organizations, and how you should handle yourself during this process. This latter review will serve two important purposes: (1) to present practical suggestions that will help you "sell yourself" during the selection process, and (2) to build on Chapter 18 by showing how sales managers go about their important task of screening, testing, selecting, and hiring the "right type of applicant" for their sales forces.

SOME STRAIGHT THINKING ABOUT JOB HUNTING

One of the first hard facts you must face as a job applicant is that, stripped of all the fancy words, you are selling your services, and the potential employer is buying your services. A high percentage of the world's business firms, organizations, and government agencies spend much time and money recruiting, especially from among university and college seniors, but they are searching for good people, not just bodies, and for potential executive talent.

In Third World countries, where really good jobs are scarce, college graduates know they must plan carefully for and fight hard to get through job interviews leading to a desirable position. Many North American and European graduates, on the other hand, often seem quite unprepared by education or outlook for the penetrating in-depth interviews and psychological testing used by many companies and organizations to screen applicants. All too often they approach such interviews without any preparation and, when rejected, are angry or demoralized, not knowing what hit them or why.

To put it bluntly, an employer buys your services at the going market price for people of your age, education, intelligence, and skills. The more desirable and sought-after the position, the tougher the competition and the more selective the employer can afford to be.

The way to "manage" this situation to your own advantage is to first find a sales position you like, and then sell yourself for it or another of your choice.

HOW DO YOU GET A DESIRABLE SALES POSITION?

The answer to this question starts by first determining what kinds of sales positions are available that look interesting. This involves learning where to look for them and how to contact the organizations that are offering them, or might offer them.

Locating a Good Sales Position

In order to get the sales position best suited to your career goals, you must start planning long before any job interviews. A good place to start is to determine the projected population and best economic opportunity growth area or areas in which you might like to live and work within your country of residence.

In the United States, for example, better job opportunities during the 1990s are likely to be plentiful in states with the fastest-growing populations and scarce in states where populations are decreasing or remaining constant.

The U.S. Census Bureau projections released in 1988 show the United States population increasing from 246 million in 1989 to 267.7 million in the year 2000, with half of this growth occuring in just three states: California, Texas, and Florida.

Other projections show that this population growth will occur in just 40 metropolitan areas. Expected to lead the way among these is the Los Angeles-Long Beach, California metro area, adding over 1,017,000 people during the period. Others, expected to add from 500,000 to 1 million people, are the Riverside-San Bernardino, Anaheim-Santa Ana, and San Diego metro areas in California, the Houston and Dallas areas in Texas, and the metro areas of Phoenix, Arizona, and Washington, D.C.

In the late 1980s population decreased in the American farm states of Iowa, Nebraska, North Dakota, Montana, and Idaho. Energy-depressed states including Louisiana, Oklahoma, West Virginia, and Wyoming also showed continued population loss during the period. Firm population gain and loss figures for American states and metro areas will result from the full-fledged official national Federal government census of 1990.

Within the geographic area or areas of your choice, you should determine the growth industry or industries in which you might like to work. The U.S. Department of Labor predicts that the leading American growth industries in the 1990s will include equipment and services, business services, electronics, synthetic fibers, computers and peripheral equipment, floor coverings, transportation services, radio and television services, aluminum and plastic, and retailing.

Once you have selected the area and industries within it that most appeal to you, you should study the potential employers within each that might offer the best vehicle for meeting your career goals. Then go after a position with them. At the same time, you may wish to check further to make certain that you haven't overlooked anything.

Further Tips on Planning the Job Hunt

Since employers seek people with specific knowledge, skills, aptitudes, and experience to help solve their problems, it pays to develop specific job-hunting goals early and to prepare yourself carefully for the contacts that lie ahead. Aimless job hunters can rarely prepare the personalized letters and focused resumés that spark employer interest and job offers, or handle themselves effectively in job interviews.

Mobilize Your Contact Network.   Relatives, friends, successful businesspeople, and acquaintances are good sources of advice about whom to contact and how to check for sales openings. Your college placement office, alumni office, and professors are also good sources. And, of course, traditional sources such as newspaper advertisements and employment agencies are still valuable. It is highly important at this stage to talk to many people, to build contacts, to investigate, *because up to eighty percent of the better sales job openings never appear in the newspapers and are never made known to any agency.* Person-to-person contact meetings are better than phone calls or letters. It's safer to ask for advice and information than for names of new contacts or job leads. Always send a thank-you note for any help.

Develop Your Professional Identity.   Start immediately to immerse yourself in your desired areas of interest. Start a file of articles, advertising, or other information about people, companies, industries, and issues of interest. Such data will prove useful in job interviews. Read the trade magazines, especially those with job-advertisement sections.

Assemble a Personal Portfolio.   Assemble any papers or work samples, letters of recommendation, lists of potential references (from whom you have obtained permission in advance), a well-prepared resumé, and any other material that might interest a prospective employer and place it in a nice-looking portfolio to take with you to interviews.

In order to determine whether you would like a sales career and to get some idea of sales work you would most enjoy, you may first try to get a part-time job in selling. Many companies offer such part-time work. Even though you are presently attending college or engaged in other work during the day, you may get a part-time sales job in the evening or on weekends. Direct or party-plan selling is one such area, and if you are successful at it, your experience will certainly help you land a permanent sales position. You can obtain a list of over 100 direct sales member companies in the United States by writing the Direct Selling Association, 1776 K Street, N.W., Suite 600, Washington, D.C. 20006. In Canada, the Direct Sellers Association is located in Toronto.

Once these planning preliminaries are completed, you are ready to make contact with prospect employers.

HOW DO YOU CONTACT COMPANIES THAT MAY HAVE DESIRABLE SALES OPENING?

Once you have decided on the area of selling that you think you would like and on the product service, cause, or idea you feel you would enjoy selling, your problem is how to contact companies or organizations you feel you might consider joining. This is done in two basic ways: (1) through an employment agency or (2) on your own.

The Employment Agency

While federal, state, or provincial national employment agencies throughout the world often list sales positions, generally speaking, they list mainly jobs in unskilled or semi-skilled categories. Private employment agencies specializing in sales or executive positions offer greater selection. These can be found listed in telephone book classified pages, in newspaper advertisements, trade journals, or at good libraries.

The problem here is to find one that will really try to help you match your interests to the most suitable openings. Some are interested only in their fee, which the employer normally pays (but not always, so ask), and not in really helping you. Check them out with friends and local businesspeople, and judge them for yourself on personal calls. You can often sense their attitude in the attention, time, and respect they pay you. Through questions, you can soon determine how well they know and handle their business.

How to Get Job Interviews on Your Own

One good source for locating sales openings in specific geographic areas is in the classified section of that area's leading local newspaper. Also, many trade associations act as clearinghouses for sales jobs in their fields. Your local library may have an *Encyclopedia of Associations* to help you locate them, or your local Chamber of Commerce may be able to help. In many cities throughout the world, local sales executives clubs offer advice. College or university placement services serve their students or graduates, and their placement officers can often prove very helpful.

Direct mail may be your best source. Simply write the president or managing director, or sales manager of any and all firms or organizations within industries that interest you; their names and addresses can be easily found through the several sources noted above. Answering newspaper or trade or professional journal or magazine ads is another good way to establish contact.

The best way to contact these sources or advertisers is to either write a letter requesting an appointment, contact them by telephone for an appointment, or simply cold-call on them in person. Whichever way you elect, prepare carefully beforehand, with a single job objective in mind and a structured sales approach to fit that objective. Prepare to "sell yourself" as a person, as you would a product, by convincing the "buyer" that your experience and talents will help him or her.

A personal letter, requesting an interview, is the most effective way to contact companies, nonbusiness organizations, or government agencies of interest to you. We mention nonbusiness organizations and government agencies as well as companies, since many employ salespeople (under another guise) to sell their cause or services. You should contact all possible organizations by personal letter. It pays to write to several if possible, since you will want to be in the position of choosing among several positions rather than just taking the first job available.

While some authorities do not recommend attaching a resumé to your personal letter, most recipients appreciate it, since it will help them evaluate you better in connection with any openings they might have available now or in the near future.

Whether sending personal letter alone, or a letter and resumé, treat and carefully prepare each as if it were the most important document you will ever write. Consider it as a sales-promotion piece. Since *prospective employers are basically interested in only one thing—what can you do for them*—concentrate on your accomplishments and not on your biography or academic or other qualifications. The more specific accomplishments you can relate to the sales position sought, the better. Use a command close in your letter. Just as in selling, if you want your prospect to buy, you have to ask for the order.

Figure 19.1 illustrates a good personal letter of application, but there is no set form to follow. Many such applications include a brief cover letter with a detailed resumé, or a listing of educational background or experience, attached on a separate sheet (as in Figure 19.2). This procedure is recommended when an applicant has a lengthy academic or job record.

If you do not have such extensive qualifications, your application can be a one-page letter.

Since this letter represents the first step in selling yourself as a desirable employee, you should do it in this way:

1. Type it neatly, being careful to avoid misspelled words or grammatical errors.
2. Present briefly and factually all important personal, educational, and work or other experience data that will enable the prospective employer to consider your potential qualifications.
3. State briefly, without being bombastic, why you feel you would like to join the organization, and what you feel you have to offer.
4. Request an appointment for a personal interview at their earliest convenience.

Upon receipt of your letter of application most companies or organizations will respond by (1) informing you that no openings are available, (2) enclosing a detailed application form for you to fill in and return for their further consideration, or (3) inviting you for a personal interview. In the event of either of the

```
                                   4632 South Bandicoot Lane
                                   Los Angeles, California 09342
                                   May 20, 1990




Mr. Colin Utterson
Vice-President, Sales
Latin American Export Corporation
178 Fifth Avenue
New York, New York 02461

Dear Mr. Utterson:

I have long been aware of the international operations of
your company and would like the opportunity to join your
organization in a sales capacity.  I have been preparing
myself for such a career in international sales/marketing
at Thunderbird Graduate School of International Management,
Phoenix, Arizona.

At Thunderbird, under professors experienced in foreign
trade, I have become familiar with the techniques of
international trade and how to apply them.  I read, write,
and speak Spanish.  I have an understanding of the social,
political, and economic situations in Latin America, both
through study and personal travel in that area of the world.

This specialized training, travel abroad, and graduation
from the University of Virginia, where I studied business
administration and marketing, are among the qualifications
I have to offer for your consideration.  They are explained
in greater detail in the enclosed resumé.

If you have any sort of a position in international sales
for which I might be considered, I would be happy to supply
further details.  If you so desire, I would also be pre-
pared to visit you for a personal interview at my expense,
any time at your convenience between September 1 and Septem-
ber 20.

Will you please write or telephone me your decision?  My
home telephone number is OR2-4168.

                            Sincerely, yours,

                            Rodney A. Molitor

                            Rodney A. Molitor
```

FIGURE 19.1

Personal Letter and Experience Resumé

PERSONAL AND EXPERIENCE RESUME

RODNEY A. MOLITOR

4632 South Bandicoot Lane   Photo
Los Angeles, CA 09342   Attached
Phone: OR2-4168

CAREER OBJECTIVE

The opportunity to participate in the growth and expansion of an
International business in the field of selling and ultimately
sales management.

QUALIFICATIONS

Through association with businessmen friends, prominent in foreign
trade, I long ago developed an intense interest in international
sales management. As a result I have oriented my academic program
toward such a career and hope to be given the opportunity to prove
my worth to your company in this field.

EDUCATION

THUNDERBIRD GRADUATE SCHOOL OF INTERNATIONAL MANAGEMENT,
Phoenix, Arizona (1988-1990) Master of Foreign Trade degree,
June 1990

> A specialized postgraduate school emphasizing the practical
> aspects of international trade. Courses of instruction
> included: international commerce and finance; international
> marketing, where I acquired first-hand experience in the
> various means of international marketing, including foreign-
> market surveys, distributions, and sale of products abroad;
> and area studies, where I became familiar with the political,
> social, and economic problems of Latin America. Through study
> under a native-born instructor, I became fluent in written and
> conversational Spanish.

Extracurricular Activities:

> Marketing Club, Spanish Club, intramural athletics,
> Phi Delta Epsilon

THE UNIVERSITY OF VIRGINIA, Charlottesville, Virginia (1984-1988),
Graduated, Bachelor of Arts degree with Honors, June, 1988.

> Majored in business administration with a minor in marketing.
> Courses of study included: Spanish, marketing, finance,
> economics, accounting, and political and economic geography.

Extracurricular Activities and Elected Offices:

> Omicron Delta Kappa (national honorary leadership fraternity),
> Dean's List every semester. Captain of varsity golf team,
> varsity soccer, advertising manager of University of Virginia
> yearbook, and second lieutenant in Army R.O.T.C.

FIGURE 19.2

HOW TO SELL YOURSELF FOR THE SALES POSITION OF YOUR CHOICE

EXPERIENCE

The Anniston Star, daily newspaper, circulation 37,000
Anniston, Alabama, 1985-1987 (summers only).

Position: Classified and display advertising salesperson. I was personally responsible for a 20 percent increase in classified space through introduction of a new technique.

I earned 25 percent of my college expenses through summer employment and through positions in college. As advertising manager of the school yearbook I increased advertising revenue 62 percent, working on a commission basis.

MILITARY SERVICE

I was commissioned second lieutenant, U.S. Army Reserve, June, 1988. I was honorably discharged, April 15, 1990.

PERSONAL DATA

Single	Born July 12, 1966
United States citizen	in Gulfstream, Alabama
6'1/2", 170 lb.	Excellent health

REFERENCES FURNISHED ON REQUEST

FIGURE 19.2 *(continued)*

latter two responses, you should follow up by telephone either to make an interview appointment or to confirm your acceptance (or to request rescheduling) of the time, date, and place they may have suggested.

Once you have been called in for an interview, you formally enter the employment process, which for the employer is first and foremost a selection process.

THE EMPLOYMENT PROCESS—STEPPING STONES TO GETTING HIRED

Between every sales job opening and applicant stands a major hurdle—the employment process with its interview or interviews and other checks. For most larger organizations, this involves a seven-step selection sequence. Before we describe these steps, however, it must be made clear that the actual process may vary between organizations; even between different levels of sales jobs the process may be confined to one interview, or an interview plus some aptitude tests and perfunctory reference checks. For high-level sales jobs the process might be quite lengthy, involving a series of progressive in-depth interviews by different executives intended to screen applicants as carefully as possible before offering to employ them. The seven steps in the complete selection sequence are

1. Completion of the application form
2. Initial screening interview
3. Testing (optional)
4. Reference checks and other background investigation
5. In-depth selection interviews
6. Physical examination
7. The job offer

In describing each of these steps, we take a two-part approach. First, as an extension of the section on selection and hiring in Chapter 18, we look at it from the employer's (and its sales management's) point of view. Second, in boxed paragraphs, we pass along practical suggestions that will enable you to anticipate and better handle each of these steps as an applicant.

Completion of the Application Form

Some employers require the application to be filled out and sent to them in advance of their confirming a first personal interview appointment. Others require it as a first step of the selection sequence at the first interview appointment. The formal application form, when completed, provides interviewers with basic information to help conduct interviews and to serve as a control personal record if the applicant is hired.

Often two such forms are used—a short one for the initial screening interview, with a longer and more comprehensive one required to be filled in prior to subsequent in-depth interviews. Legally, within the United States, questions asked on such forms must relate only to qualifications for the job itself and must avoid questions concerning race, religion, nationality, age, or the many other such questions specified by federal or state laws. Other countries may have different legal requirements for such matters.

In most cases, application forms provide information concerning personal data, educational background, employment history, experience and interests, and references applying to the specific sales position involved. Other, more detailed personal information required by federal or national and state or provincial employer reporting laws and regulations, and for insurance and other purposes, is obtained *after* the applicant has been hired.

One key purpose of the application form is to help eliminate applicants who lack qualifications or interest for the job being offered. Answers to questions such as "Are you willing to relocate?" or "Are you willing to travel two to four nights per week away from home?" help both the applicant and the prospective employer determine real applicant interest. Specific questions concerning educational background and work experience also help determine an applicant's chances for success in the job at hand. Normally, in the United States, preparation of such forms and initial selection interview use of them is done by the employer's personnel department in order to assure that all legal requirements concerning equal opportunity employment are adhered to.

Initial Screening Interview

This initial interview helps determine for both the applicant and the employer whether or not the applicant has both the basic background and interests suitable for the position. While care must be taken in the United States and some other countries not to ask personal questions of the type prohibited by law, questions can be asked relating to educational background, experience, salary expectations, travel and relocation availability, and the like.

Testing (Optional)

Job applicants may or may not be asked to take various types of psychological and aptitude tests, depending on laws of the country in which applicants are being considered, and the employer's policy concerning such tests.

In the United States, prior to the mid-1960s, many business firms and other types of organizations relied on a variety of such tests as one basis among others for selecting "most likely to succeed" sales-job applicants. Since passage of the Civil Rights Act of 1964 and subsequent regulations that required EEOC-approved validation of such tests in order to eliminate job discrimination practices, and other federal and state laws, a growing number of firms have abandoned such tests. Increasingly, they are now placing emphasis on formal educational qualifications and prior job experience as bases for selecting rather than on tests. While such tests can be, and are frequently used, they must adhere to federal and state guidelines regarding validity, and are less risky when administered by outside

Every job starts with a good interview. Here are 11 tips and techniques to improve your chances for success!

Most employers evaluate an applicant's job qualifications as well as other factors, including personality traits, attitude, interest, and ambition. The interview offers you an excellent opportunity to demonstrate these qualities and present yourself at your best. Remember: there is never a second chance to make a good "first impression." Review the following list and be prepared to make your next interview a complete success.

1. Arrive for your appointment ahead of time.

2. Good impressions include good grooming. Dress neatly—clothes pressed and shoes clean.

3. Show your enthusiasm for the job and the company. Learn all you can about the firm—your public library can help. Complete application forms neatly and answer questions openly.

4. For your reference, take along a list of previous employers' names, addresses, dates worked, and supervisors' names. If there are any gaps in your work history, you will probably be asked to account for them. Sometimes friends' names can be used for references.

5. **Any** of your skills, training, hobbies, interests, and achievements may be exactly what an employer is looking for in an applicant. List them all—completely and honestly.

6. Determine your worth to an employer realistically. Do not ask for an unreasonable salary. Rather, indicate a salary range.

7. Put your capabilities, skills, and training in writing, then "sell yourself" to your interviewer! Show how much **value** you can bring to the job, not why you need the job.

8. If you have transportation problems or job conflicts, work out solutions **before** the interview.

9. Be ready to explain why you want the job, and what you plan to be doing three to five years from now. Keep your goals in mind.

10. Relax and enjoy your interview. Always be polite and courteous. Look directly at the person and smile! If you have any questions, do not be afraid to ask.

11. When the interview is finished, thank the interviewer. Write a short letter to the person when you return home, again expressing your interest in the position.

ACME PERSONNEL SERVICE
"Where the jobs are"
Headquarters: Opportunity, WA 99214

FIGURE 19.3

Such tests help the interviewers evaluate your mentality, drive, persistence, poise, sociability, and aptitudes for the particular position under consideration. Some applicants resent such tests and either refuse to take them or quit in anger halfway through. This justifies the whole testing process to the employer, because if an applicant cannot take that little irritation, he or she certainly cannot cope with a rough business situation in which the penalties to the employer for his or her blowing up could be severe.

Many of these tests are designed merely to ask you to tell the employer more about yourself. Since you provide the answers, it is not the employer's fault if negative traits show up. Actually, you should welcome the opportunity to take such tests because they often shed a great deal of light on your suitability for the position. If they help point out that you do not have the necessary traits or aptitudes for success in selling, it is better to find it out now rather than later.

There is nothing personal involved in a prospective employer's asking you to take such tests. The company is not trying to be Big Brother; it is only trying to help you and itself to avoid a mistake. It may cheer you up to know that very few employers base their final decisions on such tests.

professional testing firms recognized by the American Psychological Association. Types of tests used include those that measure personality, mental ability or intelligence, interest, sales aptitude, mechanical ability, and social or general intelligence. Underlying all such tests and evaluations of them is the admonition of the Supreme Court of the United States, "Any tests used must measure the person for the job and not the person in the abstract."

Such tests, if required, are most often given after an applicant has filled out the application form and gone through a preliminary interview. Important in-depth interviews are usually conducted after such tests have been taken and carefully evaluated, since many questions then asked relate to the applicant's test answers and scores.

Reference Checks and Other Background Investigation

At some point during the selection process, the employer normally seeks to check the accuracy of the applicant's job application statements by contacting educational, employment, and personal references. Current employers are normally not contacted unless the applicant has first given permission for such a check.

These checks are normally conducted by personal visits or telephone calls. After the employer's representative has identified himself or herself and stated the purpose of the call, the reference source is asked to confirm the accuracy of the information the applicant has supplied and, if possible, to rate the applicant's skills and abilities. One question that is nearly always asked of your former employer is "Would you rehire this individual?"

While most employers consider it essential to check educational employment records, many consider personal references to be of little value—due to the fact that most applicants list only personal friends in that category.

More extensive background investigations, in the United States and some other countries, require careful prior checks with federal and state or provincial

Since, as has already been mentioned, key employment references are nearly always checked carefully, and frequently personal references as well, you should list them carefully and accurately on your application form. It will help to offer prewritten letters from personal references (addressed "To Whom It May Concern") attached to your application form. It may also help to notify prior employers that they may receive personal visits or phone calls from prospective employers you've contacted, so they will know in advance what the contacts will be in reference to.

agencies concerned with employment discrimination in order to stay within legal guidelines (new laws or court rulings in this area occur frequently). Additionally, in the United States, even in checking prior arrest records, the employer must be prepared to prove in a court of law the job necessity for such checks.

In-Depth Selection Interviews

Unlike the initial screening interview, which in larger organizations is usually conducted by a member of the personnel department, the in-depth interview or interviews that often follow are usually conducted by sales executives, including in most cases the field sales manager to whom the applicant will report if hired. For higher-level sales jobs, it is common for several executives, both in the field and at the head office, to interview the most promising applicants individually in order for a group consensus to be formed. Also, prior to final interviews, such applicants may be invited to spend one or more days in the field accompanying an experienced salesperson on his or her rounds.

If the applicant is married, the selection process may involve either an interview with or at least an informal dinner including the applicant's spouse in order to determine attitudes toward (and possible effects upon family life) extended periods of travel or possible relocation. If such a meeting can take place in the applicant's home, so much the better.

For many types of sales positions, this part of the selection process can be quite lengthy and time consuming. Since the employer is seeking not only the "right" person, but one who is likely to stay with the firm, reasons have to be considered why many recently hired salespeople often quit their jobs after a year or so. The leading reasons for this, in many industries, are lack of advancement, desire for higher salary, the wish to live in another locality, lack of real interest in sales work, a change in career goals, and dislike of traveling. In-depth interviews help clarify all these matters to the satisfaction of both the applicant and the employer, and help reduce the risk of costly early turnover.

Above all, and regardless of the time involved, or the number of interviews involved, the end purpose of the employer is to try to select an applicant with the "winning combination" of education, interest, motivation, employment experience, personal judgement, and maturity that best fits the needs of the specific sales position involved. The in-depth selection process helps the employers get to

SELL YOURSELF

Your success during this part of the interview lies in your ability to communicate a positive attitude about yourself and the prospective job. The interviewers will be looking for initiative and perseverance, a realistic viewpoint toward life and work, how good a team player you will make, and how customers will respond to you, so you must sell them on the fact that you possess these traits and characteristics.

As you smilingly and confidently answer their questions, you should project enthusiasm, flexibility, eagerness to face challenge, and a desire for growth. Body language counts, so sit erectly yet relaxed. Give concise answers, do not interrupt the interviewer, and don't be afraid to ask that a question be restated if you don't understand it.

HANDLE KEY QUESTIONS PROPERLY

There are certain questions that you should be prepared to answer: "Why do you want to join our organization?" "Tell me about yourself." "What are your short-/long-range career goals?"

Such questions usually mean, "What do you have to offer our organization?" so your answers should indicate aspiration and a desire to learn. Confessing that you want the job "because it offers security" or "to work with the type of people I like" doesn't show you to be a person eager to assume responsibility or constantly face new challenges.

If you are asked, "What are your greatest strengths and weaknesses?" offer negatives that are likely to be interpreted as positives. For example, "I tend to work too hard" or "I sometimes try too soon to demonstrate my abilities."

Such answers usually prove to be selling points in your favor.

AVOID TRAPS—ASK QUESTIONS YOURSELF

Interviewers are impressed when you ask them thoughtful questions about their organization and the specific prospective job. For example, "Is the job opening the result of organizational expansion, or because someone left?" If the latter, "Why did that person leave?" "What are my opportunities for advancement within the organization to sales or top executive rank?"

Avoid asking questions about salary, vacations, or benefits too early in the interview. It's always better to save these for the end, or until a firm hiring offer is made.

Keep in mind at all times that a basic purpose of in-depth interviews is to uncover any possible lack of interest in selling or basic traits and attitudes that may lead to your failure as a salesperson. An interviewer normally frames questions around such areas of potential weakness so as to further explore real interests or aptitudes. He or she may throw out unusual questions or challenges during this exploration process to get some idea of your reaction to the unexpected. Do not be surprised at anything; just meet the situation normally and cheerfully and observe how well the interviewer does his or her job.

Be patient if the in-depth interview part of the hiring process drags out and you are called in for interviews by several people. It means that they are interested in you!

At the end of each interview, when you rise to leave, thank the interviewer—by name—for having taken the time to see you. Write a short thank-you letter to each interviewer when you return home, again expressing your interest in the position.

know the applicant, and vice versa, so that if hired the applicant is regarded as, and feels, part of the "company team" working toward a common objective. Along the way, the process can involve several types of combinations of interviewing techniques, among which are the following:

Guided or Patterned Interview.   This type of interview is based on a series of predetermined questions structured to elicit a basic core of information as the applicant tells his or her own story. Penetrating questions designed to draw out the applicant's true feelings and interests run along the lines of: "What did you like best (and least) about your last job?" "What criticisms of your work were made by your last boss, and did you feel them justified?" Along with this attempt to determine the "whys" of behavior and thinking, interviewers check observable qualities such as appearance, personality, poise, communication skills, and thinking ability and judgment in handling questions. In most such interviews, impressions are recorded following the interview on some sort of a grading sheet. These grading and evaluation sheets, prepared by different interviewers, help form a "consensus picture" of the applicant. If significant differences in individual evaluation occur, this may lead to additional interviews to clarify any problem areas.

Nondirective Interview.   In this type of interview the interviewer, while asking relatively few questions, aims to encourage the applicant to speak freely about his or her experience, attitudes, interests, and future aspirations. The theory behind this type of interview is that, if encouraged to speak freely, the applicant will reveal, consciously or unconsciously, a great deal about his or her personality, true feelings, and interests. Since this type of interview requires much more skill on the part of the interviewer than the guided or patterned interview, specialized instruction in conducting and evaluating results is required.

Interaction Interview.   This type of interview often involves a "real-life" sales situation in which the applicant is asked to make a presentation to, or to handle questions or challenges posed by, one interviewer while a second interviewer (who is not a participant) observes and records the applicant's poise, judgment, and reactions.

FINAL STEPS IN THE EMPLOYMENT PROCESS

Final steps in the employment/hiring process usually involve a physical examination and in some cases, the signing of a bond or employment agreement, prior to the employer's making a final job offer.

Physical Examinations.   Since good health is important to sales success, most employers require physical examinations of successful applicants as one of the final steps in the selection process. Such an examination not only helps assure both the employer and the applicant that the latter can perform effectively in the sales position, but also, in the United States, helps protect the employer against unjust workmen's compensation claims.

The Job Offer.   As a final step to formal hiring, some business firms ask the applicant whether he or she is prepared to sign a bond that will protect the company against certain actions on the new employee's part. This procedure is usually followed only when the company plans to entrust the employee with valuable and expensive samples or demonstration equipment, or when the em-

> Once hired, you enter the company or organization training program and are officially on your way. A major step toward your ultimate career goal has thus been taken: you have obtained the position you sought. Now you have to produce in order to justify your employer's faith in you.

ployee will be handling cash. Many companies require such bonds as a matter of practice, so there is nothing unusual in their asking for one.

Some business firms also ask prospective new sales employees if they are prepared to sign an agreement to remain with the firm for a minimum period of time. They make this request most often when expensive technical training is involved. Such agreements represent an attempt to ensure that an applicant will not accept a position merely for the valuable training and then promptly resign to look for a better position elsewhere.

Once an applicant has successfully passed through all the above-mentioned selection steps and still indicates a desire for employment, the employer is ready to take the final step of making a firm job offer, based on mutual agreement as to financial compensation.

SUMMARY

Assuming that you wish to enter a sales career, we noted in this chapter how to do so; where to look for a suitable position of your choice and how to apply for it.

We suggested employment agencies or getting job interviews on your own as being the two most generally used methods of contacting prospective employers. How to prepare a personal application letter and personal resumé was explained and illustrated.

Seven basic steps of normal selection and employment process (application form, initial screening interview, testing, reference checks, in-depth selection interviews, physical exam, and job offer) were presented via a two-part approach. First, in building on Chapter 18, we looked at these steps from sales management's point of view. Second, in boxed paragraphs, suggestions were made as to how you (as an applicant) can "give them what they want" by selling yourself in terms of what you can do for them—their real buying reason.

Once hired for the position sought, you now have to produce in order to justify your employer's faith in you. How to do this is the topic of Chapter 20.

Questions for Analysis and Discussion

1.   What major thread of thought ran through our discussion of how you can best seek and land the sales position you desire? What must you always keep in mind throughout the entire application-interview process?

2. What is a hard fact of life that a job applicant should keep in mind when applying for a desirable sales position?

3. A prospective employer is basically looking for only one thing when considering sales applications. What is that one thing?

4. How should an applicant for a sales job end his or her initial personal application letter?

5. Why is it so important to prepare a personal and experience resumé so carefully?

6. What is the first step in the employment practice?

7. What key point should a sales applicant keep in mind throughout all personal interviews, no matter what the questions?

8. What is your personal opinion concerning aptitude tests for sales applicants? If you were an employer, would you use them? Why?

A Top Personnel Executive Tells What He Looks For in Applicants Seeking Sales Positions*

In our large company, the screening process consists of the appointment, a brief preliminary interview, filling out of the application blank, testing, the main interview, and, if the applicant seems promising, careful reference checks. If those prove satisfactory, he or she goes through a final selection by the responsible sales manager, and if hired, a physical examination.

We require that applicants write for an appointment and attach a resumé of their educational and employment background. We do not look for any set form of letter and resumé, but we do expect them to be neat and orderly. We are especially leery of statements that tend to oversell or statements that when challenged later in the interview turn out to have skirted the truth. We immediately notice any poor spelling, time unaccounted for, or past earnings not shown on both the resumé, and the after-employment application.

Our initial reception-room impression of applicants means a lot. Their appearance and general manner and attitude toward our secretaries or other people in the reception area give us clues on how they may fit into our company or act toward our customers. We expect them to be neat, well-dressed, courteous, and patient.

Above all, we expect them to be on time for appointments. If they cannot make it on the set date, they should call and reschedule it. We do not mind their rescheduling the interview time to suit their convenience, but since we are also busy, we expect them to be courteous enough to notify us of any such change.

Since we do observe our applicants while they are in the reception room, we notice favorably such things as their picking up our company literature from the tables and thus gaining knowledge of our company as they await their interviews.

OUR SELECTION CRITERIA REVOLVES AROUND FIVE BASIC AREAS

What Are Applicants Like Personally? During the interview, we again note applicants' appearance, manner, and decorum. We realize that their inner attitude is "What can the company do for me?" but we on our side are thinking, "We are going to spend money on you, so what can you do that merits our investment in you?" The responses they give to our questions are most important—we like positive, enthusiastic responses best. We try to judge applicants as customers would, and for salespeople, such judgments can be vitally important.

What Have They Done? We like enthusiastic yet objective responses to questions about education, training, and past work experience. For first-job applicants we like such statements as "I was editor of our school paper in high school" or "I worked my way through college but still got good grades." Our company does not view high scholastic grades as being overly important, but good grades do indicate native ability, intelligence, and willingness to apply oneself. We also like to see evidence of extracurricular activities. For those with past work histories, we look for

* Author's Note: This case study outlines candid, off-the-record comments by the top male personnel officer of a major American company who, along with his staff, interviews hundreds of sales-job applicants each year. His name must remain anonymous because he tells frankly why some applicants impress interviewers and why others fail to do so.

evidence of job-hopping, amount of past earnings, and what employers thought of them and vice versa.

What Do Applicants Know about Our Company? We expect applicants to know something about our company, its past and present operations, and our standing in the industry. We also ask and expect them to have given serious thought to where they expect to go with our company. We are looking here for evidence of clear thinking rather than for specific answers.

What Do They Want to Do? They are applying for a sales position, but we look for any signs of misguided interest. We know that applicants will not stay with us unless they are basically interested in selling, so we try to draw out their real interests during the interviews.

We like questions from applicants such as, "Where can I expect to be in two years?" or "Will I get recognition for hard work?" We dislike too many questions about money, coffee breaks, time off, and so forth. We feel our kind of salespeople want to learn about the job and where it can lead them first. We normally raise the question of money ourselves halfway through the interview.

What Are Their Potentialities? We use tests to help determine applicants' intelligence, aptitudes, and skills in reference to our particular sales requirements. We consider test results as only part of the interview process but expect applicants to take them willingly as one means of discovering to our mutual satisfaction whether they stand a good chance of being happy and successful in our sales work.

My personal peeve is the know-it-all or bombastic applicant. The ones I respect most are the very few who write follow-up notes thanking me for the interview; it can often tip the scales.

Questions for Written Reports or Class Discussion

1.   Why would this or any business firm want to hire you? Explain.

2.   When should you start planning in order to get the position you would like with this company?

3.   What key thoughts should you always keep in mind during employment interviews, as brought out in this case study?

4.   Do you consider it reasonable or fair for a prospective employer to ask you to take written tests? Why?

Sales Problem 19.1

Which of these two sales-job applicants would you hire?

Let us assume that you are an employer who has advertised for a salesperson. Introductions have been completed, the position described, and you are observing how these two applicants handle themselves during a morning's interviews.

FIRST APPLICANT

Applicant: Well, I need a job and I'd like to take a shot at yours.

Interviewer: What is it about the position that most interests you?

Applicant: The hours are good and having a company car as part of the deal sounds good, since mine has just about bombed out.

Interviewer: What makes you feel you will be successful?

Applicant: I've got a good personality and I like getting around and seeing people.

SECOND APPLICANT

Applicant: From your description, it sounds like you have some problems that a good salesperson could help you with.

Interviewer: Yes, you are right; we really are anxious to line up some new accounts.

Applicant: May I visit a couple of your type of accounts this afternoon, think overnight about how I might be able to approach new ones as your salesperson, and bring in a brief written proposal sometime tomorrow at your convenience?

Interviewer: Splendid; make it 3 P.M. What is it about this position that most interests you?

Applicant: You have problems that would be interesting to try to solve. I like challenges, and your position seems to offer great deal of opportunity for me to prove myself by getting good sales results for you.

Question for Written Report or Class Discussion

At this point, which applicant are you most likely to hire? Why?

Sales Problem 19.2	What can "Model Media Sales Reps" teach you about personal selling?

What makes ideal media sales representatives—as seen by major advertisers? The following eleven-point view of Model Media Reps evolved during a seminar sponsored by *Media Decisions* magazine at the Harvard Club in New York City in the late 1970s. It is equally applicable for the 1990s.

1. *They're honest*—not simply concerned with selling us just because it's part of their jobs.
2. *They understand us.* Something about our company, our people and the way we're structured, our products, our customers, our goals/our strategies.
3. *They understand the value of time*—and use ours *and* theirs wisely.
4. *They are idea people* (not just full of facts that are on the rate sheet which, by the way, they know well). They constantly think about how the product can best be adapted to fill our needs.
5. *They are account marketing service managers*—not "peddlers." Which means—
6. *They're prepared when they come to call on us.* They have a strategy and objective in mind.
7. *They cover all the bases*—and sell "top down" and "bottom up" including product managers, group marketing directors, and the agency—everyone involved in the planning and decision-making process.
8. *They are positive individuals*—forward-thinking individuals. They don't carp about why they might not have gotten the business last year, but how/what they can do about next year's plans.
9. *They are totally involved in the product*— and don't need a "canned" pitch to sell it (oh, they may use one occasionally, but it's always tailored to our needs).
10. *They like what they're doing* and you can tell it immediately. Their enthusiasm for the product is infectious on all contacts.
11. *They are good arbitrators,* representing their company's policies and point of view when they should and our interests when they should.

In summary: They're interested in what we're trying to do rather than what they're trying to sell. They make our life easier because *they are there to help solve our problems.* If they're only trying to solve their problems, it doesn't work. If they can help us solve our problems, we're going to do business with them.

Questions for Written Reports or Class Discussion

1. What ideas could you adapt in preparing for your own job application, resumé, or during the application interview process for any sales position, from the eleven points listed above?

2. What two key personality traits discussed in the chapter material support the inner drive and determination that would motivate Model Media Reps?

3. What are the best kinds of questions to ask (1) by our Model Media Reps during each of their calls, and (2) by applicants being interviewed for a sales position?

4. Media sales reps sell a service; job applicants seeking sales positions also have to sell. What do the latter sell, and what do they have to convince the "buyer" (the job interviewer) of?

Plan Your Work, Work Your Plan: The Self-Management of Selling

After studying this chapter, you will be able to:

Define the terms *planning, forecasting, composite inventory, territory value analysis, territory screening, programming, production requirements, production plans, scheduling, sales call patterns, follow-through* (from a managerial point of view), *controls, quantitative reports,* and *qualitative reports.*

Develop a simple four-part grouping of desirable customers or prospects for a sales territory, which will enable a salesperson to make a value analysis of that territory.

Explain why proper scheduling is so important to a salesperson and give the two most important factors involved.

Describe two types of account card systems that a salesperson can set up to quickly enable him or her to make an efficient territory analysis.

Summarize how a salesperson can set up an easy, efficient account classification system and put it to use for bigger sales.

Show how to set up sales-call patterns for both a fixed and irregular routing, and how to set up the most efficient route coverage for (1) a large territory or area, and (2) a smaller local area territory.

List six factors in a planned territory sales program that involves constant analysis and checks on progress and results, both by salesperson and by management.

We will now assume that you have successfully landed the sales position of your choice (with a medium-sized, national coverage business firm), have completed the initial training program, and have been assigned as outside real salesperson to a newly created sales territory. We are not concerned with what you are selling or to what specific type of customers; our aim is to discuss the principles, practices, and techniques that apply to any such assignment regardless of product or service, or specific types or combinations of industrial, outside retail, or end-user prospects or established customers.

Building on the concepts of modern management theory surveyed in Chapter 2, we will now start relating more specifically the four basic management functions considered there (planning, organizing, executing, and controlling) to problems you face in managing your new sales territory. We will assume you have been given an annual sales and expense budget that outlines your objectives in those areas, plus an estimate of desired profit goals. Your task now is to plan and organize your work to accomplish those objectives, like the more experienced salespeople in your company do each year. Many of the principles to be discussed are equally valid, as adapted, to sales promotion, in-store retail, or telemarketing activities.

Your assignment is the vital, responsible one of *local market* (your sales territory) *manager*. As such, you are expected to think, plan, and work from the start as a manager does.

YOU, YOUR COMPANY'S PRESIDENT, AND YOUR COMPETITION HAVE MUCH IN COMMON

Selling is a competitive profession, and competition provides half the fun of being a salesperson. The company has said you are good and has asked you to think as a manager does; so why not start by reflecting on the similarity of the problems faced by you in your sales territory and by the highly paid president (or managing director) of your company? And, think at the same time of the five (statistically average) competitors who are hard after your customers in the field every day.

As individuals you each start with native intelligence, varying degrees of education, knowledge, and experience, and the same 24 hours a day, 52 weeks, and 365 days a year. You are each positive-minded, enthusiastic, healthy, and hard workers. With so much in common basically, what secrets must *you* learn in order to become more successful than your competitors and even aim, if you so desire, toward the ultimate company position of president (or managing director)? The basic secrets are (1) to properly plan your work and (2) to work your plan effectively and efficiently.

Planning, as we first learned in Chapter 2, is predetermining a course of action; it starts with the establishing of goals and objectives. Based on company policy, your planning involves the identification of problems you logically expect to solve to accomplish objectives as efficiently as possible, and the practical actions necessary to accomplish them. We now consider this in terms of forecasting, programming, and scheduling your work. Once your work is planned, you will follow your plan, reviewing it constantly, adapting it when necessary to meet changing conditions.

Forecasting

Forecasting involves collecting facts or data upon which you try to calculate or estimate in advance what will happen within a specific time. For example, you collect all the data available from your company about past accounts in your territory and thus get a picture of past yearly sales and profits. You then assemble all available facts about new prospects, market trends, and competition sales, and any other information to get some idea of how well past yearly sales compared to actual market potential. This collection of facts should include everything you can relate to the five W's and the H of basic reporting or fact-finding: who, what, when, where, why, and how.

Once you have collected the information, you can make a composite inventory of your territory, which includes a value analysis.

A *composite inventory* involves territory screening (further described on pages 506–507), or listing all accounts, both current and potential. Only when you have done this can you determine intelligently when and where you are going to start working, what you are going to do in what order of priority, and how you are going to go about developing your territory to its full potential.

Part of this decision making involves making a *value analysis* of your territory. This analysis sorts out and classifies your desirable customers or prospects into simplified groups, based on business potential, so that you have an order of priority for calls and time to be allocated. You may set up such a simple grouping in the following four parts.

Prime potential
Better-than-average potential
Average potential
Poor potential

Normally, such a forecast indicates that you should call on customers or prospects in order of their business potential to attain greatest results. Other factors such as scheduling and time-call patterns may affect the picture, however, so forecasting up to this point is only a part of your overall planning picture.

Programming

Programming is planning the specific activities or procedures necessary to successfully accomplish the planned goals and objectives. This step involves setting *production requirements*—how many calls per day are necessary to accomplish your objectives—and making *production plans*—the breakdown of those calls (for example, 75 percent active accounts and 25 percent new ones). It is fairly easy to establish the overall goal, such as a 20 percent increase in sales and profits within the next year. It is more difficult, however, to specifically plan how to reach it.

Your action, therefore, is (1) to determine a series of attainable intermediate objectives that will enable you to systematically work your way to successful accomplishment of your overall goal, and (2) to plan the step-by-step procedures to be followed in meeting them within specified, planned time limits. These procedures are thus the step-by-step details of your overall sales plan.

By way of illustration, let us suppose that you have a sales goal of $400,000 net volume in your territory next year. Taking off two weeks vacation time leaves you 50 working weeks and weekly sales objectives of $8000. These smaller weekly objectives seem easier to attain than the $400,000, but your problem still remains—how to go about hitting that target figure each week.

It is easy to say, "I'll just go out and visit as many good prospects as possible, and if the law of averages is with me, I'll make my sales." Unfortunately, it is not that easy. Here are just some of the factors and activities you have to consider in advance of actual interview calls:

Which prospects are you going to call on? In what order? How often?

How are you going to arrange your call schedules to visit key prospects at the best time for them?

How can you best handle your travel and routing problems?

What is involved in planning good, effective interviews for different prospects in different geographical areas?

When will you be able to do all the necessary reports and paperwork?

What delays will be caused by customers who are not in or by problems they need your help in solving?

How much nonproductive selling time will you have to devote to servicing or follow-up calls?

These are some of the problems faced daily by outside salespeople. If you want to achieve sales success, you should plan your sales program well in advance, carefully anticipating as many such problems as possible and establishing procedures that will allow you to overcome all problems and still meet your sales goals and objectives on time.

Scheduling

Scheduling is arranging and managing the time necessary to carry out your sales program, and involves *planning routes* and *scheduling time* in order to cover your territory most effectively. Schedules should always be flexible enough to allow you to do unexpected things, but every successful salesperson not only schedules his or her work carefully but also tries as consistently as possible to follow this schedule.

By way of illustration, let us assume that you are planning scheduling to enable you to achieve your $8000-a-week, $400,000-a-year sales goal. You may decide to plan a six-month travel itinerary that will enable you to proceed from one geographical area to another at least cost of time and money, spending enough time in each place to see all key prospects plus a certain percentage of new ones. Within this schedule, you should plan to visit the key prospects at the time when past records indicate they are most likely to buy.

Your daily objectives call for you to visit your prime prospects first, then your next-best potential customers, planning each day (by appointment wherever possible) to make ten calls. Perhaps you have already worked out that if you can make eight such calls a day, you will be able to average four good presentations and one or two actual sales. By doing this consistently each day, you can expect $7500 sales that week. But where will the additional $500 come from? Your scheduling allows you time to visit each day perhaps two new potential customers. The extra business should come from these new customers. Such a schedule also allows you time to do your paperwork, such as sending in orders and reports, at the end of each working day.

What if the unexpected happens? You may be asked to attend a conference or meeting or be called to help a customer in a nearby city with an emergency problem. You can solve this by dropping the two end-of-the-day new-potential-customer calls. If the problem requires a longer period of time, you will most likely resume your itinerary, simply skipping those calls in between.

Scheduling should be flexible, but the most certain road to sales success lies in carefully planning your work and, through proper scheduling, in working that plan as consistently as possible.

SOME PRINCIPLES OF SUCCESSFUL WORK PLANNING AND FOLLOW-THROUGH

At this point, you may wonder how you can relate some of the managerial concepts and techniques we have been discussing to your specific sales territory and situation. There are many different sales activities, each with varying successful techniques, employment of which should bring sales success. Your own employer can provide you with training in these specific techniques. Thus it may be most helpful to you if we delve into some of the principles applicable to any form of selling. We can relate these to what we have already touched upon in the following areas:

Management of time
Efficient territory analysis
Account classification for bigger sales
Most effective territory coverage

Some basic routing plans that save time
Management of paperwork and reports

Management of Time

Let us assume that there are approximately 240 working days or 1920 working hours in a year. If on salary, divide your salary by 1920, and you can readily see what your time is worth. If your salary is $12,000 a year, each hour of your working time is worth $6.25. If you earn $24,000 a year, your time is worth $12.50 per hour. If you are paid on a commission basis at the rate of 20 percent of net sales volume, and wish to earn $40,000, you must bring in $200,000 net sales; your time will then be worth $104.12.

That is not the whole story, however, because of all the other factors involved, such as travel time, waiting time, paperwork, and nonproductive activities, even top professional salespeople find that only about one-third of their time is spent in productive, face-to-face interviews with prospects. That means you have only about 640 hours in which to make your sales. If you are earning $24,000 per year, this prime time is now worth approximately $37.50 per hour, and if you are on the above-noted commission on earnings goal basis, you have to sell $312.50 worth of goods and services each of these hours. Impossible? Not at all—thousands of professional salespeople are doing that each working day in many countries.

The lesson should be very clear: In order to achieve the success you desire, every hour of your working time must count. You should place the proper monetary value on your time and never forget how valuable it is. The late Richard Prentice Ettinger, a leading American publisher, summed it up as follows:

> "Time is the most important and valuable asset you have. You and you alone know whether you are using it in the most effective and profitable manner. The self-discipline you exercise in your use of your time determines the success you make of your life and of the organization for which you work. It will pay you to make every minute count."

Efficient Territory Analysis

Since sales results are so closely related to efficient use of time, you should concentrate on calls that pay off and eliminate as far as possible nonprofitable calls. This is true even for route calls, in which you have to regularly call back on a set customer list.

A basic step in efficient planning is to analyze your territory carefully in order to identify in advance if possible who your best prospects are and where they are located. This process is often called *territory screening*. Some salespeople do this screening by setting up two separate sets of account card files.

Current Accounts. Taken from past company records and rated (prime, good, and so on) in order of past business and future potential, current-account cards are grouped into easy-to-work geographical clusters.

Potential Accounts.   These are new, uncalled-on potential customers. Your research has indicated that, if developed properly, each could give you a certain amount of business. These cards are rated, grouped, and filed in the same way as are current accounts.

The purpose of such an account file system is to develop an efficient basic working tool; you can systematically list on these cards other information, either initially or as you learn it. For example, you may want to list the name of the key buyer, periods of the month or year when purchasing decisions are made, and bank and credit references. Maintenance of such a list is constant. You gather information on both current and potential accounts from many sources: company records, trade associations or directories, personal observation, and trade journals or newspapers, and from constantly asking questions and calling on new prospects.

All too few salespeople take the time to carefully set up and constantly use and improve such an account card file. Yet it can be a very efficient and scientific system for up-to-date *territory analysis*. Through it, you can pinpoint key potential customers and thus be able to plan the amount of time required for their maximum development. Just as importantly, your analysis can pinpoint the unprofitable segments of your customer list. Eliminating them completely or reducing call time spent on them means more time to get to the right places at the right time.

Account Classification for Bigger Sales

Once you have made your basic territory analysis and set up your account card files, you may find it extremely profitable to continually refine your analysis and classification of current and potential accounts. You will have to develop the techniques either by yourself or with the help of your sales supervisors, but basically the idea is to rate your accounts accurately as to current business and, more importantly, as to potential. This rating is important in view of two generally accepted sales principles.

1.   Up to 80 percent of profitable business in most sales areas comes from only about 20 percent of the customer list.
2.   It is easier to sell more to a current, satisfied customer than to develop new customers.

Once you have accurately classified your accounts in such a manner, you can plan your work to sell more to these better customers first and then to develop the other customers in a systematic way as time permits. Here are some suggestions for obtaining more sales than before from these prime customers you have so carefully analyzed and classified.

1.   Plan to call on at least one more good customer or potential customer per day than originally scheduled. Doing this may mean making eleven calls per day instead of ten.

ROUTE SCHEDULE

Sales Representative _____

Home Territory _____ For week beginning _____ 19 ___

Date	Time of arrival	City	State/Province and Country	Hotel and address	Time of departure	Planned calls upon

Tentative advance schedule for following week

Key objectives:

Additional comments:

FIGURE 20.1 *Example of a Typical Outside Salesperson's Route Schedule Sheet*

2. Plan to sell each one more of or a wider range of your goods or services. Do not overlook any possibility.

3. Plan to sell higher-priced items; concentrate your planning and presentations on big-ticket items. It is often just as easy to make a big sale as it is to make a small one. Start with the higher-priced items in your line; you can always work down the price scale. (Please note that this guideline applies to *outside selling*; for in-store *retail selling*, as noted in Chapter 15, the best guideline is to start in the middle price range and trade up.)

Covering Your Territory Most Effectively

Your first sales trip around your territory should further clarify your initial planning, analyzing, and forecasting of who influences purchasers and where and when the most purchases are made. The second and future trips give you fresh thoughts on how to concentrate your time and efforts where they are most likely to pay off. By recording all important information on your account cards, you learn through constant evaluation where to spend your time most profitably the next trip.

Sales call patterns usually follow either (1) a fixed routing, where customers are called on repeatedly at regular intervals, or (2) an irregular routing, where frequency of calls is left up to the salesperson. If you follow a fixed route, develop your own route sheet and list on it brief notes that will be useful references for succeeding calls. Such a route sheet may look something like the one in Figure 20.1.

If you follow an irregular-routing schedule or itinerary, you might set up a separate (different color) index card for each prospect, listing important information that you want to refer to later on. Then file the cards by date in a simplified up-file. It may look something like the one in Figure 20.2 for an office-machines salesperson. Other scheduling permitting, the salesperson can review on August

FIGURE 20.2 *Example of a Simplified Up-File Account Card*

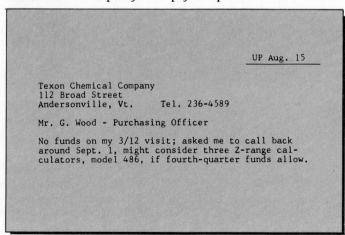

```
                                                    UP Aug. 15

    Texon Chemical Company
    112 Broad Street
    Andersonville, Vt.     Tel. 236-4589

    Mr. G. Wood - Purchasing Officer

    No funds on my 3/12 visit; asked me to call back
    around Sept. 1, might consider three Z-range cal-
    culators, model 486, if fourth-quarter funds allow.
```

15 whether to make an appointment for a personal call or at least to follow up by letter, telephone, or telegram.

Some Basic Routing Plans That Save Time

Once you have classified your accounts, determined where the best potential lies, and worked out a basic plan for most efficient coverage, you can devote some planning time to the most efficient *route coverage*. Here are a few ideas that may help you plan such a route most efficiently, depending on the type of selling you are engaged in.

1. *If you cover a large territory or area*, it may help to purchase both an overall map and detailed sectional maps (road maps are excellent) as well as maps of key cities. You can mark in symbols of your own choice the location of customers and prospects and plan an itinerary and work schedule that will enable you to see the greatest number of customers or potential prospects (based on business potential) most efficiently, at least cost, in a given area. You should keep these considerations in mind regarding trips outside your home area.

    Travel costs versus expected sales.

    Amount of time you can afford to be away at one time from your home or key area.

    The fact that it may be best to start working the outer areas first, working in toward your home or key area. Thus if you are called back there in an emergency, you will not have so far to travel to pick up the route on a future call.

    Such a simplified map may look something like the one in Figure 20.3 for a four-week itinerary involving three separate trips out of the home city and returns to it in between.

2. *If you cover a city or small territory within a two-hour radius of your home or office,* it may help you to divide it into zones, working a zone at a time, again starting with the outermost customer and working in and covering them as best you can (1) in order of business potential and (2) on the most direct route from one to the next. Such a zone and route plan may look something like the one in Figure 20.4.

3. *If you are a direct salesperson calling house-to-house or office-to-office,* the most efficient system is to work every house or every office in a given area before moving on to the next. The law of averages works for you if you hit every potential prospect in the area. This routing is most effective for cold-call, or one-call, selling.

    In area selling of this type, do not simply wander around looking for a door that appeals to you before knocking. Experienced house-to-house (or door-to-door) salespeople recommend hitting them all. A systematic house-to-house neighborhood block routing plan may look something like the one in Figure 20.5.

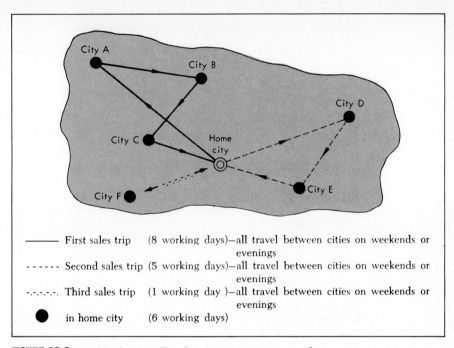

— — — First sales trip (8 working days)—all travel between cities on weekends or evenings
- - - - - Second sales trip (5 working days)—all travel between cities on weekends or evenings
-.-.-.-. Third sales trip (1 working day)—all travel between cities on weekends or evenings
● in home city (6 working days)

FIGURE 20.3 *Typical Overall Sales Territory Routing Plan*

FIGURE 20.4 *Typical Local Metropolitan Area Routing Plan*

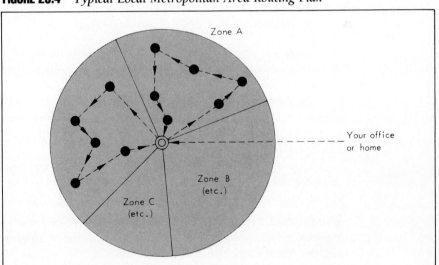

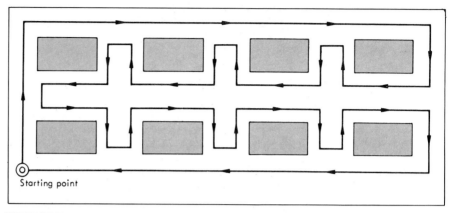

Starting point

FIGURE 20.5

WORKING THE PLAN—THE FOLLOW-THROUGH OF SELLING

Having carefully planned your work, as we have discussed, your next step is to follow through on it. *Follow-through*, in management terminology, means systematically working your planned sales program. It involves constant analysis and checks on progress and results, both by yourself and management, of these factors:

Number of calls per day
Sales-call ratio
Number of sales per day
Size of average order
Daily productivity
Profitability of productivity versus expenses

After analysis of such information over a period of time, you can evolve the most effective sales-call pattern, and after a *time-analysis review*, you can make the pattern *operationally efficient.*

Establishing controls over your activities involves making daily, weekly, monthly, quarterly, or yearly reports or summaries. Information contained in such reports provides feedback from your customers either to you, if you are self-employed, or to your company.

Company controls during the follow-through are usually based on the salesperson's field reports, which cover the above points. Such reports can be either quantitative or qualitative in nature.

Quantitative Reports. These include one or all of those listed below. Sales supervisors can compare efforts and results of one salesperson against another and thus set norms against which you can pace yourself, or they can statistically point up weaknesses in specific areas.

Daily Work Plan. This brief report, usually prepared at least a day in advance, lists the customer or prospects you plan to see and the results you expect to accomplish.

Daily Call Report. This brief report outlines daily activity along with the results. This report can be compared with your daily work plan to show how effectively you worked your plan.

Weekly Summary Report. For some companies this report takes the place of the daily call report. Others require it as a brief recap of weekly activities in addition to the more detailed daily call report. In either case, when compared with your itinerary and call objectives, it shows (1) actual results and (2) how effectively you worked your plan.

Monthly Reports. These are usually brief statistical recaps of the more detailed daily call reports. In many companies, the area manager prepares these for submission to the head office. In other companies, you, as a salesperson, are required to prepare them, as a further effort to have you constantly evaluate your own performance.

Quarterly or Semiannual Reports. These are overall progress reports. They may be only one page in length, but their purpose is to ask you to submit in writing (1) a review of your own performance to date versus your sales and expense budget, and (2) what specific plans you have to ensure that goals will be met during the next similar period.

Qualitative Reports. Required by some companies, these reports are more personalized and detailed than quantitative, factual reports in that you are asked to write your personal estimate or opinion of individual customers or other things. Such a report may be especially useful to your company credit manager if a customer is overdue in his or her accounts. Your report may indicate that the owner-manager was and still is sick, and that problems will be settled as soon as he or she is well again. Your on-the-spot opinion may thus save the credit rating of a good customer who is having temporary difficulties. Such reports may be required in many other areas, such as new product evaluation, or evaluation of new audiovisual sales aids that are being field-tested.

How to Manage Paperwork and Reports

Selling, unfortunately, involves many details. You, as a salesperson, are constantly communicating ideas to and between people and are persuading others at distant points to take action for you. The ideas you work with are frequently not your own, and, as a customer-oriented problem solver, you must report problems and facts completely and accurately to your superiors. Conversely, when a customer asks something of you in writing, you must be able to communicate intelligently and clearly. Also, in gathering market-research material, you must assemble accurate and specific details of value to you and your home office.

All these situations, plus your normal reports, follow-up letters, account card files, and the like involve paperwork. Making the sales call itself is only part of the job; you must see that the necessary follow-up steps are taken, by either yourself or others.

Salespeople in general are not known for their ability to shuffle papers across a desk. By nature they prefer to be out where the action is rather than writing reports. But if you want to achieve success in your sales career, and most certainly if you aspire to a managerial position, you have to learn to manage your paperwork efficiently. Time means money in selling, and paperwork involves nonproductive selling time. Since you have to get it done, the secret is to get it done as rapidly, thoroughly, and efficiently as possible within the least amount of time.

You can do many things to make the paperwork side of your sales job less burdensome. All of them require a certain amount of self-discipline until they become habit, but once they become fixed, they can make your work far more pleasant than it was before. Here are a few good habits that, if developed, can help you manage your paperwork efficiently.

1. *Do all routine paperwork daily!* The best technique for handling paperwork is to get it done as it comes up rather than let it accumulate. The message once again: Get today's paperwork done today! This includes the daily work plan for tomorrow and the daily call report today.

2. *Note taking.* If your prospect or customer allows you to take some notes during the interview, splendid. In those majority of cases where you cannot, you should do so immediately afterwards while the facts are still fresh in your mind. Do not wait until later and run the risk of forgetting; take a few minutes to complete it, according to your own shorthand and system, right after the interview or on any other occasion when you need to jot down facts learned.

3. *Memos.* Those to the home office or brief thank-you or follow-up notes can often be written during waiting periods in prospects' offices or during lunch. An average, brief, factual memo takes only from two to five minutes to write. There is rarely a day when you do not have ten minutes or so of free or waiting time. It makes sense to get necessary memos out of the way during those free minutes and not to have to do them at night.

4. *Weekly summary reports or weekly expense reports.* These are best done regularly late in the afternoon each Friday, at the end of the work day before returning home. If you get into this habit, you feel relaxed during the weekend. Fail to do it, and little stomach worry-knots over that undone task may actually ruin your weekend!

5. *Order forms.* These should always be carried. Fill in all details briefly, yet accurately and completely, after the sale is completed, and mail to the home office that day.

Some Tips on How to Write a Good Report

The most important part of your job is selling, but almost as important is reporting activities in the field to the home office. This reporting not only enables management to appraise and evaluate your performance and to offer advice and help wherever indicated, but also is essential for effective coordination of overall company sales activities. A success in your area may be parlayed into success in many areas, providing management receives sufficient facts to make an intelligent appraisal.

Be it a monthly report, an annual report, a special report on a particular situation, or even a plain memo, following certain guidelines will make it effective.

Be Specific. Avoid generalities and stick to facts. Explain facts with reasons. For instance, if your sales are down, the home office knows it before you do. They normally have the figures from current computer runoffs. What they do not know right away is why your sales are down; there may be a valid reason, but it has to be supplied from your end. They need to know why they are down and what you plan to do about it.

Avoid Cliches. Statements like "I will do my best" are meaningless. Substitute specifics such as "I plan to increase sales by 20 percent to a total of $1000." "The exhibition was a great success" does not convey why it was a great success. Because of the number attending or the products sold? Only facts can give the answer. Statements like "I will solve the problem by a positive sales program" are meaningless. The major advantage of specific reporting is that it forces you to supply answers rather than to rely on pulling something out of a hat. So remember the previously discussed fundamentals of good reporting—who, what, when, where, why, and how.

Comparisons Help Understanding. Figures themselves are neither good nor bad. Only comparison with other figures can breathe meaning into them. When talking about sales or potential sales, always relate them to comparative figures for the previous year and to budgets for the current year. Where possible, relate them to competitive figures and to the potential of your market.

Be Realistic. Wishful thinking is out of place in business; it is a treacherous bog into which many salespeople have fallen. Your reports are filed and thus become a matter of record at the home office. If they reflect muddled thinking, management forms a poor opinion of your judgment and your promotion potential. If your report is important, you should perhaps draft it, sleep on it, try reading it objectively the following day from the home-office point of view, and then prepare it for submission in careful, final form.

Be Brief. The best reports are concise and are written in telegraphic business style. Winston Churchill refused to read reports stretching beyond one page. Without going to that extreme, you can boil most reports down to essentials by eliminating unnecessary verbiage. People who think clearly express themselves clearly in writing. And the discipline of forcing yourself to write factually and concisely helps clarify your thinking. Muddled thinking often tries to camouflage itself in a maze of words.

Some Concluding Thoughts on Effective Planning and Working the Plan

It has been interesting comparing your planning and working activities to those of your company president, or managing director, but let us reflect once again on those five hungary competitors who, statistically at least, are also after your prime and potential prospects' business. If you do not hustle and get the business, they will! General Nathan Bedford Forrest, a famous yet somewhat illiterate Confederate calvary commander in the American Civil War (1861–65), summed up his secret for winning battles in these words: "Git there fustest with the mostest." That is not a bad strategy for sales success either, but like General Forrest, you know that a lot of planning, organization, energy, enthusiasm, and plain hard work lie behind the winning of any military or sales campaign.

You and your statistical five salesperson competitors start off with the same basic natural ingredients each day: your head, your feet, and eight average working hours. As in a long-distance foot race, victory is most likely to go to those salespeople who plan their strategy, follow their plan, pace themselves, turn on the steam at the proper moment, and are flexible enough to recognize and take advantage of unexpected opportunities.

Management judges you on your productivity, so you have to plan your activities and spend your time in selling where it will pay the greatest dividends. To repeat the central theme of this chapter: the time-tested best way to sales success is to effectively and efficiently plan your work—and work your plan!

SUMMARY

We have covered in this chapter several important concepts of how a newly hired outside salesperson can plan coverage of his or her sales territory most efficiently. Many of these principles are equally valid, as adapted, to sales promotion, in-store retail selling, or telemarketing activities.

Building on the four basic management functions of planning, organizing, executing, and controlling surveyed in Chapter 2, we first considered such topics as forecasting, programming, and scheduling—all essential to good planning. Then, as guides to most effective working of the plan, we considered the importance of management of time, efficient territory analysis, account classification for bigger sales, efficient territory coverage, and time-saving basic routing plan suggestions. Many practical illustrative examples were presented.

Yardsticks used to measure performance and evaluate progress were discussed, as were types of reports commonly required of salespeople. Several practical suggestions on how to manage paperwork and reports were offered.

Questions for Analysis and Discussion

1. All things being equal between you and a sales competitor, what is your best secret weapon to outperform him or her over any given period of time?
2. What does programming, as related to personal selling, mean to you?

3. In managerial and sales terms, what do controls mean to you?

4. Why is it so important for a salesperson to continually refine his or her analysis and classification of current and potential accounts?

5. Since sales results are so closely related to efficient use of time, what types of sales calls require greatest attention? Why?

6. Concerning account classification, what two generally accepted sales principles might help you rate your accounts most accurately, both as to current and potential business?

7. What two types of routings do sales call patterns usually follow?

8. A salesperson's call reports can be either quantitative or qualitative in nature. What is the difference between the two?

CASE STUDY 20

Best Foods Store-Procedure Selling Features Solid Objectives and Systematic Planning

CPC International, Inc., is a worldwide family of food-related businesses serving home and industry. The company has approximately 32,000 employees, and operates in 47 countries. When ranked by sales, it is one of the hundred largest industrial corporations and the tenth largest food company in the United States. Approximately 85 percent of CPC's business is concentrated in the United States, Canada, and Western Europe.

The company operates its two basic lines of business, consumer foods and corn refining, through five divisions.

Consumer foods, which account for over 80 percent of total sales, include such well-known United States packaged food and household items as Hellmann's, Best Foods, Mazola, Skippy, Thomas', Karo, Golden Griddle, Niagara, Argo, and Rit. Internationally, the company's major food products include Knorr, the world's leading brand in dry soup mixes and bouillons; Hellmann's and Best Foods mayonnaise, Mazola corn oil and margarine, Skippy peanut butter, Thomas' English muffins, Arnold breads and rolls, Mueller's pasta products, and Karo and Golden Griddle syrups.

Consumer food products are distributed primarily by the company's own sales organizations through grocery retailers and such institutions as restaurants, schools, hotels, and hospitals. Each product sold in the United States, and virtually all sold in Europe, are marketed under the company's brand names.

The success of Best Foods, a division of CPC International, Inc., is built on a solid base of (1) systematic overall marketing planning and (2) a time-tested and successful approach to retail sale calls.

Best Foods salesperson's training man-

ual terms its modern and highly successful approach to retail calls "store procedure." At the heart of this concept are the solid objectives, through planning, basic selling, and merchandising procedures, reporting, and follow-through necessary to make any call by a Best Foods salesperson a worthwhile investment of his or her time. Company insistence on careful precall planning is of chief interest to us in this case study as well as how they work that plan during the sales call itself and the follow-up preparation of records and reports.

Best Foods salespeople call basically on (1) grocery stores (independent stores, chain stores, and convenience stores—all supermarket(s) and (2) the important central buying headquarters of chain-store organizations, voluntary groups, co-ops, and other large-volume direct accounts. Planning is more detailed in the second case because of the greater potential of the call, but in both cases, salespeople carefully plan their work in advance and follow the plan during the call, as outlined below.

I. *Planning* is done the night before the call and is concerned chiefly with these items.
   A. *Account review*
      1. The overall operation and background of the account as gathered from industry sources such as *Progressive Grocer*, "Facts in the Grocery Business," other trade publications, and Best Foods' own studies.
      2. Specific information from Best Foods account records that points out previous successful promotions, distribution problems, or other such matters of record.

PLAN YOUR WORK, WORK YOUR PLAN! THE SELF-MANAGEMENT OF SELLING

3. Special factors, such as personality of dealer, competitive activity, advertising tie-ins, and what items and promotions the headquarters has authorized for the store.
   B. *Specific sales objectives.* This is important since the Best Foods sales representatives have over 120 items and sizes to sell, ranging from Mazola oil to Hellmann's Best Foods mayonnaise, dressings, Karo syrup, Mazola and Nucoa margarine, Golden Griddle pancake syrup, and Argo cornstarch. These representatives have to plan which product or group of products has to be presented to this specific store in the limited *interview time* available, which is often no more than five minutes. By studying account records and the specific items the company is pushing that week, they pinpoint key items, which thus become key sales objectives. They then relate these to advertising tie-ins and other promotional activities in effect at the time of the call.
   C. *Final presentation review.* This involves a quick personalizing and dressing up of the suggested order slip and pitch sheet as a final plan and review of the sales presentations for the next day.
II. *Basic selling procedure (or the complete presentation).* Best Foods sales training prepares sales representatives to follow a basic, step-by-step selling procedure on each call. It starts with the preapproach and continues through completion of the daily report. Careful working of the plan—following each step in the order listed below—is expected during every call.
   A. *Preapproach*
      1. Briefly review plans and fix objectives in mind before each call.
      2. Greet the dealer.
      3. Check distribution to make certain all authorized brands and items are on the shelf. Plan presentation on items not stocked or temporarily out of stock.
      4. Get into stockroom and adjust planned assortment according to stock on hand.
      5. Observe competitive store activity.
   B. *Approach*
      1. Get a friendly reception from dealer.
      2. Secure dealer's undivided attention.
      3. Obtain harmony of mind, "yes" response.
   C. *Presentation*
      1. Present promotions in logical order and in an enthusiastic and convincing manner.
      2. Make complete presentation on authorized brands and sizes not in stock.
      3. Appeal to dealer by effective use of *sales material* (brochures, flyers), pitch sheet and suggested order form; samples and dummy cartons (particularly for initial sales); demonstrations; other aids such as ad layouts (proofs, P.O.P. material).
      4. Avoid negative suggestions, such as "You don't need any, do you?"
      5. Anticipate objections and include positive selling points to counter them.
   D. *Close*
      1. Ask for the order or display and reach agreement on how to handle temporary out-of-stock conditions.
         a. Phrase close to fit dealer.
         b. Use suggested order slip to gain acceptance of suggested assortment.
         c. Keep quiet after presenting suggested order slip.
      2. Thank dealer for order.
   E. *Determine method and date of delivery.*
   F. *Place order in order guide, order book, or order form.*
III. *Follow-up records and reports* are completed and handled in this way.
   A. *Route books.* Enter complete and accurate information immediately after each call. Enter remarks as an aid to planning and selling on next call.

B. *Daily report.* Complete after each call; make sure it is accurate and legible and mail to area manager twice weekly.

Questions for Written Reports or Class Discussion

1. Are the Best Foods store-procedure planning steps outlined above concerned more with long-range or short-range planning? Explain.

2. What follow-through steps are covered in the Best Foods store-procedure plan? Outline and explain.

3. How does the Best Foods salesperson employ forecasting techniques in planning?

4. Would the Best Foods after-call daily report noted above be considered a quantitative or a qualitative report? Explain.

Sales Problem 20.1

What should salesperson Marco Garcia do in this hospital supplies sales situation?

Marco Garcia is an experienced sales professional who sells four different lines of hospital supplies to hospitals in the American states of South Carolina and Georgia. Three of these lines involve items manufactured by his own company. We shall call them Lines A, B, and C. His fourth line, which we shall call Line D, is closely comparable to his Line B. Working on a straight commission basis, Marco receives 15 percent commission on net sales of all Line A, B, and C items, and 10 percent on all Line D items.

Marco is visiting for the first time Julia Tafoya, purchasing director of a large, just-opened Charleston, South Carolina hospital. He plans to close a large initial sale on this first call, and thus set the stage for keeping that hospital as a large, profitable account for his firm.

Ms. Tafoya, indicating that she is prepared to make an immediate $30,000 purchase, expresses interest in a full-line trial order of either Line B or D, but seems to really want to order Line D—Marco's low-profit (that is, lower commission) line.

Question for Written Report or Class Discussion

Should Marco try to switch Ms. Tafoya to Line B (at the risk of losing her altogether) or give her Line D without a murmur and pass up the chance to earn a larger commission? What reasons can you give to justify your position?

How can store section sales manager Anne Phillips protect her salespeople against intruders from another section?

Anne Phillips is section sales manager in a large Melbourne, Australia department store, responsible for sales of waffle irons, toasters, mixers, and similar small appliances. She supervises four salespeople, from whom she hears this one constant complaint: "Salespeople from the neighboring section, where refrigerators, freezers, and stoves are sold, constantly invade the small appliance area and add sales of these items to orders they are taking."

Since a 10 percent commission is credited for orders written up by salespeople in each department, Anne's salespeople feel they are being cheated out of rightfully deserved commissions for themselves.

The store's general manager refuses to issue an order that will stop this situation because he thinks it would discourage salespeople from following the store sales policy of suggesting, after each sale, a second or add-on sale.

Question for Written Report or Class Discussion

Assuming that you are Anne, in the face of this urgent sales management problem, what will you do to protect the interests of your salespeople so that they will continue to accept and respect your leadership?

How to Program Your Career Toward Higher Earnings and Management

After studying this chapter, you will be able to:

Describe three basic ways to get to the top through selling.

Summarize the importance of personal goal setting and self-management as essential to career success in both personal selling and management.

Explain how one can practically go about changing any negative personal self-images or attitudes into positive ones.

Discuss several basic personal and professional qualities or characteristics one must possess in order to achieve success in management.

Cite several aspects of knowledge and performance levels expected of a manager.

Summarize what one should do in order to advance most rapidly within a company or organization.

Identify and illustrate how to put it into effect as a personal challenge the first important step in deciding how you *will* achieve your personal career ambitions.

We have now completed our study of the basic concepts, principles, practices, and applied techniques of successful personal selling. If you understand and have accepted what has been presented in the preceding chapters, then you know how to succeed in selling. From here on, achieving success depends basically on how effectively and efficiently you put into practice what you have learned.

If you have only moderate ambitions in life—if you just want to know enough to get along—then you have largely accomplished your objectives in studying this book. But if you want more than the ordinary in life and in work, if you want to earn a lot of money through selling or if you desire to reach the top in management, then this chapter is worth your special and serious consideration.

But first, a warning! Reaching the top in personal selling or through management within a company or organization requires unrelenting hard work, dedication, creative thinking, and above-average drive and determination.

FEWER THAN ONE IN FIFTY WILL REACH THE TOP

As our world edges into the twenty-first century, opportunities to rise to the top through selling have never been greater. The needs and demands of our exploding world population in this exciting age of human and technological change are unparalleled. Business and industry is expanding at an unprecedented rate to fulfill those needs and is searching avidly now for those individuals capable of leadership in the future.

Yet, from among all those who, along with you, are reading these words, fewer than one in fifty will rise to the top 10 percent in earnings or job positions. More will fail from lack of proper attitude, drive, or determination than from lack of intelligence. In the end, all things being somewhat if not altogether equal, success is up to you.

What about it? Do you want to give it a go, to try to reach the top? If you do not try, you will never know whether you can. If so, then let us put our minds and will power into high gear and consider how you can most rapidly achieve your goals.

We will start by explaining three basic ways to achieve your ambitions through selling. Since personal goal-setting is the basic key to success in each, you will be asked to put down on paper a basic outline of the short-term and long-range stages along your career-goal path. The importance of proper personal attitudes toward life and work will be considered, and practical ideas for changing negative attitudes and traits into positive ones offered. Building on earlier chapters, many new "high-gear" ideas from professional salespeople will be offered as guides to faster, larger personal sales and earnings. Finally, attention will center on the special knowledge and personal characteristics and qualities essential to managerial advancement, and how you, if you so desire, can prepare yourself toward that end.

THREE BASIC WAYS TO GET TO THE TOP THROUGH SELLING

There are basically three ways to get to the top through selling.

1. *Becoming and remaining a full-time professional salesperson either independently or within the framework of a business firm.* This means forgetting about management as a goal and striving for increased earnings and relative freedom of action through personal management of your activities. Your aim thus becomes that of obtaining more and bigger sales that directly result in higher earnings and personal accomplishment.

    Such a professional career potentially offers great freedom of action, independence, satisfaction, and the opportunity to earn a great deal of money as a direct and immediate result of your own efforts. This opportunity to realize high earnings and to remain your own boss exists in many fields: real estate, insurance, and investments to name but a few. You can also find such rewards as a manufacturer's representative or agent or in many of the service or direct-selling areas.

    You become, in effect, manager of your own business, one that you can enter without any capital investment, other than that of your own time, efforts, and intelligence. If the market and need are there, success largely depends on how hard you work and on the efficiency of your self-management.

    If you have the attributes of a good salesperson, enjoy the excitement of face-to-face selling, and either lack or dislike the analytical and impersonal requirements for top sales or corporate management positions, then this career goal could well be the one toward which you should set your sights.

2. *Personally selling a good, need-filling product or service anywhere in the world and building toward your own small, medium, or large company.* Many young men and women have done this and are doing so right now in many countries of the world. Opportunities exist everywhere to start selling even an idea that can quickly develop into a profitable and growing company.

    If you have an unusual amount of drive, ambition, and business acumen, what could be more challenging than to start your own company from nothing? The best way to start such an enterprise without much or any capital is to sell successfully something produced by someone else who needs success-minded individuals to sell or market his or her product.

    Potential gains are high in this area; for some individuals the sky is the limit. The risks of such undercapitalized efforts are great, and only a relatively few make it, but who is to stop you from trying? If you have the idea for a new product or service and if the need is there, perhaps this is the direction in which you should set your sights.

    "Great idea," you say, "but how does a 'broke person' get started?" The first-step answer: Rush to read "the book that could be worth a million dollars to you," *Think and Grow Rich* by Napoleon Hill[1]—readily available in most of the world's libraries and bookstores.

---

[1] Napoleon Hill, *Think and Grow Rich* (New York: A Fawcet Crest Book published by Ballantine Books, 1960).

3. *Working up through the sales ranks of an existing business firm or nonprofit organization to sales manager, marketing director, and even president or managing director.* If you lack that touch of business acumen or genius necessary for going it alone to form your own company, perhaps you can best reach your goals as a member of a team in an existing organization. Small or large, such organizations are seeking now those individuals who one day will, in top management capacity, guide their organizations.

By starting as a salesperson with an enlightened organization whose policy is to consider you manager of your territory and a vital member of the management team, you have the opportunity immediately to learn and put into practice the concepts and techniques of top management. This fact alone can put you potentially far ahead of the people in the financial, legal, or computer areas when the time comes for considering you for a top management position. You alone understand what your customers want, how they buy, and how they use the organization's products or services.

While there will always be room for independent operators and small and specialized companies, the worldwide overall trend is toward fewer, larger, and more highly diversified companies run by well-trained professional managers. These managers of the future will have to know not only about such things as computers and scientific decision making, but also how to use them in terms of the human element. Thus sales offers the possibility of being perhaps the fastest road to top management for you.

PERSONAL GOAL-SETTING IS THE BASIC KEY TO SUCCESS

If you are serious about "getting ahead," how about starting *right now, this second?* As a first step in deciding how you *will* achieve your career ambitions, please fill out this rough outline of the short-term and long-range stages toward your ultimate goal. You may not know exactly what you want to be right now, but you can at least insert in Table 21.1(a) what you think you might like to be doing (career position) and the income you would like to be earning. There are approximately 1920 working hours in an average working year of 240 days.[2] Divide the yearly earnings you would like to have by the number of working hours, and fill out in Table 21.1(b) what your time will be worth at each stage.

Does the filling out of these blanks seem like a silly, childish exercise to you? If so, think again! From a sound psychological point of view, the act of filling them out means that you have taken a very important self-motivational first step—the action step of getting started.

If you have said, "I'll fill in the blanks later," you have committed the most basic cause of failure to succeed—procrastination! If you've laughed off the idea of filling in the blanks, you may want to seriously evaluate your basic attitudes toward life and work—a topic that must be considered before developing "how-to" steps to accomplish the "want to" goals you have just set for yourself.

---

[2] Based on an estimated three weeks annual vacation and a one-week total of national holidays. This leaves 48 working weeks, each made up of five 8-hour working days.

TABLE 21.1(a) *Your Personal Goal-Chart to Success*

	Next Year	+5 Years	+10 Years	+20 Years
What do you want to be doing (position)?				
How much do you want to be earning per year?				

TABLE 21.1(b) *What Will Your Time Be Worth along Your Success-Path?*

	Next Year	+5 Years	+10 Years	+20 Years
How much will your time be worth per hour?				

YOUR ATTITUDE WILL MAKE THE DIFFERENCE

It is true in selling, as in most other careers, that sound philosophies, a positive attitude toward life and work, enthusiasm, and good work habits are more responsible for an individual's success than are any learned techniques. These characteristics result from a good combination of the character and human qualities listed on page 23.

Psychologists tell us that principles, beliefs, and motives are central factors in individual improvement. The question now is

> Do *you* believe that the positive principles, beliefs, and motives accepted generally by the world and specifically by the society in which you live provide a structure within which you can successfully work?

It is important to answer this question, because success in selling or in most occupations involving work with other people entails a certain amount of conformity to group values. You do not have to lose your individual personality because you work for a large business firm, nonprofit organization, or government agency, but if you want to "get ahead," you have to work within the established value norms.

In fact, to achieve real success, you not only have to accept these values, but also to believe in them. Some people believe it outmoded or square to believe in traditional values, or in anything else. But mankind's progress through the ages has been made not by quitters, but by doers and believers. Here are some questions you should ask yourself in order to determine your real feelings and attitudes toward your present or future work:

- *Your job.* Do you think that you are now in the right line of work or that the work you plan to do is or will be right for you? Do you think this work is helpful to your national economy and to society? Do you consider it to be as worthy as any other? Would you want your son or daughter to engage in it?

- *Your company or organization.* Do you believe it, or the one you hope to work for, serves a useful function? Do you believe that its management has worthwhile policies toward the public? Towards its employees? Do you make or are you prepared to make a positive contribution toward its collective effort? When a short-term decision toward accomplishment of overall goals differs from your own ideas, do you carry it out, or will you loyally try to carry it out, as well as you can?
- *The customers or public you serve.* Do you really like the people you now serve or plan to serve? Do you now or are you prepared to put forth the necessary time and effort to determine their real needs? Do you sincerely want to offer them what is best for them?
- *Your work habits.* Do you now or are you prepared to keep professional hours—to start as early and to finish as late as necessary each working day to serve your customers or the public and the organization you work for? Do you now or are you prepared to put forth your very best effort each hour of your working day? Do you believe that your determined effort, even if others around you are slackers, will ultimately lead to success; or that, if you fail for any reason, it is still worth the effort?

CAN BASIC ATTITUDES BE CHANGED?

If the answer to most of the above questions is "yes," congratulations—you have the basic positive attitudes essential to success. If your answer to many is "no," consider it a warning and examine the reasons for your negative attitudes that do not conform to the generally accepted attitudes in your society. You may find it worthwhile to change these negative attitudes.

But, you may ask, "Can one change or adjust one's innate, ingrained personality and attitudes in such a way as to achieve desired personal success?" Since few of us are perfect, you may feel the need for certain changes, but honestly wonder whether you can change. Take heart, for leading psychologists and successful men and women in every country say you can change—if you really want to! William James, the great psychologist, put it this way:

> The greatest discovery of my generation is that human beings can alter their lives by altering their attitudes of mind.

How Can You Improve Your Self-Image and Attitudes?

Psychologists tell us that each individual has a self-image—a mental picture of the kind of person he or she is. We touched on this subject in Chapter 3 (see p. 80 in particular). This private evaluation of abilities is a motivating force which the individual tends to subconsciously fulfill or live out. Often this self-image is filled with negative as well as positive thoughts. If your negative thoughts can be eliminated and positive ones substituted in their place, it is quite possible, say the psychologists, that your new attitudes can change your life and help you achieve your goals. Many excellent books offer scientific, spiritual, and practical suggestions for self-improvement in this area. Three popular ones to start with are the previously mentioned *Think and Grow Rich* by Napoleon Hill, *The Power of Positive Thinking* by Norman Vincent Peale,[3] and *Success Through a Positive Mental Attitude* by W. Clement Stone.[4]

Changing your self-image involves honestly evaluating your basic attitudes and actually changing them by replacing negative thoughts with positive ones. You fill your mind consciously each day in practical ways by thinking positive, happy, successful thoughts, and eliminating consciously and immediately any negative thoughts that produce inward tension.

If all this sounds too good to be true, remember that it is based on sound psychological theory. Since so many psychologists feel that our physical life is determined in large part by our emotional condition, and that in turn by our mental attitude, it follows that if you can fill your mind with positive or successful thoughts your personality can change for the better. Thousands of salespeople will attest that their consistent efforts to practice this positive mental thinking concept has paid off for them. Give it a serious try, and judge for yourself!

Proper Attitudes and Personality Can Improve Habits

Along with proper attitudes toward life and work, your personality is a key factor in determining the degree of success you will have in achieving your goals. Certain qualities of personality, such as those listed below, make it easier for you to succeed when working with other people, especially in selling. Very few people are blessed at birth with all the qualities of a successful personality, but fortunately many of these can be developed as can the muscles in your body—by intelligent exercise; or, as with the self-image patterns, through daily substitution of negative traits by positive ones. Through practice, these positive attributes can become habits.

Enthusiasm is certainly one of the greatest personality traits of successful salespeople, as it is of leaders and successful people in all occupations. Enthusiasm is contagious; it makes people want to buy, enables sports teams to sweep to victory, and can cause an entire nation to follow one leader.

How do you develop enthusiasm? Frank Bettger, a business failure at 40, who changed his life by switching to positive thoughts and went on to business fame and fortune in the American insurance world, puts it this way: "To become enthusiastic, act enthusiastic. Act enthusiastic about every aspect of your life and work." "Start today—now," he says in effect, "force yourself to act enthusiastically, and you'll become enthusiastic. Be alive and your enthusiasm will be catching."[5]

---

[3] Norman V. Peale, *The Power of Positive Thinking* (Englewood Cliffs, N.J.: Prentice-Hall, Inc., 1952).

[4] W. Clement Stone, *Success Through a Positive Mental Attitude* (Englewood Cliffs, N.J.: Prentice Hall, Inc., 1965).

[5] Frank Bettger, *How I Raised Myself from Failure to Success in Selling* (Englewood Cliffs, N.J.: Prentice-Hall, Inc., 1949), p. 11.

Sincerity is another necessary personality trait. You can develop it by involving yourself thoroughly in your work and by treating other people as you would like them to treat you.

Courtesy on your part stimulates courtesy on the part of the people with whom you work; this leads to mutual respect and cheerfulness, which helps make life and having friends enjoyable.

Initiative and persistence are two more personality traits essential to success. You can develop initiative each day by the way you tackle each task. You should try to do each one 10 percent better than it has been done before. This 10 percent extra effort in all tasks, every day, builds attitudes, habits, and personality traits that cannot help but lead to success.

TO GET STARTED TOWARD YOUR GOALS—TURN ON THE ENGINE OF YOUR WILL-POWER

None of the points we have just considered in terms of goal-setting, changing negative attitudes into positive ones, or trying to improve your personality will mean anything to you in selling or life in general unless you put them into effect. The time to start is *now*! As with starting the engine of a car, you have to kick over or turn on your will power to get yourself started, to get the wheels turning.

If you can force yourself to do that, you will, as James has pointed out, ". . . reach within yourself deeper levels of energy that will keep you propelled by some inner want rather than by a coercive "ought to.""[6]

The first step is to take another look at the "want-to" goals you filled out on page 526. Then, taking into account the proper attitudes, habits, and personality changes, plus new knowledge and skills you feel you will need to acquire, outline for yourself, on a piece of paper, the "how-to" steps you feel will be necessary to accomplish your goals.

Start *now*! Force yourself to outline a few realistic short-term objectives that will enable you to get where you want to be, earning the money you want to earn, a year from now. These realistic short-term objectives should be just beyond your present reach, but near enough to seem possible.

The next step is to force yourself each day to try to meet your targets. Do not wait until you feel hot or in the mood. Simply try to continue improving. Gradually you will find that your inner drives, or wheels, will be warmed up and turning and will keep up the momentum. You will work hard and efficiently because you want to, and you will accomplish more with less effort. As you accomplish your short-term steps, your confidence will increase and with it your will to win. Successful completion of your objectives and goals, step by step, will increasingly make your big goal seem possible and attainable.

[6] Robert A. Whitney, Thomas Hubin, and John D. Murphy, *New Psychology of Persuasion and Motivation in Selling* (Englewood Cliffs, N.J.: Prentice-Hall, Inc., 1965), p. 246.

Believe in yourself, have faith in your abilities, and with sound self-confidence and hard work you can and will succeed. Per ardua ad astra—"Through adversity to the stars!"

SELF-MANAGEMENT IS ESSENTIAL FOR SUCCESS NO MATTER WHAT YOUR GOAL

Proper attitudes, good personality traits, and turning on your inner will-power drives, while essential to success, cannot in themselves ensure successful goal accomplishment. You must also "manage" your career properly; that means self-management.

In order to illustrate the importance of self-management and professionalism, let us focus our attention on two specific goals you might wish to set for yourself: (1) setting your sights for high earnings as a professional salesperson and (2) programming your career for management. The first, of course, can lead into the second if you elect, or it can remain a career end in itself. To pursue a sales management or top management goal through selling requires that you first establish a superior record in personal selling.

SETTING YOUR SIGHTS FOR HIGHER SALES AND EARNINGS

Charting your career to reach the top ranks in sales and earnings success requires the same careful planning and follow-through involved in an important military or business operation. Thinking of your sales territory management problems in terms of the managerial concepts we have presented throughout these pages enables you to review and take advantage of all the latest theoretical principles and practical techniques of both management and selling developed over the years. You must now consider them professionally, and decide on your own initiative how to plan, analyze, and take advantage of every possible product and profit opportunity.

Your first step is to study and analyze such opportunities in your specific area of selling for possible application to your own sales activity. In other words, start where others have successfully left off, by putting their hard-won, effective ideas to work for you from the start. Adapt these ideas to your own problems and needs, improve them where possible, and then add your own ideas. This procedure is the quickest and most effective way to move into high-volume selling.

In starting to put this thinking into practice, keep in mind these *basic laws for success in selling*:

1. The more efficiently you work, the more you achieve.
2. The more carefully selected calls you make, the more interviews you obtain.
3. The more interviews you obtain, the more presentations you make.
4. The more presentations you make, the greater your chances of closing sales.

5. The more sales you close, the greater your volume and, if it is profitable volume, the more income for you!

6. Careful planning, efficient work habits, and setting sales goals on big potential customers and big-ticket items leads to increased volume and income.

Progressive development of these laws or principles will lead to increased sales and higher earnings. The degree of success and speed in achievement will depend on careful planning, efficient follow-through, careful analysis and controls, and proper management of time and effort. Here, from sales professionals, are some very practical, maximum-income, sales-producing ideas that fit or can be adapted to fit all types of outside selling.

High-Volume Potential Programming Tips. Effective programming involves (1) placing the proper value on your time and (2) determining the number and types of calls that enable you to reach your sales or earning goal. When planning your program, you are basically concerned with (1) making as many calls as possible within the time available, (2) trying to close a sale on every call, (3) trying to sell as much or as many extras as possible on each call. *The suggestions that follow for accomplishing these steps are worth your careful consideration.* They add to or build on those presented earlier.

1. Try to sell something on every call. This simple objective is a powerful psychological incentive to continue trying to close, even if the resulting order is small. Small, foot-in-the-door orders give you a chance to prove your claims of after-sale service and provide reasons for callbacks.

2. Sell across the board. Try to find some use for any and all of your various product lines if you carry a range. Where unsuccessful in your attempt, follow point 6 below.

3. Try for the biggest possible sale first. It is easier to come down in quantity or price than to trade up. If a customer or prospect asks for a specific item, present the benefits of your top-of-the-line product if you have one. It always pays to ask.

4. Sell selectively by giving careful attention to low-volume items that, because of higher unit price, can add up to high total sales and profits. Too many salespeople think of volume alone.

5. When programming sales calls, concentrate on selling new customers products or services that are currently successful. It is easier to sell something of proven value in most cases than to sell something entirely new. One great secret of profitable selling is to find new markets for current, successful products.

6. Whenever possible, give up or cut down on selling items that do not produce volume commensurate with the time and effort spent on their promotion.

7. Do not forget that persistence can pay off. Large sales are often made in some types of selling only after several calls. If the need, the potential, and the ability and authority to buy are there, one more call may do the trick.

8. Program your work to fill in seasonally slack periods (such as around Christmas or during vacation periods) with calls on customers or prospects

who will be available and in a position to make buying decisions at that time. To a professional salesperson, there is no slack selling time.

Scheduling Tips for Maximum Sales Results.   One great secret of maximizing profitable sales is to spend time and effort only in those areas where maximum results are obtainable. This fact seems almost too obvious to mention, yet *here are three of the greatest mistakes commonly made by salespeople.*

1. Following a milk route through habit and failing to evaluate or change that habit.
2. Failing to check past or present sales volume against the amount of time and money expended.
3. Taking it easy and continuing to call mainly on people they know or feel will pleasantly welcome them.

Scheduling is basically concerned with planning your work; it involves scheduling routing and time so that sales result. Here are some proven ideas that will help you schedule calls that produce more profitable results.

1. Sell where the money is! This involves both analysis of past sales and forecasts of future ones to determine where and how you should spend your time and concentrate your efforts. If 10 percent of past customers have given you 80 percent of past business, then perhaps you should spend more time with these prime customers to try to sell them more.
2. Keep professional hours—that is, work as early and continue as late as prospects or customers are willing to see you.
3. Because it is often just as easy to sell a complete program or system as to sell the individual parts, consider first overall needs and try for a big sale.
4. As you conclude a sale, try to think of a second sale that will make the first one even more useful. A customer who buys is in a buying mood, and it will pay you to try to take advantage of it by offering something else.
5. Use the telephone effectively to save time. You can use it as a selling instrument to help you qualify customers, handle appointments, keep in touch with small or outlying accounts, clear up misunderstandings, or relay important information rapidly. Proper use of the telephone gives you more time for that most valuable part of selling—face-to-face interviews with the best potential customers.
6. Plan to spend your *prime selling time* only with those prospects or customers with the money and authority to buy.
7. Swim with the tide; concentrate on selling the products or services that follow current industry developments or interests. And concentrate further on your current, tested, quality items.
8. Make long-term appointments with key customers who require specific visits at specific times and with key new prospects, and plan your travel or eating time around customers' work or meal habits. This procedure helps cut down waiting time.

Follow-Up and Follow-Through Tips for Even Greater Sales Success.
Some of these ideas are new; others build on earlier suggestions.

1. Be creative in your selling and try to find new uses for old products or unthought-of uses for new products.
2. See to it that, when orders are filled by your company, the customers are resold through enclosed sales material that again describes benefits.
3. Find out why your customers buy, and get evidence and endorsement from them in the form of testimonials. Then use that evidence to sell new customers.
4. Aim always to turn small, current, satisfied accounts into large accounts.
5. Evaluate results at the end of each day and learn to recognize any significant data encountered, such as why sales were lost, competition price or product changes, customers' changing needs, or new trends or developments in the industry that could affect your future sales.
6. Keep accurate, daily, personal time records so that you will know where your time was spent and how it can be spent most profitably.
7. Set up a personal, quick-reference, cross-index system to enable you to file and find information easily and rapidly. You should file brief notes jotted down immediately after a sales presentation as a matter of course. Because most people cannot retain facts for long, place every scrap of potentially useful information in your files. This information can provide the basis for specific controls, reports, analyses, forecasts, and plans.

PROGRAMMING YOUR CAREER FOR MANAGEMENT

Early in Chapter 1 it was noted that selling and sales management offer perhaps the quickest career avenue to top management ranks for ambitious young men and women. Reflecting the increased sales/marketing orientation of top business management is the fact that today, in the United States, nearly one out of every three publicly owned corporations is headed by a person who came up through the sales/marketing route. Worldwide, by some estimates, nearly 70 percent of key executives in the industrialized world's business organizations have a primary background in sales/marketing.

This increasing sales/marketing emphasis of business is no accident. In the face of the rapid economic, social, and political changes that continue to sweep the world, business firms face a more affluent and demanding market marked by subjective choices, often unpredictable consumer discretion, and impulse buying. To keep abreast of these changes, top management must be sensitive to consumer demands. This situation means that the already high ratio of sales/marketing-trained and -oriented top business managers will continue to grow. A high percentage of these top managers in future years will come from sales management ranks.

Do you aspire to sales management, or top management ranks? If so, then now is the time to start planning, programming, and managing your own career through selling toward that end. To start, here are some questions you might ask; answers in part follow in the remaining pages of this chapter.

1.   What will selling and sales management be like in the future?
2.   What are your personal chances of reaching management level?
3.   Do you have what it takes to be a manager?
4.   How do your superiors judge your managerial potential?
5.   What knowledge and performance level does a managerial role require?
6.   How can one develop managerial knowledge, skills, and abilities?
7.   How does one advance most rapidly within an organization?

WHAT WILL SELLING AND SALES MANAGEMENT BE LIKE IN THE FUTURE?

The successful professional salesperson or sales manager of 1990 may well be the failure of the year 2000 or 2020—a victim of progress! The next 10 or 20 years will be ones of rapid, even profound change, of problems, of new challenges, and of great opportunities for those companies, organizations, and individuals who can rise to the occasion.

What will these changes be? Science and technology will produce a host of new and now unthought-of products, and entire new service industries will arise as a result. Customers will be better educated and will be more sophisticated and demanding in their buying. As ever-increasing wealth and affuence spreads to more people, they will have the leisure to enjoy the desire for new and better products and service. Socioeconomic pressures and government reaction to them may cause sweeping changes in many aspects of business life.

In this fluid situation, businesses will face increasing competition in searching for new products, in lowering costs, in producing with greater efficiency, and in making higher profits. Automation will bring many changes in the way of doing business—in marketing and selling as in other functional areas. These developments will greatly affect both the professional and the personal lives of salespeople and sales managers.

Electronic Automation Will Shape Change in the 1990s

By 1990 the electronic revolution that marked the decade of the 1980s had begun to affect operations of field sales forces in many ways. Electronic mail, facsimile machines, personal computers in the office, and laptop computers for travel were just some of the new automated, electronic marvels that enabled field salespeople and their head offices to keep in close touch 24-hours a day.

Other available new electronic field sales aids included cellular automobile phones, voice mail, and ship to shore radio phones. Other new communication aids on the way include a nationwide and international digital phone network (due by the early 2000s) that will vastly improve computer communications and have the capability of transmitting full motion video.

Increasingly, the most helpful "new electronic friend" of the salesperson is the lightweight, portable laptop computer. These are well on their way to becoming standard equipment for North American field sales forces especially. By 1990, salespeople were accounting for 90 percent of their sales in the United States and Canada. Field salespeople praise them for helping optimize face-to-face selling time and minimizing administrative time.

This trend toward automation will likely be the major work-related event of the 1990s—affecting countless jobs of all types (especially those of field salespeople) and the way that corporations and other types of organizations do business.

Some Role-Changes in Store for Sales/Marketing Executives

Although the need for competent sales/marketing executives will be greater than ever, the situation will require some changes in their role. The scientific approach will become highly important, requiring mathematical and symbolic competence as well as the current creative approach to solving complex sales/marketing problems. In this situation, individual knowledge and competence will be all that counts. Like doctors, salespeople and sales managers will have to go to school or follow a constant program of self-study in order to stay abreast of the rapid changes in their field.

This study will have to extend to learning more about the other functions within the organization. Sales/marketing managers of the future will have to understand, even more deeply than today, the total corporate business picture as well as the interdependent roles of functions such as finance, personnel, production, and advertising. Global thinking, rather than that along national lines, will increasingly be the order of the day, and the most successful new managers will be internationalists in mind and heart. Ideally, they will have a good background in one or more foreign languages; certainly they will need a cultural background that allows them to understand and accept all individuals, nationalities, and races.

These sales/marketing managers will play an important role because they, and they alone of all the functional people in the organization, will be the vital link between organization and customer, representing one to the other.

WHAT ARE YOUR PERSONAL CHANCES OF REACHING MANAGEMENT LEVEL?

Since promotional opportunities through selling into sales management will be excellent during the next decade or two, if you wish to chart your career path in that direction the question becomes, "Can you make the grade?" The answer depends basically on your attitudes toward life and work, your basic human and character qualities, your aptitude for management, and how others judge your performance and capabilities.

In previous pages we have covered the attitudes, aptitudes, basic human and character qualities, professional skills, and work habits necessary to ensure success in selling. Thus we will assume that you do possess these basic ingredients and will relate them only to specific qualities needed by a manager (or leader) as constrasted to a salesperson.

Later we consider what your superiors look for in their evaluation of you as a potential manager. For the moment, however, we are concerned only with *your evaluation* of your ability to fulfill such a role. Many men and women are simply unsuited for management and would not like the role or the responsibilities it places on them even if they were given the opportunity.

Management requires some special personal characteristics. You have to set an example and lead others by demonstration as well as by talk. Thus you lose some personal freedom of action or independence, and you place the team above self. In sales management especially, since it is a line function, you have to work hard, outperform if possible, and often put the welfare of others ahead of yourself if you are to gain their respect and confidence in you as a leader. And, as you move into higher management, a staff function, certain analytical abilities are necessary in addition to those personal leadership characteristics basic to successful line management.

Here is a listing of some of the more important basic qualities or characteristics you must possess, both from a personal and professional point of view, if you hope to achieve success in management.

Personal Characteristics	Professional Characteristics
Self-confidence	Good organization
Consideration of others	Good planning abilities
Punctuality	Ability to write accurate reports
Open-mindedness	Ability to devise practical ideas
Consistency	Ability to see the company viewpoint
Creativeness	Orderliness
Initiative	Ability to produce quality work
Ambition	Ability to manage time efficiently
Enthusiasm	Good motivation

Sales management, as contrasted to pure personal selling, is more concerned with managing in the sense of planning, organizing, problem solving, and goal setting. These differences are illustrated in part by the chart shown in Table 21.2.

While this listing seems to be in part a mere restatement of earlier noted steps necessary for personal sales success, the difference is that a manager has to put them into practice even more devotedly and efficiently than does a salesperson. A sales manager must not only be professionally capable in every respect but also must possess the initiative, drive, and stamina to lead and to show others how to do an outstanding job. His or her enthusiasm and constant attempts to do the job better must rub off on others and are thus vital to success.

Merely thinking that you have most of the listed attitudes, aptitudes, characteristics, knowledge, and skills, or wanting to acquire them is not enough. Performance is the only thing that counts in selling, and outstanding perfor-

TABLE 21.2 *Area Sales Managers' Job Responsibility Chart*

To Yourself	*To Your Company or Organization*	*To Your Customers*
Increase basic selling skills.	*Be proud* of your association with your company.	*Work* closely with deciders and influencers in each account.
Develop management abilities.		
Keep pace with changes, trends, and developments in the territory.	*Maintain* company standing and standards with all customers.	*Point* out the advantages of an association with our company.
Study to be up to date on products, promotions, policies, and procedures.	*Inform* headquarters and supervisors, through established channels, of changes and developments within your territory.	*Keep* accounts current on all company advertising and promotional activities.
Stay alert for new sales and merchandising ideas.		*Suggest* ideas, methods, techniques, and tips that can stimulate their sales.
Grow so that you can assume greater responsibilities as opportunities permit.	*Be prompt* in handling records, reports, correspondence, and requests.	*Inform* customers of trends within their areas.
Maintain the appearance and deportment expected of a territory sales manager.	*Cut* selling costs by economical routing, good use of time, better planning, and greater awareness of opportunities.	*Handle* complaints efficiently and to their complete satisfaction.
Analyze your weaknesses and strong points; then do something about them.	*Check* demand and movement of products in the territory.	*Suggest* best techniques for selling our products to their customers.
	Report on the activities of competitors.	*Organize* presentations to inform and save time.
	Strive to meet and beat sales goals.	*Alert* customers to changes in company policies or procedures.
	Ask for help when you need it.	*Stimulate* and maintain enthusiasm for our products.
	Cooperate with other departments within the company.	*Build* and maintain goodwill.

mance, as judged by superiors in your company or organization, in the end determines your ability to be promoted to management level.

HOW DO YOUR SUPERIORS JUDGE YOUR MANAGERIAL POTENTIAL?

An outstanding sales record is but one of the many factors your superiors have to evaluate when considering you for promotion to a managerial position. The new role requires leadership abilities and certain other aptitudes, abilities, and qualities not essential to success in normal sales activities. Thus your superiors consider all aspects of your performance and also take into consideration your personal qualifications, knowledge, skills, and other overall abilities required for a managerial role. Here are some of the characteristics they evaluate within these areas.

Personal Qualities.   You do not have to look like a movie star to be a manager but good personal appearance does command respect. Thus good grooming and neatness are important factors. Your manner, as exemplified in your self-confidence, enthusiasm, and sincerity, leads to respect, confidence, pride, and trust in the minds of customers, subordinates, and superiors.

Perhaps the best way to consider the personal attributes or qualities others look for in you is to picture successful businesspeople or executives whom you know. What is it about them that commands your attention and respect? Your answers probably tie in fairly closely with the list of personal and professional qualities and characteristics noted earlier. Generally, as you view and evaluate their personal qualities, so do superiors evaluate yours.

Simple virtues are most likely to impress the boss—punctuality, strict observance of company or organization rules, concentration, trustworthiness, willingness, patience, and self-control. And the qualities of a team player—one who puts the welfare of the group before selfish personal interests—also are important. You do not have to give up your ambitions or individuality, but you do have to be a cooperative and willing member of the organization team.

Performance Record. A successful sales record, as noted earlier, is but one factor your superiors consider in evaluating your overall performance. They note the soundness of your opinions, your ability to profit from mistakes, your memory, and the way you put plans into action and follow through. They also consider the consistency, reliability, creativity, adaptability, and willingness you display in creating that successful sales record. They note your attendance record, how you organize your time, your ability to learn, and the neatness and accuracy of your reports. Other evaluations include these.

- How well you handle yourself in different situations.
- How well you keep management informed of competitors' activities, customer reactions, and other business and credit information.
- How neatly and how effectively you maintain and use sales manuals, visual aids, and records.

Above all, they are interested in the overall soundness of your judgment, your adherence to the organization viewpoint and methods, and the creativity of your ideas and suggestions. Your superiors are not seeking a superperson, but they do realize that a sound balance of these ingredients is essential to success at management level. It is your overall performance record that counts most to them.

Knowledge and Skill. In order to be considered for promotion to a managerial position, you have to exhibit the depth of your knowledge and skills. Some salespeople can build a good record around superficial knowledge and a few successful techniques. This background is not sufficient for sales management, since in that position you must have a depth of knowledge, theory, and practical skills in order to teach others with varied personalities and levels of experience and ability. We will consider in a moment some of the specific knowledge and skills required in a management role.

Special Management Aptitudes and Abilities. It is normally harder to show others how to sell successfully, to supervise their activities, and to motivate them than it is to do the job yourself. Therefore, in addition to normal sales skills, character qualifications, job knowledge, and a balanced, successful performance record, other special aptitudes and abilities are necessary for success in management.

A manager works at executive level, and the basic function of any executive is to get things done through subordinates who are confident of his or her abilities and talents and who trust his or her decisions. How he or she accomplishes this function is less important than that he or she possesses the gift of getting others to perform willingly under one's direction. This is perhaps the most important aptitude necessary for success. Because it is a difficult quality to pin down, your superiors have to evaluate your personality and performance record carefully to see whether you have it.

Some other special aptitudes and abilities necessary for success in management include analytical gifts, organizational and administrative talents, the ability to plan group efforts, and good communication skills.

WHAT KNOWLEDGE AND PERFORMANCE LEVEL DOES A MANAGERIAL ROLE REQUIRE?

What does being a manager entail? We have just discussed the fact that a manager has to be a leader, but what else does he or she have to know and do in order to hold this position? Management is the art, skill, or act of controlling, directing, or administering activities or affairs. Thus, a manager is a director or controller. In order to do that effectively, a manager must, in addition to the many things already noted, be able to:

Speak, write, and listen well.
Profit from mistakes.
Take calculated risks.
Simplify the task.
Tie up loose ends.
Set high standards.
Establish objectives to give a sense of direction.
Praise in public.
Criticize in private.
Be demanding yet considerate of others.

And, most importantly, beyond all this, a manager must possess the following qualities—qualities so essential to managerial success that you must honestly decide for yourself if you really possess them. These qualities are key factors to superiors who evaluate your past performance in terms of your possible managerial potential.

Judgment. A managerial role involves responsibility, and the soundness of your analyses and recommendations becomes more important the higher you rise. Do you have the ability to analyze problems calmly and objectively, and are you willing to be held accountable for your decisions?

Ability to Plan.   The higher your managerial position, the more time you must spend in planning. At the very top, the effectiveness of your planning determines the profitability of your division or company. The stakes are high—failure can even affect survival. Do you have the analytical abilities of a planner, or do you prefer to be out on the firing line, face-to-face with prospects and customers?

Communication Skills.   A manager has to be able to communicate plans effectively and persuasively, verbally or in writing. He or she has to sell his or her ideas to begin with in competition with courses of action advocated by others within the organization and to persuade others to accomplish them afterward.

The sincerity, logic, and clarity of expression in times of crisis can lead to success in spite of seemingly impossible obstacles. The best example of this is the eloquence of British Prime Minister Winston Churchill during the Battle of Britain in World War II. His verbal and written words alone at that time lifted his nation from physical and emotional defeat to ultimate victory.

Do you have the ability to think clearly and to communicate your thoughts rationally, forcefully (if not eloquently), and persuasively?

Reliability and Moral Courage.   Consistency and dependability are two very necessary qualities in management. A manager, because of the key role he or she plays, is considered one who can be depended upon by top management and subordinates alike. And consistent with reliability and dependability is the moral courage to make prompt decisions, to take prompt action, and to bravely accept the consequences of wrong decisions. Are you reliable? Do you have the moral courage to face the possibly adverse consequences of important decisions?

Ambition and Persistence.   These two qualities are also necessary for success in management. Ambition, if channeled in the right direction, is something to be proud of. It helps feed the inner drive necessary for success. Unless one is ambitious, why put up with the constant strain and risk that come with managerial responsibility? Persistence, or determination, is also essential to managerial follow-through, especially when the going is rough. Are you ambitious enough to face the risks and strains of a responsible managerial role? Are you determined and persistent enough to see every project through to the end whether it be a success or a failure?

HOW CAN YOU DEVELOP MANAGERIAL KNOWLEDGE, SKILLS, AND ABILITIES?

Up to this point, we have observed that while the door to management level is wide open, there is room at the top only for those who can produce results. Having considered what is required, do you at this point feel that you have the inner characteristics and qualities essential for success in management? Would you like a managerial job, in which you may spend most of your time in brain work at a desk, as contrasted to field sales work? If you are determined to try, then let us see how you may most rapidly develop the knowledge, skills, and abilities that will lead you to success.

Start by Programming and Managing Your Own Career.   Start by thinking like a manager about your own career, and develop a program for goal attainment. These simple four steps can form its core:

1.   Make an analysis of what has to be done to reach your objective.
2.   Plan the best way to reach it.
3.   Put the plan into action.
4.   Follow through to see that you accomplish your plan.

We will not attempt, in this brief section, to outline such a program for you. That is your responsibility. But we can dwell on three of the most important areas of growth necessary for success: knowledge, managerial and organizational skills, and communication skills.

Knowledge Comes Through Study

Basic to success at any level of management is your overall knowledge. Since the best way to learn is to see, hear, and do, the assimilation of knowledge is a never-ending, day-by-day task. Knowledge can be acquired on the job, through formal course study, and at home by joining professional associations such as Sales and Marketing Executives International (SMEI) which has approximately 10,000 members worldwide. In addition to SMEI executive offices at The Statler Office Tower (Suite 458), Cleveland, Ohio, 44115, U.S.A., the organization has affiliated chapter offices in Hong Kong, Tokyo, Mexico City, Toronto, Manila, and Kuala Lumpur (Malaysia).

It is, of course, always helpful to read professional publications such as the *Journal of Personal Selling & Sales Management* and *Sales & Marketing Management* (magazine) plus the many available good backlist books in the field, and the new ones that are constantly being published, all of which are normally available at good libraries.

Managerial and Organizational Skills

These can be learned through formal study, by observing others and asking questions, and by application. The best way to learn by doing, is to seize every opportunity to accept responsibility, to take on tasks that others may shirk because of the extra work involved, and to do as many jobs, surveys, or reports as you can.

All this responsibility involves heavy extra work, but you will be rewarded with knowledge that is difficult to get in any other way. Opportunities to learn new skills and to apply them come every day in many different ways if you look for them. Once you decide that skills are necessary for success, then you can plan how to acquire them over a period of time.

Communication Skills

These also can be learned through formal study and practice. Many books and courses are available on report writing and effective oral communication. When you make written reports, spend all the time necessary to do them carefully and properly. Then ask your superiors to constructively criticize them so that you can do a better job next time.

Joining a local Toastmaster's Club, where you can practice public speaking before friends, is one of the best ways to improve your oral communication skills. You can also tape sales presentations and play them back so that you can hear yourself as others hear you. Your spouse, friends, or business associates can help point out areas that need improvement.

HOW DO YOU ADVANCE MOST RAPIDLY WITHIN AN ORGANIZATION?

Sell yourself if you want to be considered for a management position. Let your superiors know that you are capable of performing a bigger job than the one you currently hold. As in all selling situations, you have to determine their needs and wants and present your product (you) in terms of value and benefits to them.

Since requirements for management are different from those for line selling, you have to prove that you fit the needs and requirements of the better position. The best proof you can offer is to demonstrate constantly by action and results your capabilities and potential in every aspect of your work.

Accept the fact that every task assigned to you represents opportunity. Most men and women consider difficult tasks or assignments problems. What a difference it can make in your life and career if you look upon problems as opportunity in disguise! Seek those tasks or assignments others may try to avoid, and through superior performance prove your willingness and capabilities.

Selling your own capabilities depends in part on how well you program your goals within the organization, how well you perform at each stage, and how effectively you let your superiors know of each new qualification you have. You need not be embarrassed to sell yourself if you are capable and are producing good results. Top executives are busy people and may not notice your efforts unless they are somehow called to their attention.

Find out What Your Superiors Want and Need and Give It to Them. This involves a total commitment to the organization effort, complete loyalty as a subordinate so that you are trusted, and willingness to take advantage of every opportunity offered. Opportunity to prove your abilities in a new situation may come in the form of a request to relocate anywhere within your country or the world. Many men and women fail to be promoted because they are unwilling to relocate. Yet top executives as a group are highly mobile, and, as in the military or diplomatic service, constant relocation is part of the game.

Pattern Yourself after Successful Superiors. In North American companies a newly promoted executive quite often takes two or three trusted subordinates along with him or her. If you are offered the opportunity to work with an executive on the way up and prove to be highly competent and dependable, you may help make him or her look good and even become crucial to his or her upward moves. Such an association does not mean that you have to be a yes-person or lose your individuality. Even if you do not move with him or her, you can apply his or her successful methods to your own work.

The Ability to Adapt Rapidly to New Situations Is Important to Success.   One of the main functions of executives is to solve new problems or problems subordinates for one reason or another are unable to solve. The ability you display in grasping, adapting to, and handling successfully new assignments or problems gives superiors a good clue to your managerial potential. If you can prove such competence in new assignments, your pathway to the top will be smooth.

The Ability to Be Promoted Does not Depend on Intellectual Ability Alone.   Being a poor student in school does not necessarily reduce your chances for reaching even top management. Dwight Eisenhower did not graduate in the top part of his West Point Military Academy class in the United States. Yet because of his leadership abilities, he surpassed all his classmates to become commander of the Allies in World War II and later president of his country.

You may not have to be an intellectual giant or technical expert to reach the top through sales/marketing, but you must have the executive ability to work with those who are. You must know how to meet and talk with highly intelligent experts or technicians, how to select key facts from their knowledge, and how to use these facts in making sound decisions.

The Ability to Work with Others Is Important to Any Team Effort.   This ability is just as important within the company or organization as outside it. Organization charts look good on paper, but coordination among different functional or department heads is usually achieved informally. If you know personally, get along with, and understand the problems of these individuals in your organization, you can often accomplish goals faster than you could through formal meetings. Thus, the ability to work well informally with others is an important aspect of teamwork.

How not to Get Ahead in Management!   We have delved at some length throughout this chapter into what you have to do to succeed in management. But we should note in passing some of things one should not do if he or she wants to get along with others or to be promoted to management level. Perhaps this brief listing is sufficient warning.

How Not to Get Along or Ahead

Harbor resentment	Worry all the time
Be an office politician	Criticize too quickly
Act self-important	Be a slave driver
Complain all the time	Be a crybaby
Be an apple polisher	Undermine colleagues

Strive at All Times to Think and Act Like a Professional.   A successful manager, executive, or leader is a professional. He or she has the ability to analyze problems, develop solutions, and lead others to successful conclusion of a planned action. If you can do these things in a disciplined way and can inspire trust and confidence in others, then you are a professional and certainly deserve to fill the managerial role of your ambitions.

SUMMARY

We directed this chapter to those readers who have the desire, through hard work and dedication, to reach the higher income brackets in personal selling, or to advance to sales management or top management via the sales route. Opportunities for each have never been greater.

Three basic ways to get to the top, in income or promotion, through personal selling were noted: (1) as a full-time professional salesperson, (2) as developer of one's own business, or (3) as a member of a company team. Since personal goal setting and effective self-management are essential to success in any of these areas, we challenged ambitious readers to *start now* by filling out a sample one-to-20-year "want to" goal chart.

The importance of proper attitudes toward life and work was considered, and practical ideas for changing negative attitudes and traits into positive ones were presented.

Building on previous chapters, many new, high-powered proven ideas from successful professional salespeople were offered as guides to higher sales and earnings.

Through a series of seven questions, we then discussed opportunities for promotion to management in the future and outlined the knowledge, characteristics, and qualities needed for such promotion. Discussion then centered on the level of knowledge and performance required of a manager, and we discussed how to develop the managerial knowledge, skills, and abilities necessary for success.

Our conclusion was that a managerial role requires special attributes not necessarily essential to success in selling itself. These include well-rounded knowledge, plus cited special human and character qualities, analytical abilities, reasonable intelligence, and certain basic aptitudes for management. We also noted that a natural gift for leadership is essential for success.

Reaching the top requires a total commitment to your company or organization, including, if necessary, frequent relocation. You should view such moves or the assignment of difficult tasks as opportunities to further prove your abilities. Since management is a team effort, your commitment must be that of a team player, although that need not affect your ambitions or individuality.

Questions for Analysis and Discussion

1.   Do you really believe that a total commitment to the organization one works for is necessary for a salesperson who wants to become a sales manager? Why?

2.   What does the term *programming* mean in terms of managerial planning?

3.   Increased sales volume alone is not enough to achieve high sales and earnings in selling. What else is vitally important?

4.   Think of a friend, relative, or acquaintance whom you feel demonstrates true leadership and managerial qualities. What, in your opinion, are those qualities that cause you to feel the way you do about him or her?

5.   Why is it so important, in order to achieve real sales success, for a salesperson to make every effort to find out why customers buy, and to get evidence and endorsement from them in the form of testimonials?

6.   It is easy for a salesperson to say, "I would like to sell more or extras to each of my current customers," but what can he or she do practically to accomplish this objective?

7.   What is meant by the suggestion, "One good way to increase sales is to sell across the board"?

8.   Why is it so important to personal selling for a salesperson to analyze all his or her sales in terms of what each customer purchased and the size of their purchase?

CASE STUDY 21

Trained as Problem-Solvers—A High Percentage of Today's Top IBM Executives Started Out as Marketing Representatives

International Business Machines Corporation—IBM—one of the world's largest industrial corporations, is well-known for its company slogan "THINK," coined by Thomas J. Watson, Sr., its famed chief executive from 1914 to 1956.

A more apt motto might be "SELL," for while IBM has certainly been an important innovator of new ideas and products, their explosive growth since starting corporate life in 1911 under the name Computing-Tabulating-Recording Company (renamed in 1924 as International Business Machines Corporation in the United States), has been largely due to their belief and strength in sales/marketing. Mr. Watson, who joined IBM as president in 1914, had formerly worked for National Cash Register Company, where he was a branch manager at age 25 and later general sales manager. He had great confidence that good salespeople could do almost anything, and consistantly promoted successful salespeople into jobs such as plant management, personnel, and other key nonsales positions.

TODAY'S RESULTS PROVE THE WISDOM OF THAT PROMOTIONAL POLICY

As a result of Watson's policies and faith, a high percentage of today's top IBM executives chart their success from starting out as marketing representatives. Today, more than 60,000 company sales/marketing people worldwide are involved in providing effective information, products, and services to countless IBM customers.

Their training, thinking, and efforts are focused around the long-held corporate goal of anticipating needs of the world's marketplaces, and producing innovative products and programs to meet those needs. After-sale service to ensure product reliability and long-term customer satisfaction is their second major goal. As a result of efforts like these, IBM, with 387,000 employees in 132 countries, had a worldwide revenue of $59.7 billion in 1988.

IBM Marketing Representatives Do More than Selling—They're Specialists in Problem Solving

Within the United States, IBM divides its business effort into 12 major marketplaces under an umbrella U.S. Marketing and Services organization. Area managers for both marketing and service oversee those functions in each of the 12 geographical trading areas.

Carefully selected college and university graduate applicants interested in sales join the company as marketing representatives, and begin a comprehensive training program that may last a year or more. This program prepares them to contact and work with all areas of management within business firms, government agencies, or educational institutions.

Once in the field, their sales duties include direct in-depth contact with IBM customers and prospects. They concentrate on analyzing business operations carefully in order to recommend overall systems solutions, software, and contract services.

These marketing representatives soon become specialists in problem solving and experts in providing solutions that meet specific customer needs. They learn how to conduct detailed surveys to understand how businesses and other types of organizations are structured, and how individual companies compare with others in their industries. The marketing representatives also learn how to prepare and present effective oral and written presentations on their findings, and how to make businesslike recommendations to customer, management, and executives.

Moreover, they learn to work on an IBM team with others, including specialist technical professionals. All the initial and continued training and development field work aims to prepare each marketing representative to serve his or her customers as a valued problem solver in information management.

In its constant company-wide effort to recruit sales-minded people of both sexes and all races as marketing representatives, IBM seeks individuals who look at new situations as opportunities and challenges. The company wants employees who can work well with others, develop rapport, and originate and follow through on their own projects. Above all—IBM seeks future marketing representatives with that special inner motivation—the will to win!

Questions for Written Reports or Class Discussion

1. Do you feel that IBM might be a good company to join in order to pursue a sales career? Upon what factors is your opinion based?

2. Let's assume that you have just been hired as a new IBM marketing representative, and are commencing a training class with 30 other equally intelligent, carefully selected college graduates. What will you have to do better than most of them in order to achieve your personal high promotional goals ten years from now?

3. Do you feel a woman can be as successful as a man in designing and selling expensive computer systems to government agencies, or business and industrial firms? Would a woman be equally effective in after-sale servicing? Upon what known or felt factors do you base your opinion?

4. Does IBM's sales success, as noted in the above case study, bear out the opinion of many experts that personal selling plays a vital role in large-scale systems selling? Could IBM dispense with its marketing representatives and continue to maintain its huge sales lead in the future? Explain.

| Sales Problem 21.1 | A challenge to young Americans—win personal fame and fortune by selling new types of "made in America" products abroad |

A late 1980s *Wall Street Journal* article explained why West Germany had just supplanted the United States as the world's top exporter (Japan was listed as number three) despite the deutsche mark's huge appreciation relative to the dollar. The article's headline blared the clue to success: "German Firms Stress Quality, Niches to Keep Exports High."

Nearly any red-blooded American high school football quarterback could tell his nation's business leaders that the best preemptive defense of their home market in the long term is to take on formidable competitors on their turf. Such bravado was hardly characteristic of the vast majority of American business executives as their country entered the 1990s, however, when corporate whining for a "level playing field" seemed to be the norm in face of a huge and ever-widening national trade deficit, no matter how far the dollar fell.

Even as giant American manufacturers like General Motors (which sold only 1800 cars to Japan in 1987) still refused to move car steering wheels to the right for export to Japan (the Japanese, like the British, drive on the left), a new, younger generation of Americans was starting to profit from recognizing international competition as an opportunity, not a threat.

Take Jim Koch, for example. It was nearly impossible to find an "American" brew in Munich, Germany (the beer capital of the world) until he came along. Nowadays his Samuel Adams Boston Lager can be had just around the corner from the Hofbrau Haus. It became the first (and as of early 1989 the only) American beer to be sold there, having passed the 472-year-old German beer-purity law. And take Charles Nevil of California; he's exporting good old American river bottom sand to the Middle East (a finer quality than is to be found there) for assorted uses.

Other aggressive Americans are selling frozen tuna fish and disposable chopsticks to Japan, and Fred Chao of San Francisco promoted a joint venture with the Chinese government to set up 24 Super Kleen dry cleaning shops in the city of Tianjin. These were the first modern dry-cleaning outlets in the People's Republic of China. Fred thinks big—he has plans for self-service laundries there as well. Since ten Chinese cities have populations over 8 million—these alone represent "a lot of wash," to his way of thinking!

These American entrepreneurs and their companies, and others like them, are, along with so many internationally sales-minded Japanese and West Germans, frequently "niche players." They start by finding a niche in the overseas market where quality, service, and innovation, rather than low cost, has proven to be the secret of their success.

Japanese officials keep saying that U.S. companies and those of other foreign countries have great opportunities to sell their products in Japan during the 1990s. With the Japanese consumer market alone nearly half the size of the U.S. consumer market, with about the same per capita consumption, they could be right. Imports of meat, seafood, lumber, office products, and semiconductors all increased dramatically there in the late 1980s. These officials predict that huge and largely untapped Japanese markets exist for, among other things, imported American-made alcoholic beverages, automobiles (with right side steering wheels), chemicals, and apparel. They wonder why American salespeople are not trying harder to tap these markets.

Question for Written Reports or Class Discussion

Recognizing that Japan is sincerely interested in opening its doors to more American and other foreign-made imports during the 1990s, what basic steps would you take, as sales representative for a small U.S. full-line manufacturer of specialty sportswear, on your first visit to that country, to penetrate that market?

How do you rate yourself in terms of managerial and leadership potential?

How do you determine whether you are presently qualified for sales management or high level executive authority—for administrative or emergency leadership? The following self-evaluation questions will help you analyze your potential for such. Go ahead, fill them out right now. Be honest with yourself in your answers!

1. I have the ability to analyze a complicated problem and to explain it in an orderly, logical manner.

   Yes _____ No _____

2. I respond to the stimulus of a different assignment and am fully confident that I can carry it through.

   Yes _____ No _____

3. I lack confidence in my decisions if they affect important operations and prefer to have my superior review my recommendations before I take action.

   Yes _____ No _____

4. I am a bug on details. Once I am given an assignment and am told exactly how it is to be accomplished, I carry it through to the letter.

   Yes _____ No _____

5. I seek difficult jobs. By accomplishing them I add to my reputation.

   Yes _____ No _____

6. I need my superior's approval. I am upset if he or she criticizes my performance.

   Yes _____ No _____

7. I want responsibility and diplomatically seek to enlarge my authority by acting on my own initiative when I have the chance. Usually I am successful.

   Yes _____ No _____

8. When there are several alternate approaches to accomplishing an objective, I have no hesitancy in choosing a course of action.

   Yes _____ No _____

9. I like living by a schedule and am comfortable when my responsibilities are clearly laid out for me.

   Yes _____ No _____

10. I like to complete a job once I start it. It annoys me to be asked to handle two or three important assignments simultaneously.

    Yes _____ No _____

11. I do not like to delegate. I always have a feeling of confidence when I am doing the job myself or, if it is necessary to delegate, when I am supervising the work of my subordinates.

Yes _____ **No** _____

12. I dislike details and prefer to work on broad problems and to delegate the routine to assistants.

Yes _____ **No** _____

13. I avoid arguing with my superior even when I disagree with his or decisions.

Yes _____ **No** _____

14. My subordinates respect me but consider me a middle person in the relaying of instructions.

Yes _____ **No** _____

15. I am perfectly willing to accept the responsibility for decisions I make that go wrong. After all, I want to be held accountable. That way I get credit for success.

Yes _____ **No** _____

Yes answers to seven of the above questions (1, 2, 5, 7, 8, 12, and 15) indicate that you have the temperament for successful leadership in any situation. They indicate that you have an analytical mind, are independent in your thinking, have confidence in your decisions, and do not fear criticism.

No answers to these seven and *yes* answers to the remaining ones indicate that you are probably an able administrator but shy away from ultimate responsibilities.

Questions for Written Reports or Class Discussion

1.   Do you accept the judgment that failure to answer "yes" to these seven questions indicates a lack of leadership potential on your part? Why do you feel this way?

2.   Regardless of how you judge your own characteristics in the above index, what is the value in honestly asking yourself such questions?

GLOSSARY OF SALES TERMS

The following selected terms, most of which are used in this text, are commonly used in selling. The definitions are drawn from authoritative sources, are based upon general acceptance, and are related to selling. In some instances the definitions have been extended to include the practices connected with the terms.

Not all the terms or definitions included in the text appear on this list; only the most important or commonly used ones are given.

Account classification The rating of customers according to current business and, more importantly, according to potential.

Advantage In sales, the way a feature of a product or service can help solve problems or meet needs.

Agent middleman (merchant middleman) One who negotiates purchases or sales or both, but does not take title to the goods in which he or she deals.

Annual report A printed and most often illustrated message to stockholders that is signed by the chairman of the board and president and that incorporates the company income statement and balance sheet for the latest fiscal year, usually with comparisons to previous periods, comments on past performance, and prospects for the future.

Appeal The motive toward which a sales point is directed in the hopes of stirring the prospect to favorable consideration of the product or service being presented.

Approach phase The part of the sales presentation that covers the introduction and quick selling of self, product, and company, in that order, to get and hold attention and interest and thus develop INP (Information, Need, Product).

Authority The power to make decisions and enforce them.

Automation The complete performance of a complex mechanical act without human intervention.

Bad debt An uncollectible receivable.

Balance sheet A financial statement of the condition of an enterprise as of a specified date.

Benefit In sales, a need that has been met.

Bonus An extra compensation because of high productivity, contractual agreement, or a similar reason.

Brand name The spoken trademark or part of a trademark, as contrasted to the pictorial symbol.

Budget   A financial plan of proposed expenditures for a stated period, often combined with a forecast of revenues.

Business   In the economic sense it relates to the buying and selling of goods and services; in the commercial sense it relates more to a person, partnership, or corporation engaged in manufacturing, commerce, or service. In both senses it relates to profit-seeking activities.

Business ethics   The socially accepted rules of conduct that influence businesspeople to be honest and fair in their dealings with others.

Buyer   (1) In retailing, an executive responsible for purchasing and other duties of departmental management; (2) any person who is open to acquire merchandise for monetary consideration; thus, one who buys.

Buyer's market   Where goods and services are plentiful and prices relatively low.

Buying signals   Any words, facial expressions, or physical actions on the part of a prospect, at any time during the sales interview, which may indicate that he or she feels psychologically compelled to buy.

Callback   The approach that a sales representative makes on the second or subsequent attempt to sell a prospect.

Canned presentation   A prewritten and memorized sales presentation which is verbally presented word for word.

Canvass   To call on individuals personally or by telephone to make a survey or to sell goods or services.

Capitalism   An economic system based on the freedoms of ownership, production, exchange, acquisition, work, movement, and competition.

Cash discounts   Discounts off the list price offered to buyer in return for prompt payment for merchandise bought.

Catalogue   Printed matter listing items for sale, usually with descriptions, illustrations, and prices.

Chain stores   A group of retail outlets which may or may not have the same ownership, but which operate under the same central management and business policy.

Channel of distribution (*see* **marketing channel**)

Close or closing   In sales, the prospect's verbal or signed agreement to buy the product or service being offered.

Cold call   The act of going to see a prospect without an appointment, in the hope of either getting an interview on the spot or of making an appointment for one.

Cold-canvassing   Finding leads independently, such as following up a telephone book Yellow Pages listing of specific potential users.

Commission   A percentage of a sale price paid to a sales representative, broker, or agent.

Composite inventory   A collection of facts about customers or prospects, including everything that can be related to the who, what, where, why, and how of basic reporting or fact-finding.

Consignment   Goods on which title is conveyed to the consignee only when he or she resells and pays, with the consignee retaining the right to return the unsold portion of the goods.

Consumer   One who consumes or uses up.

Consumer goods (or products)   Those goods, products, or services bought by consumers for their own personal use.

Consumer market (*see* **market**)   Consumers who buy for personal or household consumption.

Consumerism   The interaction of consumers, politicians, consumer advocates, business, and industry toward the achievement of consumer rights.

Consumerist movement   Social action to achieve consumerism.

Controls   The checks employed by both the sales representative and management to compare progress or results against the preplanned sales program.

Convenience goods   Those consumer goods that are normally bought at nearby or convenient outlets without shopping for better prices, styles, or other features.

Cooperative advertising   Advertising placed by retailers and paid for at least in part by the manufacturers or suppliers whose products are advertised.

Cost of sales   (1) To a trading business, the cost of goods purchased less the excess of inventory at the end of the period over inventory at the beginning; (2) to a manufacturing business, the cost of goods manufactured less the excess of the inventory of finished goods at the end of the period over the inventory of finished goods at the beginning.

Current accounts Those customer names taken from past records and rated (prime, good, etc.) in order of past business and future potential.

Customer-oriented In sales, the attempt to understand problems, wants, and needs from the customer's point of view and to help him fulfill his or her desires.

Customer/society-oriented marketing concept (*see* **marketing concept**) A sales/marketing orientation backed by integrated marketing aimed at fulfilling consumer needs with something of value and benefit that will bring lasting satisfaction and provide as well for net improvement in the quality of life for all consumers and to the long-term benefit of society.

Dealer One who confers quantity utility (breaks lots into smaller quantities for resale) and other utilities on goods or services.

Decision maker In sales, the individual or key individual in a group who either has the authority to make a decision or the ability to influence others.

Decision making The process of resolving open choices into one opinion or course of action so that, when backed by authority, it becomes policy.

Decision-making group Individual decision makers, often specialists, who share responsibility for purchase decisions. (The final decision is usually a consensus of the individual decisions.)

Direct, or door-to-door, or house-to-house, selling The sales representative's taking of a product or service directly from the manufacturer or supplier to the customer's home or office, thus cutting out all middlemen in the process.

Direct mail Advertisements sent to prospects or customers (printed pieces, catalogues, circular letters, postcards, and telegrams).

Discount To offer something for sale at a reduced price below the normal list price.

Distribution In marketing, the separation, breaking down, or spreading out of units or parts to apportion them among different layers and levels of groups.

Drummer An old-fashioned American sales representative who called on retailers of soft goods or greeted them as they went into buying centers.

Emotional buying motives Nonrational motives, such as impulses, habits, and drives.

Empathy In sales, the ability to detect by perception how a prospect feels and what his attitudes and opinions are.

Ethical responsibility The professional standards of a sales representative as related to moral character, motives, and actions.

Exclusive (1) Obtainable only at certain stores or from a limited number of designated distributors or dealers; (2) an agreement to confine sales in an area to a single retailer.

Executive A person whose position calls for the making of decisions and the exercise of power over others in the conduct of the affairs of a company or organization.

Expense account Monies which are advanced by a company to a sales representative to meet travel, entertainment, or other specified costs and for which he or she is held accountable.

Feature In sales, the characteristic of a product or service that produces a benefit.

Feedback In sales, market information from the field obtained from interviews or surveys.

Field survey A sampling of opinion or facts among industry members, dealers, or consumers that is assembled from interviews on the premises of those interviewed.

Firm order A definite order, either verbal or written, that cannot be canceled.

Fixed routing A sales-call pattern whereby customers are called on repeatedly or at regular intervals.

FOB price Most merchandise is sold FOB (Free On Board) shipping point. This means the seller pays transportation costs to that point, and the buyer pays charges from that point.

Follow-up or follow-through (1) In management, the systematic working of a preplanned sales program both up to and following a closing attempt; (2) in sales, actions taken after the closing of the sale to ensure delivery, satisfaction, etc.

Forecasting The collection of facts or data upon which one tries to calculate or estimate what will happen within a specific time.

Forestalling objections The incorporation into the planned sales presentation of some commonly expressed objections and the answering of them in the course of the presentation, before they can be raised as objections.

Free enterprise The freedom of a business or an individual to organize and operate competitively for profit without undue government interference.

Fringe benefits Compensation for labor in a form other than wages, such as health insurance, pensions, paid vacations, etc.

Goal-setting The stages leading to or including the end of one's aims or objectives.

Goods (*see* **product**).

Goods and services The output of industry and labor, equaling, in economic terms, the gross national product of a nation for any given year.

Group selling Involves selling to a group of two or more individuals as contrasted to a single person.

Hard sell (high-pressure selling) A method of selling which is direct, forceful, and insistent (the opposite of **soft sell**).

House organ A publication of a business concern that contains articles of interest to its employees and customers.

Impulse buying The purchasing of goods or services on impulse rather than by plan or according to need.

Inducement An additional consideration to persuade a person to make an agreement.

Industrial goods (*or* products) Those goods, products, or services consumed by businesses, and those used in the manufacture of other goods.

Industrial market (*see* **market**) Consumers who buy to further production of other goods and services.

Industry An industry represents a level in the Standard Industrial Classification (SIC) system developed by the United States Bureau of the Census to cover all commercial activity.

INP Abbreviation for Information-Need-Product; a "sales handle" often taught to sales trainees to help them remember the simple, logical, step-by-step progressive development of a sales presentation in any common sales situation.

Interaction In sales, the reciprocal action, influence, or understanding between the sales represen-

tative and the prospect or customer and between him or her and the company.

Irregular routing A sales-call pattern in which frequency of calls is left up to the sales representative.

Jobber A marketing middleman or company that buys in quantity from wholesalers and resells in smaller lots to retailers.

Lead (sales lead) A possible but unqualified prospect or customer.

Lead-in That part of a discussion that allows a salesperson to move into a sales presentation; or, during a presentation, into a close.

Leadership The exercise of qualities of guidance and command in a resourceful and responsible manner in a company or organization.

Line and staff A form of organization characterized by direct-line authority, with staff assistants provided to those in the higher ranks.

List price Published, basic prices; normally found in sellers' price lists, catalogues, and advertisements. Normally considered the highest price on a product, since it is often subject to discounts.

Management The process whereby resources are combined into an integrated system in order to accomplish the objectives of the system. Management, at its many levels, plans and sets objectives and strives to ensure that they are met.

Management by objectives (MBO) A way of practicing the four basic management functions of planning, organizing, executing, and controlling—a way of managing.

Management functions There are four generally accepted action processes essential to meeting objectives: planning, organizing, executing, and controlling. They may occur simultaneously in different ways, at different managerial levels, at different times.

Manager A person charged with the control or direction (all or in assigned part) of a business, an organization, or the like.

Managerially oriented One who thinks like a manager in terms of setting and controlling efforts toward a predetermined goal or objective.

Mannerisms Peculiarities of speaking or acting or in one's bearing.

Mark-down To fix the selling price of an item by adding seller's cost price and selling expenses to reach desired profit level.

Market The total or aggregate demand of the potential buyers for a product or service; *aggregate* is the composite demands of many consumers for a specific item. From a sales/marketing viewpoint, there are two broad market divisions—the consumer market and the organizational market.

Market research Research to gather the facts upon which a marketing decision can be made.

Market segment Groups of potential buyers who demand specific different requirements for the same item.

Marketing The performance of business activities that direct the flow of goods and services from producer to consumer or user.

Marketing channel A path traced in the direct or indirect transfer of ownership to a product, as it moves from a producer to ultimate consumers or industrial users. (This same definition also applies to **channel of distribution**.)

Marketing concept (*see* **customer/society-oriented marketing concept**) A customer orientation backed by integrated marketing aimed at generating customer satisfaction as the key to satisfying organizational goals.

Marketing mix The combination of four elements to achieve sales/marketing strategic objectives: the product, channels of distribution, pricing policies, and promotional methods.

Marketplace Relates, in the commercial sense, to the activities of business and trade.

Merchandising The planning and promotion of sales by presenting a product to the right market at the proper time, by carrying out organized, skillful advertising and sales promotion. It includes nearly every activity that influences consumers to buy the product except personal selling (but even here a sales representative often sells merchandising plans).

Merchant One who takes title to (that is, buys) and resells merchandise.

Middlemen Those who specialize in performing activities that are directly involved in the purchase and sale of goods in the process of their flow from producer to final buyer. Middlemen can also fall into categories such as agent middlemen, merchant middlemen, retailers, and wholesalers.

Motivational needs Basic common denominators of desire, such as psychological, biological, social, or self-fulfillment needs.

Net price When the list price is reduced by the discounts applicable, the net price is the result.

No sale final A management policy meaning that no sale is final until a customer is completely satisfied with his or her purchase.

Objections Questions or doubts in the prospect's mind which the salesperson is happy to answer.

Objective (*or* goal) Something specific to be achieved.

Order form A previously prepared or printed form containing information about a product or service being offered for sale which, to save time, the sales representative often fills out in front of the customer, often asking for an approval signature.

Peddler One who travels and retails or hawks small quantities of goods.

Personal leadership qualities The ability to persuade others to work under one's direction as a team to accomplish certain designated objectives.

Personal selling The art/skill/science of persuading someone to accept or follow ideas and thus to take the action desired (buying).

Persuasion To move a person or persons to a belief, a position, a point of view, or a course of action.

Physical inventory An inventory taken by actual count of merchandise rather than from existing records.

Planned presentation A preplanned, structured sales message in which only key points are memorized and presented in word-for-word sequence, the parts in between being presented more informally as the situation requires.

Planning A predetermined course of action that starts with the establishment of goals and objectives.

Point-of-purchase (POP) advertising Interior store displays and literature distributed at retail counters or for window displays.

Preapproach Involves (1) finding out as much as possible about the prospect prior to the interview, and (2) determining how to get the specific interview—through prior appointment or without an appointment.

President or managing director The highest-ranking operating company official, who is responsible to the board of directors for company policy and management.

Price control When a manufacturer exercises price control, the buyer-for-resale is not permitted to determine his or her own selling price.

Product (goods) A product is what a seller has to sell; it can be goods, services, ideas, or anything else of value. *Goods* and *products mean the same thing in a sales/marketing sense.*

Professional standards In sales, the conduct, aims, and qualities generally agreed on as opposed to amateur or nonprofessional standards.

Profit The difference between income received from sales and all costs or expenses.

Profitability The ability of a business to earn a profit and the extent of the profit it can earn.

Programming The specific activities or procedures necessary to accomplish planned goals or objectives.

Promotional mix In attempting to communicate with, inform, persuade, and sell goods, services, or ideas to consumers, a firm or organization employs a four-part promotional mix consisting of advertising, publicity, sales promotion, and personal selling.

Proposal A verbal or written recommendation or offer.

Prospect A potential customer.

Prospecting The process of looking up and checking out sales leads.

Purchasing agent An officially appointed buyer for a large company or organization.

Put-off (or stall) A pretext, ruse, or trick often expressed by prospects in the form of objections to delay or avoid a buying decision.

Qualified prospect A prospect who has a need or want for any given product or service, is able to afford it, and is able to make the decision to purchase it.

Qualitative reports More personalized and detailed than quantitative reports in that a personal estimate or opinion is included.

Quantitative reports Brief factual reports that help compare efforts expended versus results in the preplanned sales program.

Quantity discounts Discounts off list price offered to buyers in return for buying in large volume.

Question technique The sales technique of directing questions to prospects in order to find out what they know, think, or feel about what is being offered, and to secure their agreement on various sales points made.

Radiation (selling) methods Involves exploiting a single sale as a center from which to attempt other sales out from it in a widening circle or area based on using it as an example.

Rapport In sales, the affinity, understanding, accord, or harmony between sales representative and prospect.

Rational buying motives All costs affecting the buyer, including cost in money, cost of use, length of usage, degree of labor, and ultimate benefit.

Real salespeople (or sales representatives) Those specialty (outside) salespeople who are vitally concerned with closing sales on most calls.

Referral leads Names of potential prospects given by satisfied users, unsold prospects, or other individuals.

Results-oriented In sales, the understanding by salespeople that they are paid to sell products in the marketplace and that they will be judged on results.

Retail (inside) salesperson One who normally works inside stores and has customers come to him or her.

Retailer A merchant, or occasionally an agent, whose main business is selling directly to ultimate consumer.

Retailing Consists of the activities involved in selling directly to the ultimate consumer. Retailers, of course, are engaged in retailing, but so is any other institution, organization, or individual that sells directly to ultimate consumers.

Rifle technique A sales concept that concentrates on a few items of greatest interest to the prospect in a planned, systematic, effective manner which, through involving him or her in the buying process, leads directly, rapidly, and persuasively to a buying decision (the opposite of **shotgun approach**).

Sale   The transfer of title to goods or property or the agreement to perform a service in return for payment of cash or for the promise to pay.

Sales anchors   Planned statements kept in mind, ready for use at any time, to help sales representatives handle certain standard objections, especially those of a stalling nature.

Sales aptitude   The natural potential, capacity, or ability to achieve success as a sales representative according to the qualities, characteristics, and demands of the sales profession.

Sales manual (sales kit)   A handbook or manual offering details about a product or service; can be employed for instructional uses only, or as a visual sales tool, or a combination thereof.

Sales/marketing   A term often used to describe the modern interrelationship of marketing and personal selling, perhaps the most important of the four marketing functions.

Salesperson (sales representative)   One who sells goods, services, or ideas. The term *salesperson* is often used to describe those who sell goods in a retail store; *sales representative* (replacing the older term *salesman*) is often used to describe those men and women engaged in outside selling, where they call on prospects in their homes, offices, or places of business.

Sales pitch   A line of reasoning or persuasive argument intended to persuade someone to buy, accept, or do something.

Sales presentation   The complete sales process of telling a prospect or a group about a product or service, from personal introduction to asking for the order.

Sales promotion   Those elements of marketing that embrace display, selling schemes, publicity-winning ploys, and advertising other than in regularly paid, space-and-time media.

Sales representative (*see* **salesperson**).

Sales trainee   A newly hired salesperson or sales representative engaged in basic sales training.

Sample or sampling   The distribution of small lots of a product to permit prospective buyers to become familiar with it, thus promoting its sale, or, simply, a model used for sales demonstrations and booking orders.

Scheduling   In sales, the arrangement and management of the time necessary to carry out a sales program.

Second sale   When a customer has just made a purchase, he or she is in a buying mood. This offers an opportunity to suggest something else which he or she might purchase readily as a second item.

Self-image   The private evaluation of one's abilities or what one would like to be seen as; thus, the inner, personal, mental picture of the kind of person one is.

Self-management   The personal organization of planning, time, and work.

Seller's market   Where goods and services are scarce and prices relatively high.

Selling   The personal or impersonal process of assisting and/or persuading a prospective customer to buy a commodity or service and to act favorably upon an idea that has commercial significance to the seller.

Shopping center   An area that is planned and engineered as a place for retail trade, free from manufacturing and residential dilution, with stores, shops, and parking in one specialized location away from the heart of an urban area but readily reached by automobile.

Shopping goods   The products a consumer buys infrequently after shopping around to compare price, style, and other features.

Shotgun approach   A sales approach that covers a wide area in an irregular, ineffective, haphazard way based on the hope that by sheer luck something might be said or done that will interest or persuade a prospective buyer.

Soft sell   A method of selling which is quietly persuasive, subtle, and indirect (the opposite of **hard sell**).

Specialty (outside) sales representative   One who goes outside to call on prospects in their homes, offices, or places of business.

Telephone sales itinerary   A plan outlining in advance exactly which prospects or accounts will be called, and in what frequency.

Territory screening   An analysis of a customer or prospect list to identify in advance the best customers in terms of potential and of location.

Testimonial A statement in praise of a product or service made by a satisfied user and publicized by a company through advertising or sales promotion.

Tickler file A follow-up folder in which correspondence, memoranda, etc. are filed by future dates and reviewed on the respective dates.

Trade discount A deduction from the list price of an item granted by manufacturer or supplier to a retailer.

Trade reference An individual or company in business to which a seller is referred for information concerning an applicant's credit standing.

Trade show A public exhibition or showing of products offered by sellers to prospective buyers.

Trade up To show or move up to items of higher quality or price.

Traveling salesperson (*or* sales representative) **or commercial traveler** A firm's traveling representative who solicits orders.

Trial close An attempt, based on listening or observation, to induce action (to buy) at any stage of the sales presentation prior to the final, planned closing attempt.

Turnover The number of times a stock of merchandise is replaced in one year.

User calls The callbacks a sales representative makes on a customer who has made a purchase through him or her or through the company.

Value The worth of any property, good, service, right, or thing: (1) at market; (2) as agreed; (3) as determined by legislation; (4) at the owner's minimum selling price; (5) as determined in a dispute or by judicial decree; (6) intrinsically; (7) in the long run; (8) at par or face; or (9) at maturity.

Value analysis The sorting out and classifying of customers or prospects into a simplified grouping to establish an order of priority for calls and for time to be allocated.

Warranty or guarantee A seller's declaration, enforceable in a suit for damages, that merchandise is as represented.

Wholesale The level of marketing between manufacturing and retailing.

Wholesaler One who buys and resells merchandise to retailers and other merchants and to industrial, institutional, and commercial users, but does not sell in significant amounts to ultimate consumers.

Wholesaling Involves selling to buyers other than to ultimate customers.

INDEX

Four major factors that affect consumer buying behavior:
cultural, 76–77
personal, 76, 78–81
psychological, 76, 81–85
social, 76–77
France, 13, 43, 412
Free enterprise, benefits of American system of, 39, 429
Fuller Brush Company, 241

G

Gap, The (American specialty store chain), 377
General Electric Corporation (GE), 358, 472
General Motors Corporation (GM), 8, 358, 548
Germany, Federal Republic of (West Germany), 13, 54, 70, 547–48
Goals (and objectives) in selling:
definition of, 4, 48
importance to success of salespeople, 48
personal decisions for setting, 48, 52
planning of, 48, 52, 63–64, 405–406, 451, 462–63
working toward, 48–52
Great Britain, (see United Kingdom)
Greeter (see Drummer)
Grolier, Inc., 412
Grooming, personal, of salespeople, importance of, 161–62, 206–207
Groups, selling to, 389–90, 359–60

H

Hamilton, Alexander, 44
Hierarchy of Needs, Maslow's Theory of, 82–83
High-pressure selling (see also Low-pressure selling), 318, 320–21
Hobbies, noting prospect's or customer's, 150–51
Holland America Line Westours, Inc., 423–24
Home Depot (American home improvement store chain), 20
Hong Kong, 13, 395–96
House-to-house selling (see Door-to-door selling)
How a salesperson can motivate buying action:
by logical reasoning, 261–62
by suggestion, 262–63
Hudson's Bay Company, 376, 379

I

Independent agent sales organizations, advantages and disadvantages of using, 453–59
India, 53
Indonesia, 13
Information, obtaining:
about competition, 116–17
on companies, 104–10, 153–54
on industry data and trends, 153
on people, 151–53
through "yes-building" question technique, 230–32
Inside-outside salespeople, 12
Inside selling, 10
In-store retail salespeople, 12
International Business Machines Corporation (IBM), 472, 546–47
Interest, prospect:
changing, into desire, 258–60
creating and holding, principles of, 227–28, 235–38
holding, in different personality types, 235–38
Interview, sales:
average length of, 178
building on atmosphere of warmth and confidence during, 217–28
controlling, 227–28
for a sales position (see Jobs, sales)
how to obtain (see Preapproach, sales)
ideal, the, 178, 204–205
interruption of, how to handle, 238–39
introduction (see Leads, sales)
Ireland, 13
Italy, 13, 44

J

Japan, 13, 19, 28–29, 54, 70, 76, 412, 472–73, 547–48
Jobbers (see Wholesaler's salesperson)
Jobs, sales (see also Sales careers), 7, 10–14, 480–83
Journal of Personal Selling & Sales Management, 541
Judgment, necessary for promotion to management, 539–43

K

K Mart (American retail chain), 377, 379
Keys to business success, the two major:
controls, 452
planning, 452
Keys to goal attainment, 4
Knowledge, in selling:
how to develop, 539–42
importance of, to success, 102–103, 539–42
of company, 103–10
of competition, 116–17
of market/territory, 34–37, 502–503
of product, 103, 105
of promotional support, 112–16
Kotler, Philip, 35, 38

L

Landers, Ann (columnist), 425–26
Laws affecting American business and selling (see Business)
Leadership abilities, required of sales managers, 469–70, 533–42
Leads, sales (see also Prospect and Prospecting)
definition of, 126
how to obtain, 127–35
qualification of, 135–36
referral, 130–33, 337
Limited, The (American specialty store chain), 376
Lipton, Sir Thomas J., 119
Thomas J. Lipton, Inc., 119–24
Listening, in selling:
importance of, 232–33
techniques of, 233–35

Objectives (and goals) in selling (*see* Goals)
Order form, handling of, 309
Order-takers (in selling), 10
Organizational markets, 35–36
Organizations, how to advance within, 542–44
Organizations, selling to, 360–68
Overselling, 92, 429–32, 442–43

P

Paperwork, in selling:
  how to manage, 513–14
  how to prepare, 512–15
  salesperson's attitude toward, 513–14
Party-plan selling, 14, 413–14
Peddler, 45
Penney, J.C. Co., 376, 378–79
Peoples Republic of China, 54, 548
Personal goal-setting in selling (*see* Goals and objectives)
Personal selling:
  definition of, 6
  historical development of, 43–45
  importance of in marketing mix, 40, 43
Personality, prospect's, types of, 149, 217–18, 235–38
Persuasion:
  definition of, 6
  central role of in selling, 6, 261
  logic in, importance of, 261–62
  suggestion in, importance of, 262–63
Philippines, The, 13
Pi Sigma Epsilon, 5
Planned (or formula) sales presentation, 171–72, 196
Planning in selling:
  controls, establishing of, 49–52, 63–64, 512–13, 531
  definition of, 50, 503
  forecasting in, 53, 503
  goals and objectives of, 48–49, 516
  management of time, importance in, 506
  mental outlining of, 177–79
  organization of:
    around eight basic elements, 173
    around features, advantages, benefits, 121, 139, 251–53, 386–87
    around five decisions prospect

makes before buying, 226–27
    around four basic steps, 174–76
    around negative facts and words, 184
    around positive facts and words, 184
  planned type of, 171–72
  planning of, how to start, 171–73
  programming in, 504
  proper development of selling points for, 173
  recognizing interest changing into desire during, 227–28, 258–61
  reports, as tools of, 512–13
  routing in, 510–11
  strategic objectives of, 247–48, 276
  survey-proposal type of, 172
  use of demonstration and sales tools during, 239, 255–57
Preapproach, sales:
  definition of, 148
  elements involved in, 148–49
  getting the interview:
    by appointment, 154–60
    steps in, 155–57
    without an appointment, 160–64
Presentation, complete sales:
  anatomy of, 174–77
  approach phase of, 205–208
  attention, arousing and holding throughout, 175, 251–57
  automated (or audiovisual type of), 172
  basic steps (four) of, 174–77
  body language during, 180–81
  canned (or memorized) type of, 171
  clarity of, 178–79, 184
  closing of, 177
  creating and holding interest during, 227–28
  definition of, 173
  demonstration during, 182–83, 251–57
  desire, arousing and securing conviction during, 175–77, 248–61
  discussion (talking) during, 181–82, 184
  essentials of (six), 247–48
  handling interruptions during, 238–39
  handling questions, objections,

or challenges during, 275–83
  how to develop an outline for, 177–80, 184
  ideal, the, 204–205
  interest, creating and holding during, 181–83, 185–86
  length of, 178
  listening (feedback) during, importance of, 178, 228–29, 232–35
  objectives of a good, 185–86
  planned (or formula) type of, 171
  survey (or problem-solution) type of, 172
  use of sales aids during, 181–82
Pricing, company:
  considerations by, 62
  importance to buyers of, 106
  strategies of, 106
Problems (in selling):
  faced by salespeople, 18, 21–23
  of overcoming tension and fear, 214–16, 308–309
  with put-offs, handling of, 289–91, 294–96
  with repeated negative replies, 18, 160–64
Product knowledge, importance of in selling, 110–11
Product (or service) salesperson, 12
Profit, as business and sales objective, 8
Programming, of sales work, 504, 531–32
Promotion and selling, within the "promotional mix" of marketing, 40–41, 112–16
Prospect (*see also* Prospecting and Qualification of prospects):
  definition of, 7, 11, 126
  getting information about, 150–52
  handling different types of, 149, 235–38
  holding interest of, 235–38
  how to communicate effectively with, 177–84
  how to find, 127–35
  how to qualify, 126, 135–36
  importance of, 126–27
  impressions of, concerning salesperson, 205–207
  needs, wants, problems of, 172–73, 174–77
  types of, 217–18, 235–38

Prospecting:
  definition of, 127
  methods of, 127–35
Psychological factors in selling:
  attitudes and beliefs, 84–85
  learning, 84
  Maslow's "Hierarchy of Needs,"
    82–83
  motivation, theories of, 81
  needs:
    acquired, 82
    innate, 81
  perception, 83–84
Publicity (in selling), 40–41

Q

Qualified prospect, definition of,
  126, 135–36
Qualification of prospects:
  how to qualify, 135–36
  three tests of, 135–36
  using the telephone for, 137–40
Qualities necessary for sales suc-
    cess, 23–24, 536–37
Questioning (in selling):
  importance of, 229
  techniques of, 229–30
  "yes-building," technique of,
    230–32

R

Rapport, how to establish, 216–17
Rational buying motives, 73
Real salespeople, 10–11
Records, personal sales, 512–16
Reid, R.T. Associates, Inc., 267–68
Reports, sales (see also Follow-
    through, sales)
  how to manage, 513–14
  preparation and writing of, 512–
    15
  qualitative, 513
  quantitative, 512–13
  tips on how to prepare, 514–15
Retailing and retail selling:
  changing scene, the, 43–5, 375–
    80
  compensation, retail salesperson,
    380
  greeting the retail customer,
    383–84
  handling special sales problems
    in, 388–90
  knowledge of merchandise
    essential, 390–92

making second (or add-on)
    sales, 391–92
  presenting merchandise specials,
    391
  retail salespeople, 12, 376, 380–
    82
  retail sales presentation, the,
    385–88
  sales fundamentals that apply to,
    382–83
  salesperson as a host, 383
  selling substitute items, 392
  trading up for bigger sales, 392
  training of retail salespeople,
    381–82
  two separate areas of:
    in-store (inside), 375
    nonstore (outside), 375
Reference groups, as affecting
    buying decisions, 77–78
Relationship selling, 358–59
Revlon, Inc., 96
Role-playing in selling, 253–55
Route salesperson, 11
Routing plans and scheduling,
    507–11
Rubenstein, Helena, Company, 96

S

Sales aids, use of, 181–82
Sales and Marketing Executives
    International (SMEI), 541
Sales & Marketing Management
    (magazine), 17–18, 541
Sales aptitude, self-evaluation of,
    23–24
Sales call patterns:
  fixed routing, 509
  irregular routing, 509
Sales call ratio, 512
Sales careers (see also Salesperson,
    and Selling)
  advantage of, 14–15, 23
  application letter and experience
    resumé for, 454–87
  applying for a sales position,
    480–87
  career opportunities in selling
    for American:
    blacks, 18
    handicapped, 18
    Hispanics, 18
    mature adults, 18–19
    part-time workers, 19
    women, 18–19
  disadvantages of, 21–23
  how to sell yourself for

planning the job hunt, 481–
    82
  preparing experience resumé,
    484–87
  steps in the employment
    process, 487–95
Sales concept (or selling concept),
    37
Sales, costs, and expense of get-
    ting, 8
Sales force (see also Sales manage-
    ment):
  communication with, 465–66
  morale and motivation of, 465–
    66
  organizational structures of:
    functional, 455
    line, 455
    line and staff, 455
    other specialized types, 456–
      58
  recruitment, selection, hiring
    for, 459–61
  role and objectives for, 63
  sales meetings and contests
    for, 466
  sales territory assignment,
    routing, and scheduling
    of, 463–65
  supervision control, and
    performance evaluation
    of, 466–67
Sales interview, the ideal, 204
Sales letters, 157–58
Salesmanship, 6
Sales management:
  definition of, 450
  earning potential in, 469
  knowledge and skills necessary
    for success in, 535–42
  opportunities for reaching, 533
  personal characteristics neces-
    sary for success in, 536–
    40
  responsibilities of, 452–70
Sales managers, duties and respon-
    sibilities of:
  budgeting, 462–64
  establishing quotas, 462–63
  as a leader, 469–70
  motivation and communication,
    465–66
  planning and conducting sales
    meetings and contests,
    466
  "real life" activities of, 468–69
  recruitment, selection, hiring,
    459–61
  sales territory assignment,
    routing, and scheduling,
    463–65